THE AVENGERS

CELESTIAL QUEST

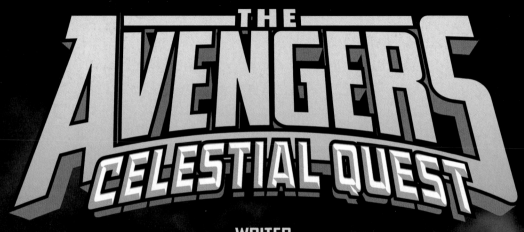

THE AVENGERS
CELESTIAL QUEST

WRITER
STEVE ENGLEHART

PENCILERS
JORGE SANTAMARIA & JOE STATON

INKERS
SCOTT HANNA
with SCOTT KOBLISH & RICH PERROTTA

COLORIST
HIFI DESIGN

LETTERER
SHARPEFONT'S PAUL TUTRONE

ASSISTANT EDITOR
MARC SUMERAK

EDITOR
TOM BREVOORT

FRONT COVER ARTISTS
JORGE SANTAMARIA,
SCOTT HANNA & HIFI DESIGN

COLLECTION EDITOR: Nelson Ribeiro • ASSISTANT EDITOR: Alex Starbuck • EDITORS, SPECIAL PROJECTS: Jennifer Grünwald & Mark D. Beazley
SENIOR EDITOR, SPECIAL PROJECTS: Jeff Youngquist • RESEARCH: Dugan Trodglen • LAYOUT: Jeph York • BOOK DESIGN: Jeff Powell
SENIOR VICE PRESIDENT OF SALES: David Gabriel • SVP OF BRAND PLANNING & COMMUNICATIONS: Michael Pasciullo

EDITOR IN CHIEF: Axel Alonso • CHIEF CREATIVE OFFICER: Joe Quesada • PUBLISHER: Dan Buckley • EXECUTIVE PRODUCER: Alan Fine

AVENGERS: CELESTIAL QUEST. Contains material originally published in magazine form as AVENGERS: CELESTIAL QUEST #1-8. First printing 2012. ISBN# 978-0-7851-6233-9. Published by MARVEL WORLDWIDE, INC., a subsidiary of MARVEL ENTERTAINMENT, LLC. OFFICE OF PUBLICATION: 135 West 50th Street, New York, NY 10020. $24.99 per copy in the U.S. and $27.99 in Canada (GST #R127032852); Canadian Agreement #40668537. Printed in the U.S.A. ALAN FINE, EVP - Office of the President, Marvel Worldwide, Inc. and EVP & CMO Marvel Characters B.V.; DAN BUCKLEY, Publisher & President - Print, Animation & Digital Divisions; JOE QUESADA, Chief Creative Officer; TOM BREVOORT, SVP of Publishing; DAVID BOGART, SVP of Operations & Procurement, Publishing; RUWAN JAYATILLEKE, SVP & Associate Publisher, Publishing; C.B. CEBULSKI, SVP of Creator & Content Development; DAVID GABRIEL, SVP of Publishing Sales & Circulation; MICHAEL PASCIULLO, SVP of Brand Planning & Communications; JIM O'KEEFE, VP of Operations & Logistics; DAN CARR, Executive Director of Publishing Technology; SUSAN CRESPI, Editorial Operations Manager; ALEX MORALES, Publishing Operations Manager; STAN LEE, Chairman Emeritus. For information regarding advertising in Marvel Comics or on Marvel.com, please contact Niza Disla, Director of Marvel Partnerships, at ndisla@marvel.com. For Marvel subscription inquiries, please call 800-217-9158. Manufactured between 7/19/2012 and 8/21/2012 by QUAD/GRAPHICS, DUBUQUE, IA, USA.

10 9 8 7 6 5 4 3 2 1

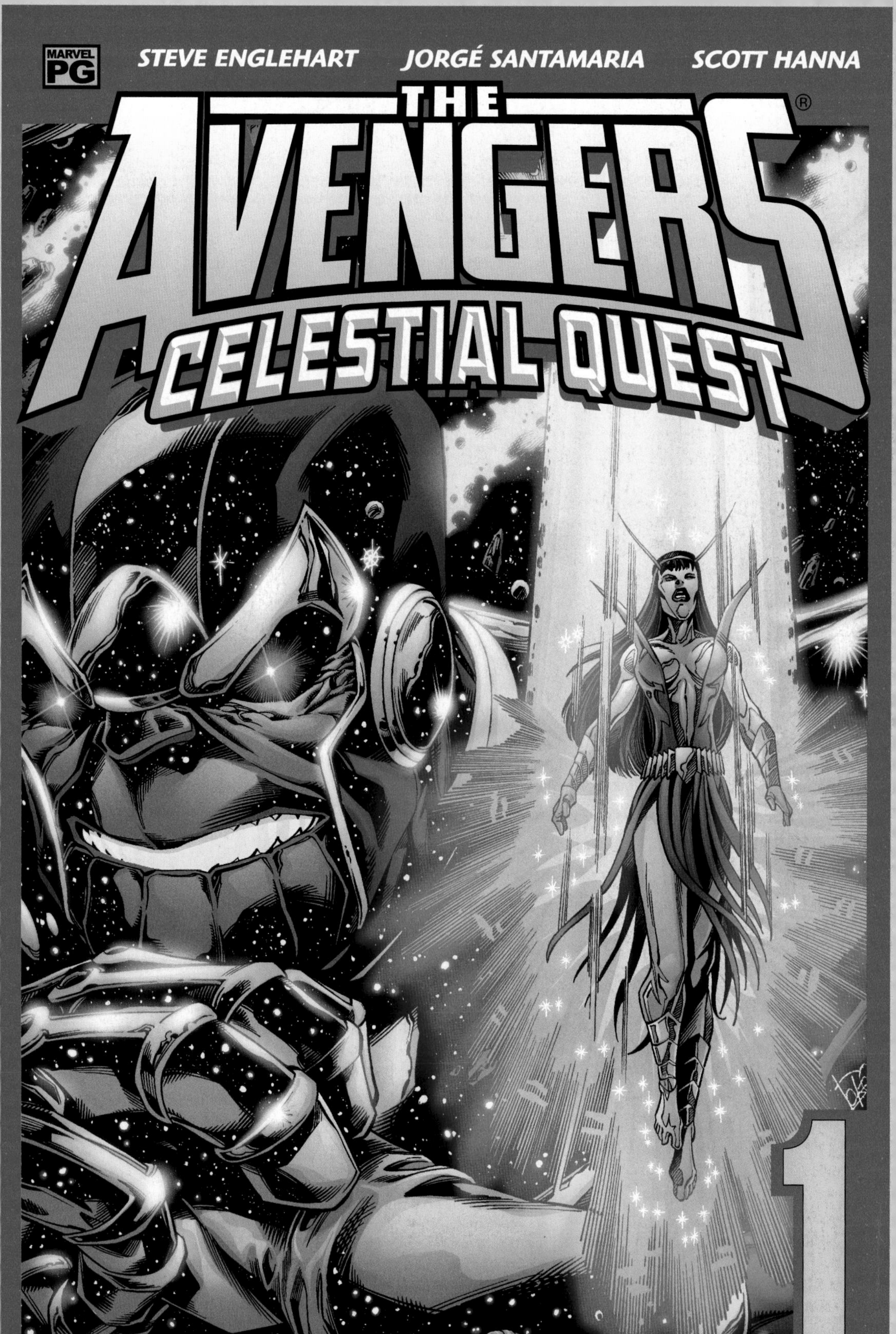

MARVEL PG
STEVE ENGLEHART
JORGÉ SANTAMARIA
SCOTT HANNA
THE AVENGERS®
CELESTIAL QUEST
1
of 8

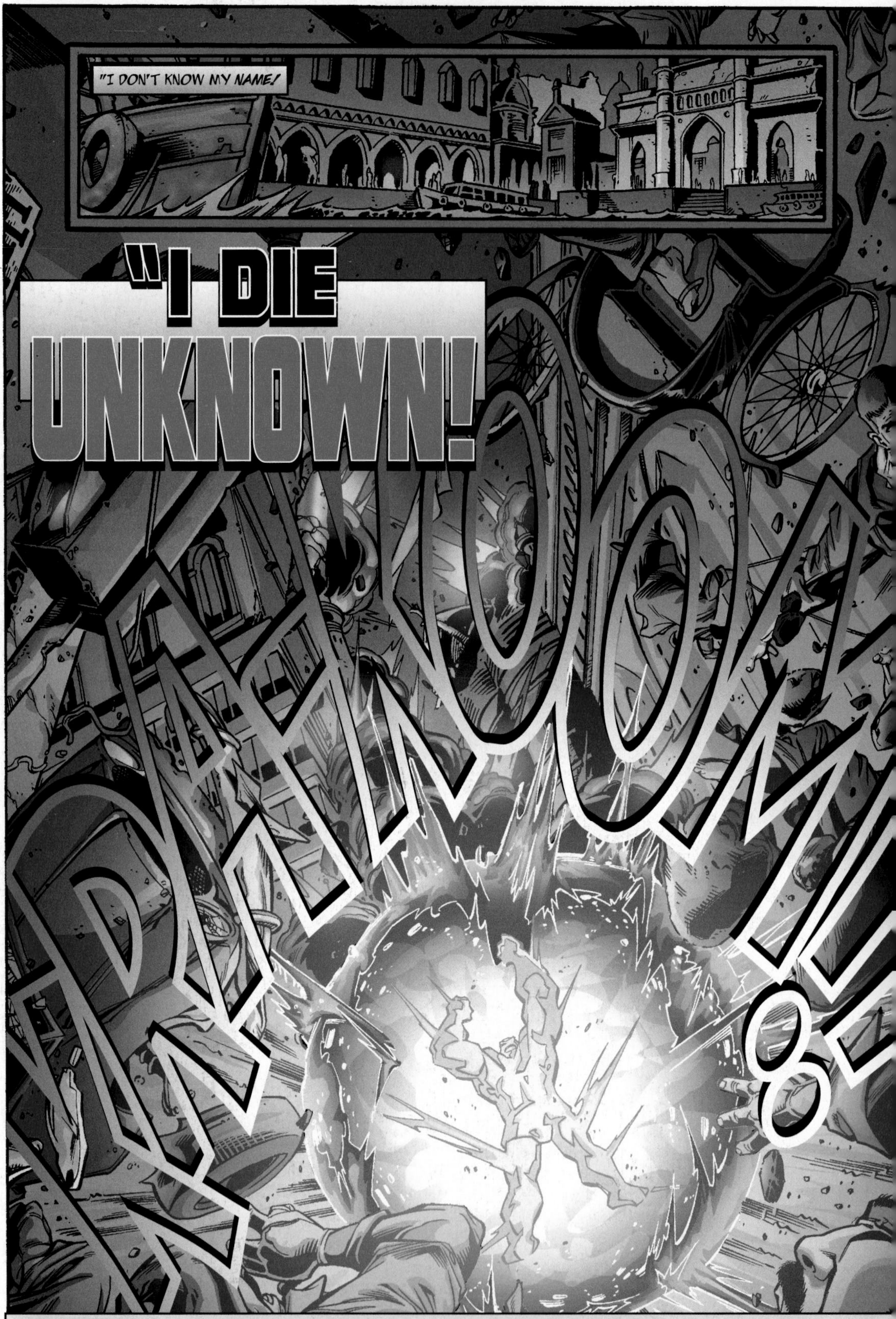
"I DON'T KNOW MY NAME!
"I DIE UNKNOWN!

STAINLESS STEVE ENGLEHART · AUTHOR JORGE SANTAMARÍA · PENCIL ARTIST SCOTT HANNA · INK ARTIST
COLOR HIFI · COLORIST SHARPEFONT & PT · LETTERER MARC SUMERAK · ASSISTANT EDITOR TOM BREVOORT · EDITOR
JOE QUESADA · EDITOR IN CHIEF BILL JEMAS · PRESIDENT JAMMIN' JIM STARLIN · CREATOR OF THANOS

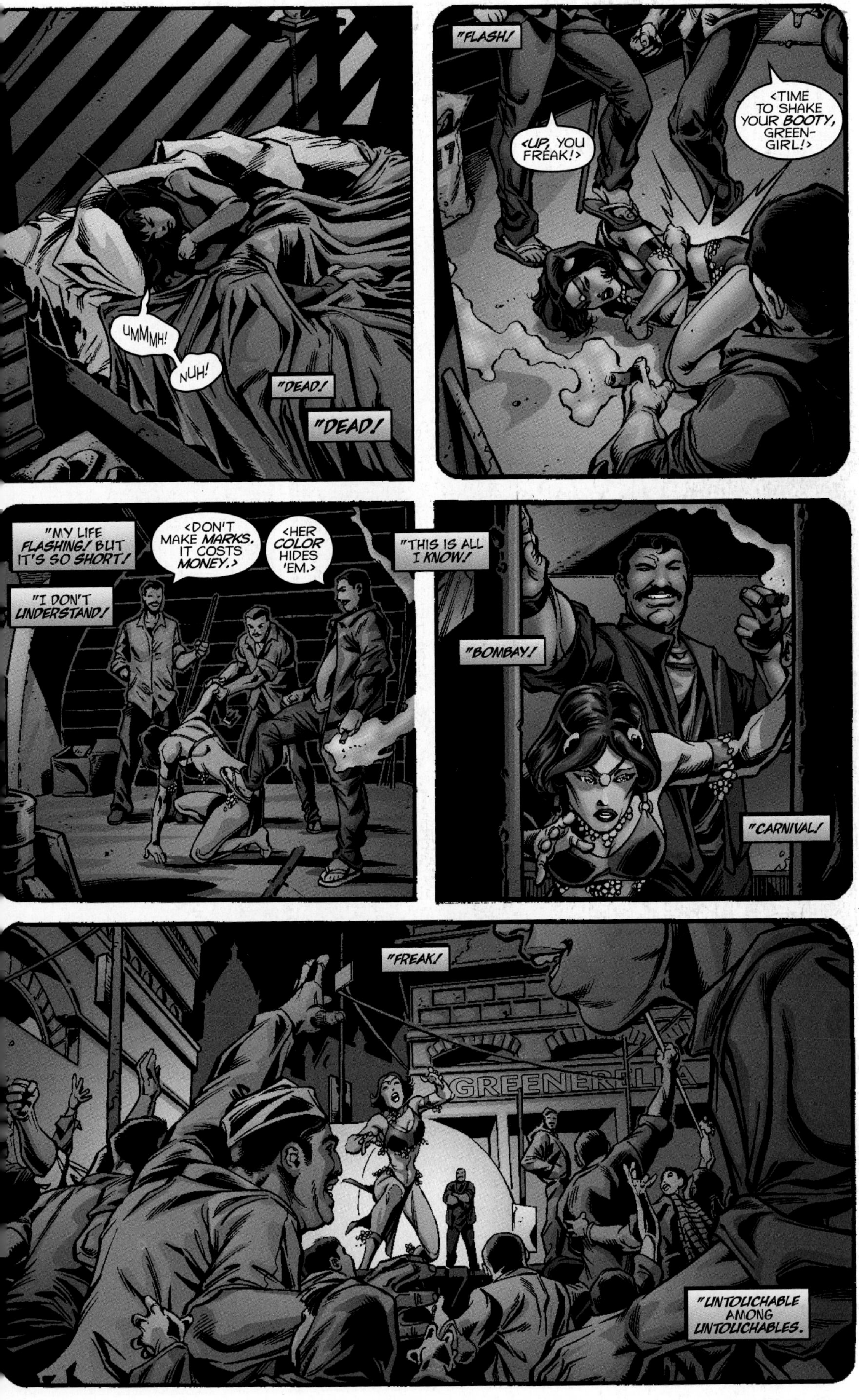
UMMMH!
NUH!
"DEAD!
"DEAD!
"FLASH!
<UP, YOU FREAK!>
<TIME TO SHAKE YOUR BOOTY, GREEN-GIRL!>
"MY LIFE FLASHING! BUT IT'S SO SHORT!
"I DON'T UNDERSTAND!
<DON'T MAKE MARKS. IT COSTS MONEY.>
<HER COLOR HIDES 'EM.>
"THIS IS ALL I KNOW!
"BOMBAY!
"CARNIVAL!
"FREAK!
GREENERELLA
"UNTOUCHABLE AMONG UNTOUCHABLES.

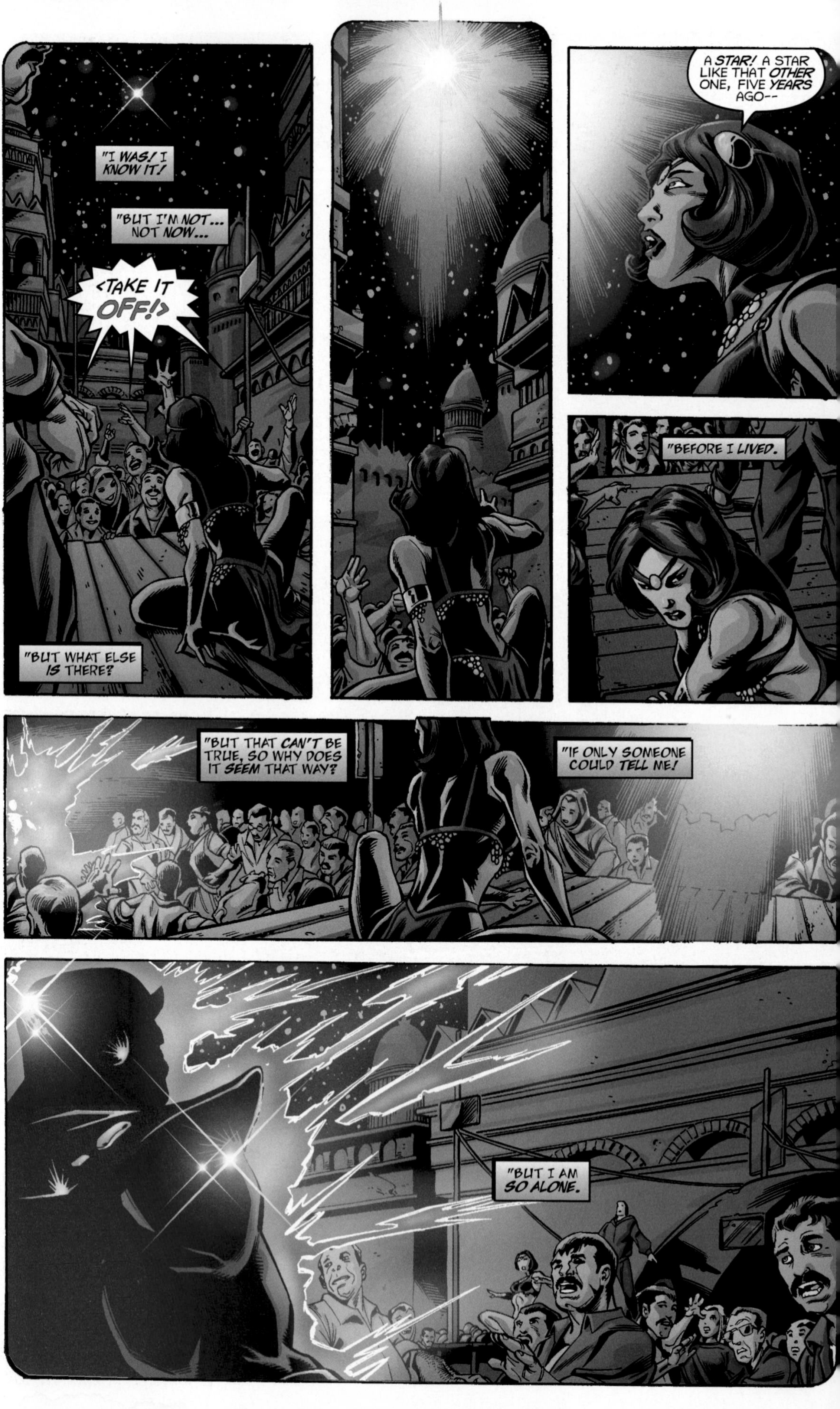
"I WAS! I KNOW IT!
"BUT I'M NOT... NOT NOW...
<TAKE IT OFF!>
"BUT WHAT ELSE IS THERE?
A STAR! A STAR LIKE THAT OTHER ONE, FIVE YEARS AGO--
"BEFORE I LIVED.
"BUT THAT CAN'T BE TRUE, SO WHY DOES IT SEEM THAT WAY?
"IF ONLY SOMEONE COULD TELL ME!
"BUT I AM SO ALONE.

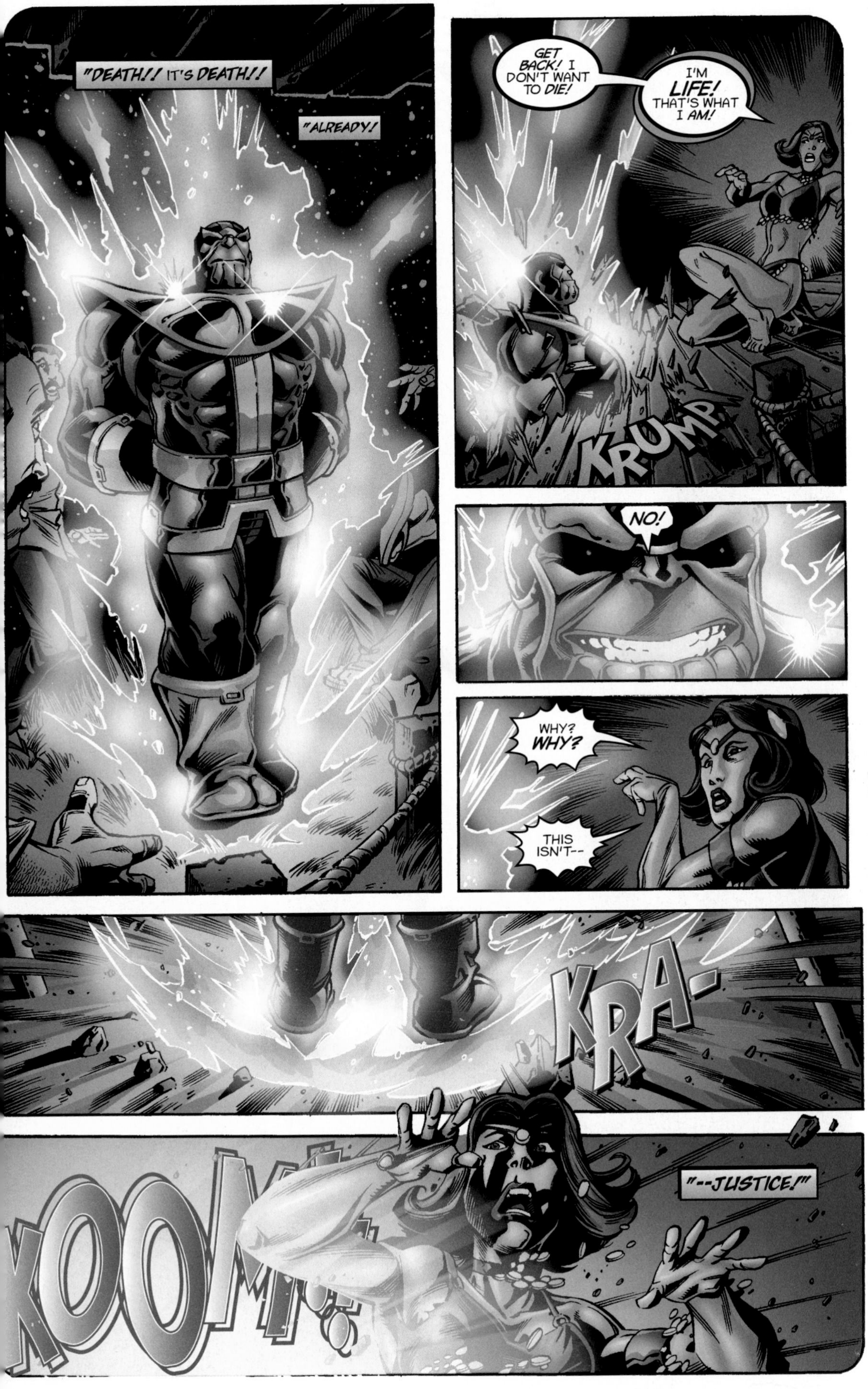
"DEATH!! IT'S DEATH!!
"ALREADY!
GET BACK! I DON'T WANT TO DIE!
I'M LIFE! THAT'S WHAT I AM!
KRUMP
NO!
WHY? WHY?
THIS ISN'T--
KRA-
KOOM
"--JUSTICE!"

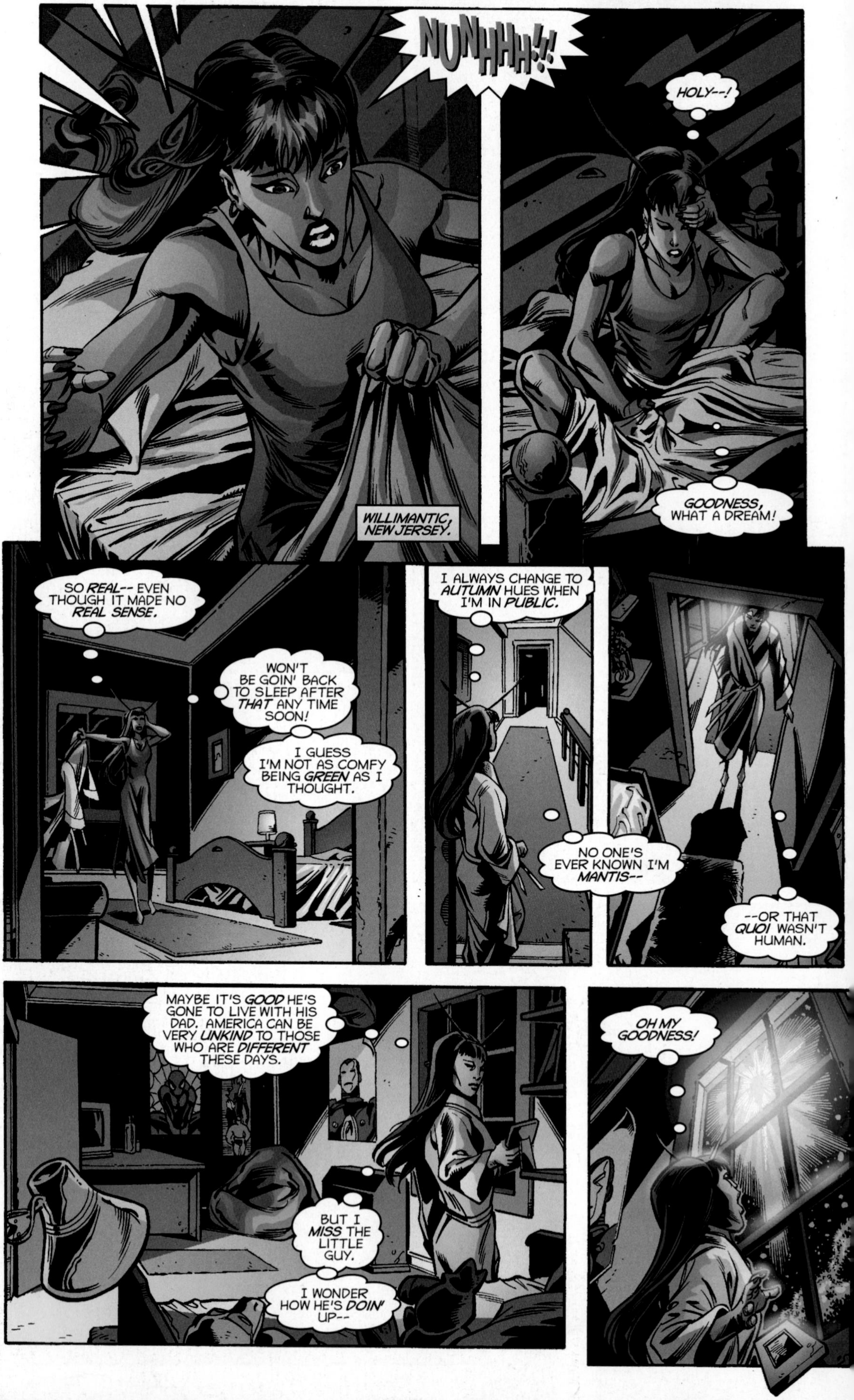
NUNHHH!!!
WILLIMANTIC, NEW JERSEY.
HOLY--!
GOODNESS, WHAT A DREAM!
SO REAL-- EVEN THOUGH IT MADE NO REAL SENSE.
WON'T BE GOIN' BACK TO SLEEP AFTER THAT ANY TIME SOON!
I GUESS I'M NOT AS COMFY BEING GREEN AS I THOUGHT.
I ALWAYS CHANGE TO AUTUMN HUES WHEN I'M IN PUBLIC.
NO ONE'S EVER KNOWN I'M MANTIS--
--OR THAT QUOI WASN'T HUMAN.
MAYBE IT'S GOOD HE'S GONE TO LIVE WITH HIS DAD. AMERICA CAN BE VERY UNKIND TO THOSE WHO ARE DIFFERENT THESE DAYS.
BUT I MISS THE LITTLE GUY.
I WONDER HOW HE'S DOIN' UP--
OH MY GOODNESS!

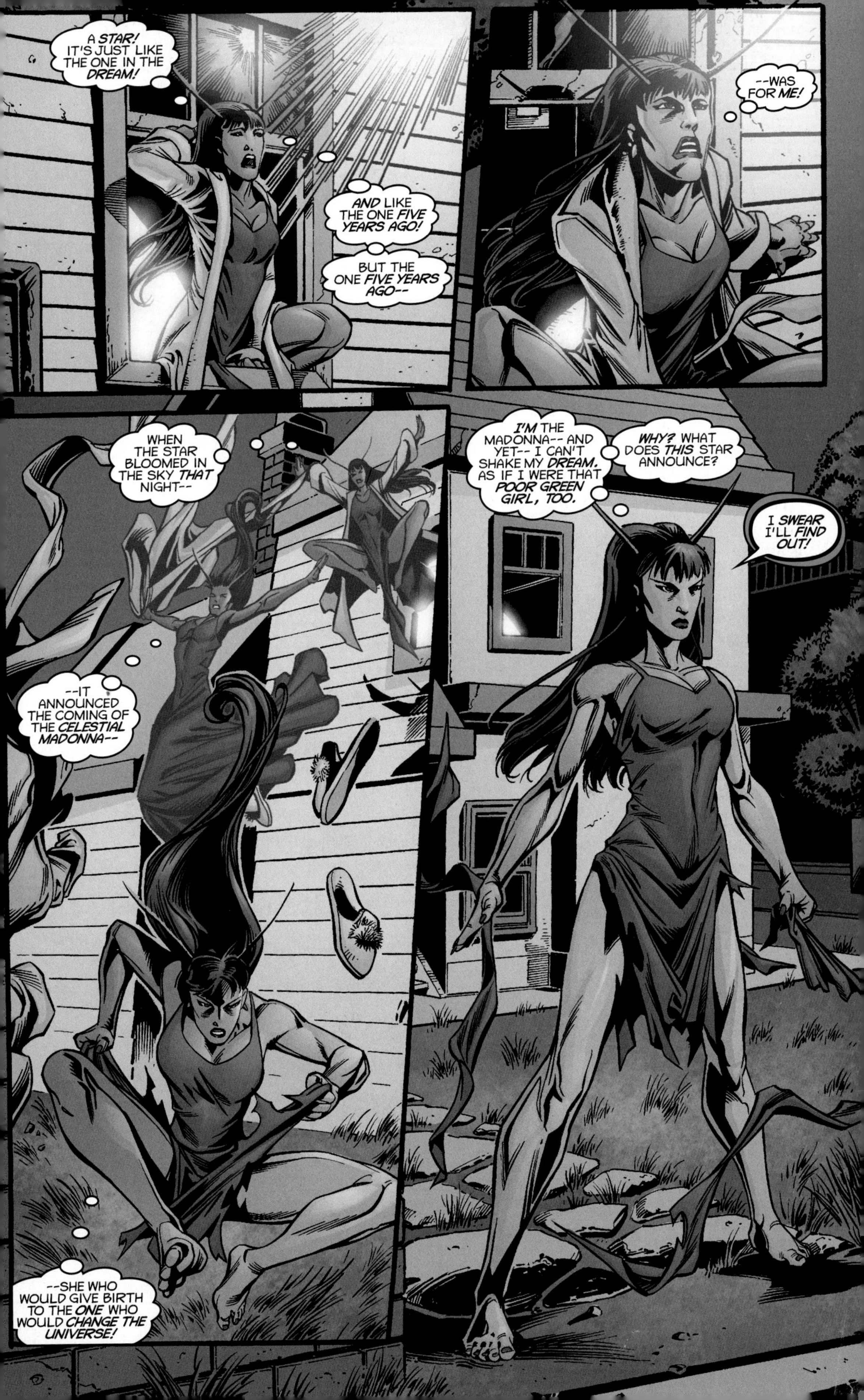
A STAR! IT'S JUST LIKE THE ONE IN THE DREAM!
AND LIKE THE ONE FIVE YEARS AGO!
BUT THE ONE FIVE YEARS AGO--
--WAS FOR ME!
WHEN THE STAR BLOOMED IN THE SKY THAT NIGHT--
--IT ANNOUNCED THE COMING OF THE CELESTIAL MADONNA--
--SHE WHO WOULD GIVE BIRTH TO THE ONE WHO WOULD CHANGE THE UNIVERSE!
I'M THE MADONNA-- AND YET-- I CAN'T SHAKE MY DREAM. AS IF I WERE THAT POOR GREEN GIRL, TOO.
WHY? WHAT DOES THIS STAR ANNOUNCE?
I SWEAR I'LL FIND OUT!

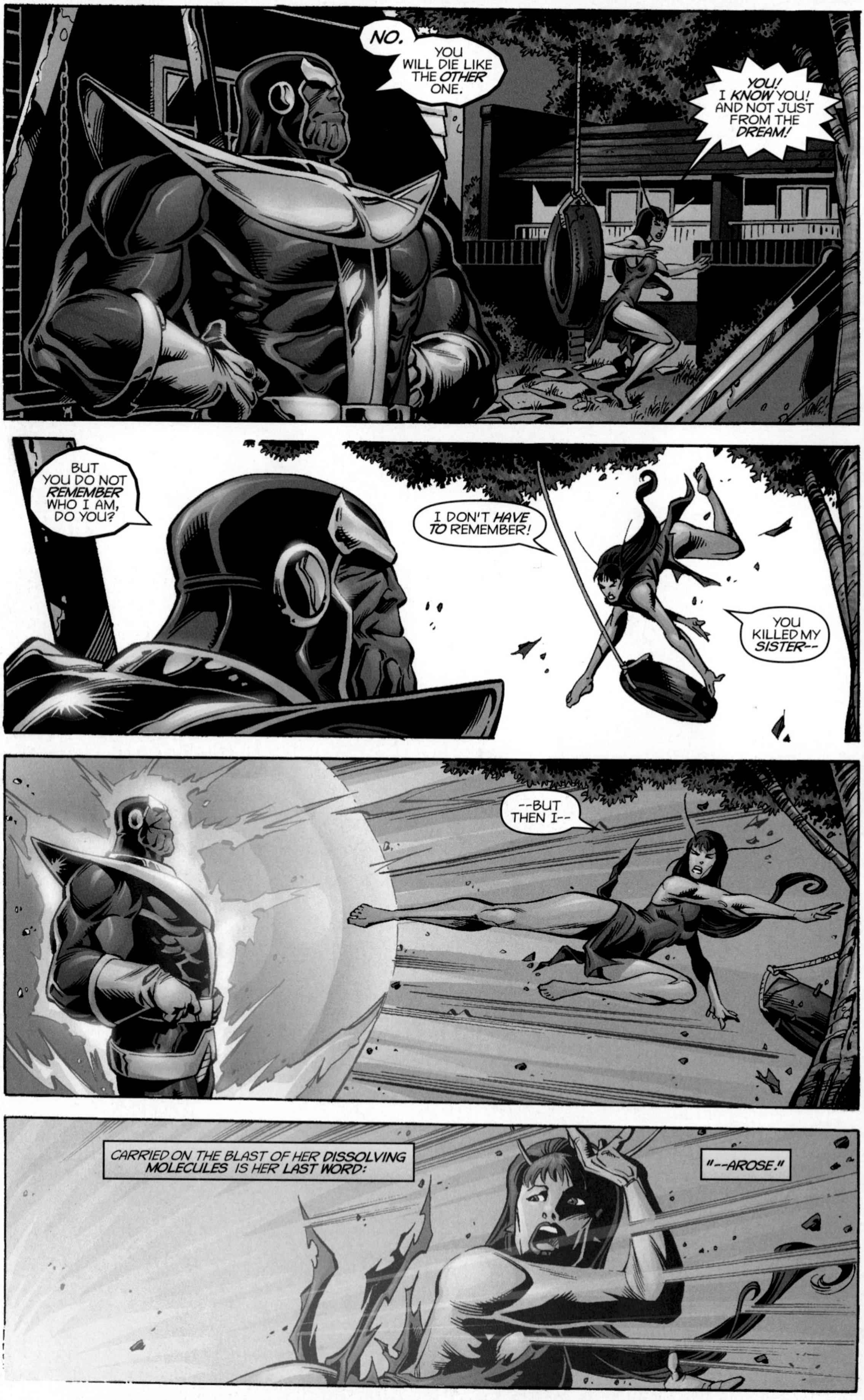
NO.
YOU WILL DIE LIKE THE OTHER ONE.
YOU! I KNOW YOU! AND NOT JUST FROM THE DREAM!
BUT YOU DO NOT REMEMBER WHO I AM, DO YOU?
I DON'T HAVE TO REMEMBER!
YOU KILLED MY SISTER--
--BUT THEN I--
CARRIED ON THE BLAST OF HER DISSOLVING MOLECULES IS HER LAST WORD:
"--AROSE."

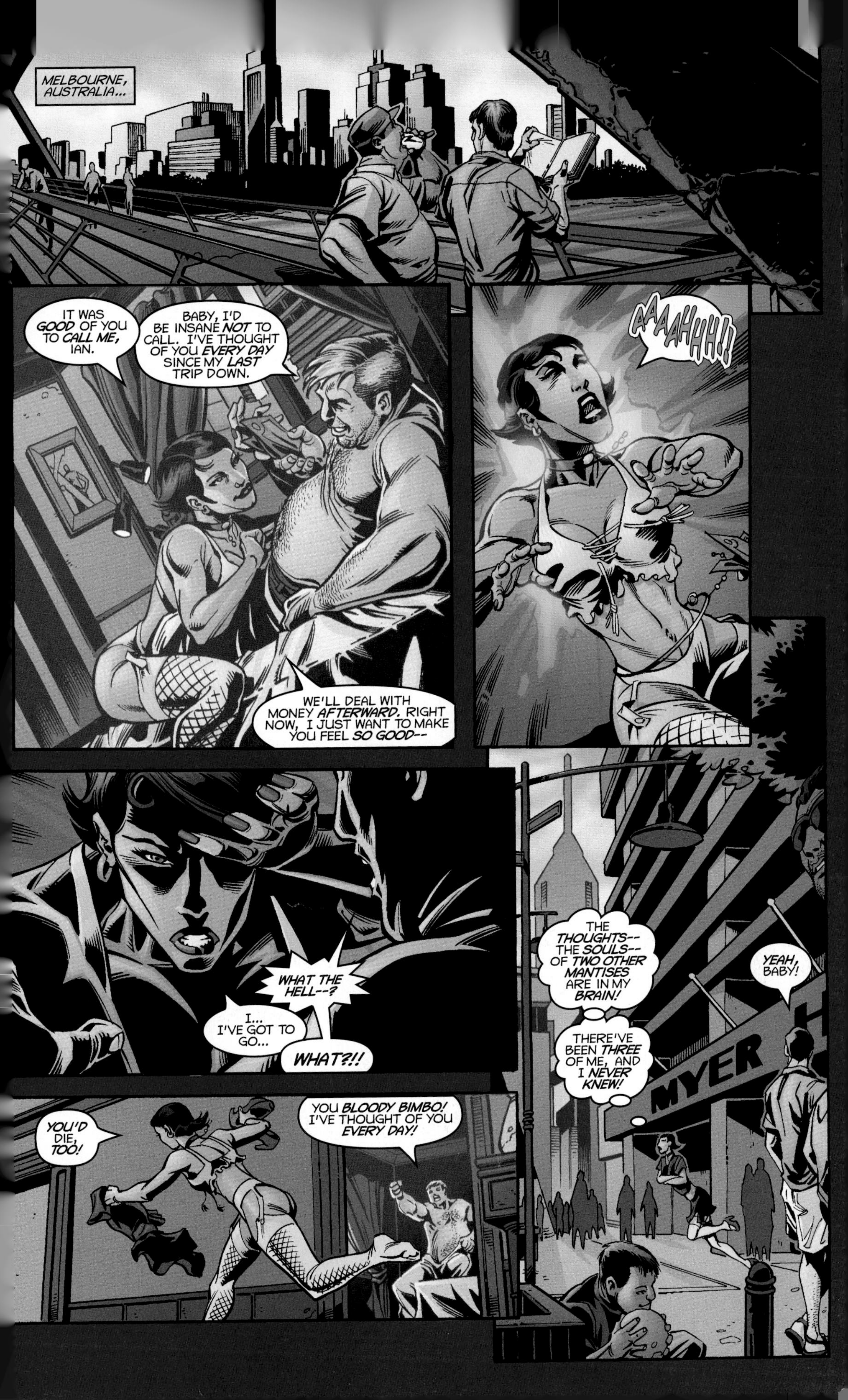
MELBOURNE, AUSTRALIA...
IT WAS GOOD OF YOU TO CALL ME, IAN.
BABY, I'D BE INSANE NOT TO CALL. I'VE THOUGHT OF YOU EVERY DAY SINCE MY LAST TRIP DOWN.
WE'LL DEAL WITH MONEY AFTERWARD. RIGHT NOW, I JUST WANT TO MAKE YOU FEEL SO GOOD--
AAAHHH!!
WHAT THE HELL--?
I... I'VE GOT TO GO...
WHAT?!!
YOU'D DIE, TOO!
YOU BLOODY BIMBO! I'VE THOUGHT OF YOU EVERY DAY!
THE THOUGHTS-- THE SOULS-- OF TWO OTHER MANTISES ARE IN MY BRAIN!
THERE'VE BEEN THREE OF ME, AND I NEVER KNEW!
YEAH, BABY!
MYER

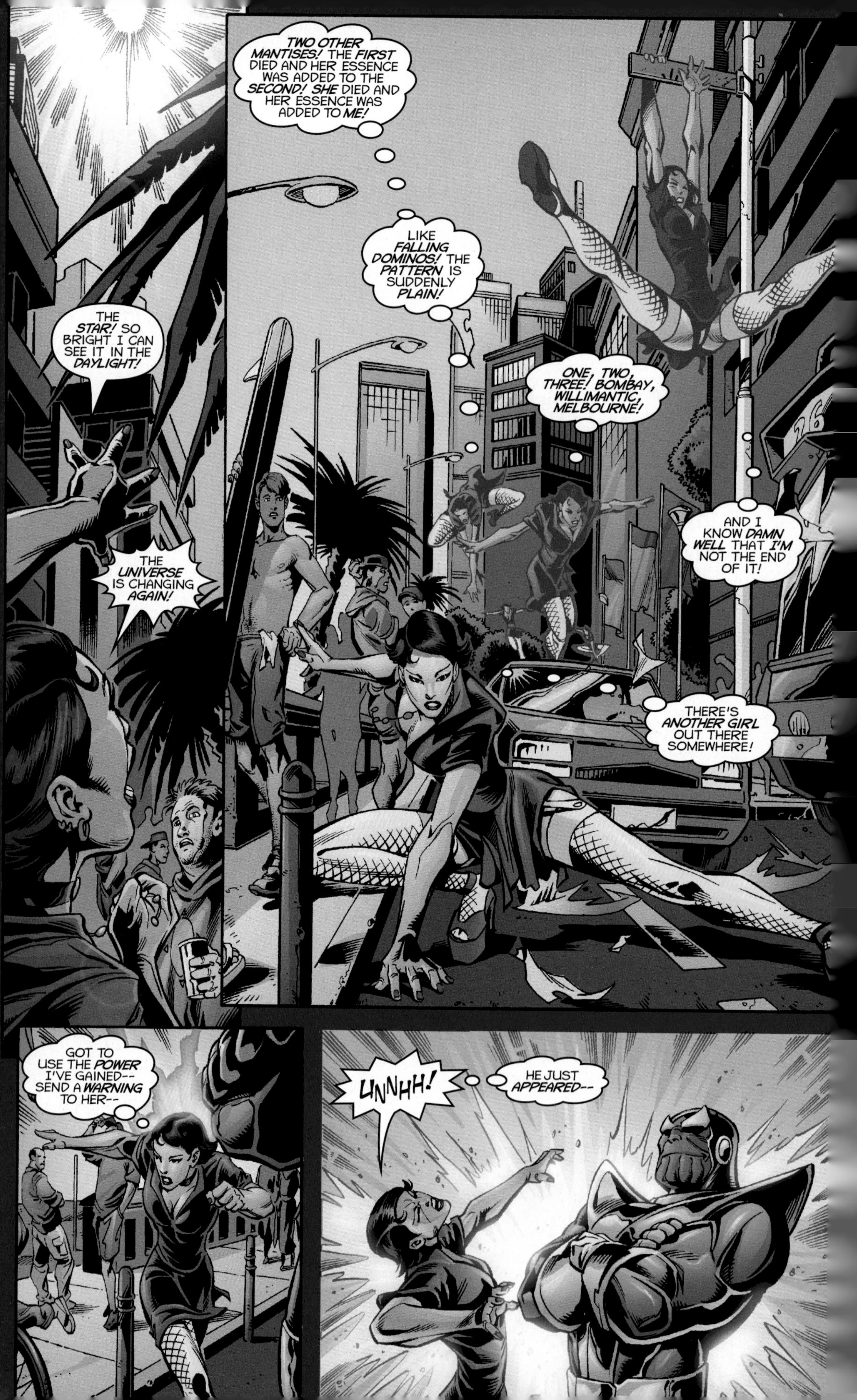
THE STAR! SO BRIGHT I CAN SEE IT IN THE DAYLIGHT!
THE UNIVERSE IS CHANGING AGAIN!
TWO OTHER MANTISES! THE FIRST DIED AND HER ESSENCE WAS ADDED TO THE SECOND! SHE DIED AND HER ESSENCE WAS ADDED TO ME!
LIKE FALLING DOMINOS! THE PATTERN IS SUDDENLY PLAIN!
ONE, TWO, THREE! BOMBAY, WILLIMANTIC, MELBOURNE!
AND I KNOW DAMN WELL THAT I'M NOT THE END OF IT!
THERE'S ANOTHER GIRL OUT THERE SOMEWHERE!
GOT TO USE THE POWER I'VE GAINED-- SEND A WARNING TO HER--
UNNHH!
HE JUST APPEARED--

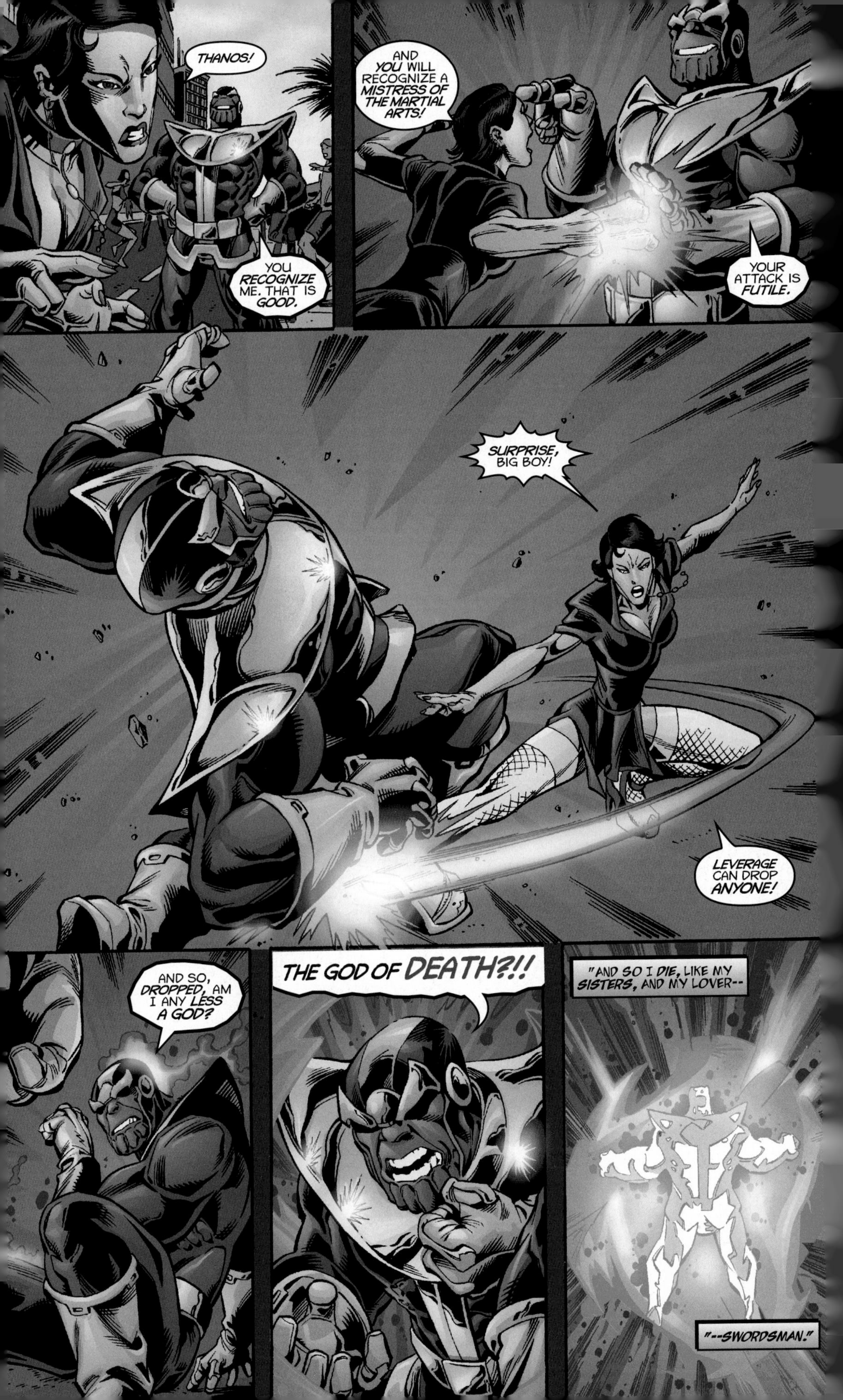
THANOS!
YOU RECOGNIZE ME. THAT IS GOOD.
AND YOU WILL RECOGNIZE A MISTRESS OF THE MARTIAL ARTS!
YOUR ATTACK IS FUTILE.
SURPRISE, BIG BOY!
LEVERAGE CAN DROP ANYONE!
AND SO, DROPPED, AM I ANY LESS A GOD?
THE GOD OF DEATH?!!
"AND SO I DIE, LIKE MY SISTERS, AND MY LOVER--
"--SWORDSMAN."

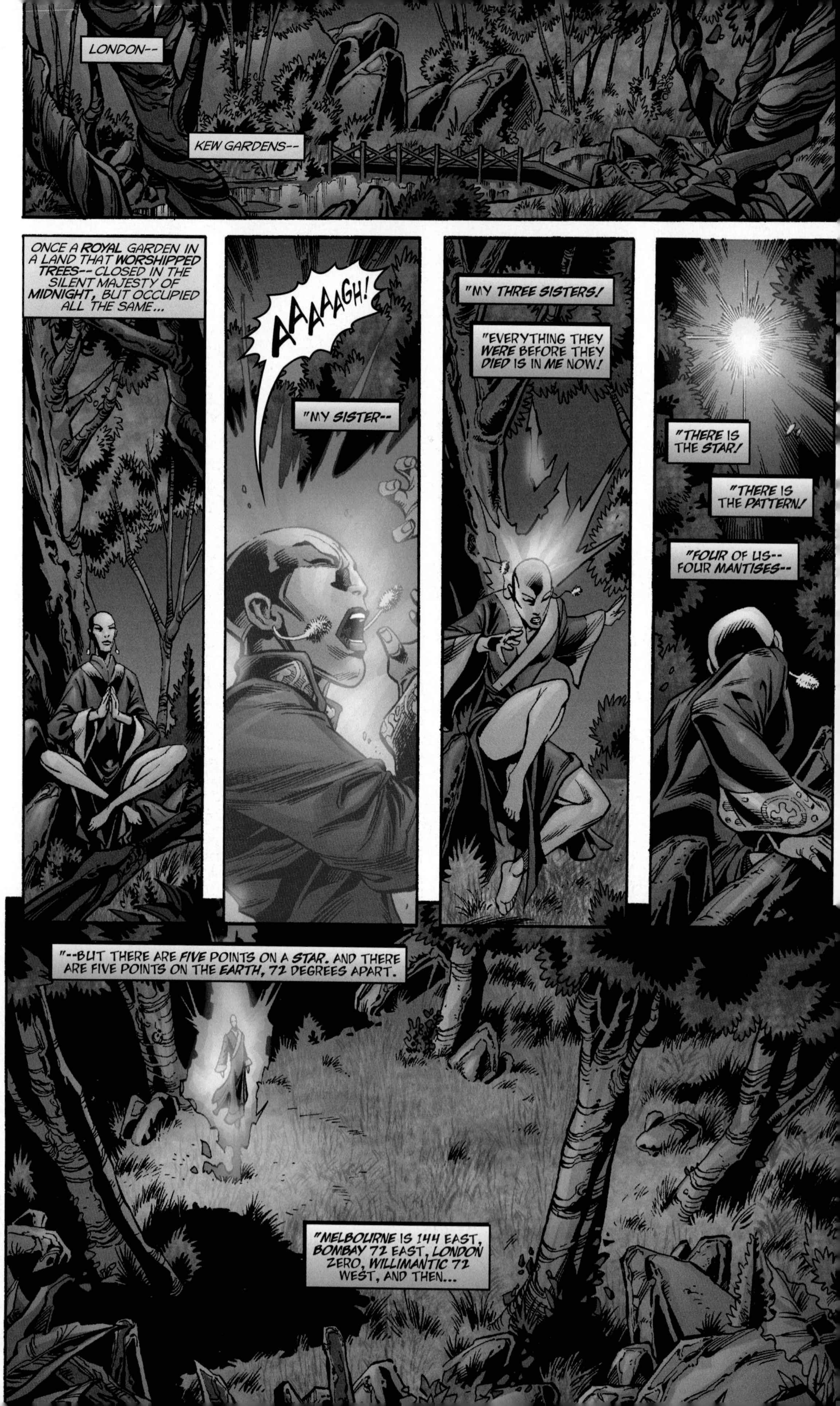

LONDON--
KEW GARDENS--
ONCE A ROYAL GARDEN IN A LAND THAT WORSHIPPED TREES--CLOSED IN THE SILENT MAJESTY OF MIDNIGHT, BUT OCCUPIED ALL THE SAME...
AAAAAGH!
"MY SISTER--
"MY THREE SISTERS!
"EVERYTHING THEY WERE BEFORE THEY DIED IS IN ME NOW!
"THERE IS THE STAR!
"THERE IS THE PATTERN!
"FOUR OF US-- FOUR MANTISES--
"--BUT THERE ARE FIVE POINTS ON A STAR. AND THERE ARE FIVE POINTS ON THE EARTH, 72 DEGREES APART.
"MELBOURNE IS 144 EAST, BOMBAY 72 EAST, LONDON ZERO, WILLIMANTIC 72 WEST, AND THEN...

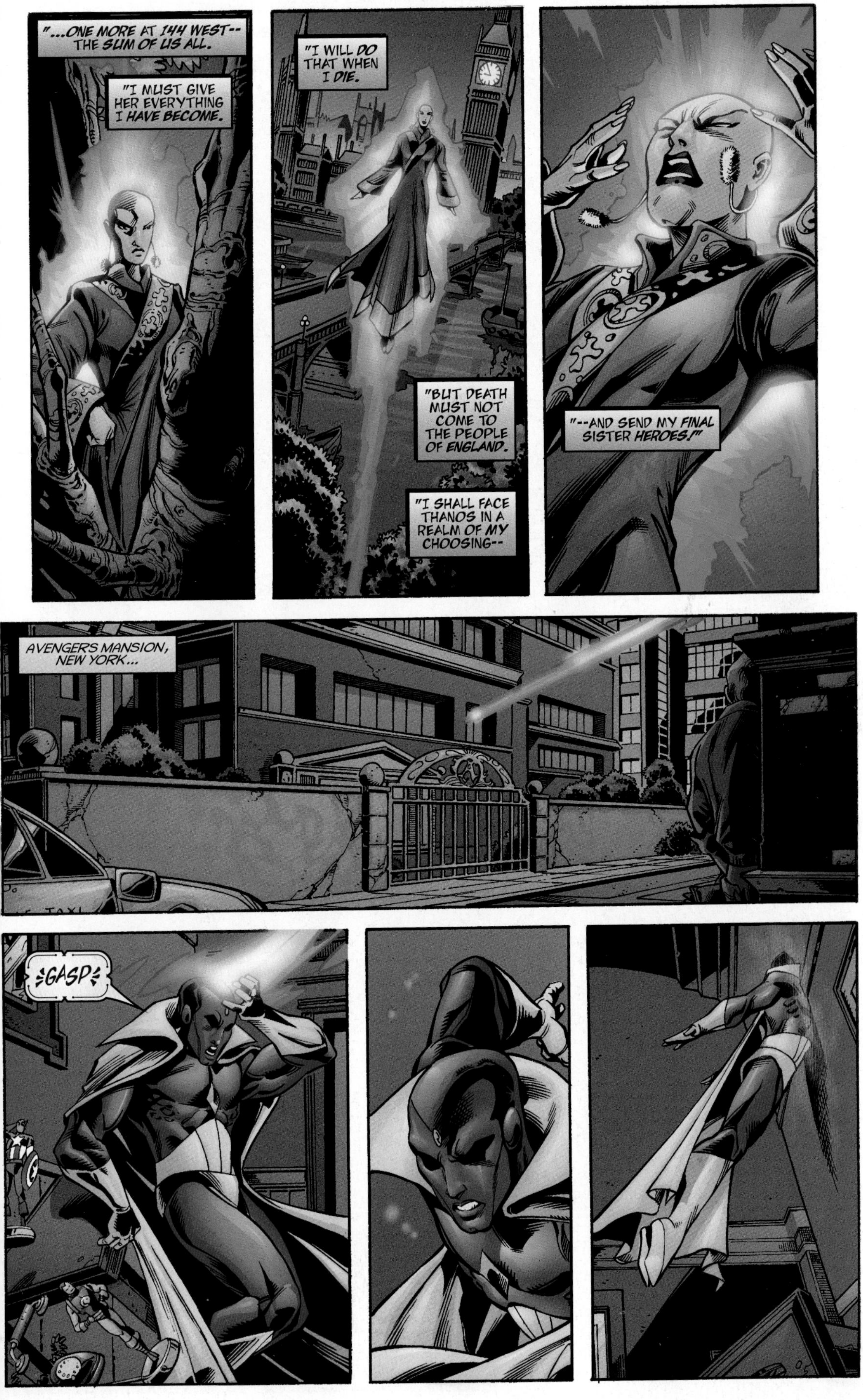
"...ONE MORE AT 144 WEST--
THE SUM OF US ALL.
"I MUST GIVE HER EVERYTHING I HAVE BECOME.
"I WILL DO THAT WHEN I DIE.
"BUT DEATH MUST NOT COME TO THE PEOPLE OF ENGLAND.
"I SHALL FACE THANOS IN A REALM OF MY CHOOSING--
"--AND SEND MY FINAL SISTER HEROES!"
AVENGERS MANSION, NEW YORK...
TAXI
GASP

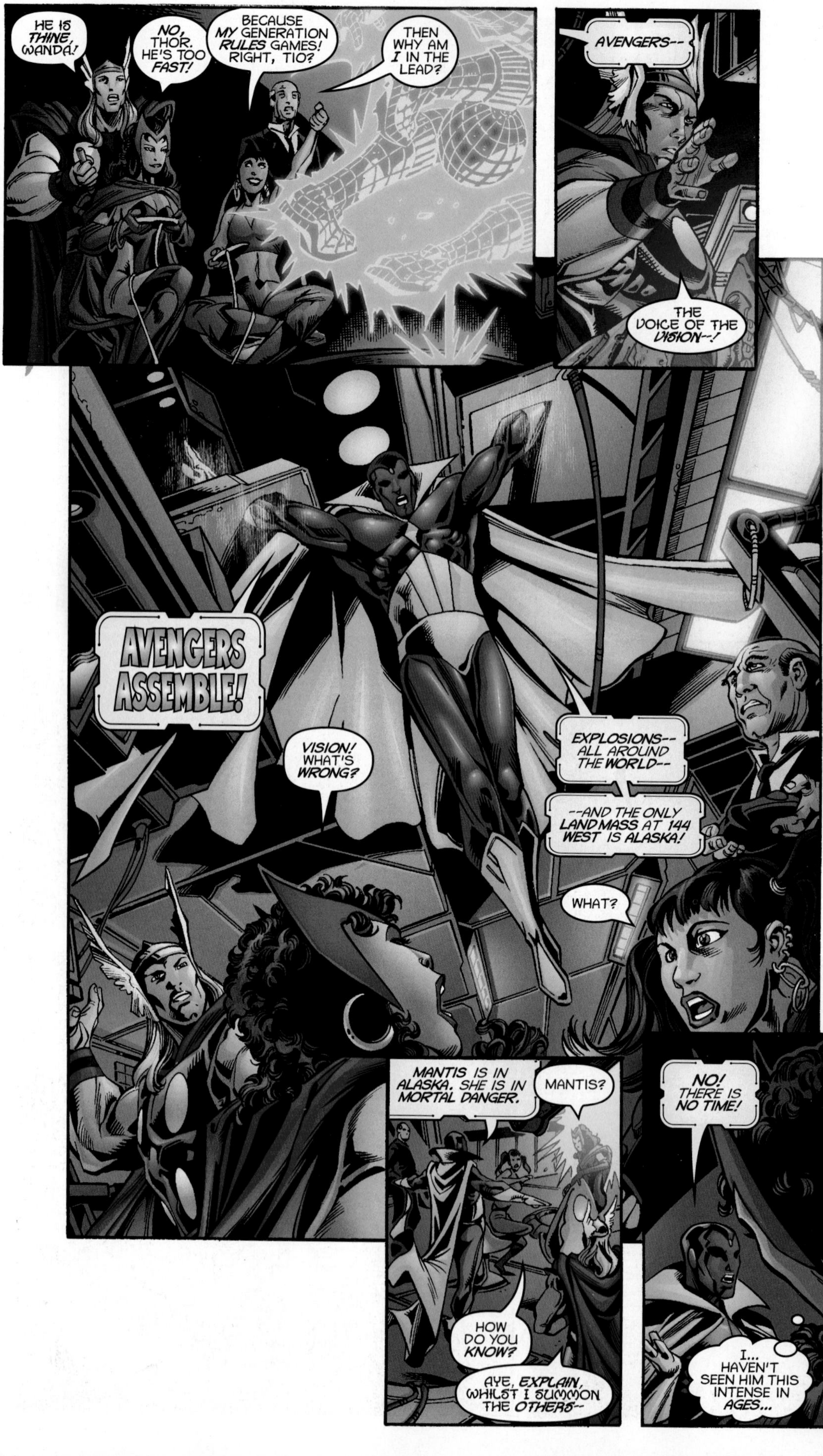
HE IS THINE, WANDA!
NO, THOR. HE'S TOO FAST!
BECAUSE MY GENERATION RULES GAMES! RIGHT, TIO?
THEN WHY AM I IN THE LEAD?
AVENGERS--
THE VOICE OF THE VISION--!
AVENGERS ASSEMBLE!
VISION! WHAT'S WRONG?
EXPLOSIONS-- ALL AROUND THE WORLD--
--AND THE ONLY LAND MASS AT 144 WEST IS ALASKA!
WHAT?
MANTIS IS IN ALASKA. SHE IS IN MORTAL DANGER.
MANTIS?
HOW DO YOU KNOW?
AYE, EXPLAIN, WHILST I SUMMON THE OTHERS--
NO! THERE IS NO TIME!
I... HAVEN'T SEEN HIM THIS INTENSE IN AGES...

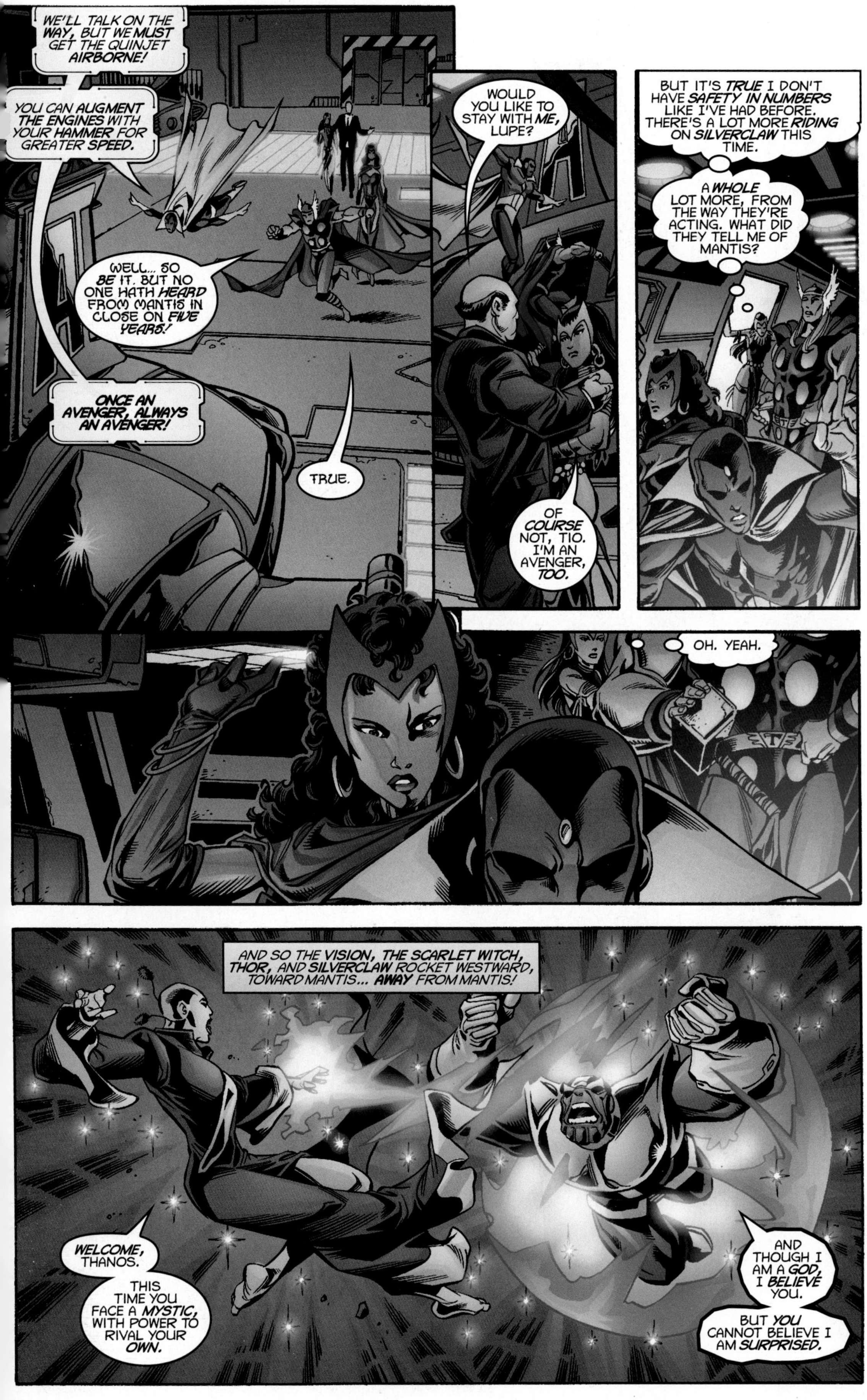
WE'LL TALK ON THE WAY, BUT WE MUST GET THE QUINJET AIRBORNE!
YOU CAN AUGMENT THE ENGINES WITH YOUR HAMMER FOR GREATER SPEED.
WELL... SO BE IT. BUT NO ONE HATH HEARD FROM MANTIS IN CLOSE ON FIVE YEARS!
ONCE AN AVENGER, ALWAYS AN AVENGER!
TRUE.
WOULD YOU LIKE TO STAY WITH ME, LUPE?
OF COURSE NOT, TIO. I'M AN AVENGER, TOO.
BUT IT'S TRUE I DON'T HAVE SAFETY IN NUMBERS LIKE I'VE HAD BEFORE. THERE'S A LOT MORE RIDING ON SILVERCLAW THIS TIME.
A WHOLE LOT MORE, FROM THE WAY THEY'RE ACTING. WHAT DID THEY TELL ME OF MANTIS?
OH. YEAH.
AND SO THE VISION, THE SCARLET WITCH, THOR, AND SILVERCLAW ROCKET WESTWARD, TOWARD MANTIS... AWAY FROM MANTIS!
WELCOME, THANOS.
THIS TIME YOU FACE A MYSTIC, WITH POWER TO RIVAL YOUR OWN.
AND THOUGH I AM A GOD, I BELIEVE YOU.
BUT YOU CANNOT BELIEVE I AM SURPRISED.

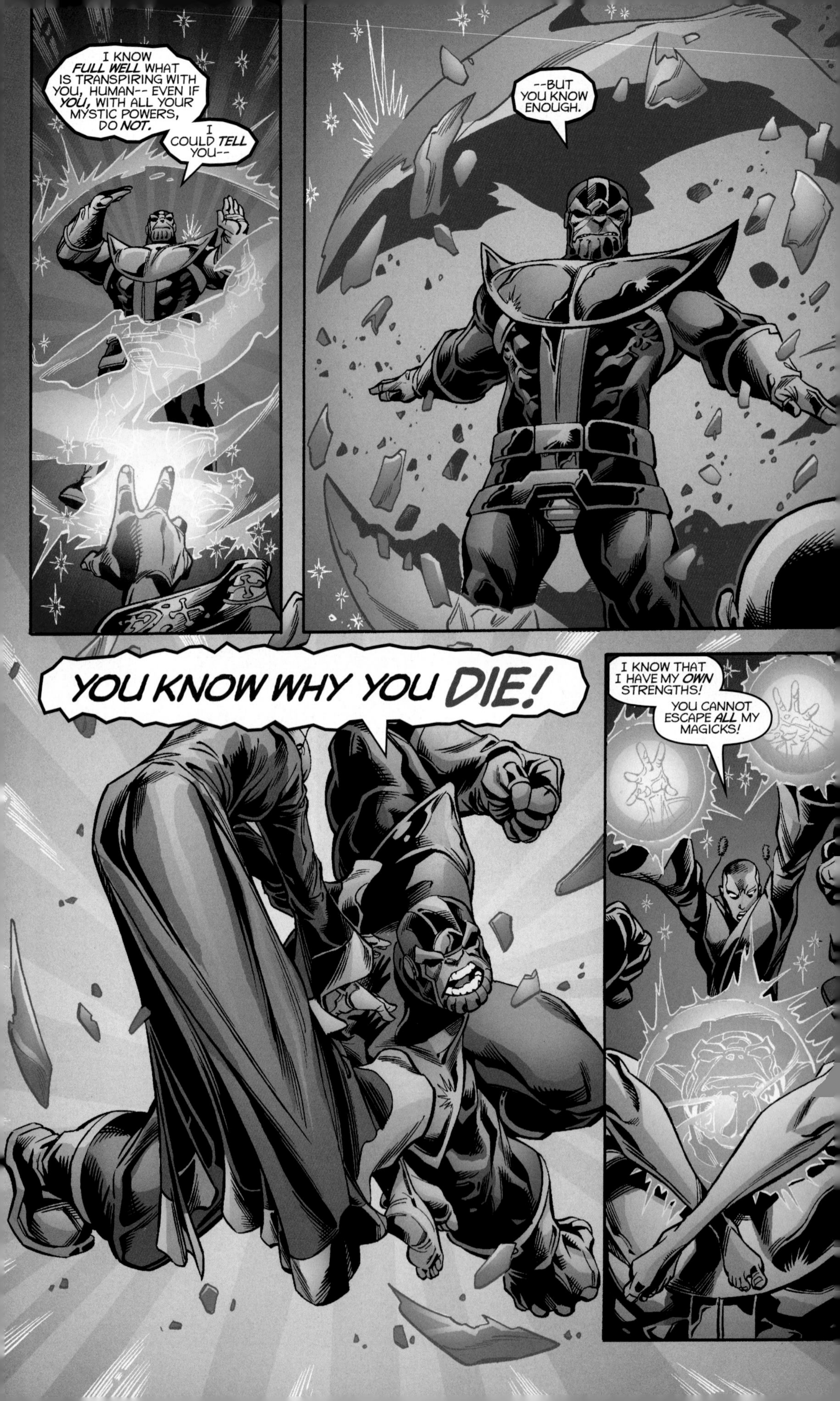
I KNOW FULL WELL WHAT IS TRANSPIRING WITH YOU, HUMAN-- EVEN IF YOU, WITH ALL YOUR MYSTIC POWERS, DO NOT.
I COULD TELL YOU--
--BUT YOU KNOW ENOUGH.
YOU KNOW WHY YOU DIE!
I KNOW THAT I HAVE MY OWN STRENGTHS!
YOU CANNOT ESCAPE ALL MY MAGICKS!

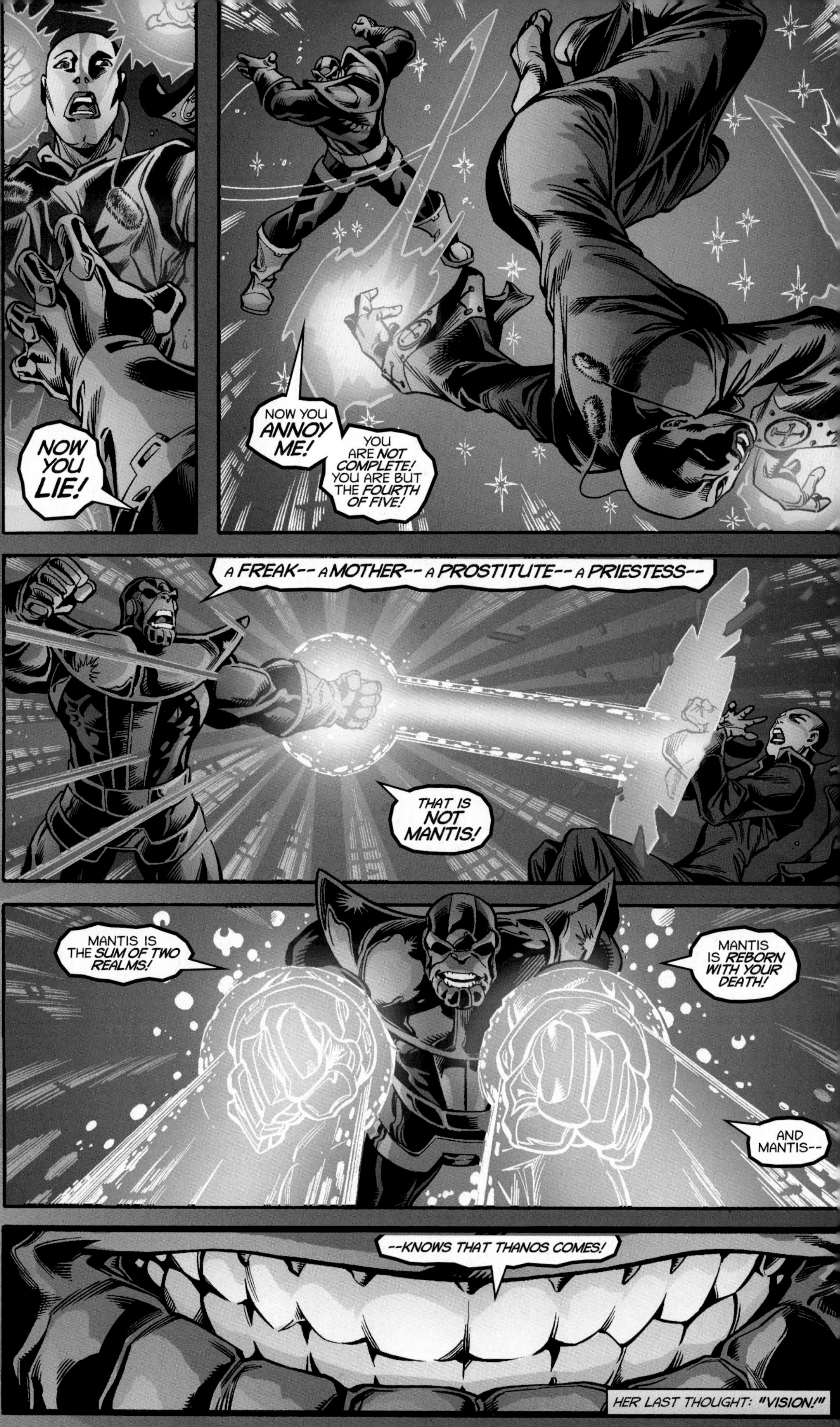
NOW YOU LIE!
NOW YOU ANNOY ME!
YOU ARE NOT COMPLETE! YOU ARE BUT THE FOURTH OF FIVE!
A FREAK-- A MOTHER-- A PROSTITUTE-- A PRIESTESS--
THAT IS NOT MANTIS!
MANTIS IS THE SUM OF TWO REALMS!
MANTIS IS REBORN WITH YOUR DEATH!
AND MANTIS--
--KNOWS THAT THANOS COMES!
HER LAST THOUGHT: "VISION!"

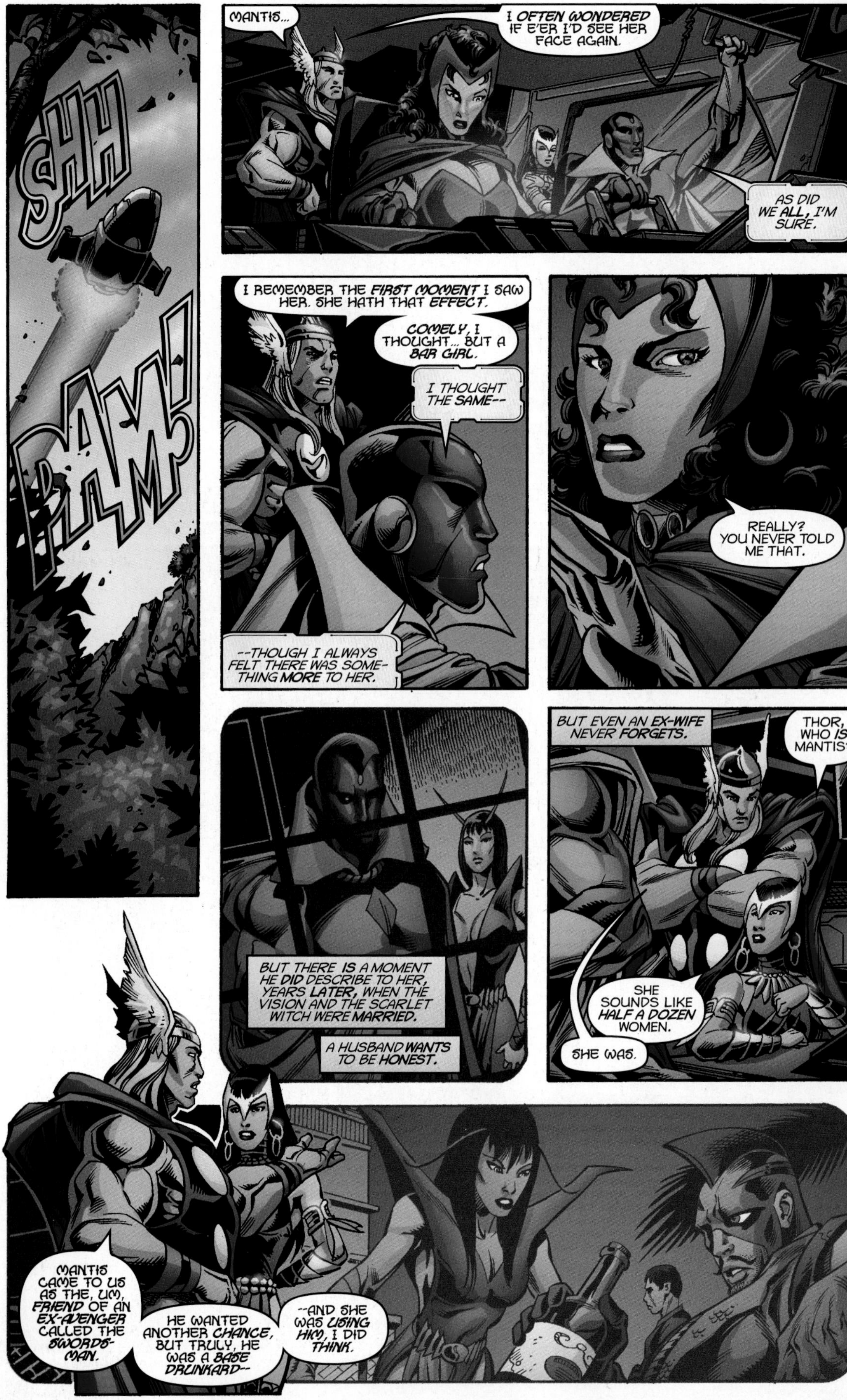
SHH
BAM!
BLAM!
MANTIS...
I OFTEN WONDERED IF E'ER I'D SEE HER FACE AGAIN.
AS DID WE ALL, I'M SURE.
I REMEMBER THE FIRST MOMENT I SAW HER. SHE HATH THAT EFFECT.
COMELY, I THOUGHT... BUT A BAR GIRL.
I THOUGHT THE SAME--
--THOUGH I ALWAYS FELT THERE WAS SOMETHING MORE TO HER.
REALLY? YOU NEVER TOLD ME THAT.
BUT THERE IS A MOMENT HE DID DESCRIBE TO HER, YEARS LATER, WHEN THE VISION AND THE SCARLET WITCH WERE MARRIED.
A HUSBAND WANTS TO BE HONEST.
BUT EVEN AN EX-WIFE NEVER FORGETS.
THOR, WHO IS MANTIS?
SHE SOUNDS LIKE HALF A DOZEN WOMEN.
SHE WAS.
MANTIS CAME TO US AS THE, UM, FRIEND OF AN EX-AVENGER CALLED THE SWORDSMAN.
HE WANTED ANOTHER CHANCE, BUT TRULY, HE WAS A BASE DRUNKARD--
--AND SHE WAS USING HIM, I DID THINK.

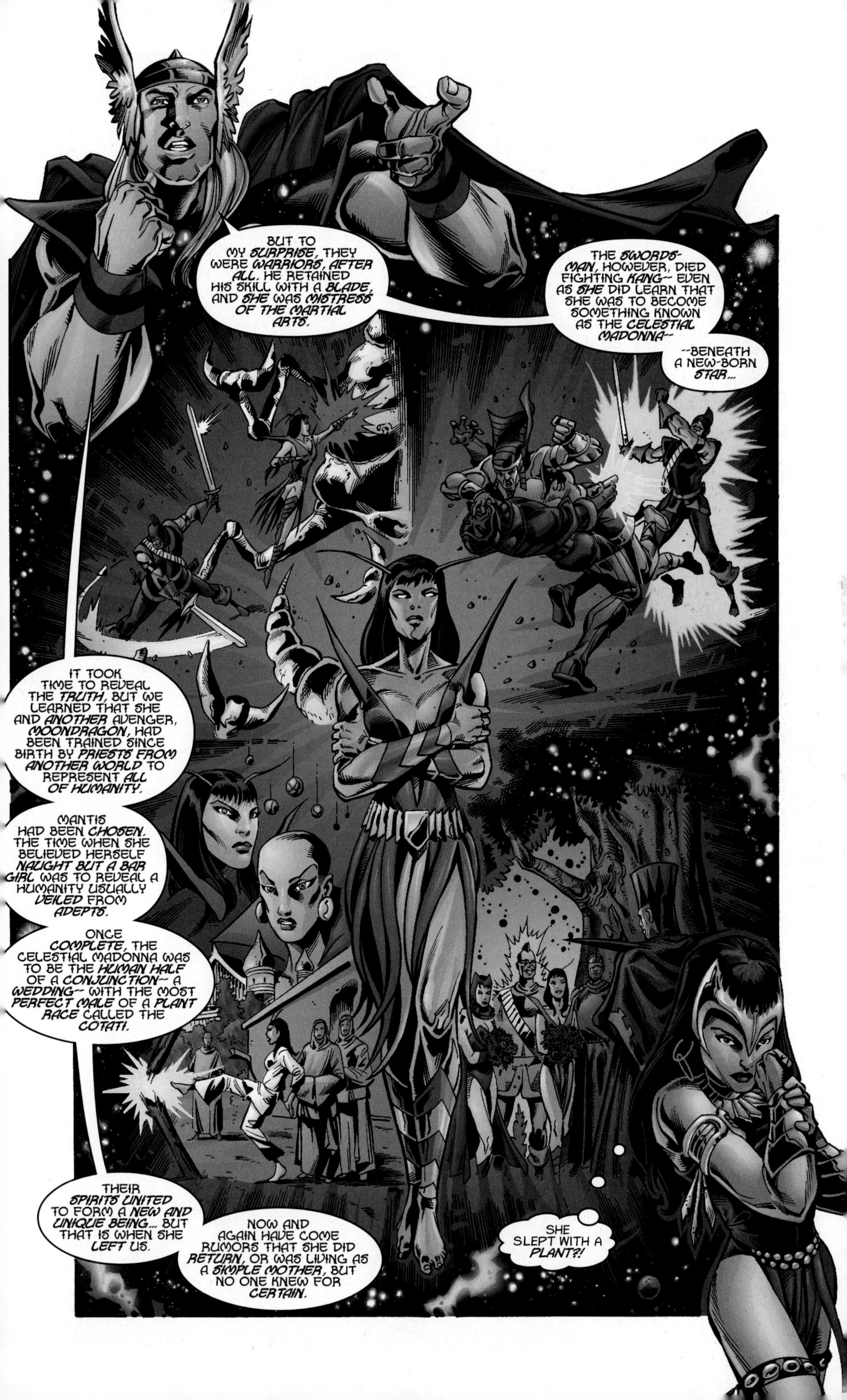
BUT TO MY SURPRISE, THEY WERE WARRIORS, AFTER ALL. HE RETAINED HIS SKILL WITH A BLADE, AND SHE WAS MISTRESS OF THE MARTIAL ARTS.
THE SWORDS-MAN, HOWEVER, DIED FIGHTING KANG-- EVEN AS SHE DID LEARN THAT SHE WAS TO BECOME SOMETHING KNOWN AS THE CELESTIAL MADONNA--
--BENEATH A NEW-BORN STAR...
IT TOOK TIME TO REVEAL THE TRUTH, BUT WE LEARNED THAT SHE AND ANOTHER AVENGER, MOONDRAGON, HAD BEEN TRAINED SINCE BIRTH BY PRIESTS FROM ANOTHER WORLD TO REPRESENT ALL OF HUMANITY.
MANTIS HAD BEEN CHOSEN. THE TIME WHEN SHE BELIEVED HERSELF NAUGHT BUT A BAR GIRL WAS TO REVEAL A HUMANITY USUALLY VEILED FROM ADEPTS.
ONCE COMPLETE, THE CELESTIAL MADONNA WAS TO BE THE HUMAN HALF OF A CONJUNCTION-- A WEDDING-- WITH THE MOST PERFECT MALE OF A PLANT RACE CALLED THE COTATI.
THEIR SPIRITS UNITED TO FORM A NEW AND UNIQUE BEING... BUT THAT IS WHEN SHE LEFT US.
NOW AND AGAIN HAVE COME RUMORS THAT SHE DID RETURN, OR WAS LIVING AS A SIMPLE MOTHER, BUT NO ONE KNEW FOR CERTAIN.
SHE SLEPT WITH A PLANT?!

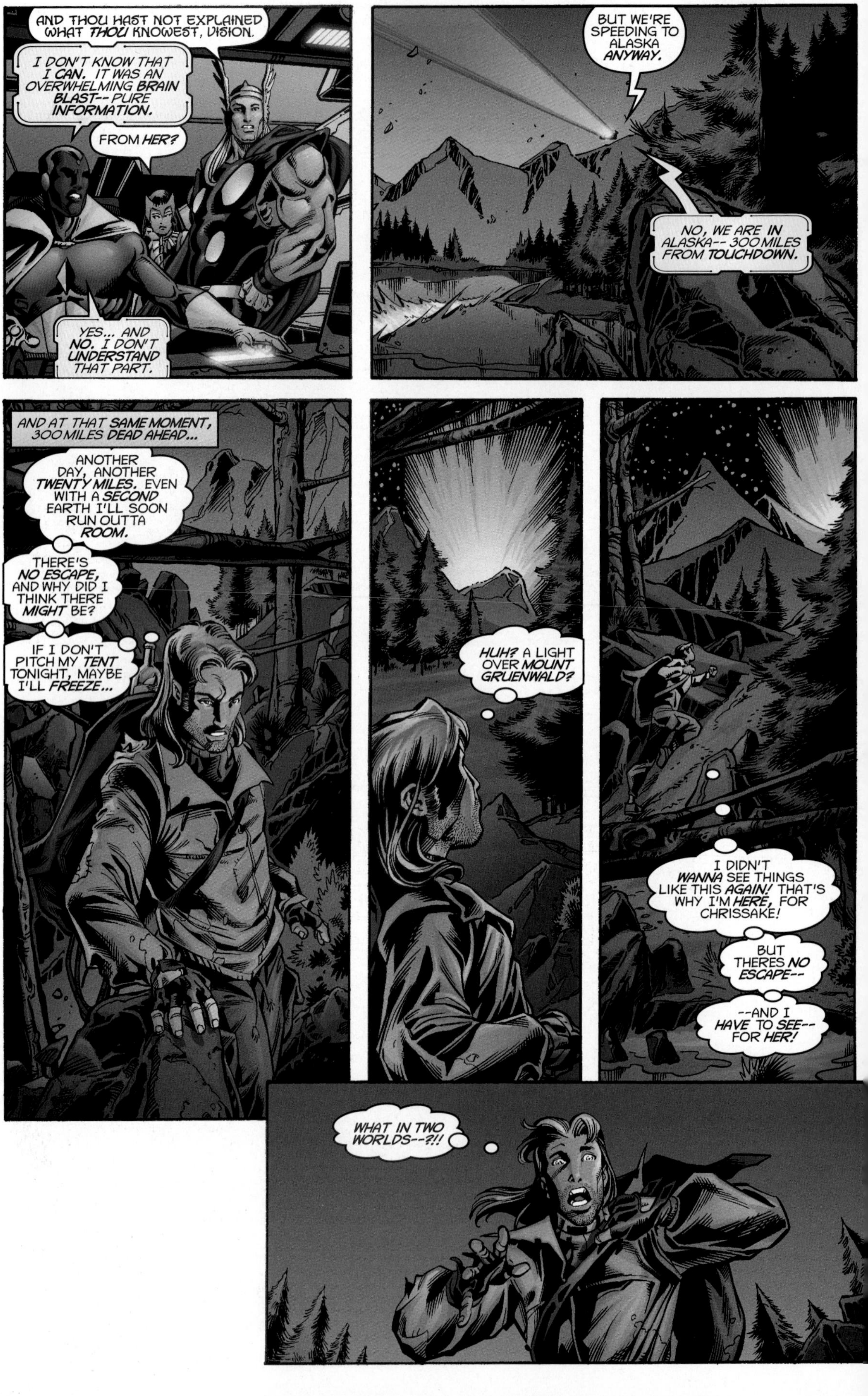
AND THOU HAST NOT EXPLAINED WHAT THOU KNOWEST, VISION.
I DON'T KNOW THAT I CAN. IT WAS AN OVERWHELMING BRAIN BLAST--PURE INFORMATION.
FROM HER?
YES... AND NO. I DON'T UNDERSTAND THAT PART.
BUT WE'RE SPEEDING TO ALASKA ANYWAY.
NO, WE ARE IN ALASKA-- 300 MILES FROM TOUCHDOWN.
AND AT THAT SAME MOMENT, 300 MILES DEAD AHEAD...
ANOTHER DAY, ANOTHER TWENTY MILES. EVEN WITH A SECOND EARTH I'LL SOON RUN OUTTA ROOM.
THERE'S NO ESCAPE, AND WHY DID I THINK THERE MIGHT BE?
IF I DON'T PITCH MY TENT TONIGHT, MAYBE I'LL FREEZE...
HUH? A LIGHT OVER MOUNT GRUENWALD?
I DIDN'T WANNA SEE THINGS LIKE THIS AGAIN! THAT'S WHY I'M HERE, FOR CHRISSAKE!
BUT THERES NO ESCAPE--
--AND I HAVE TO SEE-- FOR HER!
WHAT IN TWO WORLDS--?!!

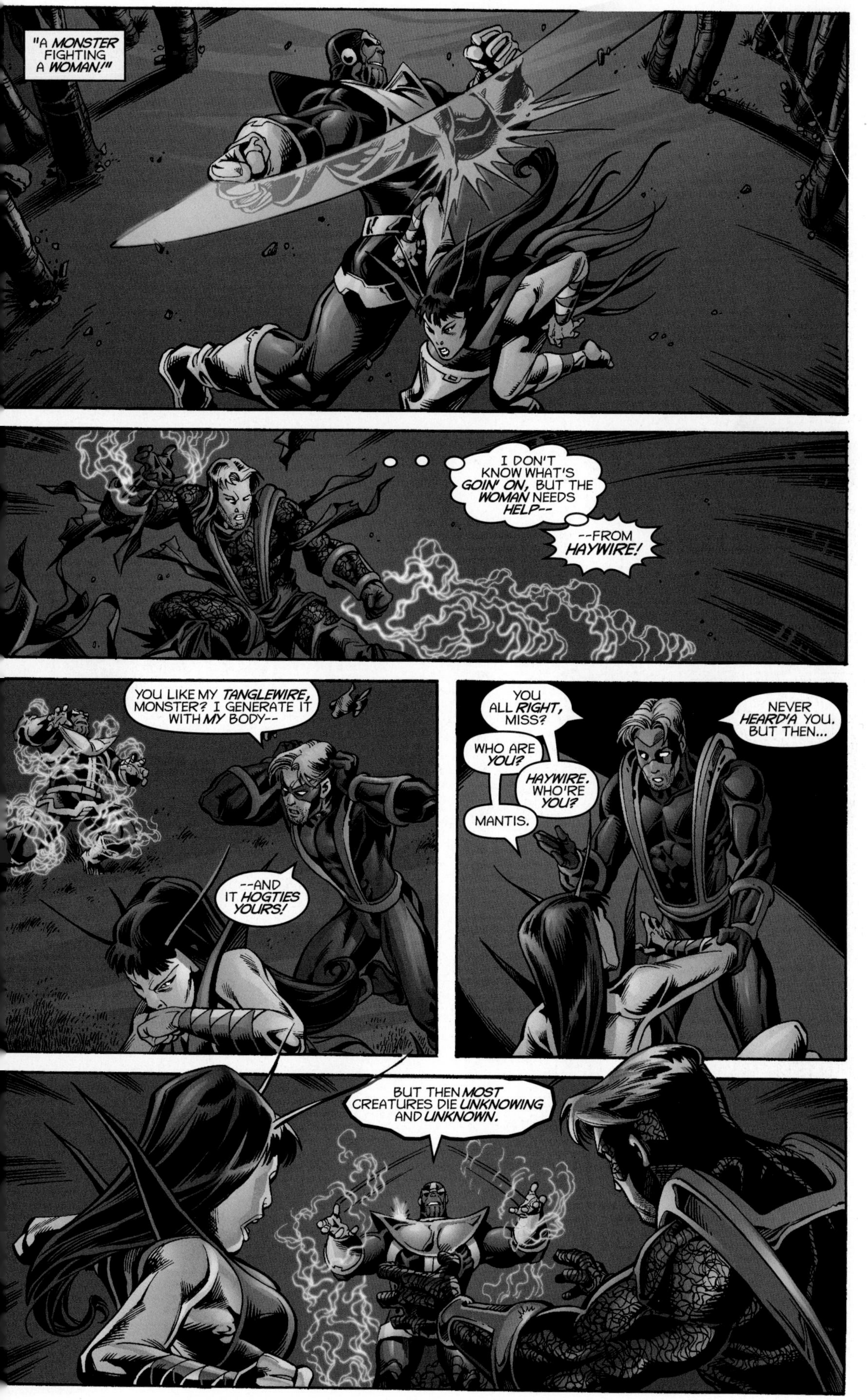
"A MONSTER FIGHTING A WOMAN!"
I DON'T KNOW WHAT'S GOIN' ON, BUT THE WOMAN NEEDS HELP--
--FROM HAYWIRE!
YOU LIKE MY TANGLEWIRE, MONSTER? I GENERATE IT WITH MY BODY--
--AND IT HOGTIES YOURS!
YOU ALL RIGHT, MISS?
WHO ARE YOU?
HAYWIRE. WHO'RE YOU?
MANTIS.
NEVER HEARD'A YOU. BUT THEN...
BUT THEN MOST CREATURES DIE UNKNOWING AND UNKNOWN.

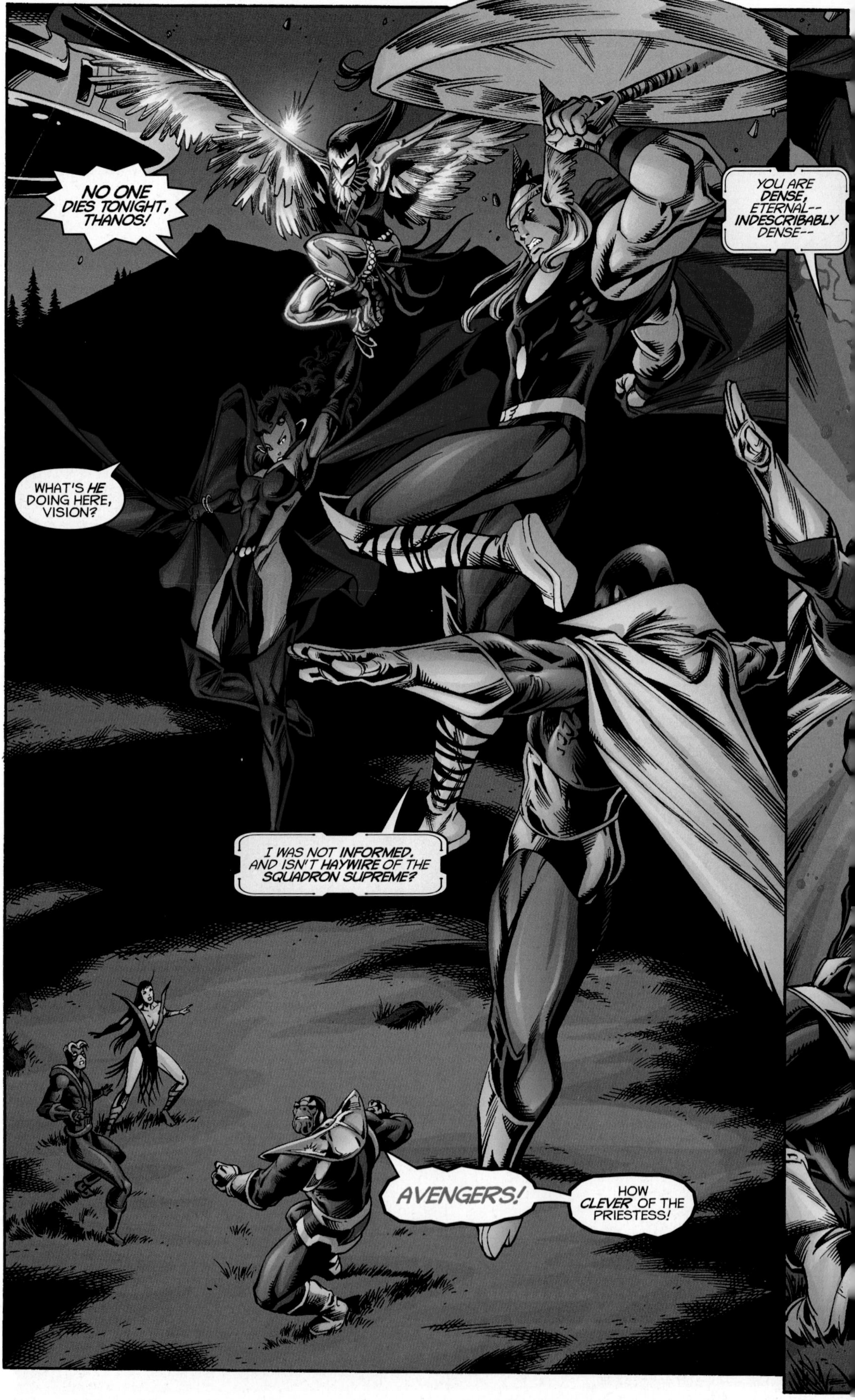

NO ONE DIES TONIGHT, THANOS!
YOU ARE DENSE, ETERNAL-- INDESCRIBABLY DENSE--
WHAT'S HE DOING HERE, VISION?
I WAS NOT INFORMED. AND ISN'T HAYWIRE OF THE SQUADRON SUPREME?
AVENGERS!
HOW CLEVER OF THE PRIESTESS!

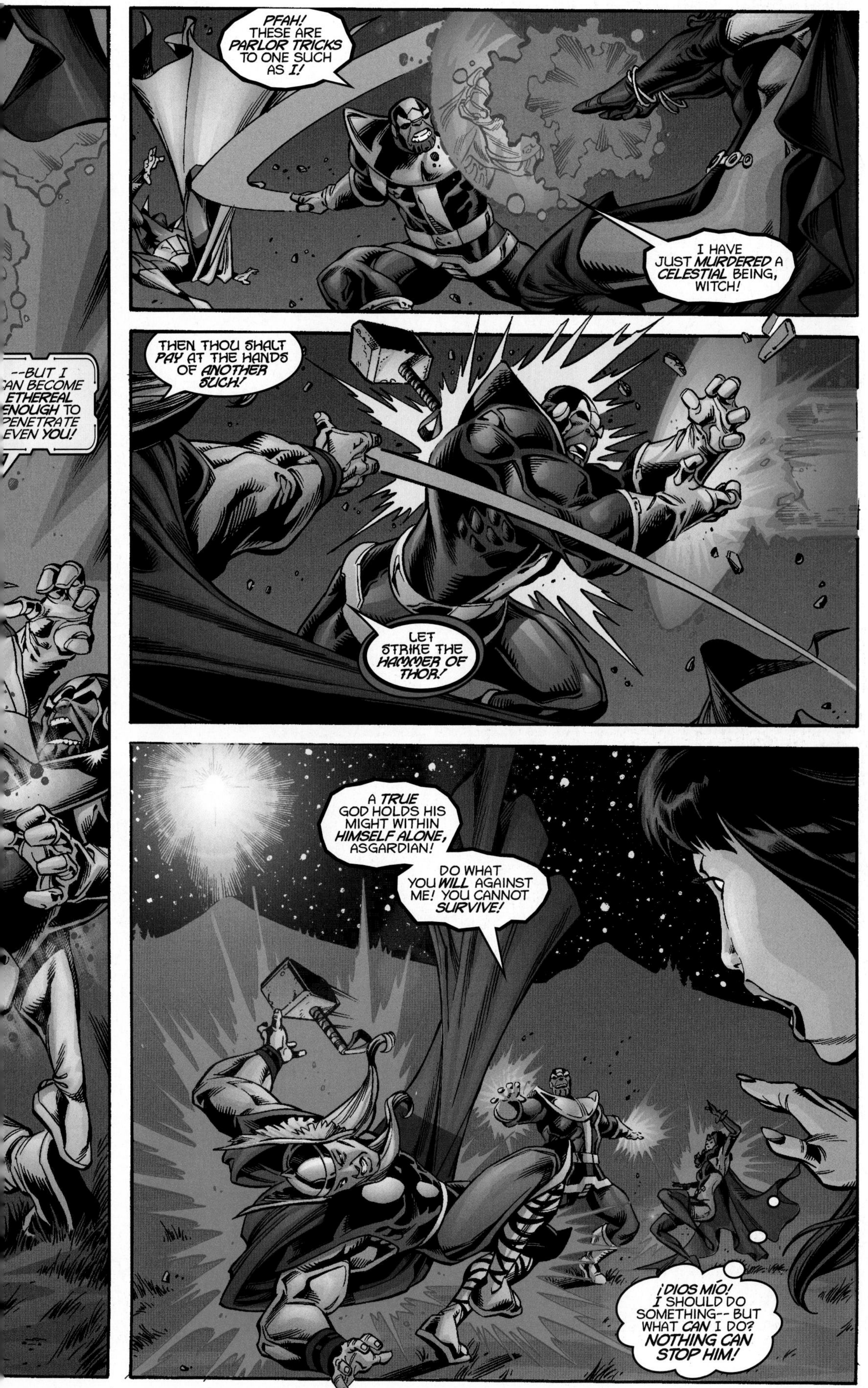

PFAH! THESE ARE PARLOR TRICKS TO ONE SUCH AS I!
I HAVE JUST MURDERED A CELESTIAL BEING, WITCH!
--BUT I CAN BECOME ETHEREAL ENOUGH TO PENETRATE EVEN YOU!
THEN THOU SHALT PAY AT THE HANDS OF ANOTHER SUCH!
LET STRIKE THE HAMMER OF THOR!
A TRUE GOD HOLDS HIS MIGHT WITHIN HIMSELF ALONE, ASGARDIAN!
DO WHAT YOU WILL AGAINST ME! YOU CANNOT SURVIVE!
¡DIOS MÍO! I SHOULD DO SOMETHING-- BUT WHAT CAN I DO? NOTHING CAN STOP HIM!

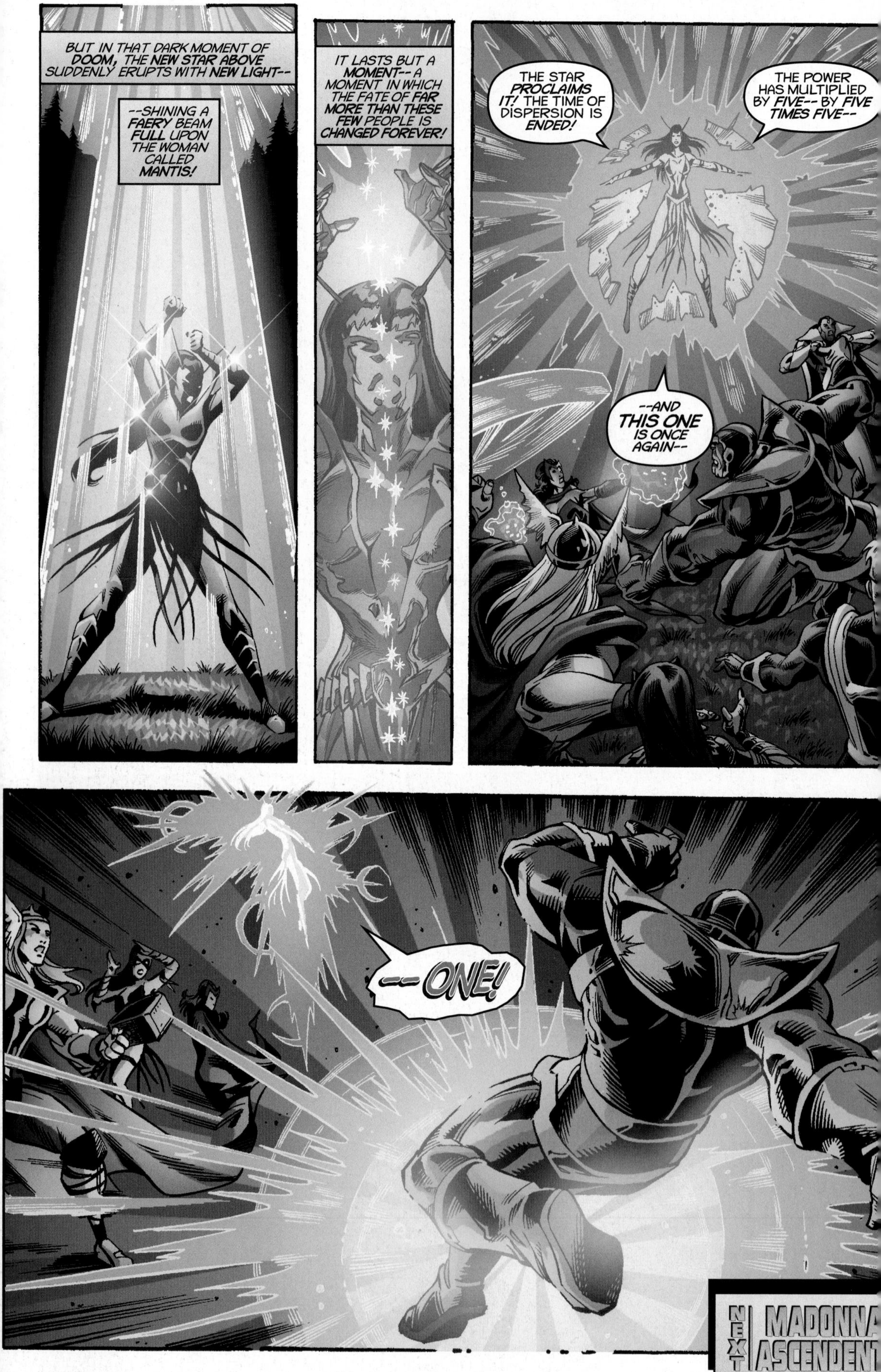
BUT IN THAT DARK MOMENT OF DOOM, THE NEW STAR ABOVE SUDDENLY ERUPTS WITH NEW LIGHT--
--SHINING A FAERY BEAM FULL UPON THE WOMAN CALLED MANTIS!
IT LASTS BUT A MOMENT-- A MOMENT IN WHICH THE FATE OF FAR MORE THAN THESE FEW PEOPLE IS CHANGED FOREVER!
THE STAR PROCLAIMS IT! THE TIME OF DISPERSION IS ENDED!
THE POWER HAS MULTIPLIED BY FIVE-- BY FIVE TIMES FIVE--
--AND THIS ONE IS ONCE AGAIN--
--ONE!
NEXT
MADONNA ASCENDENT

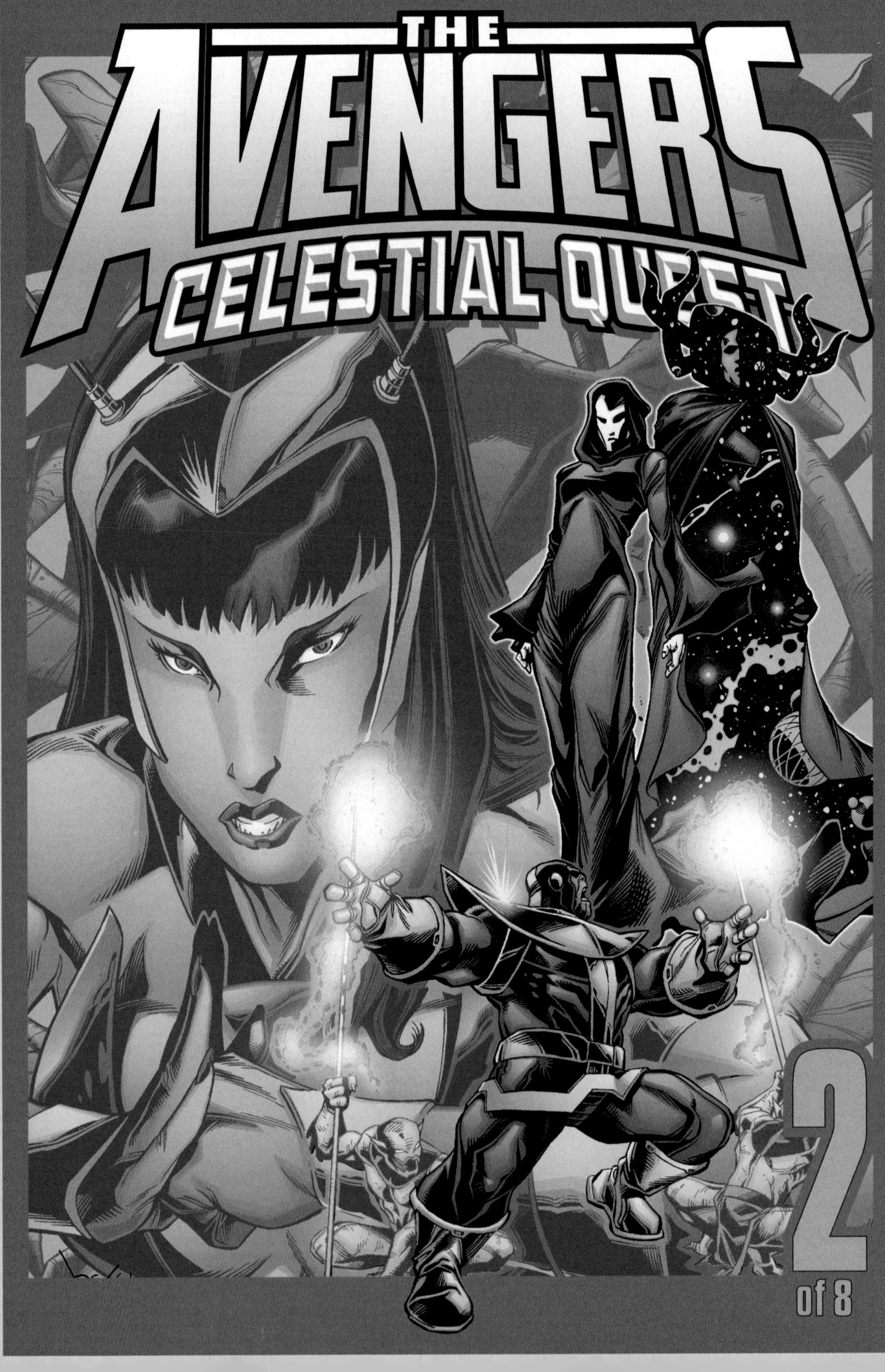
THE AVENGERS
CELESTIAL QUEST
2
of 8

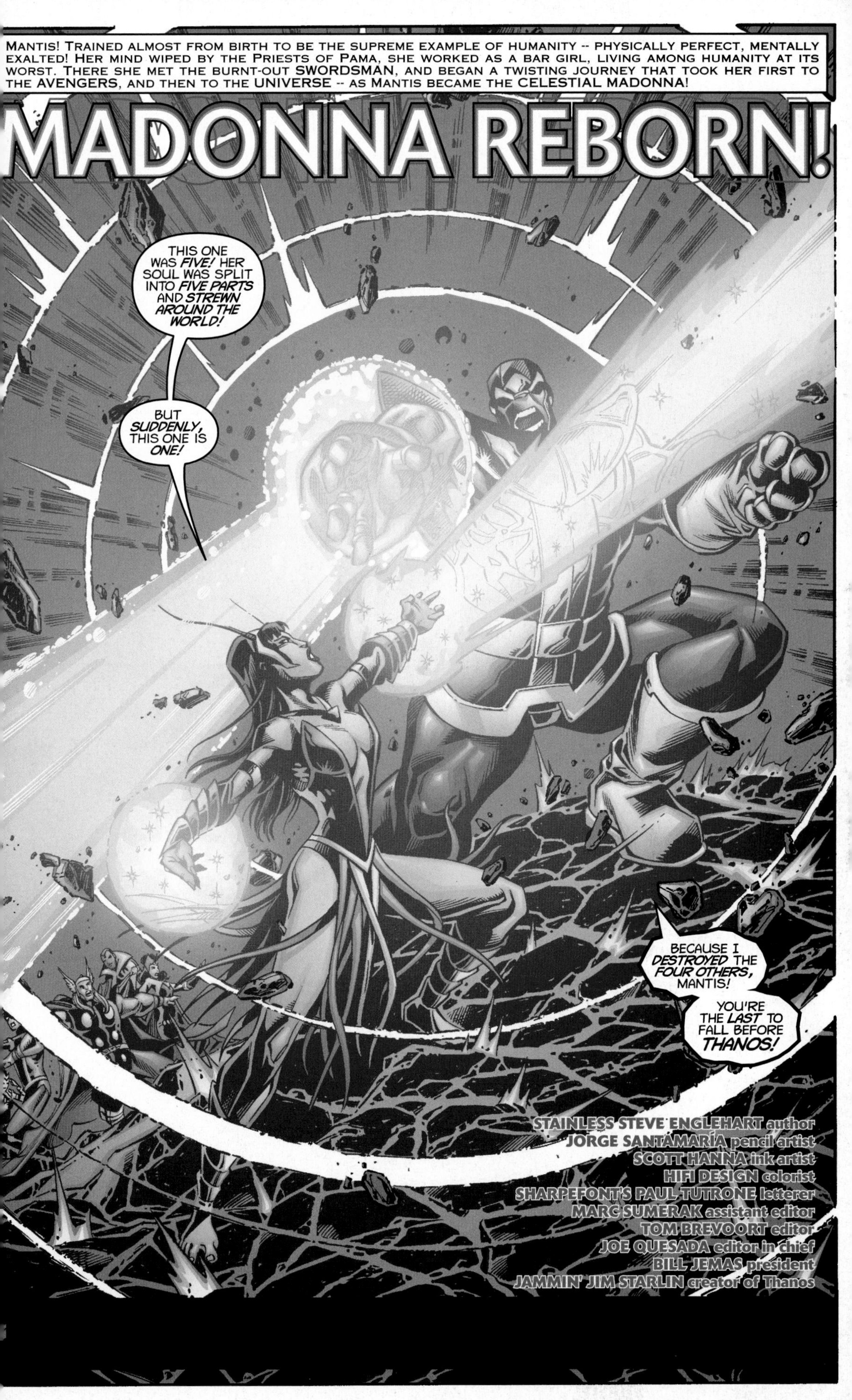

MANTIS! TRAINED ALMOST FROM BIRTH TO BE THE SUPREME EXAMPLE OF HUMANITY -- PHYSICALLY PERFECT, MENTALLY EXALTED! HER MIND WIPED BY THE PRIESTS OF PAMA, SHE WORKED AS A BAR GIRL, LIVING AMONG HUMANITY AT ITS WORST. THERE SHE MET THE BURNT-OUT SWORDSMAN, AND BEGAN A TWISTING JOURNEY THAT TOOK HER FIRST TO THE AVENGERS, AND THEN TO THE UNIVERSE -- AS MANTIS BECAME THE CELESTIAL MADONNA!
MADONNA REBORN!
THIS ONE WAS FIVE! HER SOUL WAS SPLIT INTO FIVE PARTS AND STREWN AROUND THE WORLD!
BUT SUDDENLY, THIS ONE IS ONE!
BECAUSE I DESTROYED THE FOUR OTHERS, MANTIS!
YOU'RE THE LAST TO FALL BEFORE THANOS!
STAINLESS STEVE ENGLEHART author
JORGE SANTAMARÍA pencil artist
SCOTT HANNA ink artist
HIFI DESIGN colorist
SHARPEFONT'S PAUL TUTRONE letterer
MARC SUMERAK assistant editor
TOM BREVOORT editor
JOE QUESADA editor in chief
BILL JEMAS president
JAMMIN' JIM STARLIN creator of Thanos

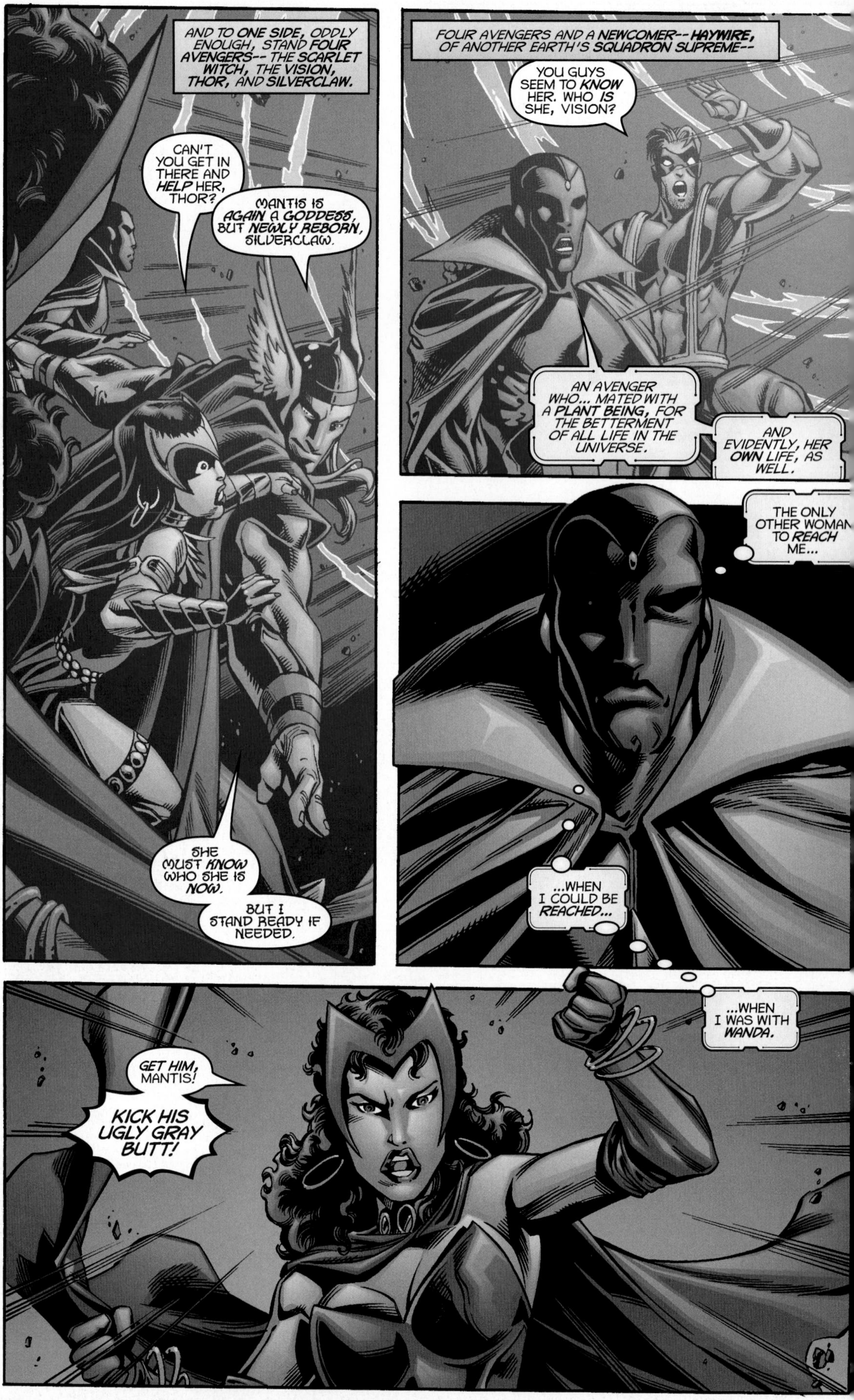
AND TO ONE SIDE, ODDLY ENOUGH, STAND FOUR AVENGERS-- THE SCARLET WITCH, THE VISION, THOR, AND SILVERCLAW.
CAN'T YOU GET IN THERE AND HELP HER, THOR?
MANTIS IS AGAIN A GODDESS, BUT NEWLY REBORN, SILVERCLAW.
SHE MUST KNOW WHO SHE IS NOW.
BUT I STAND READY IF NEEDED.
FOUR AVENGERS AND A NEWCOMER-- HAYWIRE, OF ANOTHER EARTH'S SQUADRON SUPREME--
YOU GUYS SEEM TO KNOW HER. WHO IS SHE, VISION?
AN AVENGER WHO... MATED WITH A PLANT BEING, FOR THE BETTERMENT OF ALL LIFE IN THE UNIVERSE.
AND EVIDENTLY, HER OWN LIFE, AS WELL.
THE ONLY OTHER WOMAN TO REACH ME...
...WHEN I COULD BE REACHED...
...WHEN I WAS WITH WANDA.
GET HIM, MANTIS!
KICK HIS UGLY GRAY BUTT!

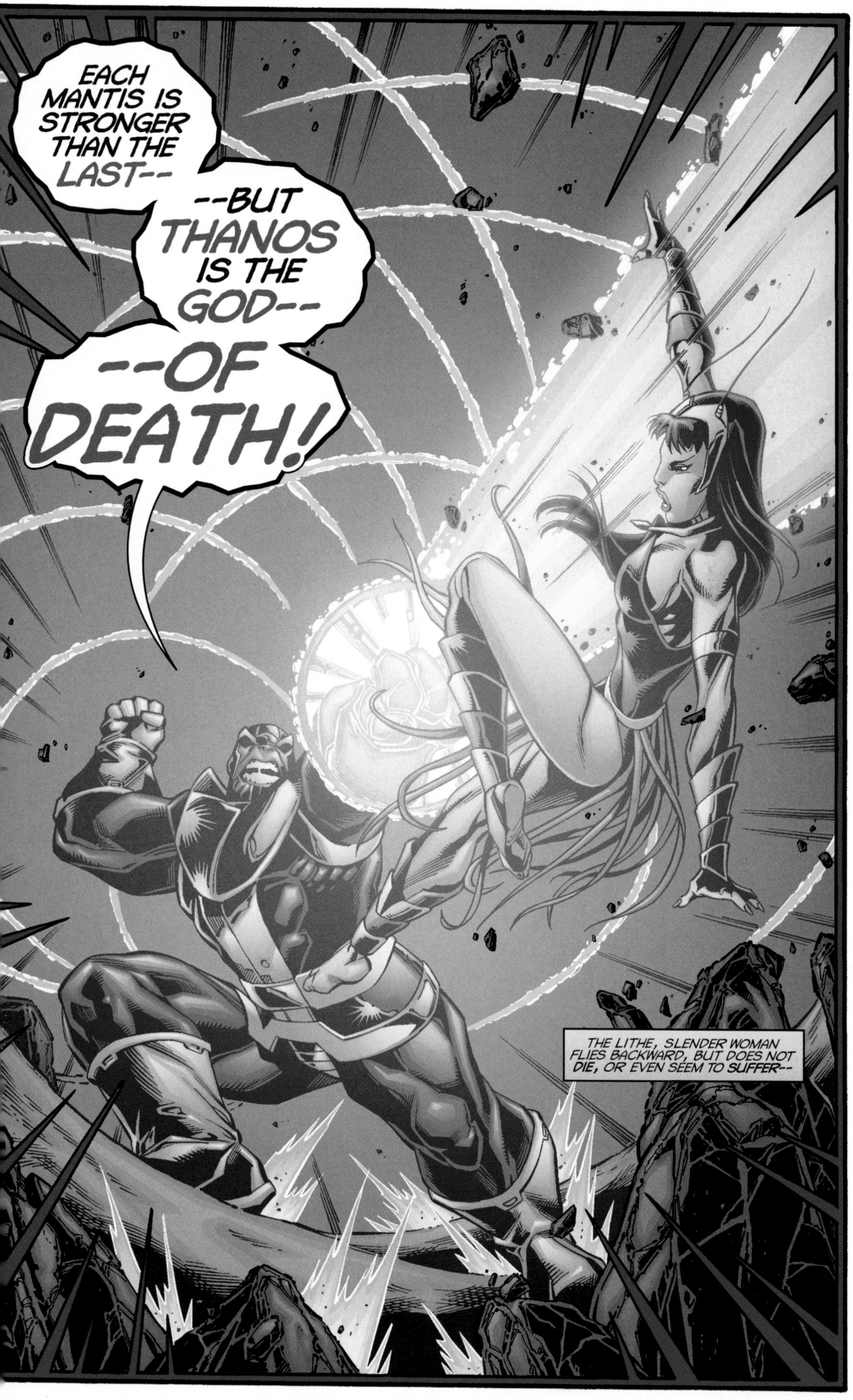
EACH MANTIS IS STRONGER THAN THE LAST--
--BUT THANOS IS THE GOD--
--OF DEATH!
THE LITHE, SLENDER WOMAN FLIES BACKWARD, BUT DOES NOT DIE, OR EVEN SEEM TO SUFFER--

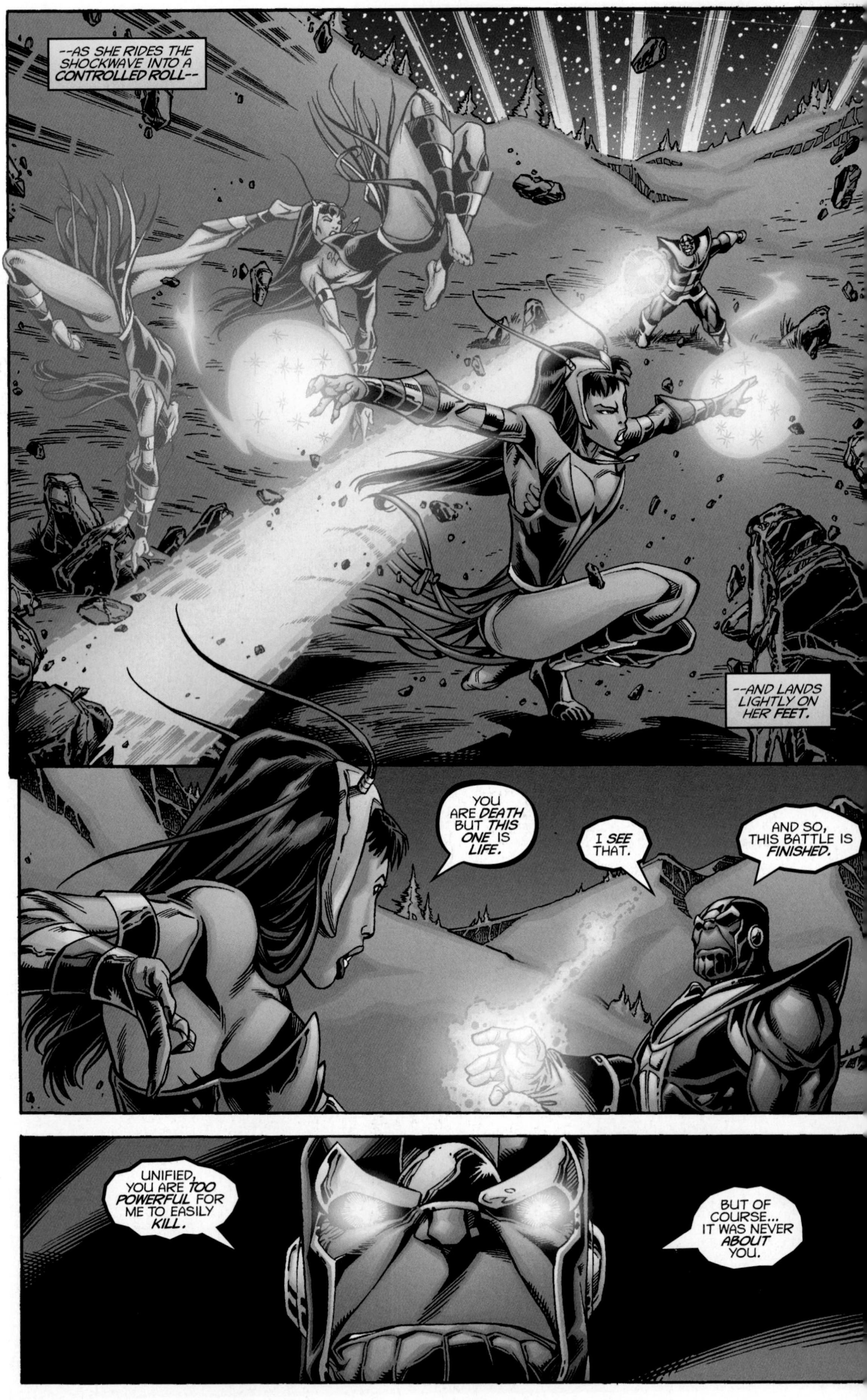
--AS SHE RIDES THE SHOCKWAVE INTO A CONTROLLED ROLL--
--AND LANDS LIGHTLY ON HER FEET.
YOU ARE DEATH BUT THIS ONE IS LIFE.
I SEE THAT.
AND SO, THIS BATTLE IS FINISHED.
UNIFIED, YOU ARE TOO POWERFUL FOR ME TO EASILY KILL.
BUT OF COURSE... IT WAS NEVER ABOUT YOU.

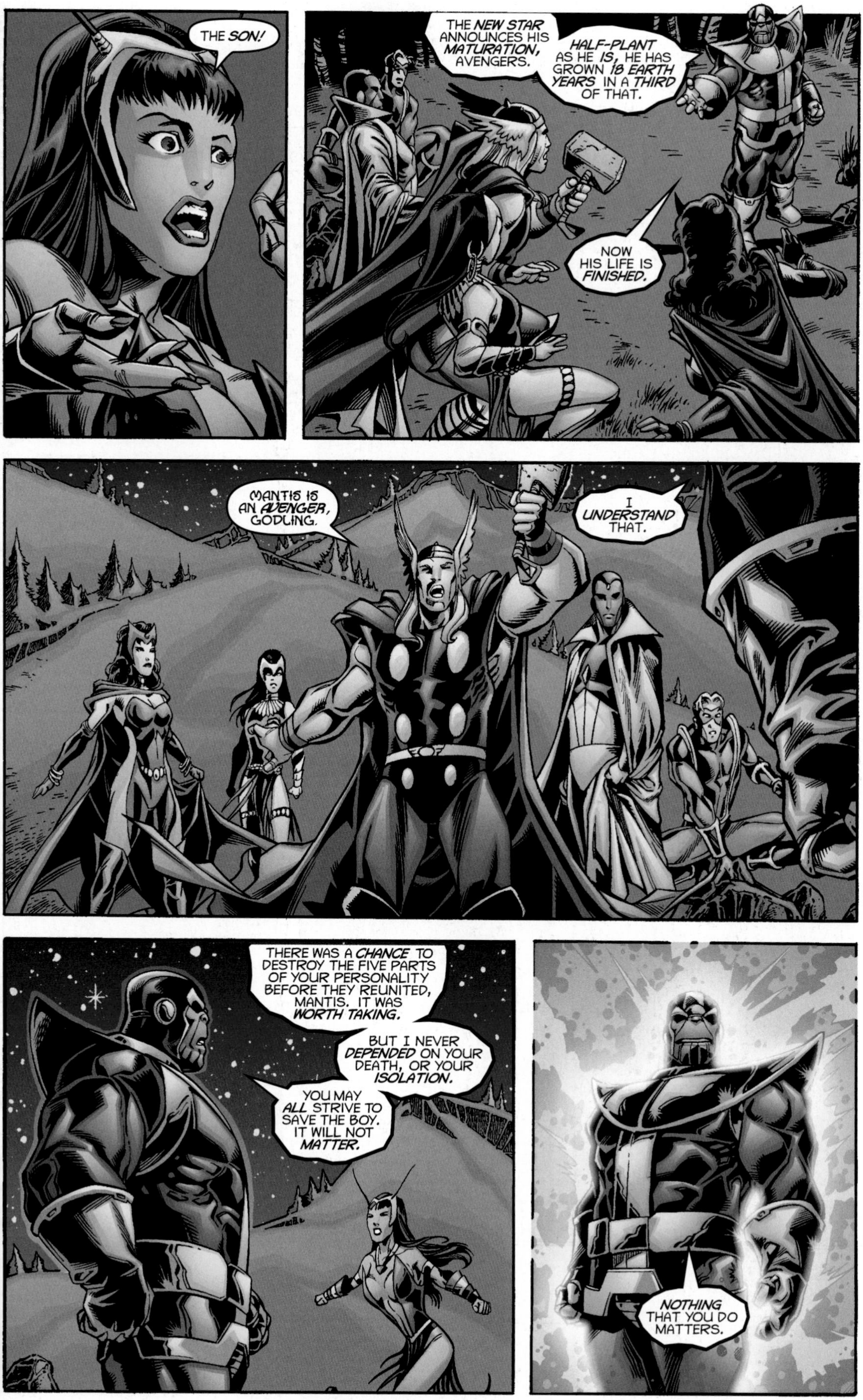
THE SON!
THE NEW STAR ANNOUNCES HIS MATURATION, AVENGERS.
HALF-PLANT AS HE IS, HE HAS GROWN 18 EARTH YEARS IN A THIRD OF THAT.
NOW HIS LIFE IS FINISHED.
MANTIS IS AN AVENGER, GODLING.
I UNDERSTAND THAT.
THERE WAS A CHANCE TO DESTROY THE FIVE PARTS OF YOUR PERSONALITY BEFORE THEY REUNITED, MANTIS. IT WAS WORTH TAKING.
BUT I NEVER DEPENDED ON YOUR DEATH, OR YOUR ISOLATION.
YOU MAY ALL STRIVE TO SAVE THE BOY. IT WILL NOT MATTER.
NOTHING THAT YOU DO MATTERS.

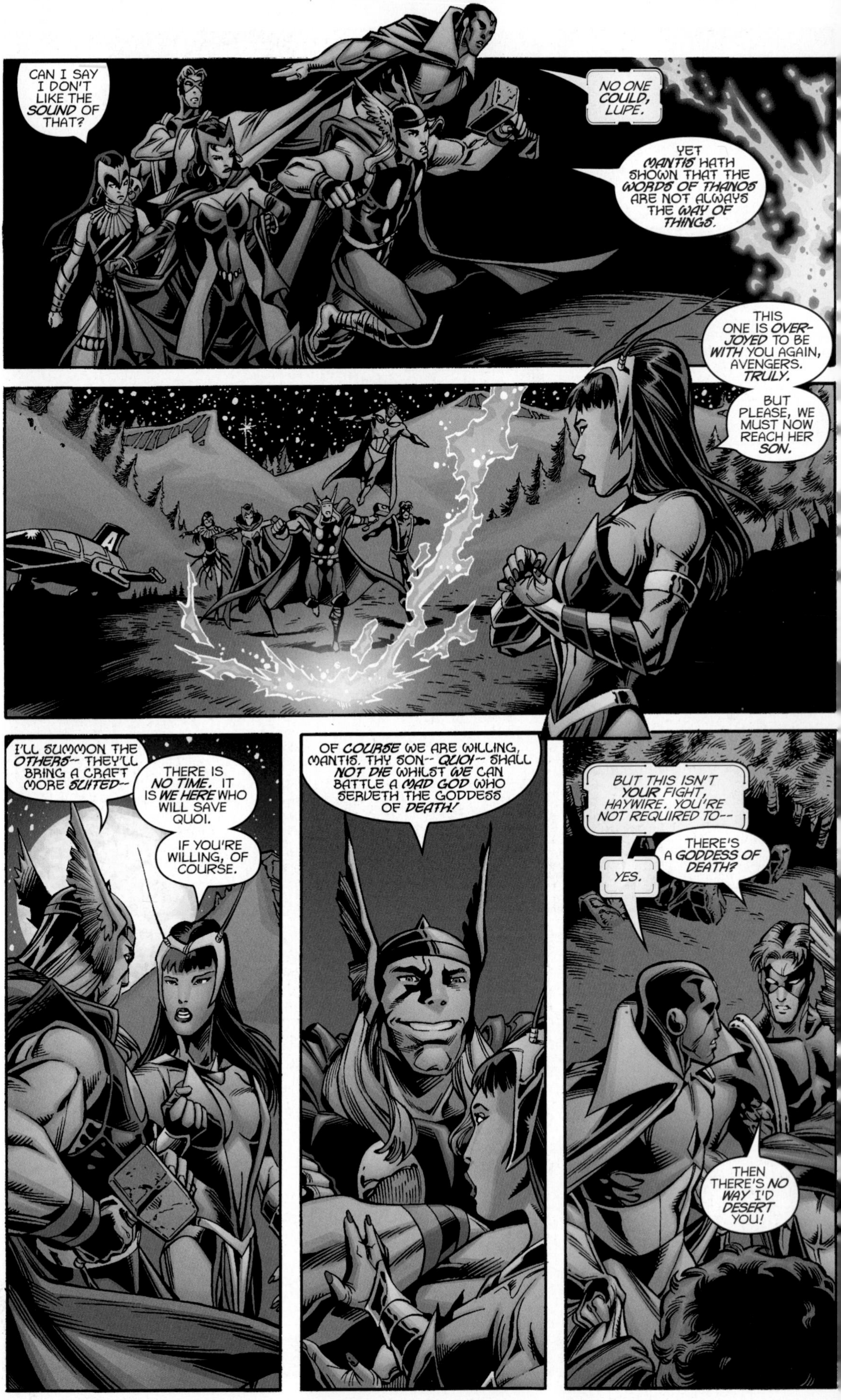
CAN I SAY I DON'T LIKE THE SOUND OF THAT?
NO ONE COULD, LUPE.
YET MANTIS HATH SHOWN THAT THE WORDS OF THANOS ARE NOT ALWAYS THE WAY OF THINGS.
THIS ONE IS OVERJOYED TO BE WITH YOU AGAIN, AVENGERS. TRULY.
BUT PLEASE, WE MUST NOW REACH HER SON.
I'LL SUMMON THE OTHERS-- THEY'LL BRING A CRAFT MORE SUITED--
THERE IS NO TIME. IT IS WE HERE WHO WILL SAVE QUOI.
IF YOU'RE WILLING, OF COURSE.
OF COURSE WE ARE WILLING, MANTIS. THY SON-- QUOI-- SHALL NOT DIE WHILST WE CAN BATTLE A MAD GOD WHO SERVETH THE GODDESS OF DEATH!
BUT THIS ISN'T YOUR FIGHT, HAYWIRE. YOU'RE NOT REQUIRED TO--
THERE'S A GODDESS OF DEATH?
YES.
THEN THERE'S NO WAY I'D DESERT YOU!

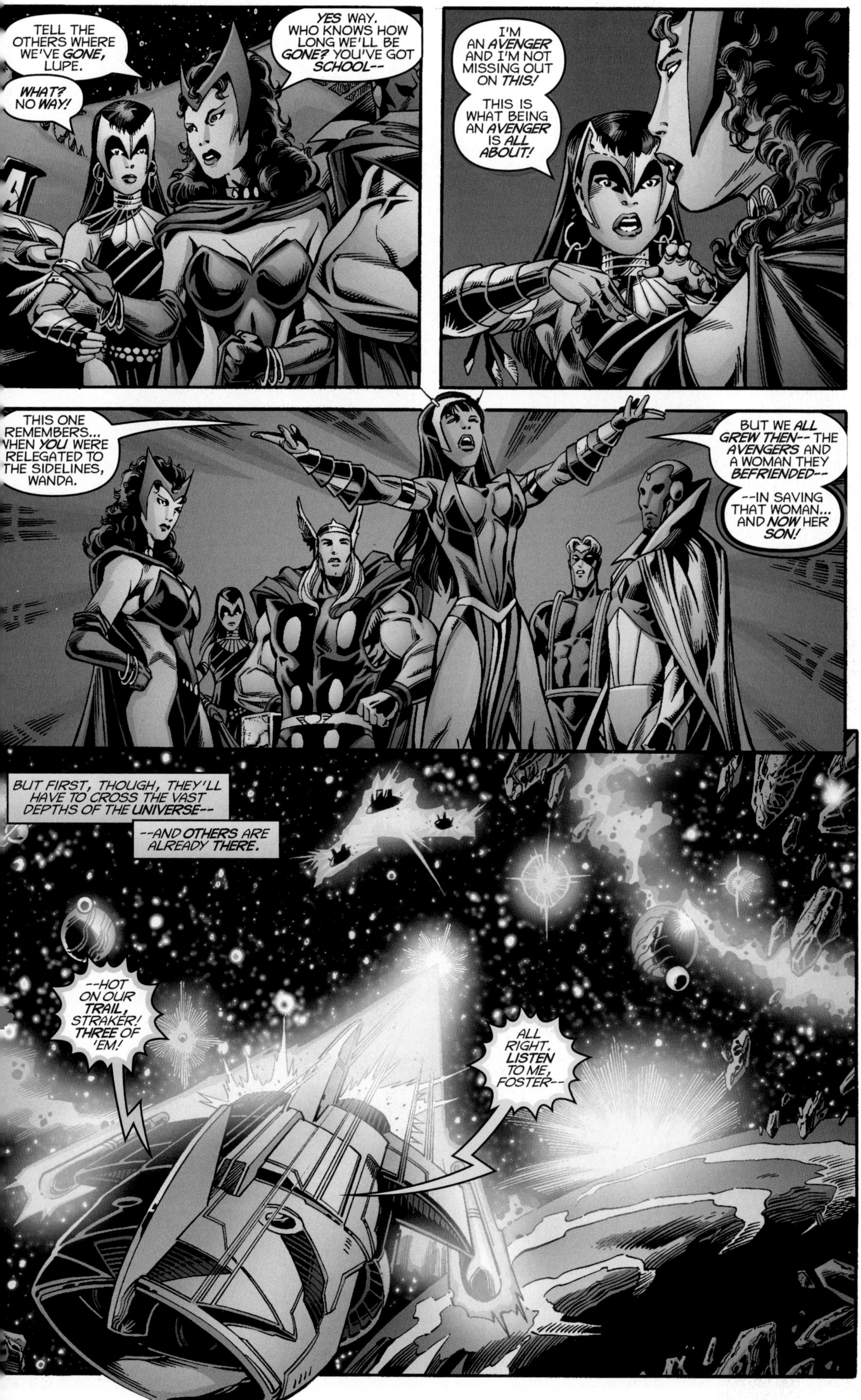
TELL THE OTHERS WHERE WE'VE GONE, LUPE.
WHAT? NO WAY!
YES WAY. WHO KNOWS HOW LONG WE'LL BE GONE? YOU'VE GOT SCHOOL--
I'M AN AVENGER AND I'M NOT MISSING OUT ON THIS!
THIS IS WHAT BEING AN AVENGER IS ALL ABOUT!
THIS ONE REMEMBERS... WHEN YOU WERE RELEGATED TO THE SIDELINES, WANDA.
BUT WE ALL GREW THEN-- THE AVENGERS AND A WOMAN THEY BEFRIENDED--
--IN SAVING THAT WOMAN... AND NOW HER SON!
BUT FIRST, THOUGH, THEY'LL HAVE TO CROSS THE VAST DEPTHS OF THE UNIVERSE--
--AND OTHERS ARE ALREADY THERE.
--HOT ON OUR TRAIL, STRAKER! THREE OF 'EM!
ALL RIGHT. LISTEN TO ME, FOSTER--

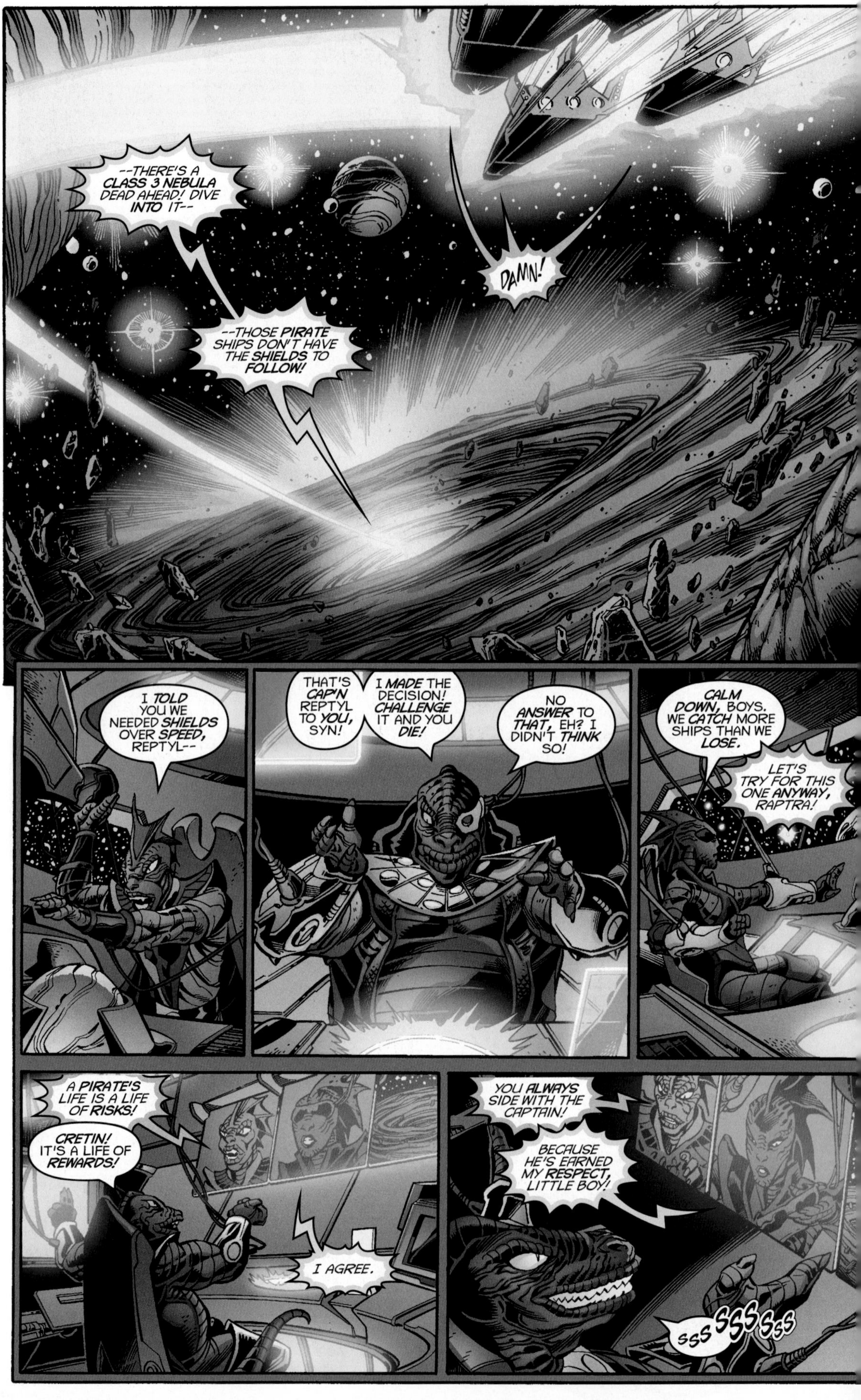
--THERE'S A CLASS 3 NEBULA DEAD AHEAD! DIVE INTO IT--
DAMN!
--THOSE PIRATE SHIPS DON'T HAVE THE SHIELDS TO FOLLOW!
I TOLD YOU WE NEEDED SHIELDS OVER SPEED, REPTYL--
THAT'S CAP'N REPTYL TO YOU, SYN!
I MADE THE DECISION! CHALLENGE IT AND YOU DIE!
NO ANSWER TO THAT, EH? I DIDN'T THINK SO!
CALM DOWN, BOYS. WE CATCH MORE SHIPS THAN WE LOSE.
LET'S TRY FOR THIS ONE ANYWAY, RAPTRA!
A PIRATE'S LIFE IS A LIFE OF RISKS!
CRETIN! IT'S A LIFE OF REWARDS!
I AGREE.
YOU ALWAYS SIDE WITH THE CAPTAIN!
BECAUSE HE'S EARNED MY RESPECT, LITTLE BOY!
SSS SSS SSS

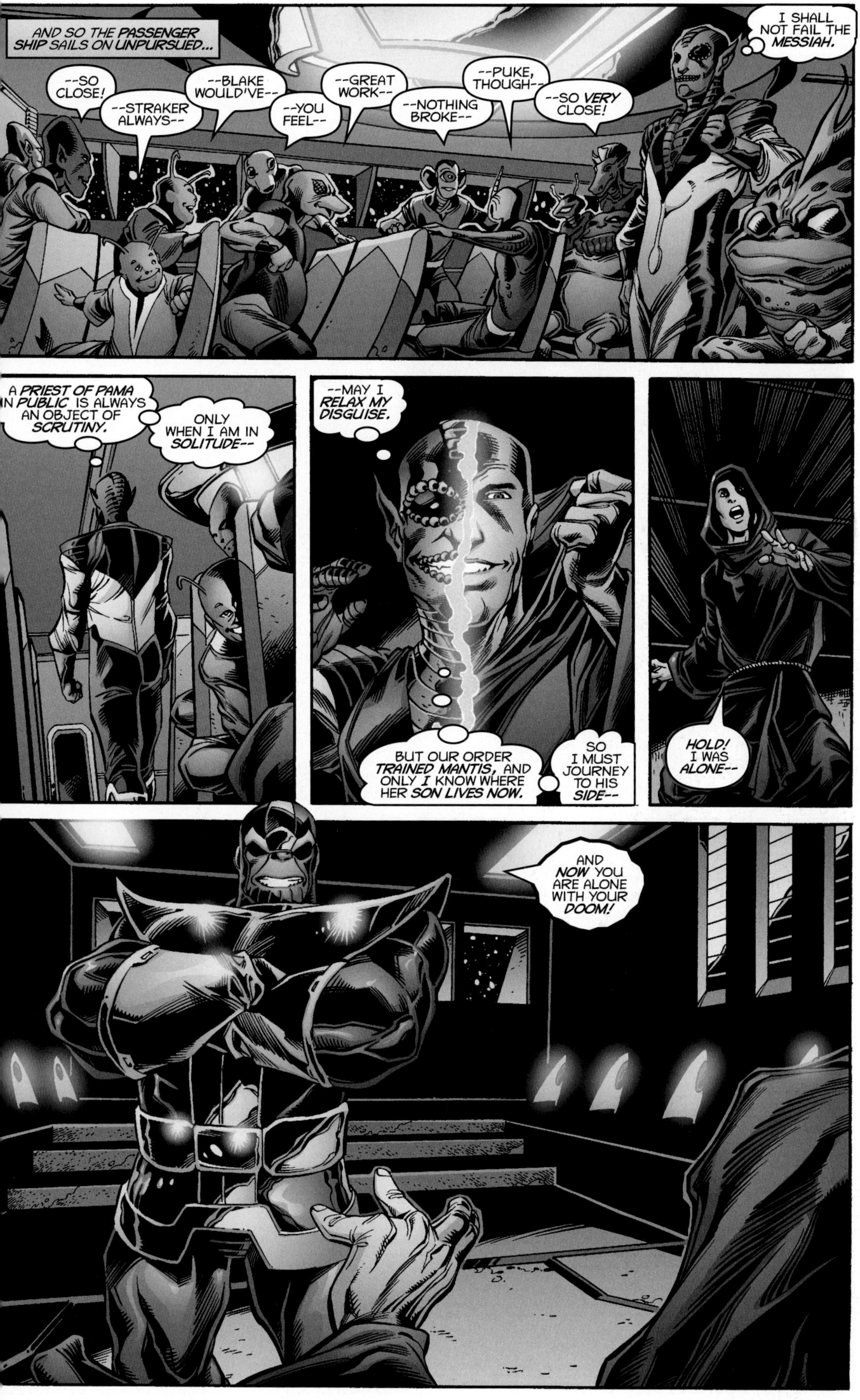
AND SO THE PASSENGER SHIP SAILS ON UNPURSUED...
--SO CLOSE!
--STRAKER ALWAYS--
--BLAKE WOULD'VE--
--YOU FEEL--
--GREAT WORK--
--NOTHING BROKE--
--PUKE, THOUGH--
--SO VERY CLOSE!
I SHALL NOT FAIL THE MESSIAH.
A PRIEST OF PAMA N PUBLIC IS ALWAYS AN OBJECT OF SCRUTINY.
ONLY WHEN I AM IN SOLITUDE--
--MAY I RELAX MY DISGUISE.
BUT OUR ORDER TRAINED MANTIS, AND ONLY I KNOW WHERE HER SON LIVES NOW.
SO I MUST JOURNEY TO HIS SIDE--
HOLD! I WAS ALONE--
AND NOW YOU ARE ALONE WITH YOUR DOOM!

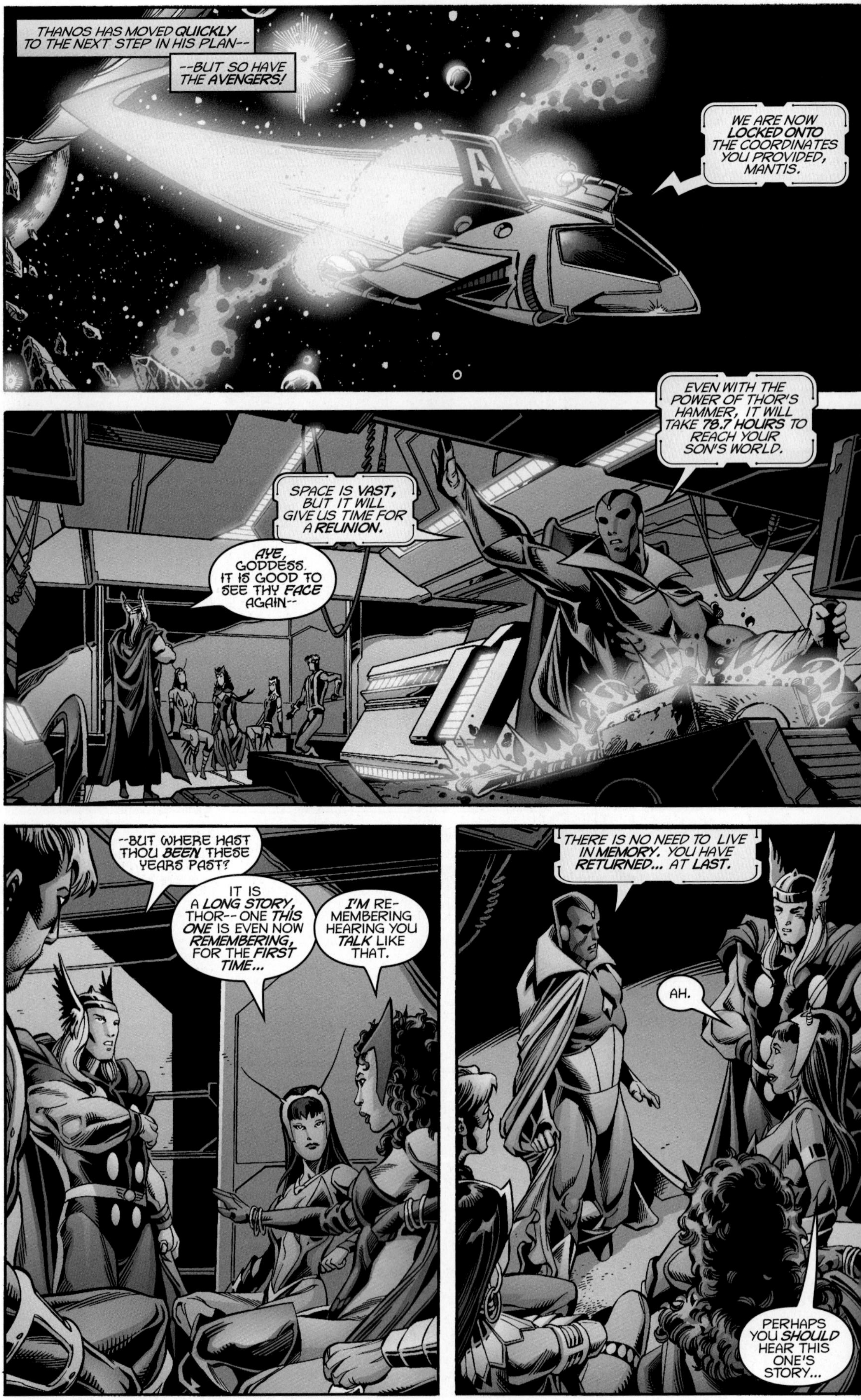
THANOS HAS MOVED QUICKLY TO THE NEXT STEP IN HIS PLAN--
--BUT SO HAVE THE AVENGERS!
WE ARE NOW LOCKED ONTO THE COORDINATES YOU PROVIDED, MANTIS.
EVEN WITH THE POWER OF THOR'S HAMMER, IT WILL TAKE 78.7 HOURS TO REACH YOUR SON'S WORLD.
SPACE IS VAST, BUT IT WILL GIVE US TIME FOR A REUNION.
AYE, GODDESS. IT IS GOOD TO SEE THY FACE AGAIN--
--BUT WHERE HAST THOU BEEN THESE YEARS PAST?
IT IS A LONG STORY, THOR-- ONE THIS ONE IS EVEN NOW REMEMBERING, FOR THE FIRST TIME...
I'M RE-MEMBERING HEARING YOU TALK LIKE THAT.
THERE IS NO NEED TO LIVE IN MEMORY. YOU HAVE RETURNED... AT LAST.
AH.
PERHAPS YOU SHOULD HEAR THIS ONE'S STORY...

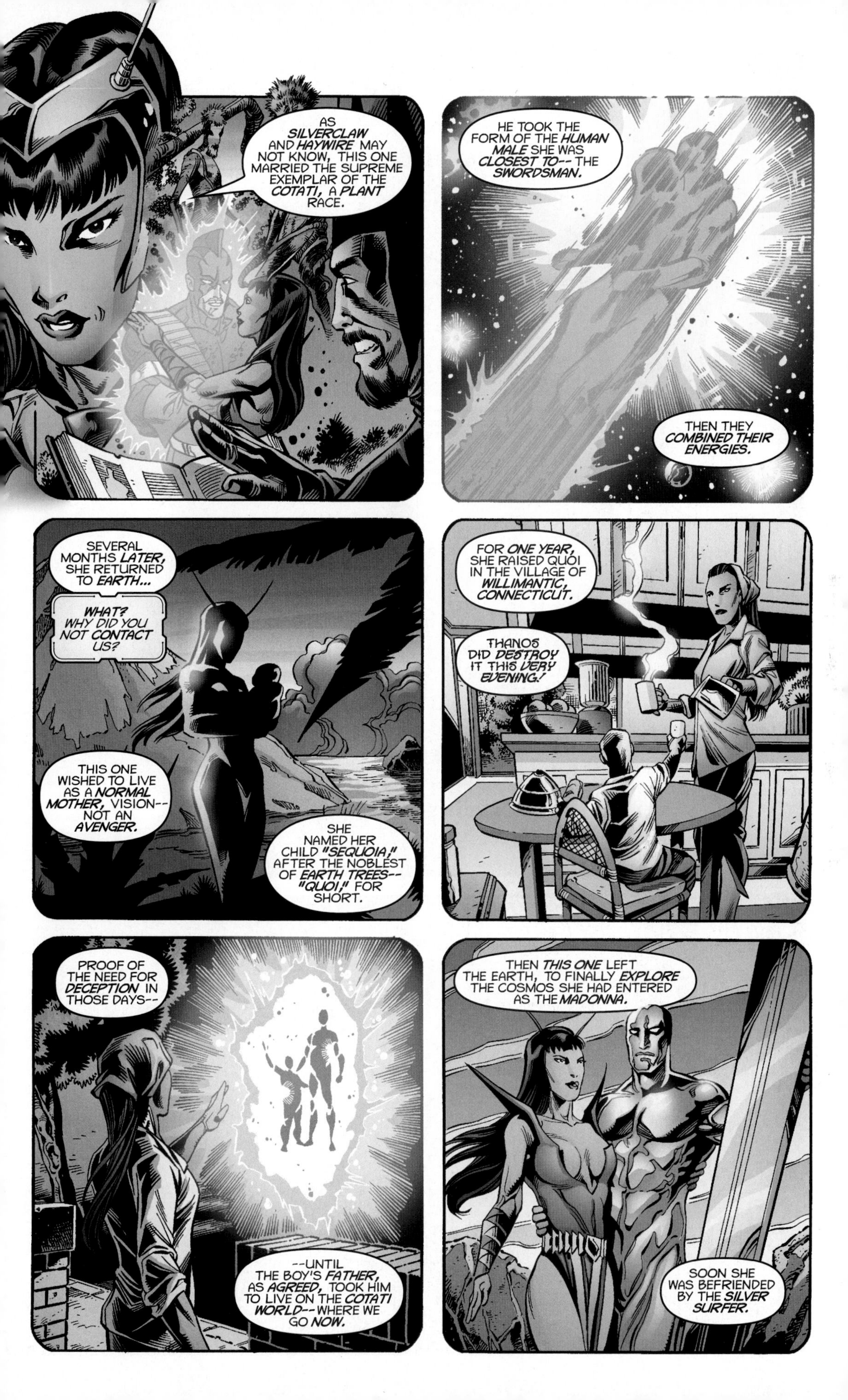
AS SILVERCLAW AND HAYWIRE MAY NOT KNOW, THIS ONE MARRIED THE SUPREME EXEMPLAR OF THE COTATI, A PLANT RACE.
HE TOOK THE FORM OF THE HUMAN MALE SHE WAS CLOSEST TO-- THE SWORDSMAN.
THEN THEY COMBINED THEIR ENERGIES.
SEVERAL MONTHS LATER, SHE RETURNED TO EARTH...
WHAT? WHY DID YOU NOT CONTACT US?
THIS ONE WISHED TO LIVE AS A NORMAL MOTHER, VISION-- NOT AN AVENGER.
SHE NAMED HER CHILD "SEQUOIA," AFTER THE NOBLEST OF EARTH TREES-- "QUOI," FOR SHORT.
FOR ONE YEAR, SHE RAISED QUOI IN THE VILLAGE OF WILLIMANTIC, CONNECTICUT.
THANOS DID DESTROY IT THIS VERY EVENING!
PROOF OF THE NEED FOR DECEPTION IN THOSE DAYS--
--UNTIL THE BOY'S FATHER, AS AGREED, TOOK HIM TO LIVE ON THE COTATI WORLD-- WHERE WE GO NOW.
THEN THIS ONE LEFT THE EARTH, TO FINALLY EXPLORE THE COSMOS SHE HAD ENTERED AS THE MADONNA.
SOON SHE WAS BEFRIENDED BY THE SILVER SURFER.

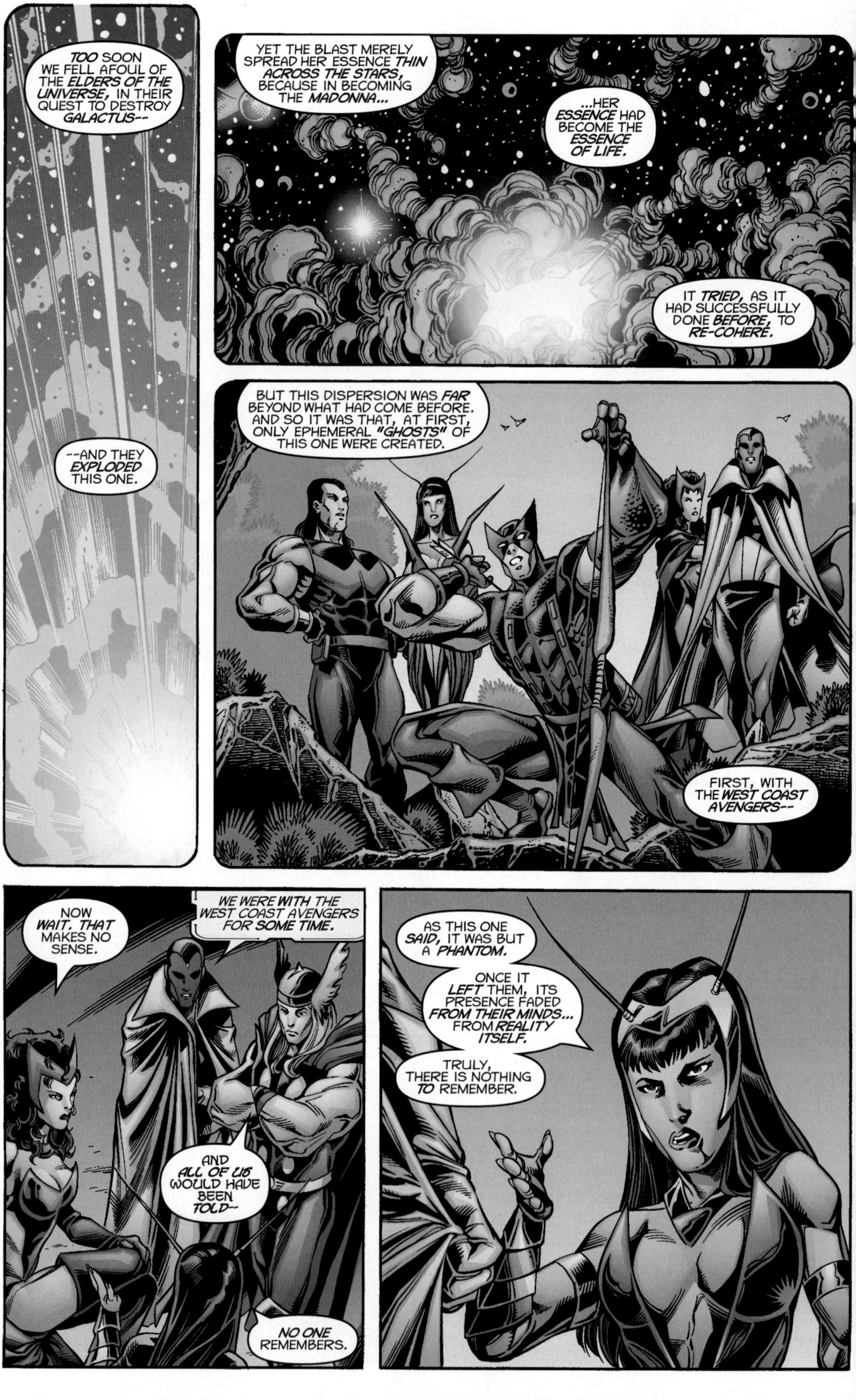
TOO SOON WE FELL AFOUL OF THE ELDERS OF THE UNIVERSE, IN THEIR QUEST TO DESTROY GALACTUS--
--AND THEY EXPLODED THIS ONE.
YET THE BLAST MERELY SPREAD HER ESSENCE THIN ACROSS THE STARS, BECAUSE IN BECOMING THE MADONNA...
...HER ESSENCE HAD BECOME THE ESSENCE OF LIFE.
IT TRIED, AS IT HAD SUCCESSFULLY DONE BEFORE, TO RE-COHERE.
BUT THIS DISPERSION WAS FAR BEYOND WHAT HAD COME BEFORE. AND SO IT WAS THAT, AT FIRST, ONLY EPHEMERAL "GHOSTS" OF THIS ONE WERE CREATED.
FIRST, WITH THE WEST COAST AVENGERS--
NOW WAIT. THAT MAKES NO SENSE.
WE WERE WITH THE WEST COAST AVENGERS FOR SOME TIME.
AND ALL OF US WOULD HAVE BEEN TOLD--
NO ONE REMEMBERS.
AS THIS ONE SAID, IT WAS BUT A PHANTOM.
ONCE IT LEFT THEM, ITS PRESENCE FADED FROM THEIR MINDS... FROM REALITY ITSELF.
TRULY, THERE IS NOTHING TO REMEMBER.

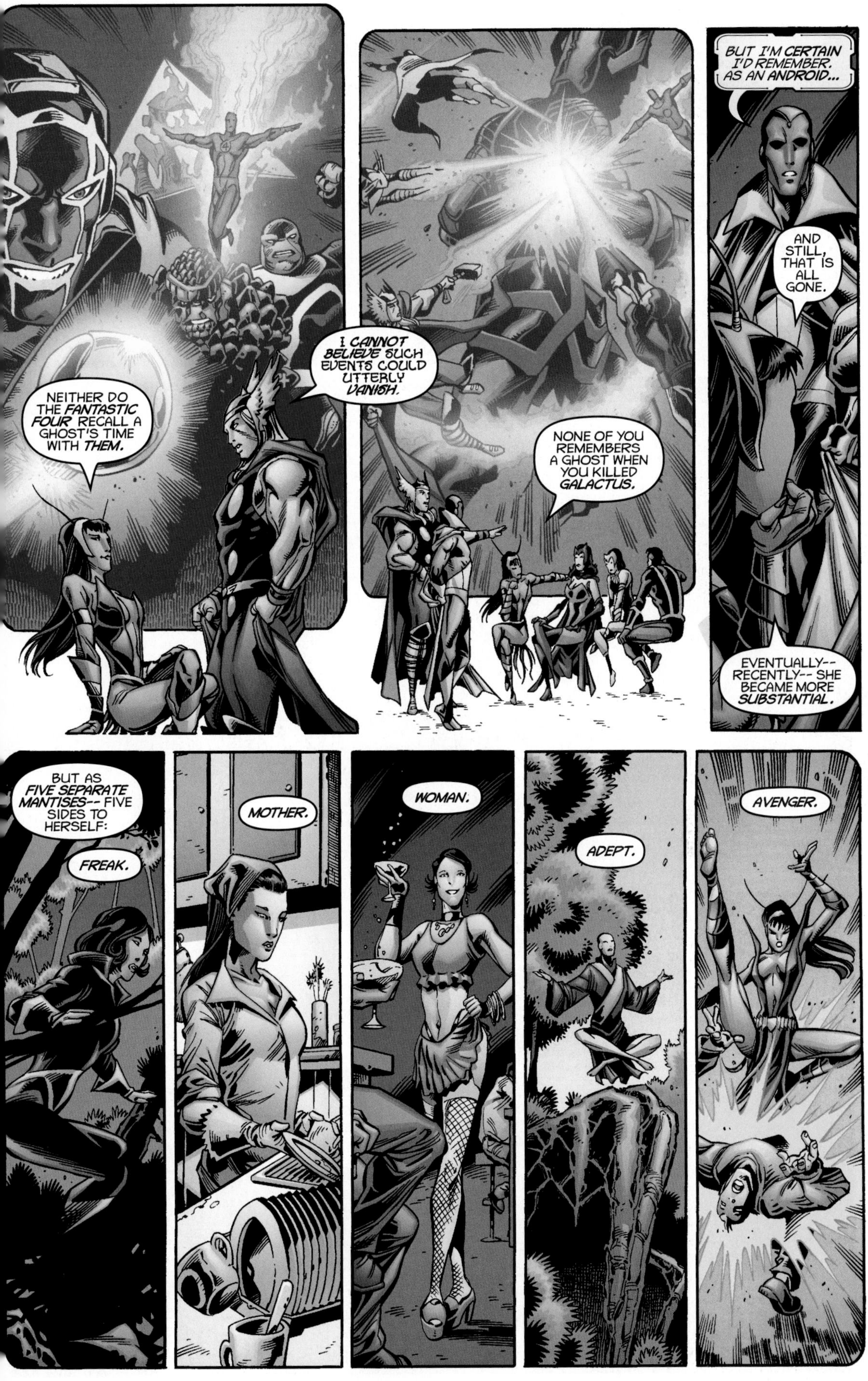
NEITHER DO THE FANTASTIC FOUR RECALL A GHOST'S TIME WITH THEM.
I CANNOT BELIEVE SUCH EVENTS COULD UTTERLY VANISH.
NONE OF YOU REMEMBERS A GHOST WHEN YOU KILLED GALACTUS.
BUT I'M CERTAIN I'D REMEMBER. AS AN ANDROID...
AND STILL, THAT IS ALL GONE.
EVENTUALLY-- RECENTLY-- SHE BECAME MORE SUBSTANTIAL.
BUT AS FIVE SEPARATE MANTISES-- FIVE SIDES TO HERSELF:
FREAK.
MOTHER.
WOMAN.
ADEPT.
AVENGER.

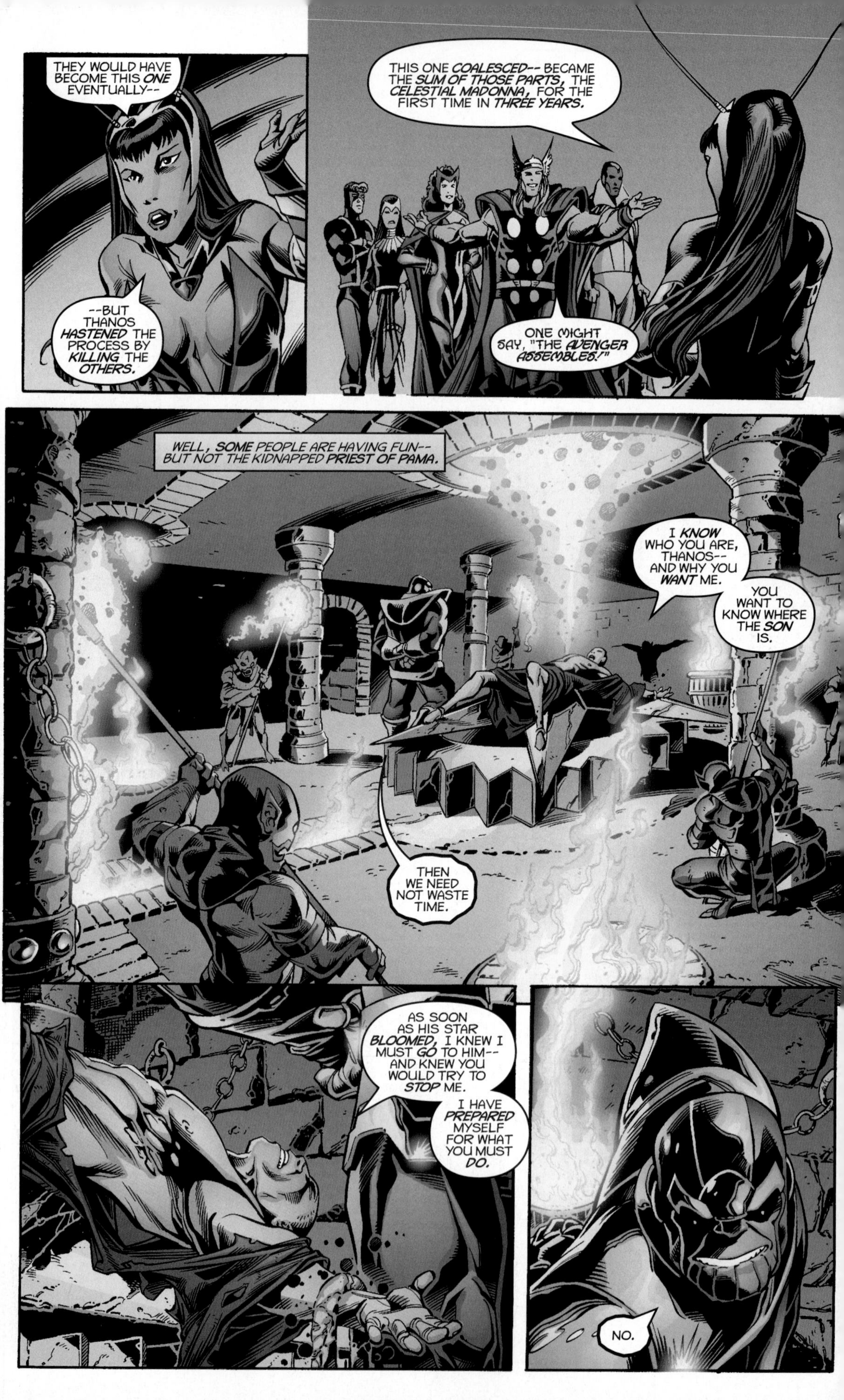
THEY WOULD HAVE BECOME THIS ONE EVENTUALLY--
--BUT THANOS HASTENED THE PROCESS BY KILLING THE OTHERS.
THIS ONE COALESCED-- BECAME THE SUM OF THOSE PARTS, THE CELESTIAL MADONNA, FOR THE FIRST TIME IN THREE YEARS.
ONE MIGHT SAY, "THE AVENGER ASSEMBLES!"
WELL, SOME PEOPLE ARE HAVING FUN-- BUT NOT THE KIDNAPPED PRIEST OF PAMA.
I KNOW WHO YOU ARE, THANOS-- AND WHY YOU WANT ME.
YOU WANT TO KNOW WHERE THE SON IS.
THEN WE NEED NOT WASTE TIME.
AS SOON AS HIS STAR BLOOMED, I KNEW I MUST GO TO HIM-- AND KNEW YOU WOULD TRY TO STOP ME.
I HAVE PREPARED MYSELF FOR WHAT YOU MUST DO.
NO.

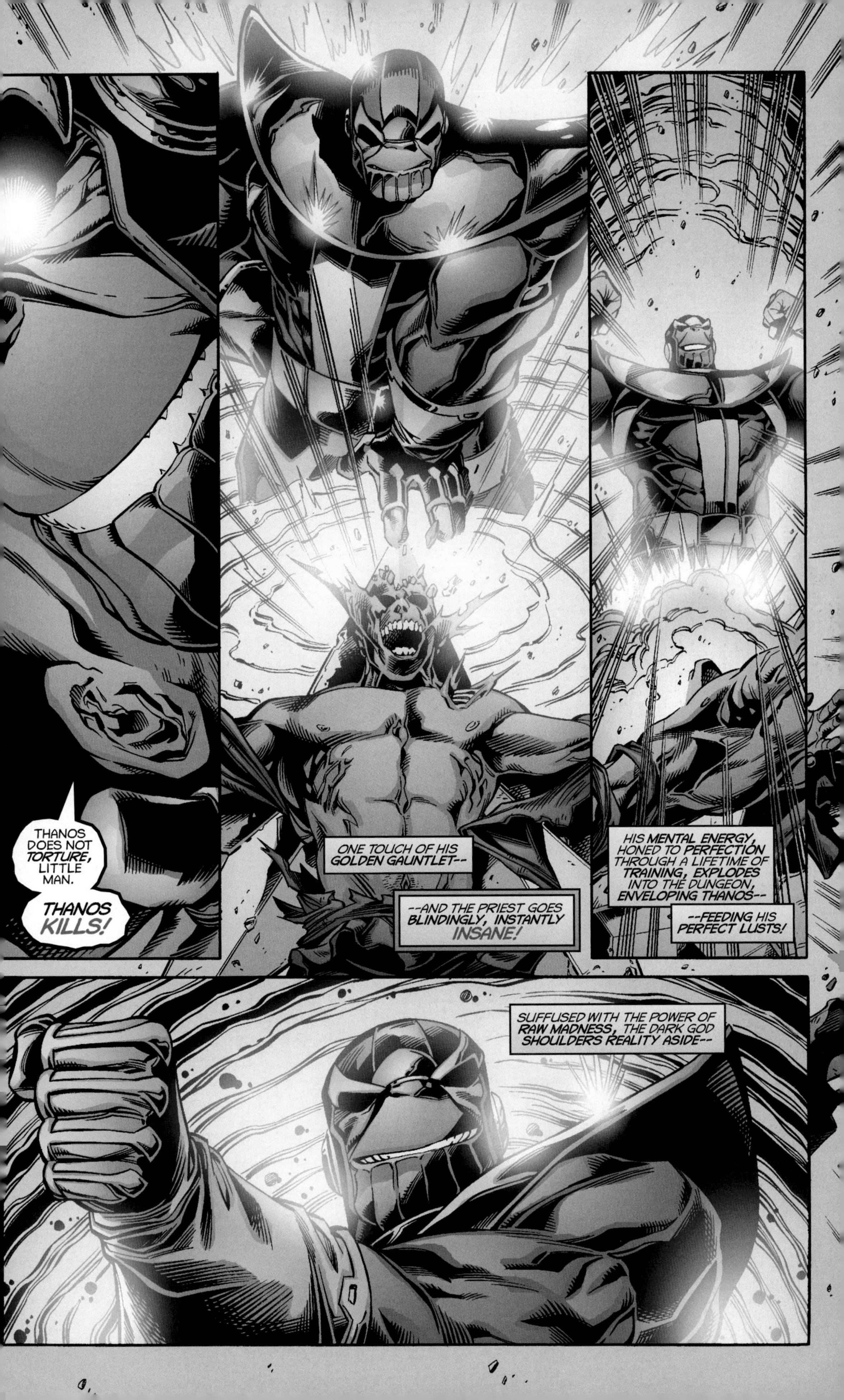
THANOS DOES NOT TORTURE, LITTLE MAN.
THANOS KILLS!
ONE TOUCH OF HIS GOLDEN GAUNTLET--
--AND THE PRIEST GOES BLINDINGLY, INSTANTLY INSANE!
HIS MENTAL ENERGY, HONED TO PERFECTION THROUGH A LIFETIME OF TRAINING, EXPLODES INTO THE DUNGEON, ENVELOPING THANOS--
--FEEDING HIS PERFECT LUSTS!
SUFFUSED WITH THE POWER OF RAW MADNESS, THE DARK GOD SHOULDERS REALITY ASIDE--

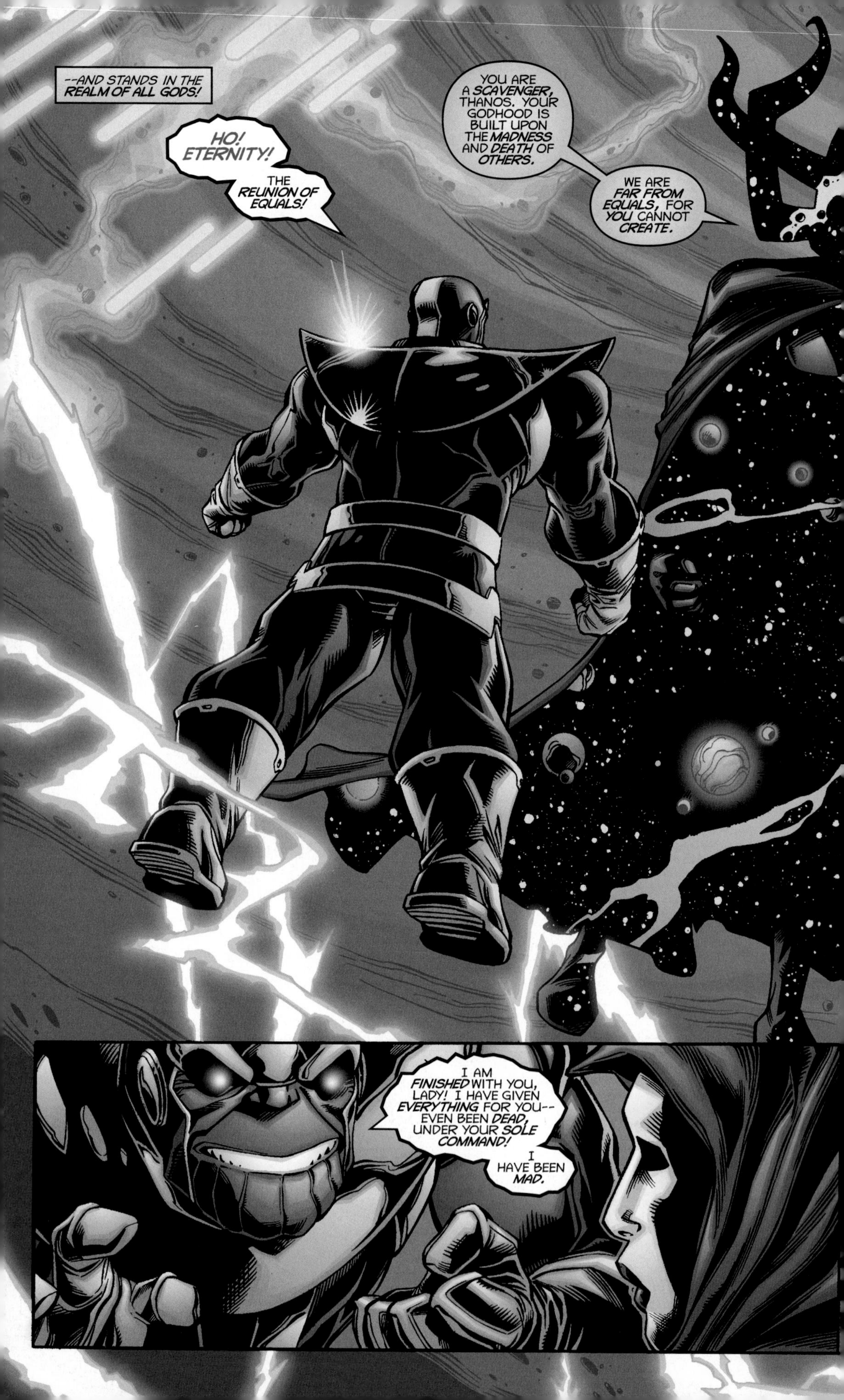
--AND STANDS IN THE REALM OF ALL GODS!
HO! ETERNITY!
THE REUNION OF EQUALS!
YOU ARE A SCAVENGER, THANOS. YOUR GODHOOD IS BUILT UPON THE MADNESS AND DEATH OF OTHERS.
WE ARE FAR FROM EQUALS, FOR YOU CANNOT CREATE.
I AM FINISHED WITH YOU, LADY! I HAVE GIVEN EVERYTHING FOR YOU-- EVEN BEEN DEAD, UNDER YOUR SOLE COMMAND!
I HAVE BEEN MAD.

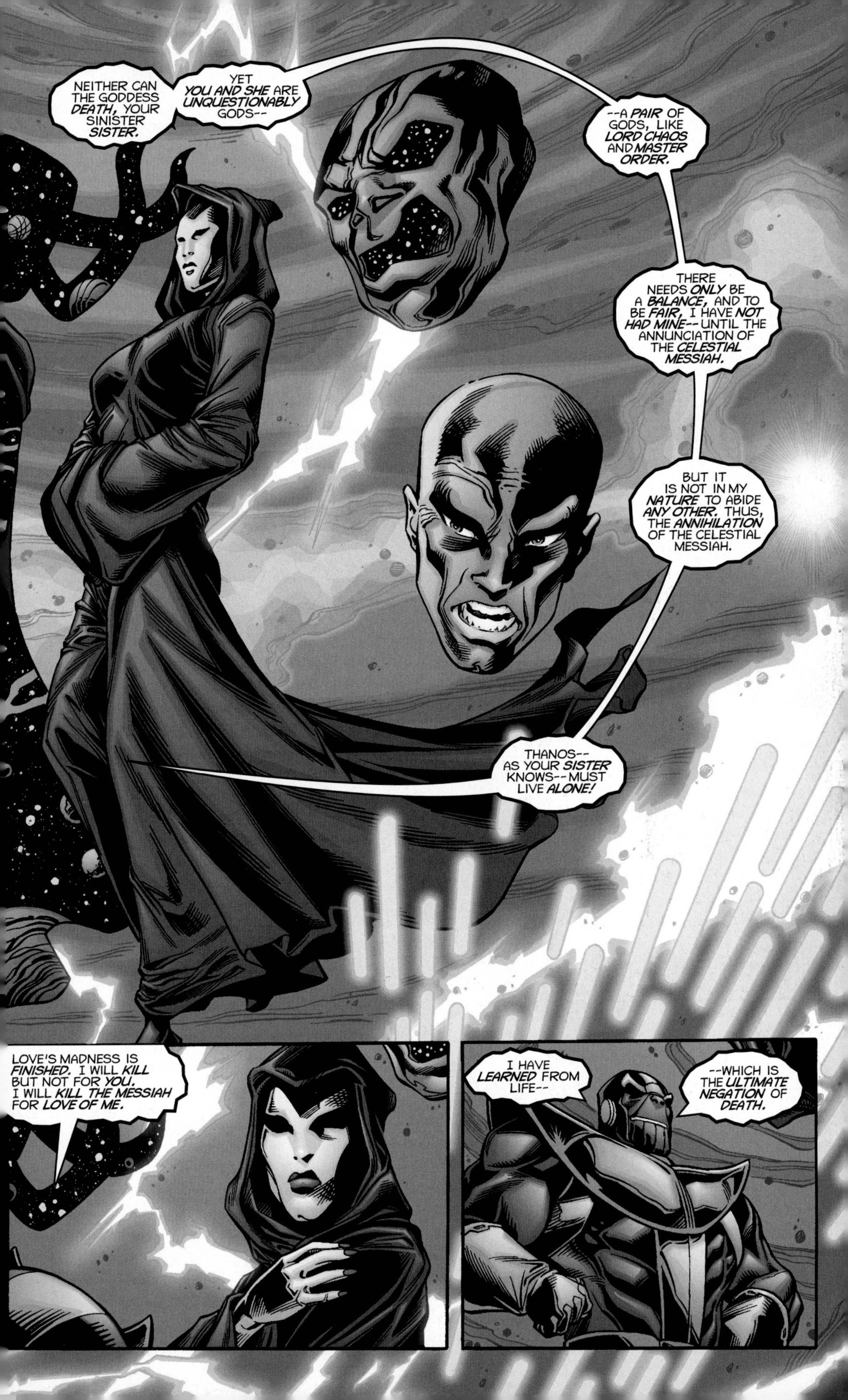
NEITHER CAN THE GODDESS DEATH, YOUR SINISTER SISTER.
YET YOU AND SHE ARE UNQUESTIONABLY GODS--
--A PAIR OF GODS, LIKE LORD CHAOS AND MASTER ORDER.
THERE NEEDS ONLY BE A BALANCE, AND TO BE FAIR, I HAVE NOT HAD MINE-- UNTIL THE ANNUNCIATION OF THE CELESTIAL MESSIAH.
BUT IT IS NOT IN MY NATURE TO ABIDE ANY OTHER. THUS, THE ANNIHILATION OF THE CELESTIAL MESSIAH.
THANOS-- AS YOUR SISTER KNOWS--MUST LIVE ALONE!
LOVE'S MADNESS IS FINISHED. I WILL KILL BUT NOT FOR YOU. I WILL KILL THE MESSIAH FOR LOVE OF ME.
I HAVE LEARNED FROM LIFE--
--WHICH IS THE ULTIMATE NEGATION OF DEATH.

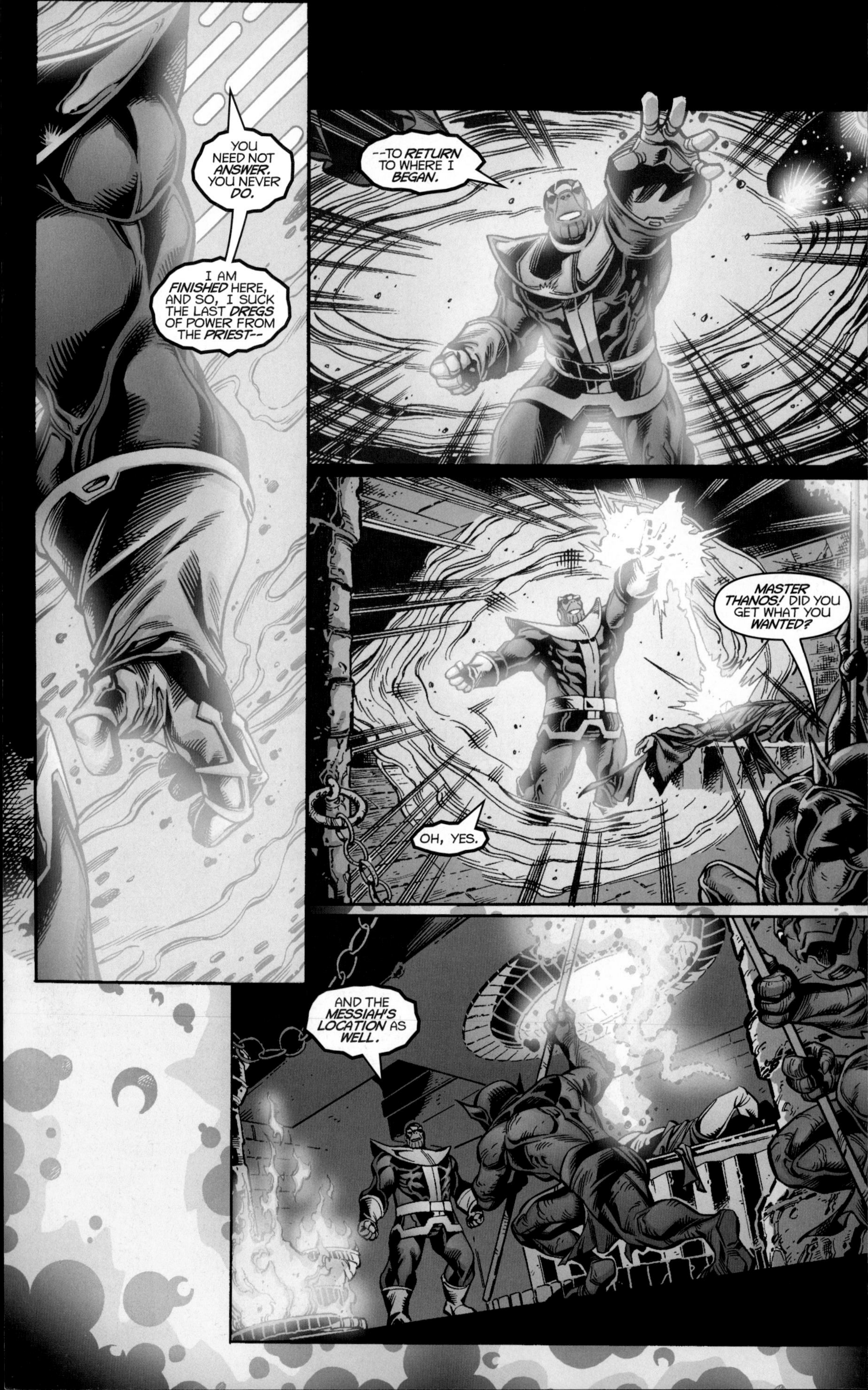
YOU NEED NOT ANSWER. YOU NEVER DO.
I AM FINISHED HERE, AND SO, I SUCK THE LAST DREGS OF POWER FROM THE PRIEST--
--TO RETURN TO WHERE I BEGAN.
MASTER THANOS! DID YOU GET WHAT YOU WANTED?
OH, YES.
AND THE MESSIAH'S LOCATION AS WELL.

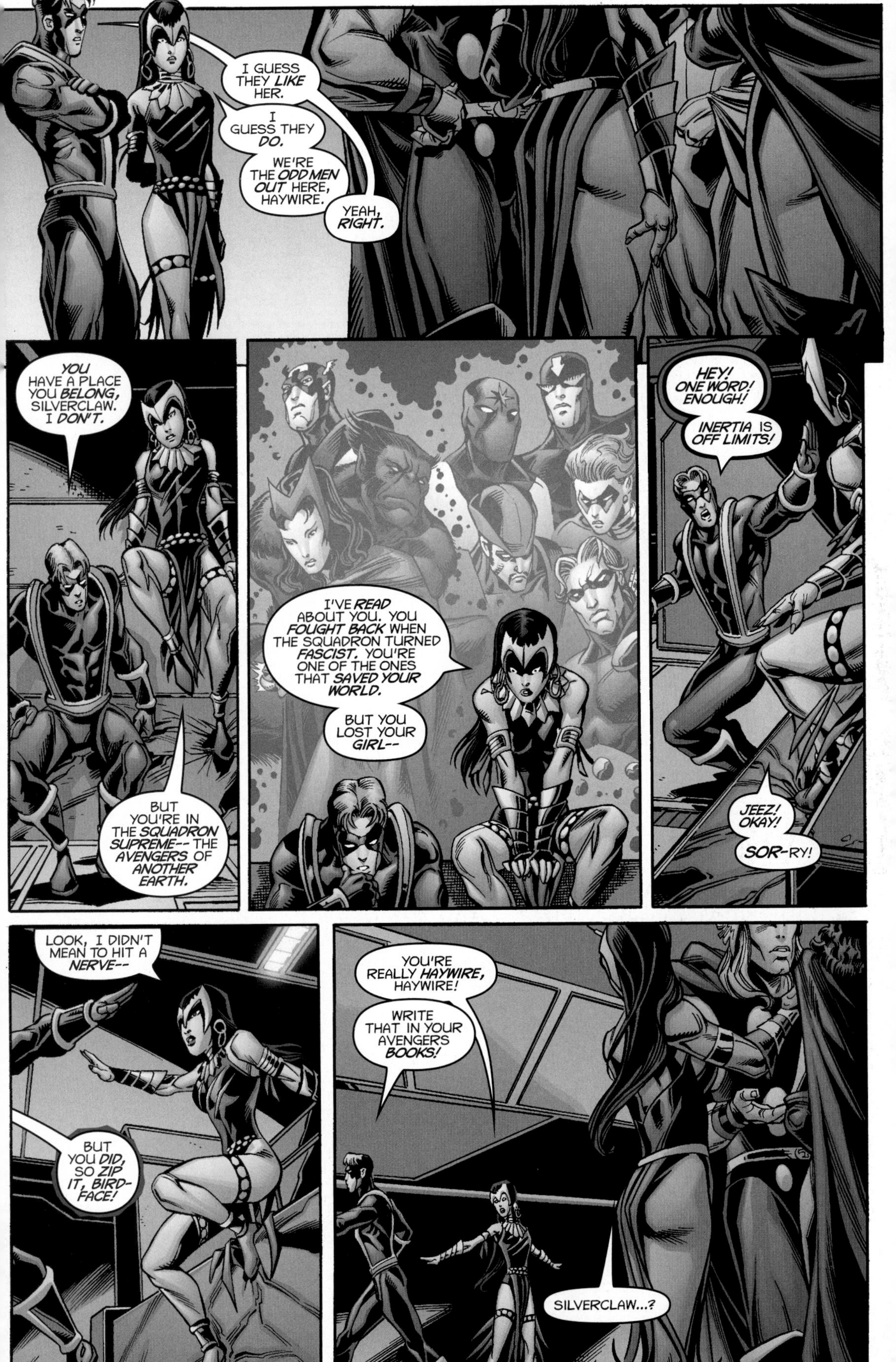

I GUESS THEY LIKE HER.
I GUESS THEY DO.
WE'RE THE ODD MEN OUT HERE, HAYWIRE.
YEAH, RIGHT.
YOU HAVE A PLACE YOU BELONG, SILVERCLAW. I DON'T.
BUT YOU'RE IN THE SQUADRON SUPREME-- THE AVENGERS OF ANOTHER EARTH.
I'VE READ ABOUT YOU. YOU FOUGHT BACK WHEN THE SQUADRON TURNED FASCIST. YOU'RE ONE OF THE ONES THAT SAVED YOUR WORLD.
BUT YOU LOST YOUR GIRL--
HEY! ONE WORD! ENOUGH!
INERTIA IS OFF LIMITS!
JEEZ! OKAY!
SOR-RY!
LOOK, I DIDN'T MEAN TO HIT A NERVE--
BUT YOU DID, SO ZIP IT, BIRD-FACE!
YOU'RE REALLY HAYWIRE, HAYWIRE!
WRITE THAT IN YOUR AVENGERS BOOKS!
SILVERCLAW...?

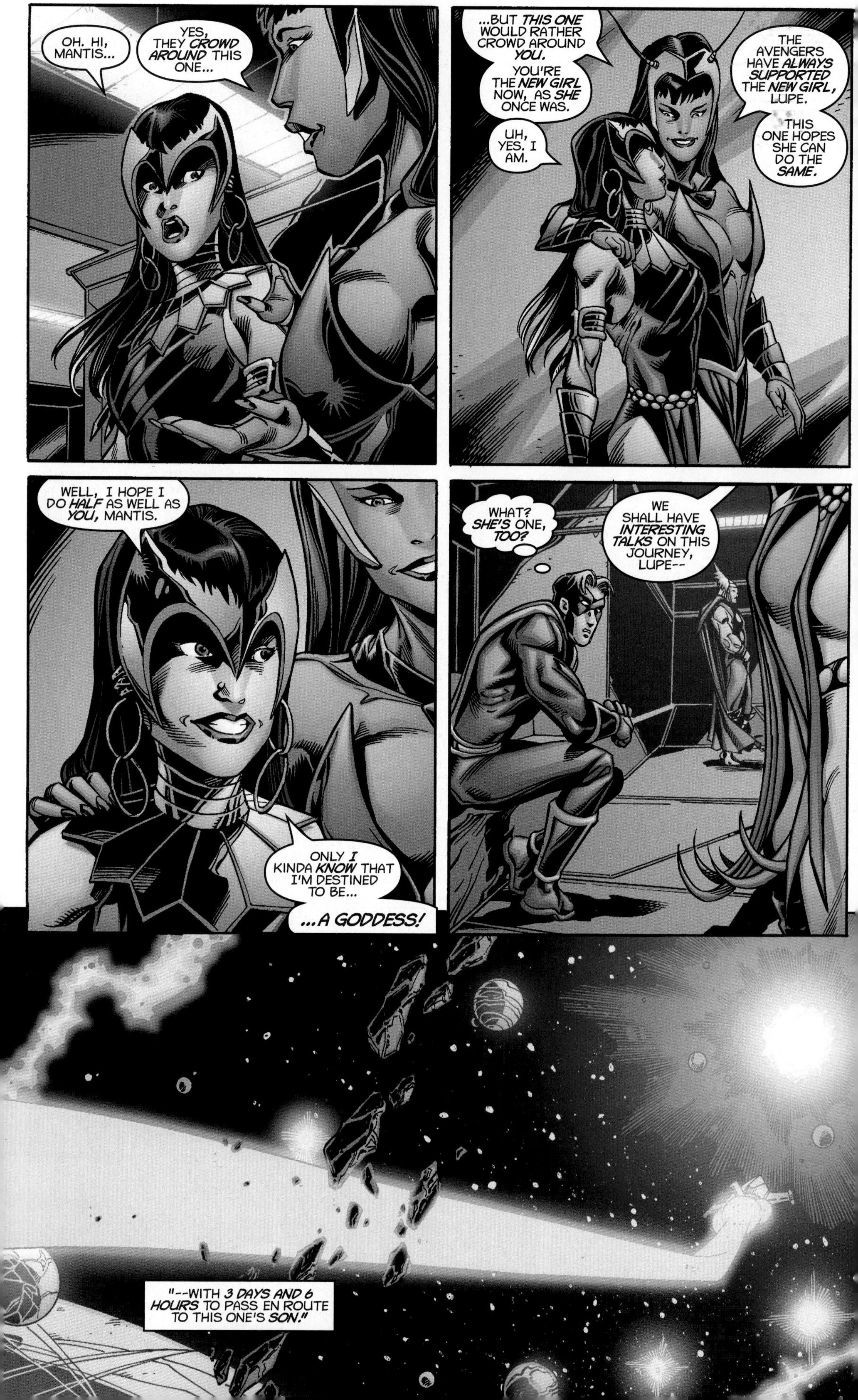

OH. HI, MANTIS...
YES, THEY CROWD AROUND THIS ONE...
...BUT THIS ONE WOULD RATHER CROWD AROUND YOU.
YOU'RE THE NEW GIRL NOW, AS SHE ONCE WAS.
UH, YES. I AM.
THE AVENGERS HAVE ALWAYS SUPPORTED THE NEW GIRL, LUPE.
THIS ONE HOPES SHE CAN DO THE SAME.
WELL, I HOPE I DO HALF AS WELL AS YOU, MANTIS.
ONLY I KINDA KNOW THAT I'M DESTINED TO BE...
...A GODDESS!
WHAT? SHE'S ONE, TOO?
WE SHALL HAVE INTERESTING TALKS ON THIS JOURNEY, LUPE--
"--WITH 3 DAYS AND 6 HOURS TO PASS EN ROUTE TO THIS ONE'S SON."

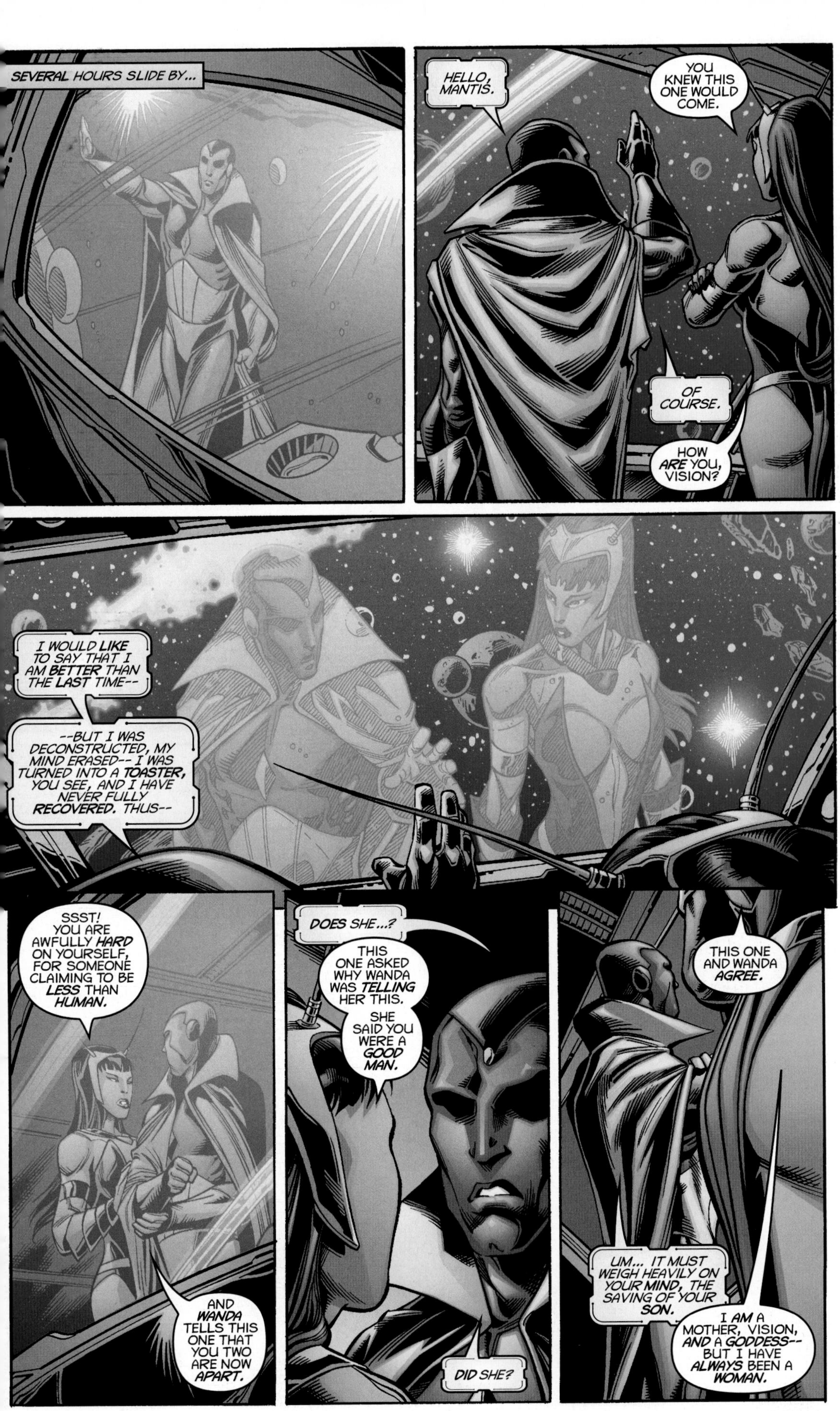
SEVERAL HOURS SLIDE BY...
HELLO, MANTIS.
YOU KNEW THIS ONE WOULD COME.
OF COURSE.
HOW ARE YOU, VISION?
I WOULD LIKE TO SAY THAT I AM BETTER THAN THE LAST TIME--
--BUT I WAS DECONSTRUCTED, MY MIND ERASED-- I WAS TURNED INTO A TOASTER, YOU SEE, AND I HAVE NEVER FULLY RECOVERED. THUS--
SSST! YOU ARE AWFULLY HARD ON YOURSELF, FOR SOMEONE CLAIMING TO BE LESS THAN HUMAN.
AND WANDA TELLS THIS ONE THAT YOU TWO ARE NOW APART.
DOES SHE...?
THIS ONE ASKED WHY WANDA WAS TELLING HER THIS.
SHE SAID YOU WERE A GOOD MAN.
DID SHE?
THIS ONE AND WANDA AGREE.
UM... IT MUST WEIGH HEAVILY ON YOUR MIND, THE SAVING OF YOUR SON.
I AM A MOTHER, VISION, AND A GODDESS-- BUT I HAVE ALWAYS BEEN A WOMAN.

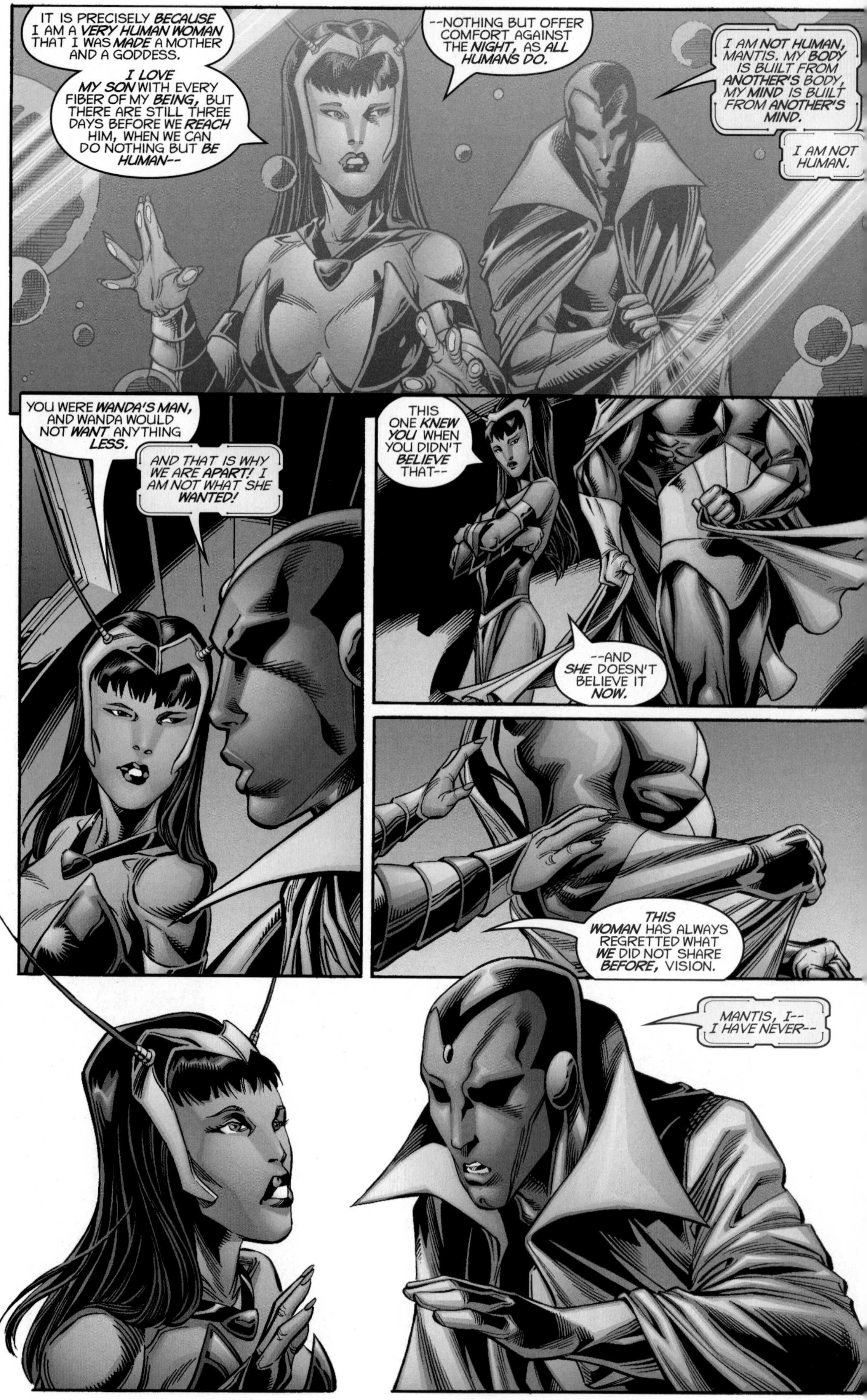

IT IS PRECISELY BECAUSE I AM A VERY HUMAN WOMAN THAT I WAS MADE A MOTHER AND A GODDESS.
I LOVE MY SON WITH EVERY FIBER OF MY BEING, BUT THERE ARE STILL THREE DAYS BEFORE WE REACH HIM, WHEN WE CAN DO NOTHING BUT BE HUMAN--
--NOTHING BUT OFFER COMFORT AGAINST THE NIGHT, AS ALL HUMANS DO.
I AM NOT HUMAN, MANTIS. MY BODY IS BUILT FROM ANOTHER'S BODY, MY MIND IS BUILT FROM ANOTHER'S MIND.
I AM NOT HUMAN.
YOU WERE WANDA'S MAN, AND WANDA WOULD NOT WANT ANYTHING LESS.
AND THAT IS WHY WE ARE APART! I AM NOT WHAT SHE WANTED!
THIS ONE KNEW YOU WHEN YOU DIDN'T BELIEVE THAT--
--AND SHE DOESN'T BELIEVE IT NOW.
THIS WOMAN HAS ALWAYS REGRETTED WHAT WE DID NOT SHARE BEFORE, VISION.
MANTIS, I-- I HAVE NEVER--

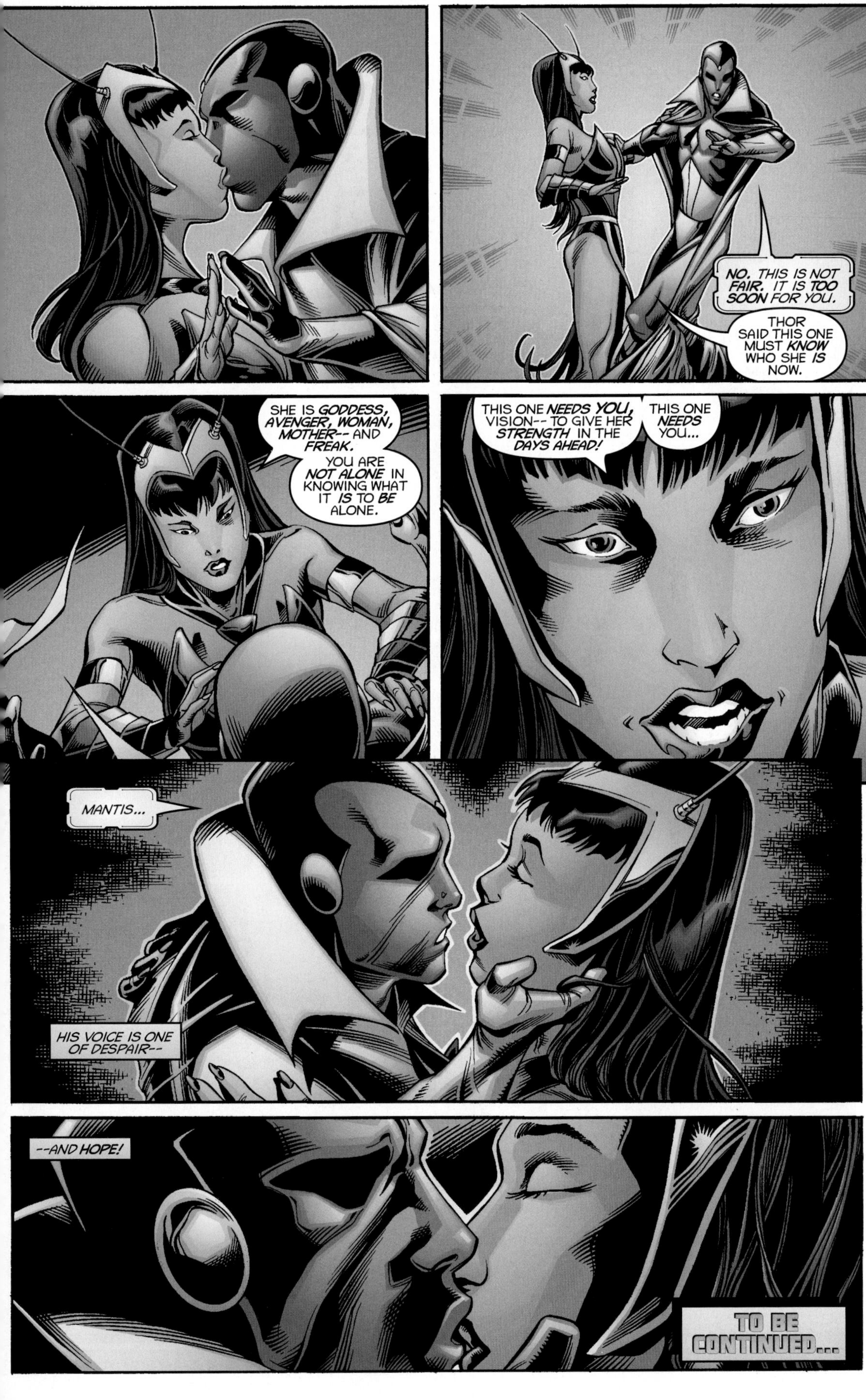
NO. THIS IS NOT FAIR. IT IS TOO SOON FOR YOU.
THOR SAID THIS ONE MUST KNOW WHO SHE IS NOW.
SHE IS GODDESS, AVENGER, WOMAN, MOTHER-- AND FREAK.
YOU ARE NOT ALONE IN KNOWING WHAT IT IS TO BE ALONE.
THIS ONE NEEDS YOU, VISION-- TO GIVE HER STRENGTH IN THE DAYS AHEAD!
THIS ONE NEEDS YOU...
MANTIS...
HIS VOICE IS ONE OF DESPAIR--
--AND HOPE!
TO BE CONTINUED...

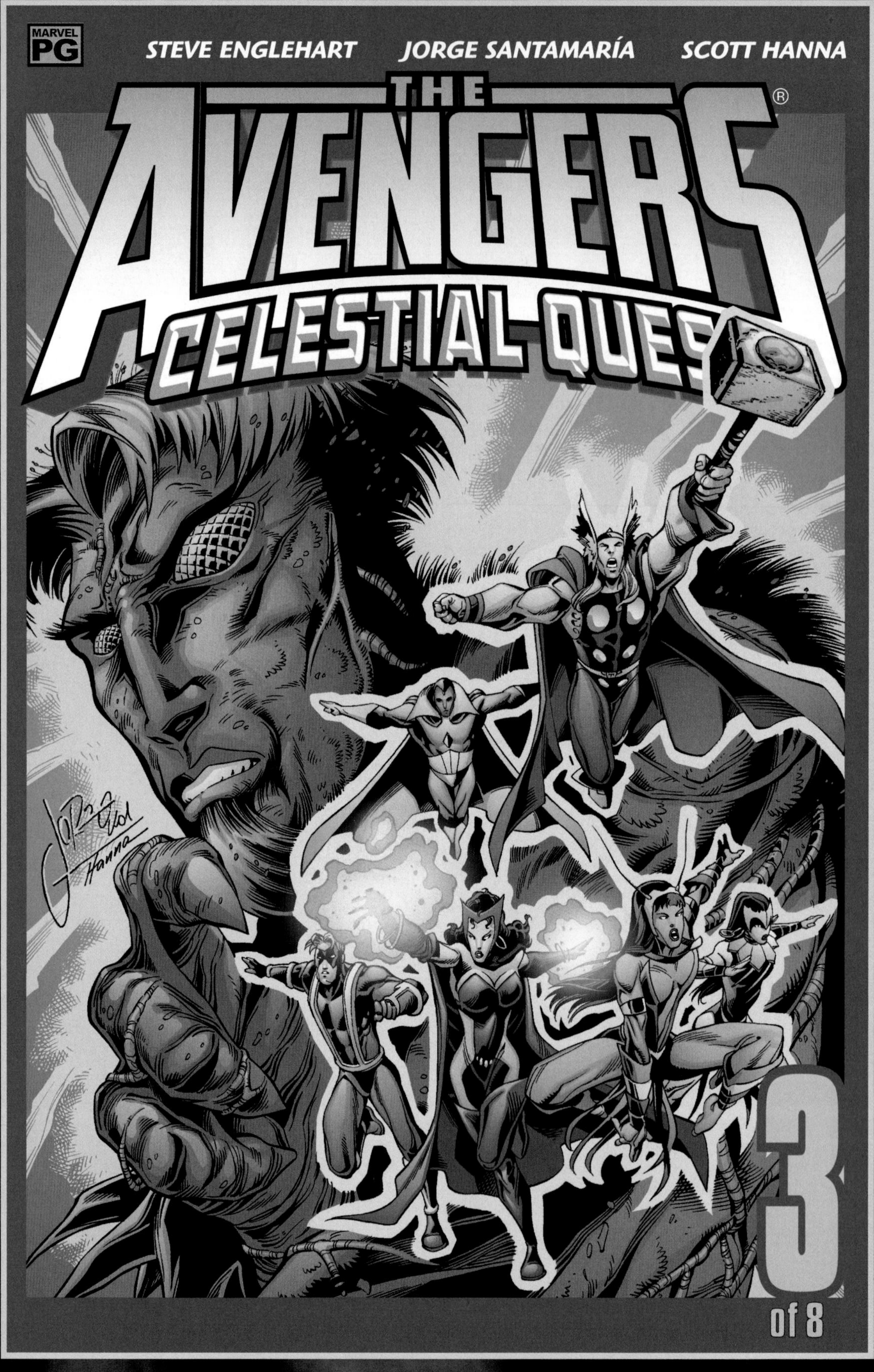

MARVEL PG
STEVE ENGLEHART
JORGE SANTAMARÍA
SCOTT HANNA
THE AVENGERS®
CELESTIAL QUES
3
of 8

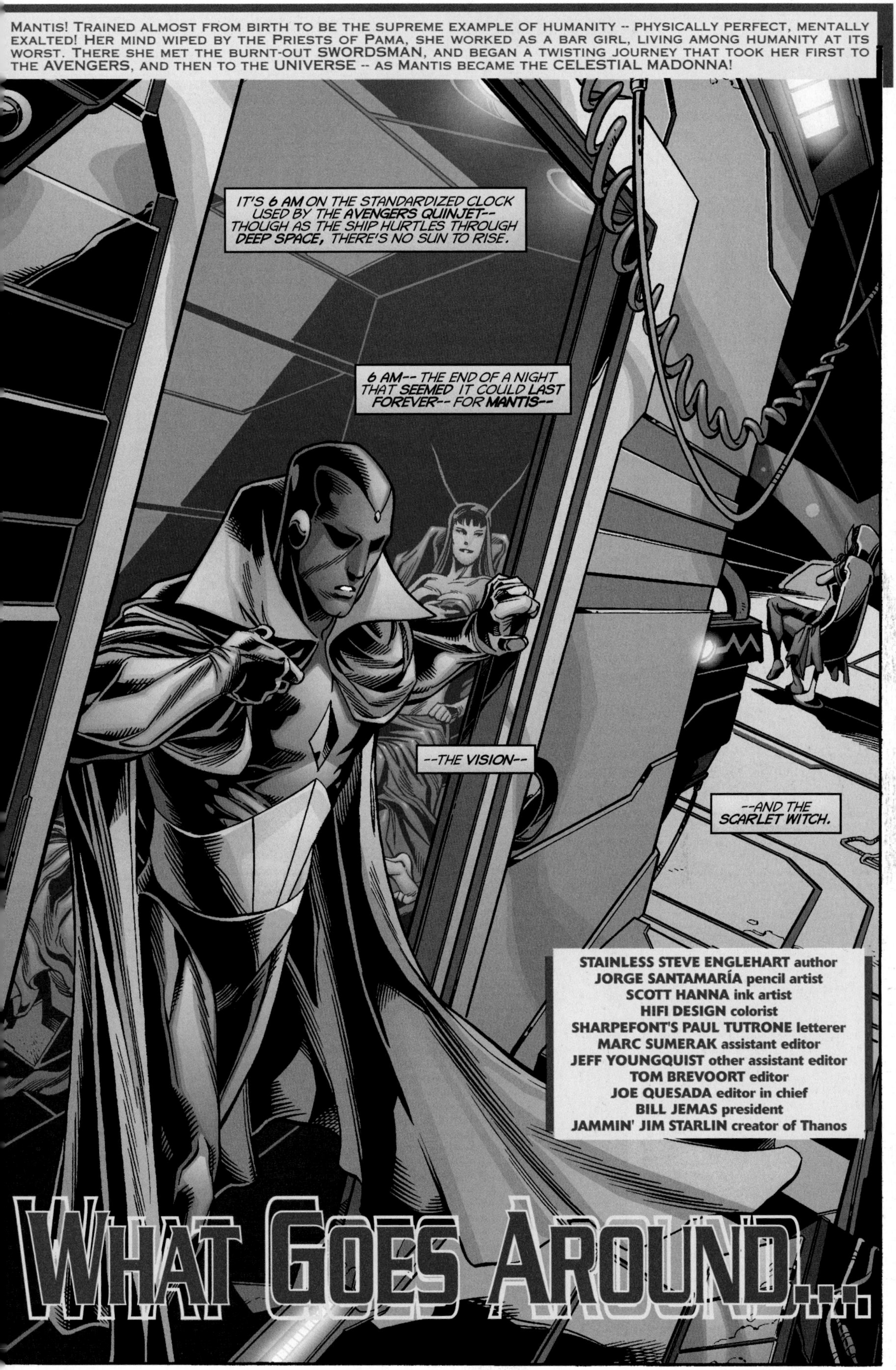
MANTIS! TRAINED ALMOST FROM BIRTH TO BE THE SUPREME EXAMPLE OF HUMANITY -- PHYSICALLY PERFECT, MENTALLY EXALTED! HER MIND WIPED BY THE PRIESTS OF PAMA, SHE WORKED AS A BAR GIRL, LIVING AMONG HUMANITY AT ITS WORST. THERE SHE MET THE BURNT-OUT SWORDSMAN, AND BEGAN A TWISTING JOURNEY THAT TOOK HER FIRST TO THE AVENGERS, AND THEN TO THE UNIVERSE -- AS MANTIS BECAME THE CELESTIAL MADONNA!
IT'S 6 AM ON THE STANDARDIZED CLOCK USED BY THE AVENGERS QUINJET-- THOUGH AS THE SHIP HURTLES THROUGH DEEP SPACE, THERE'S NO SUN TO RISE.
6 AM-- THE END OF A NIGHT THAT SEEMED IT COULD LAST FOREVER-- FOR MANTIS--
--THE VISION--
--AND THE SCARLET WITCH.
STAINLESS STEVE ENGLEHART author
JORGE SANTAMARÍA pencil artist
SCOTT HANNA ink artist
HIFI DESIGN colorist
SHARPEFONT'S PAUL TUTRONE letterer
MARC SUMERAK assistant editor
JEFF YOUNGQUIST other assistant editor
TOM BREVOORT editor
JOE QUESADA editor in chief
BILL JEMAS president
JAMMIN' JIM STARLIN creator of Thanos
WHAT GOES AROUND...

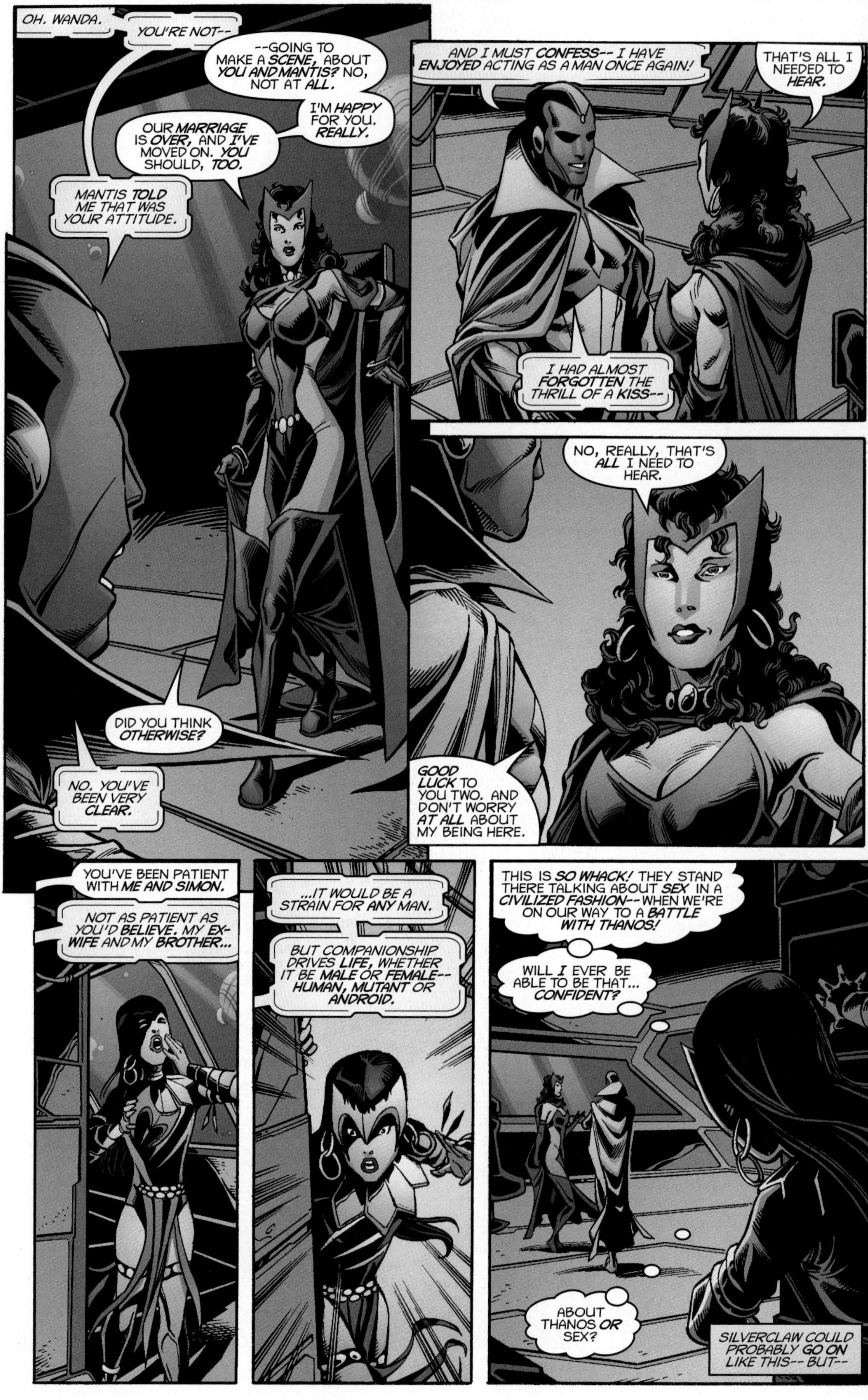

OH. WANDA.
YOU'RE NOT--
--GOING TO MAKE A SCENE, ABOUT YOU AND MANTIS? NO, NOT AT ALL.
I'M HAPPY FOR YOU. REALLY.
OUR MARRIAGE IS OVER, AND I'VE MOVED ON. YOU SHOULD, TOO.
MANTIS TOLD ME THAT WAS YOUR ATTITUDE.
DID YOU THINK OTHERWISE?
NO. YOU'VE BEEN VERY CLEAR.
AND I MUST CONFESS-- I HAVE ENJOYED ACTING AS A MAN ONCE AGAIN!
I HAD ALMOST FORGOTTEN THE THRILL OF A KISS--
THAT'S ALL I NEEDED TO HEAR.
NO, REALLY, THAT'S ALL I NEED TO HEAR.
GOOD LUCK TO YOU TWO. AND DON'T WORRY AT ALL ABOUT MY BEING HERE.
YOU'VE BEEN PATIENT WITH ME AND SIMON.
NOT AS PATIENT AS YOU'D BELIEVE. MY EX-WIFE AND MY BROTHER...
...IT WOULD BE A STRAIN FOR ANY MAN.
BUT COMPANIONSHIP DRIVES LIFE, WHETHER IT BE MALE OR FEMALE-- HUMAN, MUTANT OR ANDROID.
THIS IS SO WHACK! THEY STAND THERE TALKING ABOUT SEX IN A CIVILIZED FASHION-- WHEN WE'RE ON OUR WAY TO A BATTLE WITH THANOS!
WILL I EVER BE ABLE TO BE THAT... CONFIDENT?
ABOUT THANOS OR SEX?
SILVERCLAW COULD PROBABLY GO ON LIKE THIS-- BUT--

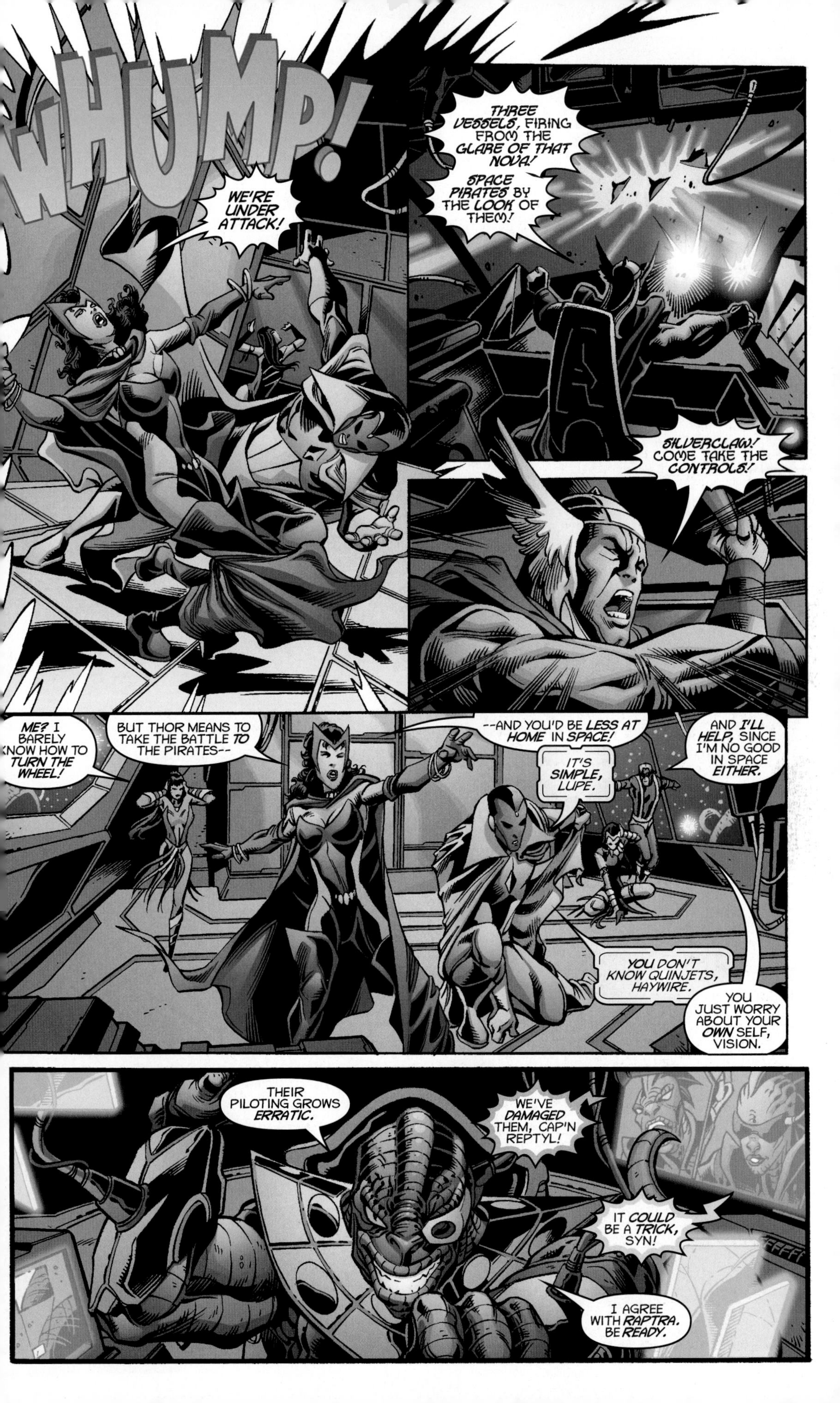
WHUMP!
WE'RE UNDER ATTACK!
THREE VESSELS, FIRING FROM THE GLARE OF THAT NOVA!
SPACE PIRATES BY THE LOOK OF THEM!
SILVERCLAW! COME TAKE THE CONTROLS!
ME? I BARELY KNOW HOW TO TURN THE WHEEL!
BUT THOR MEANS TO TAKE THE BATTLE TO THE PIRATES--
--AND YOU'D BE LESS AT HOME IN SPACE!
IT'S SIMPLE, LUPE.
AND I'LL HELP, SINCE I'M NO GOOD IN SPACE EITHER.
YOU DON'T KNOW QUINJETS, HAYWIRE.
YOU JUST WORRY ABOUT YOUR OWN SELF, VISION.
THEIR PILOTING GROWS ERRATIC.
WE'VE DAMAGED THEM, CAP'N REPTYL!
IT COULD BE A TRICK, SYN!
I AGREE WITH RAPTRA. BE READY.

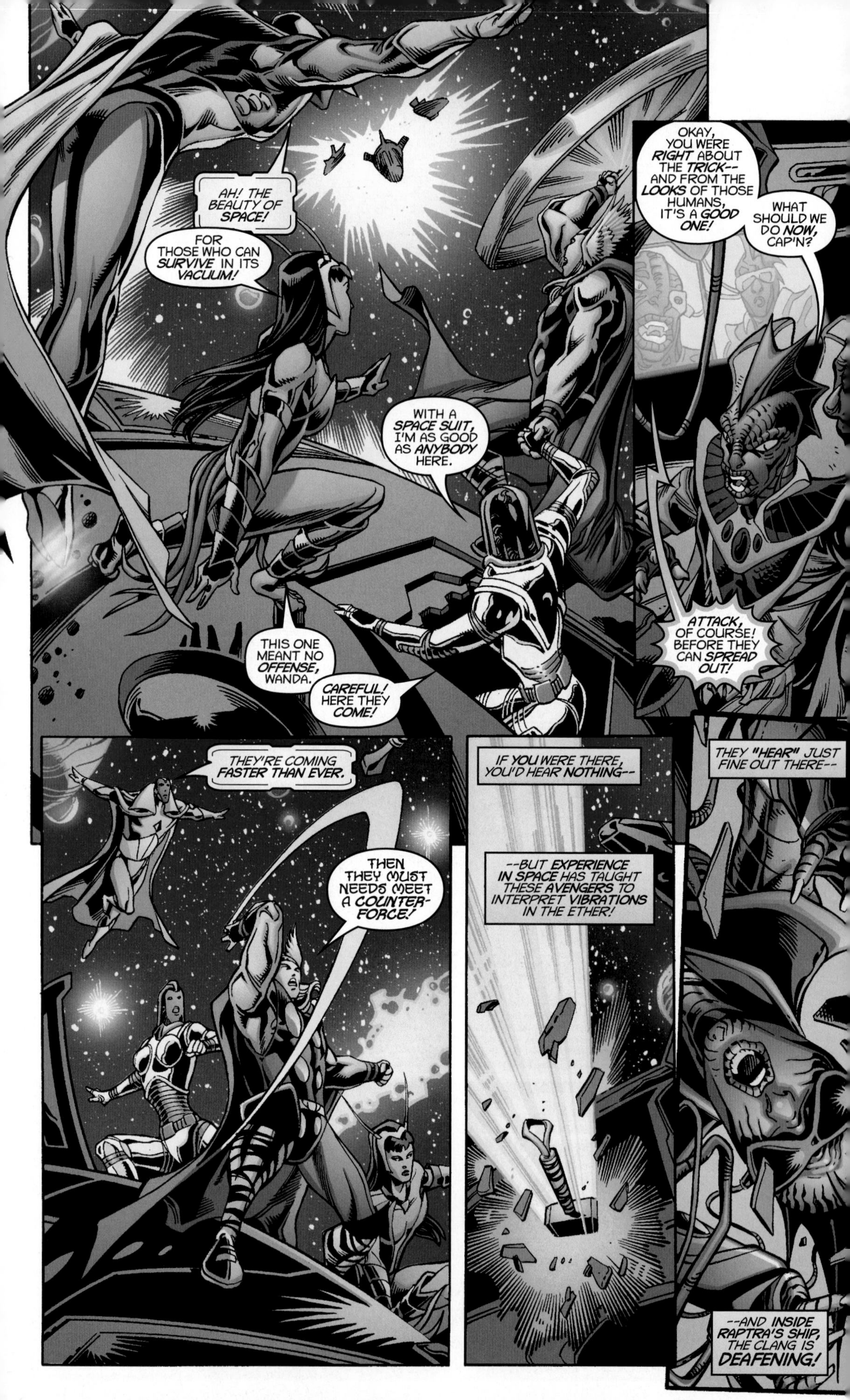
AH! THE BEAUTY OF SPACE!
FOR THOSE WHO CAN SURVIVE IN ITS VACUUM!
OKAY, YOU WERE RIGHT ABOUT THE TRICK-- AND FROM THE LOOKS OF THOSE HUMANS, IT'S A GOOD ONE!
WHAT SHOULD WE DO NOW, CAP'N?
WITH A SPACE SUIT, I'M AS GOOD AS ANYBODY HERE.
THIS ONE MEANT NO OFFENSE, WANDA.
CAREFUL! HERE THEY COME!
ATTACK, OF COURSE! BEFORE THEY CAN SPREAD OUT!
THEY'RE COMING FASTER THAN EVER.
THEN THEY MUST NEEDS MEET A COUNTER-FORCE!
IF YOU WERE THERE, YOU'D HEAR NOTHING--
--BUT EXPERIENCE IN SPACE HAS TAUGHT THESE AVENGERS TO INTERPRET VIBRATIONS IN THE ETHER!
THEY "HEAR" JUST FINE OUT THERE--
--AND INSIDE RAPTRA'S SHIP, THE CLANG IS DEAFENING!

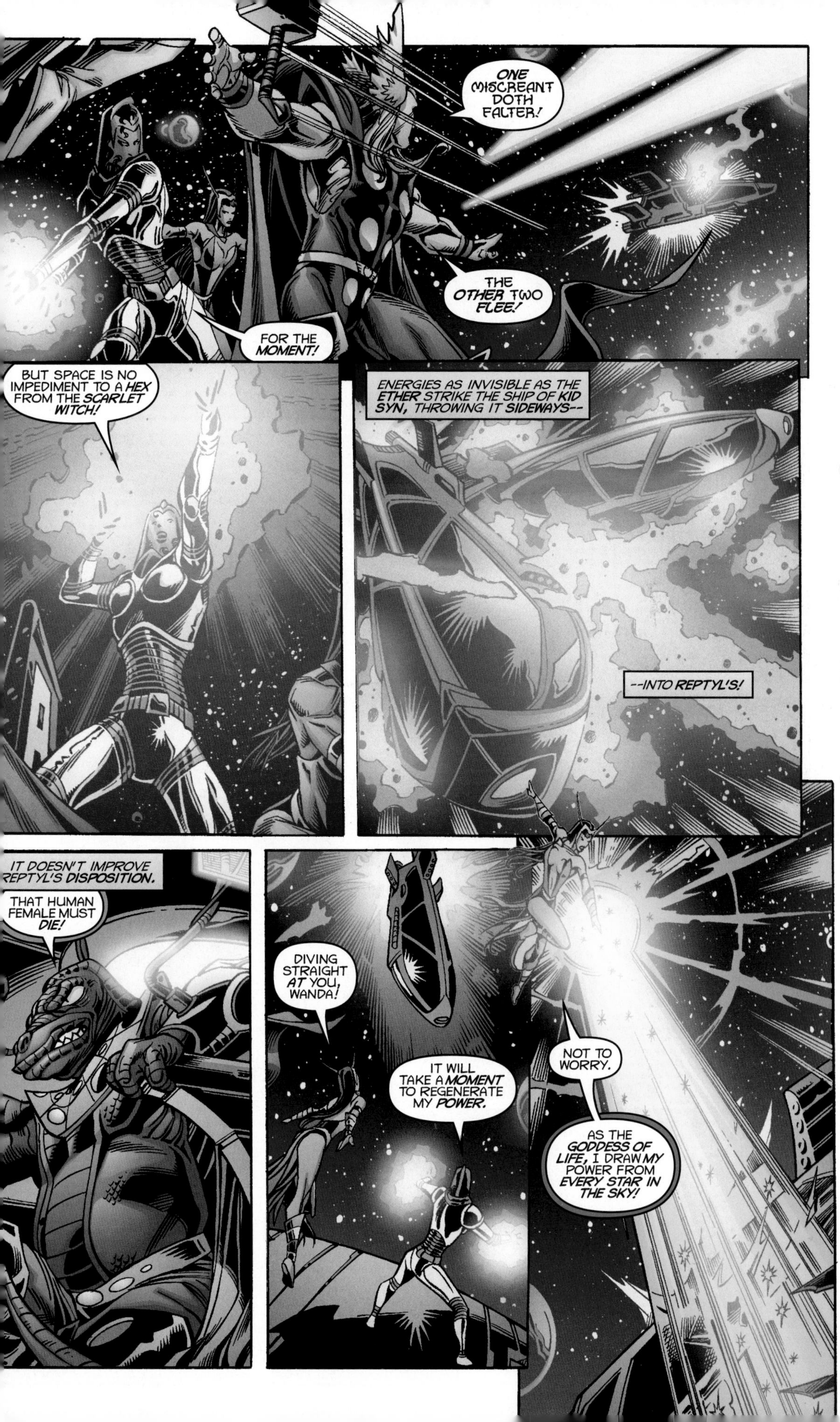

ONE MISCREANT DOTH FALTER!
THE OTHER TWO FLEE!
FOR THE MOMENT!
BUT SPACE IS NO IMPEDIMENT TO A HEX FROM THE SCARLET WITCH!
ENERGIES AS INVISIBLE AS THE ETHER STRIKE THE SHIP OF KID SYN, THROWING IT SIDEWAYS--
--INTO REPTYL'S!
IT DOESN'T IMPROVE REPTYL'S DISPOSITION.
THAT HUMAN FEMALE MUST DIE!
DIVING STRAIGHT AT YOU, WANDA!
IT WILL TAKE A MOMENT TO REGENERATE MY POWER.
NOT TO WORRY.
AS THE GODDESS OF LIFE, I DRAW MY POWER FROM EVERY STAR IN THE SKY!

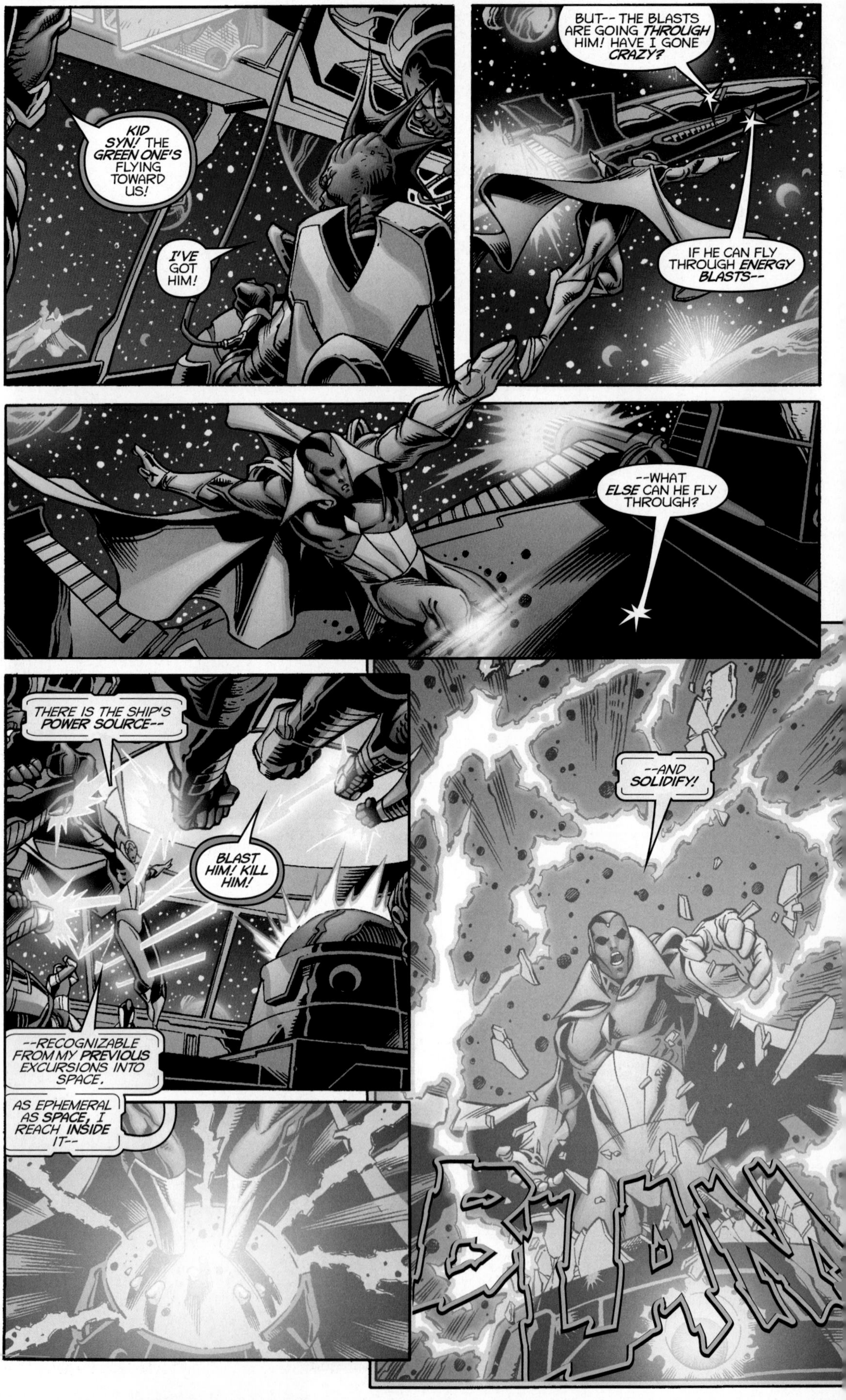

KID SYN! THE GREEN ONE'S FLYING TOWARD US!
I'VE GOT HIM!
BUT-- THE BLASTS ARE GOING THROUGH HIM! HAVE I GONE CRAZY?
IF HE CAN FLY THROUGH ENERGY BLASTS--
--WHAT ELSE CAN HE FLY THROUGH?
THERE IS THE SHIP'S POWER SOURCE--
BLAST HIM! KILL HIM!
--RECOGNIZABLE FROM MY PREVIOUS EXCURSIONS INTO SPACE.
AS EPHEMERAL AS SPACE, I REACH INSIDE IT--
--AND SOLIDIFY!

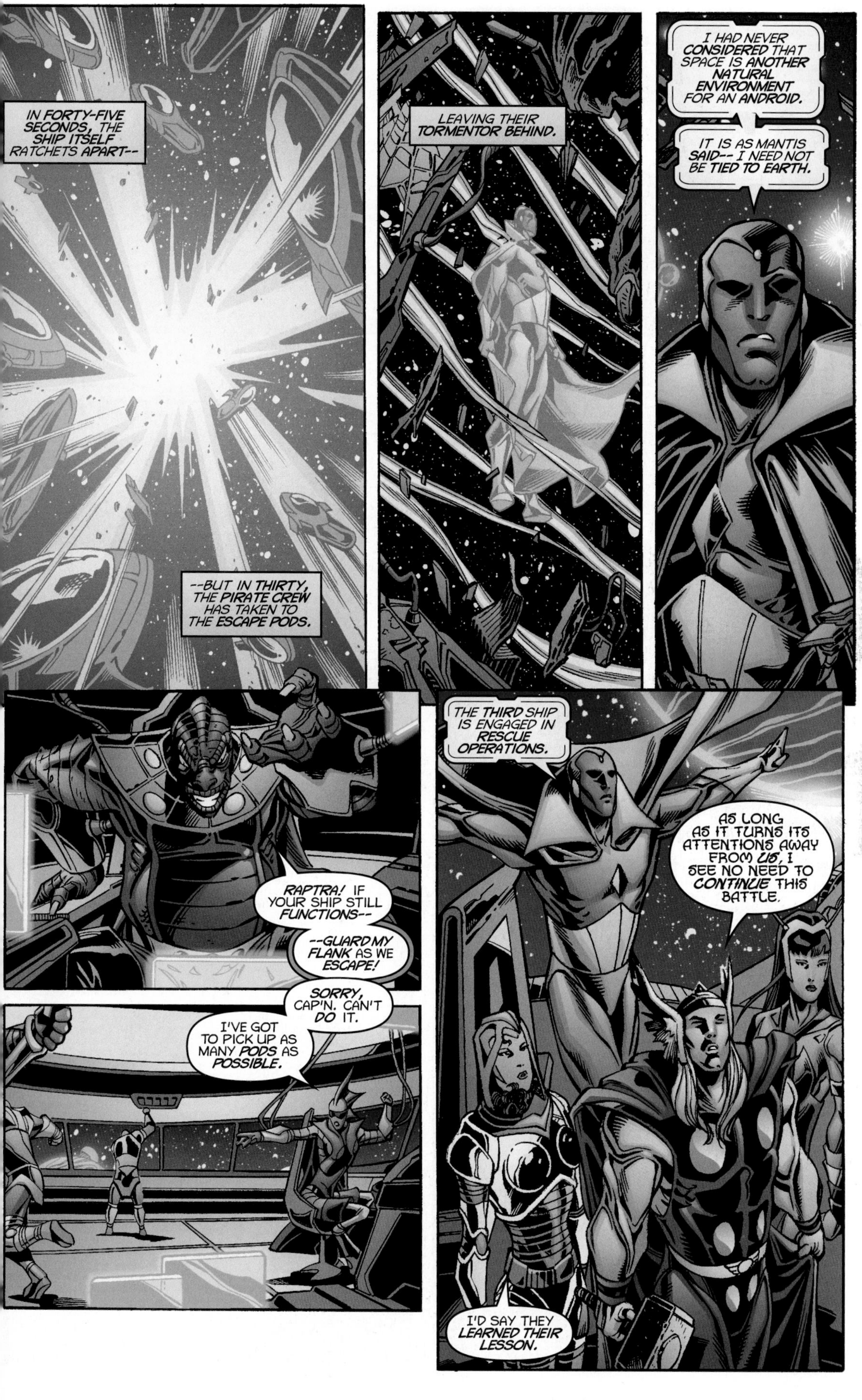
IN FORTY-FIVE SECONDS, THE SHIP ITSELF RATCHETS APART--
--BUT IN THIRTY, THE PIRATE CREW HAS TAKEN TO THE ESCAPE PODS.
LEAVING THEIR TORMENTOR BEHIND.
I HAD NEVER CONSIDERED THAT SPACE IS ANOTHER NATURAL ENVIRONMENT FOR AN ANDROID.
IT IS AS MANTIS SAID-- I NEED NOT BE TIED TO EARTH.
RAPTRA! IF YOUR SHIP STILL FUNCTIONS--
--GUARD MY FLANK AS WE ESCAPE!
SORRY, CAP'N. CAN'T DO IT.
I'VE GOT TO PICK UP AS MANY PODS AS POSSIBLE.
THE THIRD SHIP IS ENGAGED IN RESCUE OPERATIONS.
AS LONG AS IT TURNS ITS ATTENTIONS AWAY FROM US, I SEE NO NEED TO CONTINUE THIS BATTLE.
I'D SAY THEY LEARNED THEIR LESSON.

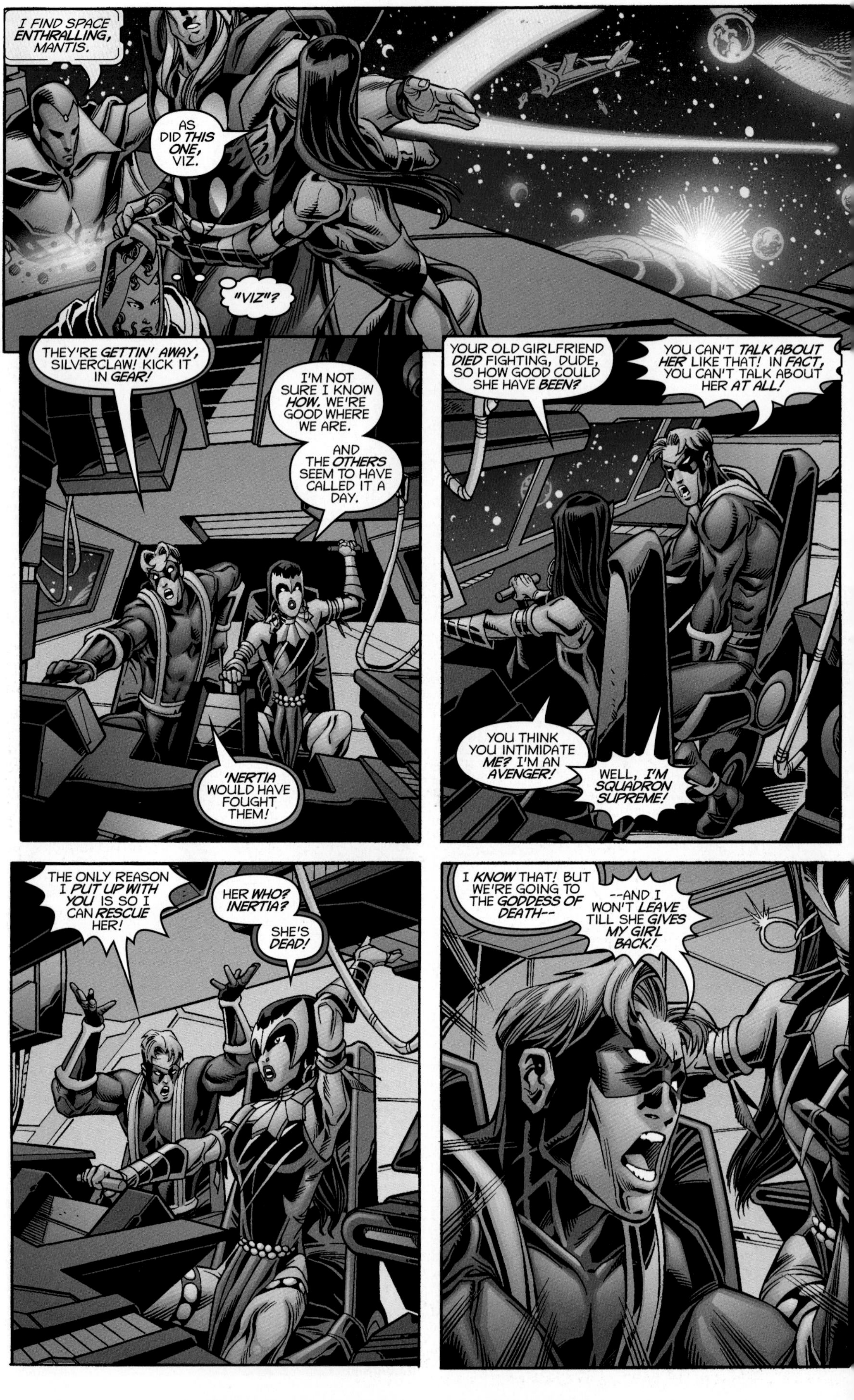

I FIND SPACE ENTHRALLING, MANTIS.
AS DID THIS ONE, VIZ.
"VIZ"?
THEY'RE GETTIN' AWAY, SILVERCLAW! KICK IT IN GEAR!
I'M NOT SURE I KNOW HOW. WE'RE GOOD WHERE WE ARE.
AND THE OTHERS SEEM TO HAVE CALLED IT A DAY.
'NERTIA WOULD HAVE FOUGHT THEM!
YOUR OLD GIRLFRIEND DIED FIGHTING, DUDE, SO HOW GOOD COULD SHE HAVE BEEN?
YOU CAN'T TALK ABOUT HER LIKE THAT! IN FACT, YOU CAN'T TALK ABOUT HER AT ALL!
YOU THINK YOU INTIMIDATE ME? I'M AN AVENGER!
WELL, I'M SQUADRON SUPREME!
THE ONLY REASON I PUT UP WITH YOU IS SO I CAN RESCUE HER!
HER WHO? INERTIA?
SHE'S DEAD!
I KNOW THAT! BUT WE'RE GOING TO THE GODDESS OF DEATH--
--AND I WON'T LEAVE TILL SHE GIVES MY GIRL BACK!

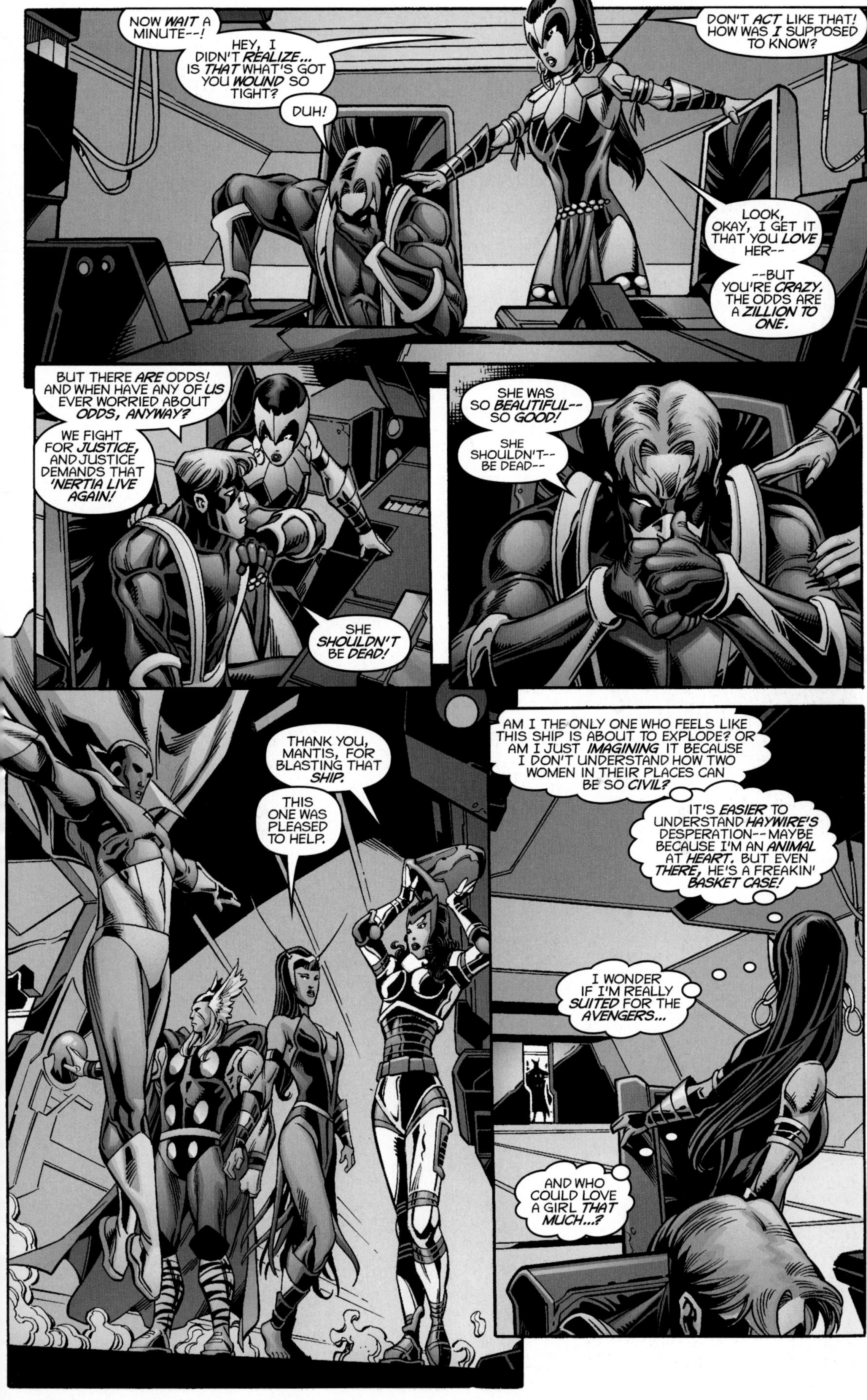

NOW WAIT A MINUTE--!
HEY, I DIDN'T REALIZE... IS THAT WHAT'S GOT YOU WOUND SO TIGHT?
DUH!
DON'T ACT LIKE THAT! HOW WAS I SUPPOSED TO KNOW?
LOOK, OKAY, I GET IT THAT YOU LOVE HER--
--BUT YOU'RE CRAZY. THE ODDS ARE A ZILLION TO ONE.
BUT THERE ARE ODDS! AND WHEN HAVE ANY OF US EVER WORRIED ABOUT ODDS, ANYWAY?
WE FIGHT FOR JUSTICE, AND JUSTICE DEMANDS THAT 'NERTIA LIVE AGAIN!
SHE SHOULDN'T BE DEAD!
SHE WAS SO BEAUTIFUL-- SO GOOD!
SHE SHOULDN'T-- BE DEAD--
THANK YOU, MANTIS, FOR BLASTING THAT SHIP.
THIS ONE WAS PLEASED TO HELP.
AM I THE ONLY ONE WHO FEELS LIKE THIS SHIP IS ABOUT TO EXPLODE? OR AM I JUST IMAGINING IT BECAUSE I DON'T UNDERSTAND HOW TWO WOMEN IN THEIR PLACES CAN BE SO CIVIL?
IT'S EASIER TO UNDERSTAND HAYWIRE'S DESPERATION-- MAYBE BECAUSE I'M AN ANIMAL AT HEART. BUT EVEN THERE, HE'S A FREAKIN' BASKET CASE!
I WONDER IF I'M REALLY SUITED FOR THE AVENGERS...
AND WHO COULD LOVE A GIRL THAT MUCH...?

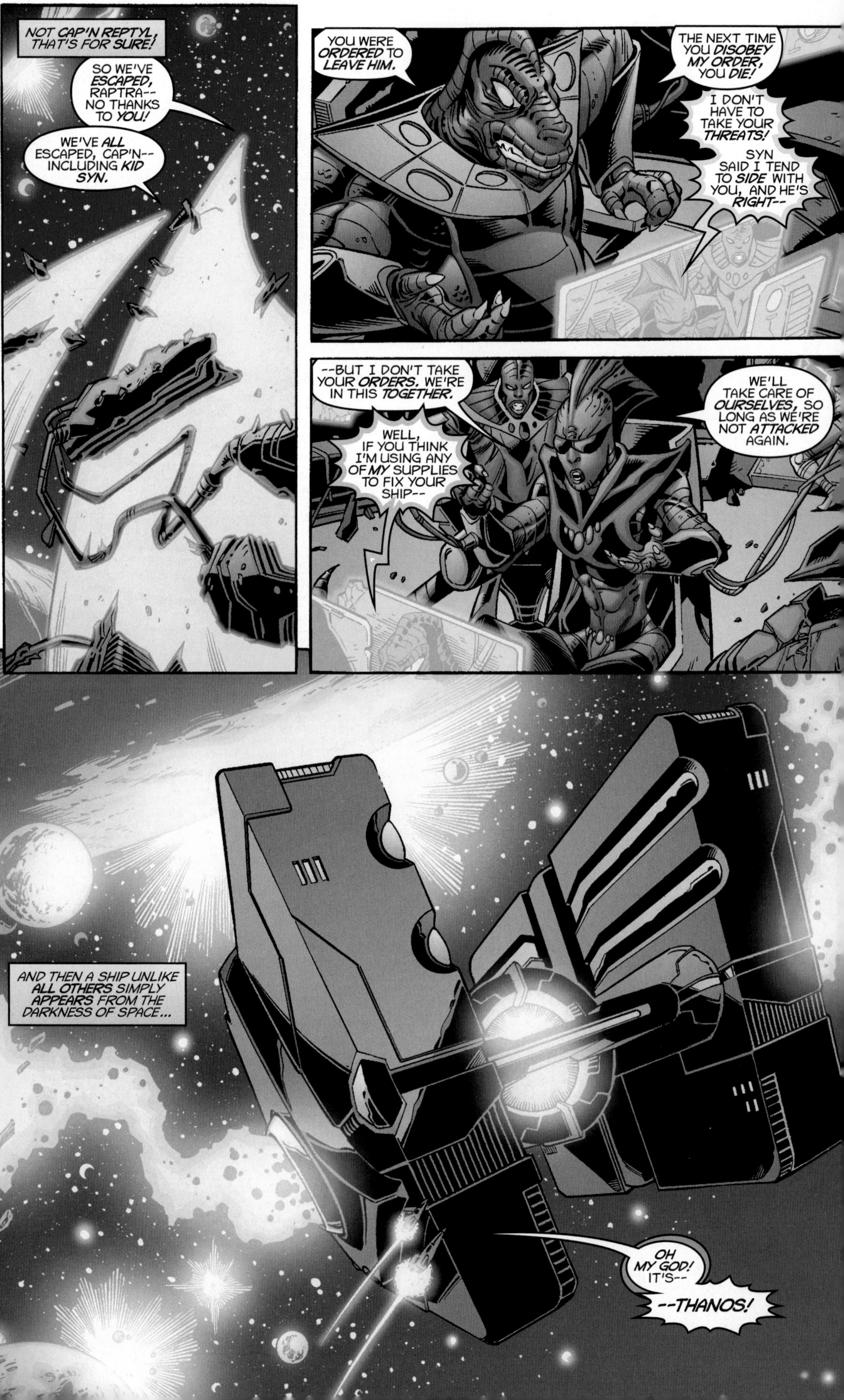
NOT CAP'N REPTYL, THAT'S FOR SURE!
SO WE'VE ESCAPED, RAPTRA-- NO THANKS TO YOU!
WE'VE ALL ESCAPED, CAP'N-- INCLUDING KID SYN.
YOU WERE ORDERED TO LEAVE HIM.
THE NEXT TIME YOU DISOBEY MY ORDER, YOU DIE!
I DON'T HAVE TO TAKE YOUR THREATS!
SYN SAID I TEND TO SIDE WITH YOU, AND HE'S RIGHT--
--BUT I DON'T TAKE YOUR ORDERS. WE'RE IN THIS TOGETHER.
WELL, IF YOU THINK I'M USING ANY OF MY SUPPLIES TO FIX YOUR SHIP--
WE'LL TAKE CARE OF OURSELVES, SO LONG AS WE'RE NOT ATTACKED AGAIN.
AND THEN A SHIP UNLIKE ALL OTHERS SIMPLY APPEARS FROM THE DARKNESS OF SPACE...
OH MY GOD! IT'S--
--THANOS!

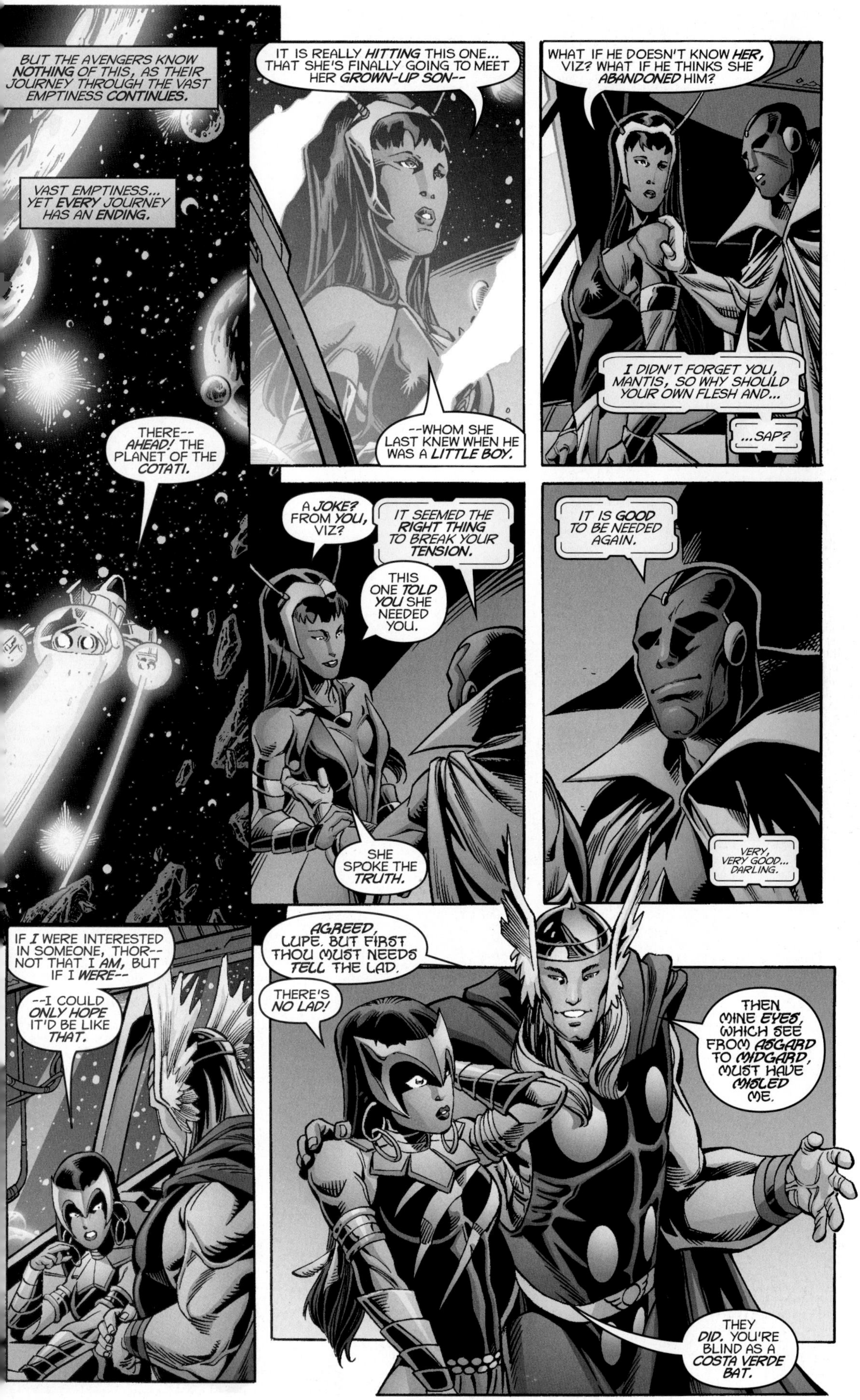

BUT THE AVENGERS KNOW NOTHING OF THIS, AS THEIR JOURNEY THROUGH THE VAST EMPTINESS CONTINUES.
VAST EMPTINESS... YET EVERY JOURNEY HAS AN ENDING.
THERE--AHEAD! THE PLANET OF THE COTATI.
IT IS REALLY HITTING THIS ONE... THAT SHE'S FINALLY GOING TO MEET HER GROWN-UP SON--
--WHOM SHE LAST KNEW WHEN HE WAS A LITTLE BOY.
WHAT IF HE DOESN'T KNOW HER, VIZ? WHAT IF HE THINKS SHE ABANDONED HIM?
I DIDN'T FORGET YOU, MANTIS, SO WHY SHOULD YOUR OWN FLESH AND...
...SAP?
A JOKE? FROM YOU, VIZ?
IT SEEMED THE RIGHT THING TO BREAK YOUR TENSION.
THIS ONE TOLD YOU SHE NEEDED YOU.
SHE SPOKE THE TRUTH.
IT IS GOOD TO BE NEEDED AGAIN.
VERY, VERY GOOD... DARLING.
IF I WERE INTERESTED IN SOMEONE, THOR--NOT THAT I AM, BUT IF I WERE--
--I COULD ONLY HOPE IT'D BE LIKE THAT.
AGREED, LUPE. BUT FIRST THOU MUST NEEDS TELL THE LAD.
THERE'S NO LAD!
THEN MINE EYES, WHICH SEE FROM ASGARD TO MIDGARD, MUST HAVE MISLED ME.
THEY DID. YOU'RE BLIND AS A COSTA VERDE BAT.

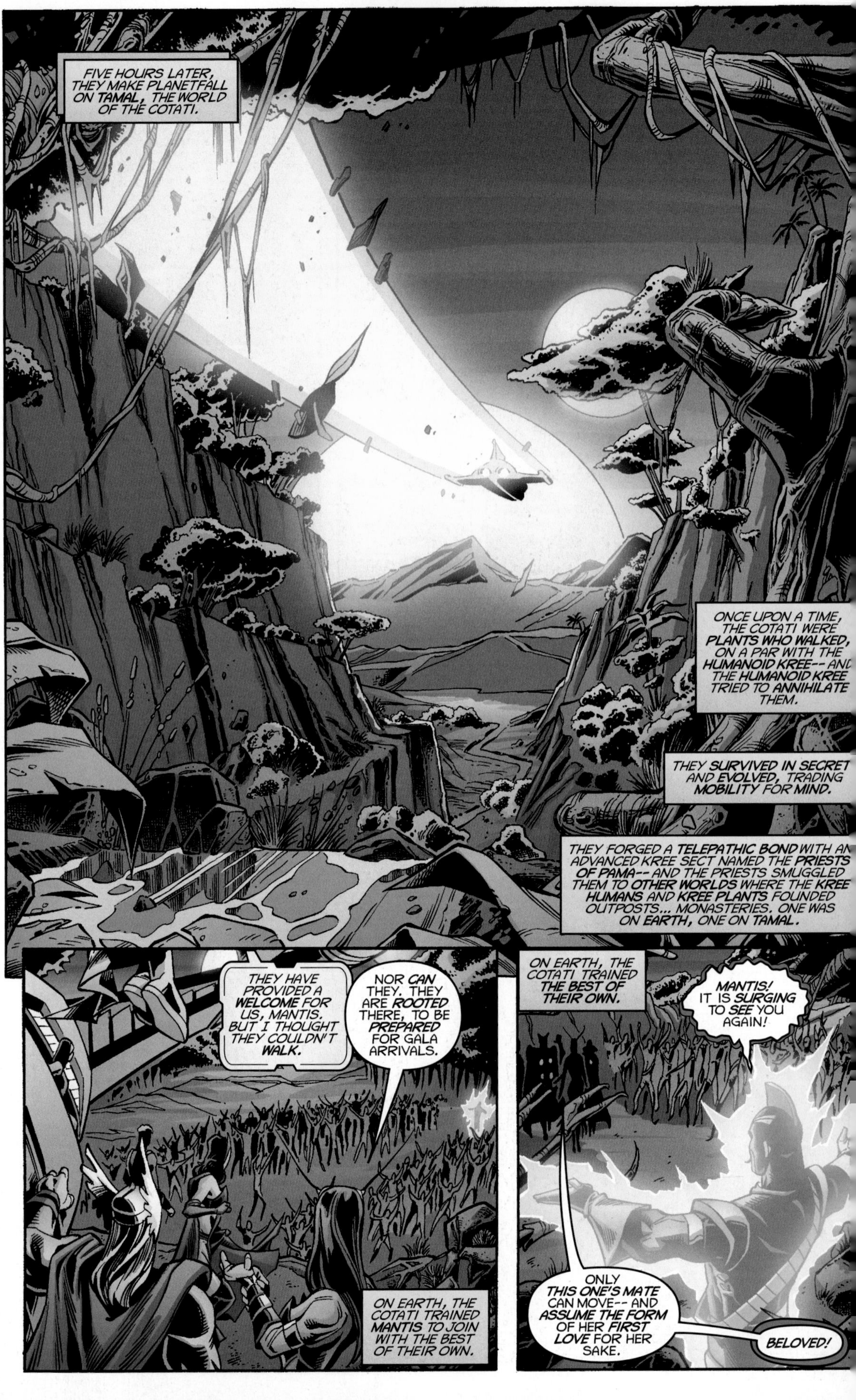
FIVE HOURS LATER, THEY MAKE PLANETFALL ON TAMAL, THE WORLD OF THE COTATI.
ONCE UPON A TIME, THE COTATI WERE PLANTS WHO WALKED, ON A PAR WITH THE HUMANOID KREE-- AND THE HUMANOID KREE TRIED TO ANNIHILATE THEM.
THEY SURVIVED IN SECRET AND EVOLVED, TRADING MOBILITY FOR MIND.
THEY FORGED A TELEPATHIC BOND WITH AN ADVANCED KREE SECT NAMED THE PRIESTS OF PAMA-- AND THE PRIESTS SMUGGLED THEM TO OTHER WORLDS WHERE THE KREE HUMANS AND KREE PLANTS FOUNDED OUTPOSTS... MONASTERIES. ONE WAS ON EARTH, ONE ON TAMAL.
THEY HAVE PROVIDED A WELCOME FOR US, MANTIS. BUT I THOUGHT THEY COULDN'T WALK.
NOR CAN THEY. THEY ARE ROOTED THERE, TO BE PREPARED FOR GALA ARRIVALS.
ON EARTH, THE COTATI TRAINED MANTIS TO JOIN WITH THE BEST OF THEIR OWN.
ON EARTH, THE COTATI TRAINED THE BEST OF THEIR OWN.
MANTIS! IT IS SURGING TO SEE YOU AGAIN!
ONLY THIS ONE'S MATE CAN MOVE-- AND ASSUME THE FORM OF HER FIRST LOVE FOR HER SAKE.
BELOVED!

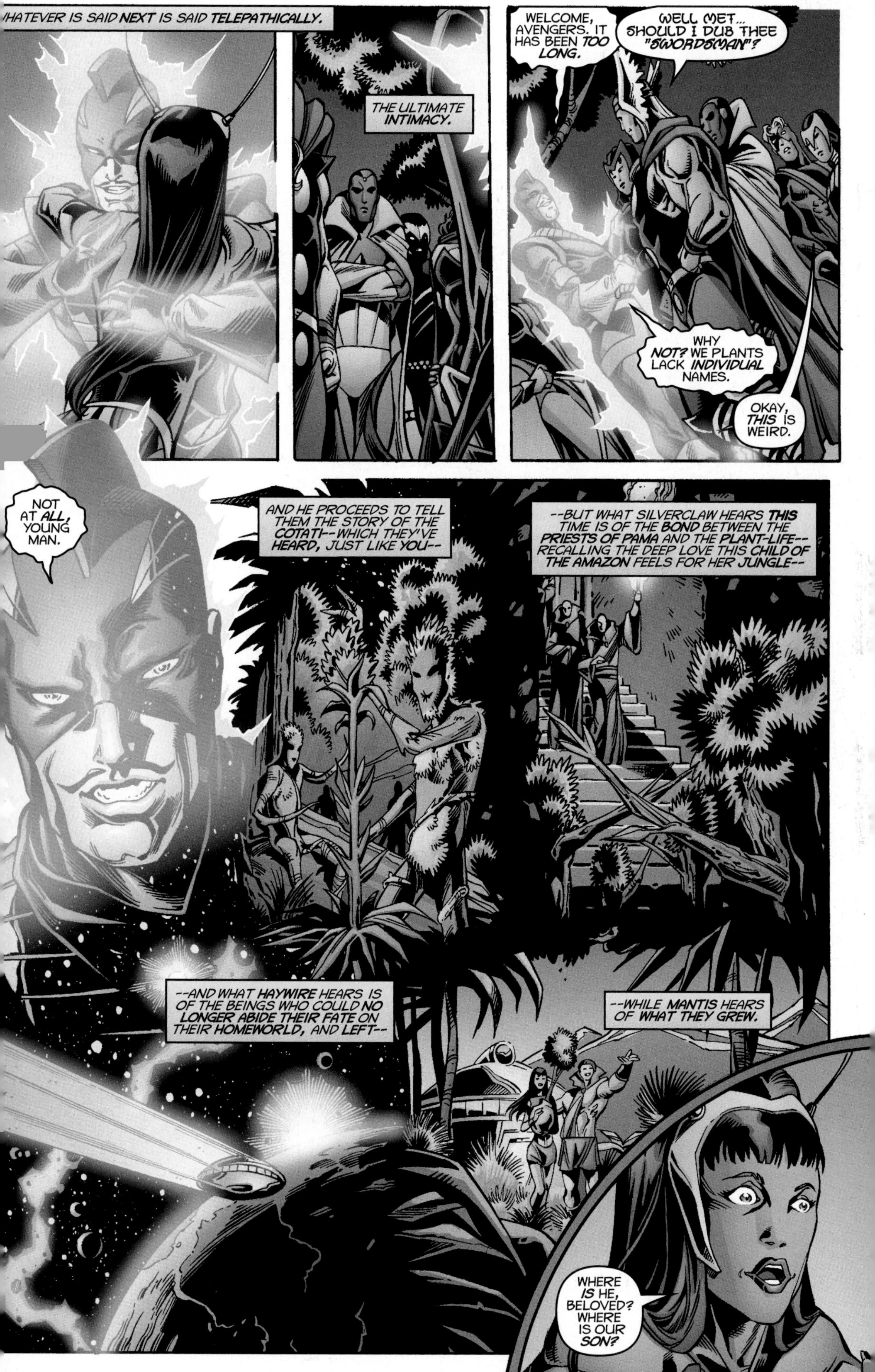

WHATEVER IS SAID NEXT IS SAID TELEPATHICALLY.
THE ULTIMATE INTIMACY.
WELCOME, AVENGERS. IT HAS BEEN TOO LONG.
WELL MET... SHOULD I DUB THEE "SWORDSMAN"?
WHY NOT? WE PLANTS LACK INDIVIDUAL NAMES.
OKAY, THIS IS WEIRD.
NOT AT ALL, YOUNG MAN.
AND HE PROCEEDS TO TELL THEM THE STORY OF THE COTATI--WHICH THEY'VE HEARD, JUST LIKE YOU--
--BUT WHAT SILVERCLAW HEARS THIS TIME IS OF THE BOND BETWEEN THE PRIESTS OF PAMA AND THE PLANT-LIFE--RECALLING THE DEEP LOVE THIS CHILD OF THE AMAZON FEELS FOR HER JUNGLE--
--AND WHAT HAYWIRE HEARS IS OF THE BEINGS WHO COULD NO LONGER ABIDE THEIR FATE ON THEIR HOMEWORLD, AND LEFT--
--WHILE MANTIS HEARS OF WHAT THEY GREW.
WHERE IS HE, BELOVED? WHERE IS OUR SON?

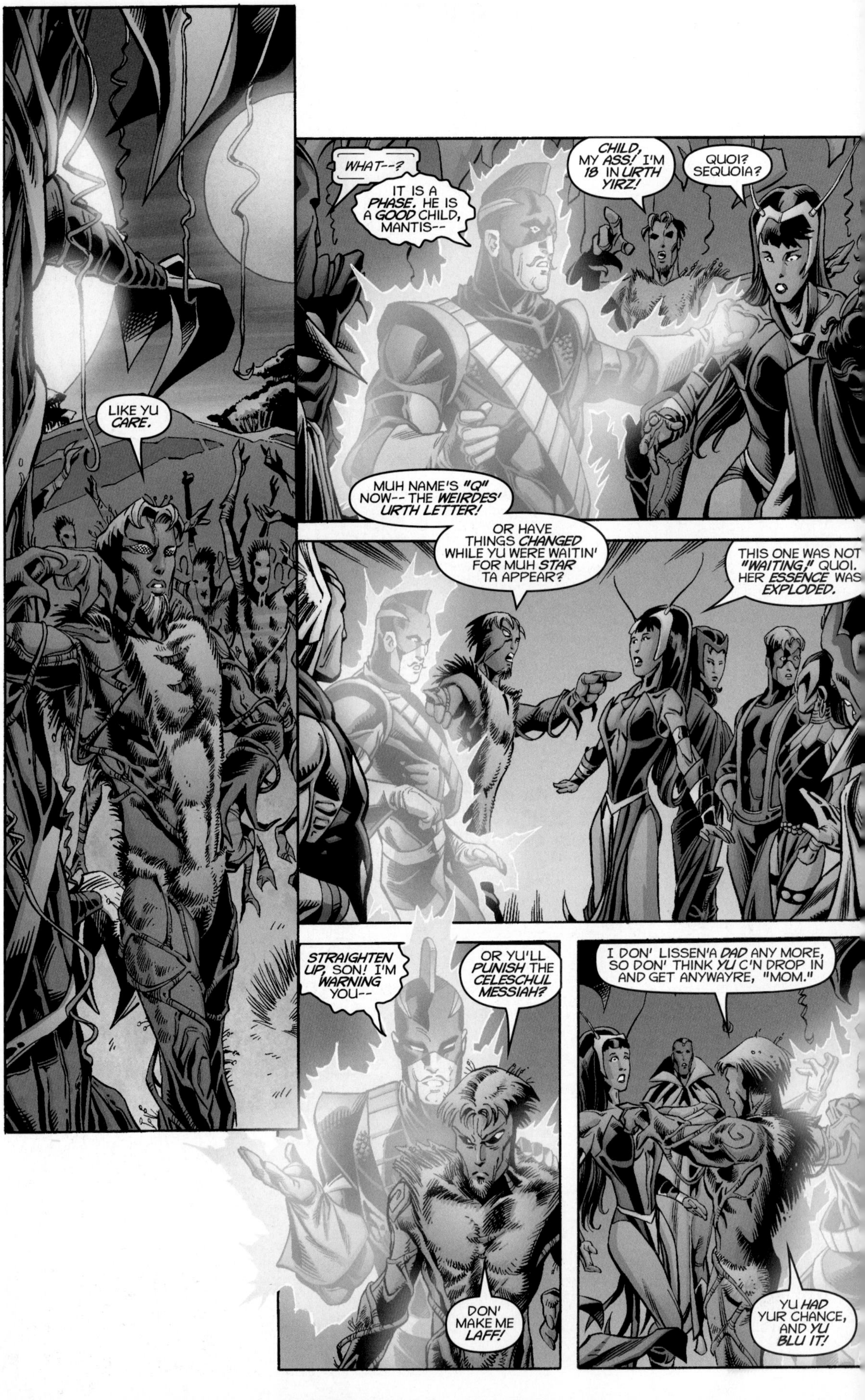
LIKE YU CARE.
WHAT--?
IT IS A PHASE. HE IS A GOOD CHILD, MANTIS--
CHILD, MY ASS! I'M 18 IN URTH YIRZ!
QUOI? SEQUOIA?
MUH NAME'S "Q" NOW-- THE WEIRDES' URTH LETTER!
OR HAVE THINGS CHANGED WHILE YU WERE WAITIN' FOR MUH STAR TA APPEAR?
THIS ONE WAS NOT "WAITING," QUOI. HER ESSENCE WAS EXPLODED.
STRAIGHTEN UP, SON! I'M WARNING YOU--
OR YU'LL PUNISH THE CELESCHUL MESSIAH?
DON' MAKE ME LAFF!
I DON' LISSEN'A DAD ANY MORE, SO DON' THINK YU C'N DROP IN AND GET ANYWAYRE, "MOM."
YU HAD YUR CHANCE, AND YU BLU IT!

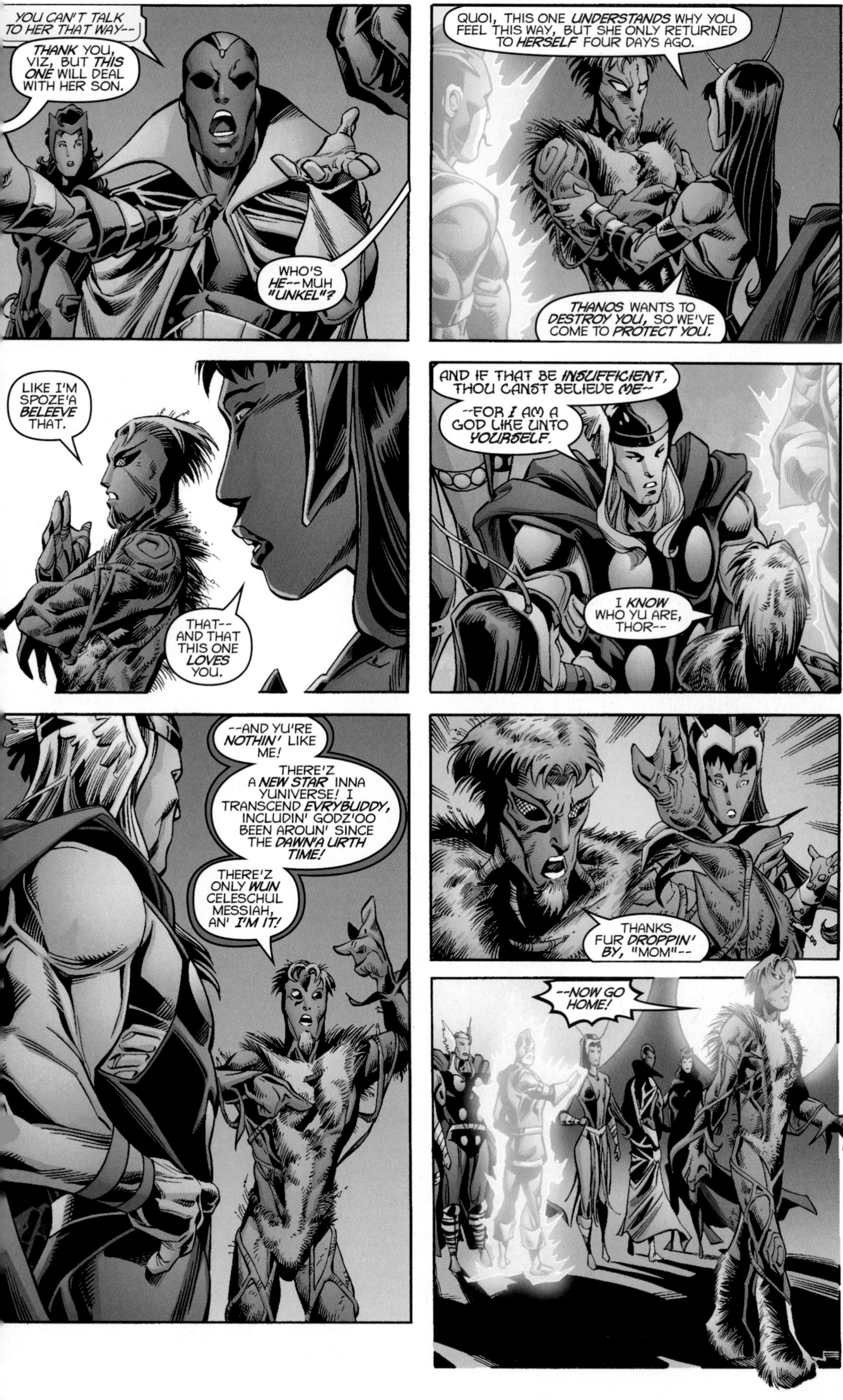
YOU CAN'T TALK TO HER THAT WAY--
THANK YOU, VIZ, BUT THIS ONE WILL DEAL WITH HER SON.
WHO'S HE--MUH "UNKEL"?
QUOI, THIS ONE UNDERSTANDS WHY YOU FEEL THIS WAY, BUT SHE ONLY RETURNED TO HERSELF FOUR DAYS AGO.
THANOS WANTS TO DESTROY YOU, SO WE'VE COME TO PROTECT YOU.
LIKE I'M SPOZE'A BELEEVE THAT.
THAT-- AND THAT THIS ONE LOVES YOU.
AND IF THAT BE INSUFFICIENT, THOU CANST BELIEVE ME--
--FOR I AM A GOD LIKE UNTO YOURSELF.
I KNOW WHO YU ARE, THOR--
--AND YU'RE NOTHIN' LIKE ME!
THERE'Z A NEW STAR INNA YUNIVERSE! I TRANSCEND EVRYBUDDY, INCLUDIN' GODZ'OO BEEN AROUN' SINCE THE DAWN'A URTH TIME!
THERE'Z ONLY WUN CELESCHUL MESSIAH, AN' I'M IT!
THANKS FUR DROPPIN' BY, "MOM"--
--NOW GO HOME!

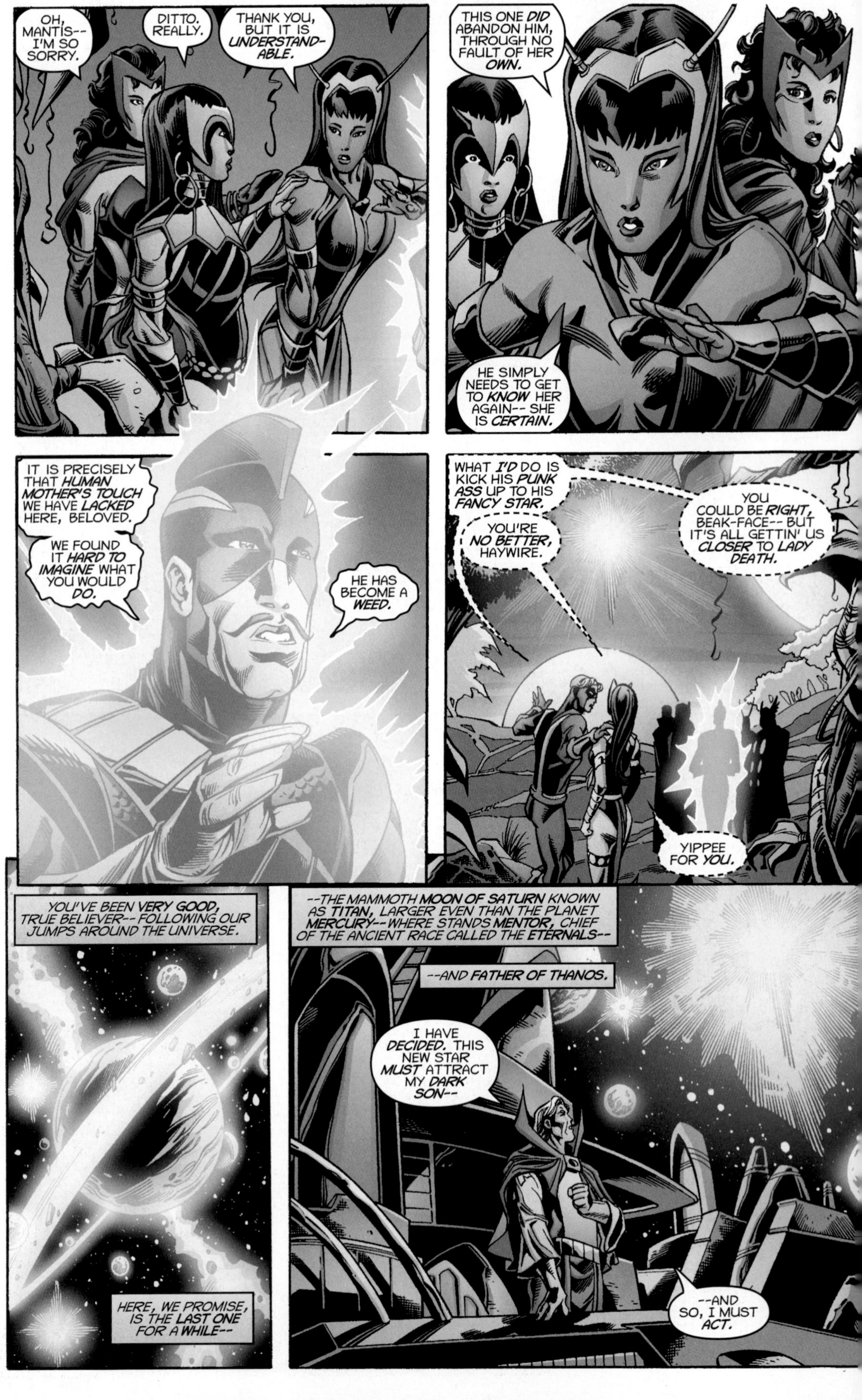
OH, MANTIS-- I'M SO SORRY.
DITTO. REALLY.
THANK YOU, BUT IT IS UNDERSTANDABLE.
THIS ONE DID ABANDON HIM, THROUGH NO FAULT OF HER OWN.
HE SIMPLY NEEDS TO GET TO KNOW HER AGAIN-- SHE IS CERTAIN.
IT IS PRECISELY THAT HUMAN MOTHER'S TOUCH WE HAVE LACKED HERE, BELOVED.
WE FOUND IT HARD TO IMAGINE WHAT YOU WOULD DO.
HE HAS BECOME A WEED.
WHAT I'D DO IS KICK HIS PUNK ASS UP TO HIS FANCY STAR.
YOU'RE NO BETTER, HAYWIRE.
YOU COULD BE RIGHT, BEAK-FACE-- BUT IT'S ALL GETTIN' US CLOSER TO LADY DEATH.
YIPPEE FOR YOU.
YOU'VE BEEN VERY GOOD, TRUE BELIEVER-- FOLLOWING OUR JUMPS AROUND THE UNIVERSE.
HERE, WE PROMISE, IS THE LAST ONE FOR A WHILE--
--THE MAMMOTH MOON OF SATURN KNOWN AS TITAN, LARGER EVEN THAN THE PLANET MERCURY-- WHERE STANDS MENTOR, CHIEF OF THE ANCIENT RACE CALLED THE ETERNALS--
--AND FATHER OF THANOS.
I HAVE DECIDED. THIS NEW STAR MUST ATTRACT MY DARK SON--
--AND SO, I MUST ACT.

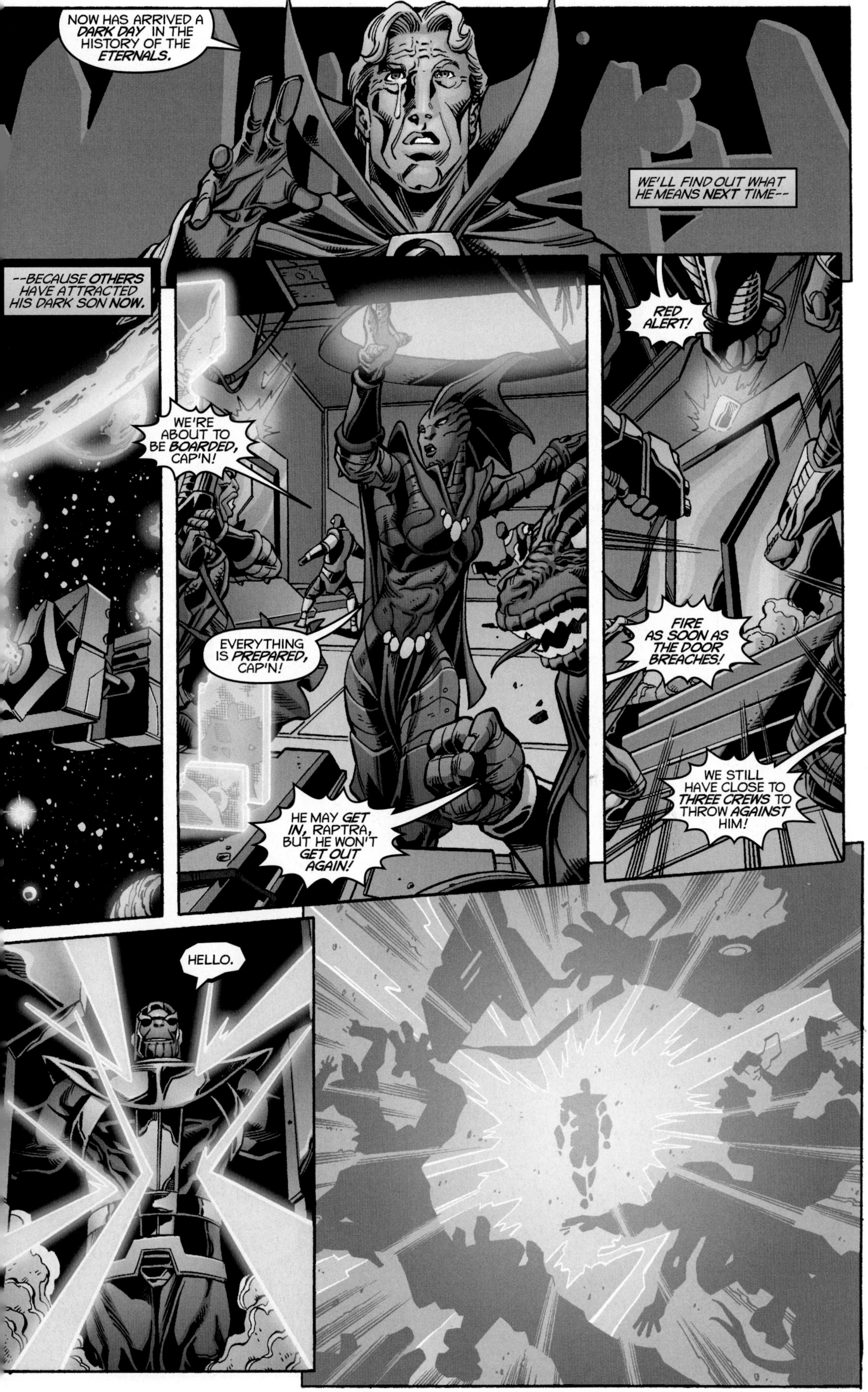
NOW HAS ARRIVED A DARK DAY IN THE HISTORY OF THE ETERNALS.
WE'LL FIND OUT WHAT HE MEANS NEXT TIME--
--BECAUSE OTHERS HAVE ATTRACTED HIS DARK SON NOW.
RED ALERT!
WE'RE ABOUT TO BE BOARDED, CAP'N!
EVERYTHING IS PREPARED, CAP'N!
FIRE AS SOON AS THE DOOR BREACHES!
WE STILL HAVE CLOSE TO THREE CREWS TO THROW AGAINST HIM!
HE MAY GET IN, RAPTRA, BUT HE WON'T GET OUT AGAIN!
HELLO.

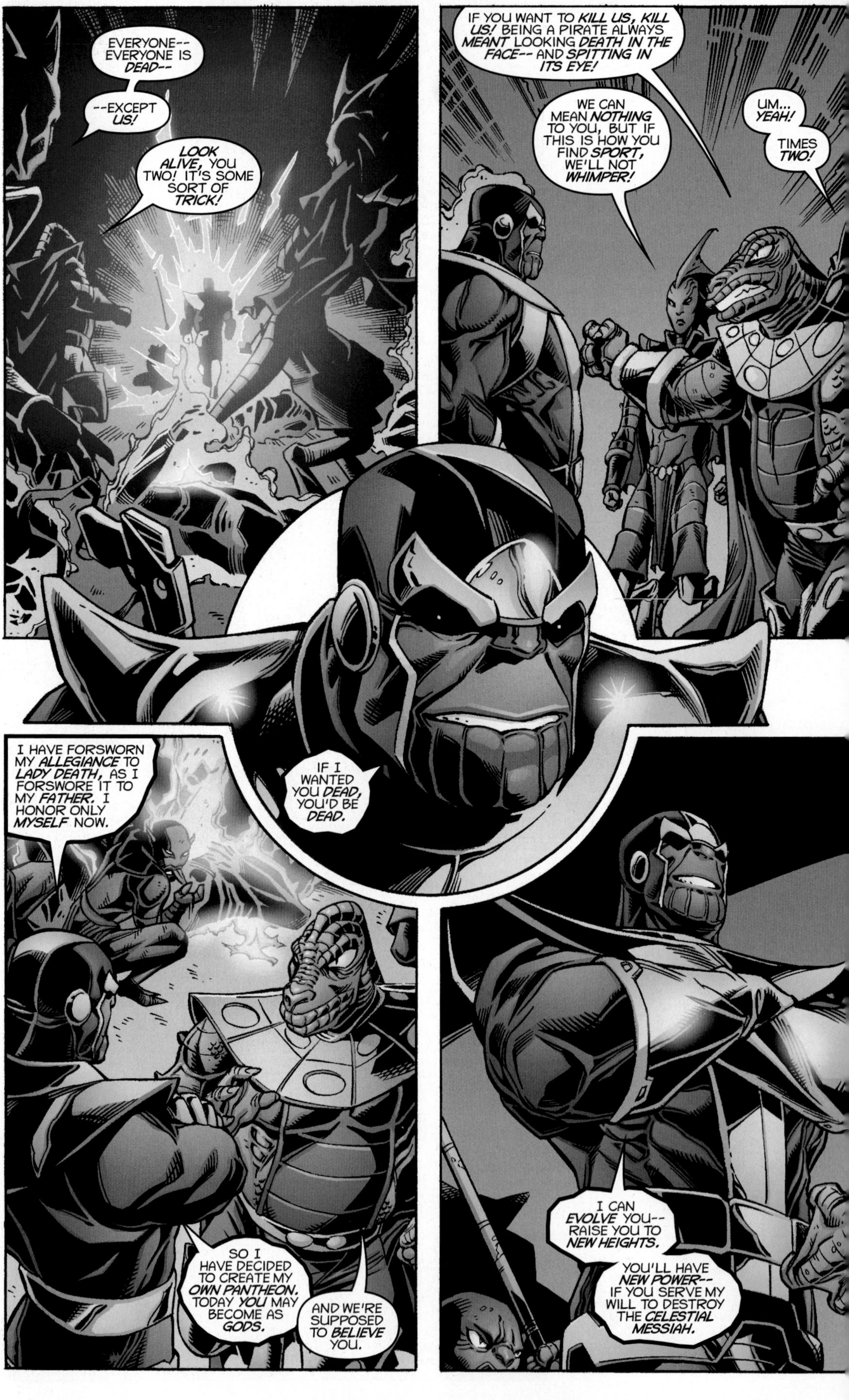
EVERYONE-- EVERYONE IS DEAD--
--EXCEPT US!
LOOK ALIVE, YOU TWO! IT'S SOME SORT OF TRICK!
IF YOU WANT TO KILL US, KILL US! BEING A PIRATE ALWAYS MEANT LOOKING DEATH IN THE FACE-- AND SPITTING IN ITS EYE!
WE CAN MEAN NOTHING TO YOU, BUT IF THIS IS HOW YOU FIND SPORT, WE'LL NOT WHIMPER!
UM... YEAH!
TIMES TWO!
IF I WANTED YOU DEAD, YOU'D BE DEAD.
I HAVE FORSWORN MY ALLEGIANCE TO LADY DEATH, AS I FORSWORE IT TO MY FATHER. I HONOR ONLY MYSELF NOW.
SO I HAVE DECIDED TO CREATE MY OWN PANTHEON. TODAY YOU MAY BECOME AS GODS.
AND WE'RE SUPPOSED TO BELIEVE YOU.
I CAN EVOLVE YOU-- RAISE YOU TO NEW HEIGHTS.
YOU'LL HAVE NEW POWER-- IF YOU SERVE MY WILL TO DESTROY THE CELESTIAL MESSIAH.

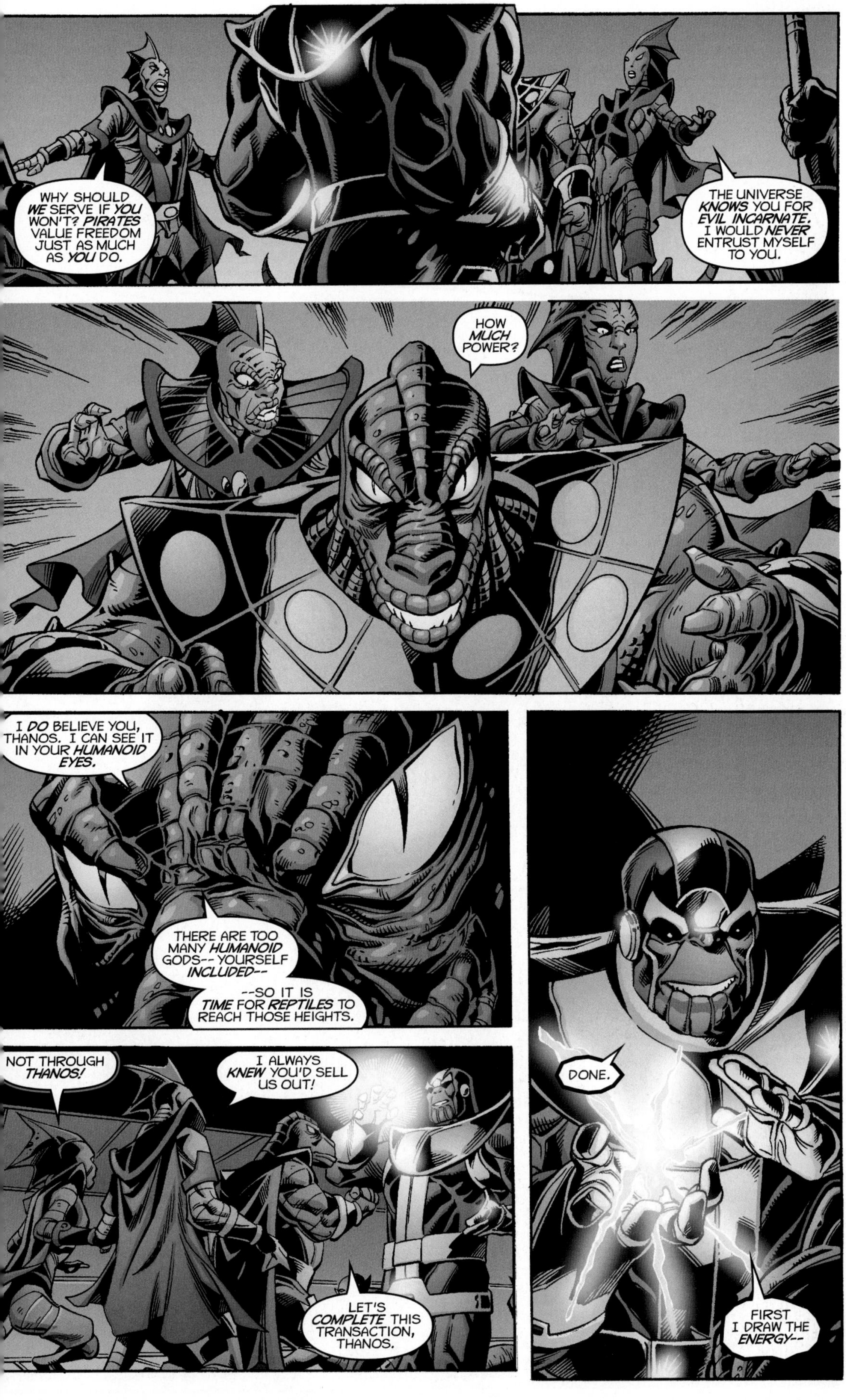
WHY SHOULD WE SERVE IF YOU WON'T? PIRATES VALUE FREEDOM JUST AS MUCH AS YOU DO.
THE UNIVERSE KNOWS YOU FOR EVIL INCARNATE. I WOULD NEVER ENTRUST MYSELF TO YOU.
HOW MUCH POWER?
I DO BELIEVE YOU, THANOS. I CAN SEE IT IN YOUR HUMANOID EYES.
THERE ARE TOO MANY HUMANOID GODS-- YOURSELF INCLUDED--
--SO IT IS TIME FOR REPTILES TO REACH THOSE HEIGHTS.
NOT THROUGH THANOS!
I ALWAYS KNEW YOU'D SELL US OUT!
LET'S COMPLETE THIS TRANSACTION, THANOS.
DONE.
FIRST I DRAW THE ENERGY--

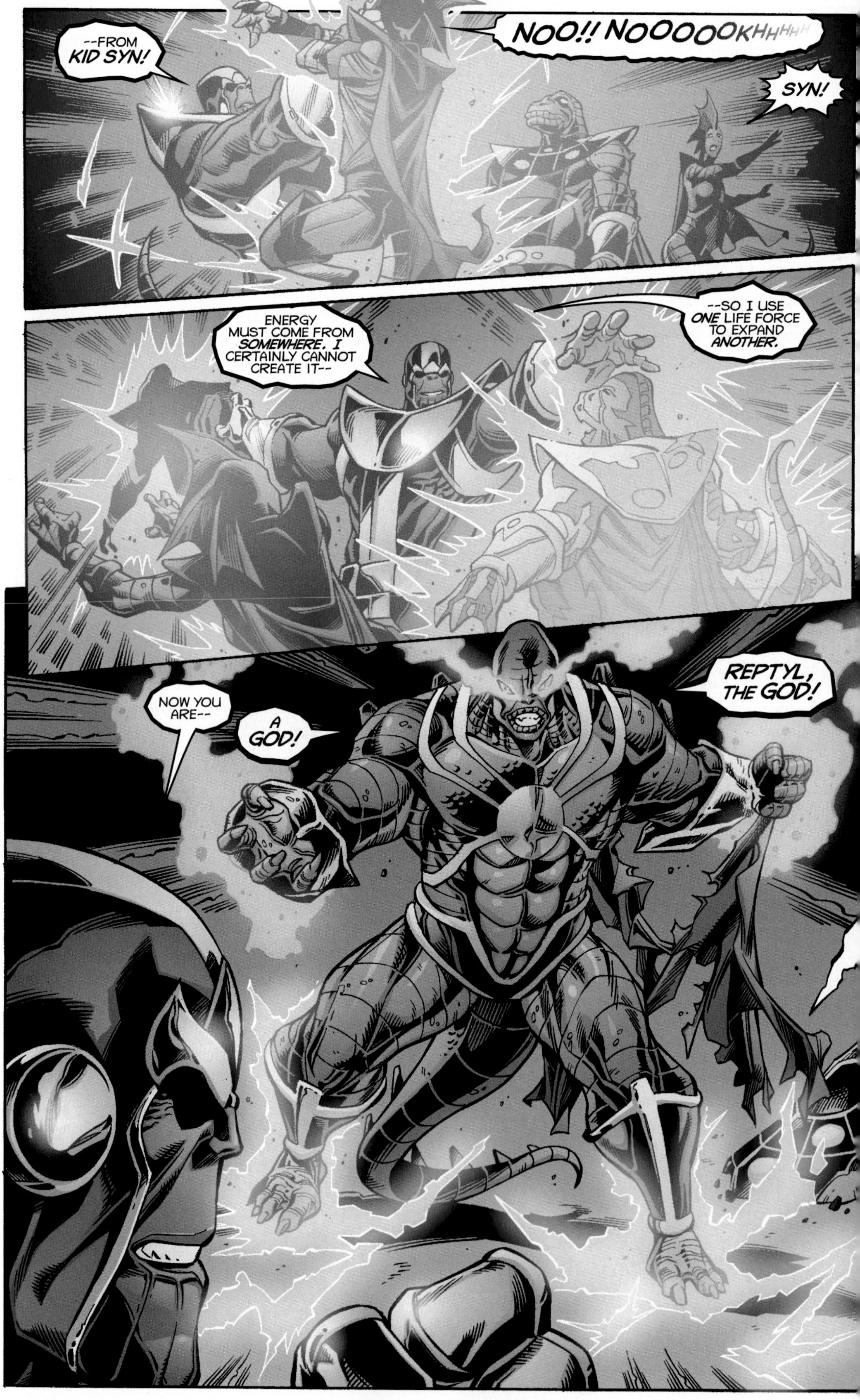
--FROM KID SYN!
NOO!! NOOOOOKHHHHH
SYN!
ENERGY MUST COME FROM SOMEWHERE. I CERTAINLY CANNOT CREATE IT--
--SO I USE ONE LIFE FORCE TO EXPAND ANOTHER.
NOW YOU ARE--
A GOD!
REPTYL, THE GOD!

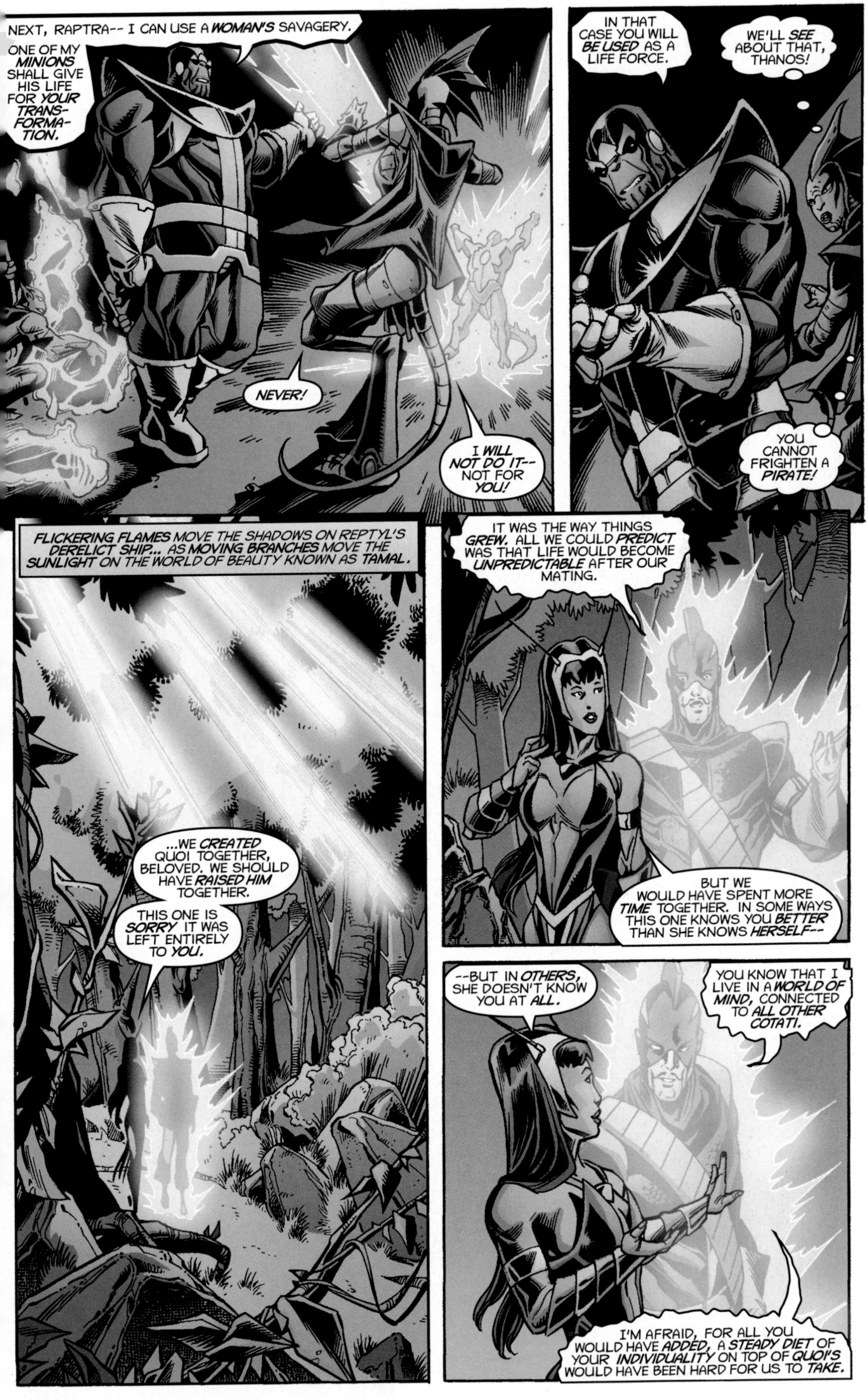
NEXT, RAPTRA-- I CAN USE A WOMAN'S SAVAGERY.
ONE OF MY MINIONS SHALL GIVE HIS LIFE FOR YOUR TRANSFORMATION.
NEVER!
I WILL NOT DO IT-- NOT FOR YOU!
IN THAT CASE YOU WILL BE USED AS A LIFE FORCE.
WE'LL SEE ABOUT THAT, THANOS!
YOU CANNOT FRIGHTEN A PIRATE!
FLICKERING FLAMES MOVE THE SHADOWS ON REPTYL'S DERELICT SHIP... AS MOVING BRANCHES MOVE THE SUNLIGHT ON THE WORLD OF BEAUTY KNOWN AS TAMAL.
...WE CREATED QUOI TOGETHER, BELOVED. WE SHOULD HAVE RAISED HIM TOGETHER.
THIS ONE IS SORRY IT WAS LEFT ENTIRELY TO YOU.
IT WAS THE WAY THINGS GREW. ALL WE COULD PREDICT WAS THAT LIFE WOULD BECOME UNPREDICTABLE AFTER OUR MATING.
BUT WE WOULD HAVE SPENT MORE TIME TOGETHER. IN SOME WAYS THIS ONE KNOWS YOU BETTER THAN SHE KNOWS HERSELF--
--BUT IN OTHERS, SHE DOESN'T KNOW YOU AT ALL.
YOU KNOW THAT I LIVE IN A WORLD OF MIND, CONNECTED TO ALL OTHER COTATI.
I'M AFRAID, FOR ALL YOU WOULD HAVE ADDED, A STEADY DIET OF YOUR INDIVIDUALITY ON TOP OF QUOI'S WOULD HAVE BEEN HARD FOR US TO TAKE.

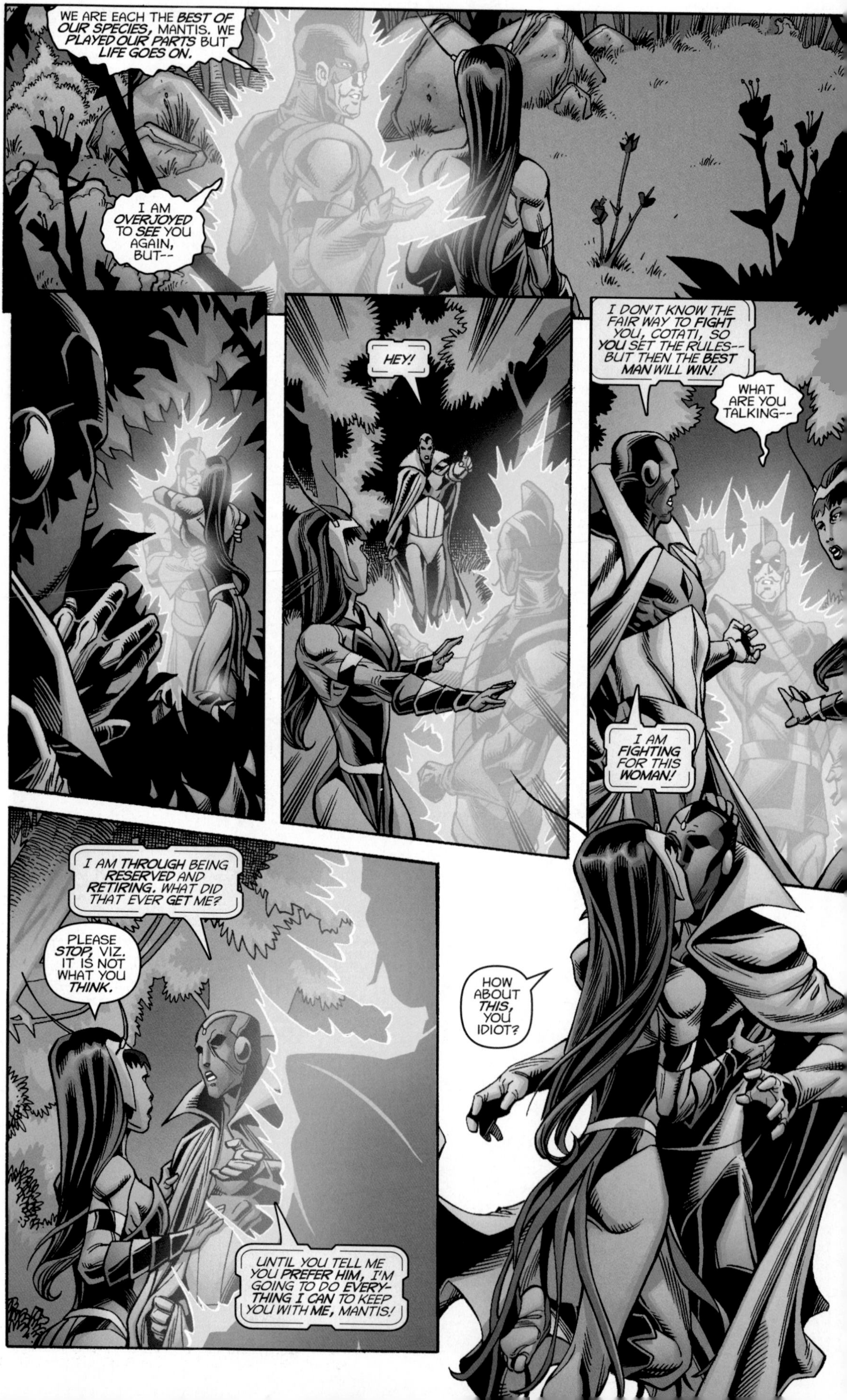
WE ARE EACH THE BEST OF OUR SPECIES, MANTIS. WE PLAYED OUR PARTS BUT LIFE GOES ON.
I AM OVERJOYED TO SEE YOU AGAIN, BUT--
HEY!
I DON'T KNOW THE FAIR WAY TO FIGHT YOU, COTATI, SO YOU SET THE RULES-- BUT THEN THE BEST MAN WILL WIN!
WHAT ARE YOU TALKING--
I AM FIGHTING FOR THIS WOMAN!
I AM THROUGH BEING RESERVED AND RETIRING. WHAT DID THAT EVER GET ME?
PLEASE STOP, VIZ. IT IS NOT WHAT YOU THINK.
UNTIL YOU TELL ME YOU PREFER HIM, I'M GOING TO DO EVERYTHING I CAN TO KEEP YOU WITH ME, MANTIS!
HOW ABOUT THIS, YOU IDIOT?

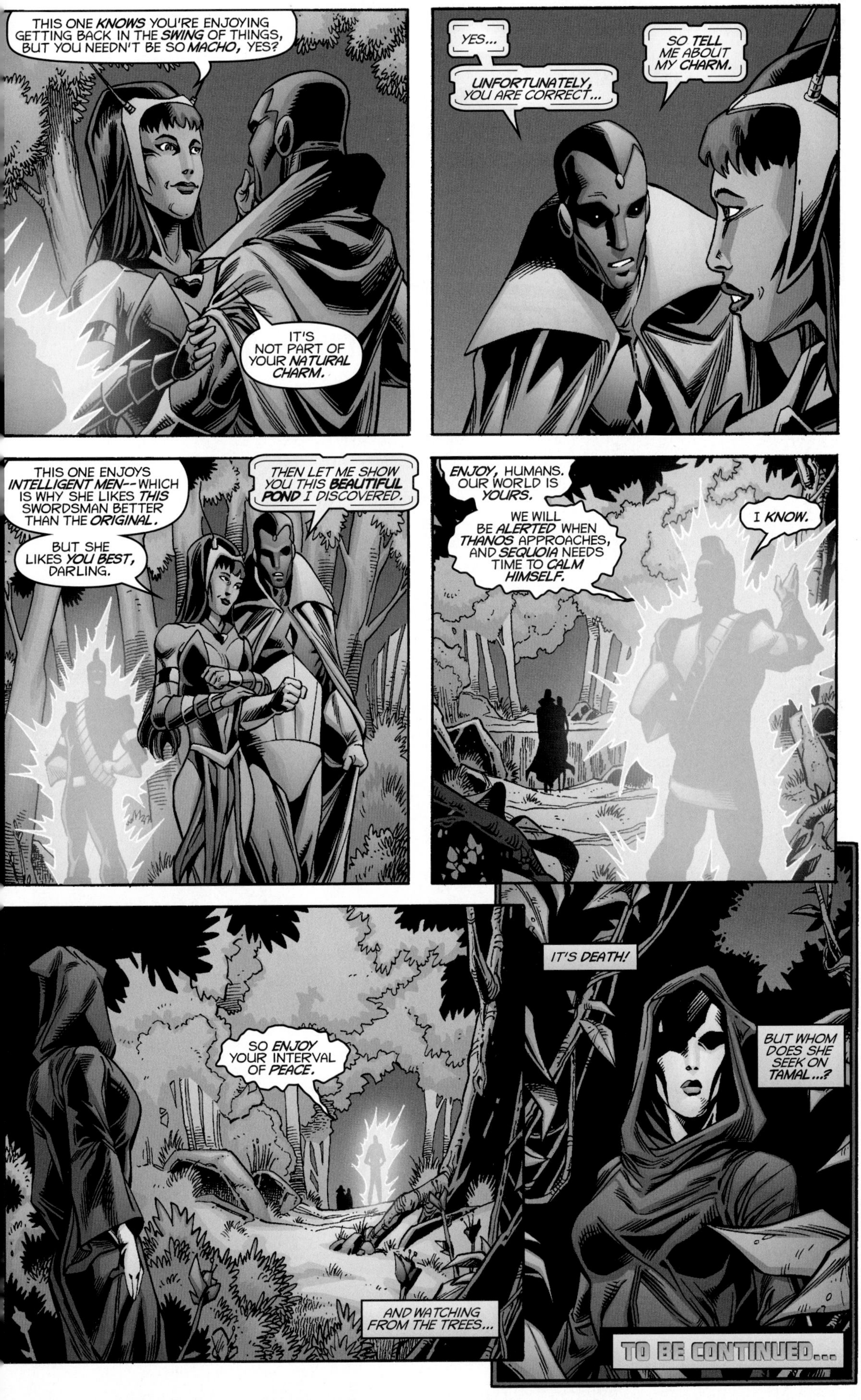
THIS ONE KNOWS YOU'RE ENJOYING GETTING BACK IN THE SWING OF THINGS, BUT YOU NEEDN'T BE SO MACHO, YES?
IT'S NOT PART OF YOUR NATURAL CHARM.
YES...
UNFORTUNATELY, YOU ARE CORRECT...
SO TELL ME ABOUT MY CHARM.
THIS ONE ENJOYS INTELLIGENT MEN--WHICH IS WHY SHE LIKES THIS SWORDSMAN BETTER THAN THE ORIGINAL.
BUT SHE LIKES YOU BEST, DARLING.
THEN LET ME SHOW YOU THIS BEAUTIFUL POND I DISCOVERED.
ENJOY, HUMANS. OUR WORLD IS YOURS.
WE WILL BE ALERTED WHEN THANOS APPROACHES, AND SEQUOIA NEEDS TIME TO CALM HIMSELF.
I KNOW.
SO ENJOY YOUR INTERVAL OF PEACE.
AND WATCHING FROM THE TREES...
IT'S DEATH!
BUT WHOM DOES SHE SEEK ON TAMAL...?
TO BE CONTINUED...

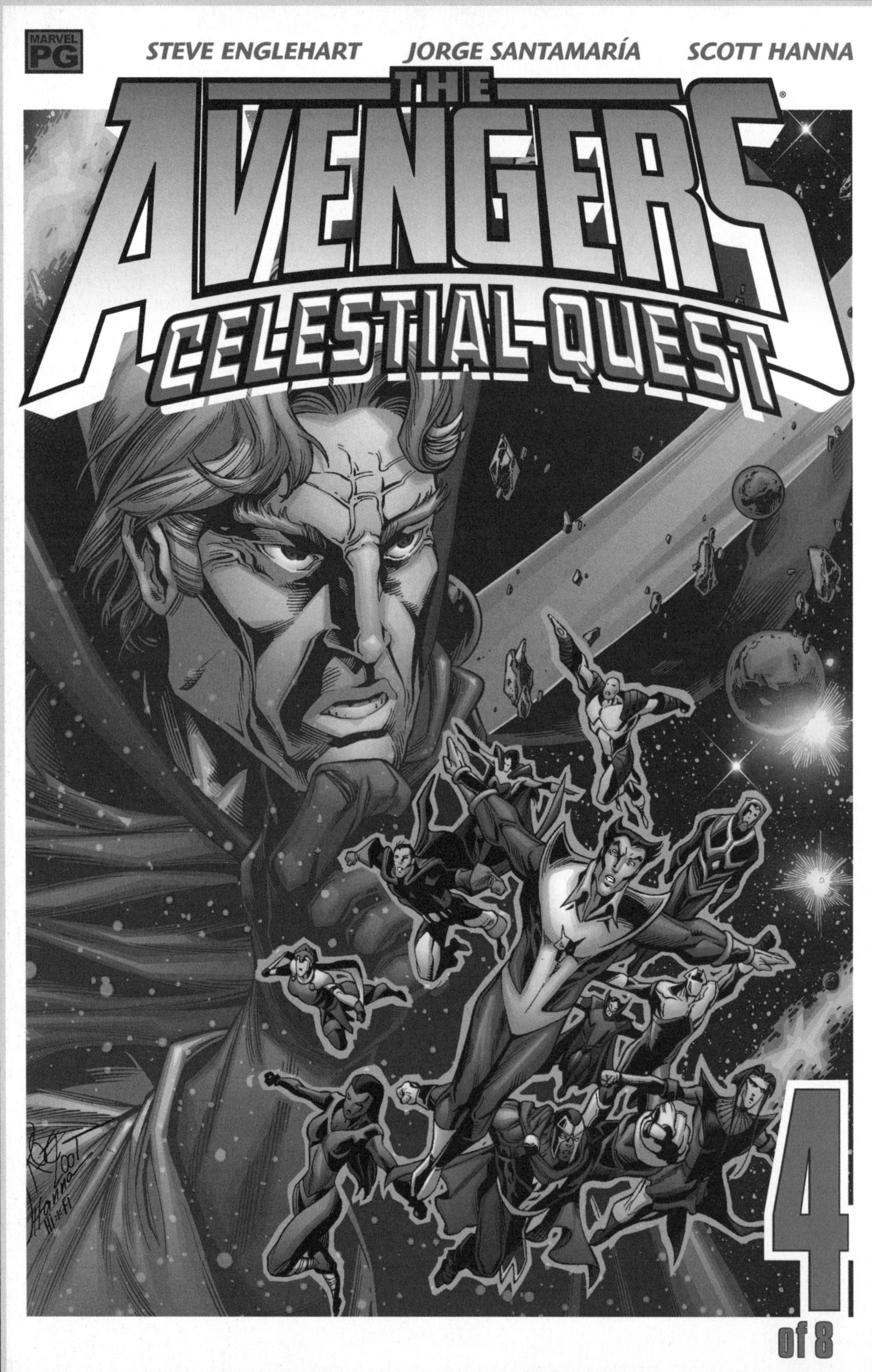
MARVEL PG
STEVE ENGLEHART
JORGE SANTAMARÍA
SCOTT HANNA
THE AVENGERS
CELESTIAL QUEST
4
of 8

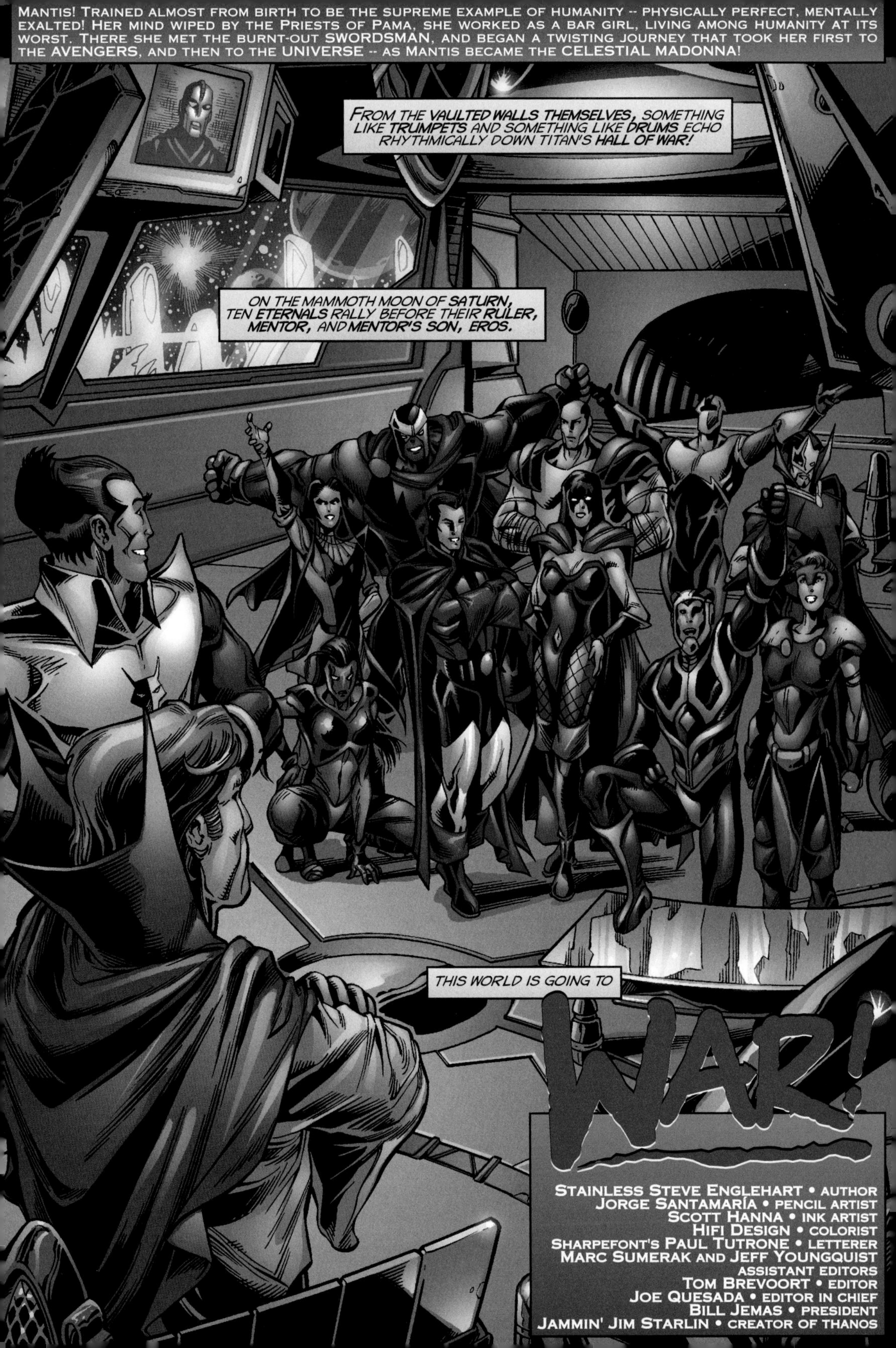
Mantis! Trained almost from birth to be the supreme example of humanity -- physically perfect, mentally exalted! Her mind wiped by the Priests of Pama, she worked as a bar girl, living among humanity at its worst. There she met the burnt-out SWORDSMAN, and began a twisting journey that took her first to the AVENGERS, and then to the UNIVERSE -- as Mantis became the CELESTIAL MADONNA!
FROM THE VAULTED WALLS THEMSELVES, SOMETHING LIKE TRUMPETS AND SOMETHING LIKE DRUMS ECHO RHYTHMICALLY DOWN TITAN'S HALL OF WAR!
ON THE MAMMOTH MOON OF SATURN, TEN ETERNALS RALLY BEFORE THEIR RULER, MENTOR, AND MENTOR'S SON, EROS.
THIS WORLD IS GOING TO
WAR!
Stainless Steve Englehart • author
Jorge Santamaría • pencil artist
Scott Hanna • ink artist
Hifi Design • colorist
Sharpefont's Paul Tutrone • letterer
Marc Sumerak and Jeff Youngquist
assistant editors
Tom Brevoort • editor
Joe Quesada • editor in chief
Bill Jemas • president
Jammin' Jim Starlin • creator of Thanos

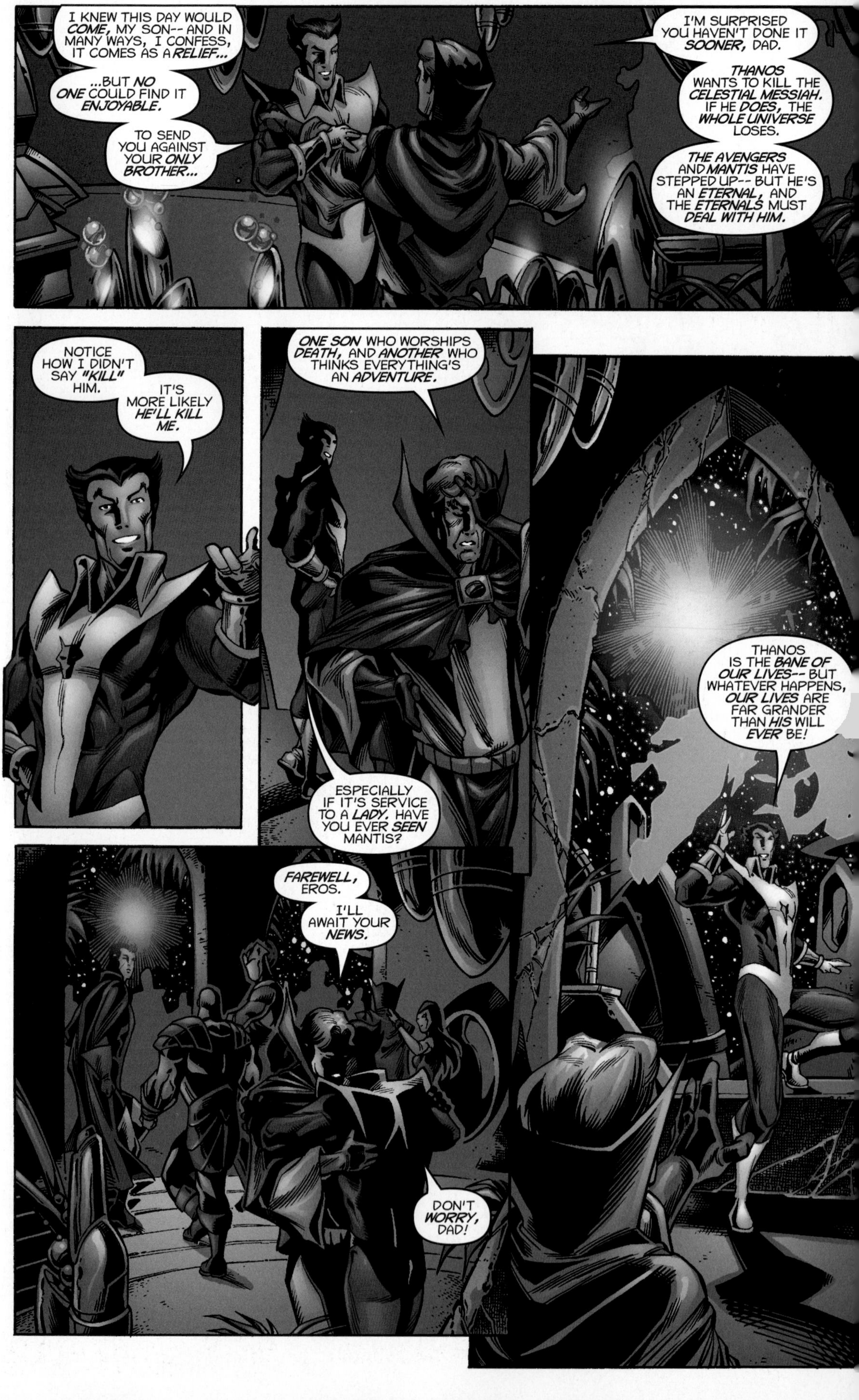
I KNEW THIS DAY WOULD COME, MY SON-- AND IN MANY WAYS, I CONFESS, IT COMES AS A RELIEF...
...BUT NO ONE COULD FIND IT ENJOYABLE.
TO SEND YOU AGAINST YOUR ONLY BROTHER...
I'M SURPRISED YOU HAVEN'T DONE IT SOONER, DAD.
THANOS WANTS TO KILL THE CELESTIAL MESSIAH. IF HE DOES, THE WHOLE UNIVERSE LOSES.
THE AVENGERS AND MANTIS HAVE STEPPED UP-- BUT HE'S AN ETERNAL, AND THE ETERNALS MUST DEAL WITH HIM.
NOTICE HOW I DIDN'T SAY "KILL" HIM.
IT'S MORE LIKELY HE'LL KILL ME.
ONE SON WHO WORSHIPS DEATH, AND ANOTHER WHO THINKS EVERYTHING'S AN ADVENTURE.
ESPECIALLY IF IT'S SERVICE TO A LADY. HAVE YOU EVER SEEN MANTIS?
THANOS IS THE BANE OF OUR LIVES-- BUT WHATEVER HAPPENS, OUR LIVES ARE FAR GRANDER THAN HIS WILL EVER BE!
FAREWELL, EROS.
I'LL AWAIT YOUR NEWS.
DON'T WORRY, DAD!

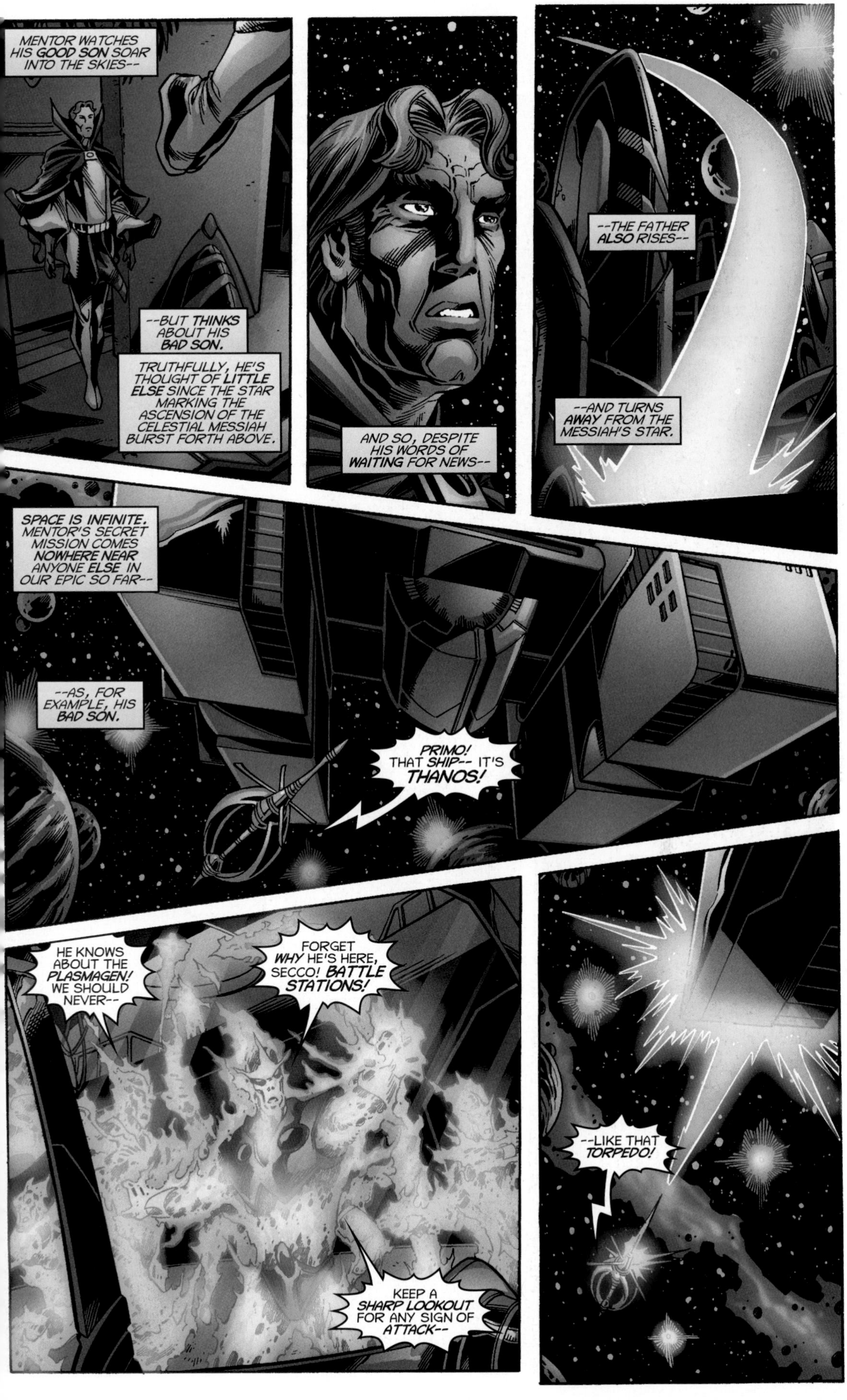
MENTOR WATCHES HIS GOOD SON SOAR INTO THE SKIES--
--BUT THINKS ABOUT HIS BAD SON.
TRUTHFULLY, HE'S THOUGHT OF LITTLE ELSE SINCE THE STAR MARKING THE ASCENSION OF THE CELESTIAL MESSIAH BURST FORTH ABOVE.
AND SO, DESPITE HIS WORDS OF WAITING FOR NEWS--
--THE FATHER ALSO RISES--
--AND TURNS AWAY FROM THE MESSIAH'S STAR.
SPACE IS INFINITE. MENTOR'S SECRET MISSION COMES NOWHERE NEAR ANYONE ELSE IN OUR EPIC SO FAR--
--AS, FOR EXAMPLE, HIS BAD SON.
PRIMO! THAT SHIP-- IT'S THANOS!
HE KNOWS ABOUT THE PLASMAGEN! WE SHOULD NEVER--
FORGET WHY HE'S HERE, SECCO! BATTLE STATIONS!
KEEP A SHARP LOOKOUT FOR ANY SIGN OF ATTACK--
--LIKE THAT TORPEDO!

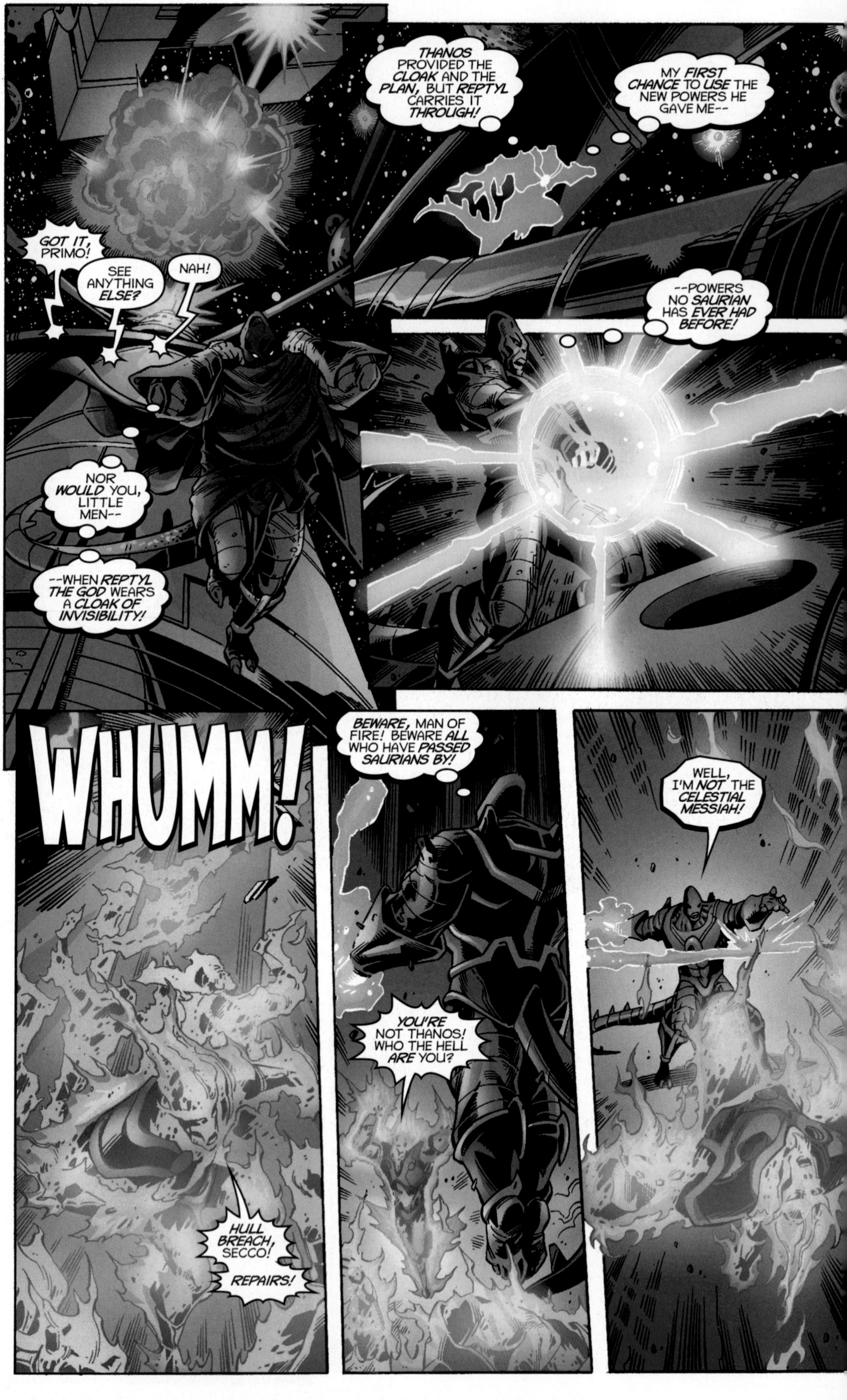

THANOS PROVIDED THE CLOAK AND THE PLAN, BUT REPTYL CARRIES IT THROUGH!
MY FIRST CHANCE TO USE THE NEW POWERS HE GAVE ME--
GOT IT, PRIMO!
SEE ANYTHING ELSE?
NAH!
NOR WOULD YOU, LITTLE MEN--
--WHEN REPTYL THE GOD WEARS A CLOAK OF INVISIBILITY!
--POWERS NO SAURIAN HAS EVER HAD BEFORE!
WHUMM!
HULL BREACH, SECCO!
REPAIRS!
BEWARE, MAN OF FIRE! BEWARE ALL WHO HAVE PASSED SAURIANS BY!
YOU'RE NOT THANOS! WHO THE HELL ARE YOU?
WELL, I'M NOT THE CELESTIAL MESSIAH!

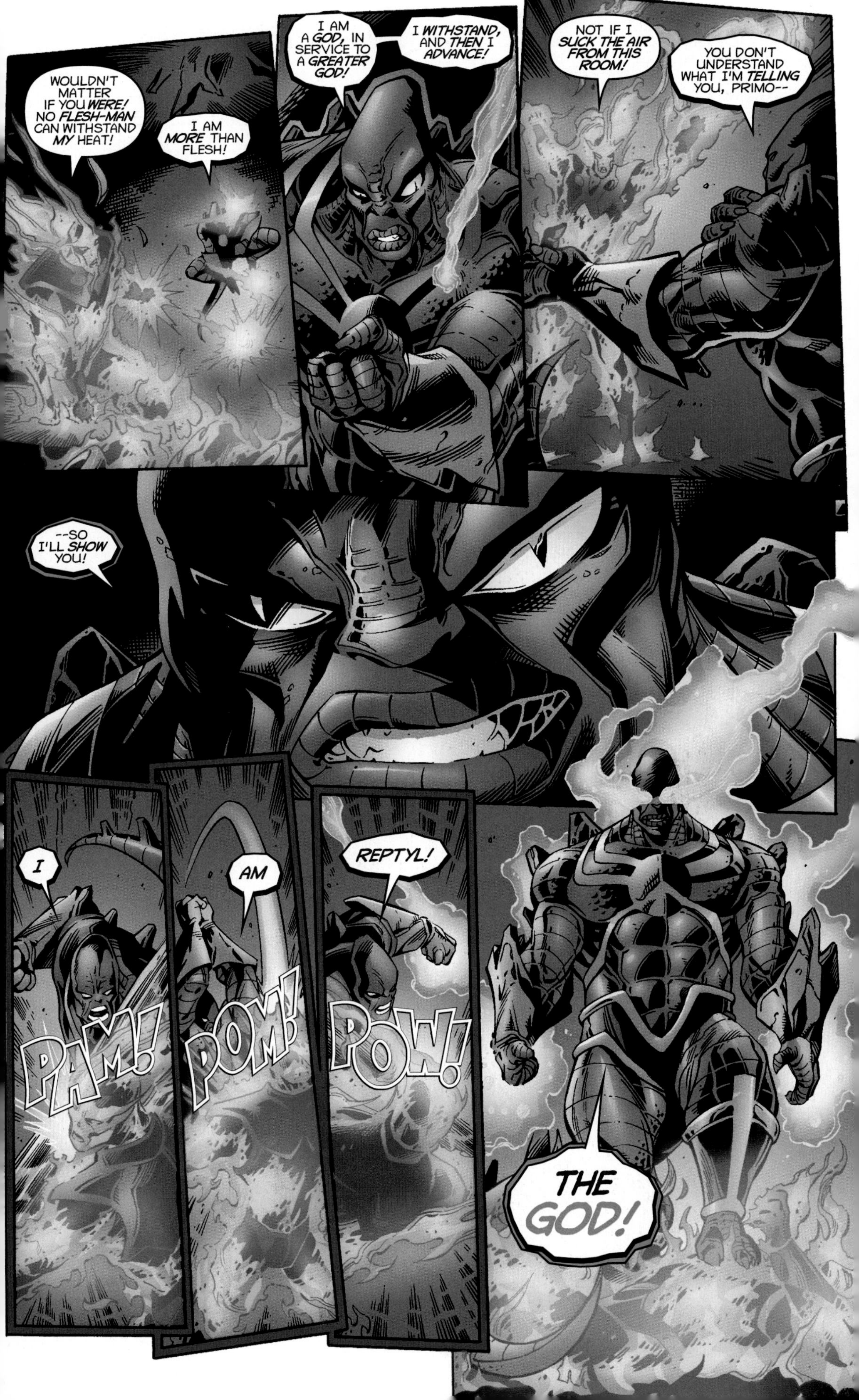

WOULDN'T MATTER IF YOU *WERE!* NO *FLESH-MAN* CAN WITHSTAND *MY* HEAT!
I AM *MORE* THAN FLESH!
I AM A *GOD*, IN SERVICE TO A *GREATER GOD!*
I *WITHSTAND*, AND *THEN* I *ADVANCE!*
NOT IF I *SUCK THE AIR FROM THIS ROOM!*
YOU DON'T UNDERSTAND WHAT I'M *TELLING* YOU, PRIMO--
--SO I'LL *SHOW* YOU!
I
PAM!
AM
POM!
REPTYL!
POW!
THE GOD!

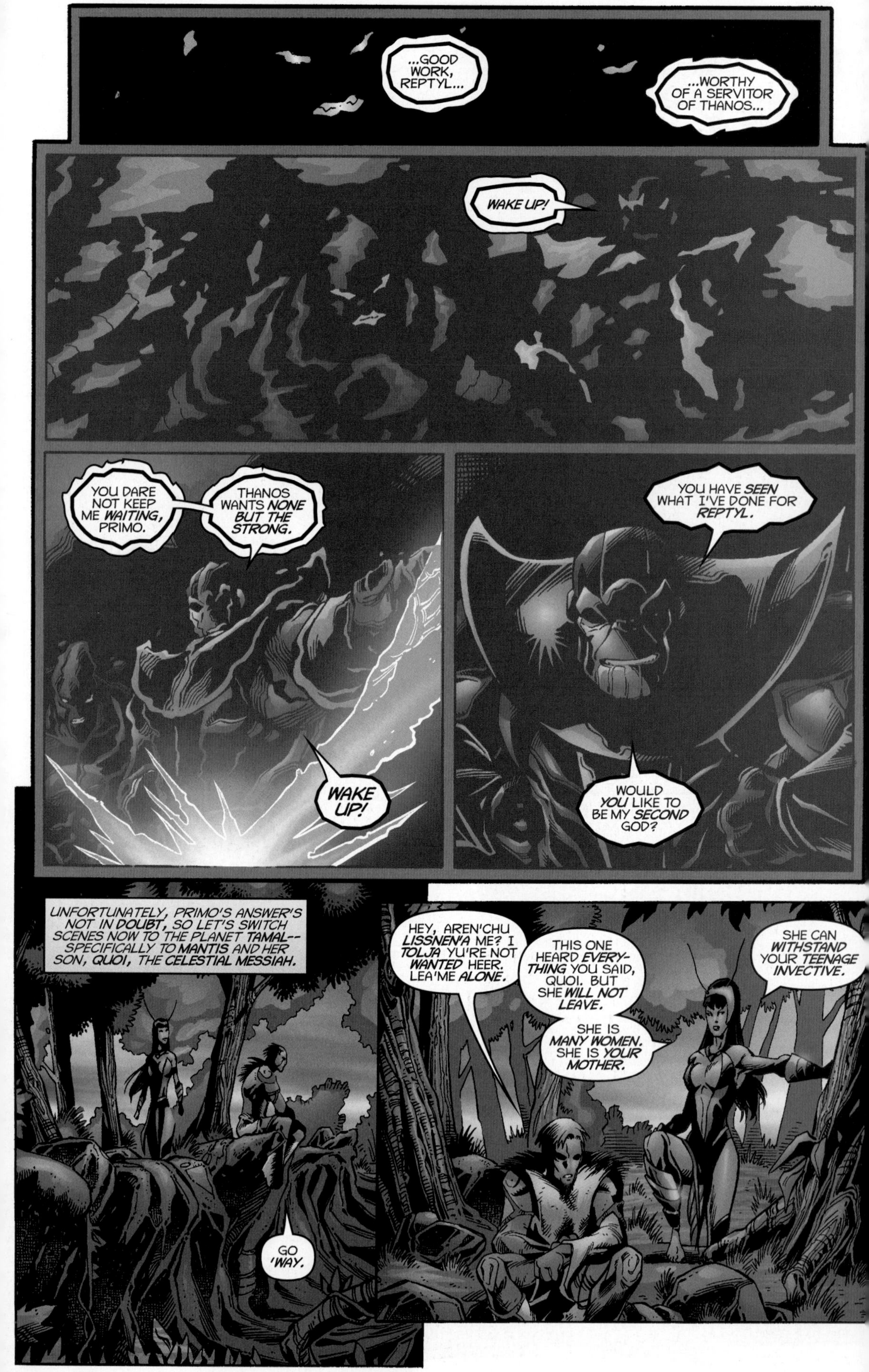
...GOOD WORK, REPTYL...
...WORTHY OF A SERVITOR OF THANOS...
WAKE UP!
YOU DARE NOT KEEP ME WAITING, PRIMO.
THANOS WANTS NONE BUT THE STRONG.
WAKE UP!
YOU HAVE SEEN WHAT I'VE DONE FOR REPTYL.
WOULD YOU LIKE TO BE MY SECOND GOD?
UNFORTUNATELY, PRIMO'S ANSWER'S NOT IN DOUBT, SO LET'S SWITCH SCENES NOW TO THE PLANET TAMAL-- SPECIFICALLY TO MANTIS AND HER SON, QUOI, THE CELESTIAL MESSIAH.
GO 'WAY.
HEY, AREN'CHU LISSNEN'A ME? I TOLJA YU'RE NOT WANTED HEER. LEA'ME ALONE.
THIS ONE HEARD EVERYTHING YOU SAID, QUOI. BUT SHE WILL NOT LEAVE.
SHE IS MANY WOMEN. SHE IS YOUR MOTHER.
SHE CAN WITHSTAND YOUR TEENAGE INVECTIVE.

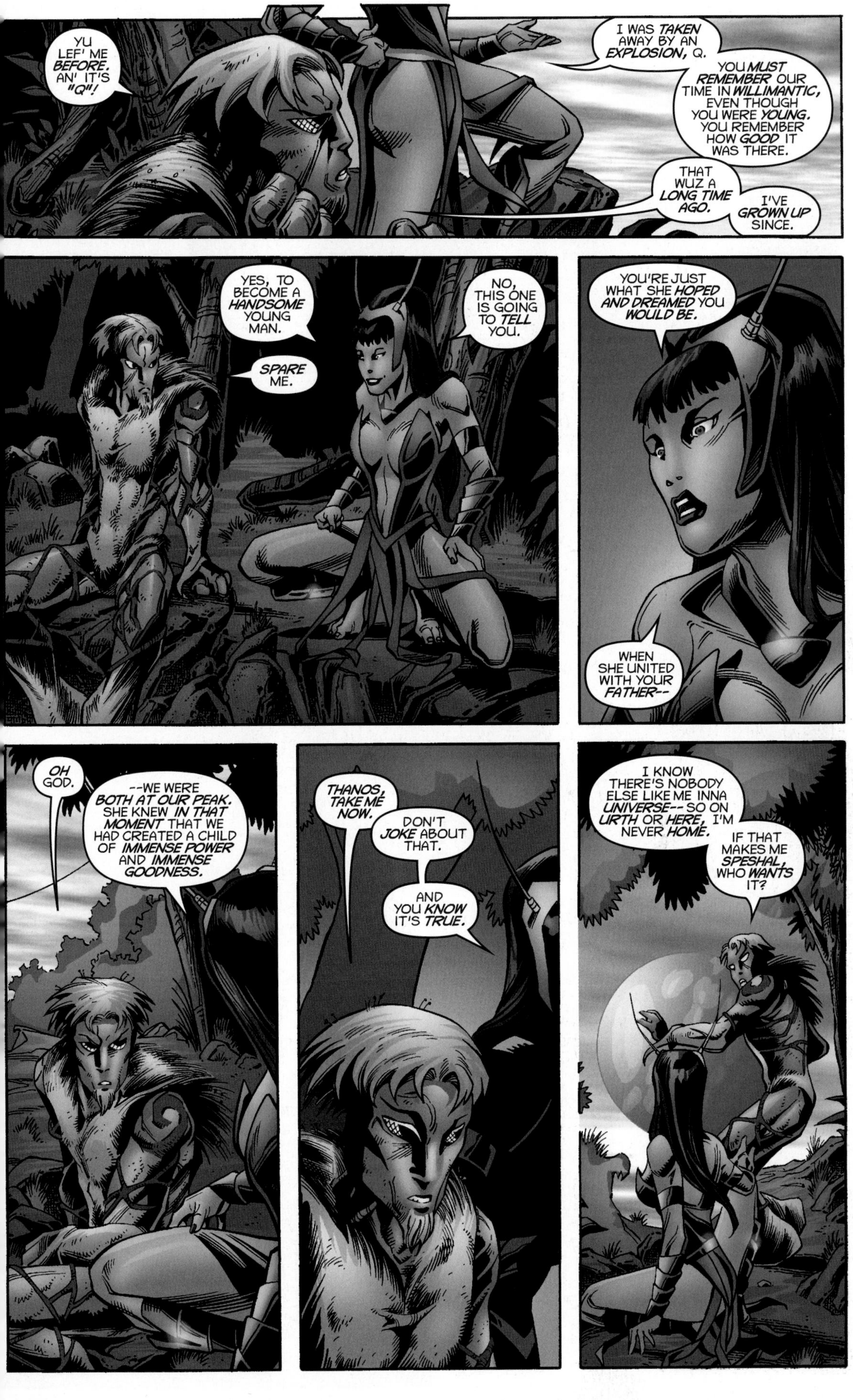

YU LEF' ME BEFORE. AN' IT'S "Q"!
I WAS TAKEN AWAY BY AN EXPLOSION, Q.
YOU MUST REMEMBER OUR TIME IN WILLIMANTIC, EVEN THOUGH YOU WERE YOUNG. YOU REMEMBER HOW GOOD IT WAS THERE.
THAT WUZ A LONG TIME AGO.
I'VE GROWN UP SINCE.
YES, TO BECOME A HANDSOME YOUNG MAN.
SPARE ME.
NO, THIS ONE IS GOING TO TELL YOU.
YOU'RE JUST WHAT SHE HOPED AND DREAMED YOU WOULD BE.
WHEN SHE UNITED WITH YOUR FATHER--
OH GOD.
--WE WERE BOTH AT OUR PEAK. SHE KNEW IN THAT MOMENT THAT WE HAD CREATED A CHILD OF IMMENSE POWER AND IMMENSE GOODNESS.
THANOS, TAKE ME NOW.
DON'T JOKE ABOUT THAT.
AND YOU KNOW IT'S TRUE.
I KNOW THERE'S NOBODY ELSE LIKE ME INNA UNIVERSE-- SO ON URTH OR HERE, I'M NEVER HOME.
IF THAT MAKES ME SPESHAL, WHO WANTS IT?

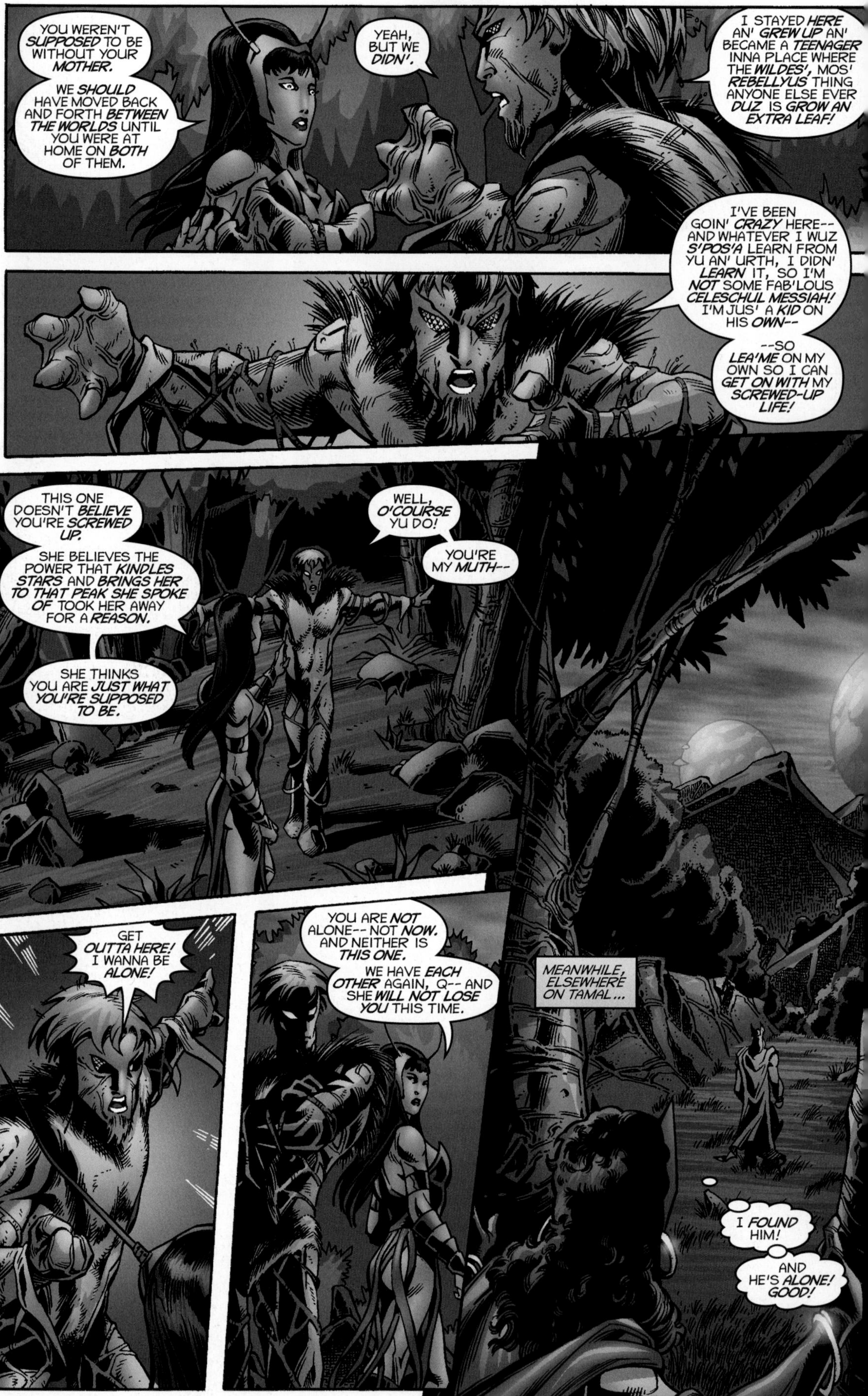
YOU WEREN'T SUPPOSED TO BE WITHOUT YOUR MOTHER.
WE SHOULD HAVE MOVED BACK AND FORTH BETWEEN THE WORLDS UNTIL YOU WERE AT HOME ON BOTH OF THEM.
YEAH, BUT WE DIDN'.
I STAYED HERE AN' GREW UP AN' BECAME A TEENAGER INNA PLACE WHERE THE WILDES', MOS' REBELLYUS THING ANYONE ELSE EVER DUZ IS GROW AN EXTRA LEAF!
I'VE BEEN GOIN' CRAZY HERE-- AND WHATEVER I WUZ S'POS'A LEARN FROM YU AN' URTH, I DIDN' LEARN IT, SO I'M NOT SOME FAB'LOUS CELESCHUL MESSIAH! I'M JUS' A KID ON HIS OWN--
--SO LEA'ME ON MY OWN SO I CAN GET ON WITH MY SCREWED-UP LIFE!
THIS ONE DOESN'T BELIEVE YOU'RE SCREWED UP.
SHE BELIEVES THE POWER THAT KINDLES STARS AND BRINGS HER TO THAT PEAK SHE SPOKE OF TOOK HER AWAY FOR A REASON.
SHE THINKS YOU ARE JUST WHAT YOU'RE SUPPOSED TO BE.
WELL, O'COURSE YU DO!
YOU'RE MY MUTH--
GET OUTTA HERE! I WANNA BE ALONE!
YOU ARE NOT ALONE-- NOT NOW. AND NEITHER IS THIS ONE.
WE HAVE EACH OTHER AGAIN, Q-- AND SHE WILL NOT LOSE YOU THIS TIME.
MEANWHILE, ELSEWHERE ON TAMAL...
I FOUND HIM!
AND HE'S ALONE! GOOD!

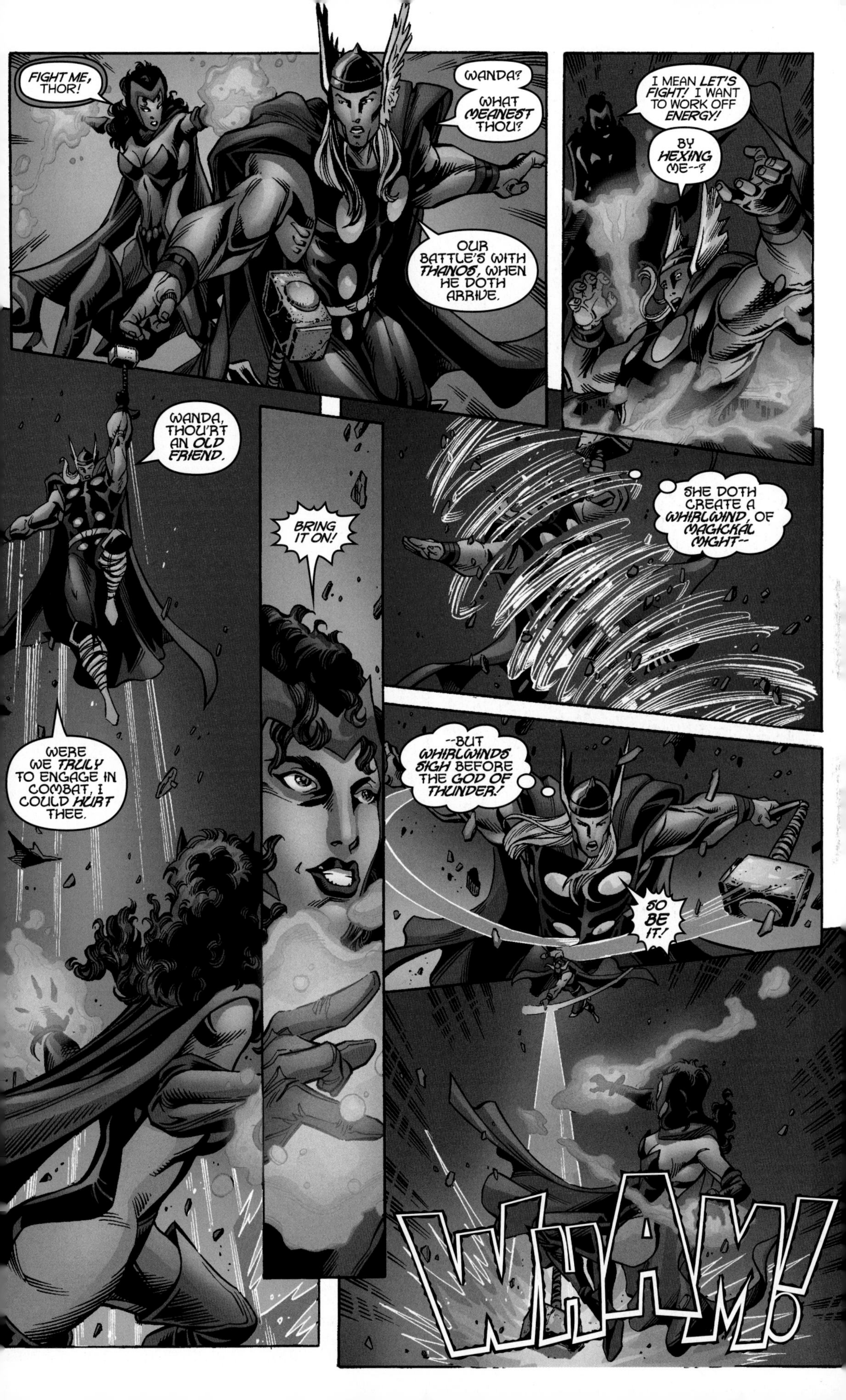

FIGHT ME, THOR!
WANDA?
WHAT MEANEST THOU?
OUR BATTLE'S WITH THANOS, WHEN HE DOTH ARRIVE.
I MEAN LET'S FIGHT! I WANT TO WORK OFF ENERGY!
BY HEXING ME--?
WANDA, THOU'RT AN OLD FRIEND.
WERE WE TRULY TO ENGAGE IN COMBAT, I COULD HURT THEE.
BRING IT ON!
SHE DOTH CREATE A WHIRLWIND, OF MAGICKAL MIGHT--
--BUT WHIRLWINDS SIGH BEFORE THE GOD OF THUNDER!
SO BE IT!
WHAM!

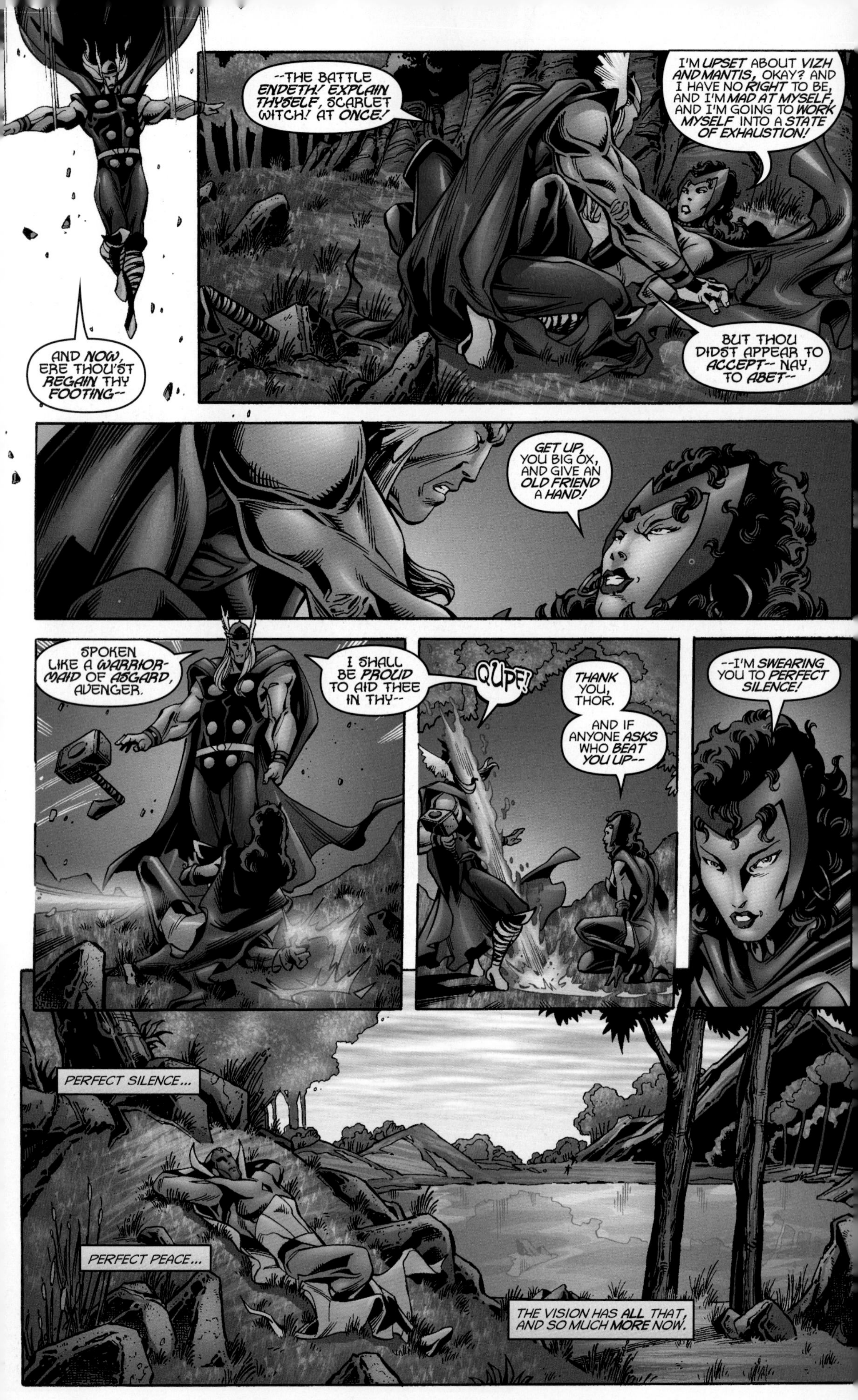
AND NOW, ERE THOU'ST REGAIN THY FOOTING--
--THE BATTLE ENDETH! EXPLAIN THYSELF, SCARLET WITCH! AT ONCE!
I'M UPSET ABOUT VIZH AND MANTIS, OKAY? AND I HAVE NO RIGHT TO BE, AND I'M MAD AT MYSELF, AND I'M GOING TO WORK MYSELF INTO A STATE OF EXHAUSTION!
BUT THOU DIDST APPEAR TO ACCEPT-- NAY, TO ABET--
GET UP, YOU BIG OX, AND GIVE AN OLD FRIEND A HAND!
SPOKEN LIKE A WARRIOR-MAID OF ASGARD, AVENGER.
I SHALL BE PROUD TO AID THEE IN THY--
QUPE!
THANK YOU, THOR.
AND IF ANYONE ASKS WHO BEAT YOU UP--
--I'M SWEARING YOU TO PERFECT SILENCE!
PERFECT SILENCE...
PERFECT PEACE...
THE VISION HAS ALL THAT, AND SO MUCH MORE NOW.

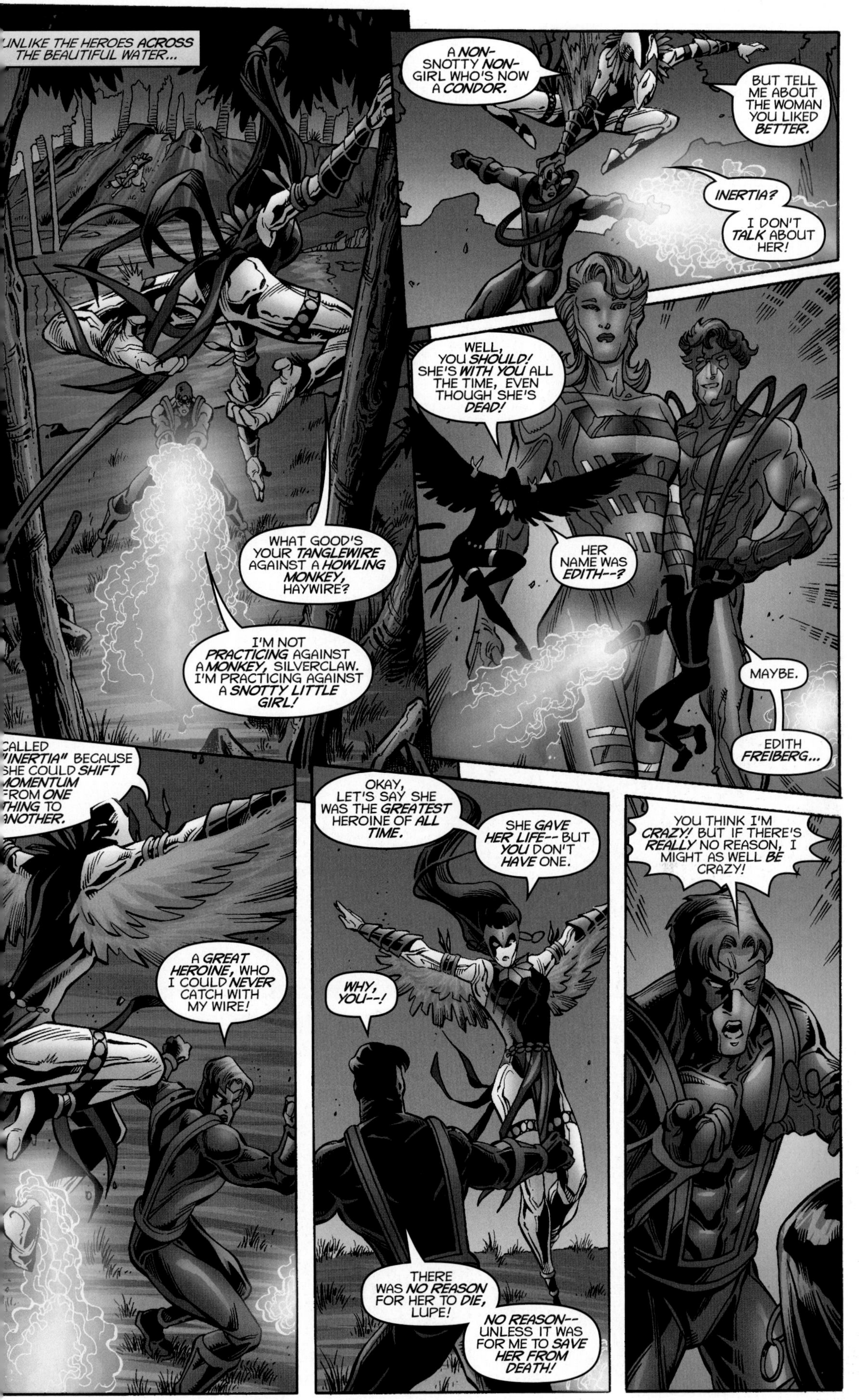
UNLIKE THE HEROES ACROSS THE BEAUTIFUL WATER...
WHAT GOOD'S YOUR TANGLEWIRE AGAINST A HOWLING MONKEY, HAYWIRE?
I'M NOT PRACTICING AGAINST A MONKEY, SILVERCLAW. I'M PRACTICING AGAINST A SNOTTY LITTLE GIRL!
A NON-SNOTTY NON-GIRL WHO'S NOW A CONDOR.
BUT TELL ME ABOUT THE WOMAN YOU LIKED BETTER.
INERTIA?
I DON'T TALK ABOUT HER!
WELL, YOU SHOULD! SHE'S WITH YOU ALL THE TIME, EVEN THOUGH SHE'S DEAD!
HER NAME WAS EDITH--?
MAYBE.
EDITH FREIBERG...
CALLED "INERTIA" BECAUSE SHE COULD SHIFT MOMENTUM FROM ONE THING TO ANOTHER.
A GREAT HEROINE, WHO I COULD NEVER CATCH WITH MY WIRE!
OKAY, LET'S SAY SHE WAS THE GREATEST HEROINE OF ALL TIME.
SHE GAVE HER LIFE-- BUT YOU DON'T HAVE ONE.
WHY, YOU--!
THERE WAS NO REASON FOR HER TO DIE, LUPE!
NO REASON-- UNLESS IT WAS FOR ME TO SAVE HER FROM DEATH!
YOU THINK I'M CRAZY! BUT IF THERE'S REALLY NO REASON, I MIGHT AS WELL BE CRAZY!

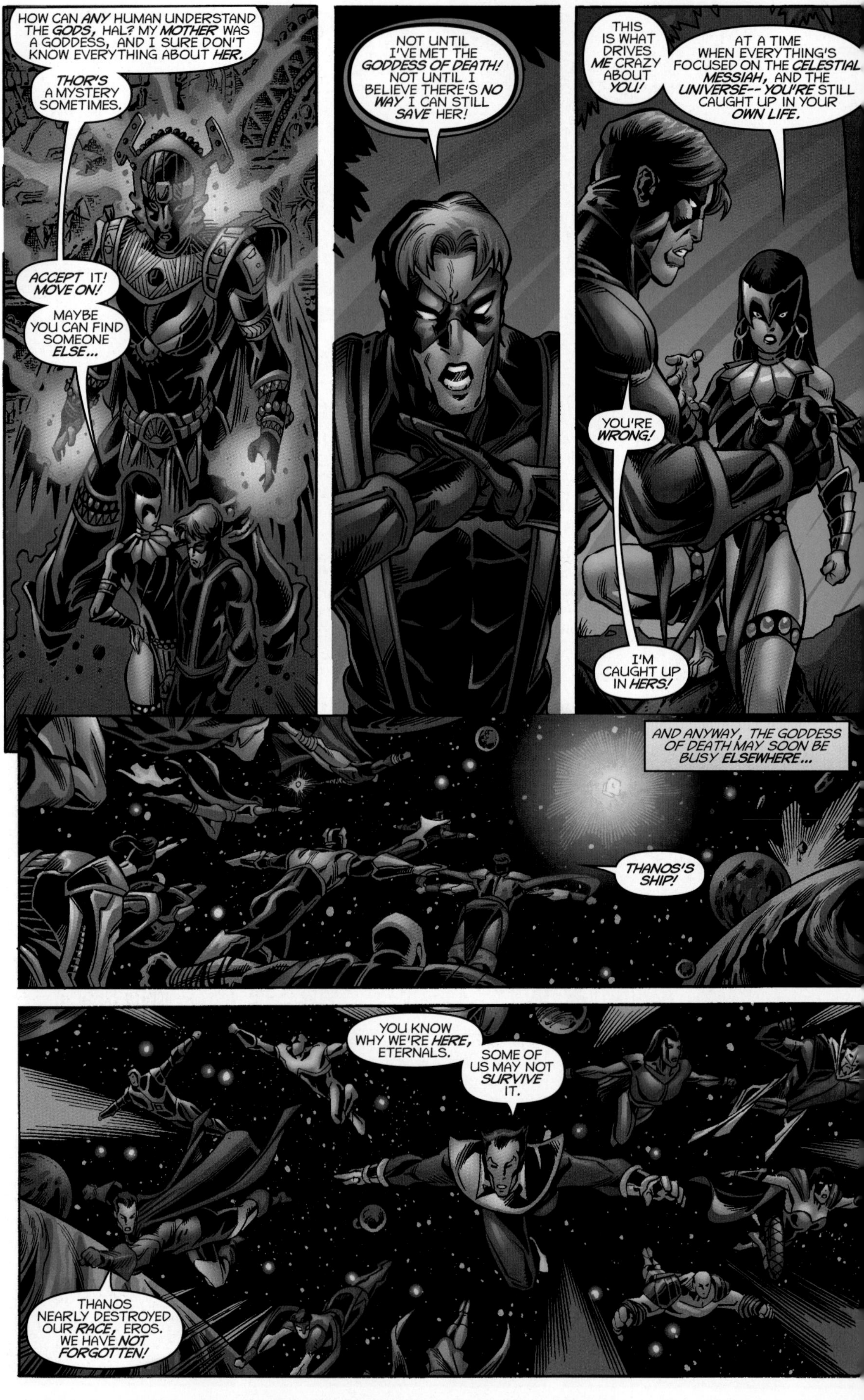
HOW CAN ANY HUMAN UNDERSTAND THE GODS, HAL? MY MOTHER WAS A GODDESS, AND I SURE DON'T KNOW EVERYTHING ABOUT HER.
THOR'S A MYSTERY SOMETIMES.
ACCEPT IT! MOVE ON!
MAYBE YOU CAN FIND SOMEONE ELSE...
NOT UNTIL I'VE MET THE GODDESS OF DEATH! NOT UNTIL I BELIEVE THERE'S NO WAY I CAN STILL SAVE HER!
THIS IS WHAT DRIVES ME CRAZY ABOUT YOU!
AT A TIME WHEN EVERYTHING'S FOCUSED ON THE CELESTIAL MESSIAH, AND THE UNIVERSE-- YOU'RE STILL CAUGHT UP IN YOUR OWN LIFE.
YOU'RE WRONG!
I'M CAUGHT UP IN HERS!
AND ANYWAY, THE GODDESS OF DEATH MAY SOON BE BUSY ELSEWHERE...
THANOS'S SHIP!
YOU KNOW WHY WE'RE HERE, ETERNALS.
SOME OF US MAY NOT SURVIVE IT.
THANOS NEARLY DESTROYED OUR RACE, EROS. WE HAVE NOT FORGOTTEN!

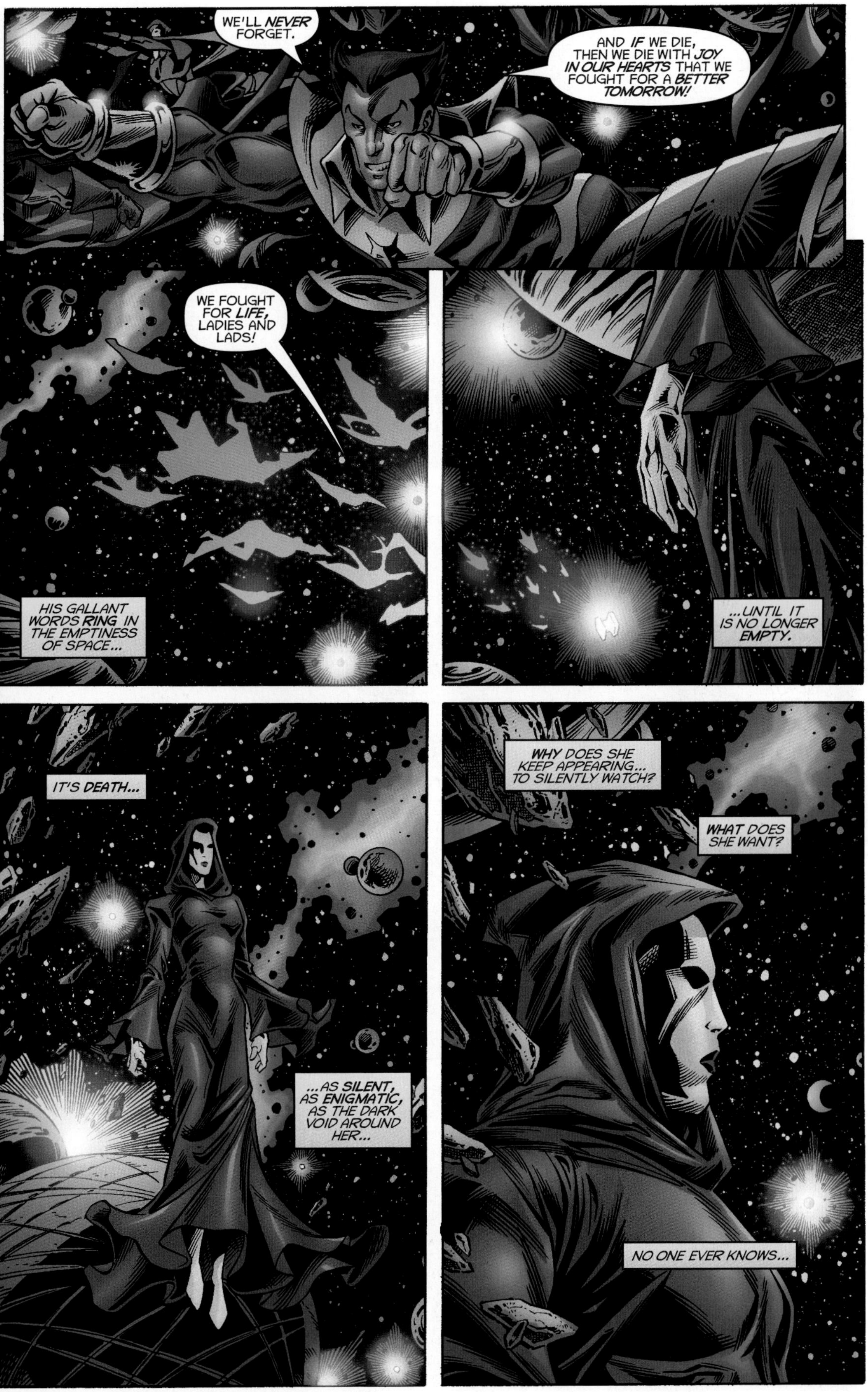
WE'LL NEVER FORGET.
AND IF WE DIE, THEN WE DIE WITH JOY IN OUR HEARTS THAT WE FOUGHT FOR A BETTER TOMORROW!
WE FOUGHT FOR LIFE, LADIES AND LADS!
HIS GALLANT WORDS RING IN THE EMPTINESS OF SPACE...
...UNTIL IT IS NO LONGER EMPTY.
IT'S DEATH...
...AS SILENT, AS ENIGMATIC, AS THE DARK VOID AROUND HER...
WHY DOES SHE KEEP APPEARING... TO SILENTLY WATCH?
WHAT DOES SHE WANT?
NO ONE EVER KNOWS...

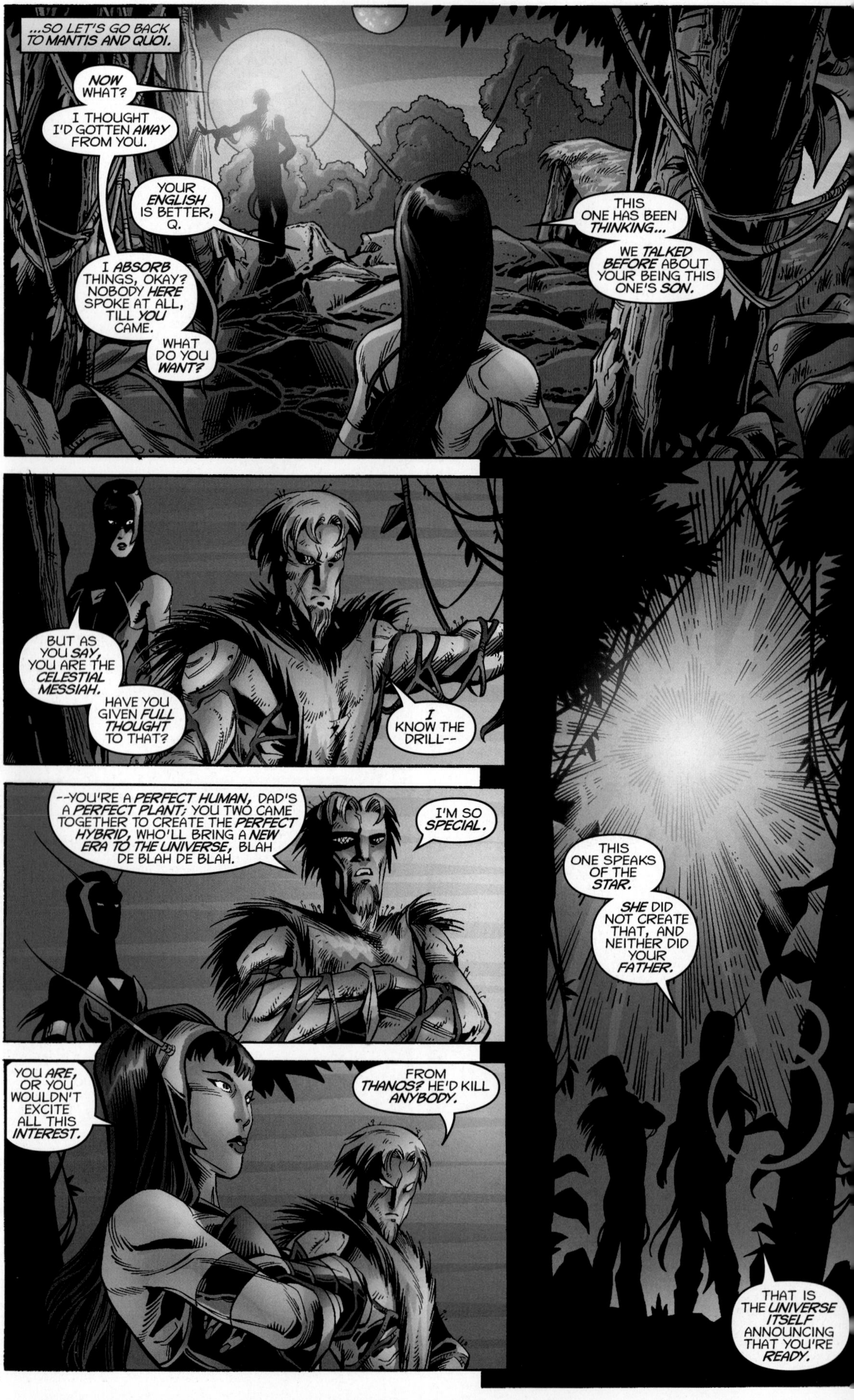
...SO LET'S GO BACK TO MANTIS AND QUOI.
NOW WHAT?
I THOUGHT I'D GOTTEN AWAY FROM YOU.
YOUR ENGLISH IS BETTER, Q.
I ABSORB THINGS, OKAY? NOBODY HERE SPOKE AT ALL, TILL YOU CAME.
WHAT DO YOU WANT?
THIS ONE HAS BEEN THINKING...
WE TALKED BEFORE ABOUT YOUR BEING THIS ONE'S SON.
BUT AS YOU SAY, YOU ARE THE CELESTIAL MESSIAH.
HAVE YOU GIVEN FULL THOUGHT TO THAT?
I KNOW THE DRILL--
--YOU'RE A PERFECT HUMAN, DAD'S A PERFECT PLANT; YOU TWO CAME TOGETHER TO CREATE THE PERFECT HYBRID, WHO'LL BRING A NEW ERA TO THE UNIVERSE, BLAH DE BLAH DE BLAH.
I'M SO SPECIAL.
YOU ARE, OR YOU WOULDN'T EXCITE ALL THIS INTEREST.
FROM THANOS? HE'D KILL ANYBODY.
THIS ONE SPEAKS OF THE STAR.
SHE DID NOT CREATE THAT, AND NEITHER DID YOUR FATHER.
THAT IS THE UNIVERSE ITSELF ANNOUNCING THAT YOU'RE READY.

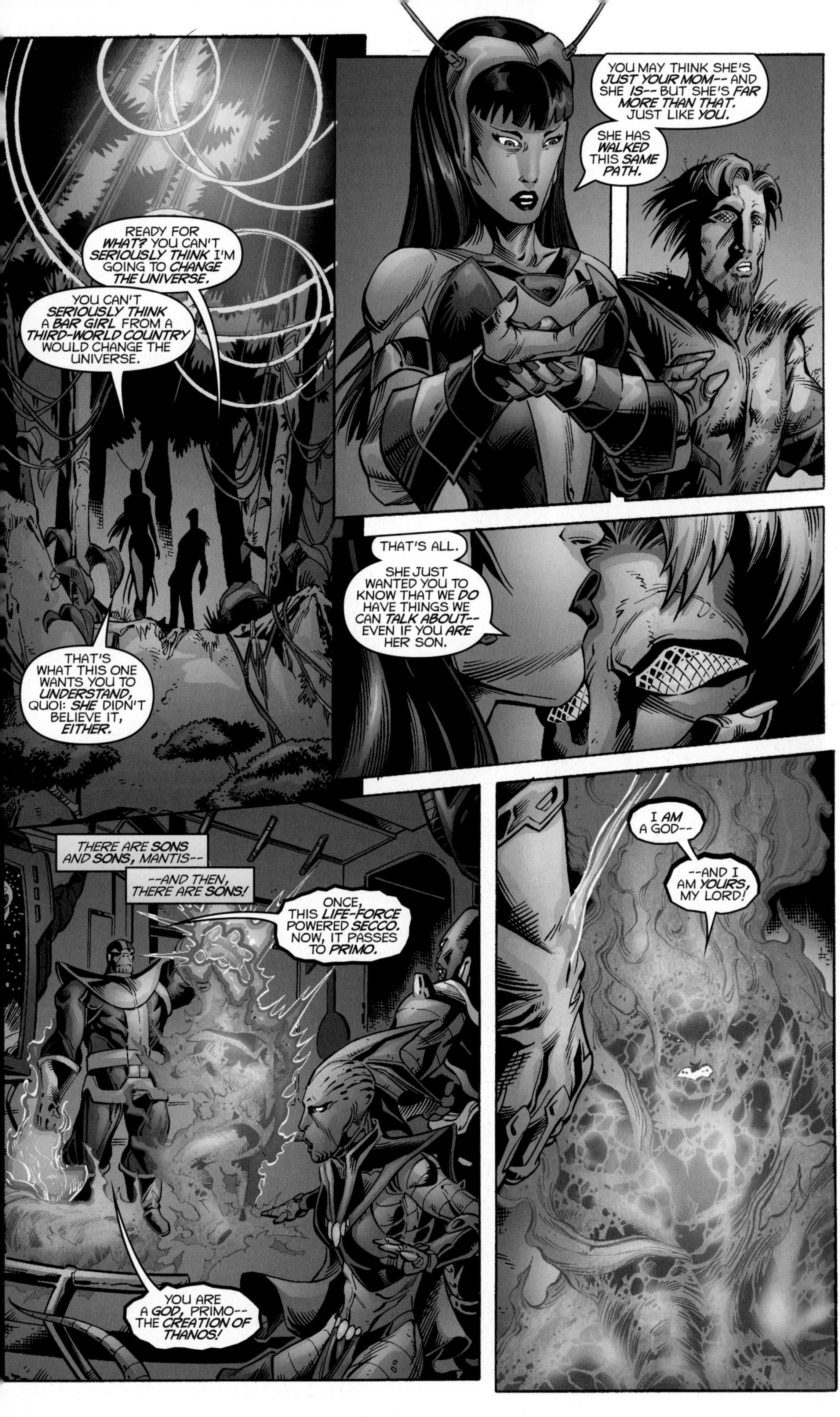

YOU MAY THINK SHE'S JUST YOUR MOM-- AND SHE IS-- BUT SHE'S FAR MORE THAN THAT. JUST LIKE YOU.
SHE HAS WALKED THIS SAME PATH.
READY FOR WHAT? YOU CAN'T SERIOUSLY THINK I'M GOING TO CHANGE THE UNIVERSE.
YOU CAN'T SERIOUSLY THINK A BAR GIRL FROM A THIRD-WORLD COUNTRY WOULD CHANGE THE UNIVERSE.
THAT'S WHAT THIS ONE WANTS YOU TO UNDERSTAND, QUOI: SHE DIDN'T BELIEVE IT, EITHER.
THAT'S ALL.
SHE JUST WANTED YOU TO KNOW THAT WE DO HAVE THINGS WE CAN TALK ABOUT-- EVEN IF YOU ARE HER SON.
THERE ARE SONS AND SONS, MANTIS--
--AND THEN, THERE ARE SONS!
ONCE, THIS LIFE-FORCE POWERED SECCO. NOW, IT PASSES TO PRIMO.
YOU ARE A GOD, PRIMO-- THE CREATION OF THANOS!
I AM A GOD--
--AND I AM YOURS, MY LORD!

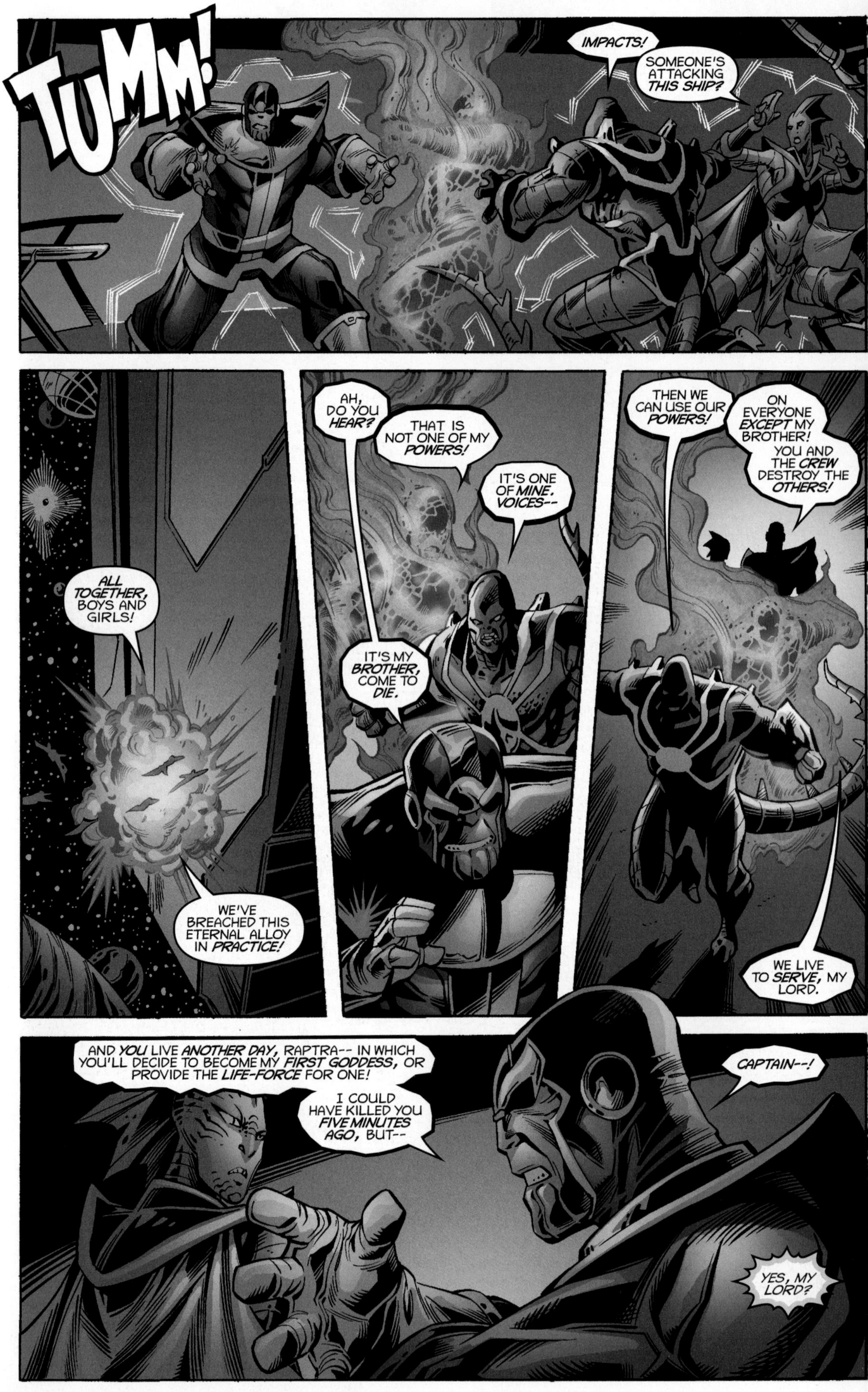
TUMM!
IMPACTS!
SOMEONE'S ATTACKING THIS SHIP?
ALL TOGETHER, BOYS AND GIRLS!
WE'VE BREACHED THIS ETERNAL ALLOY IN PRACTICE!
AH, DO YOU HEAR?
THAT IS NOT ONE OF MY POWERS!
IT'S ONE OF MINE. VOICES--
IT'S MY BROTHER, COME TO DIE.
THEN WE CAN USE OUR POWERS!
ON EVERYONE EXCEPT MY BROTHER!
YOU AND THE CREW DESTROY THE OTHERS!
WE LIVE TO SERVE, MY LORD.
AND YOU LIVE ANOTHER DAY, RAPTRA-- IN WHICH YOU'LL DECIDE TO BECOME MY FIRST GODDESS, OR PROVIDE THE LIFE-FORCE FOR ONE!
I COULD HAVE KILLED YOU FIVE MINUTES AGO, BUT--
CAPTAIN--!
YES, MY LORD?

"ON MY *MARK,* CAPTAIN--

"--FIRE!"

"THE ETERNALS HAVEN'T ENCOUNTERED *PLASMAGEN* BEFORE."

FOUR OF US DOWN IN THE FIRST MOMENTS!

BUT NO ONE WILL *FALTER!*

THANOS WON'T SURPRISE US *TWICE!* WE SEVEN WHO *SURVIVE* SCATTER TO *SAFETY!*

AND *I*--

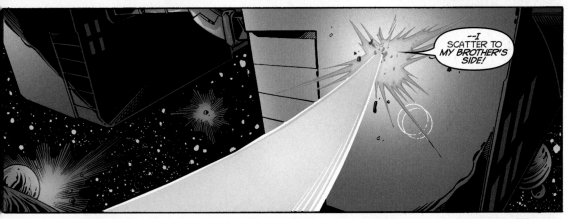

--*I* SCATTER TO *MY BROTHER'S SIDE!*

FOR THE SAKE OF THE *UNIVERSE,* ONE OF US *DIES* TODAY!

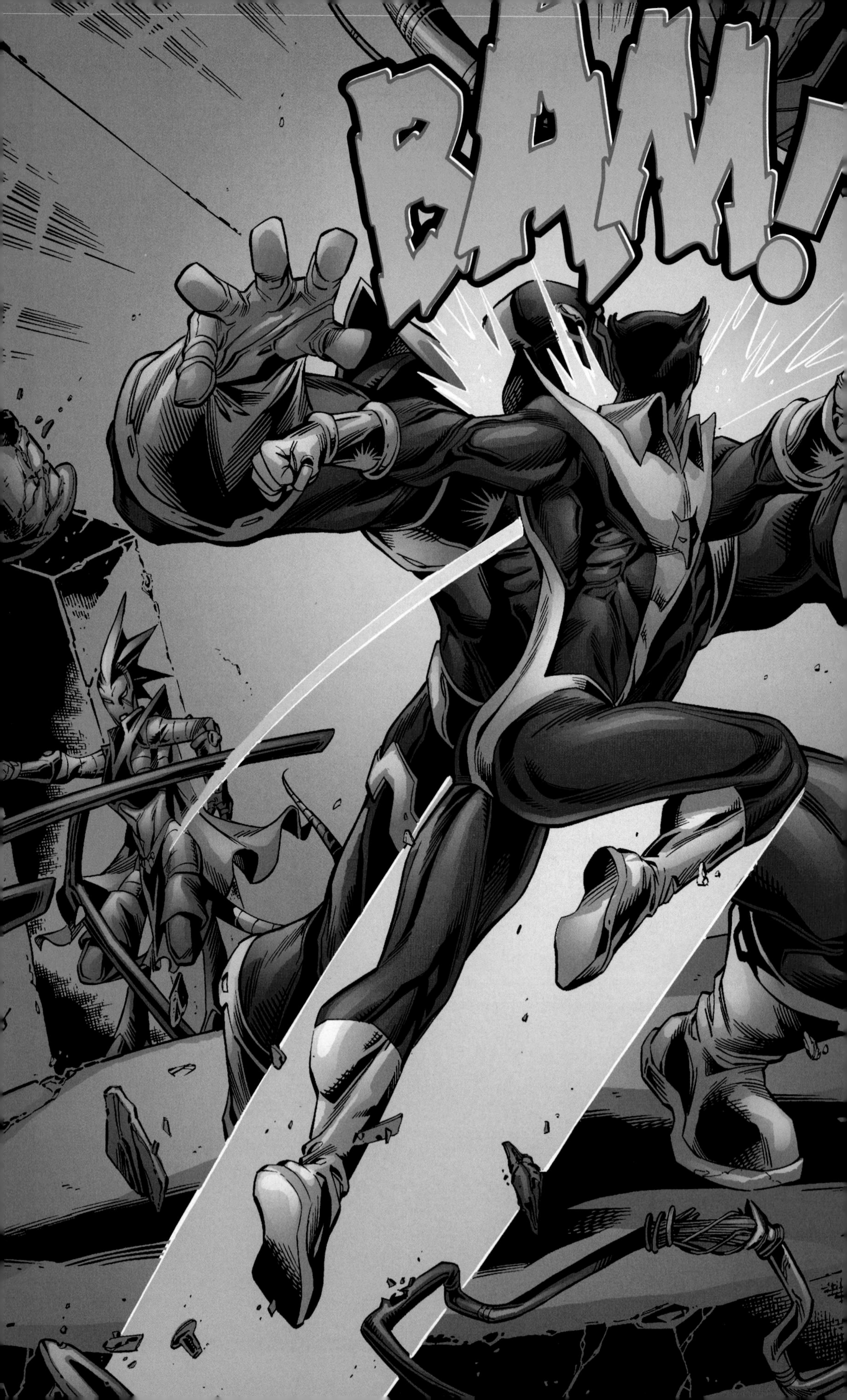
BAM!

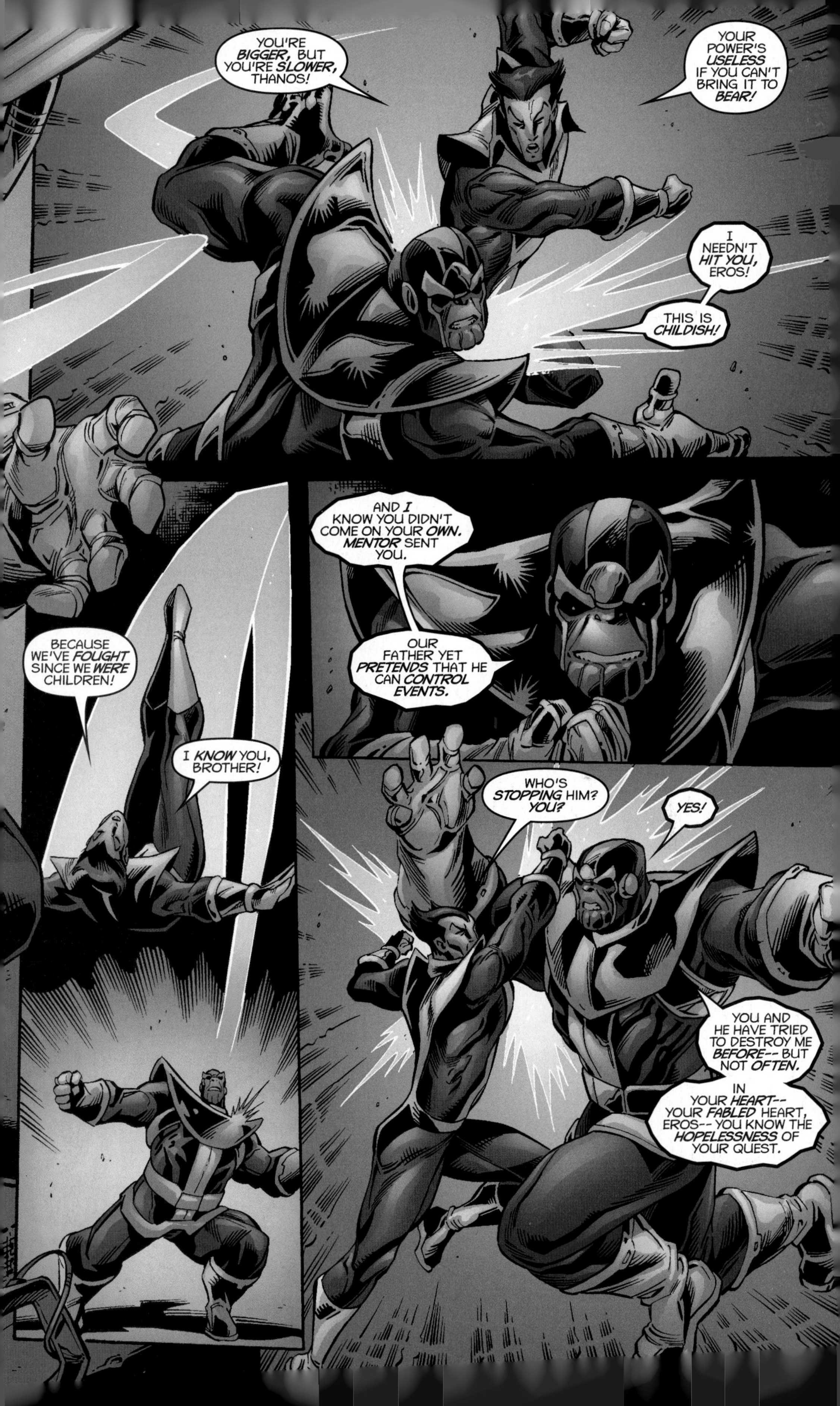

YOU'RE *BIGGER*, BUT YOU'RE *SLOWER*, THANOS!
YOUR POWER'S *USELESS* IF YOU CAN'T BRING IT TO *BEAR!*
I NEEDN'T *HIT YOU*, EROS!
THIS IS *CHILDISH!*
BECAUSE WE'VE *FOUGHT* SINCE WE *WERE* CHILDREN!
I *KNOW* YOU, BROTHER!
AND *I* KNOW YOU DIDN'T COME ON YOUR *OWN*. *MENTOR* SENT YOU.
OUR FATHER YET *PRETENDS* THAT HE CAN *CONTROL EVENTS*.
WHO'S *STOPPING* HIM? *YOU?*
YES!
YOU AND HE HAVE TRIED TO DESTROY ME *BEFORE*-- BUT NOT *OFTEN*.
IN YOUR *HEART*-- YOUR *FABLED* HEART, EROS-- YOU KNOW THE *HOPELESSNESS* OF YOUR QUEST.

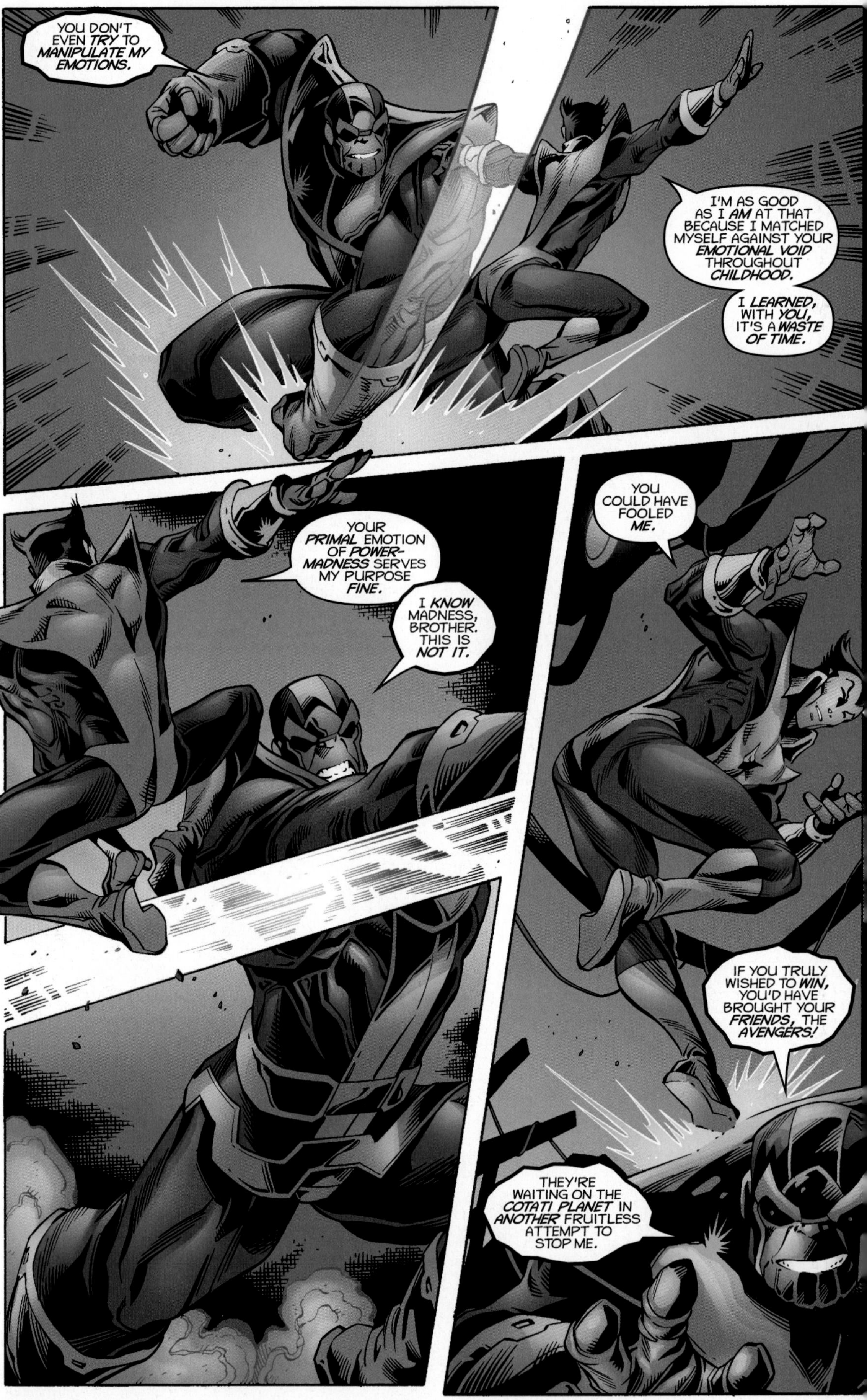
YOU DON'T EVEN TRY TO MANIPULATE MY EMOTIONS.
I'M AS GOOD AS I AM AT THAT BECAUSE I MATCHED MYSELF AGAINST YOUR EMOTIONAL VOID THROUGHOUT CHILDHOOD.
I LEARNED, WITH YOU, IT'S A WASTE OF TIME.
YOUR PRIMAL EMOTION OF POWER-MADNESS SERVES MY PURPOSE FINE.
I KNOW MADNESS, BROTHER. THIS IS NOT IT.
YOU COULD HAVE FOOLED ME.
IF YOU TRULY WISHED TO WIN, YOU'D HAVE BROUGHT YOUR FRIENDS, THE AVENGERS!
THEY'RE WAITING ON THE COTATI PLANET IN ANOTHER FRUITLESS ATTEMPT TO STOP ME.

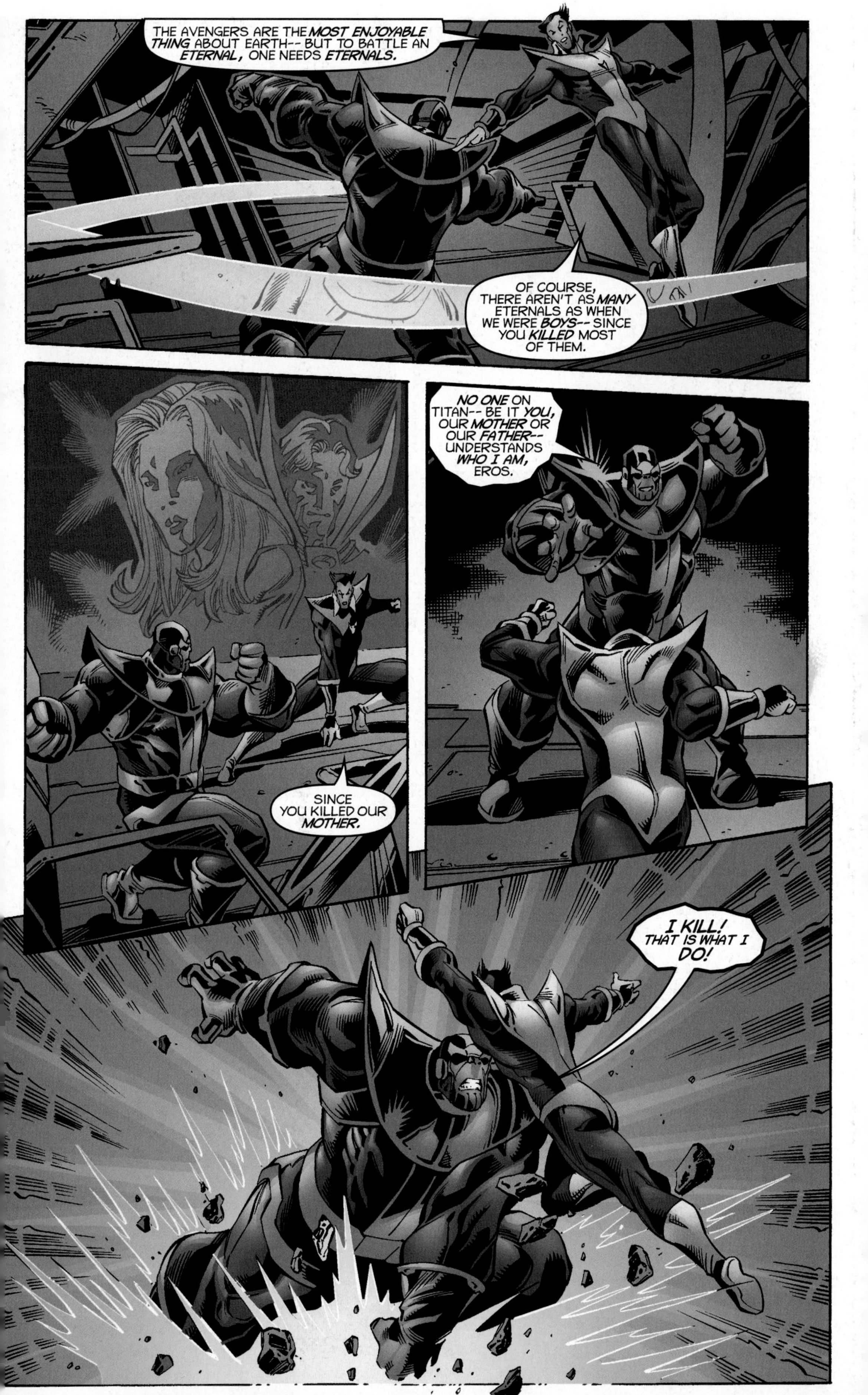

THE AVENGERS ARE THE MOST ENJOYABLE THING ABOUT EARTH-- BUT TO BATTLE AN ETERNAL, ONE NEEDS ETERNALS.
OF COURSE, THERE AREN'T AS MANY ETERNALS AS WHEN WE WERE BOYS-- SINCE YOU KILLED MOST OF THEM.
SINCE YOU KILLED OUR MOTHER.
NO ONE ON TITAN-- BE IT YOU, OUR MOTHER OR OUR FATHER-- UNDERSTANDS WHO I AM, EROS.
I KILL! THAT IS WHAT I DO!

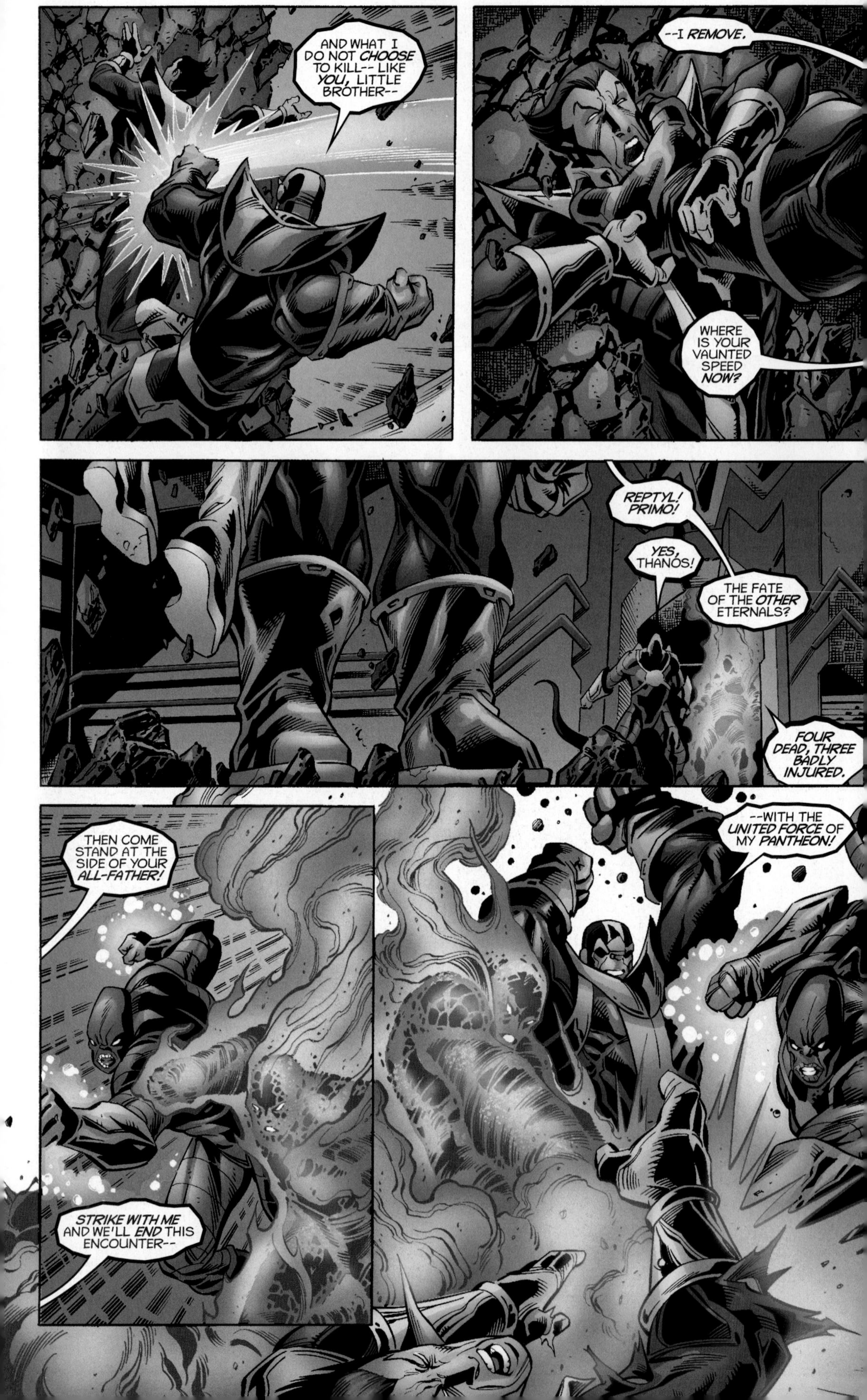
AND WHAT I DO NOT CHOOSE TO KILL-- LIKE YOU, LITTLE BROTHER--
--I REMOVE.
WHERE IS YOUR VAUNTED SPEED NOW?
REPTYL! PRIMO!
YES, THANOS!
THE FATE OF THE OTHER ETERNALS?
FOUR DEAD, THREE BADLY INJURED.
THEN COME STAND AT THE SIDE OF YOUR ALL-FATHER!
STRIKE WITH ME AND WE'LL END THIS ENCOUNTER--
--WITH THE UNITED FORCE OF MY PANTHEON!

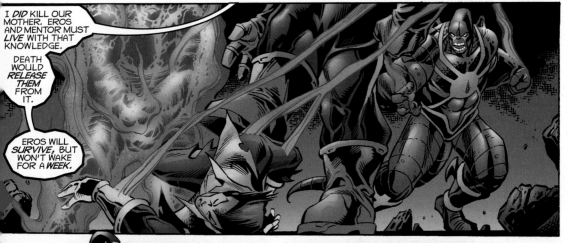

I *DID* KILL OUR MOTHER. EROS AND MENTOR MUST *LIVE* WITH THAT KNOWLEDGE.

DEATH WOULD *RELEASE THEM* FROM IT.

EROS WILL *SURVIVE*, BUT WON'T WAKE FOR A *WEEK*.

THROW HIM INTO *SPACE* WITH THE *REST* OF THE GARBAGE--

--WHILE *WE CONQUER* TAMAL.

THEN *YOU* MUST *DECIDE*, RAPTRA--

WHERE *IS* SHE? SHE WAS *HERE...*

THAT *ONE* ALWAYS *WAS* A *SURVIVOR!* I'LL BET SHE *RAN FOR HER LIFE!*

EXACTLY RIGHT.

AND HOW LONG TILL THEY DISCOVER I TOOK THE *CLOAK OF INVISIBILITY* WITH ME?

STAYING ON THAT SHIP WAS *SUICIDE*. I HAVE JUST *ONE* CHANCE TO BEAT THANOS *NOW*.

I'VE GOT TO GET THE *MESSIAH* FIRST!

TO BE CONTINUED!

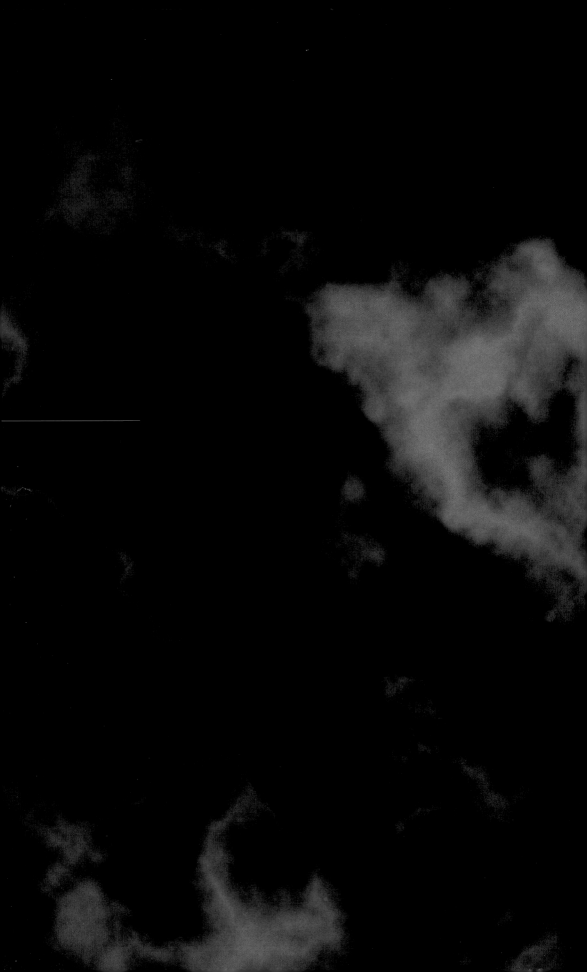

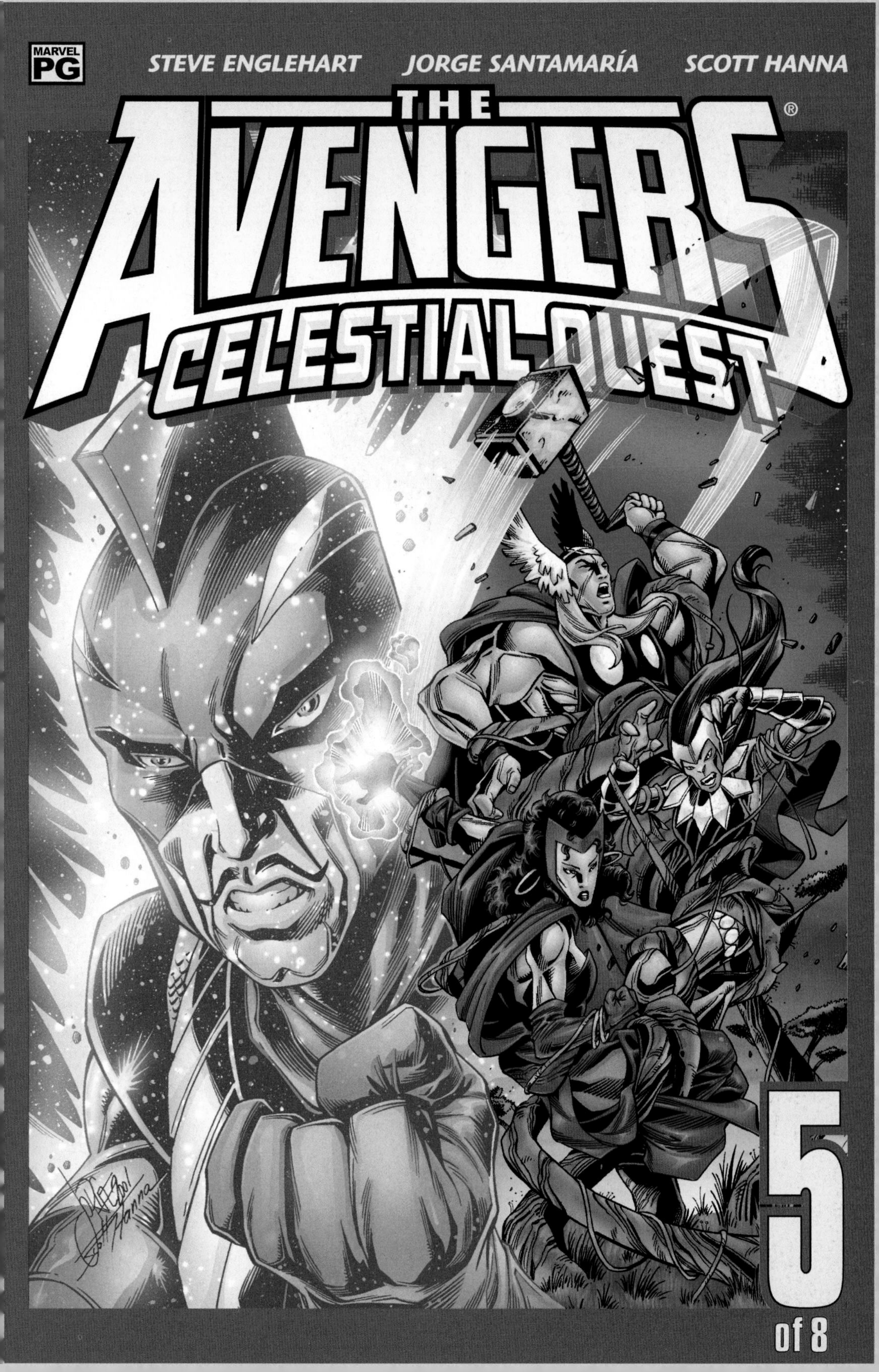
MARVEL PG
STEVE ENGLEHART
JORGE SANTAMARÍA
SCOTT HANNA
THE AVENGERS®
CELESTIAL QUEST
5
of 8

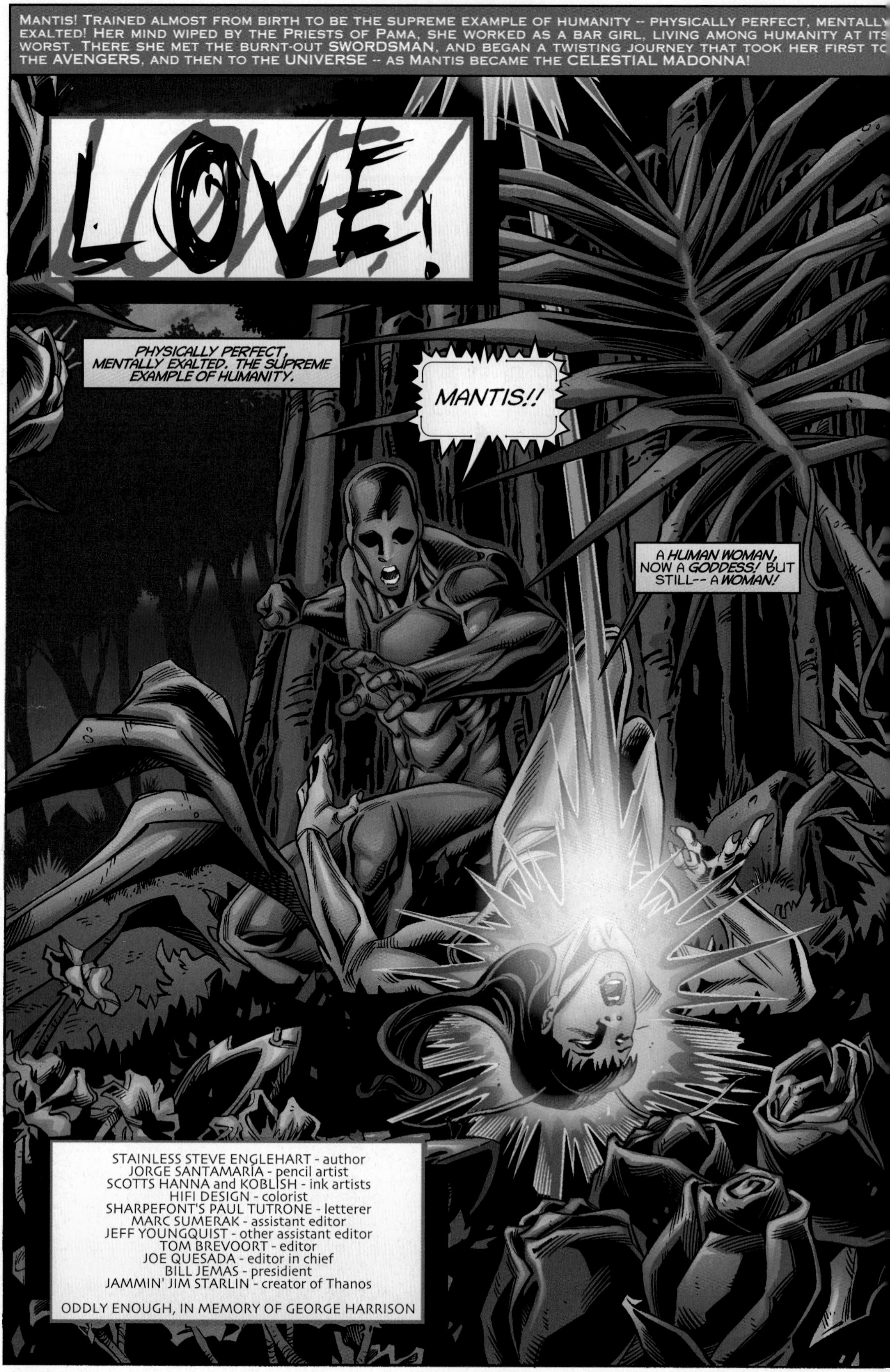
MANTIS! TRAINED ALMOST FROM BIRTH TO BE THE SUPREME EXAMPLE OF HUMANITY -- PHYSICALLY PERFECT, MENTALLY EXALTED! HER MIND WIPED BY THE PRIESTS OF PAMA, SHE WORKED AS A BAR GIRL, LIVING AMONG HUMANITY AT ITS WORST. THERE SHE MET THE BURNT-OUT SWORDSMAN, AND BEGAN A TWISTING JOURNEY THAT TOOK HER FIRST TO THE AVENGERS, AND THEN TO THE UNIVERSE -- AS MANTIS BECAME THE CELESTIAL MADONNA!
LOVE!
PHYSICALLY PERFECT, MENTALLY EXALTED. THE SUPREME EXAMPLE OF HUMANITY.
MANTIS!!
A HUMAN WOMAN, NOW A GODDESS! BUT STILL-- A WOMAN!
STAINLESS STEVE ENGLEHART - author
JORGE SANTAMARIA - pencil artist
SCOTTS HANNA and KOBLISH - ink artists
HIFI DESIGN - colorist
SHARPEFONT'S PAUL TUTRONE - letterer
MARC SUMERAK - assistant editor
JEFF YOUNGQUIST - other assistant editor
TOM BREVOORT - editor
JOE QUESADA - editor in chief
BILL JEMAS - presidient
JAMMIN' JIM STARLIN - creator of Thanos
ODDLY ENOUGH, IN MEMORY OF GEORGE HARRISON

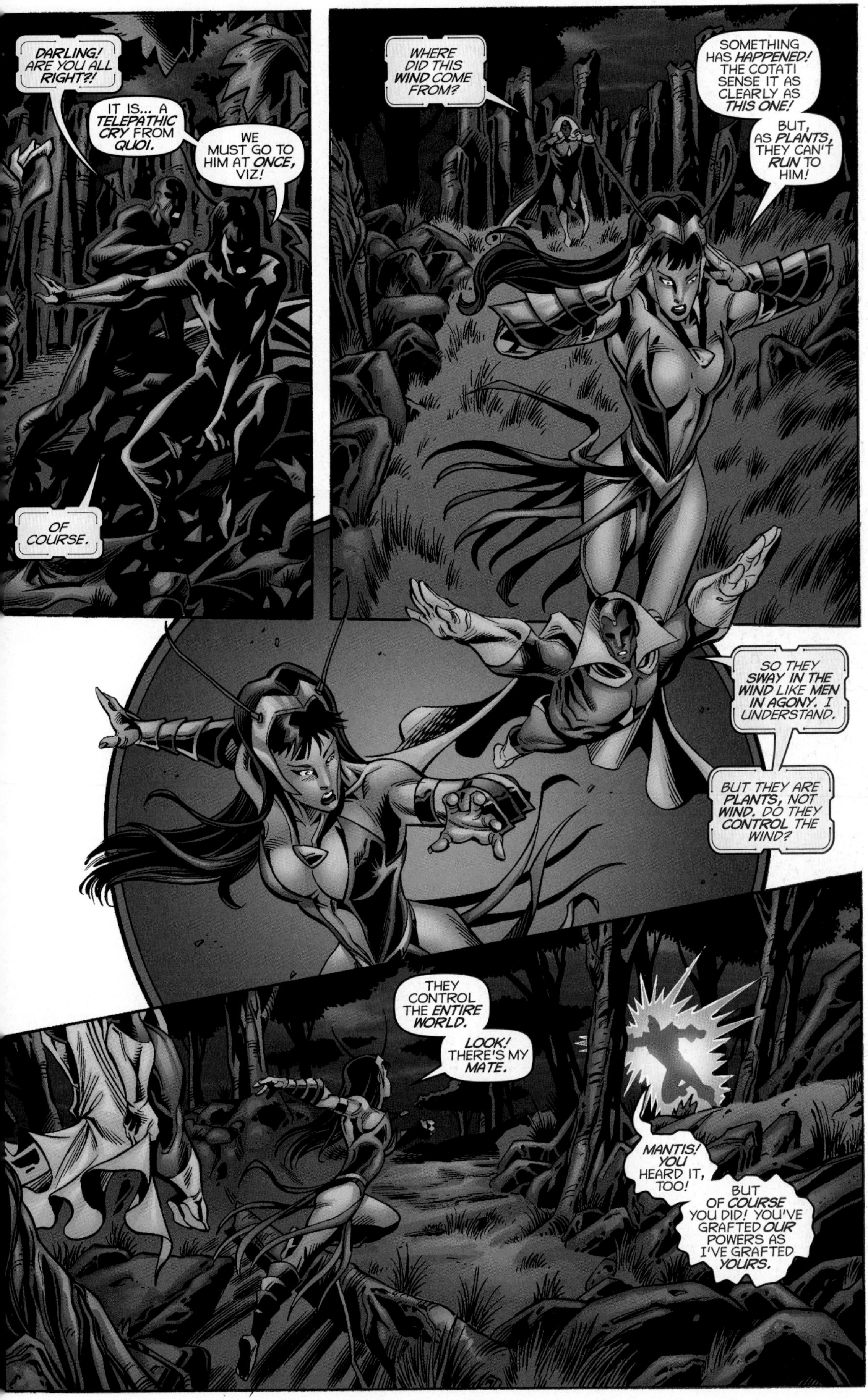
DARLING! ARE YOU ALL RIGHT?!
IT IS... A TELEPATHIC CRY FROM QUOI.
WE MUST GO TO HIM AT ONCE, VIZ!
OF COURSE.
WHERE DID THIS WIND COME FROM?
SOMETHING HAS HAPPENED! THE COTATI SENSE IT AS CLEARLY AS THIS ONE!
BUT, AS PLANTS, THEY CAN'T RUN TO HIM!
SO THEY SWAY IN THE WIND LIKE MEN IN AGONY. I UNDERSTAND.
BUT THEY ARE PLANTS, NOT WIND. DO THEY CONTROL THE WIND?
THEY CONTROL THE ENTIRE WORLD.
LOOK! THERE'S MY MATE.
MANTIS! YOU HEARD IT, TOO!
BUT OF COURSE YOU DID! YOU'VE GRAFTED OUR POWERS AS I'VE GRAFTED YOURS.

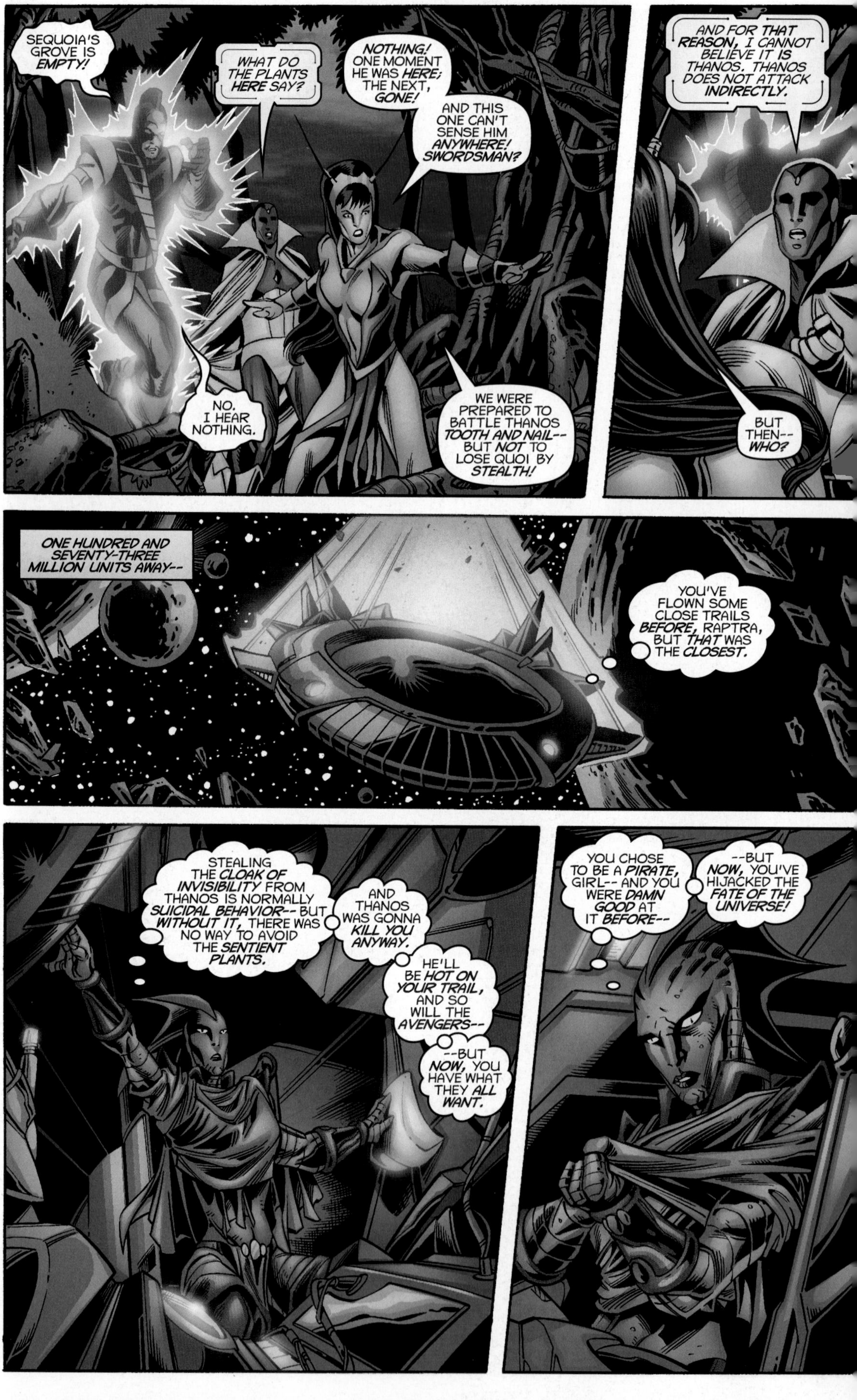
SEQUOIA'S GROVE IS *EMPTY!*
WHAT DO THE PLANTS HERE SAY?
NOTHING! ONE MOMENT HE WAS *HERE;* THE NEXT, *GONE!*
AND THIS ONE CAN'T SENSE HIM *ANYWHERE! SWORDSMAN?*
NO. I HEAR NOTHING.
WE WERE PREPARED TO BATTLE THANOS *TOOTH AND NAIL--* BUT *NOT* TO LOSE QUOI BY *STEALTH!*
AND FOR THAT REASON, I CANNOT BELIEVE IT IS THANOS. THANOS DOES NOT ATTACK INDIRECTLY.
BUT THEN-- *WHO?*
ONE HUNDRED AND SEVENTY-THREE MILLION UNITS AWAY--
YOU'VE FLOWN SOME CLOSE TRAILS *BEFORE,* RAPTRA, BUT *THAT* WAS THE *CLOSEST.*
STEALING THE *CLOAK OF INVISIBILITY* FROM THANOS IS NORMALLY *SUICIDAL BEHAVIOR--* BUT *WITHOUT IT,* THERE WAS NO WAY TO AVOID THE *SENTIENT PLANTS.*
AND THANOS WAS GONNA *KILL YOU ANYWAY.*
HE'LL BE *HOT ON YOUR TRAIL,* AND SO WILL THE *AVENGERS--*
--BUT *NOW,* YOU HAVE WHAT THEY *ALL WANT.*
YOU CHOSE TO BE A *PIRATE,* GIRL-- AND YOU WERE *DAMN GOOD* AT IT *BEFORE--*
--BUT *NOW,* YOU'VE HIJACKED THE *FATE OF THE UNIVERSE!*

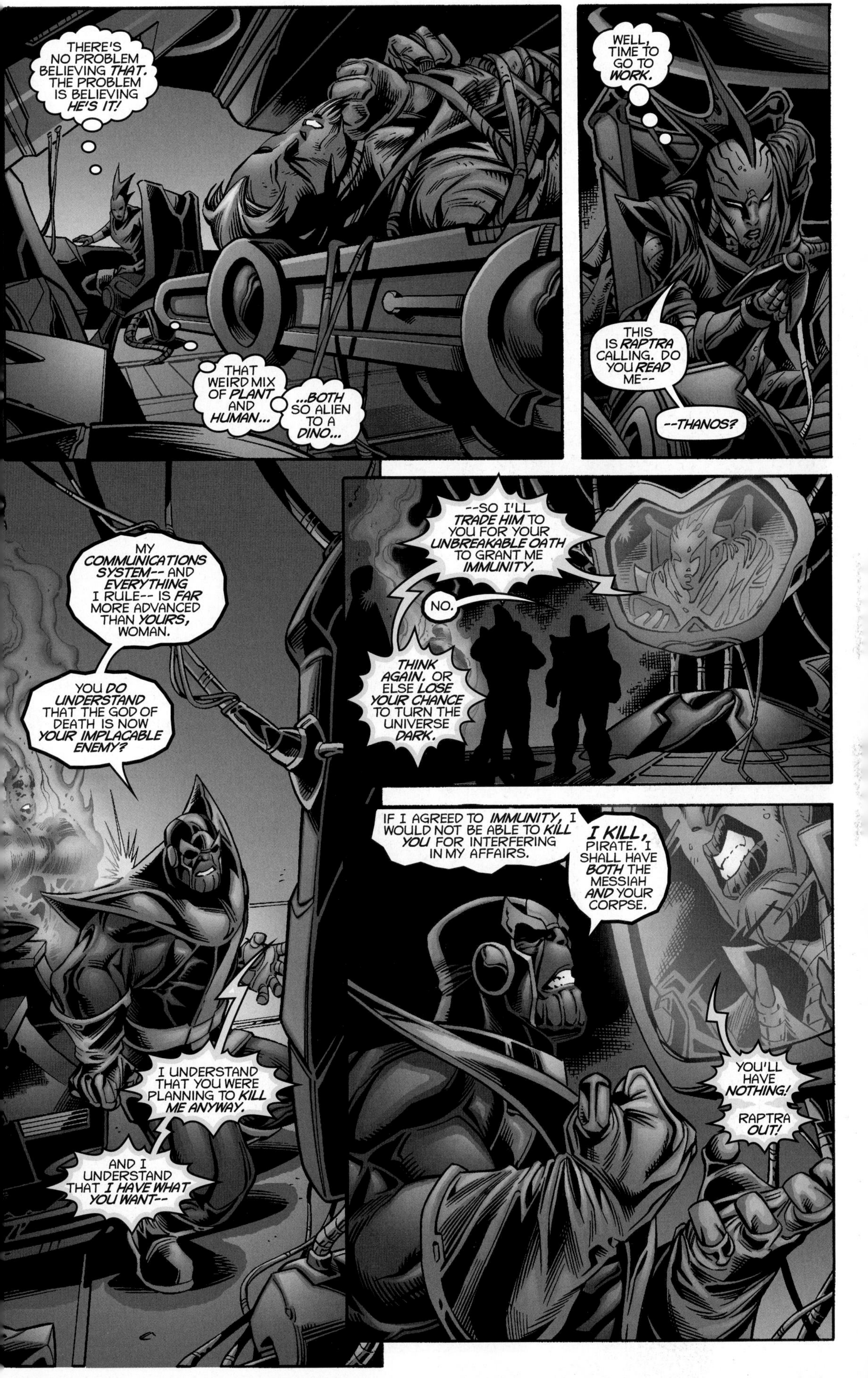

THERE'S NO PROBLEM BELIEVING THAT. THE PROBLEM IS BELIEVING HE'S IT!
THAT WEIRD MIX OF PLANT AND HUMAN...
...BOTH SO ALIEN TO A DINO...
WELL, TIME TO GO TO WORK.
THIS IS RAPTRA CALLING. DO YOU READ ME--
--THANOS?
MY COMMUNICATIONS SYSTEM-- AND EVERYTHING I RULE-- IS FAR MORE ADVANCED THAN YOURS, WOMAN.
YOU DO UNDERSTAND THAT THE GOD OF DEATH IS NOW YOUR IMPLACABLE ENEMY?
I UNDERSTAND THAT YOU WERE PLANNING TO KILL ME ANYWAY.
AND I UNDERSTAND THAT I HAVE WHAT YOU WANT--
--SO I'LL TRADE HIM TO YOU FOR YOUR UNBREAKABLE OATH TO GRANT ME IMMUNITY.
NO.
THINK AGAIN. OR ELSE LOSE YOUR CHANCE TO TURN THE UNIVERSE DARK.
IF I AGREED TO IMMUNITY, I WOULD NOT BE ABLE TO KILL YOU FOR INTERFERING IN MY AFFAIRS.
I KILL, PIRATE. I SHALL HAVE BOTH THE MESSIAH AND YOUR CORPSE.
YOU'LL HAVE NOTHING!
RAPTRA OUT!

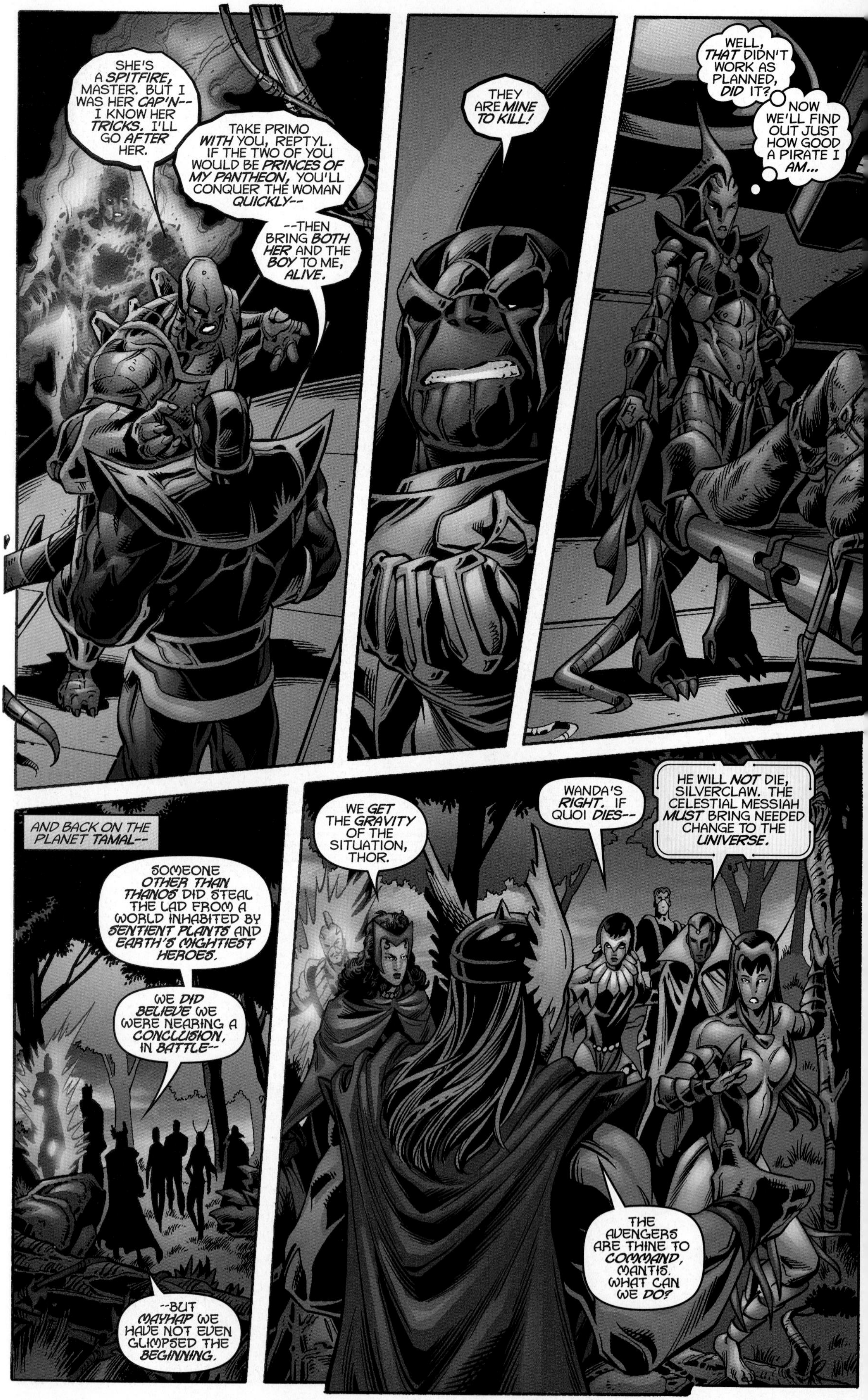
SHE'S A SPITFIRE, MASTER. BUT I WAS HER CAP'N-- I KNOW HER TRICKS. I'LL GO AFTER HER.
TAKE PRIMO WITH YOU, REPTYL. IF THE TWO OF YOU WOULD BE PRINCES OF MY PANTHEON, YOU'LL CONQUER THE WOMAN QUICKLY--
--THEN BRING BOTH HER AND THE BOY TO ME, ALIVE.
THEY ARE MINE TO KILL!
WELL, THAT DIDN'T WORK AS PLANNED, DID IT?
NOW WE'LL FIND OUT JUST HOW GOOD A PIRATE I AM...
AND BACK ON THE PLANET TAMAL--
SOMEONE OTHER THAN THANOS DID STEAL THE LAD FROM A WORLD INHABITED BY SENTIENT PLANTS AND EARTH'S MIGHTIEST HEROES.
WE DID BELIEVE WE WERE NEARING A CONCLUSION, IN BATTLE--
--BUT MAYHAP WE HAVE NOT EVEN GLIMPSED THE BEGINNING.
WE GET THE GRAVITY OF THE SITUATION, THOR.
WANDA'S RIGHT. IF QUOI DIES--
HE WILL NOT DIE, SILVERCLAW. THE CELESTIAL MESSIAH MUST BRING NEEDED CHANGE TO THE UNIVERSE.
THE AVENGERS ARE THINE TO COMMAND, MANTIS. WHAT CAN WE DO?

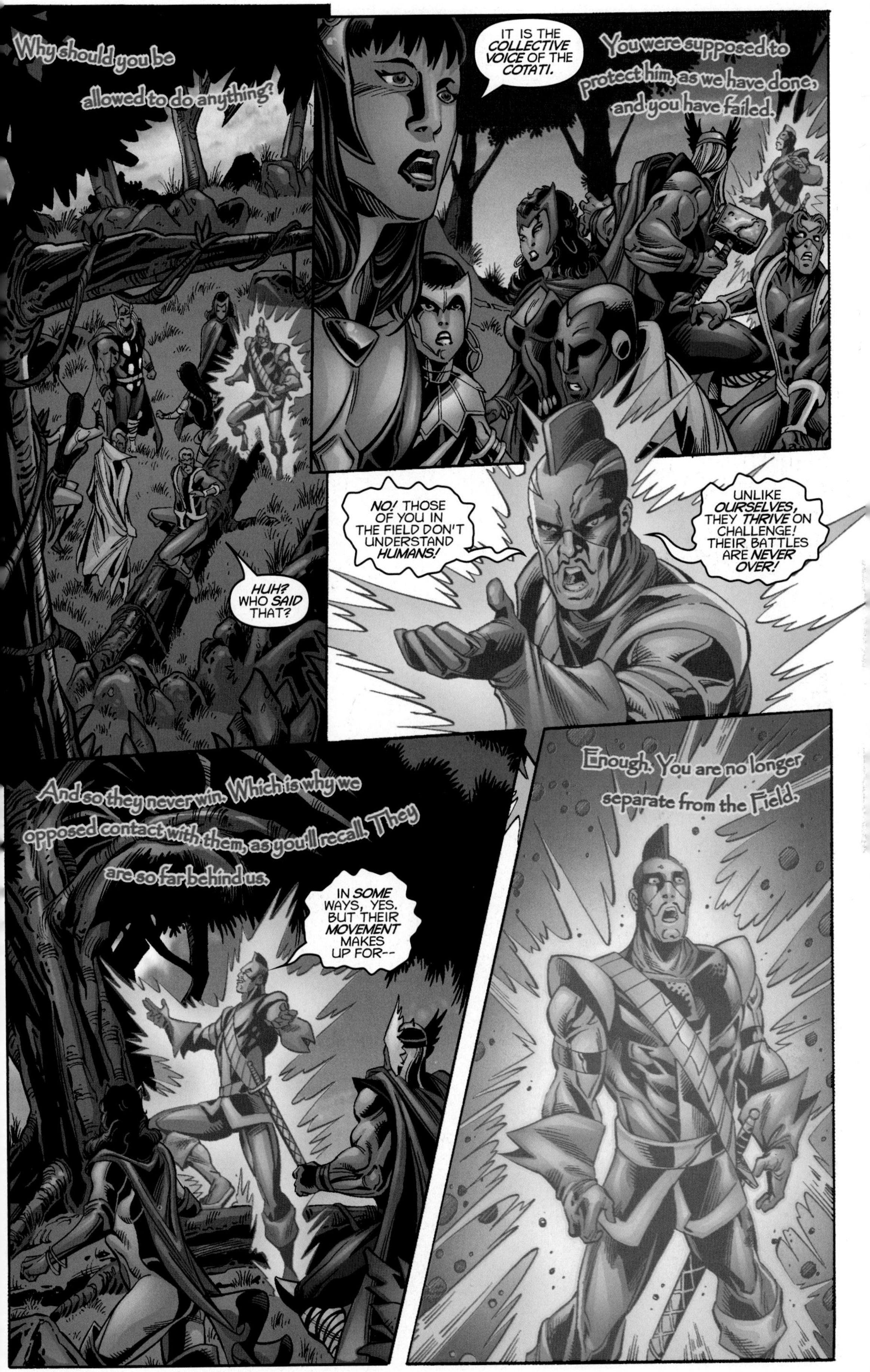

Why should you be allowed to do anything?
IT IS THE COLLECTIVE VOICE OF THE COTATI.
You were supposed to protect him, as we have done, and you have failed.
HUH? WHO SAID THAT?
NO! THOSE OF YOU IN THE FIELD DON'T UNDERSTAND HUMANS!
UNLIKE OURSELVES, THEY THRIVE ON CHALLENGE! THEIR BATTLES ARE NEVER OVER!
And so they never win. Which is why we opposed contact with them, as you'll recall. They are so far behind us.
IN SOME WAYS, YES. BUT THEIR MOVEMENT MAKES UP FOR--
Enough. You are no longer separate from the Field.

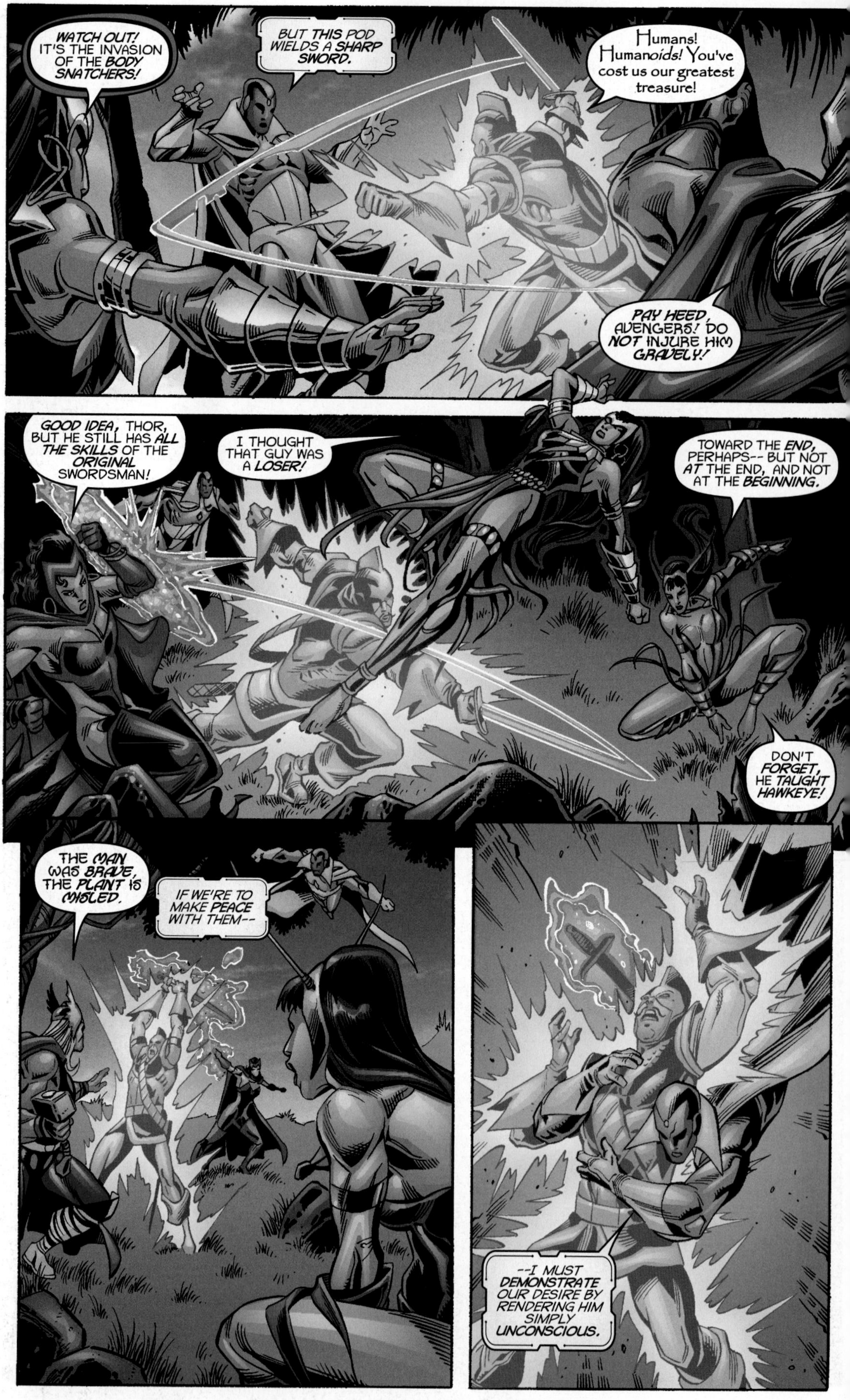
WATCH OUT! IT'S THE INVASION OF THE BODY SNATCHERS!
BUT THIS POD WIELDS A SHARP SWORD.
Humans! Humanoids! You've cost us our greatest treasure!
PAY HEED, AVENGERS! DO NOT INJURE HIM GRAVELY!
GOOD IDEA, THOR, BUT HE STILL HAS ALL THE SKILLS OF THE ORIGINAL SWORDSMAN!
I THOUGHT THAT GUY WAS A LOSER!
TOWARD THE END, PERHAPS-- BUT NOT AT THE END, AND NOT AT THE BEGINNING.
DON'T FORGET, HE TAUGHT HAWKEYE!
THE MAN WAS BRAVE, THE PLANT IS MISLED.
IF WE'RE TO MAKE PEACE WITH THEM--
--I MUST DEMONSTRATE OUR DESIRE BY RENDERING HIM SIMPLY UNCONSCIOUS.

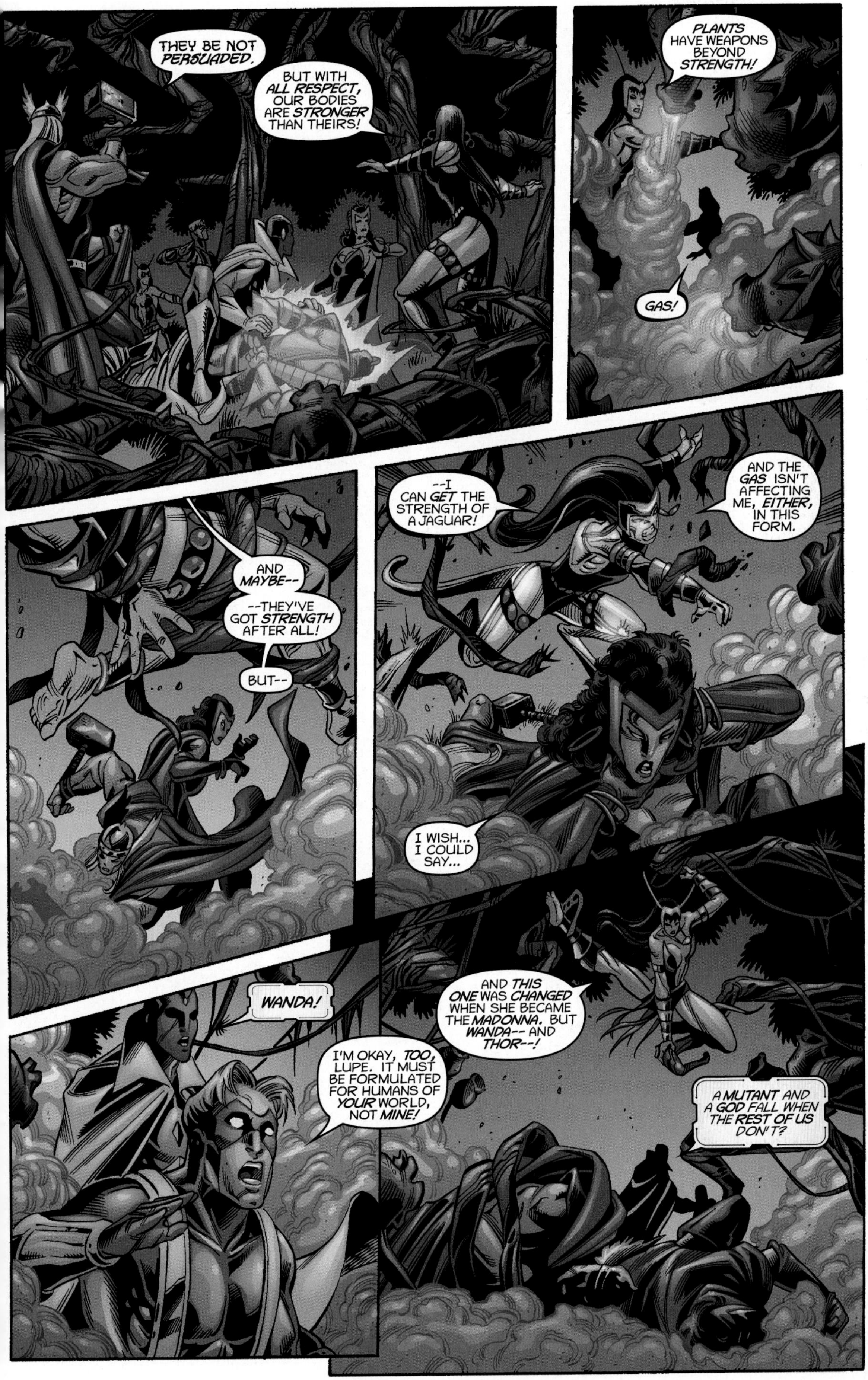
THEY BE NOT PERSUADED.
BUT WITH ALL RESPECT, OUR BODIES ARE STRONGER THAN THEIRS!
PLANTS HAVE WEAPONS BEYOND STRENGTH!
GAS!
AND MAYBE--
--THEY'VE GOT STRENGTH AFTER ALL!
BUT--
--I CAN GET THE STRENGTH OF A JAGUAR!
AND THE GAS ISN'T AFFECTING ME, EITHER, IN THIS FORM.
I WISH... I COULD SAY...
WANDA!
I'M OKAY, TOO, LUPE. IT MUST BE FORMULATED FOR HUMANS OF YOUR WORLD, NOT MINE!
AND THIS ONE WAS CHANGED WHEN SHE BECAME THE MADONNA. BUT WANDA-- AND THOR--!
A MUTANT AND A GOD FALL WHEN THE REST OF US DON'T?

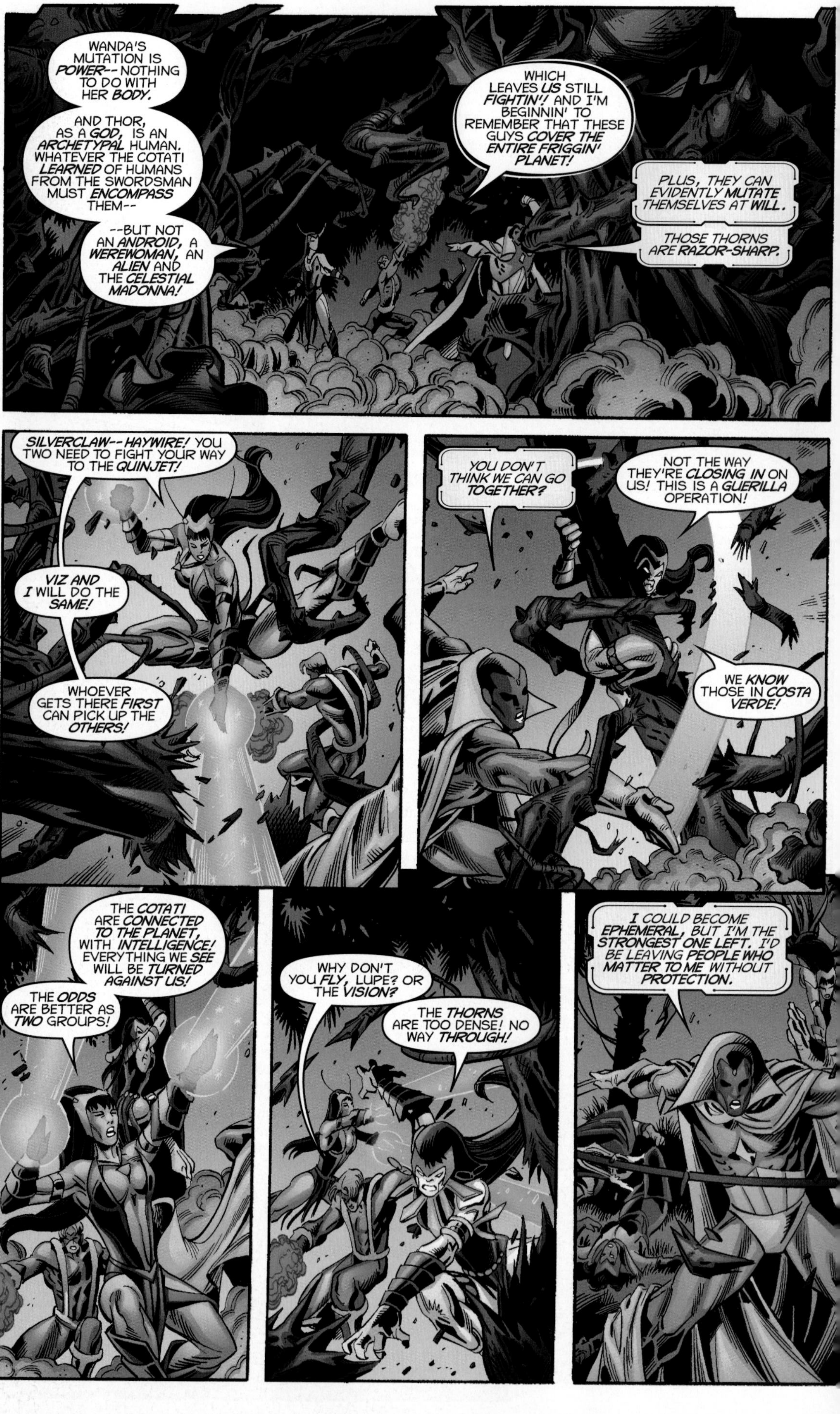
WANDA'S MUTATION IS POWER-- NOTHING TO DO WITH HER BODY.
AND THOR, AS A GOD, IS AN ARCHETYPAL HUMAN. WHATEVER THE COTATI LEARNED OF HUMANS FROM THE SWORDSMAN MUST ENCOMPASS THEM--
--BUT NOT AN ANDROID, A WEREWOMAN, AN ALIEN AND THE CELESTIAL MADONNA!
WHICH LEAVES US STILL FIGHTIN'! AND I'M BEGINNIN' TO REMEMBER THAT THESE GUYS COVER THE ENTIRE FRIGGIN' PLANET!
PLUS, THEY CAN EVIDENTLY MUTATE THEMSELVES AT WILL.
THOSE THORNS ARE RAZOR-SHARP.
SILVERCLAW-- HAYWIRE! YOU TWO NEED TO FIGHT YOUR WAY TO THE QUINJET!
VIZ AND I WILL DO THE SAME!
WHOEVER GETS THERE FIRST CAN PICK UP THE OTHERS!
YOU DON'T THINK WE CAN GO TOGETHER?
NOT THE WAY THEY'RE CLOSING IN ON US! THIS IS A GUERILLA OPERATION!
WE KNOW THOSE IN COSTA VERDE!
THE COTATI ARE CONNECTED TO THE PLANET, WITH INTELLIGENCE! EVERYTHING WE SEE WILL BE TURNED AGAINST US!
THE ODDS ARE BETTER AS TWO GROUPS!
WHY DON'T YOU FLY, LUPE? OR THE VISION?
THE THORNS ARE TOO DENSE! NO WAY THROUGH!
I COULD BECOME EPHEMERAL, BUT I'M THE STRONGEST ONE LEFT. I'D BE LEAVING PEOPLE WHO MATTER TO ME WITHOUT PROTECTION.

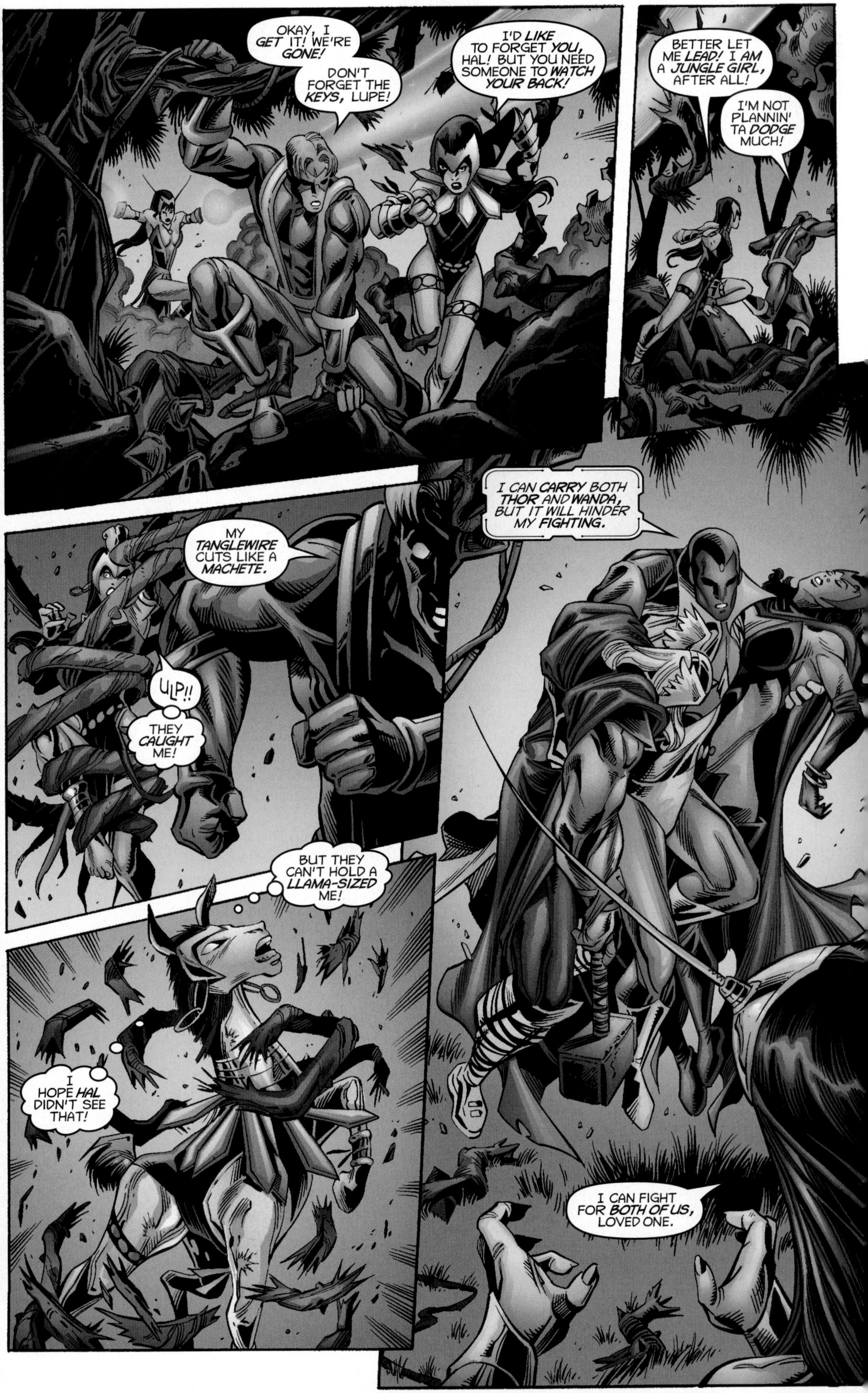
OKAY, I GET IT! WE'RE GONE!
DON'T FORGET THE KEYS, LUPE!
I'D LIKE TO FORGET YOU, HAL! BUT YOU NEED SOMEONE TO WATCH YOUR BACK!
BETTER LET ME LEAD! I AM A JUNGLE GIRL, AFTER ALL!
I'M NOT PLANNIN' TA DODGE MUCH!
MY TANGLEWIRE CUTS LIKE A MACHETE.
ULP!!
THEY CAUGHT ME!
I CAN CARRY BOTH THOR AND WANDA, BUT IT WILL HINDER MY FIGHTING.
BUT THEY CAN'T HOLD A LLAMA-SIZED ME!
I HOPE HAL DIDN'T SEE THAT!
I CAN FIGHT FOR BOTH OF US, LOVED ONE.

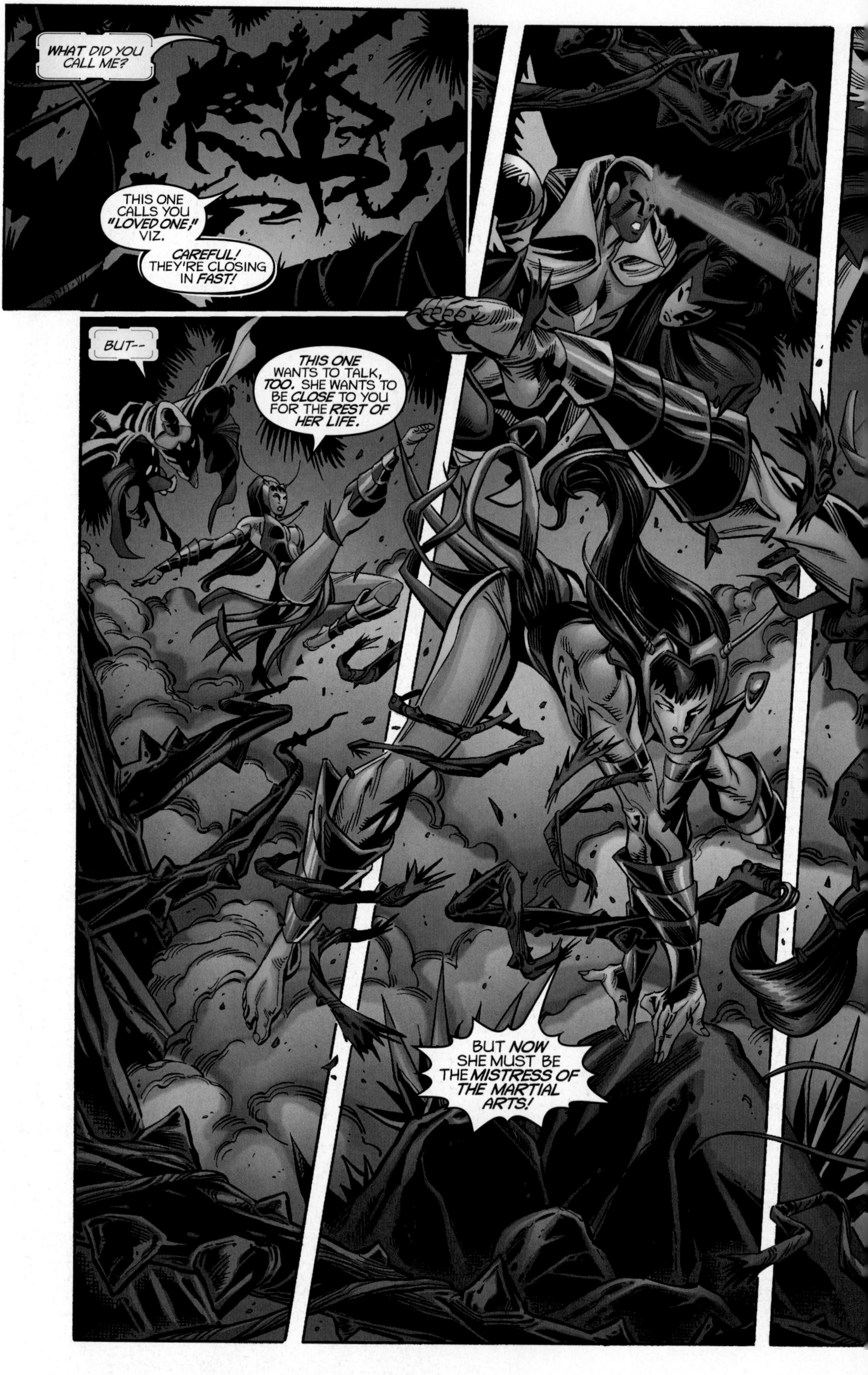
WHAT DID YOU CALL ME?
THIS ONE CALLS YOU "LOVED ONE!" VIZ.
CAREFUL! THEY'RE CLOSING IN FAST!
BUT--
THIS ONE WANTS TO TALK, TOO. SHE WANTS TO BE CLOSE TO YOU FOR THE REST OF HER LIFE.
BUT NOW SHE MUST BE THE MISTRESS OF THE MARTIAL ARTS!

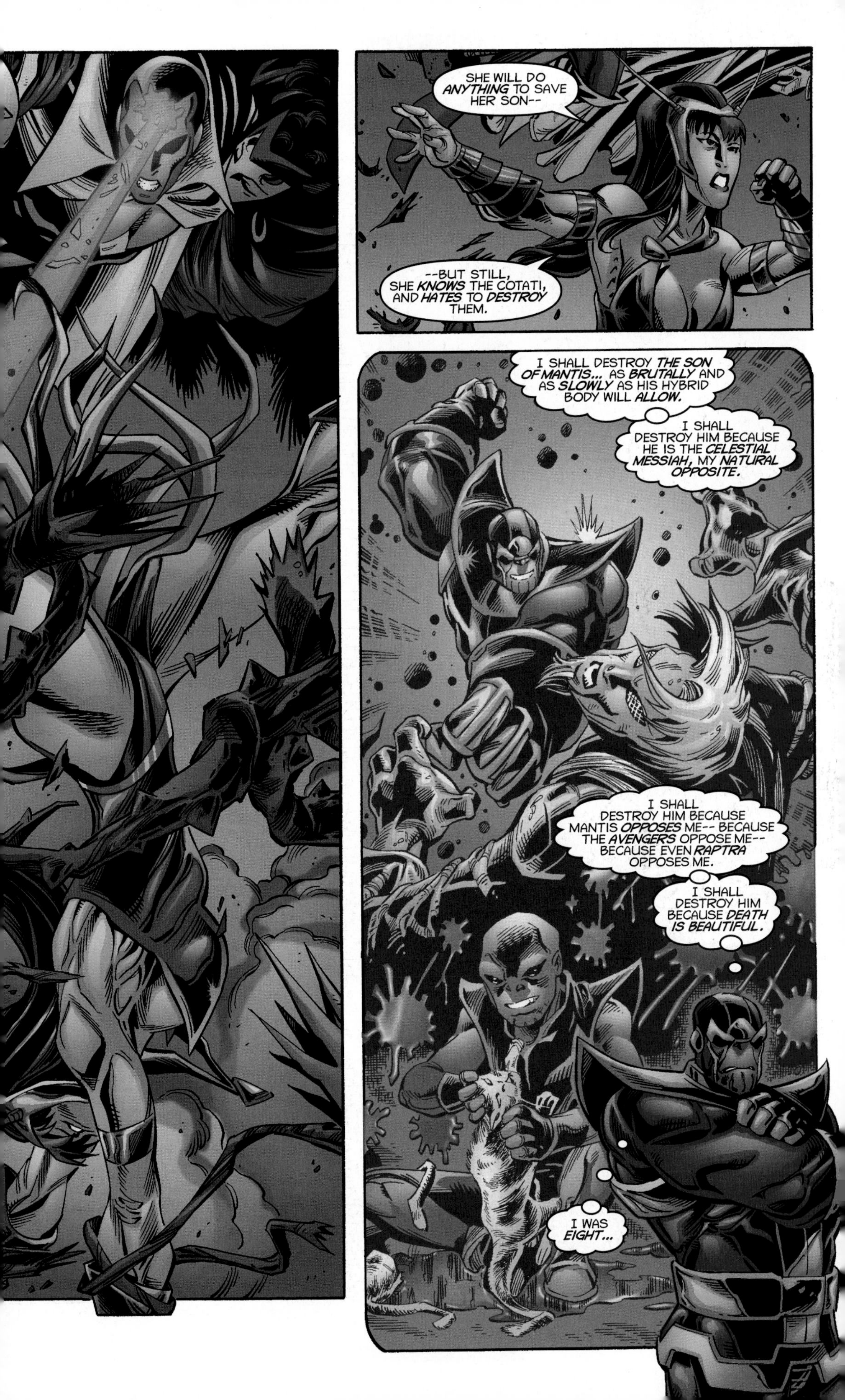
SHE WILL DO ANYTHING TO SAVE HER SON--
--BUT STILL, SHE KNOWS THE COTATI, AND HATES TO DESTROY THEM.
I SHALL DESTROY THE SON OF MANTIS... AS BRUTALLY AND AS SLOWLY AS HIS HYBRID BODY WILL ALLOW.
I SHALL DESTROY HIM BECAUSE HE IS THE CELESTIAL MESSIAH, MY NATURAL OPPOSITE.
I SHALL DESTROY HIM BECAUSE MANTIS OPPOSES ME-- BECAUSE THE AVENGERS OPPOSE ME-- BECAUSE EVEN RAPTRA OPPOSES ME.
I SHALL DESTROY HIM BECAUSE DEATH IS BEAUTIFUL.
I WAS EIGHT...

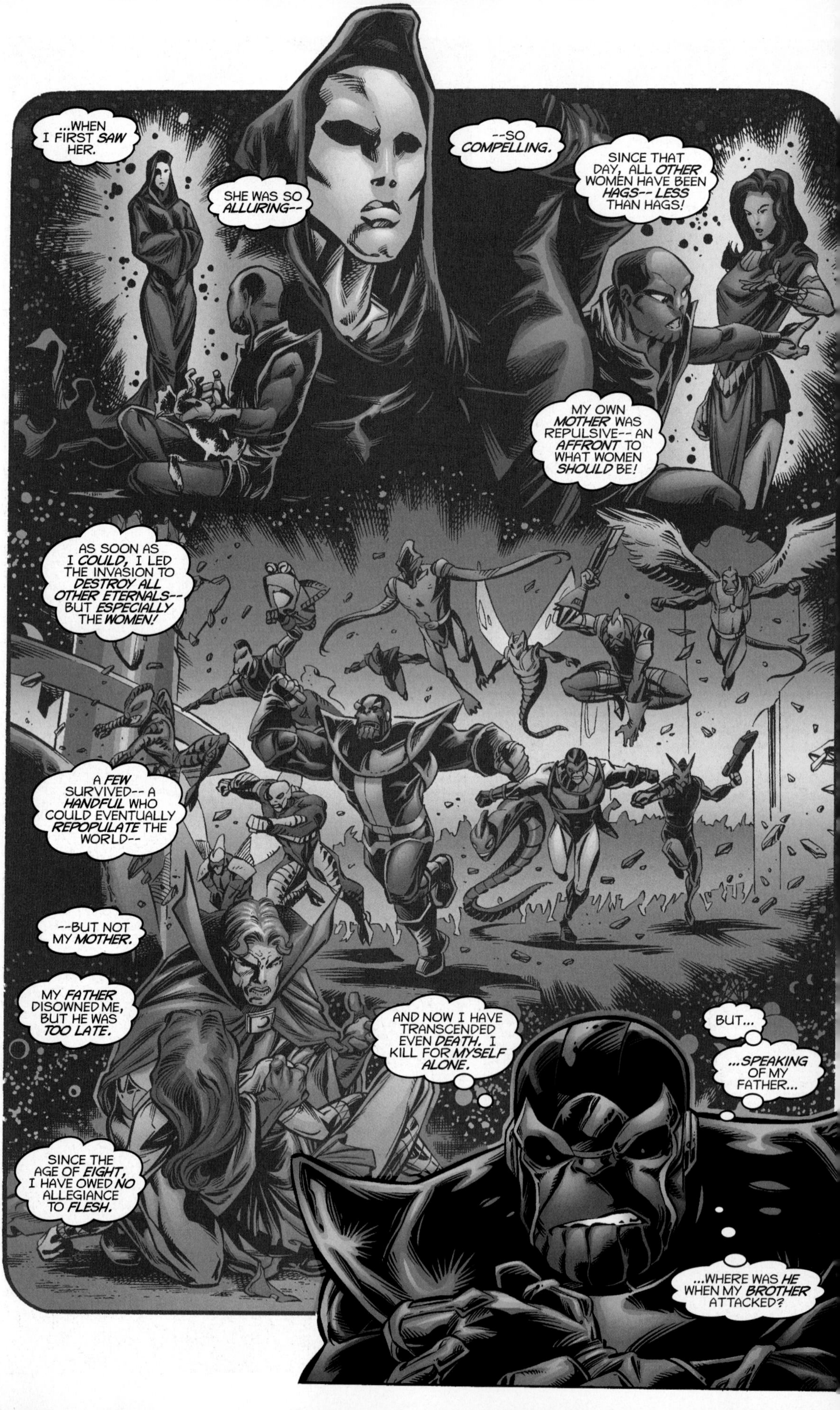

...WHEN I FIRST SAW HER.
SHE WAS SO ALLURING--
--SO COMPELLING.
SINCE THAT DAY, ALL OTHER WOMEN HAVE BEEN HAGS-- LESS THAN HAGS!
MY OWN MOTHER WAS REPULSIVE-- AN AFFRONT TO WHAT WOMEN SHOULD BE!
AS SOON AS I COULD, I LED THE INVASION TO DESTROY ALL OTHER ETERNALS-- BUT ESPECIALLY THE WOMEN!
A FEW SURVIVED-- A HANDFUL WHO COULD EVENTUALLY REPOPULATE THE WORLD--
--BUT NOT MY MOTHER.
MY FATHER DISOWNED ME, BUT HE WAS TOO LATE.
SINCE THE AGE OF EIGHT, I HAVE OWED NO ALLEGIANCE TO FLESH.
AND NOW I HAVE TRANSCENDED EVEN DEATH. I KILL FOR MYSELF ALONE.
BUT...
...SPEAKING OF MY FATHER...
...WHERE WAS HE WHEN MY BROTHER ATTACKED?

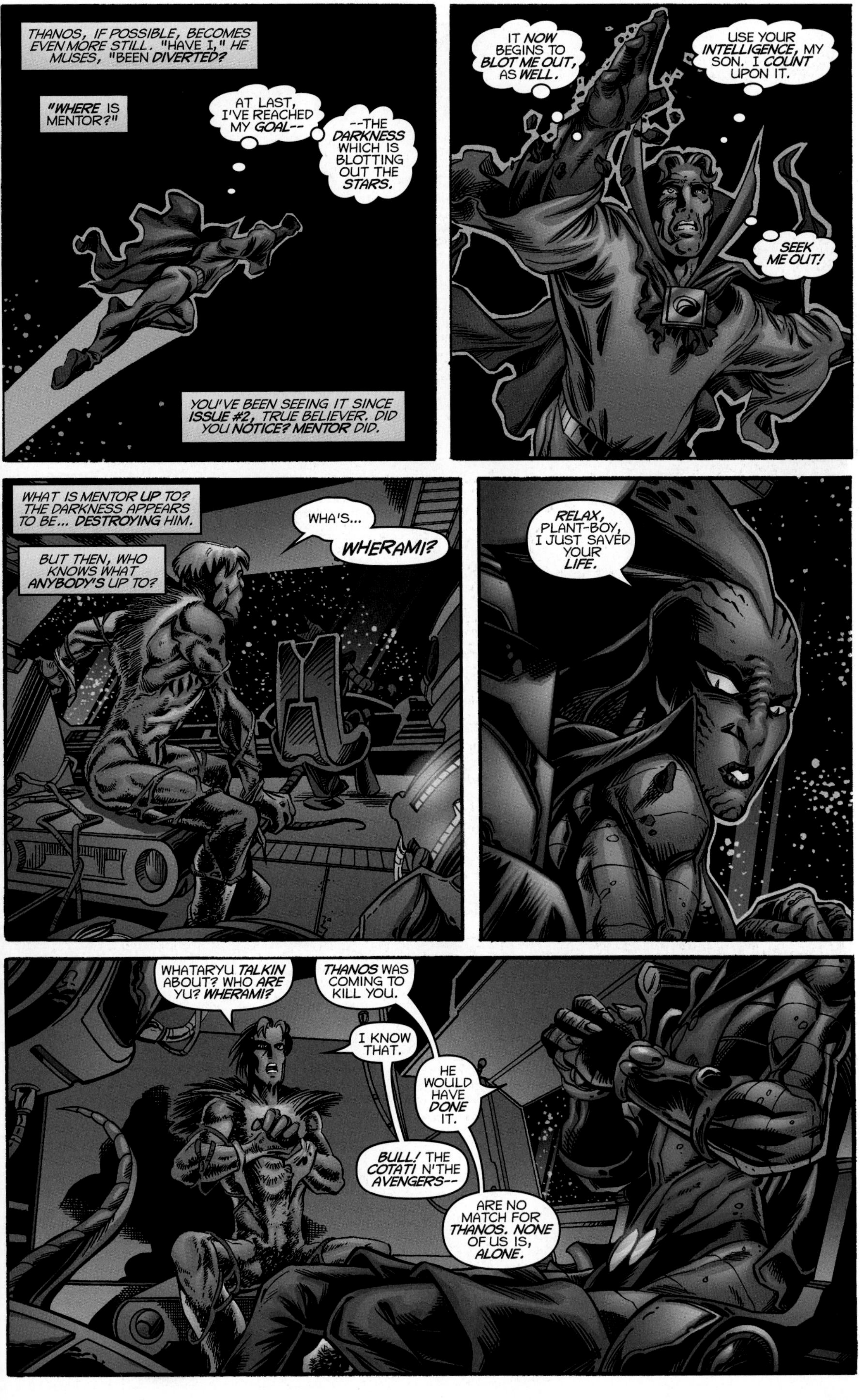
THANOS, IF POSSIBLE, BECOMES EVEN MORE STILL. "HAVE I," HE MUSES, "BEEN DIVERTED?
"WHERE IS MENTOR?"
AT LAST, I'VE REACHED MY GOAL--
--THE DARKNESS WHICH IS BLOTTING OUT THE STARS.
YOU'VE BEEN SEEING IT SINCE ISSUE #2, TRUE BELIEVER. DID YOU NOTICE? MENTOR DID.
IT NOW BEGINS TO BLOT ME OUT, AS WELL.
USE YOUR INTELLIGENCE, MY SON. I COUNT UPON IT.
SEEK ME OUT!
WHAT IS MENTOR UP TO? THE DARKNESS APPEARS TO BE... DESTROYING HIM.
BUT THEN, WHO KNOWS WHAT ANYBODY'S UP TO?
WHA'S... WHERAMI?
RELAX, PLANT-BOY, I JUST SAVED YOUR LIFE.
WHATARYU TALKIN ABOUT? WHO ARE YU? WHERAMI?
THANOS WAS COMING TO KILL YOU.
I KNOW THAT.
HE WOULD HAVE DONE IT.
BULL! THE COTATI N'THE AVENGERS--
ARE NO MATCH FOR THANOS. NONE OF US IS, ALONE.

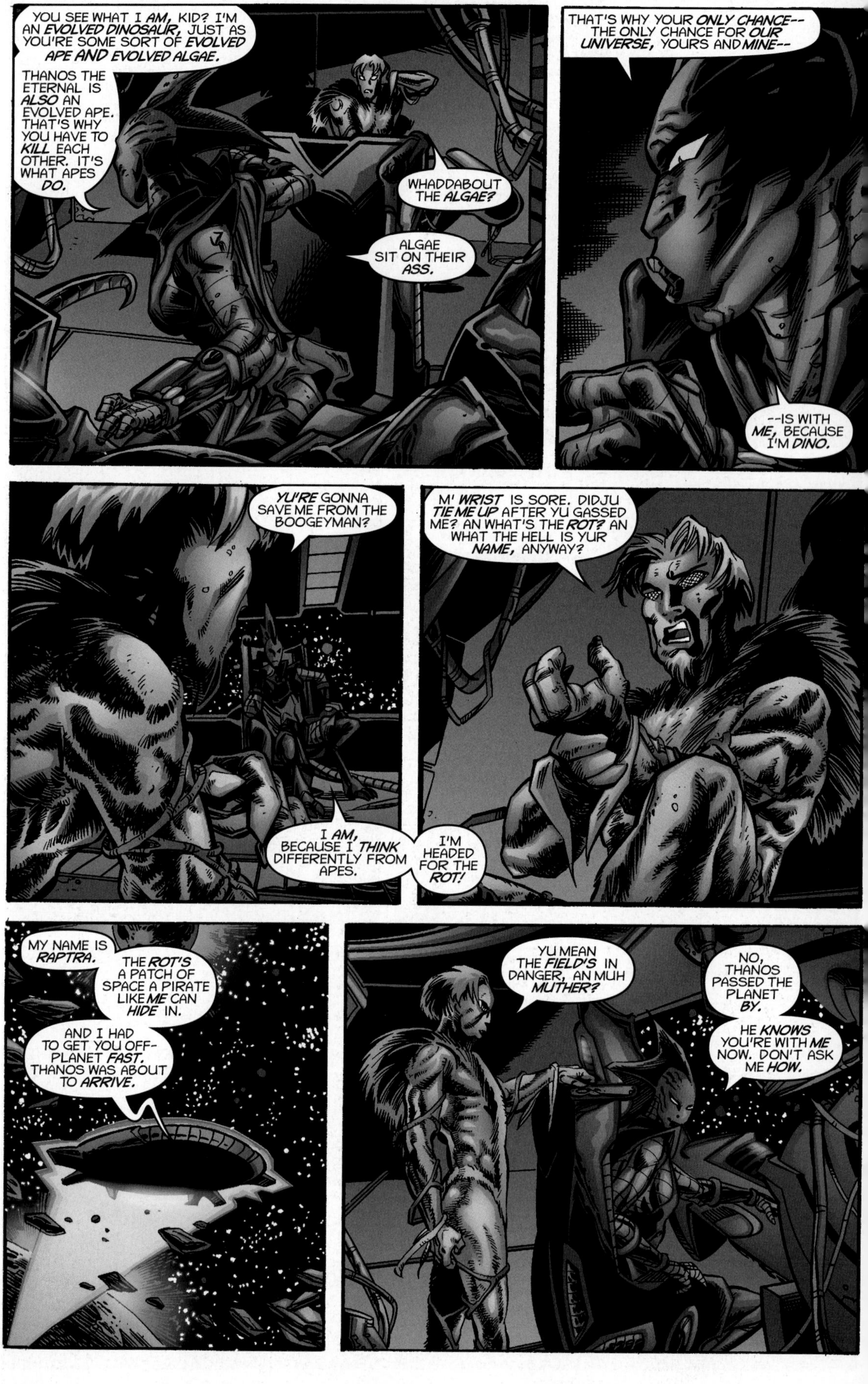

YOU SEE WHAT I AM, KID? I'M AN EVOLVED DINOSAUR, JUST AS YOU'RE SOME SORT OF EVOLVED APE AND EVOLVED ALGAE.
THANOS THE ETERNAL IS ALSO AN EVOLVED APE. THAT'S WHY YOU HAVE TO KILL EACH OTHER. IT'S WHAT APES DO.
WHADDABOUT THE ALGAE?
ALGAE SIT ON THEIR ASS.
THAT'S WHY YOUR ONLY CHANCE-- THE ONLY CHANCE FOR OUR UNIVERSE, YOURS AND MINE--
--IS WITH ME, BECAUSE I'M DINO.
YU'RE GONNA SAVE ME FROM THE BOOGEYMAN?
I AM, BECAUSE I THINK DIFFERENTLY FROM APES.
M' WRIST IS SORE. DIDJU TIE ME UP AFTER YU GASSED ME? AN WHAT'S THE ROT? AN WHAT THE HELL IS YUR NAME, ANYWAY?
I'M HEADED FOR THE ROT!
MY NAME IS RAPTRA.
THE ROT'S A PATCH OF SPACE A PIRATE LIKE ME CAN HIDE IN.
AND I HAD TO GET YOU OFF-PLANET FAST. THANOS WAS ABOUT TO ARRIVE.
YU MEAN THE FIELD'S IN DANGER, AN MUH MUTHER?
NO, THANOS PASSED THE PLANET BY.
HE KNOWS YOU'RE WITH ME NOW. DON'T ASK ME HOW.

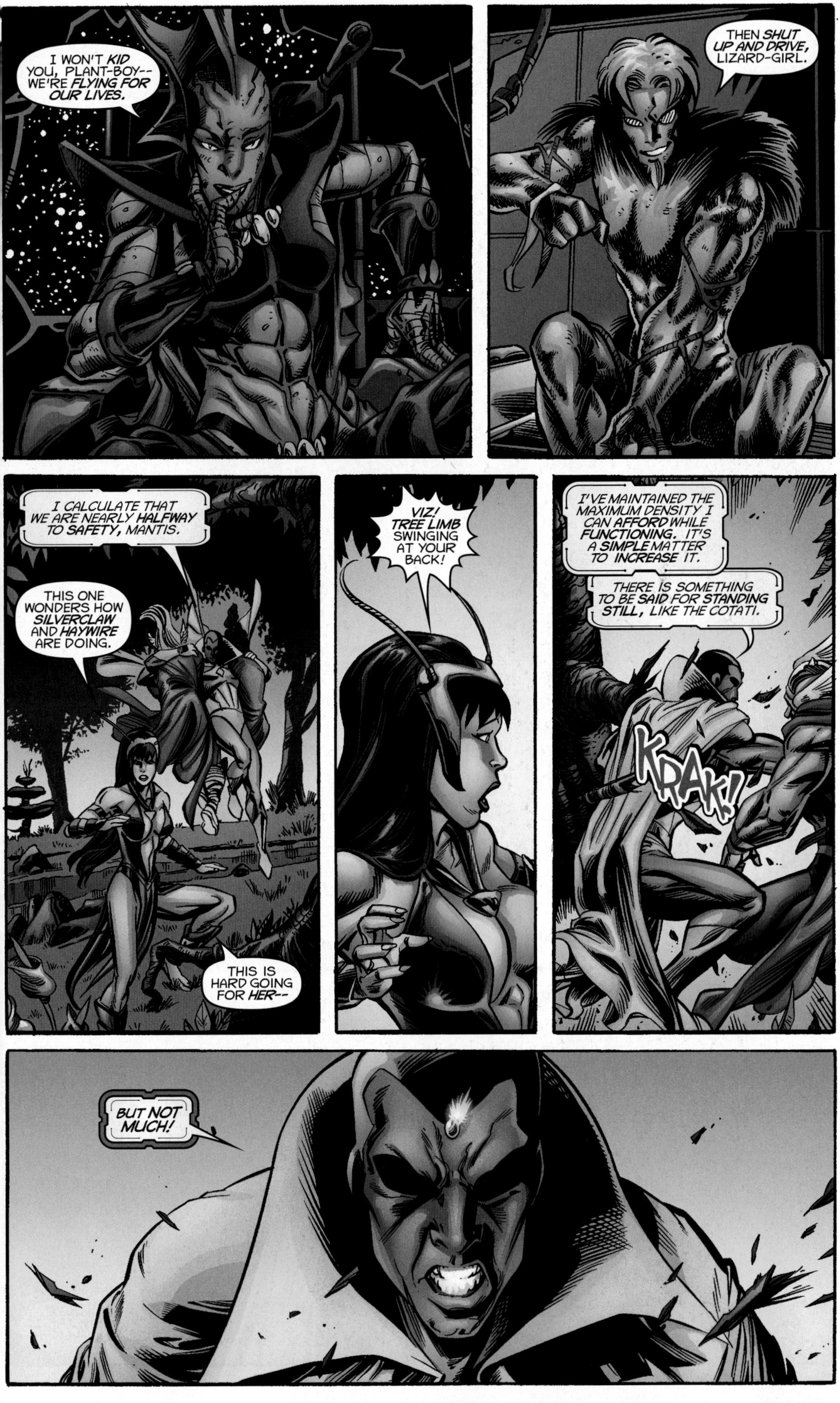
I WON'T KID YOU, PLANT-BOY--WE'RE FLYING FOR OUR LIVES.
THEN SHUT UP AND DRIVE, LIZARD-GIRL.
I CALCULATE THAT WE ARE NEARLY HALFWAY TO SAFETY, MANTIS.
THIS ONE WONDERS HOW SILVERCLAW AND HAYWIRE ARE DOING.
THIS IS HARD GOING FOR HER--
VIZ! TREE LIMB SWINGING AT YOUR BACK!
I'VE MAINTAINED THE MAXIMUM DENSITY I CAN AFFORD WHILE FUNCTIONING. IT'S A SIMPLE MATTER TO INCREASE IT.
THERE IS SOMETHING TO BE SAID FOR STANDING STILL, LIKE THE COTATI.
KRAK!
BUT NOT MUCH!

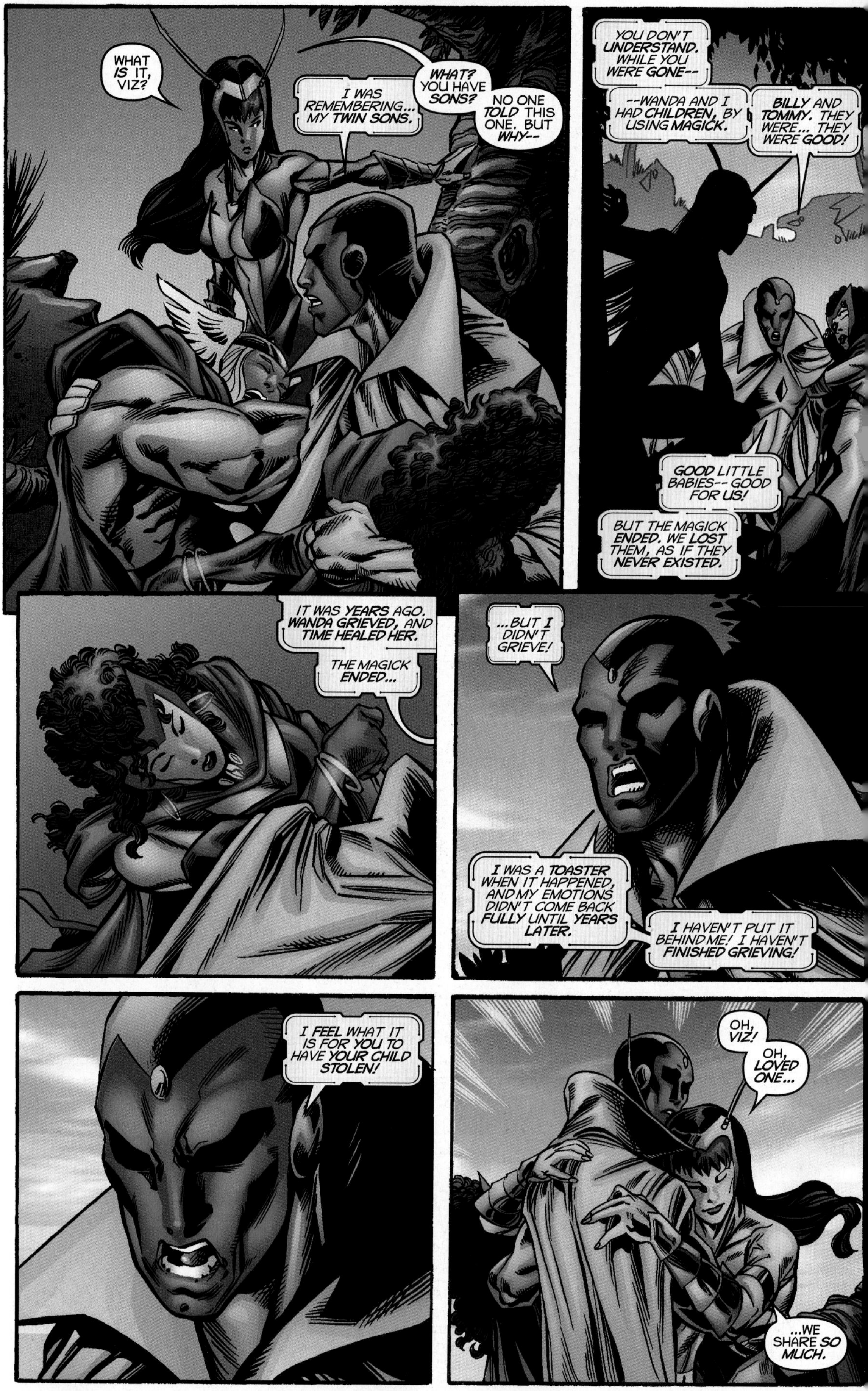
WHAT IS IT, VIZ?
I WAS REMEMBERING... MY TWIN SONS.
WHAT? YOU HAVE SONS?
NO ONE TOLD THIS ONE. BUT WHY--
YOU DON'T UNDERSTAND. WHILE YOU WERE GONE--
--WANDA AND I HAD CHILDREN, BY USING MAGICK.
BILLY AND TOMMY. THEY WERE... THEY WERE GOOD!
GOOD LITTLE BABIES-- GOOD FOR US!
BUT THE MAGICK ENDED. WE LOST THEM, AS IF THEY NEVER EXISTED.
IT WAS YEARS AGO. WANDA GRIEVED, AND TIME HEALED HER.
THE MAGICK ENDED...
...BUT I DIDN'T GRIEVE!
I WAS A TOASTER WHEN IT HAPPENED, AND MY EMOTIONS DIDN'T COME BACK FULLY UNTIL YEARS LATER.
I HAVEN'T PUT IT BEHIND ME! I HAVEN'T FINISHED GRIEVING!
I FEEL WHAT IT IS FOR YOU TO HAVE YOUR CHILD STOLEN!
OH, VIZ!
OH, LOVED ONE...
...WE SHARE SO MUCH.

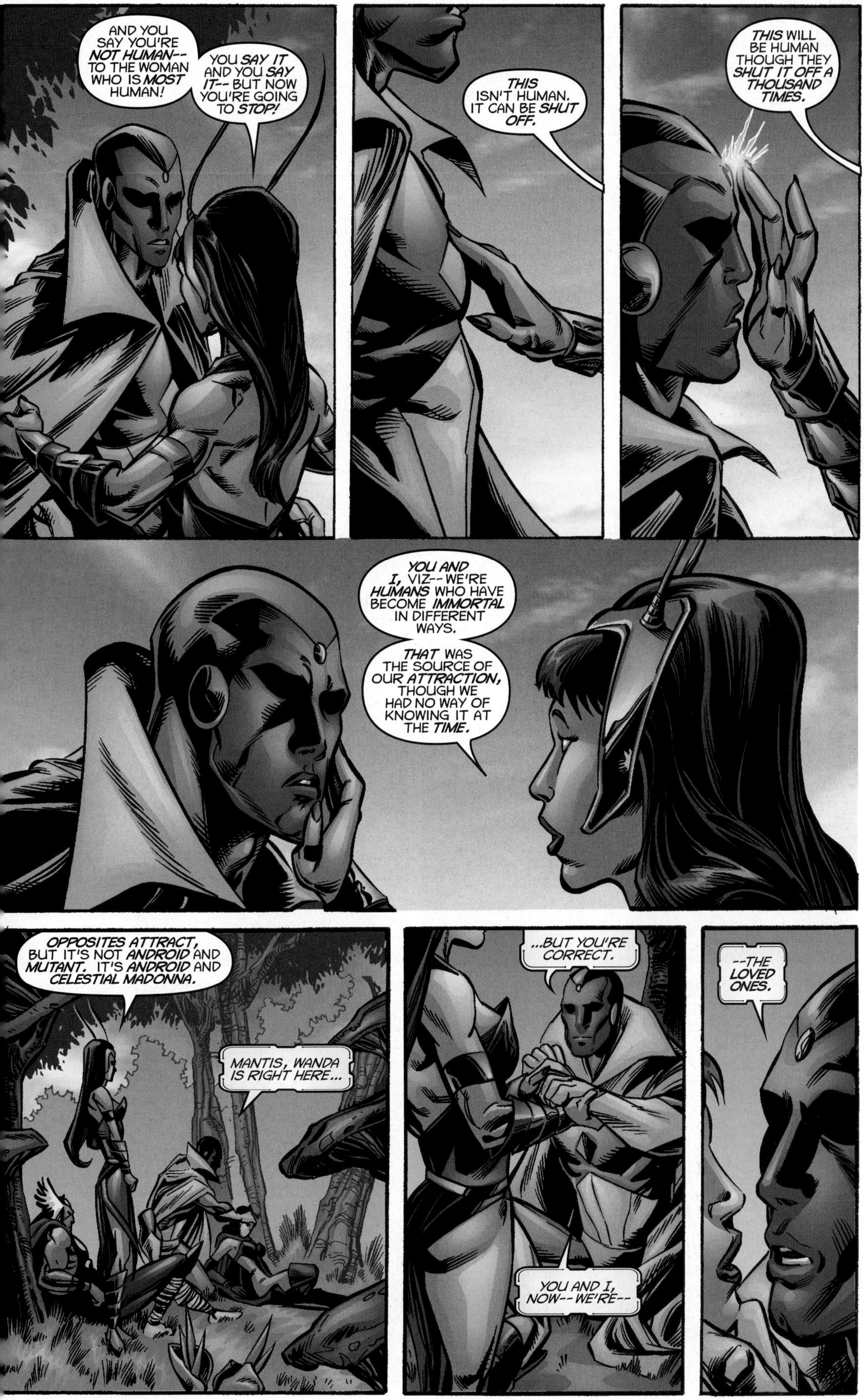
AND YOU SAY YOU'RE NOT HUMAN-- TO THE WOMAN WHO IS MOST HUMAN!
YOU SAY IT AND YOU SAY IT-- BUT NOW YOU'RE GOING TO STOP!
THIS ISN'T HUMAN. IT CAN BE SHUT OFF.
THIS WILL BE HUMAN THOUGH THEY SHUT IT OFF A THOUSAND TIMES.
YOU AND I, VIZ--WE'RE HUMANS WHO HAVE BECOME IMMORTAL IN DIFFERENT WAYS.
THAT WAS THE SOURCE OF OUR ATTRACTION, THOUGH WE HAD NO WAY OF KNOWING IT AT THE TIME.
OPPOSITES ATTRACT, BUT IT'S NOT ANDROID AND MUTANT. IT'S ANDROID AND CELESTIAL MADONNA.
MANTIS, WANDA IS RIGHT HERE...
...BUT YOU'RE CORRECT.
YOU AND I, NOW--WE'RE--
--THE LOVED ONES.

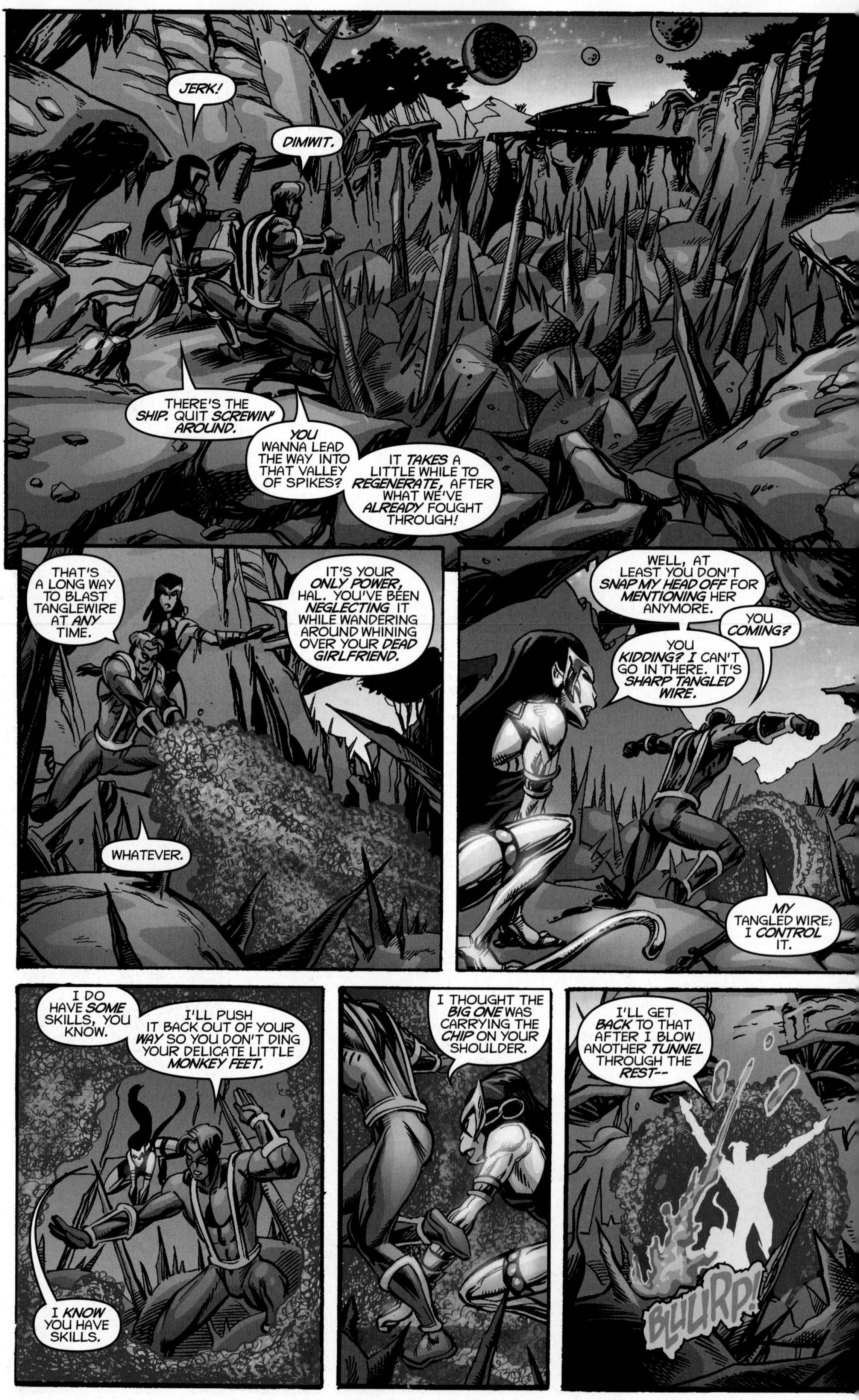
JERK!
DIMWIT.
THERE'S THE SHIP. QUIT SCREWIN' AROUND.
YOU WANNA LEAD THE WAY INTO THAT VALLEY OF SPIKES?
IT TAKES A LITTLE WHILE TO REGENERATE, AFTER WHAT WE'VE ALREADY FOUGHT THROUGH!
THAT'S A LONG WAY TO BLAST TANGLEWIRE AT ANY TIME.
IT'S YOUR ONLY POWER, HAL. YOU'VE BEEN NEGLECTING IT WHILE WANDERING AROUND WHINING OVER YOUR DEAD GIRLFRIEND.
WHATEVER.
WELL, AT LEAST YOU DON'T SNAP MY HEAD OFF FOR MENTIONING HER ANYMORE.
YOU COMING?
YOU KIDDING? I CAN'T GO IN THERE. IT'S SHARP TANGLED WIRE.
MY TANGLED WIRE; I CONTROL IT.
I DO HAVE SOME SKILLS, YOU KNOW.
I'LL PUSH IT BACK OUT OF YOUR WAY SO YOU DON'T DING YOUR DELICATE LITTLE MONKEY FEET.
I KNOW YOU HAVE SKILLS.
I THOUGHT THE BIG ONE WAS CARRYING THE CHIP ON YOUR SHOULDER.
I'LL GET BACK TO THAT AFTER I BLOW ANOTHER TUNNEL THROUGH THE REST--
BLUURP!

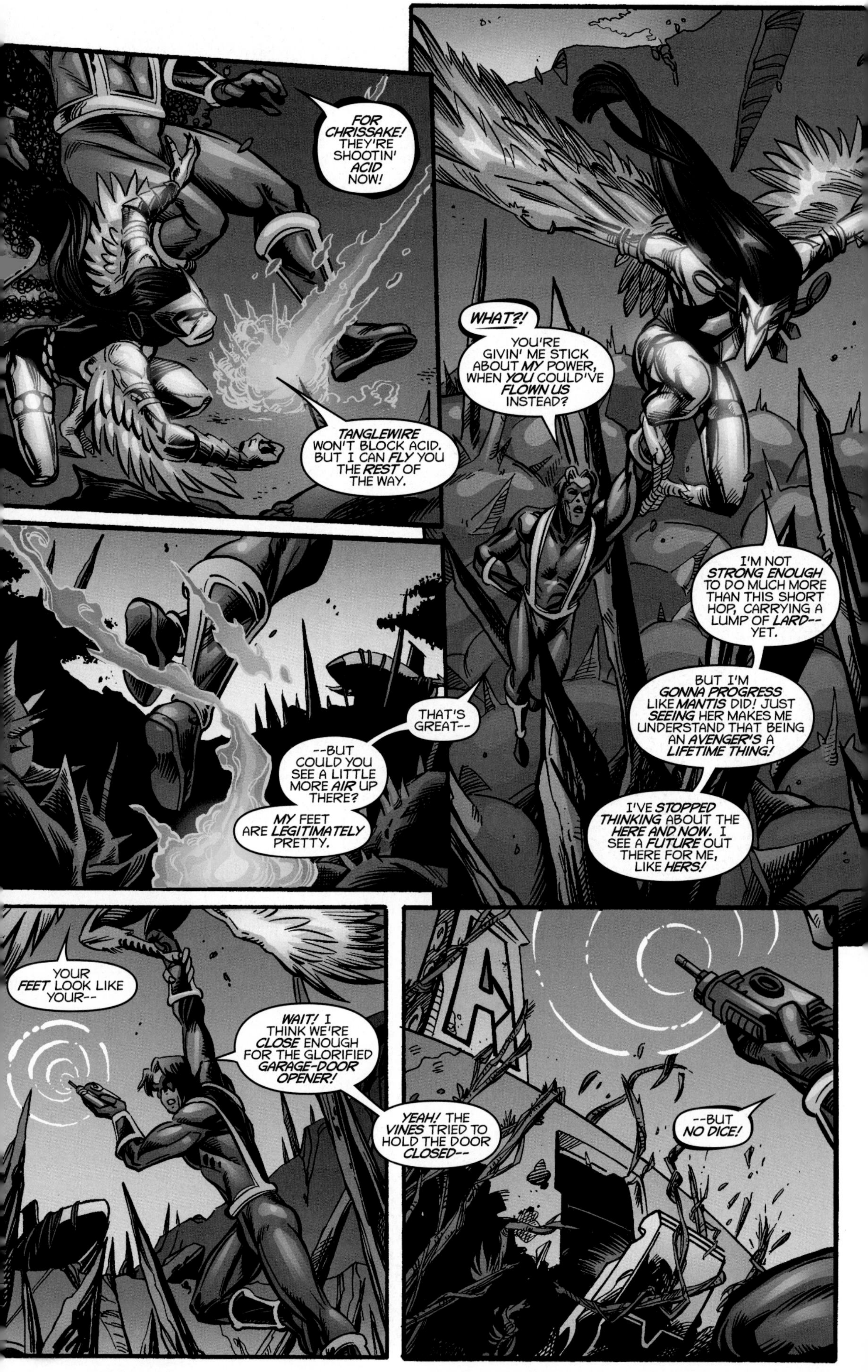
FOR CHRISSAKE! THEY'RE SHOOTIN' ACID NOW!
TANGLEWIRE WON'T BLOCK ACID. BUT I CAN FLY YOU THE REST OF THE WAY.
WHAT?!
YOU'RE GIVIN' ME STICK ABOUT MY POWER, WHEN YOU COULD'VE FLOWN US INSTEAD?
I'M NOT STRONG ENOUGH TO DO MUCH MORE THAN THIS SHORT HOP, CARRYING A LUMP OF LARD-- YET.
BUT I'M GONNA PROGRESS LIKE MANTIS DID! JUST SEEING HER MAKES ME UNDERSTAND THAT BEING AN AVENGER'S A LIFETIME THING!
I'VE STOPPED THINKING ABOUT THE HERE AND NOW. I SEE A FUTURE OUT THERE FOR ME, LIKE HERS!
THAT'S GREAT--
--BUT COULD YOU SEE A LITTLE MORE AIR UP THERE?
MY FEET ARE LEGITIMATELY PRETTY.
YOUR FEET LOOK LIKE YOUR--
WAIT! I THINK WE'RE CLOSE ENOUGH FOR THE GLORIFIED GARAGE-DOOR OPENER!
YEAH! THE VINES TRIED TO HOLD THE DOOR CLOSED--
--BUT NO DICE!

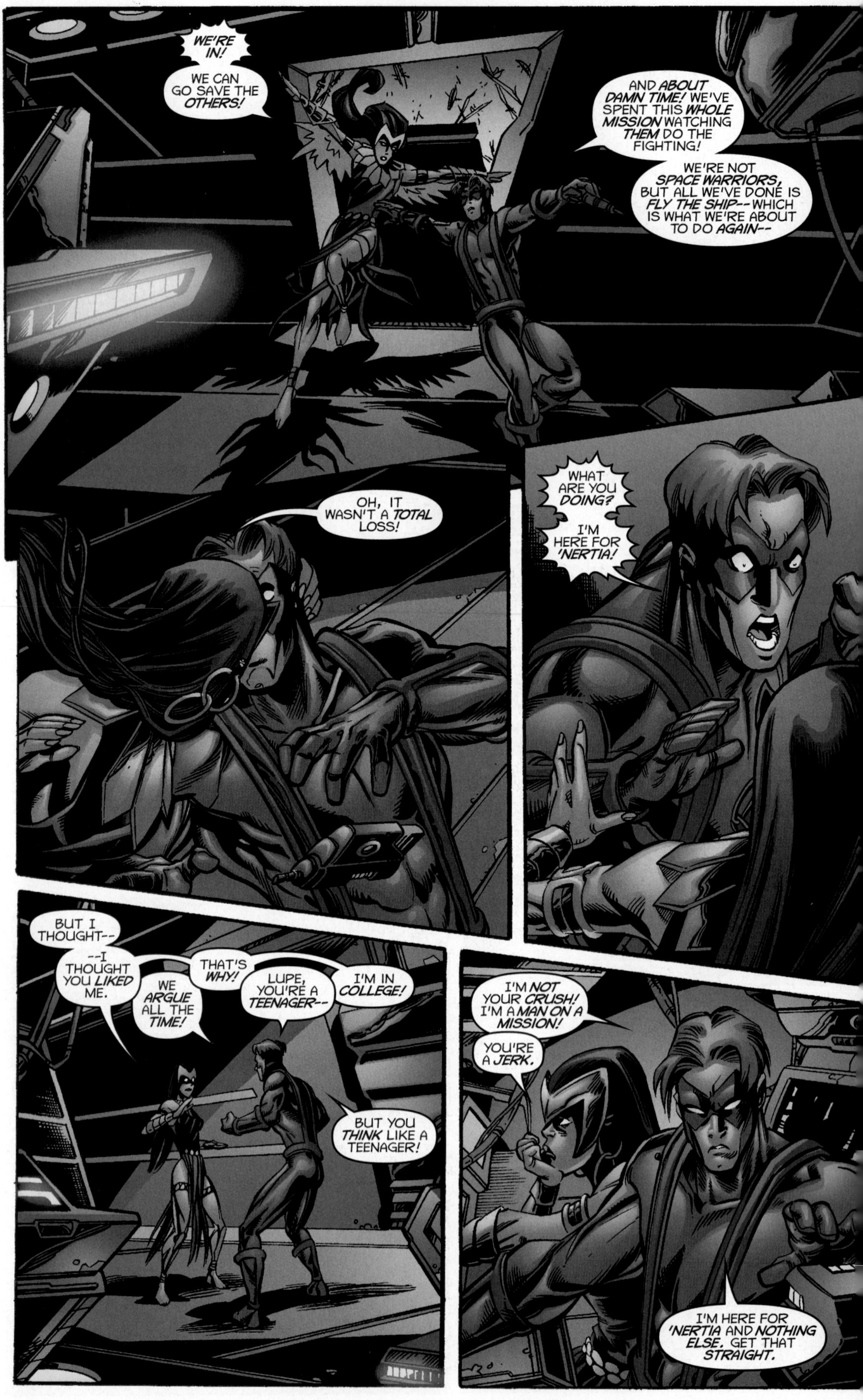

WE'RE IN!
WE CAN GO SAVE THE OTHERS!
AND ABOUT DAMN TIME! WE'VE SPENT THIS WHOLE MISSION WATCHING THEM DO THE FIGHTING!
WE'RE NOT SPACE WARRIORS, BUT ALL WE'VE DONE IS FLY THE SHIP-- WHICH IS WHAT WE'RE ABOUT TO DO AGAIN--
OH, IT WASN'T A TOTAL LOSS!
WHAT ARE YOU DOING?
I'M HERE FOR 'NERTIA!
BUT I THOUGHT--
--I THOUGHT YOU LIKED ME.
WE ARGUE ALL THE TIME!
THAT'S WHY!
LUPE, YOU'RE A TEENAGER--
I'M IN COLLEGE!
BUT YOU THINK LIKE A TEENAGER!
I'M NOT YOUR CRUSH! I'M A MAN ON A MISSION!
YOU'RE A JERK.
I'M HERE FOR 'NERTIA AND NOTHING ELSE. GET THAT STRAIGHT.

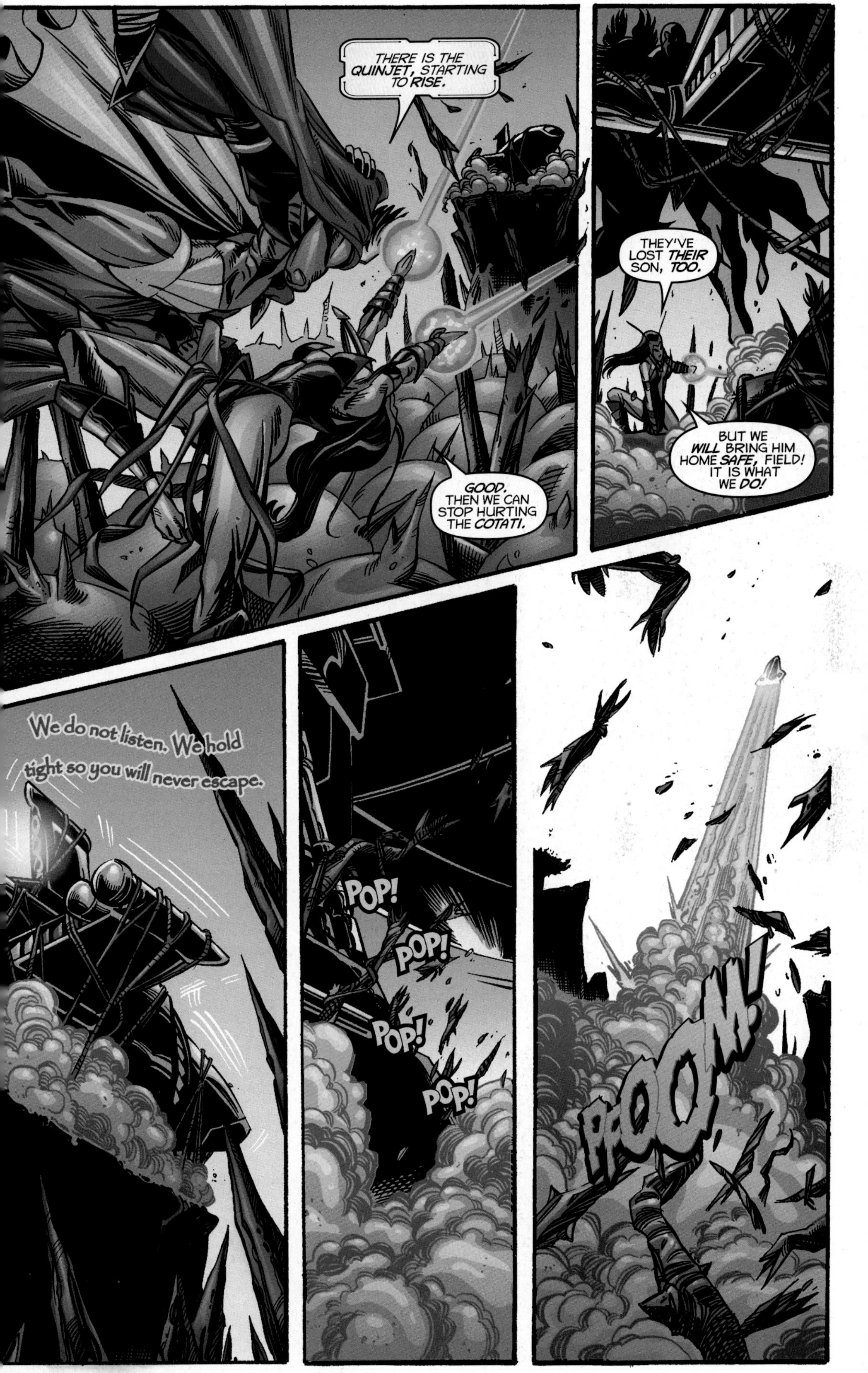
THERE IS THE QUINJET, STARTING TO RISE.
GOOD. THEN WE CAN STOP HURTING THE COTATI.
THEY'VE LOST THEIR SON, TOO.
BUT WE WILL BRING HIM HOME SAFE, FIELD! IT IS WHAT WE DO!
We do not listen. We hold tight so you will never escape.
POP!
POP!
POP!
POP!
PFOOM!

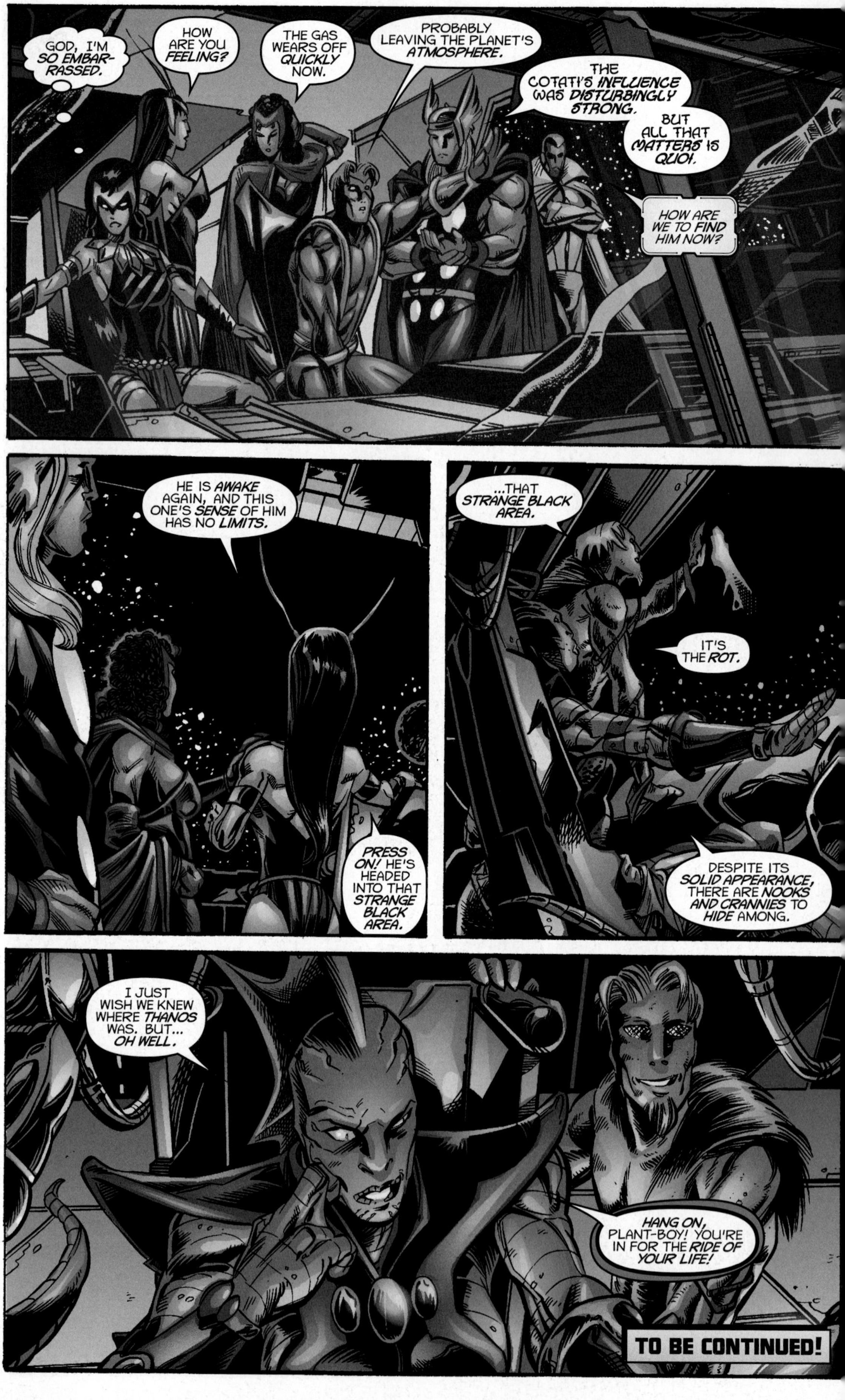
GOD, I'M SO EMBARRASSED.
HOW ARE YOU FEELING?
THE GAS WEARS OFF QUICKLY NOW.
PROBABLY LEAVING THE PLANET'S ATMOSPHERE.
THE COTATI'S INFLUENCE WAS DISTURBINGLY STRONG.
BUT ALL THAT MATTERS IS QUOI.
HOW ARE WE TO FIND HIM NOW?
HE IS AWAKE AGAIN, AND THIS ONE'S SENSE OF HIM HAS NO LIMITS.
PRESS ON! HE'S HEADED INTO THAT STRANGE BLACK AREA.
...THAT STRANGE BLACK AREA.
IT'S THE ROT.
DESPITE ITS SOLID APPEARANCE, THERE ARE NOOKS AND CRANNIES TO HIDE AMONG.
I JUST WISH WE KNEW WHERE THANOS WAS. BUT... OH WELL.
HANG ON, PLANT-BOY! YOU'RE IN FOR THE RIDE OF YOUR LIFE!
TO BE CONTINUED!

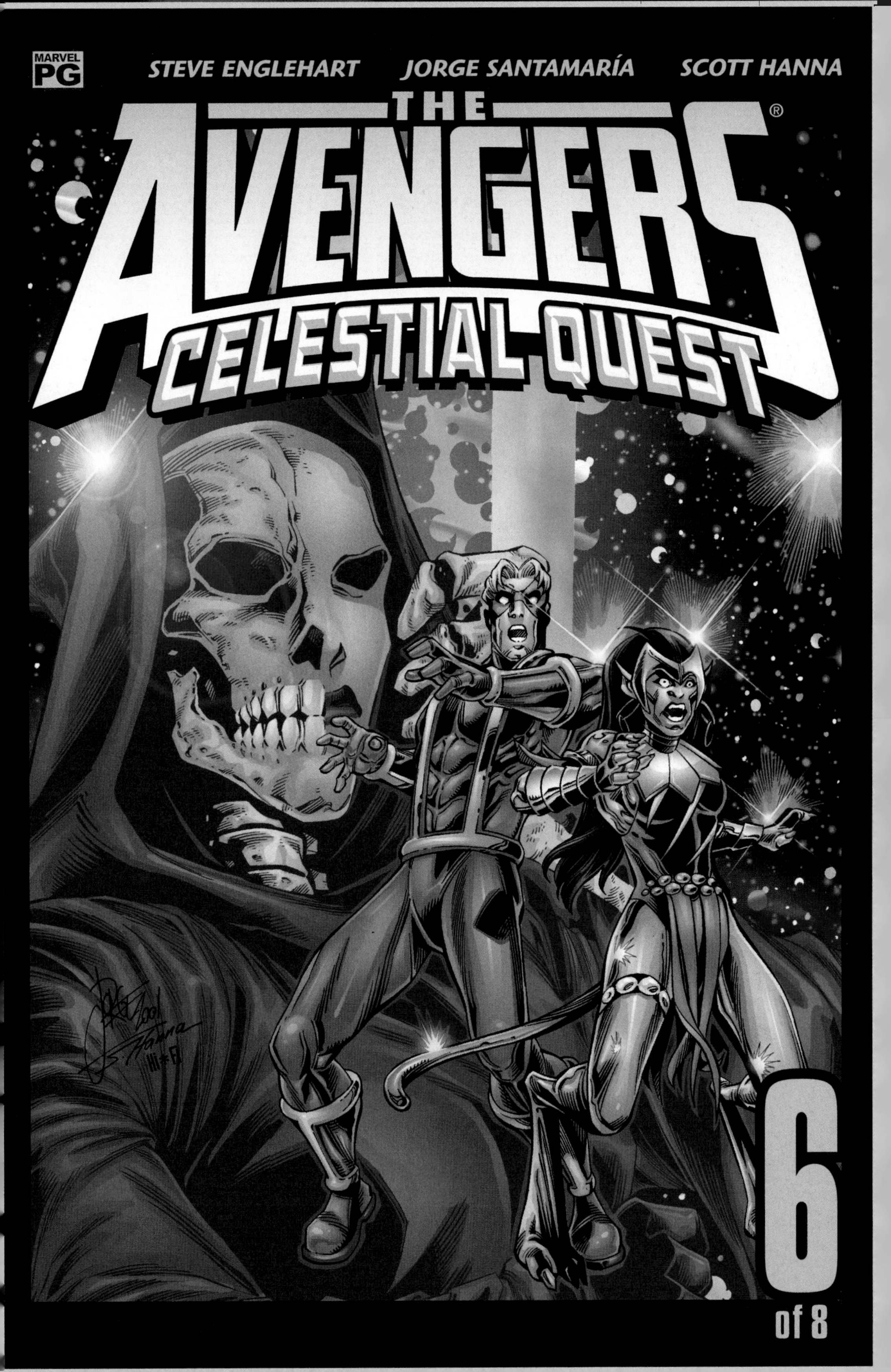
MARVEL PG
STEVE ENGLEHART
JORGE SANTAMARÍA
SCOTT HANNA
THE AVENGERS®
CELESTIAL QUEST
6
of 8

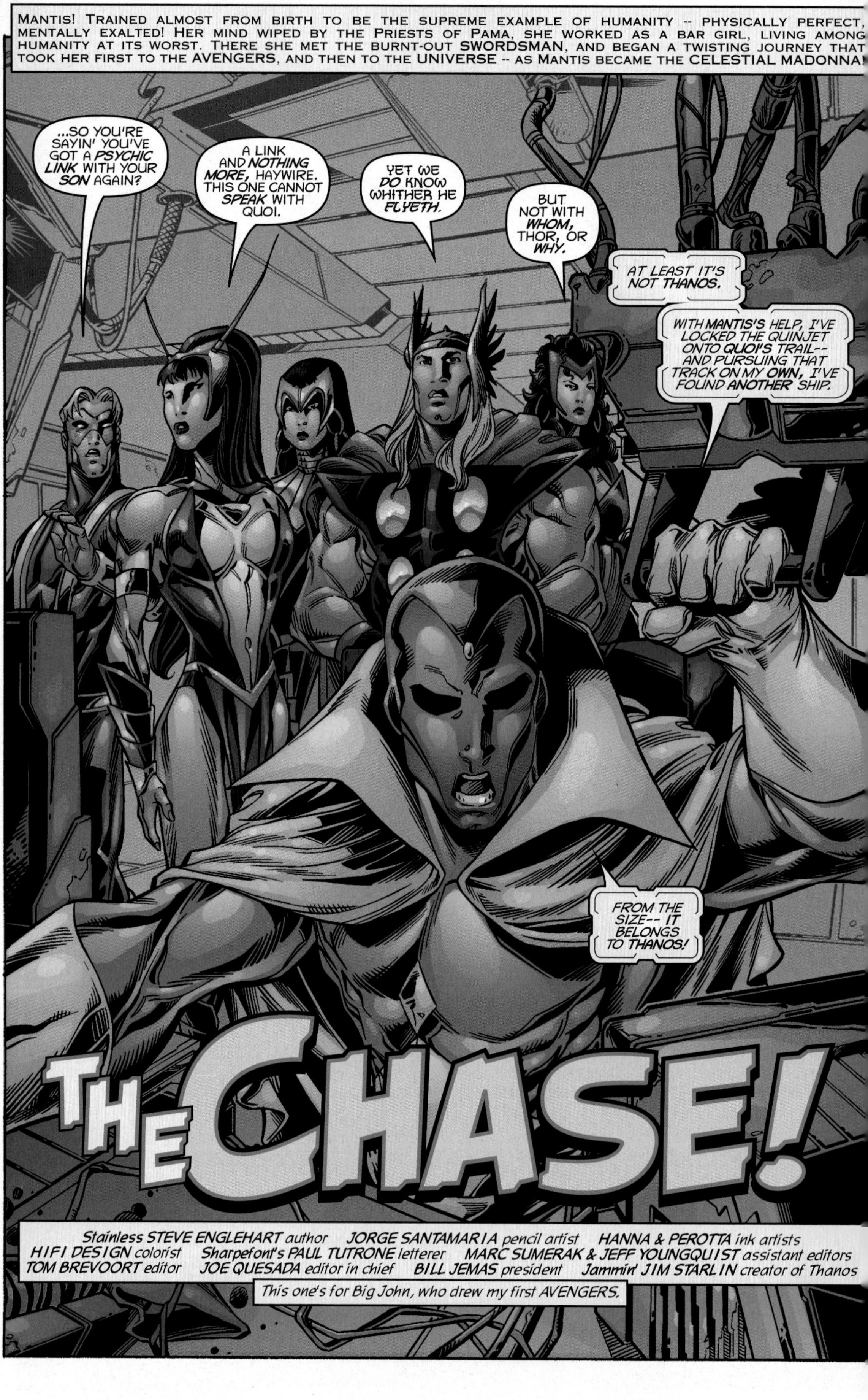
MANTIS! TRAINED ALMOST FROM BIRTH TO BE THE SUPREME EXAMPLE OF HUMANITY -- PHYSICALLY PERFECT, MENTALLY EXALTED! HER MIND WIPED BY THE PRIESTS OF PAMA, SHE WORKED AS A BAR GIRL, LIVING AMONG HUMANITY AT ITS WORST. THERE SHE MET THE BURNT-OUT SWORDSMAN, AND BEGAN A TWISTING JOURNEY THAT TOOK HER FIRST TO THE AVENGERS, AND THEN TO THE UNIVERSE -- AS MANTIS BECAME THE CELESTIAL MADONNA!
...SO YOU'RE SAYIN' YOU'VE GOT A PSYCHIC LINK WITH YOUR SON AGAIN?
A LINK AND NOTHING MORE, HAYWIRE. THIS ONE CANNOT SPEAK WITH QUOI.
YET WE DO KNOW WHITHER HE FLYETH.
BUT NOT WITH WHOM, THOR, OR WHY.
AT LEAST IT'S NOT THANOS.
WITH MANTIS'S HELP, I'VE LOCKED THE QUINJET ONTO QUOI'S TRAIL-- AND PURSUING THAT TRACK ON MY OWN, I'VE FOUND ANOTHER SHIP.
FROM THE SIZE-- IT BELONGS TO THANOS!
THE CHASE!
Stainless STEVE ENGLEHART author JORGE SANTAMARIA pencil artist HANNA & PEROTTA ink artists HIFI DESIGN colorist Sharpefont's PAUL TUTRONE letterer MARC SUMERAK & JEFF YOUNGQUIST assistant editors TOM BREVOORT editor JOE QUESADA editor in chief BILL JEMAS president Jammin' JIM STARLIN creator of Thanos
This one's for Big John, who drew my first AVENGERS.

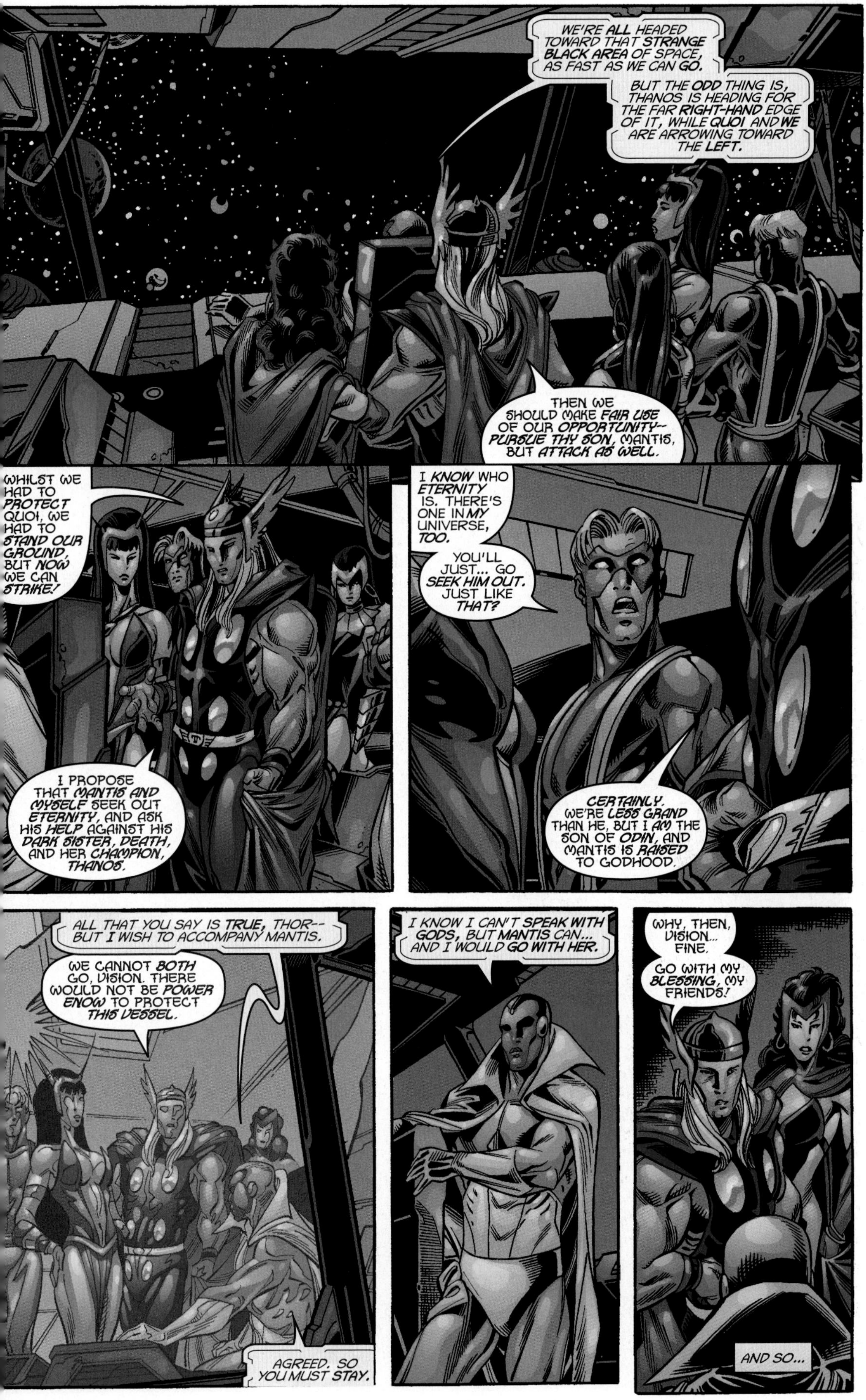
WE'RE ALL HEADED TOWARD THAT STRANGE BLACK AREA OF SPACE, AS FAST AS WE CAN GO.
BUT THE ODD THING IS, THANOS IS HEADING FOR THE FAR RIGHT-HAND EDGE OF IT, WHILE QUOI AND WE ARE ARROWING TOWARD THE LEFT.
THEN WE SHOULD MAKE FAIR USE OF OUR OPPORTUNITY-- PURSUE THY SON, MANTIS, BUT ATTACK AS WELL.
WHILST WE HAD TO PROTECT QUOI, WE HAD TO STAND OUR GROUND, BUT NOW WE CAN STRIKE!
I PROPOSE THAT MANTIS AND MYSELF SEEK OUT ETERNITY, AND ASK HIS HELP AGAINST HIS DARK SISTER, DEATH, AND HER CHAMPION, THANOS.
I KNOW WHO ETERNITY IS. THERE'S ONE IN MY UNIVERSE, TOO.
YOU'LL JUST... GO SEEK HIM OUT. JUST LIKE THAT?
CERTAINLY. WE'RE LESS GRAND THAN HE, BUT I AM THE SON OF ODIN, AND MANTIS IS RAISED TO GODHOOD.
ALL THAT YOU SAY IS TRUE, THOR-- BUT I WISH TO ACCOMPANY MANTIS.
WE CANNOT BOTH GO, VISION. THERE WOULD NOT BE POWER ENOW TO PROTECT THIS VESSEL.
AGREED. SO YOU MUST STAY.
I KNOW I CAN'T SPEAK WITH GODS, BUT MANTIS CAN... AND I WOULD GO WITH HER.
WHY, THEN, VISION... FINE.
GO WITH MY BLESSING, MY FRIENDS!
AND SO...

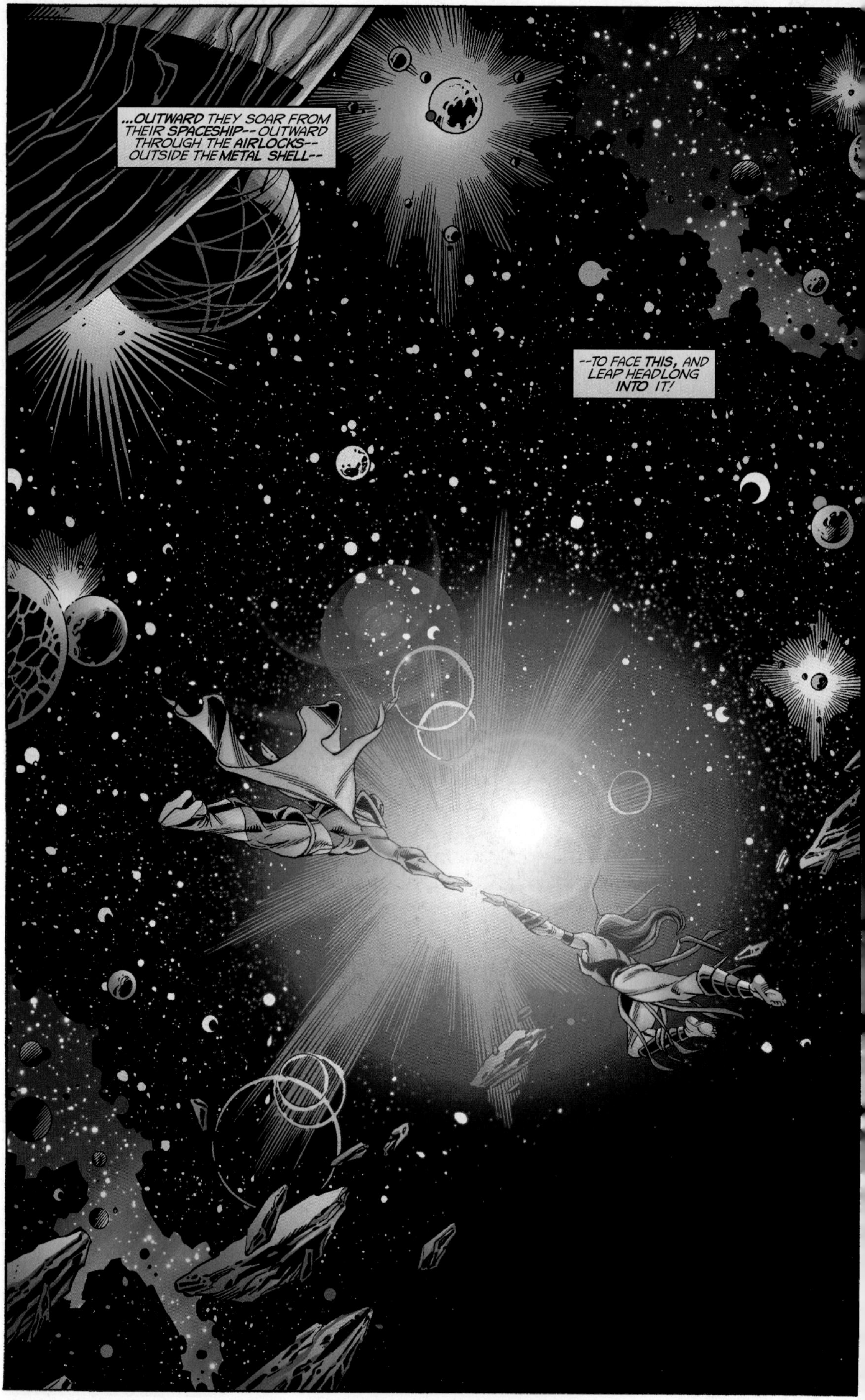
...OUTWARD THEY SOAR FROM THEIR SPACESHIP--OUTWARD THROUGH THE AIRLOCKS--OUTSIDE THE METAL SHELL--
--TO FACE THIS, AND LEAP HEADLONG INTO IT!

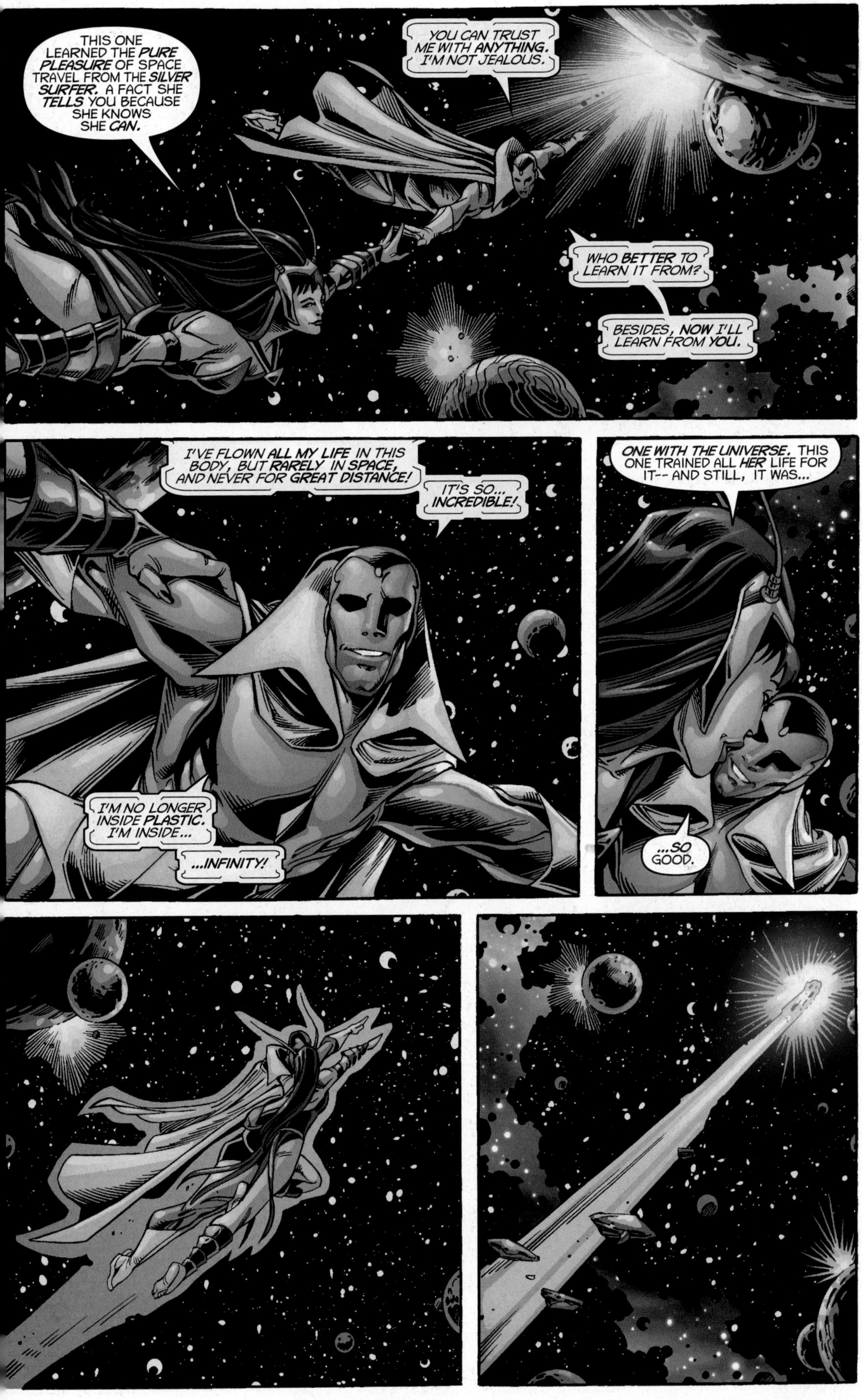
THIS ONE LEARNED THE PURE PLEASURE OF SPACE TRAVEL FROM THE SILVER SURFER. A FACT SHE TELLS YOU BECAUSE SHE KNOWS SHE CAN.
YOU CAN TRUST ME WITH ANYTHING. I'M NOT JEALOUS.
WHO BETTER TO LEARN IT FROM?
BESIDES, NOW I'LL LEARN FROM YOU.
I'VE FLOWN ALL MY LIFE IN THIS BODY, BUT RARELY IN SPACE, AND NEVER FOR GREAT DISTANCE!
IT'S SO... INCREDIBLE!
I'M NO LONGER INSIDE PLASTIC. I'M INSIDE...
...INFINITY!
ONE WITH THE UNIVERSE. THIS ONE TRAINED ALL HER LIFE FOR IT-- AND STILL, IT WAS...
...SO GOOD.

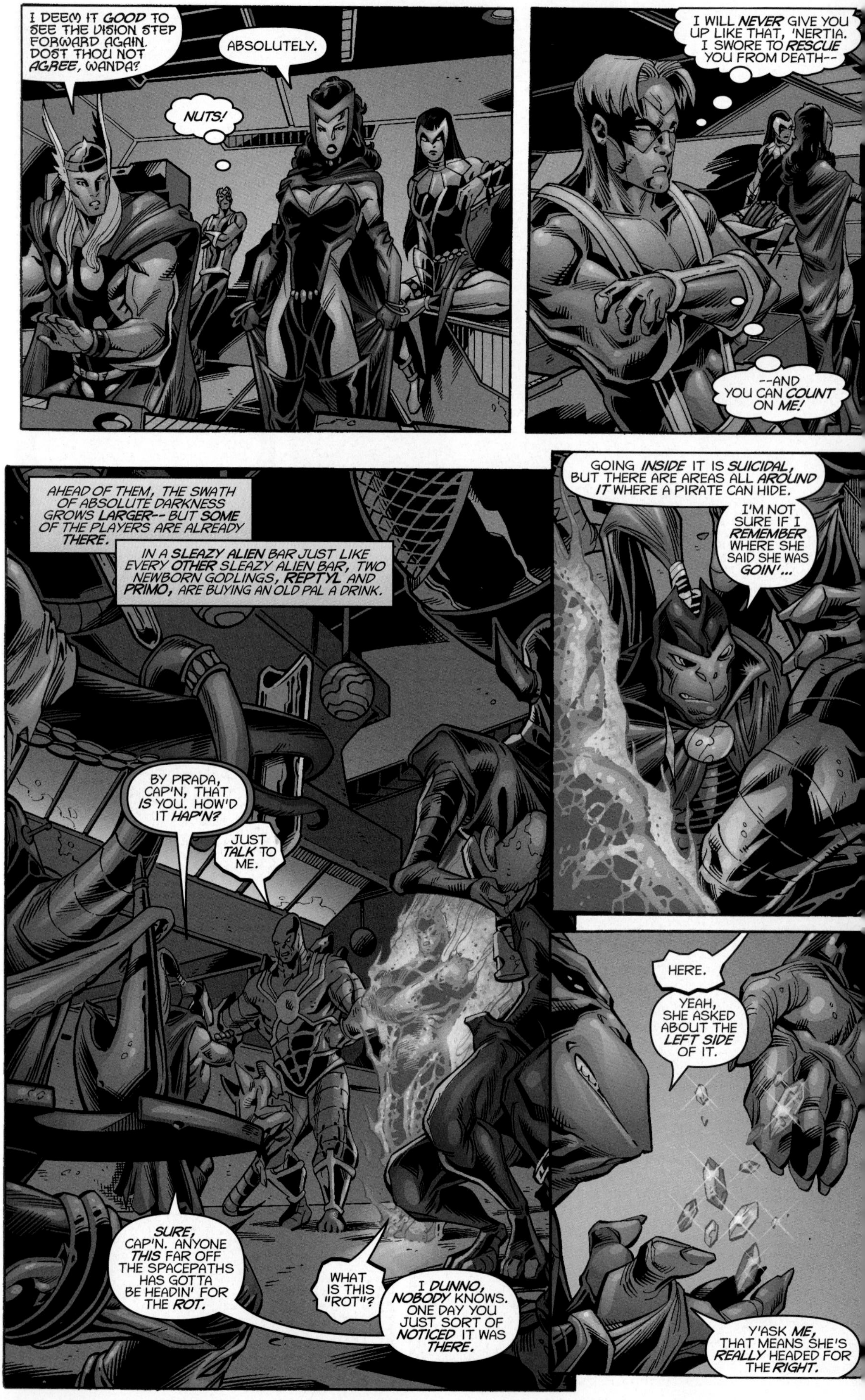
I DEEM IT GOOD TO SEE THE VISION STEP FORWARD AGAIN. DOST THOU NOT AGREE, WANDA?
ABSOLUTELY.
NUTS!
I WILL NEVER GIVE YOU UP LIKE THAT, 'NERTIA. I SWORE TO RESCUE YOU FROM DEATH--
--AND YOU CAN COUNT ON ME!
AHEAD OF THEM, THE SWATH OF ABSOLUTE DARKNESS GROWS LARGER-- BUT SOME OF THE PLAYERS ARE ALREADY THERE.
IN A SLEAZY ALIEN BAR JUST LIKE EVERY OTHER SLEAZY ALIEN BAR, TWO NEWBORN GODLINGS, REPTYL AND PRIMO, ARE BUYING AN OLD PAL A DRINK.
BY PRADA, CAP'N, THAT IS YOU. HOW'D IT HAP'N?
JUST TALK TO ME.
SURE, CAP'N. ANYONE THIS FAR OFF THE SPACEPATHS HAS GOTTA BE HEADIN' FOR THE ROT.
WHAT IS THIS "ROT"?
I DUNNO, NOBODY KNOWS. ONE DAY YOU JUST SORT OF NOTICED IT WAS THERE.
GOING INSIDE IT IS SUICIDAL, BUT THERE ARE AREAS ALL AROUND IT WHERE A PIRATE CAN HIDE.
I'M NOT SURE IF I REMEMBER WHERE SHE SAID SHE WAS GOIN'...
HERE.
YEAH, SHE ASKED ABOUT THE LEFT SIDE OF IT.
Y'ASK ME, THAT MEANS SHE'S REALLY HEADED FOR THE RIGHT.

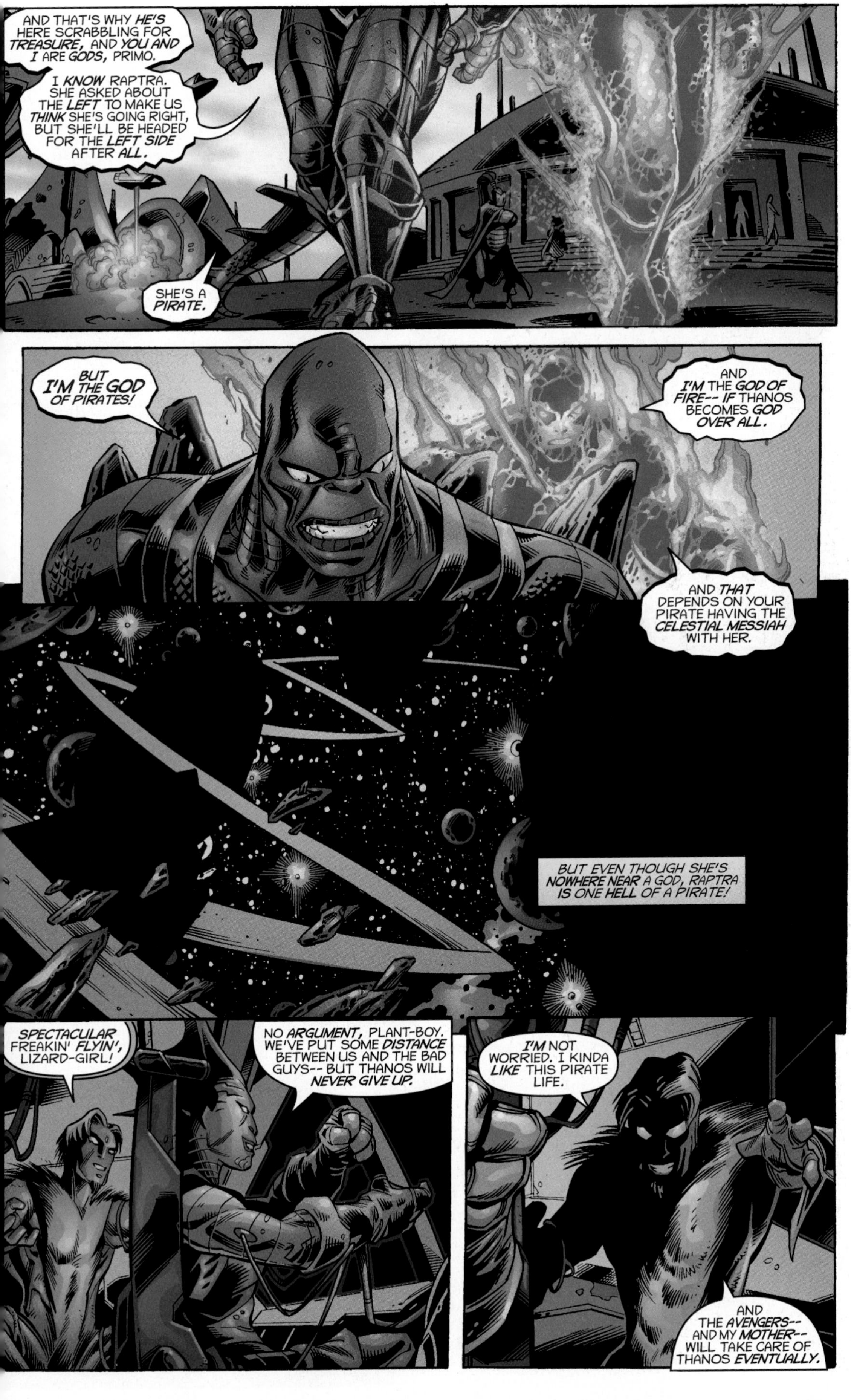
AND THAT'S WHY HE'S HERE SCRABBLING FOR TREASURE, AND YOU AND I ARE GODS, PRIMO.
I KNOW RAPTRA. SHE ASKED ABOUT THE LEFT TO MAKE US THINK SHE'S GOING RIGHT, BUT SHE'LL BE HEADED FOR THE LEFT SIDE AFTER ALL.
SHE'S A PIRATE.
BUT I'M THE GOD OF PIRATES!
AND I'M THE GOD OF FIRE-- IF THANOS BECOMES GOD OVER ALL.
AND THAT DEPENDS ON YOUR PIRATE HAVING THE CELESTIAL MESSIAH WITH HER.
BUT EVEN THOUGH SHE'S NOWHERE NEAR A GOD, RAPTRA IS ONE HELL OF A PIRATE!
SPECTACULAR FREAKIN' FLYIN', LIZARD-GIRL!
NO ARGUMENT, PLANT-BOY. WE'VE PUT SOME DISTANCE BETWEEN US AND THE BAD GUYS-- BUT THANOS WILL NEVER GIVE UP.
I'M NOT WORRIED. I KINDA LIKE THIS PIRATE LIFE.
AND THE AVENGERS-- AND MY MOTHER-- WILL TAKE CARE OF THANOS EVENTUALLY.

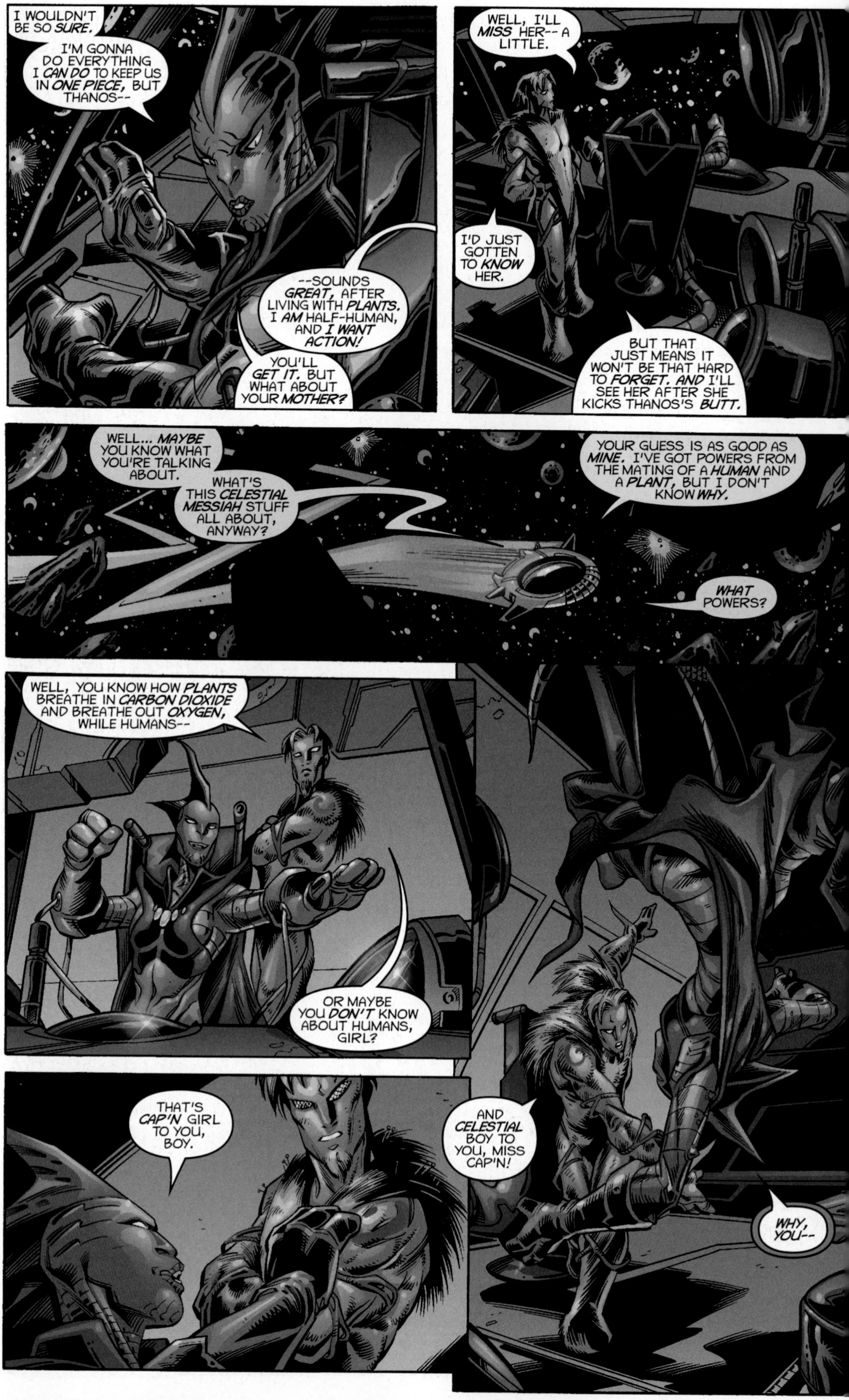
I WOULDN'T BE SO SURE.
I'M GONNA DO EVERYTHING I CAN DO TO KEEP US IN ONE PIECE, BUT THANOS--
--SOUNDS GREAT, AFTER LIVING WITH PLANTS. I AM HALF-HUMAN, AND I WANT ACTION!
YOU'LL GET IT. BUT WHAT ABOUT YOUR MOTHER?
WELL, I'LL MISS HER-- A LITTLE.
I'D JUST GOTTEN TO KNOW HER.
BUT THAT JUST MEANS IT WON'T BE THAT HARD TO FORGET. AND I'LL SEE HER AFTER SHE KICKS THANOS'S BUTT.
WELL... MAYBE YOU KNOW WHAT YOU'RE TALKING ABOUT.
WHAT'S THIS CELESTIAL MESSIAH STUFF ALL ABOUT, ANYWAY?
YOUR GUESS IS AS GOOD AS MINE. I'VE GOT POWERS FROM THE MATING OF A HUMAN AND A PLANT, BUT I DON'T KNOW WHY.
WHAT POWERS?
WELL, YOU KNOW HOW PLANTS BREATHE IN CARBON DIOXIDE AND BREATHE OUT OXYGEN, WHILE HUMANS--
OR MAYBE YOU DON'T KNOW ABOUT HUMANS, GIRL?
THAT'S CAP'N GIRL TO YOU, BOY.
AND CELESTIAL BOY TO YOU, MISS CAP'N!
WHY, YOU--

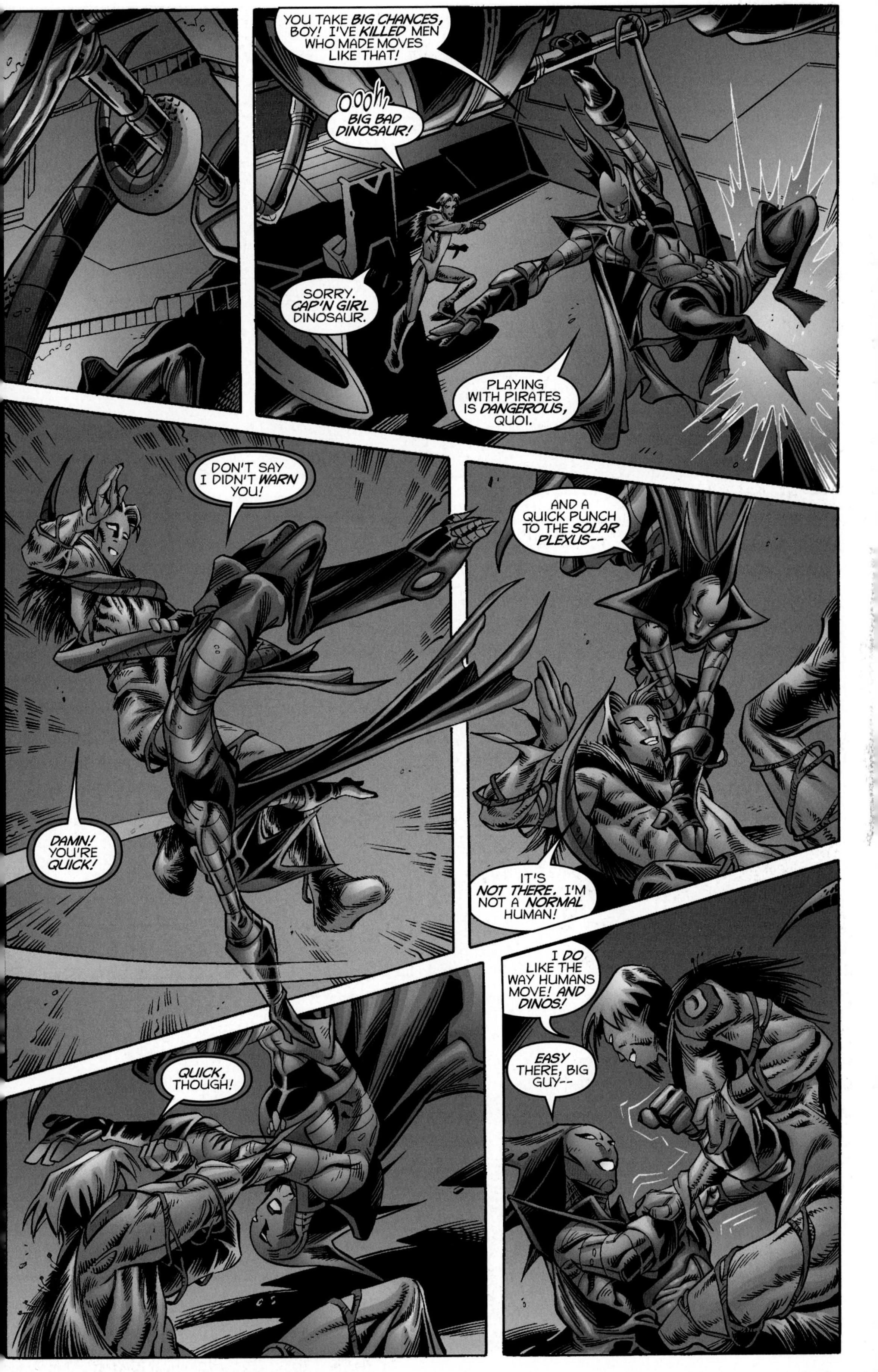
YOU TAKE BIG CHANCES, BOY! I'VE KILLED MEN WHO MADE MOVES LIKE THAT!
OOOH! BIG BAD DINOSAUR!
SORRY. CAP'N GIRL DINOSAUR.
PLAYING WITH PIRATES IS DANGEROUS, QUOI.
DON'T SAY I DIDN'T WARN YOU!
DAMN! YOU'RE QUICK!
AND A QUICK PUNCH TO THE SOLAR PLEXUS--
IT'S NOT THERE. I'M NOT A NORMAL HUMAN!
QUICK, THOUGH!
I DO LIKE THE WAY HUMANS MOVE! AND DINOS!
EASY THERE, BIG GUY--

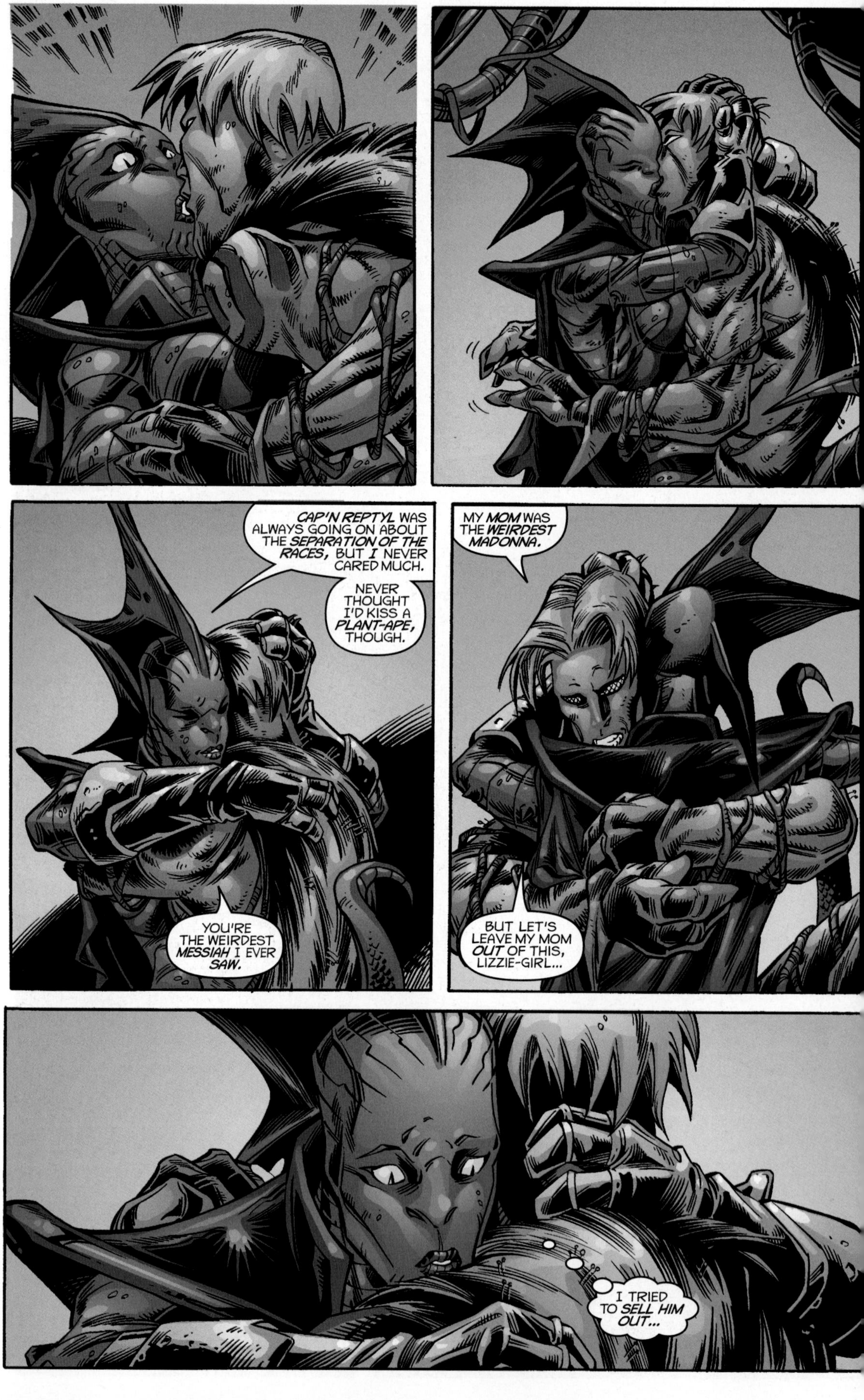
CAP'N REPTYL WAS ALWAYS GOING ON ABOUT THE SEPARATION OF THE RACES, BUT I NEVER CARED MUCH.
NEVER THOUGHT I'D KISS A PLANT-APE, THOUGH.
YOU'RE THE WEIRDEST MESSIAH I EVER SAW.
MY MOM WAS THE WEIRDEST MADONNA.
BUT LET'S LEAVE MY MOM OUT OF THIS, LIZZIE-GIRL...
I TRIED TO SELL HIM OUT...

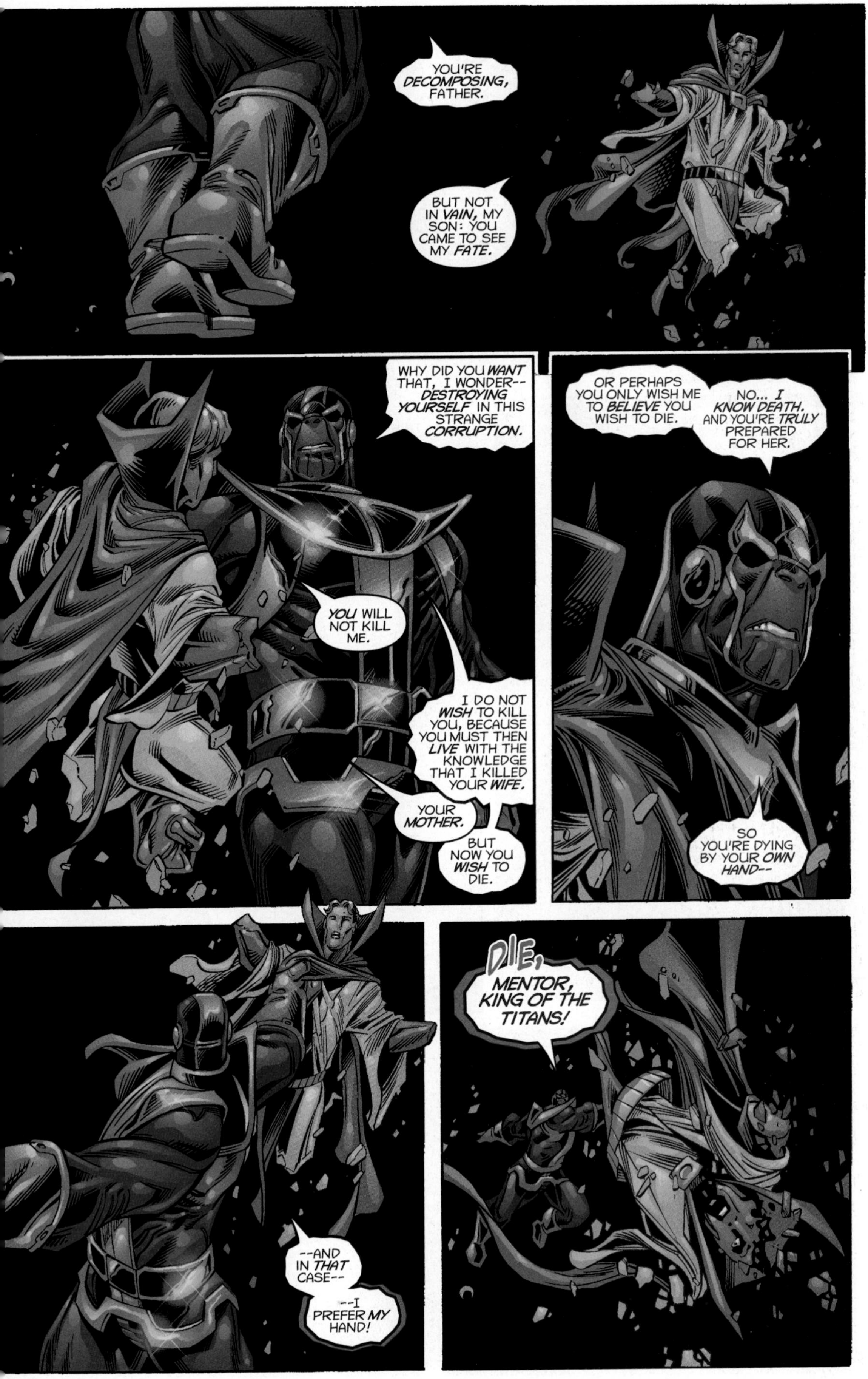
YOU'RE DECOMPOSING, FATHER.
BUT NOT IN VAIN, MY SON: YOU CAME TO SEE MY FATE.
WHY DID YOU WANT THAT, I WONDER-- DESTROYING YOURSELF IN THIS STRANGE CORRUPTION.
YOU WILL NOT KILL ME.
I DO NOT WISH TO KILL YOU, BECAUSE YOU MUST THEN LIVE WITH THE KNOWLEDGE THAT I KILLED YOUR WIFE.
YOUR MOTHER.
BUT NOW YOU WISH TO DIE.
OR PERHAPS YOU ONLY WISH ME TO BELIEVE YOU WISH TO DIE.
NO... I KNOW DEATH. AND YOU'RE TRULY PREPARED FOR HER.
SO YOU'RE DYING BY YOUR OWN HAND--
--AND IN THAT CASE--
--I PREFER MY HAND!
DIE, MENTOR, KING OF THE TITANS!

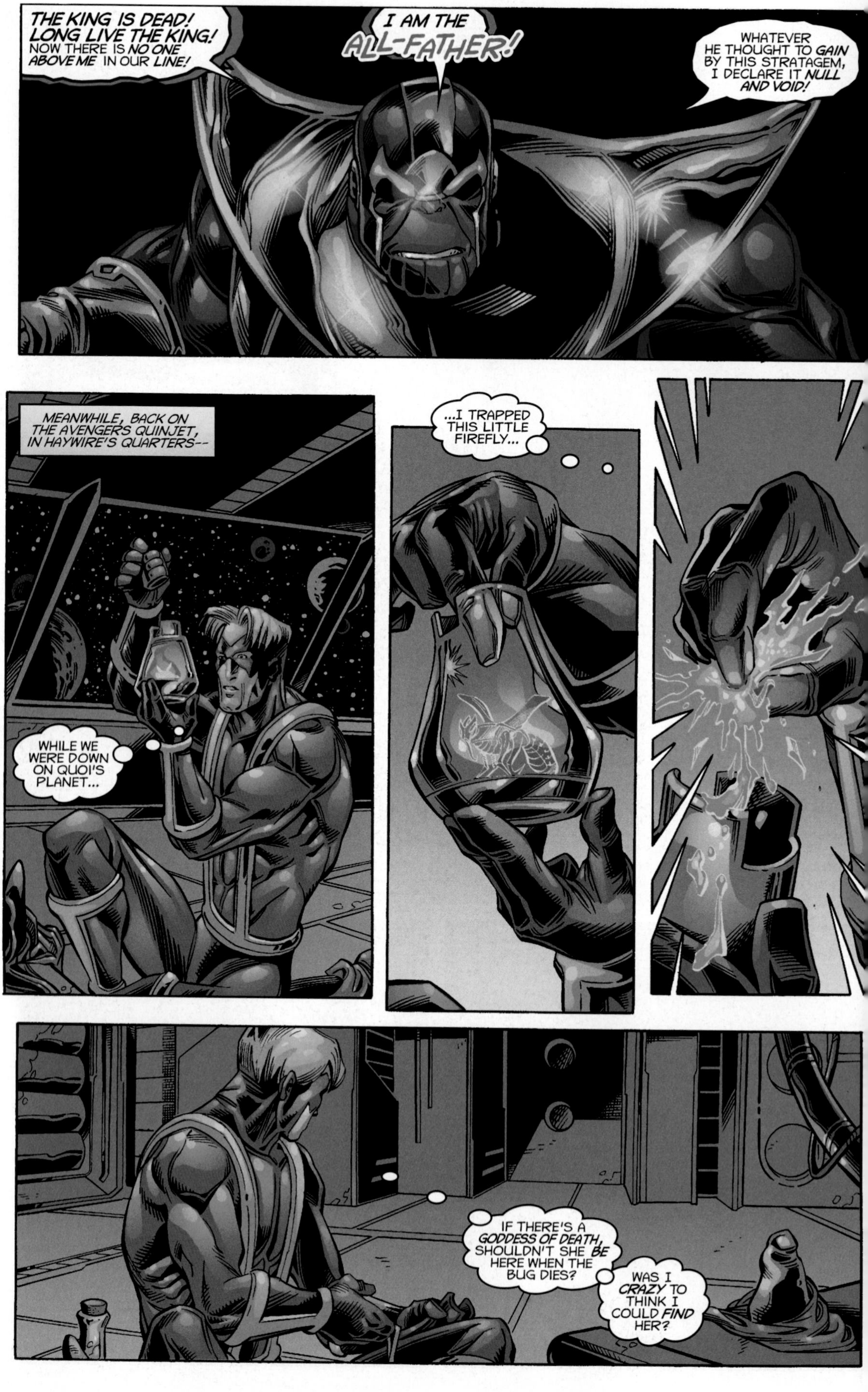
THE KING IS DEAD! LONG LIVE THE KING! NOW THERE IS NO ONE ABOVE ME IN OUR LINE!
I AM THE ALL-FATHER!
WHATEVER HE THOUGHT TO GAIN BY THIS STRATAGEM, I DECLARE IT NULL AND VOID!
MEANWHILE, BACK ON THE AVENGERS QUINJET, IN HAYWIRE'S QUARTERS--
WHILE WE WERE DOWN ON QUOI'S PLANET...
...I TRAPPED THIS LITTLE FIREFLY...
IF THERE'S A GODDESS OF DEATH, SHOULDN'T SHE BE HERE WHEN THE BUG DIES?
WAS I CRAZY TO THINK I COULD FIND HER?

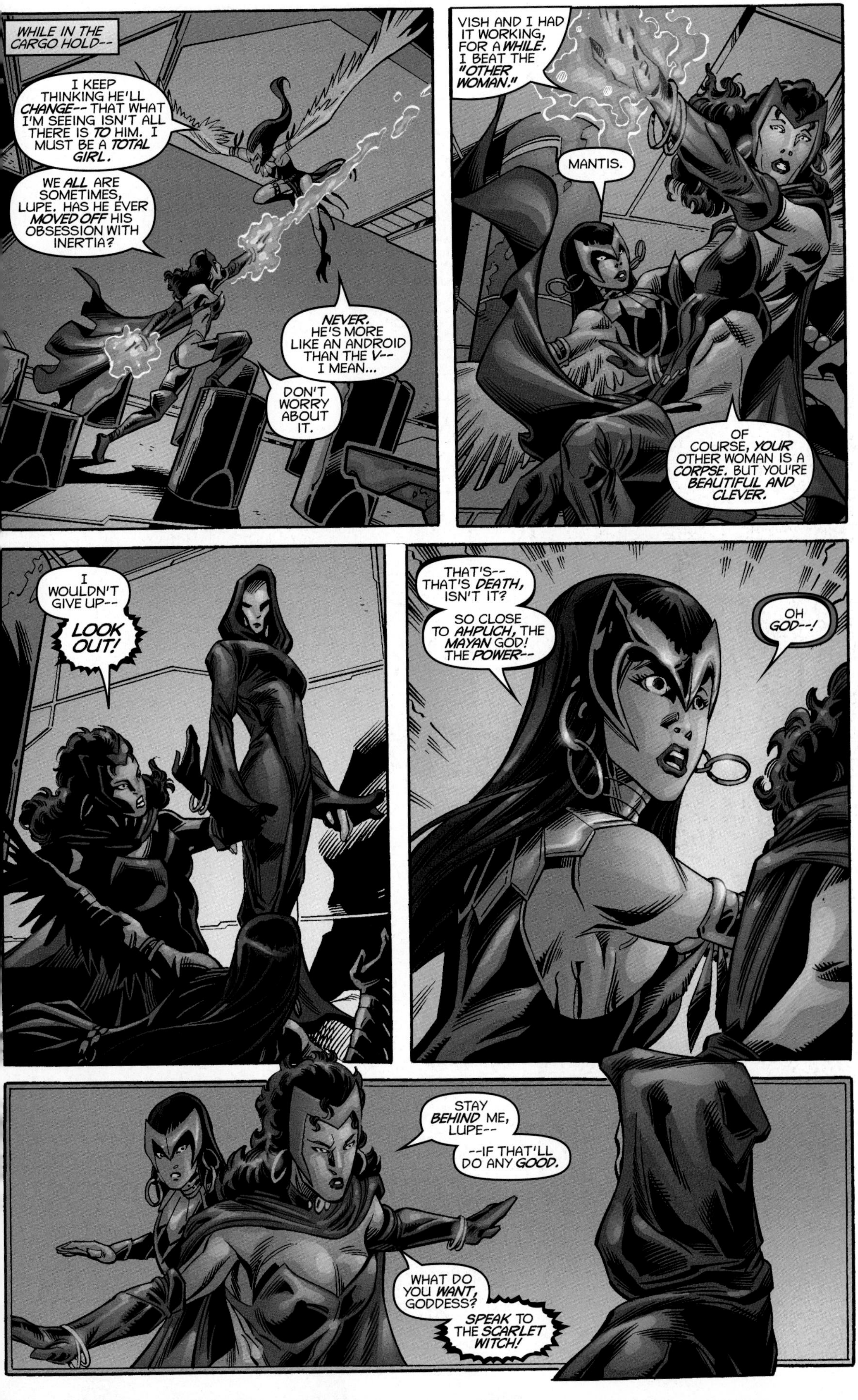

WHILE IN THE CARGO HOLD--
I KEEP THINKING HE'LL CHANGE-- THAT WHAT I'M SEEING ISN'T ALL THERE IS TO HIM. I MUST BE A TOTAL GIRL.
WE ALL ARE SOMETIMES, LUPE. HAS HE EVER MOVED OFF HIS OBSESSION WITH INERTIA?
NEVER. HE'S MORE LIKE AN ANDROID THAN THE V-- I MEAN...
DON'T WORRY ABOUT IT.
VISH AND I HAD IT WORKING, FOR A WHILE. I BEAT THE "OTHER WOMAN."
MANTIS.
OF COURSE, YOUR OTHER WOMAN IS A CORPSE. BUT YOU'RE BEAUTIFUL AND CLEVER.
I WOULDN'T GIVE UP--
LOOK OUT!
THAT'S-- THAT'S DEATH, ISN'T IT?
SO CLOSE TO AHPUCH, THE MAYAN GOD! THE POWER--
OH GOD--!
STAY BEHIND ME, LUPE--
--IF THAT'LL DO ANY GOOD.
WHAT DO YOU WANT, GODDESS?
SPEAK TO THE SCARLET WITCH!

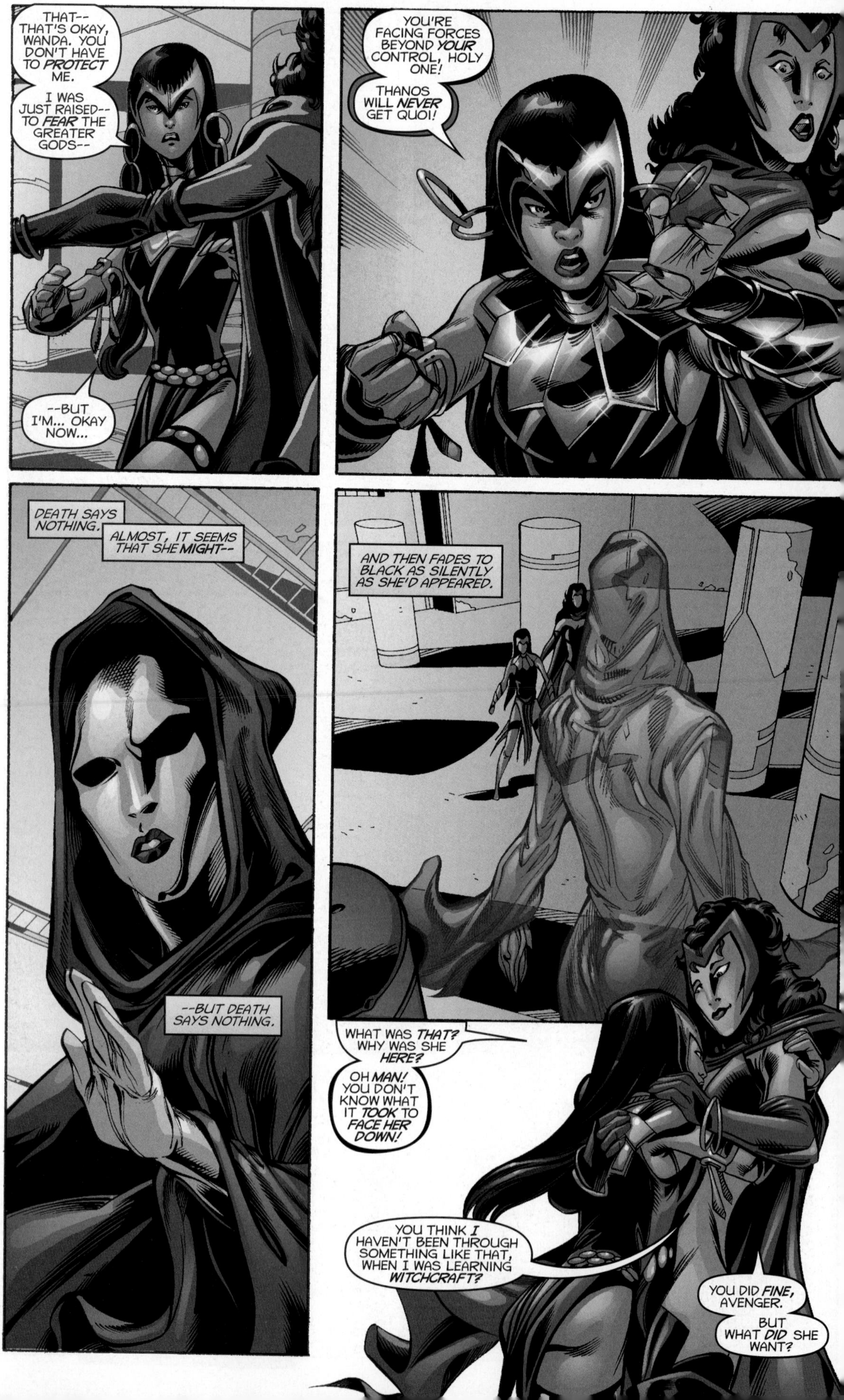
THAT-- THAT'S OKAY, WANDA. YOU DON'T HAVE TO PROTECT ME.
I WAS JUST RAISED-- TO FEAR THE GREATER GODS--
--BUT I'M... OKAY NOW...
YOU'RE FACING FORCES BEYOND YOUR CONTROL, HOLY ONE!
THANOS WILL NEVER GET QUOI!
DEATH SAYS NOTHING.
ALMOST, IT SEEMS THAT SHE MIGHT--
--BUT DEATH SAYS NOTHING.
AND THEN FADES TO BLACK AS SILENTLY AS SHE'D APPEARED.
WHAT WAS THAT? WHY WAS SHE HERE?
OH MAN! YOU DON'T KNOW WHAT IT TOOK TO FACE HER DOWN!
YOU THINK I HAVEN'T BEEN THROUGH SOMETHING LIKE THAT, WHEN I WAS LEARNING WITCHCRAFT?
YOU DID FINE, AVENGER.
BUT WHAT DID SHE WANT?

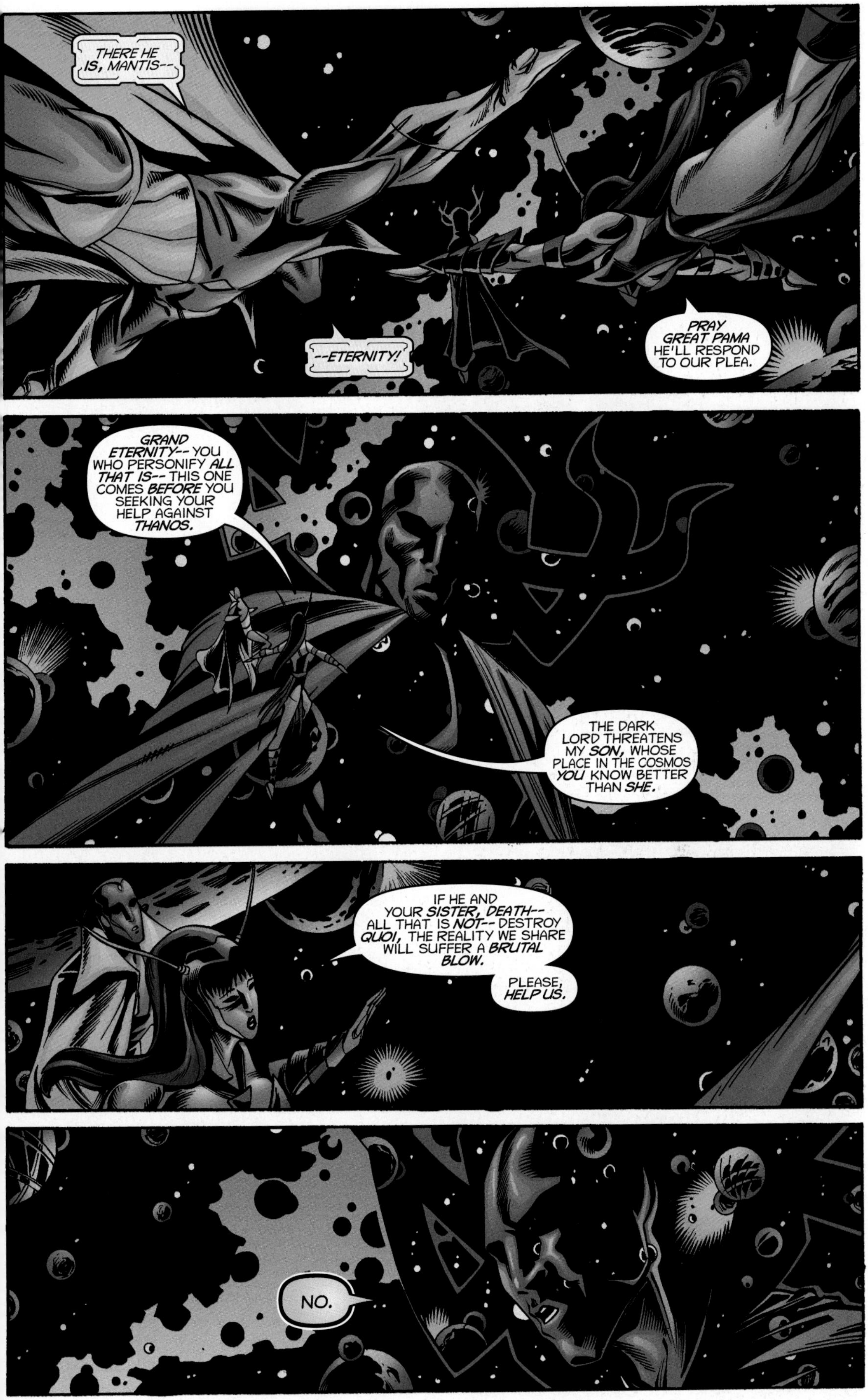
THERE HE IS, MANTIS--
--ETERNITY!
PRAY GREAT PAMA HE'LL RESPOND TO OUR PLEA.
GRAND ETERNITY-- YOU WHO PERSONIFY ALL THAT IS-- THIS ONE COMES BEFORE YOU SEEKING YOUR HELP AGAINST THANOS.
THE DARK LORD THREATENS MY SON, WHOSE PLACE IN THE COSMOS YOU KNOW BETTER THAN SHE.
IF HE AND YOUR SISTER, DEATH-- ALL THAT IS NOT-- DESTROY QUOI, THE REALITY WE SHARE WILL SUFFER A BRUTAL BLOW.
PLEASE, HELP US.
NO.

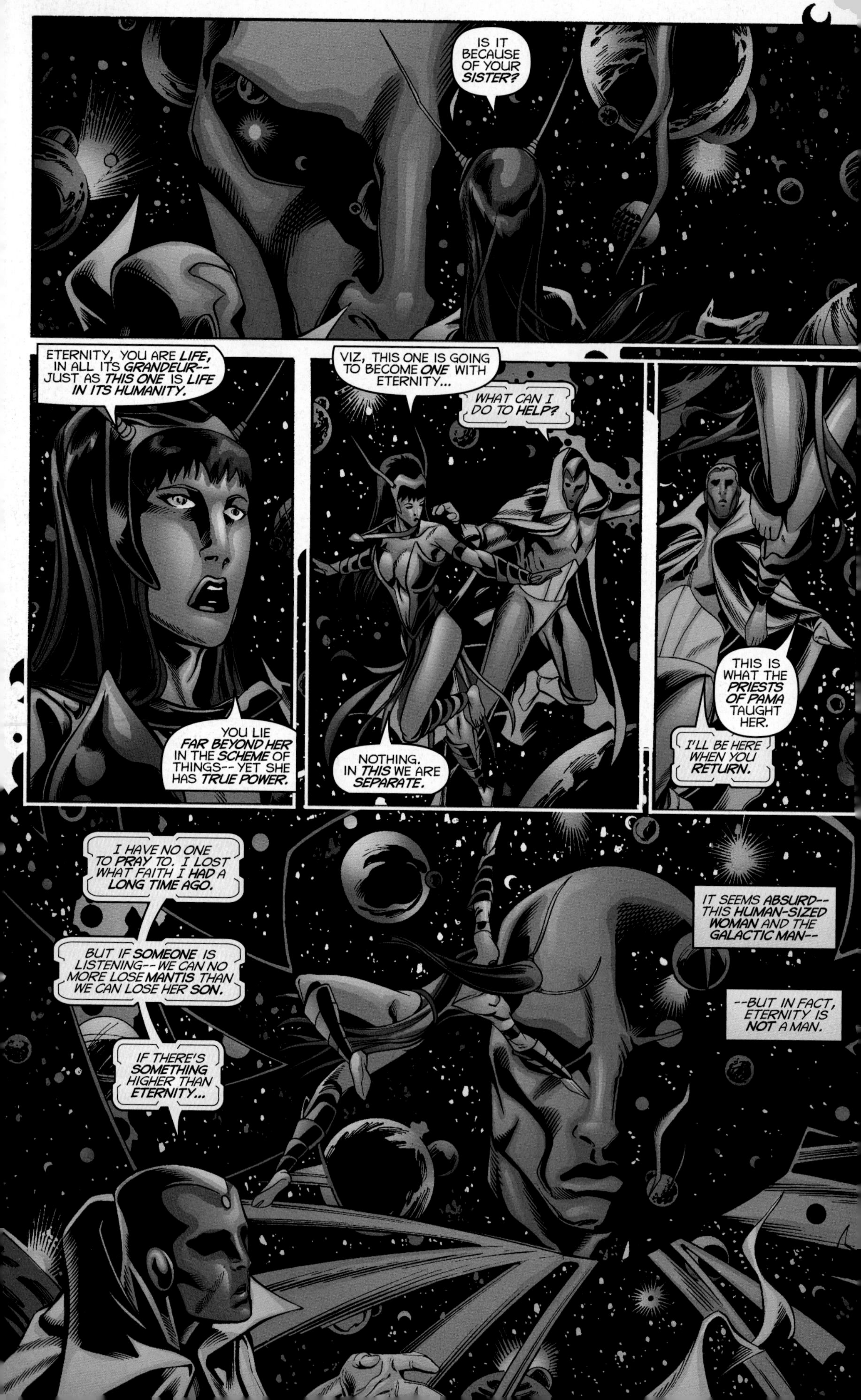
IS IT BECAUSE OF YOUR SISTER?
ETERNITY, YOU ARE LIFE, IN ALL ITS GRANDEUR-- JUST AS THIS ONE IS LIFE IN ITS HUMANITY.
YOU LIE FAR BEYOND HER IN THE SCHEME OF THINGS-- YET SHE HAS TRUE POWER.
VIZ, THIS ONE IS GOING TO BECOME ONE WITH ETERNITY...
WHAT CAN I DO TO HELP?
NOTHING. IN THIS WE ARE SEPARATE.
THIS IS WHAT THE PRIESTS OF PAMA TAUGHT HER.
I'LL BE HERE WHEN YOU RETURN.
I HAVE NO ONE TO PRAY TO. I LOST WHAT FAITH I HAD A LONG TIME AGO.
BUT IF SOMEONE IS LISTENING-- WE CAN NO MORE LOSE MANTIS THAN WE CAN LOSE HER SON.
IF THERE'S SOMETHING HIGHER THAN ETERNITY...
IT SEEMS ABSURD-- THIS HUMAN-SIZED WOMAN AND THE GALACTIC MAN--
--BUT IN FACT, ETERNITY IS NOT A MAN.

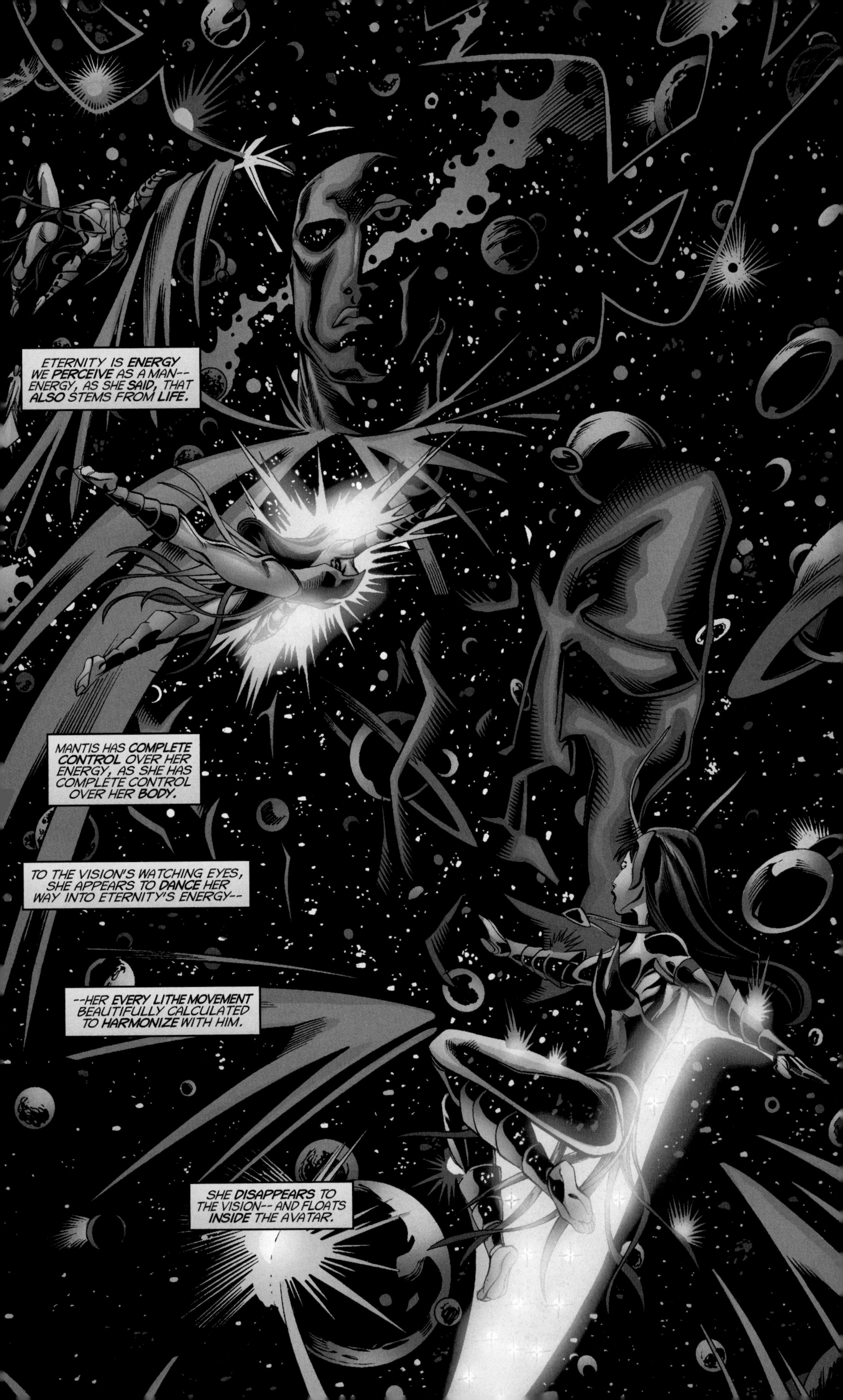

ETERNITY IS ENERGY WE PERCEIVE AS A MAN-- ENERGY, AS SHE SAID, THAT ALSO STEMS FROM LIFE.
MANTIS HAS COMPLETE CONTROL OVER HER ENERGY, AS SHE HAS COMPLETE CONTROL OVER HER BODY.
TO THE VISION'S WATCHING EYES, SHE APPEARS TO DANCE HER WAY INTO ETERNITY'S ENERGY--
--HER EVERY LITHE MOVEMENT BEAUTIFULLY CALCULATED TO HARMONIZE WITH HIM.
SHE DISAPPEARS TO THE VISION-- AND FLOATS INSIDE THE AVATAR.

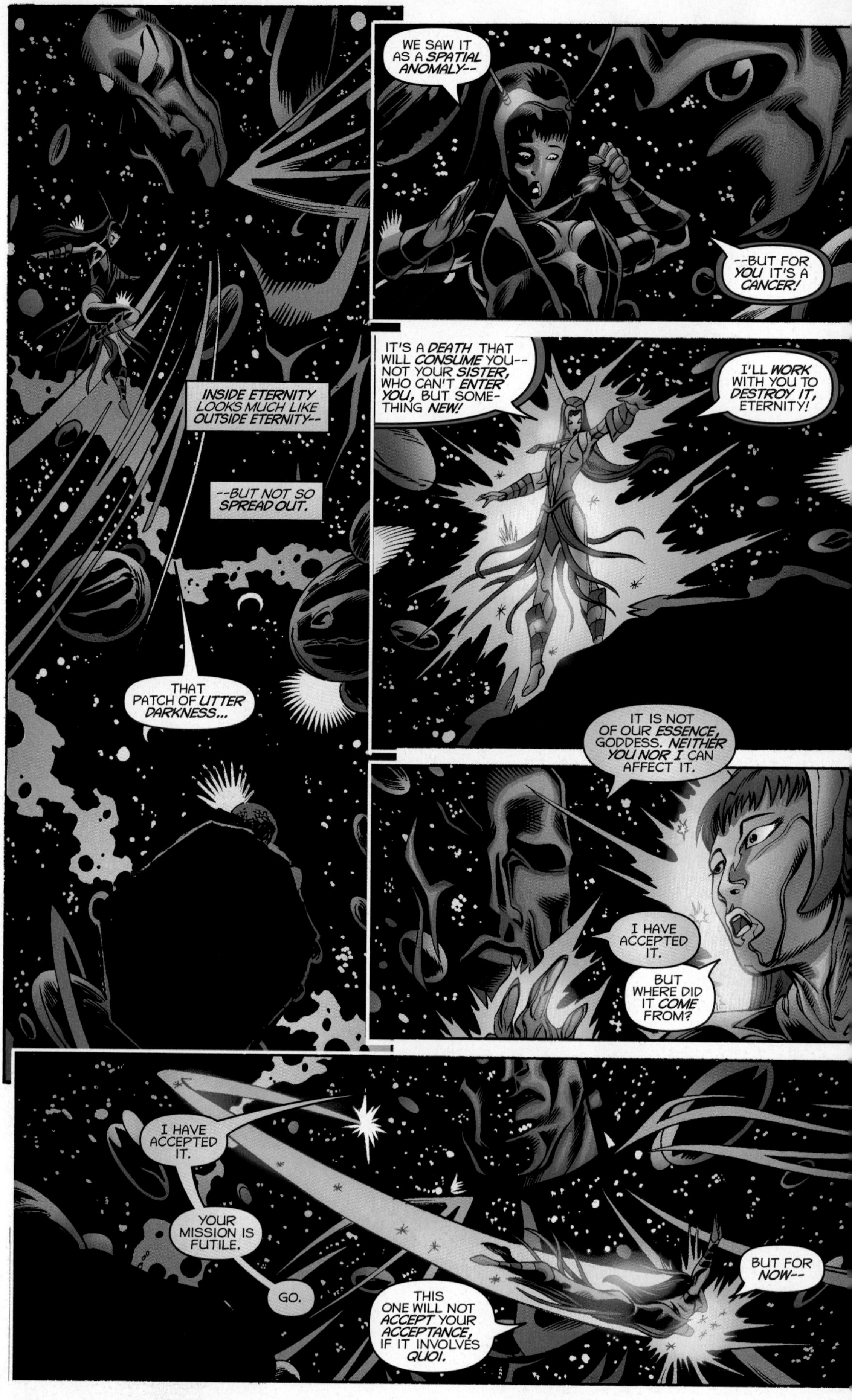
INSIDE ETERNITY LOOKS MUCH LIKE OUTSIDE ETERNITY--
--BUT NOT SO SPREAD OUT.
THAT PATCH OF UTTER DARKNESS...
WE SAW IT AS A SPATIAL ANOMALY--
--BUT FOR YOU IT'S A CANCER!
IT'S A DEATH THAT WILL CONSUME YOU-- NOT YOUR SISTER, WHO CAN'T ENTER YOU, BUT SOMETHING NEW!
I'LL WORK WITH YOU TO DESTROY IT, ETERNITY!
IT IS NOT OF OUR ESSENCE, GODDESS. NEITHER YOU NOR I CAN AFFECT IT.
I HAVE ACCEPTED IT.
BUT WHERE DID IT COME FROM?
I HAVE ACCEPTED IT.
YOUR MISSION IS FUTILE.
GO.
THIS ONE WILL NOT ACCEPT YOUR ACCEPTANCE, IF IT INVOLVES QUOI.
BUT FOR NOW--

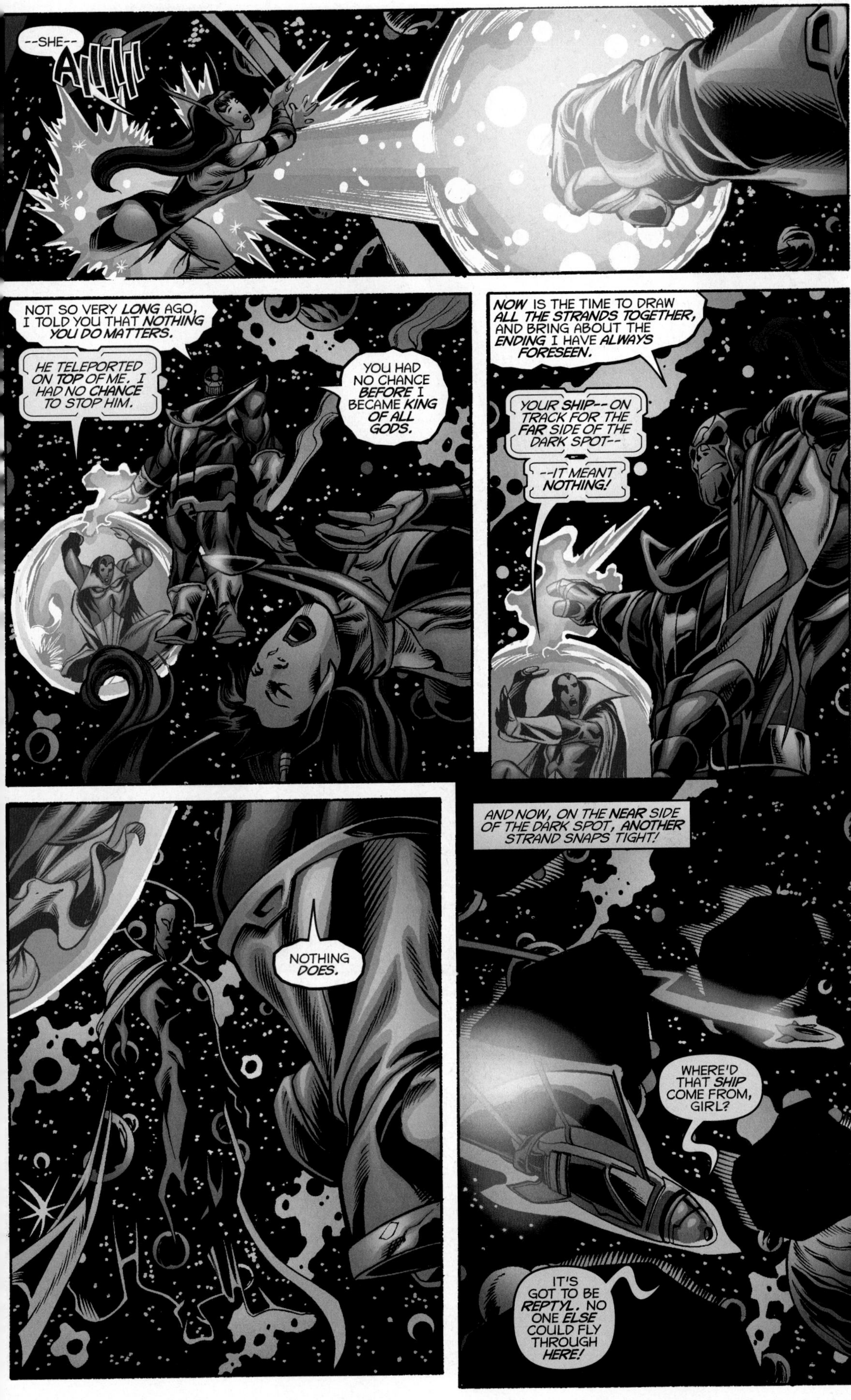
--SHE--
AIIIIII
NOT SO VERY LONG AGO, I TOLD YOU THAT NOTHING YOU DO MATTERS.
HE TELEPORTED ON TOP OF ME. I HAD NO CHANCE TO STOP HIM.
YOU HAD NO CHANCE BEFORE I BECAME KING OF ALL GODS.
NOW IS THE TIME TO DRAW ALL THE STRANDS TOGETHER, AND BRING ABOUT THE ENDING I HAVE ALWAYS FORESEEN.
YOUR SHIP--ON TRACK FOR THE FAR SIDE OF THE DARK SPOT--
--IT MEANT NOTHING!
NOTHING DOES.
AND NOW, ON THE NEAR SIDE OF THE DARK SPOT, ANOTHER STRAND SNAPS TIGHT!
WHERE'D THAT SHIP COME FROM, GIRL?
IT'S GOT TO BE REPTYL. NO ONE ELSE COULD FLY THROUGH HERE!

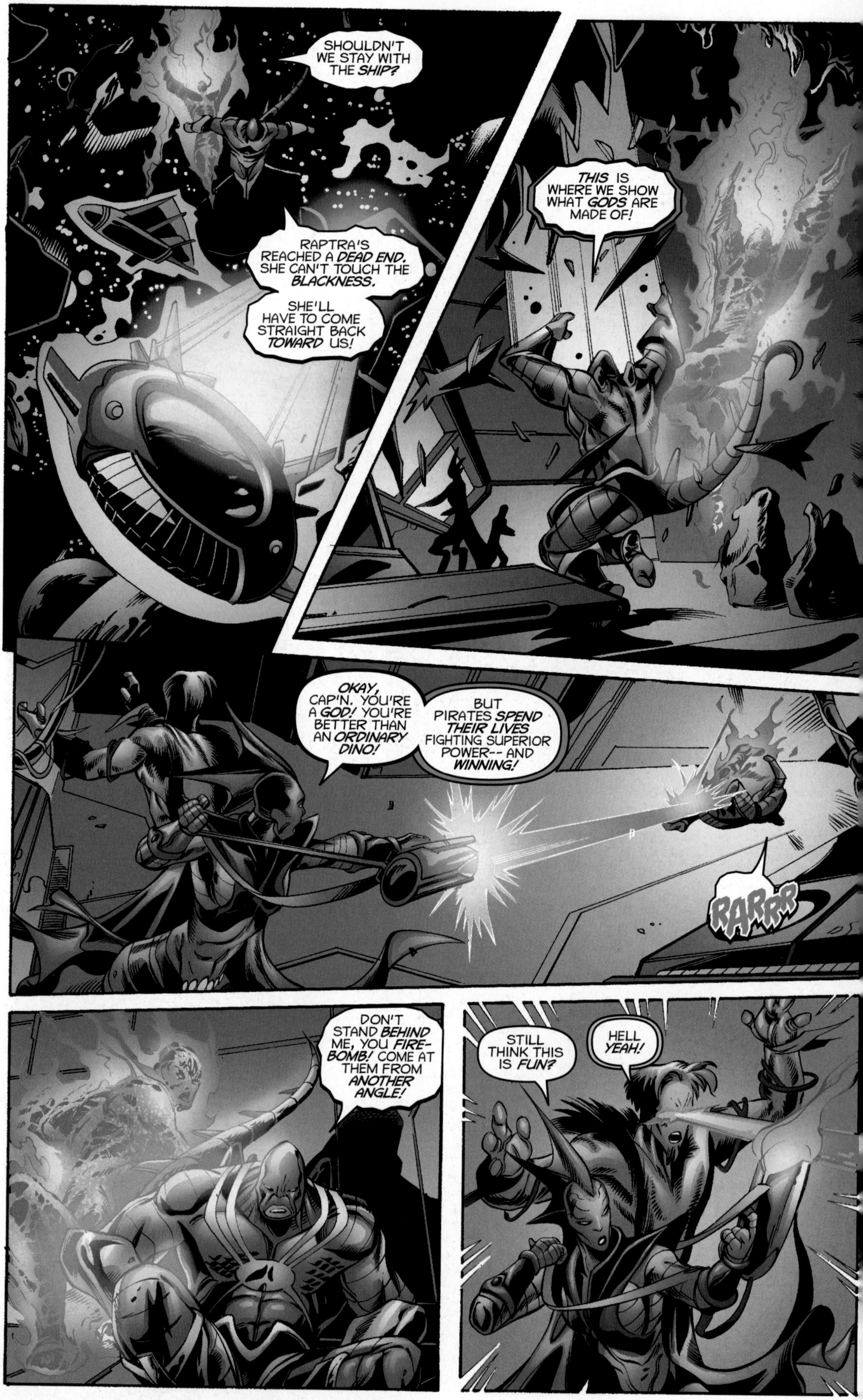
SHOULDN'T WE STAY WITH THE *SHIP?*
RAPTRA'S REACHED A *DEAD END.* SHE CAN'T TOUCH THE *BLACKNESS.*
SHE'LL HAVE TO COME STRAIGHT BACK *TOWARD* US!
THIS IS WHERE WE SHOW WHAT *GODS* ARE MADE OF!
OKAY, CAP'N. YOU'RE A *GOD!* YOU'RE BETTER THAN AN *ORDINARY DINO!*
BUT PIRATES *SPEND THEIR LIVES* FIGHTING SUPERIOR POWER-- AND *WINNING!*
RARRR
DON'T STAND *BEHIND* ME, YOU *FIRE-BOMB!* COME AT THEM FROM *ANOTHER ANGLE!*
STILL THINK THIS IS *FUN?*
HELL *YEAH!*

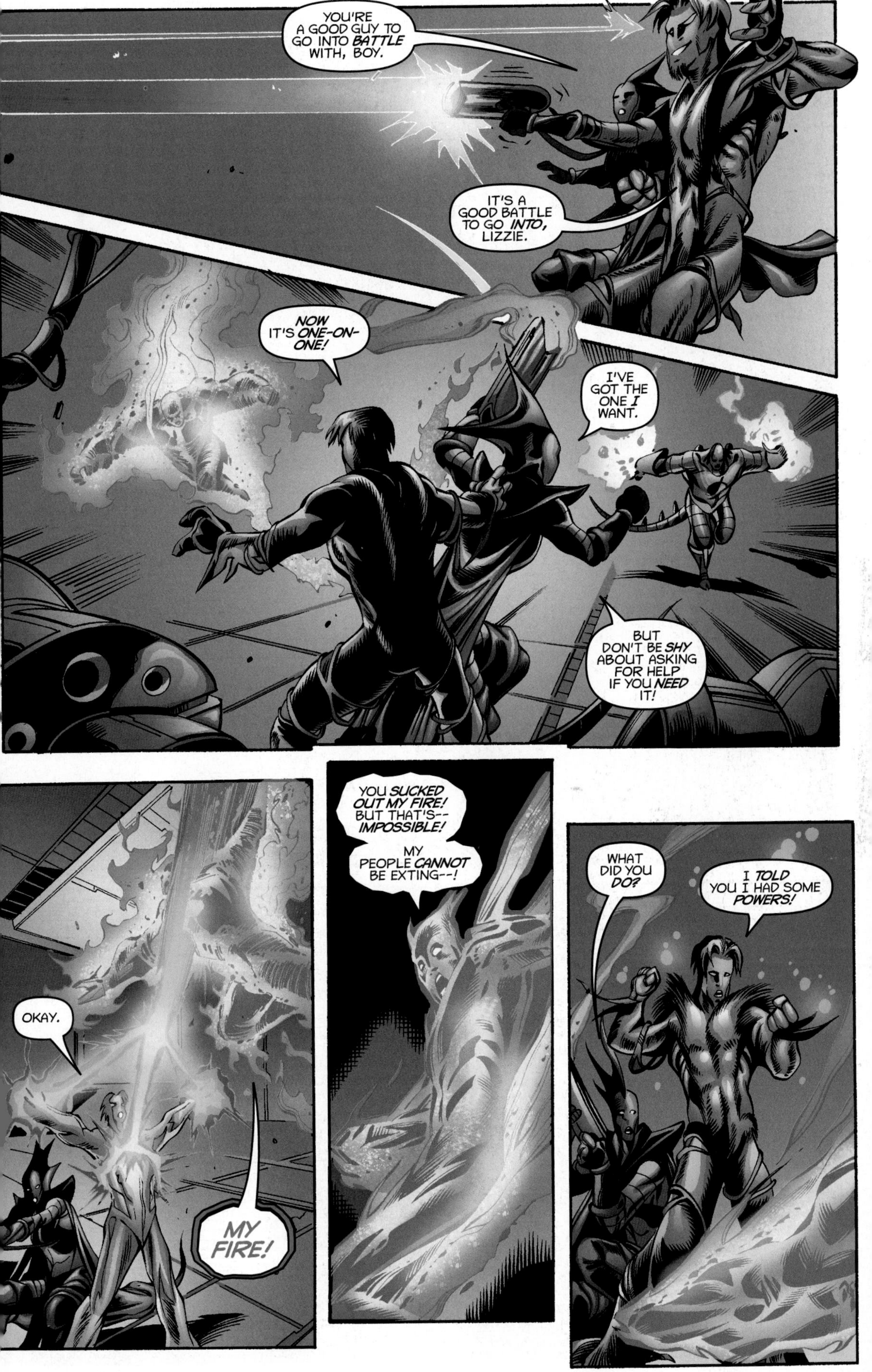

YOU'RE A GOOD GUY TO GO INTO *BATTLE* WITH, BOY.
IT'S A GOOD BATTLE TO GO *INTO*, LIZZIE.
NOW IT'S *ONE-ON-ONE!*
I'VE GOT THE ONE *I* WANT.
BUT DON'T BE *SHY* ABOUT ASKING FOR HELP IF YOU *NEED* IT!
OKAY.
MY FIRE!
YOU *SUCKED OUT MY FIRE!* BUT THAT'S-- *IMPOSSIBLE!*
MY PEOPLE *CANNOT* BE EXTING--!
WHAT DID YOU *DO?*
I *TOLD* YOU I HAD SOME *POWERS!*

PLANTS *BREATHE IN CARBON DIOXIDE* AND *BREATHE OUT OXYGEN*, WHILE HUMANS *BREATHE IN OXYGEN* AND *BREATHE OUT CARBON DIOXIDE*. THEY *ABSORB* AND *TRANSMUTE* FOR EACH OTHER.

SINCE I'M *BOTH,* I ABSORB AND TRANSMUTE *EVERYTHING.* IT'S *NO*--

YOU *DISGUSTING MUTANT FOOL!* YOU DON'T GIVE *ME* CREDIT FOR MY SPEED--

--AND *POWER!*

UNNGH!

QUOI!

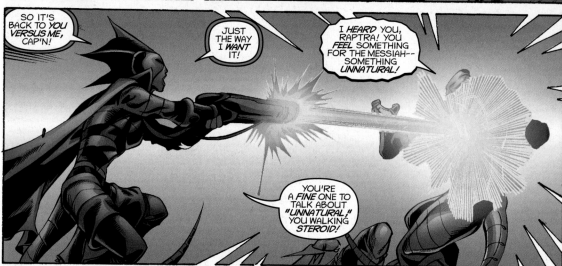

SO IT'S *YOU VERSUS ME,* CAP'N!

JUST THE WAY I *WANT* IT!

I *HEARD* YOU, *RAPTRA!* YOU *FEEL* SOMETHING FOR THE MESSIAH-- SOMETHING *UNNATURAL!*

YOU'RE A *FINE* ONE TO TALK ABOUT "*UNNATURAL,*" YOU WALKING *STEROID!*

IF *SERVING THANOS* WEREN'T *ENOUGH* REASON TO DESTROY YOU--

--*MIXING* WITH A *SLIMY HUMAN*--

ARRRR!

I DIDN'T SPEND *ALL* MY TIME RUNNING AWAY FROM YOU, CAP'N. I RECALIBRATED MY *CANNONS* TOWARD WHAT I'D SEEN YOU *BECOME!*

WHAT I'VE *BECOME*--

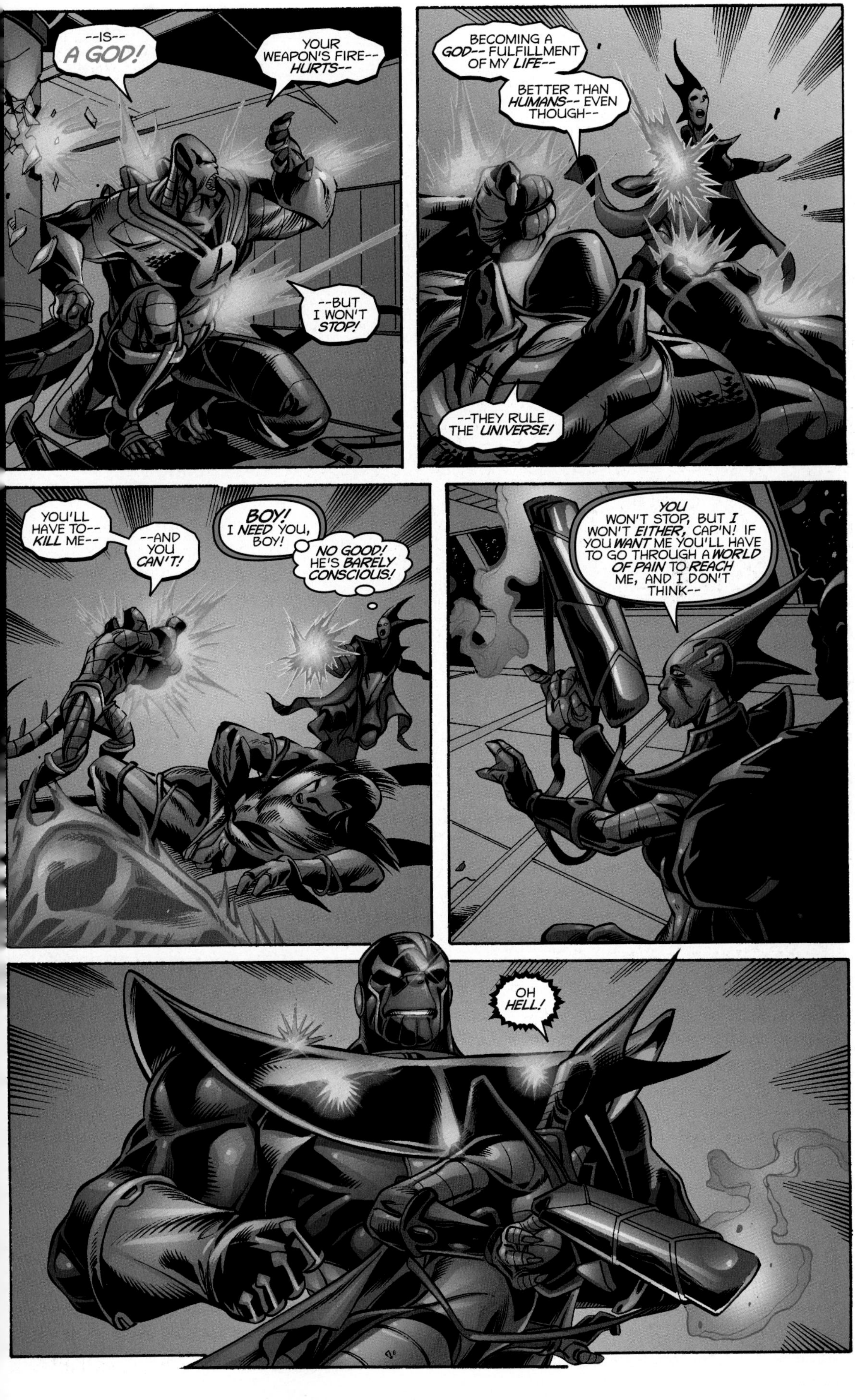
--IS--
A GOD!
YOUR WEAPON'S FIRE-- HURTS--
--BUT I WON'T STOP!
BECOMING A GOD-- FULFILLMENT OF MY LIFE--
BETTER THAN HUMANS-- EVEN THOUGH--
--THEY RULE THE UNIVERSE!
YOU'LL HAVE TO-- KILL ME--
--AND YOU CAN'T!
BOY! I NEED YOU, BOY!
NO GOOD! HE'S BARELY CONSCIOUS!
YOU WON'T STOP, BUT I WON'T EITHER, CAP'N! IF YOU WANT ME YOU'LL HAVE TO GO THROUGH A WORLD OF PAIN TO REACH ME, AND I DON'T THINK--
OH HELL!

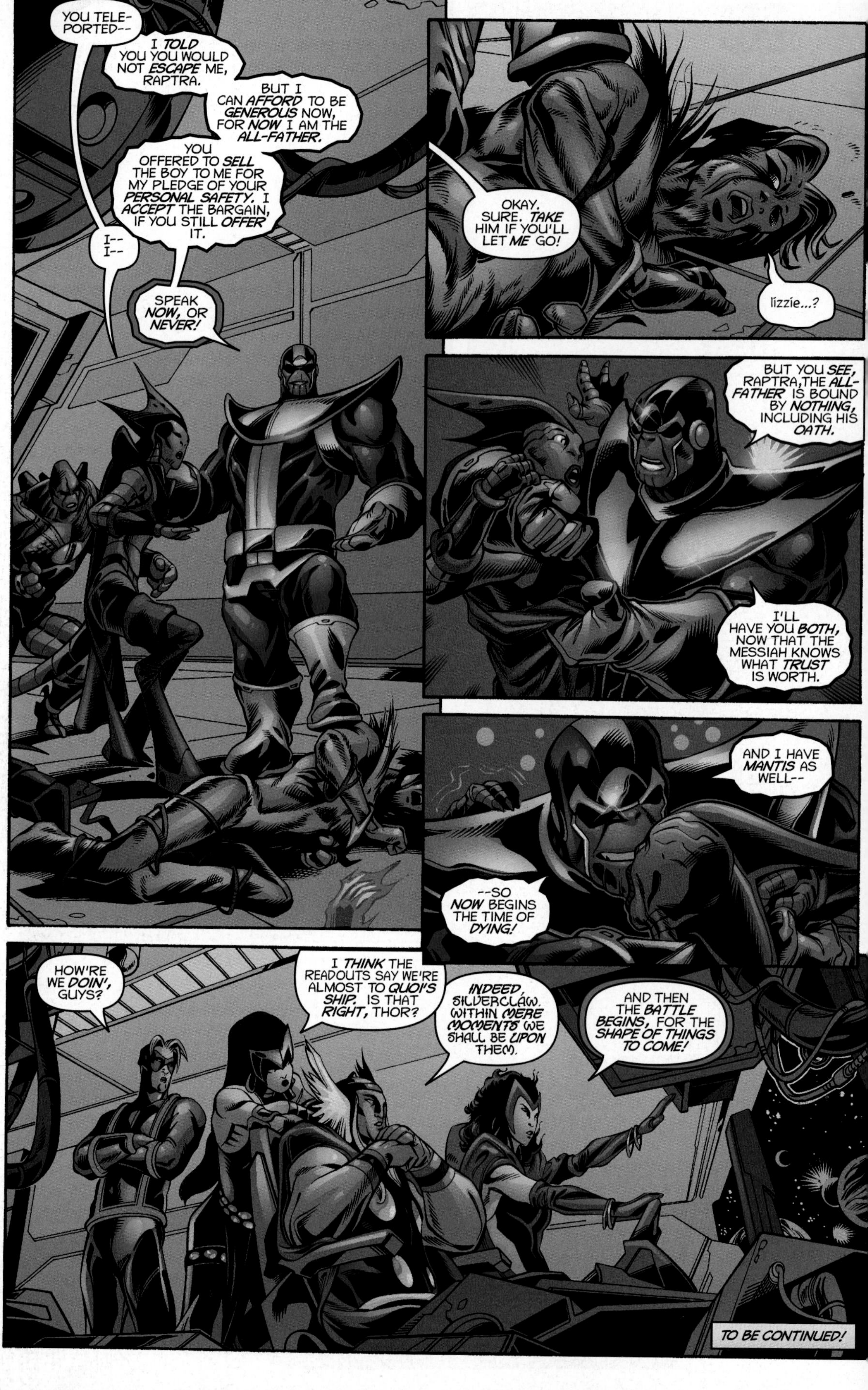
YOU TELE-PORTED--
I TOLD YOU YOU WOULD NOT ESCAPE ME, RAPTRA.
BUT I CAN AFFORD TO BE GENEROUS NOW, FOR NOW I AM THE ALL-FATHER.
YOU OFFERED TO SELL THE BOY TO ME FOR MY PLEDGE OF YOUR PERSONAL SAFETY. I ACCEPT THE BARGAIN, IF YOU STILL OFFER IT.
I-- I--
SPEAK NOW, OR NEVER!
OKAY. SURE. TAKE HIM IF YOU'LL LET ME GO!
lizzie...?
BUT YOU SEE, RAPTRA, THE ALL-FATHER IS BOUND BY NOTHING, INCLUDING HIS OATH.
I'LL HAVE YOU BOTH, NOW THAT THE MESSIAH KNOWS WHAT TRUST IS WORTH.
AND I HAVE MANTIS AS WELL--
--SO NOW BEGINS THE TIME OF DYING!
HOW'RE WE DOIN', GUYS?
I THINK THE READOUTS SAY WE'RE ALMOST TO QUOI'S SHIP. IS THAT RIGHT, THOR?
INDEED, SILVERCLAW. WITHIN MERE MOMENTS WE SHALL BE UPON THEM.
AND THEN THE BATTLE BEGINS, FOR THE SHAPE OF THINGS TO COME!
TO BE CONTINUED!

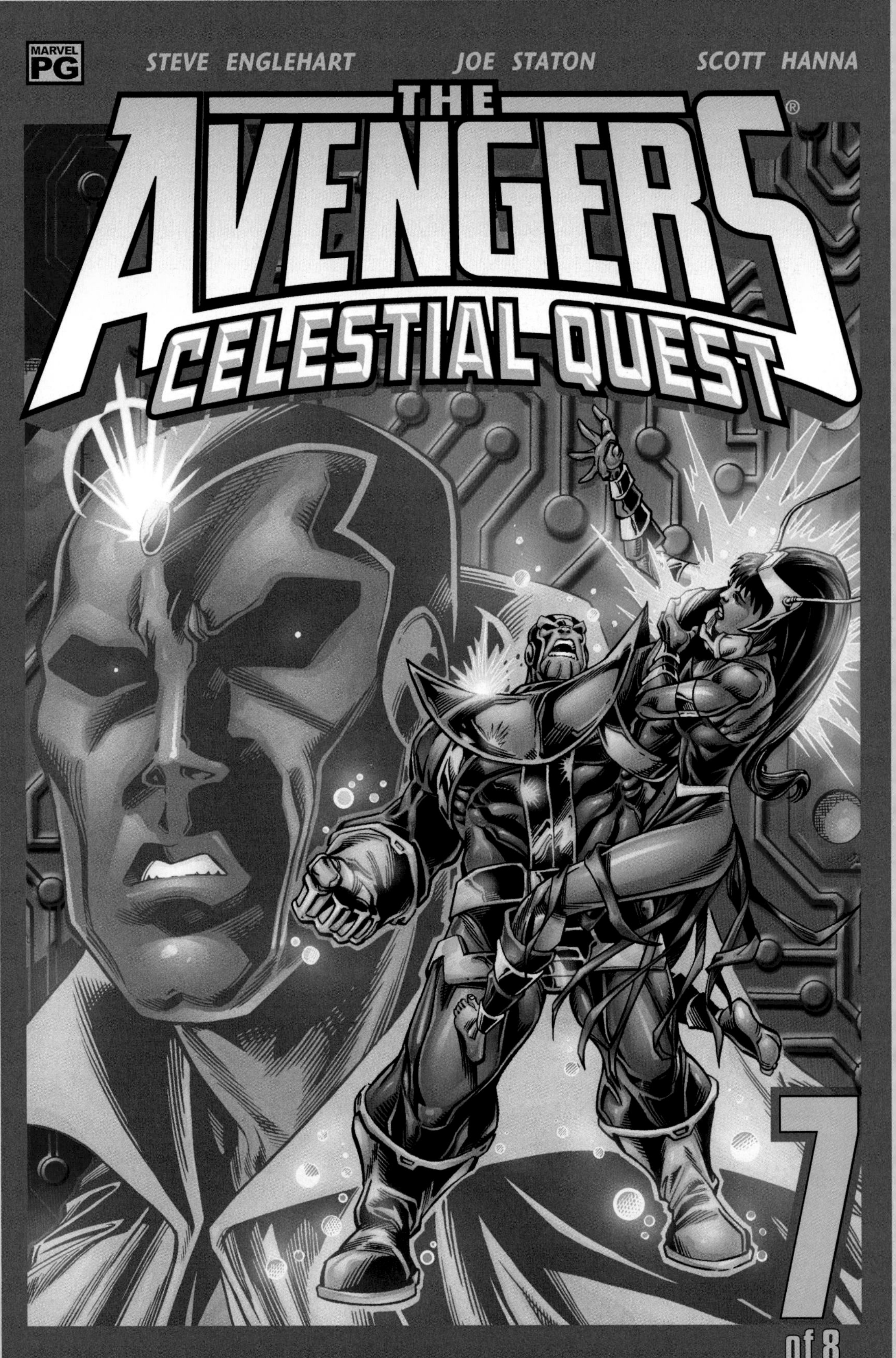
MARVEL PG
STEVE ENGLEHART
JOE STATON
SCOTT HANNA
THE AVENGERS®
CELESTIAL QUEST
7
of 8

MANTIS! TRAINED ALMOST FROM BIRTH TO BE THE SUPREME EXAMPLE OF HUMANITY -- PHYSICALLY PERFECT, MENTALLY EXALTED! HER MIND WIPED BY THE PRIESTS OF PAMA, SHE WORKED AS A BAR GIRL, LIVING AMONG HUMANITY AT ITS WORST. THERE SHE MET THE BURNT-OUT **SWORDSMAN**, AND BEGAN A TWISTING JOURNEY THAT TOOK HER FIRST TO THE **AVENGERS**, AND THEN TO THE **UNIVERSE** -- AS MANTIS BECAME THE **CELESTIAL MADONNA**!

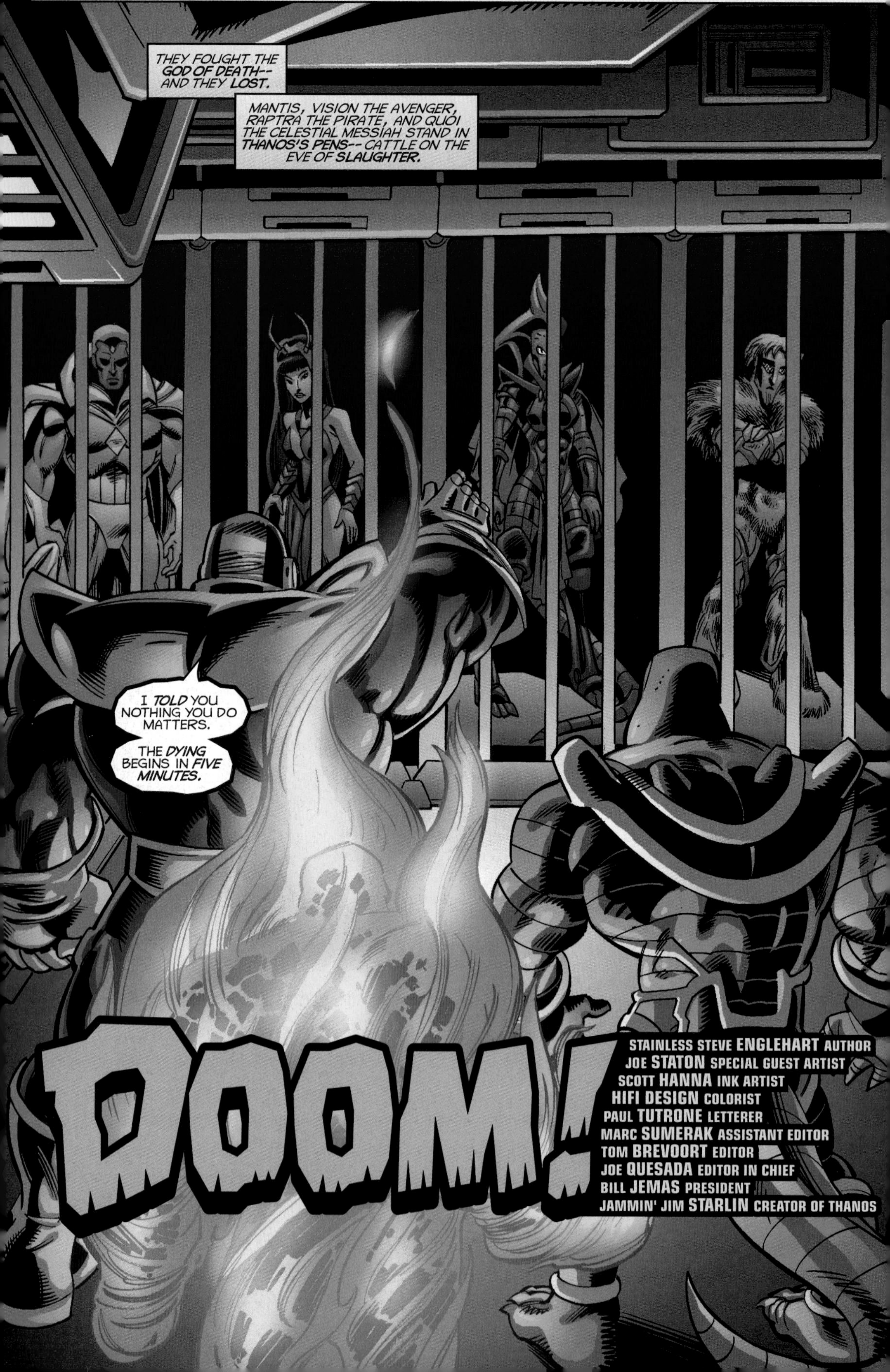
THEY FOUGHT THE GOD OF DEATH-- AND THEY LOST.
MANTIS, VISION THE AVENGER, RAPTRA THE PIRATE, AND QUOI THE CELESTIAL MESSIAH STAND IN THANOS'S PENS-- CATTLE ON THE EVE OF SLAUGHTER.
I TOLD YOU NOTHING YOU DO MATTERS.
THE DYING BEGINS IN FIVE MINUTES.
DOOM!
STAINLESS STEVE ENGLEHART AUTHOR
JOE STATON SPECIAL GUEST ARTIST
SCOTT HANNA INK ARTIST
HIFI DESIGN COLORIST
PAUL TUTRONE LETTERER
MARC SUMERAK ASSISTANT EDITOR
TOM BREVOORT EDITOR
JOE QUESADA EDITOR IN CHIEF
BILL JEMAS PRESIDENT
JAMMIN' JIM STARLIN CREATOR OF THANOS

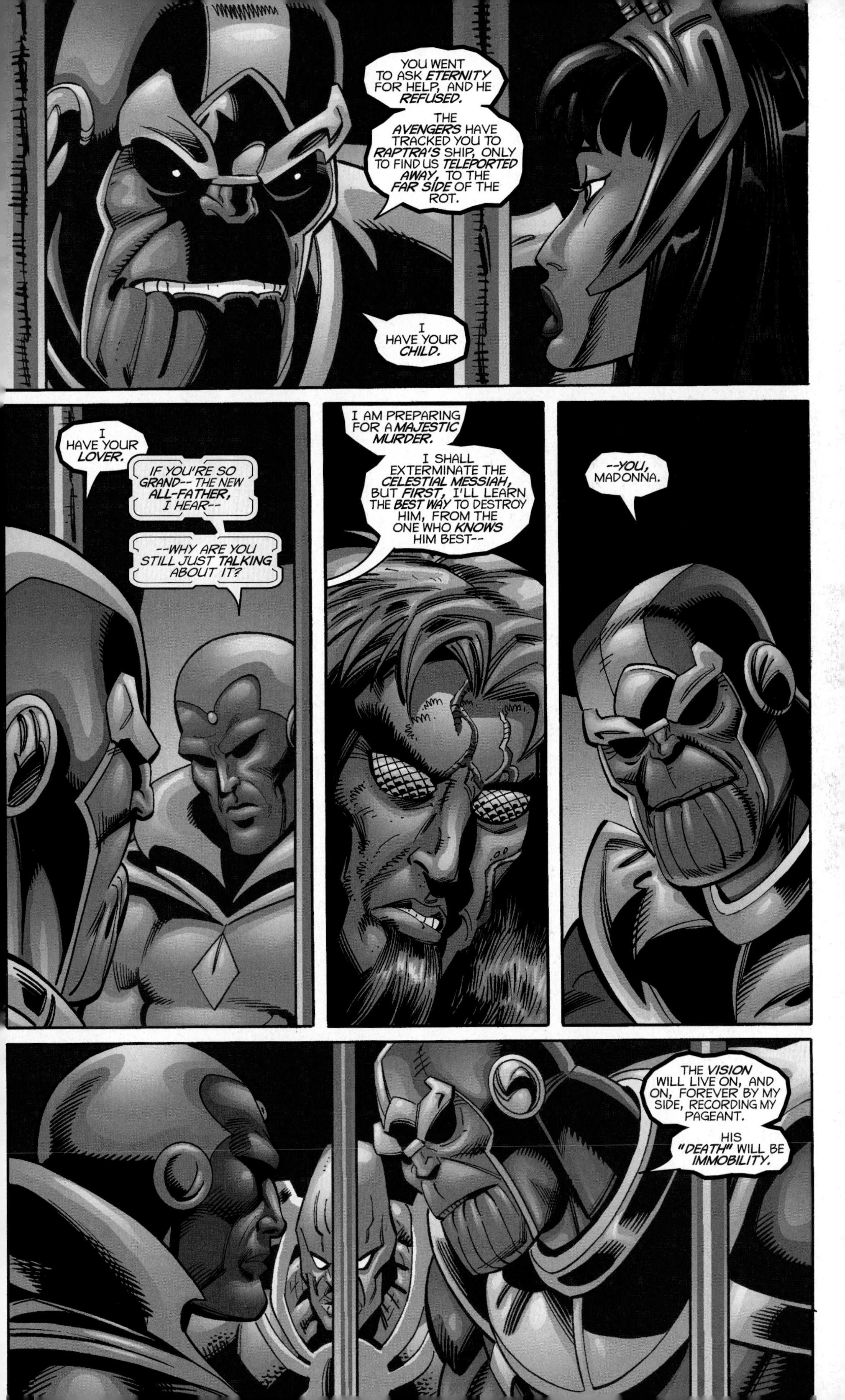
YOU WENT TO ASK ETERNITY FOR HELP, AND HE REFUSED.
THE AVENGERS HAVE TRACKED YOU TO RAPTRA'S SHIP, ONLY TO FIND US TELEPORTED AWAY, TO THE FAR SIDE OF THE ROT.
I HAVE YOUR CHILD.
I HAVE YOUR LOVER.
IF YOU'RE SO GRAND-- THE NEW ALL-FATHER, I HEAR--
--WHY ARE YOU STILL JUST TALKING ABOUT IT?
I AM PREPARING FOR A MAJESTIC MURDER.
I SHALL EXTERMINATE THE CELESTIAL MESSIAH, BUT FIRST, I'LL LEARN THE BEST WAY TO DESTROY HIM, FROM THE ONE WHO KNOWS HIM BEST--
--YOU, MADONNA.
THE VISION WILL LIVE ON, AND ON, FOREVER BY MY SIDE, RECORDING MY PAGEANT.
HIS "DEATH" WILL BE IMMOBILITY.

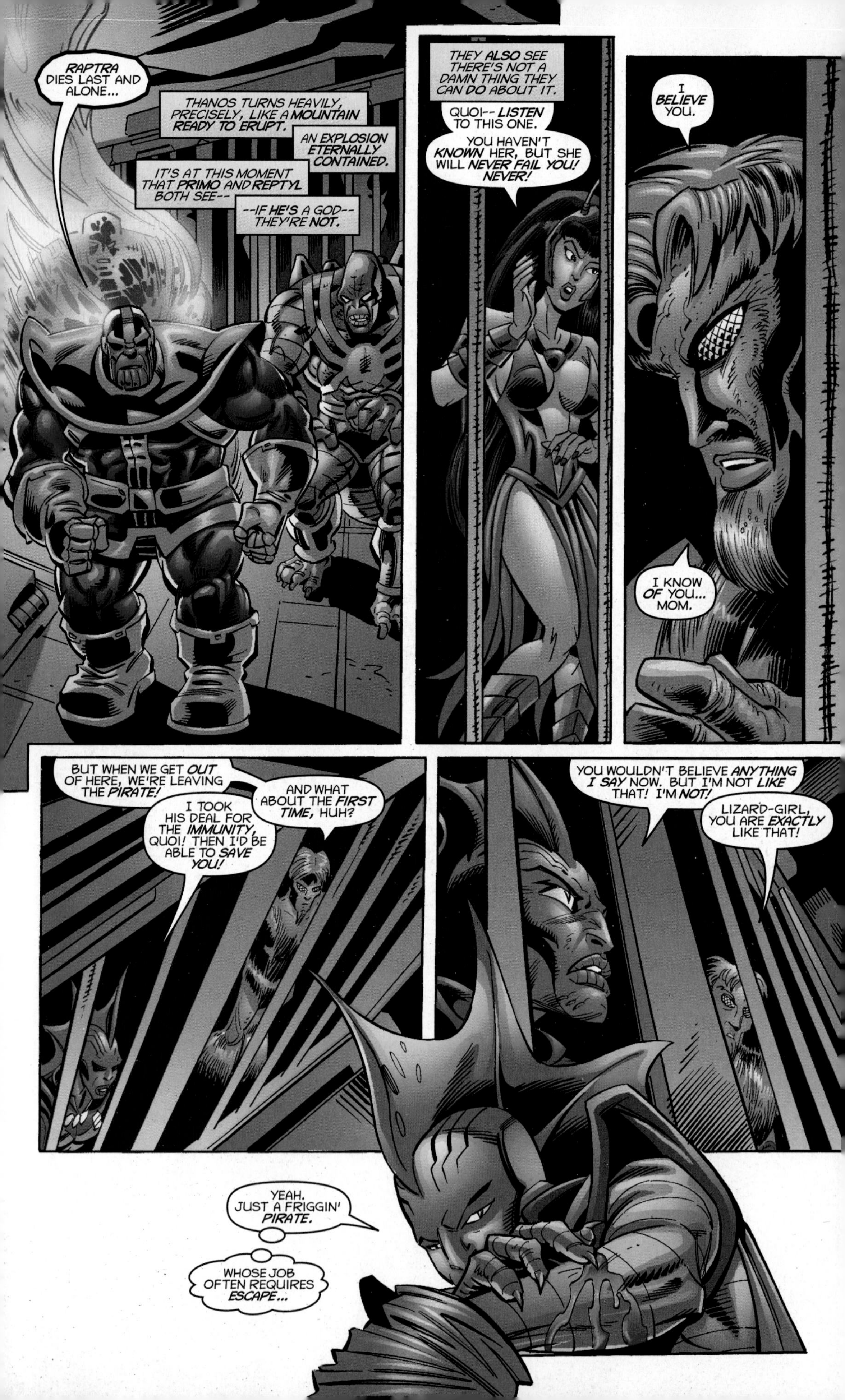

RAPTRA DIES LAST AND ALONE...
THANOS TURNS HEAVILY, PRECISELY, LIKE A MOUNTAIN READY TO ERUPT.
AN EXPLOSION ETERNALLY CONTAINED.
IT'S AT THIS MOMENT THAT PRIMO AND REPTYL BOTH SEE--
--IF HE'S A GOD-- THEY'RE NOT.
THEY ALSO SEE THERE'S NOT A DAMN THING THEY CAN DO ABOUT IT.
QUOI-- LISTEN TO THIS ONE.
YOU HAVEN'T KNOWN HER, BUT SHE WILL NEVER FAIL YOU! NEVER!
I BELIEVE YOU.
I KNOW OF YOU... MOM.
BUT WHEN WE GET OUT OF HERE, WE'RE LEAVING THE PIRATE!
I TOOK HIS DEAL FOR THE IMMUNITY, QUOI! THEN I'D BE ABLE TO SAVE YOU!
AND WHAT ABOUT THE FIRST TIME, HUH?
YOU WOULDN'T BELIEVE ANYTHING I SAY NOW. BUT I'M NOT LIKE THAT! I'M NOT!
LIZARD-GIRL, YOU ARE EXACTLY LIKE THAT!
YEAH. JUST A FRIGGIN' PIRATE.
WHOSE JOB OFTEN REQUIRES ESCAPE...

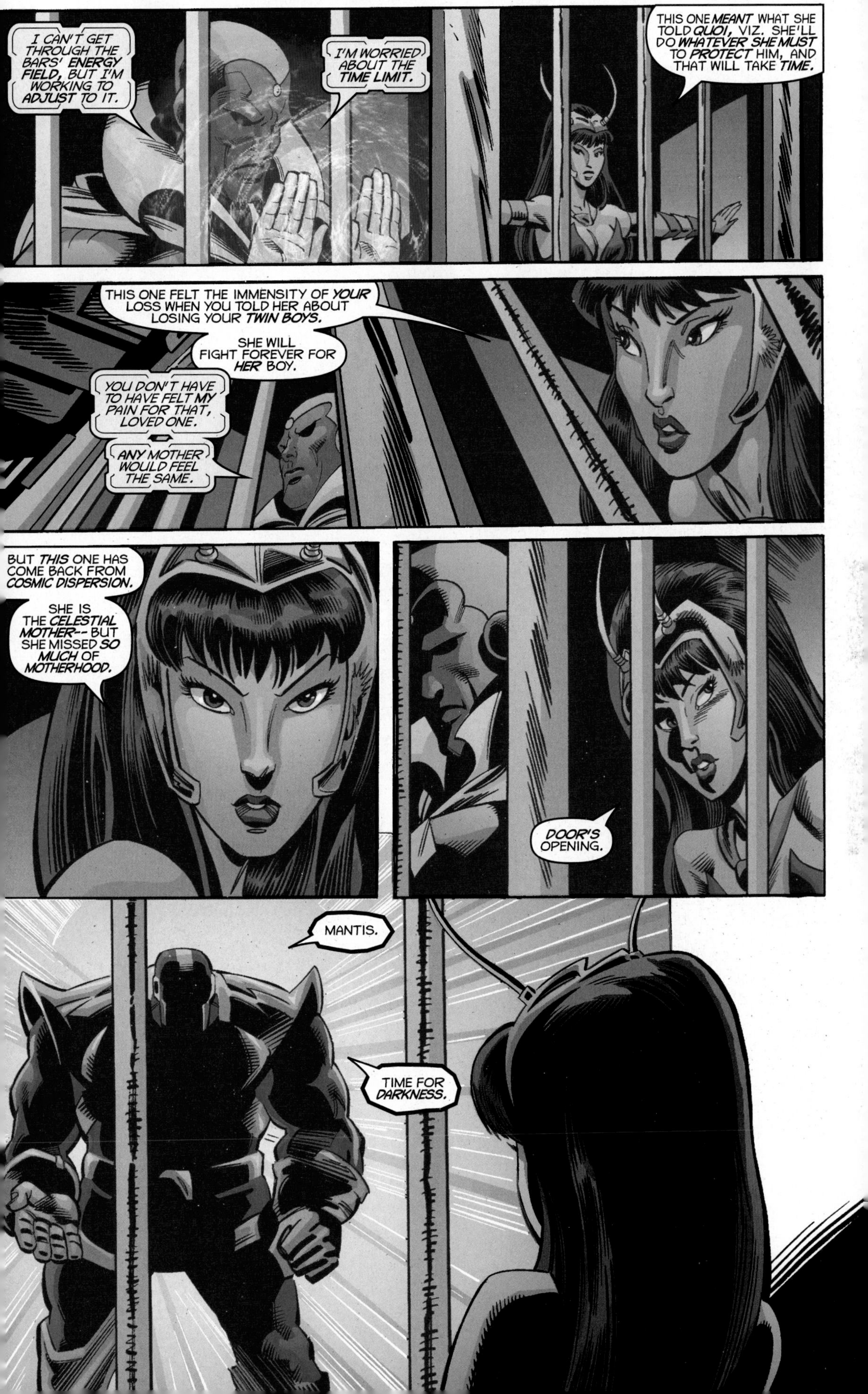

I CAN'T GET THROUGH THE BARS' ENERGY FIELD, BUT I'M WORKING TO ADJUST TO IT.
I'M WORRIED ABOUT THE TIME LIMIT.
THIS ONE MEANT WHAT SHE TOLD QUOI, VIZ. SHE'LL DO WHATEVER SHE MUST TO PROTECT HIM, AND THAT WILL TAKE TIME.
THIS ONE FELT THE IMMENSITY OF YOUR LOSS WHEN YOU TOLD HER ABOUT LOSING YOUR TWIN BOYS.
SHE WILL FIGHT FOREVER FOR HER BOY.
YOU DON'T HAVE TO HAVE FELT MY PAIN FOR THAT, LOVED ONE.
ANY MOTHER WOULD FEEL THE SAME.
BUT THIS ONE HAS COME BACK FROM COSMIC DISPERSION.
SHE IS THE CELESTIAL MOTHER-- BUT SHE MISSED SO MUCH OF MOTHERHOOD.
DOOR'S OPENING.
MANTIS.
TIME FOR DARKNESS.

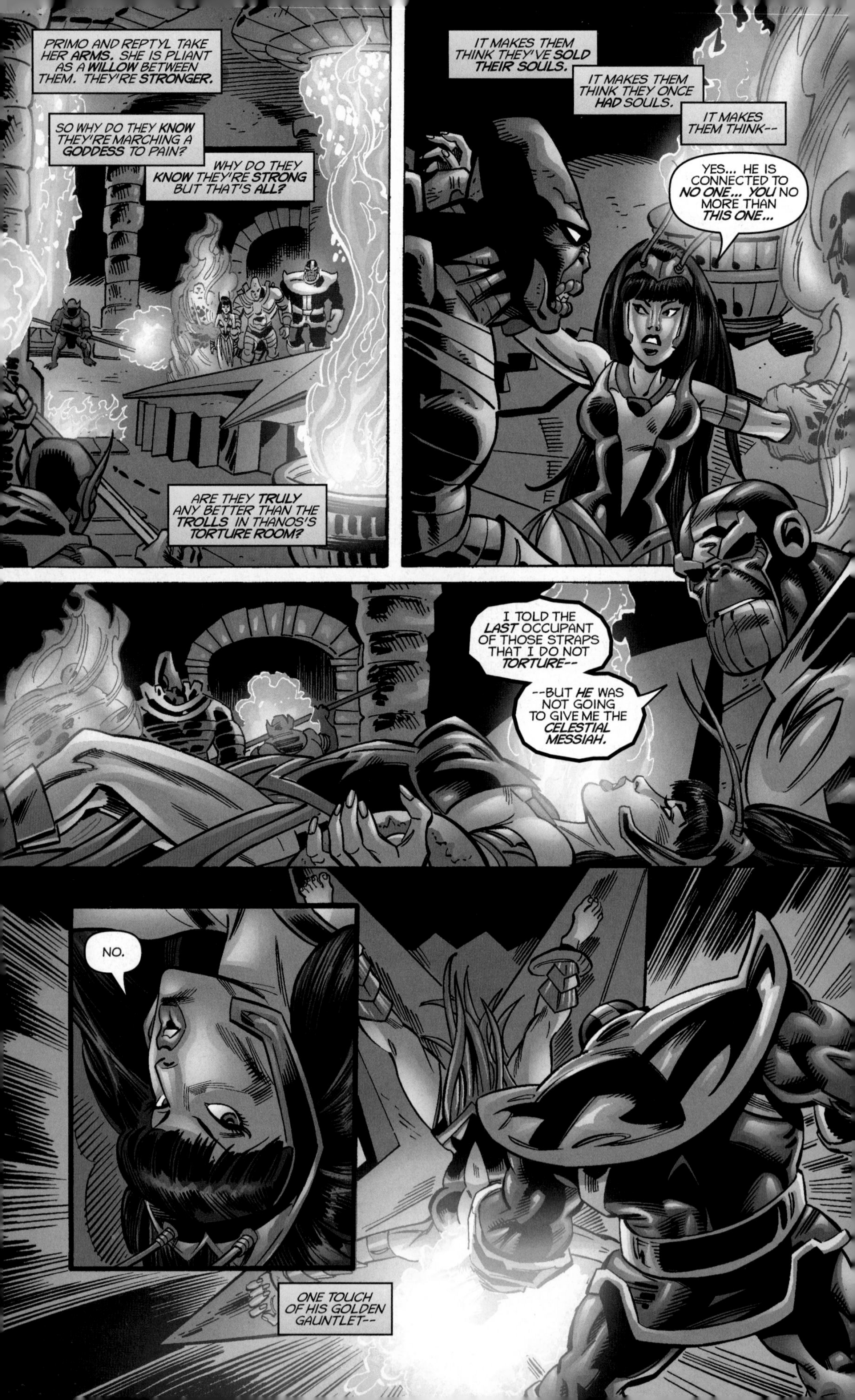

PRIMO AND REPTYL TAKE HER ARMS. SHE IS PLIANT AS A WILLOW BETWEEN THEM. THEY'RE STRONGER.
SO WHY DO THEY KNOW THEY'RE MARCHING A GODDESS TO PAIN?
WHY DO THEY KNOW THEY'RE STRONG BUT THAT'S ALL?
ARE THEY TRULY ANY BETTER THAN THE TROLLS IN THANOS'S TORTURE ROOM?
IT MAKES THEM THINK THEY'VE SOLD THEIR SOULS.
IT MAKES THEM THINK THEY ONCE HAD SOULS.
IT MAKES THEM THINK--
YES... HE IS CONNECTED TO NO ONE... YOU NO MORE THAN THIS ONE...
I TOLD THE LAST OCCUPANT OF THOSE STRAPS THAT I DO NOT TORTURE--
--BUT HE WAS NOT GOING TO GIVE ME THE CELESTIAL MESSIAH.
NO.
ONE TOUCH OF HIS GOLDEN GAUNTLET--

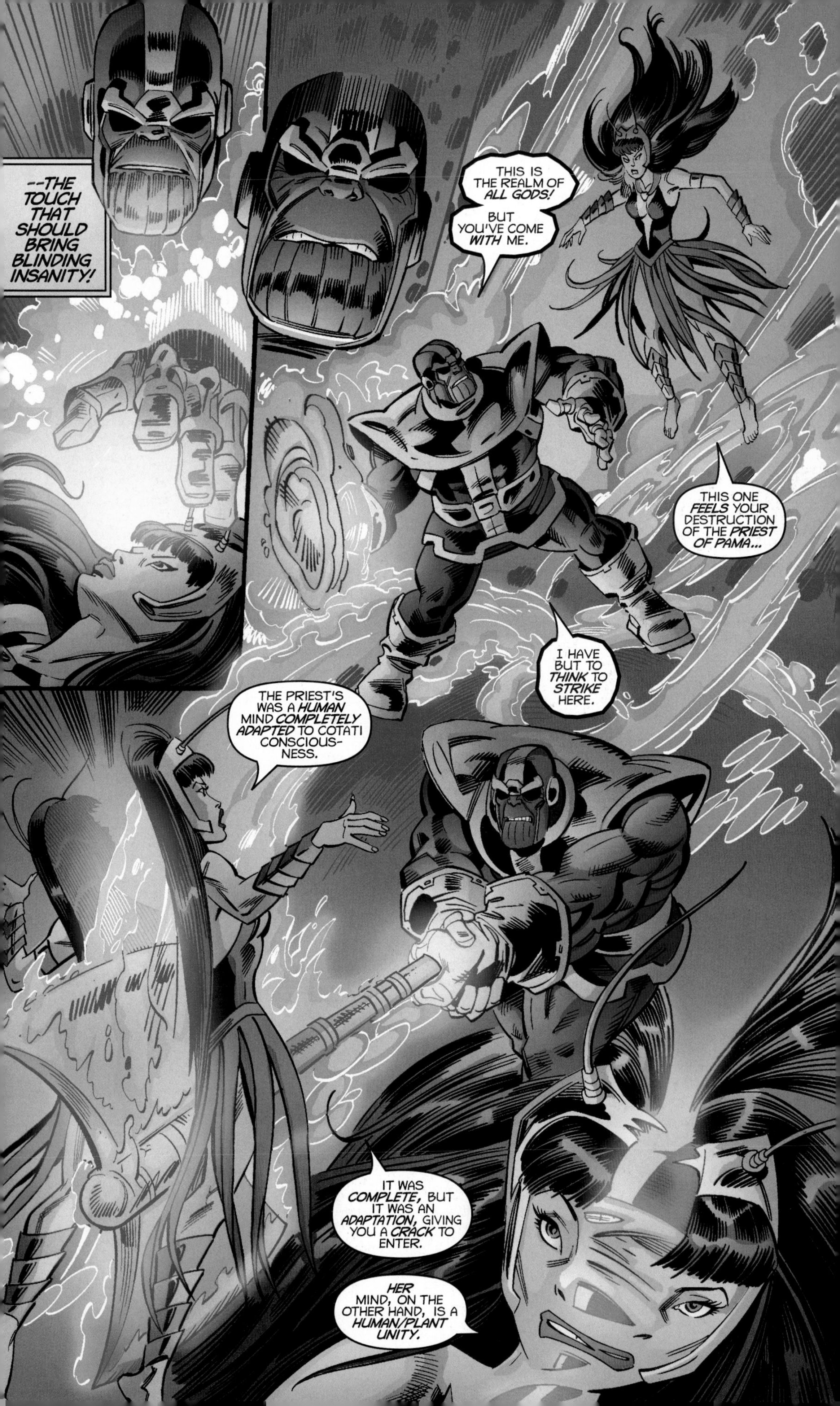
--THE TOUCH THAT SHOULD BRING BLINDING INSANITY!
THIS IS THE REALM OF ALL GODS!
BUT YOU'VE COME WITH ME.
THIS ONE FEELS YOUR DESTRUCTION OF THE PRIEST OF PAMA...
I HAVE BUT TO THINK TO STRIKE HERE.
THE PRIEST'S WAS A HUMAN MIND COMPLETELY ADAPTED TO COTATI CONSCIOUS-NESS.
IT WAS COMPLETE, BUT IT WAS AN ADAPTATION, GIVING YOU A CRACK TO ENTER.
HER MIND, ON THE OTHER HAND, IS A HUMAN/PLANT UNITY.

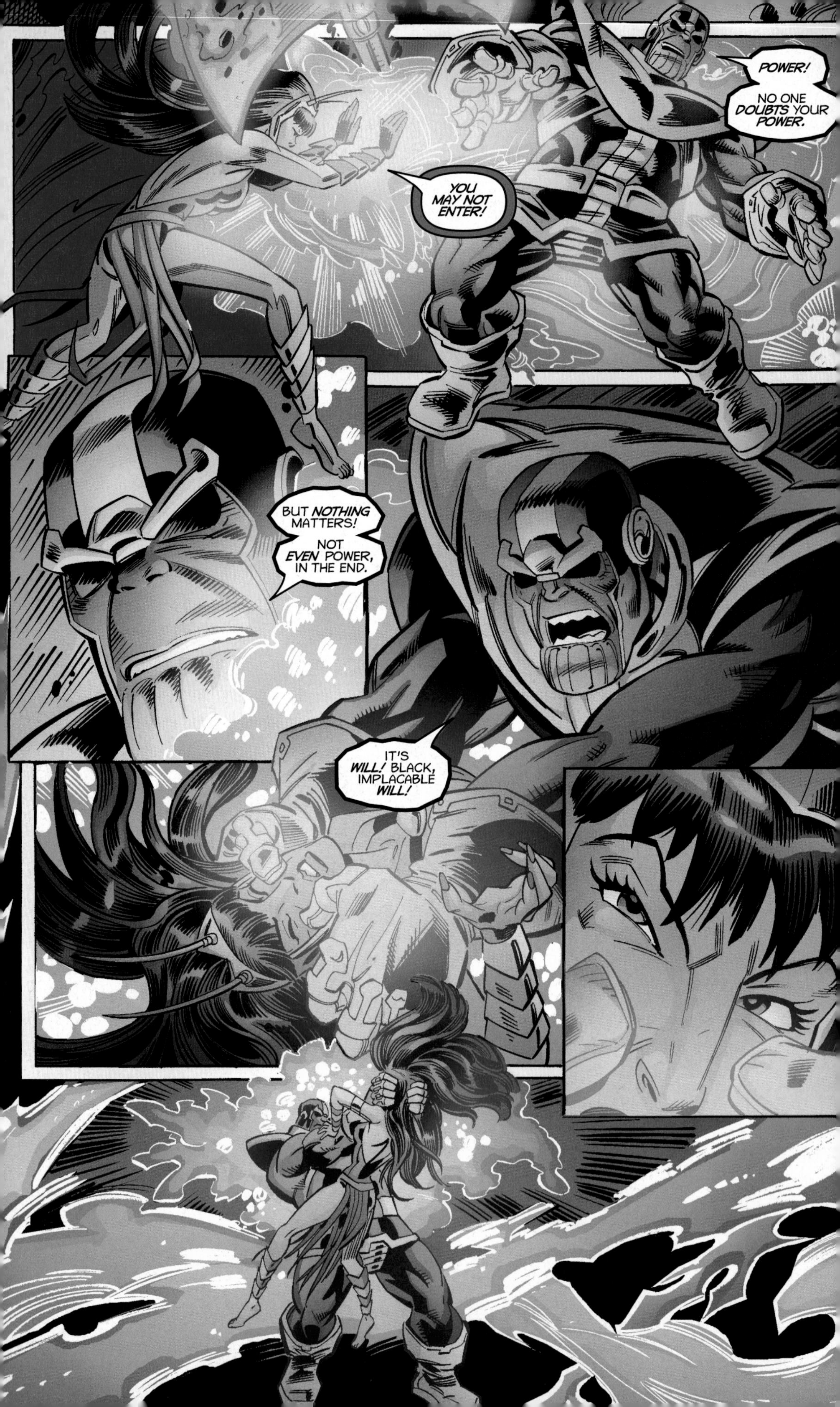
POWER!
NO ONE DOUBTS YOUR POWER.
YOU MAY NOT ENTER!
BUT NOTHING MATTERS!
NOT EVEN POWER, IN THE END.
IT'S WILL! BLACK, IMPLACABLE WILL!

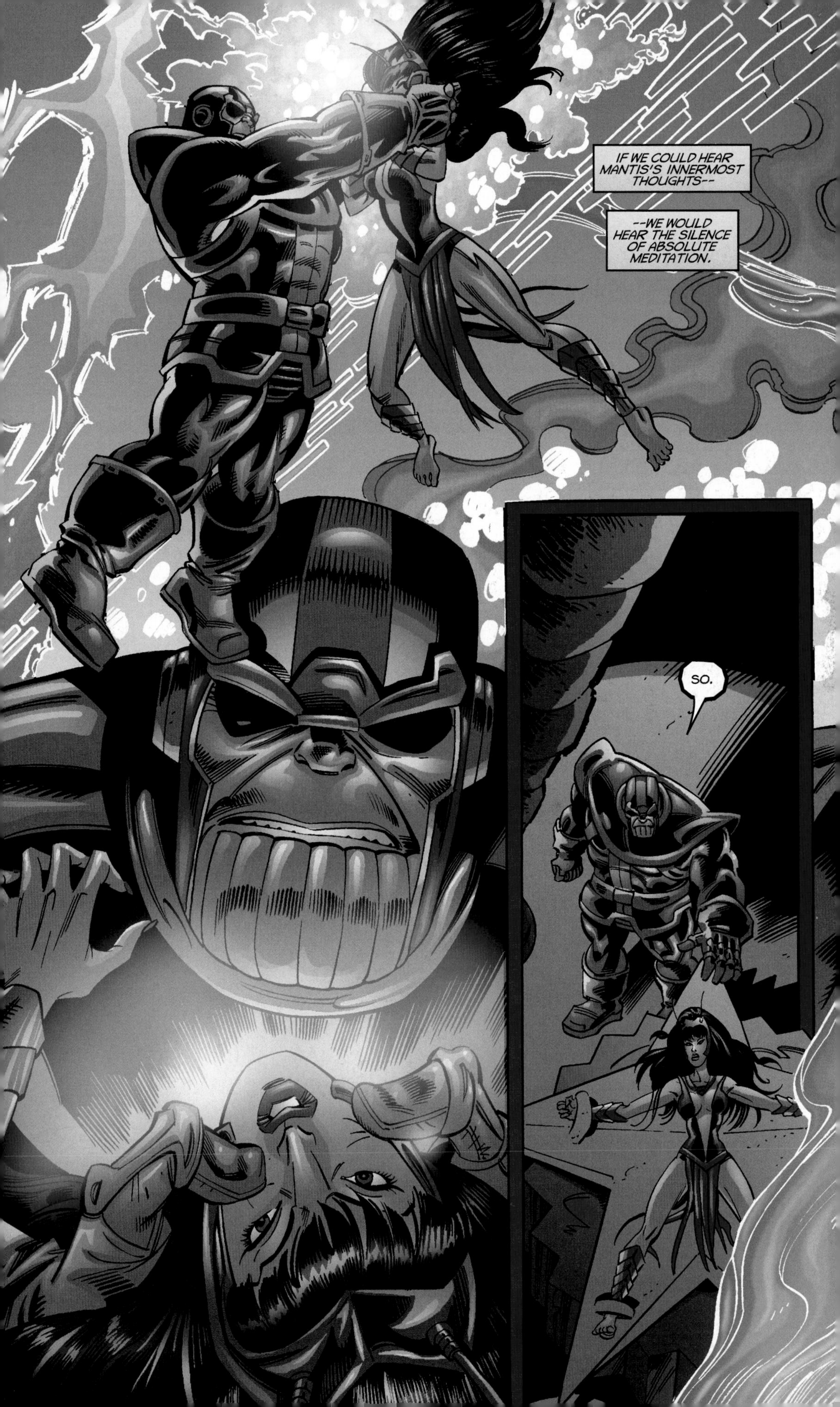

IF WE COULD HEAR MANTIS'S INNERMOST THOUGHTS--
--WE WOULD HEAR THE SILENCE OF ABSOLUTE MEDITATION.
SO.

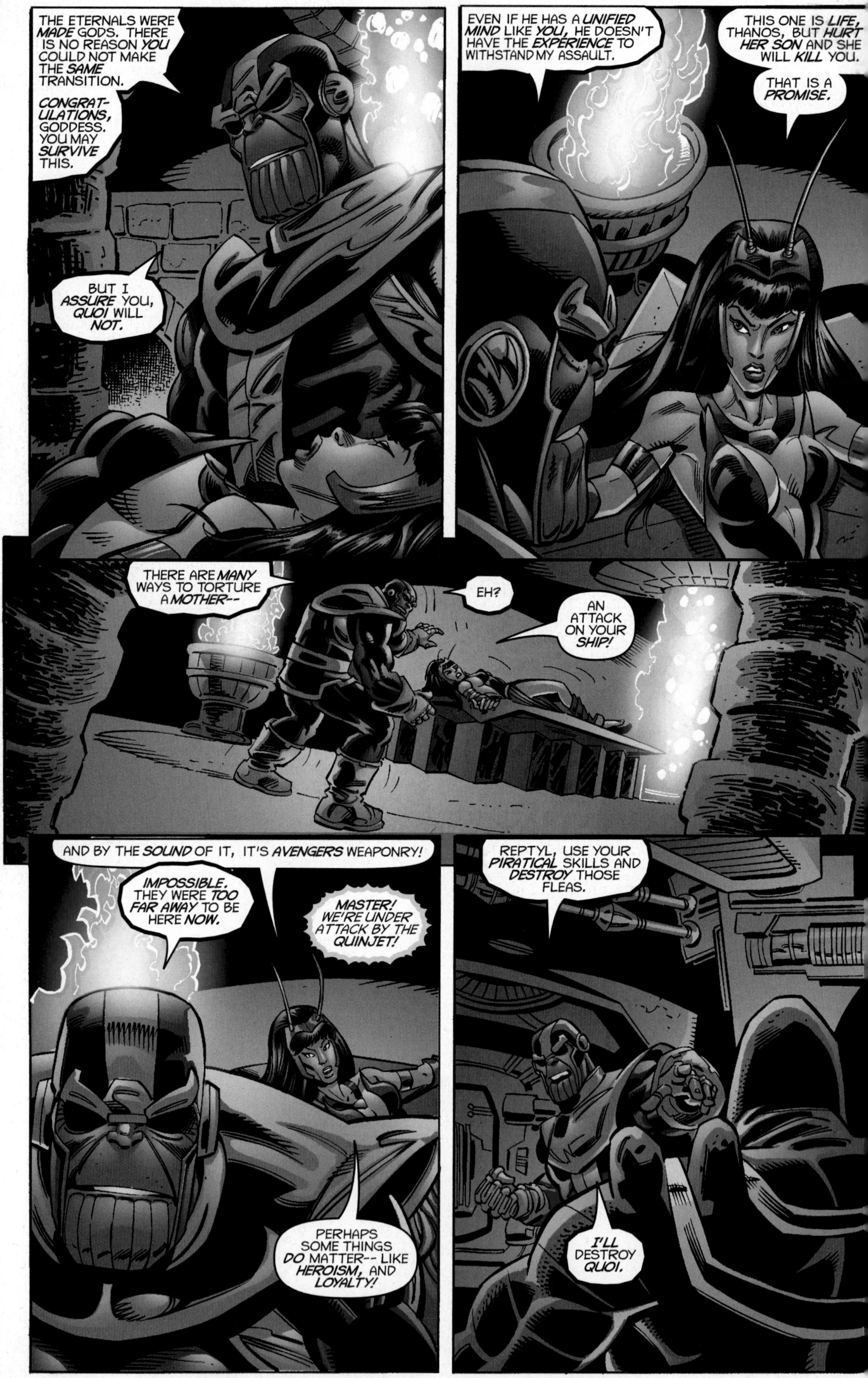
THE ETERNALS WERE *MADE* GODS. THERE IS NO REASON *YOU* COULD NOT MAKE THE *SAME* TRANSITION.
CONGRATULATIONS, GODDESS. YOU MAY *SURVIVE* THIS.
BUT I *ASSURE* YOU, *QUOI* WILL *NOT.*
EVEN IF HE HAS A *UNIFIED MIND* LIKE *YOU,* HE DOESN'T HAVE THE *EXPERIENCE* TO WITHSTAND MY ASSAULT.
THIS ONE IS *LIFE,* THANOS, BUT *HURT HER SON* AND SHE WILL *KILL* YOU.
THAT IS A *PROMISE.*
THERE ARE *MANY* WAYS TO TORTURE A *MOTHER--*
EH?
AN ATTACK ON YOUR *SHIP!*
AND BY THE *SOUND* OF IT, IT'S *AVENGERS* WEAPONRY!
IMPOSSIBLE. THEY WERE *TOO FAR AWAY* TO BE HERE *NOW.*
MASTER! WE'RE UNDER ATTACK BY THE QUINJET!
PERHAPS SOME THINGS *DO* MATTER-- LIKE *HEROISM,* AND *LOYALTY!*
REPTYL, USE YOUR *PIRATICAL* SKILLS AND *DESTROY* THOSE FLEAS.
I'LL DESTROY *QUOI.*

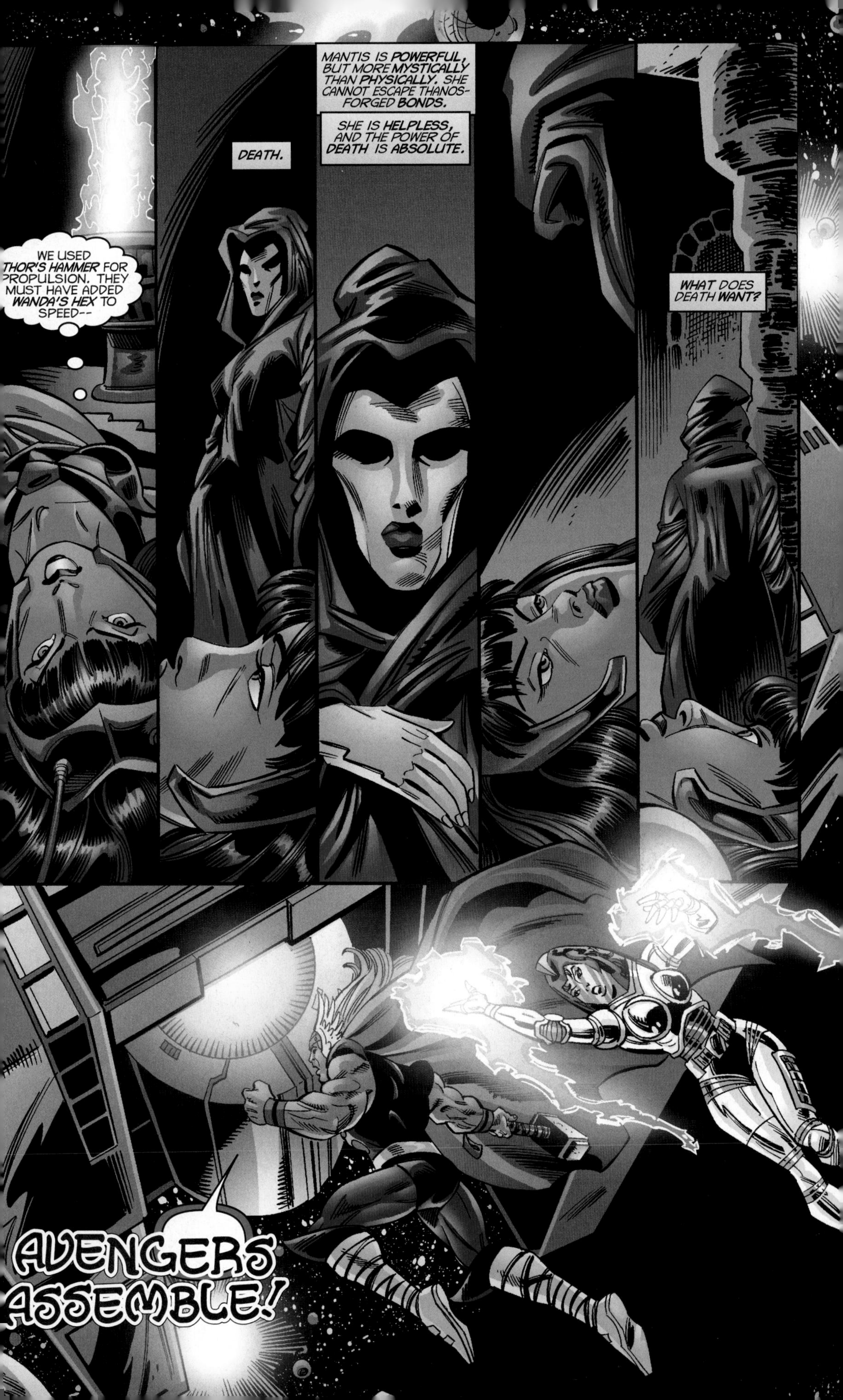
WE USED THOR'S HAMMER FOR PROPULSION. THEY MUST HAVE ADDED WANDA'S HEX TO SPEED--
DEATH.
MANTIS IS POWERFUL, BUT MORE MYSTICALLY THAN PHYSICALLY. SHE CANNOT ESCAPE THANOS-FORGED BONDS.
SHE IS HELPLESS, AND THE POWER OF DEATH IS ABSOLUTE.
WHAT DOES DEATH WANT?
AVENGERS ASSEMBLE!

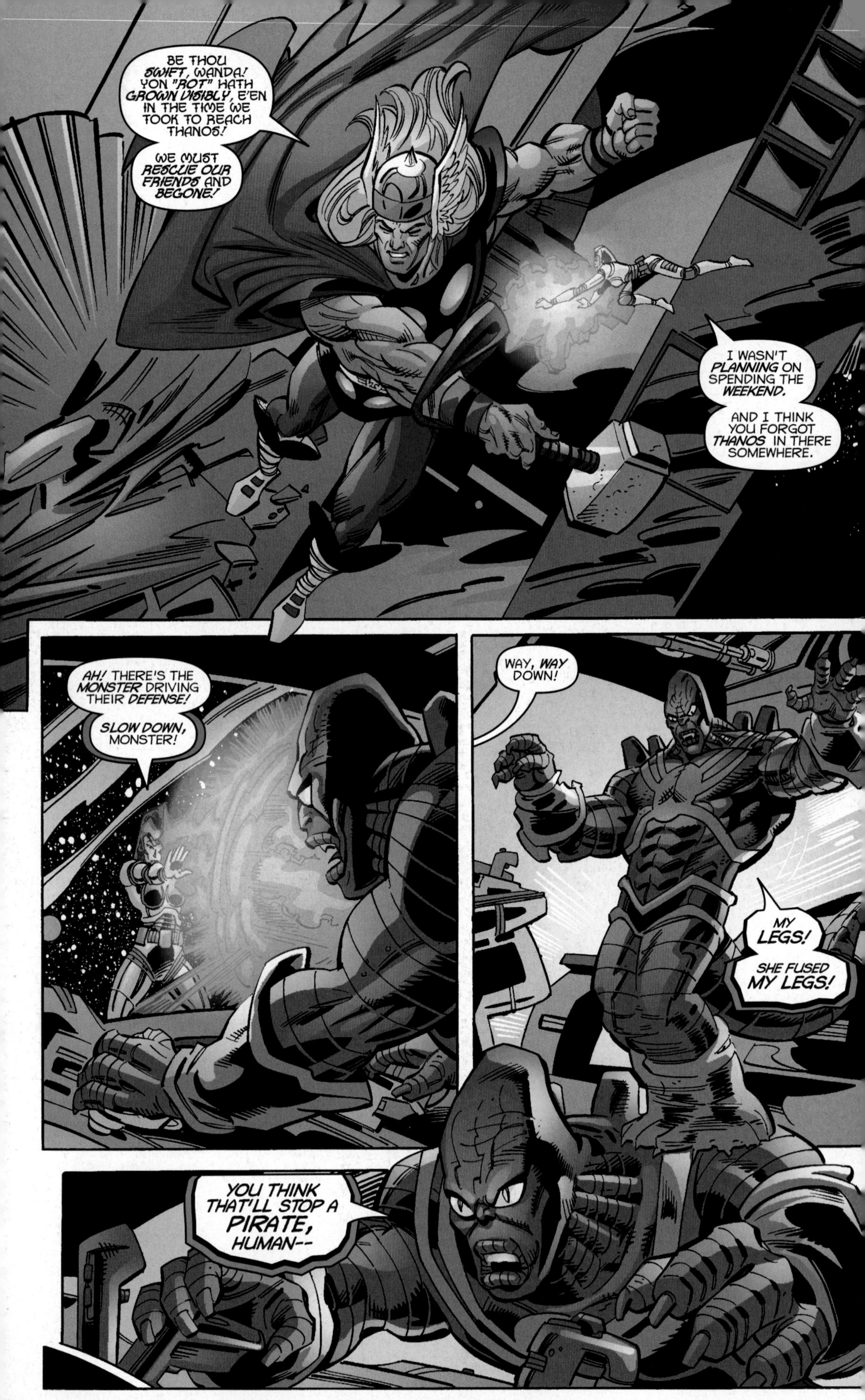
BE THOU SWIFT, WANDA! YON "ROT" HATH GROWN VISIBLY, E'EN IN THE TIME WE TOOK TO REACH THANOS!
WE MUST RESCUE OUR FRIENDS AND BEGONE!
I WASN'T PLANNING ON SPENDING THE WEEKEND.
AND I THINK YOU FORGOT THANOS IN THERE SOMEWHERE.
AH! THERE'S THE MONSTER DRIVING THEIR DEFENSE!
SLOW DOWN, MONSTER!
WAY, WAY DOWN!
MY LEGS!
SHE FUSED MY LEGS!
YOU THINK THAT'LL STOP A PIRATE, HUMAN--

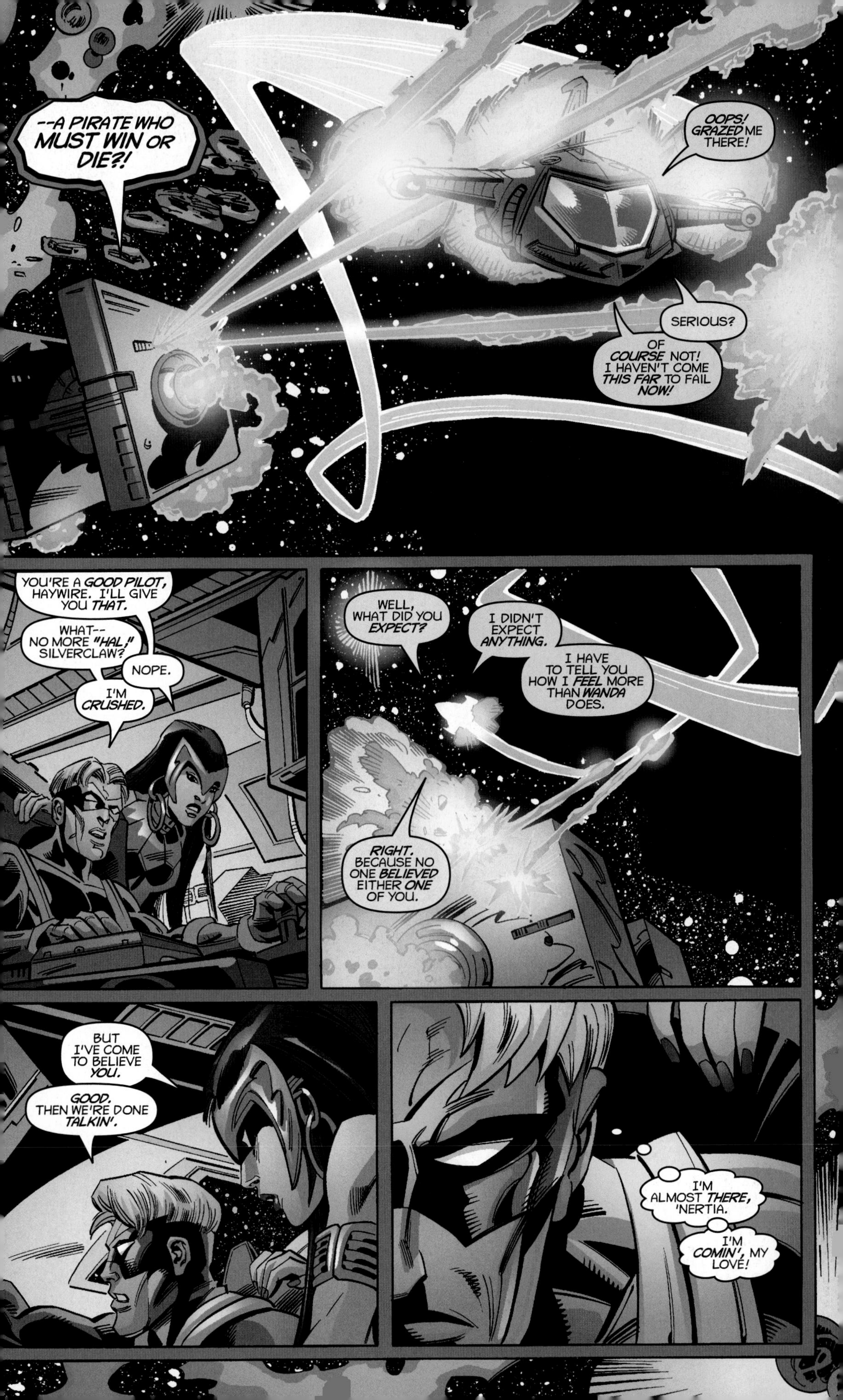

--A PIRATE WHO MUST WIN OR DIE?!
OOPS! GRAZED ME THERE!
SERIOUS?
OF COURSE NOT! I HAVEN'T COME THIS FAR TO FAIL NOW!
YOU'RE A GOOD PILOT, HAYWIRE. I'LL GIVE YOU THAT.
WHAT-- NO MORE "HAL," SILVERCLAW?
NOPE.
I'M CRUSHED.
WELL, WHAT DID YOU EXPECT?
I DIDN'T EXPECT ANYTHING.
I HAVE TO TELL YOU HOW I FEEL MORE THAN WANDA DOES.
RIGHT. BECAUSE NO ONE BELIEVED EITHER ONE OF YOU.
BUT I'VE COME TO BELIEVE YOU.
GOOD. THEN WE'RE DONE TALKIN'.
I'M ALMOST THERE, 'NERTIA.
I'M COMIN', MY LOVE!

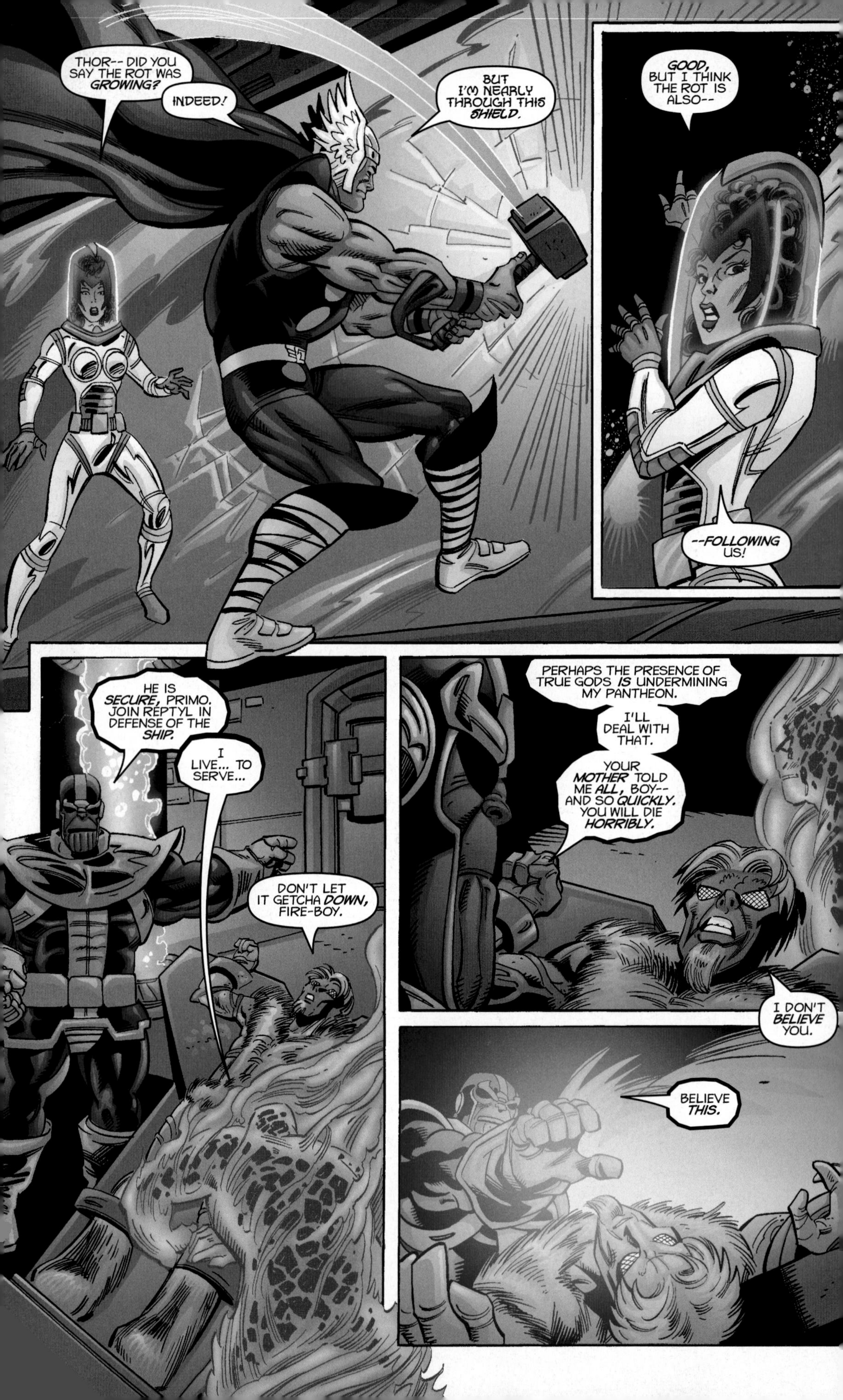
THOR-- DID YOU SAY THE ROT WAS GROWING?
INDEED!
BUT I'M NEARLY THROUGH THIS SHIELD.
GOOD, BUT I THINK THE ROT IS ALSO--
--FOLLOWING US!
HE IS SECURE, PRIMO. JOIN REPTYL IN DEFENSE OF THE SHIP.
I LIVE... TO SERVE...
DON'T LET IT GETCHA DOWN, FIRE-BOY.
PERHAPS THE PRESENCE OF TRUE GODS IS UNDERMINING MY PANTHEON.
I'LL DEAL WITH THAT.
YOUR MOTHER TOLD ME ALL, BOY-- AND SO QUICKLY. YOU WILL DIE HORRIBLY.
I DON'T BELIEVE YOU.
BELIEVE THIS.

GOT IT!

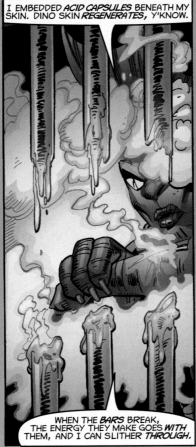

I EMBEDDED *ACID CAPSULES* BENEATH MY SKIN. DINO SKIN *REGENERATES,* Y'KNOW.

WHEN THE *BARS* BREAK, THE ENERGY THEY MAKE GOES *WITH* THEM, AND I CAN SLITHER *THROUGH.*

I DON'T HAVE ANY ACID FOR *YOUR* CELL, BUT I NEED YOU TO SAVE *QUOI,* SO JUST HOLD TIGHT.

BE CAREFUL!

YEAH. "CAREFUL"-- MY *MIDDLE* NAME.

GUARD! HEY, GUA-ARD!

SHUT UP IN THERE! WE HAVEN'T GOT *TIME* FOR Y--

HEY!

YOU'RE *OUT!*

THANOS USES GUYS LIKE YOU FOR YOUR *BRAINS,* HUH?

NO! BLOODLUST!

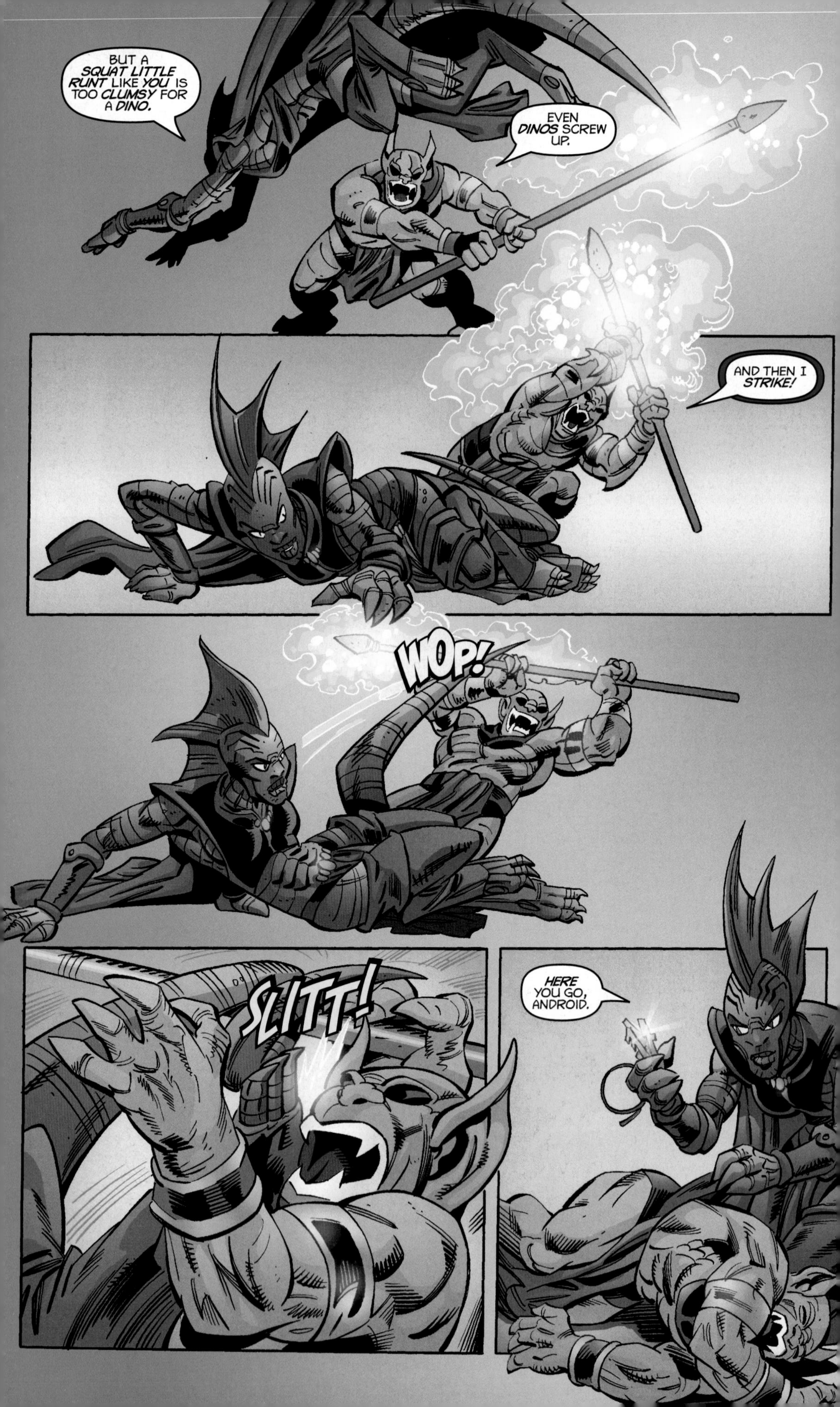
BUT A SQUAT LITTLE RUNT LIKE YOU IS TOO CLUMSY FOR A DINO.
EVEN DINOS SCREW UP.
AND THEN I STRIKE!
WOP!
SLITT!
HERE YOU GO, ANDROID.

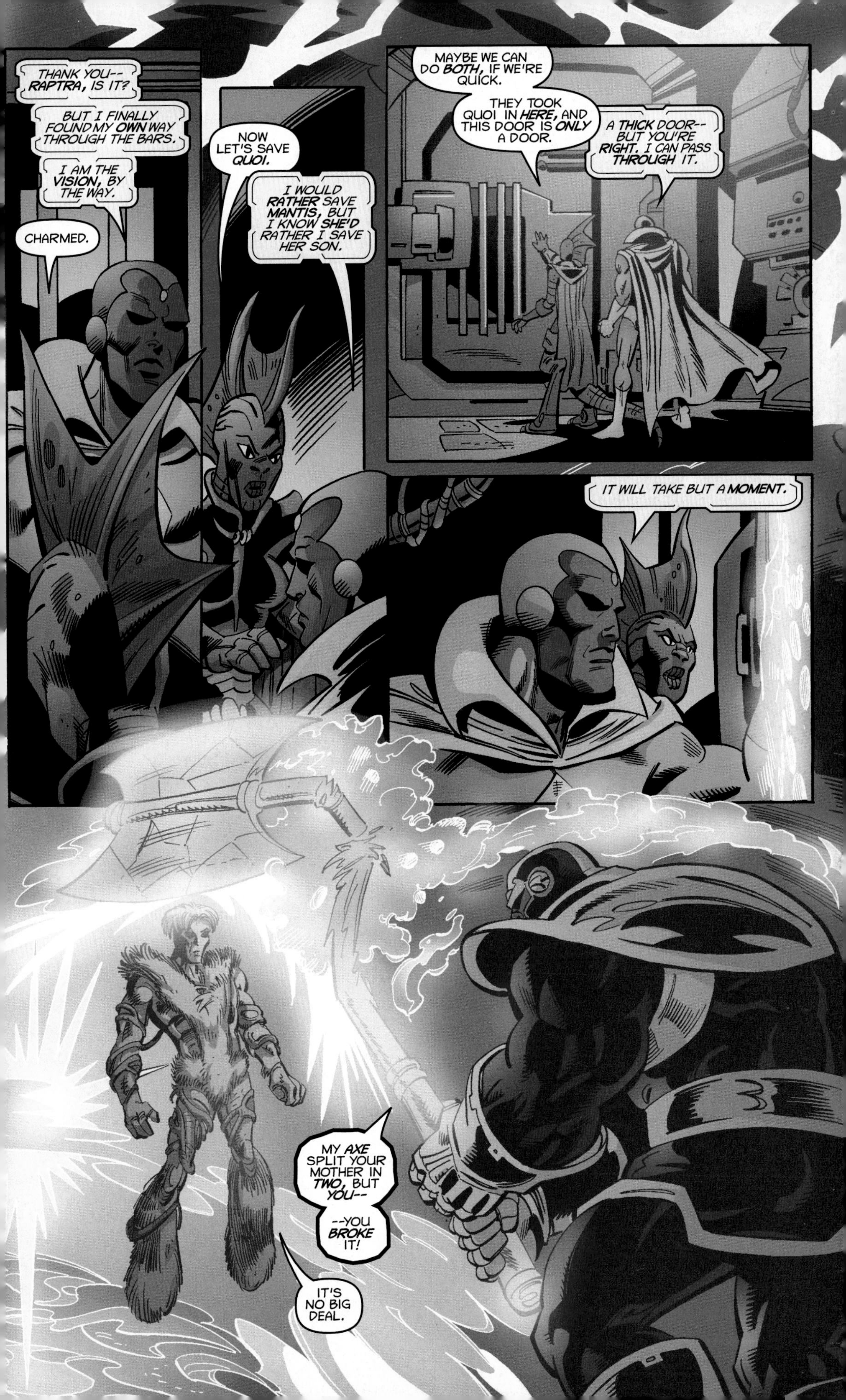
THANK YOU--RAPTRA, IS IT?
BUT I FINALLY FOUND MY OWN WAY THROUGH THE BARS.
I AM THE VISION, BY THE WAY.
CHARMED.
NOW LET'S SAVE QUOI.
I WOULD RATHER SAVE MANTIS, BUT I KNOW SHE'D RATHER I SAVE HER SON.
MAYBE WE CAN DO BOTH, IF WE'RE QUICK.
THEY TOOK QUOI IN HERE, AND THIS DOOR IS ONLY A DOOR.
A THICK DOOR--BUT YOU'RE RIGHT. I CAN PASS THROUGH IT.
IT WILL TAKE BUT A MOMENT.
MY AXE SPLIT YOUR MOTHER IN TWO, BUT YOU--
--YOU BROKE IT!
IT'S NO BIG DEAL.

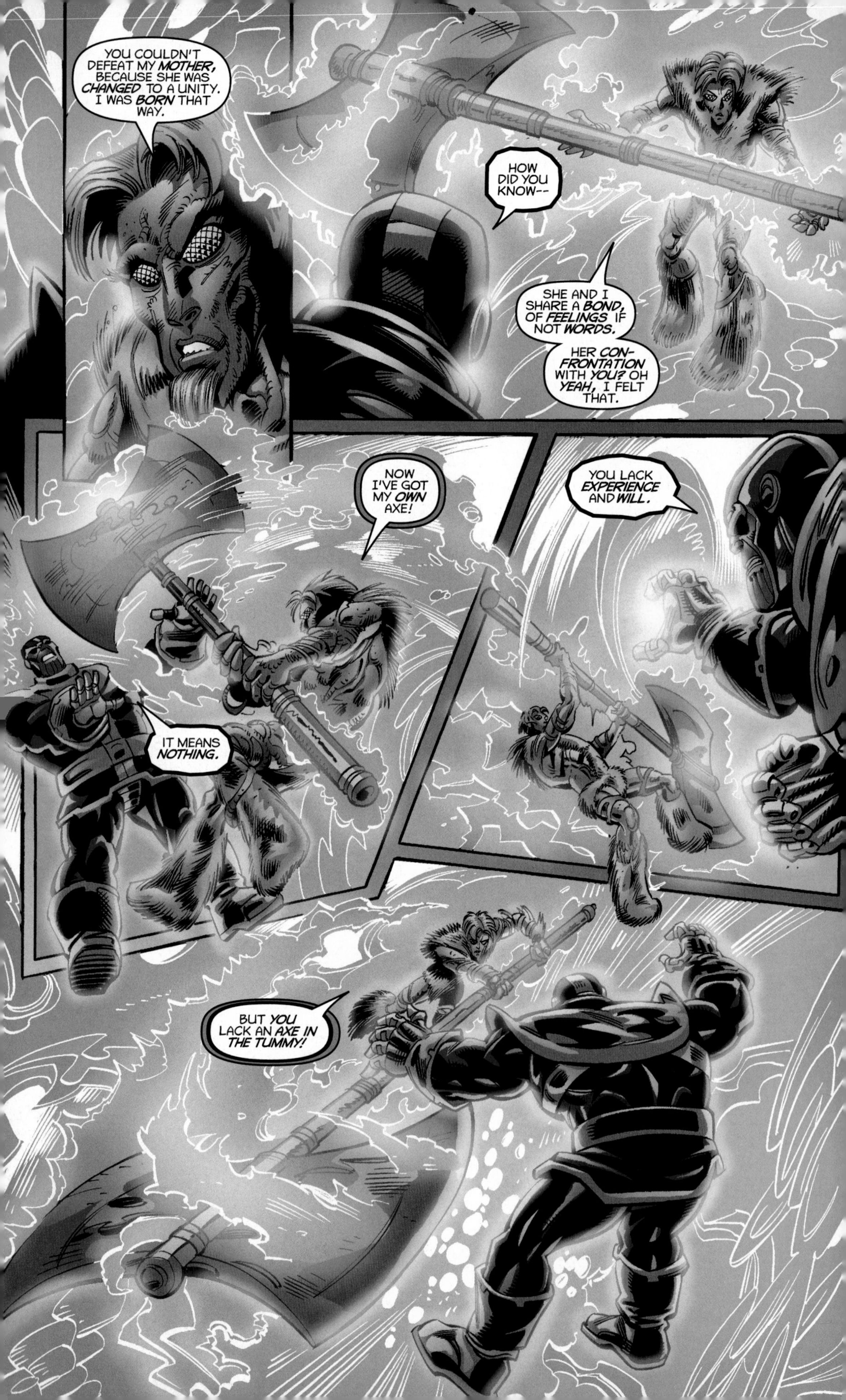

YOU COULDN'T DEFEAT MY *MOTHER*, BECAUSE SHE WAS *CHANGED* TO A UNITY. I WAS *BORN* THAT WAY.
HOW DID YOU KNOW--
SHE AND I SHARE A *BOND*, OF *FEELINGS* IF NOT *WORDS*.
HER *CONFRONTATION* WITH *YOU?* OH *YEAH*, I FELT THAT.
NOW I'VE GOT MY *OWN* AXE!
IT MEANS *NOTHING*.
YOU LACK *EXPERIENCE* AND *WILL*.
BUT *YOU* LACK AN *AXE IN THE TUMMY!*

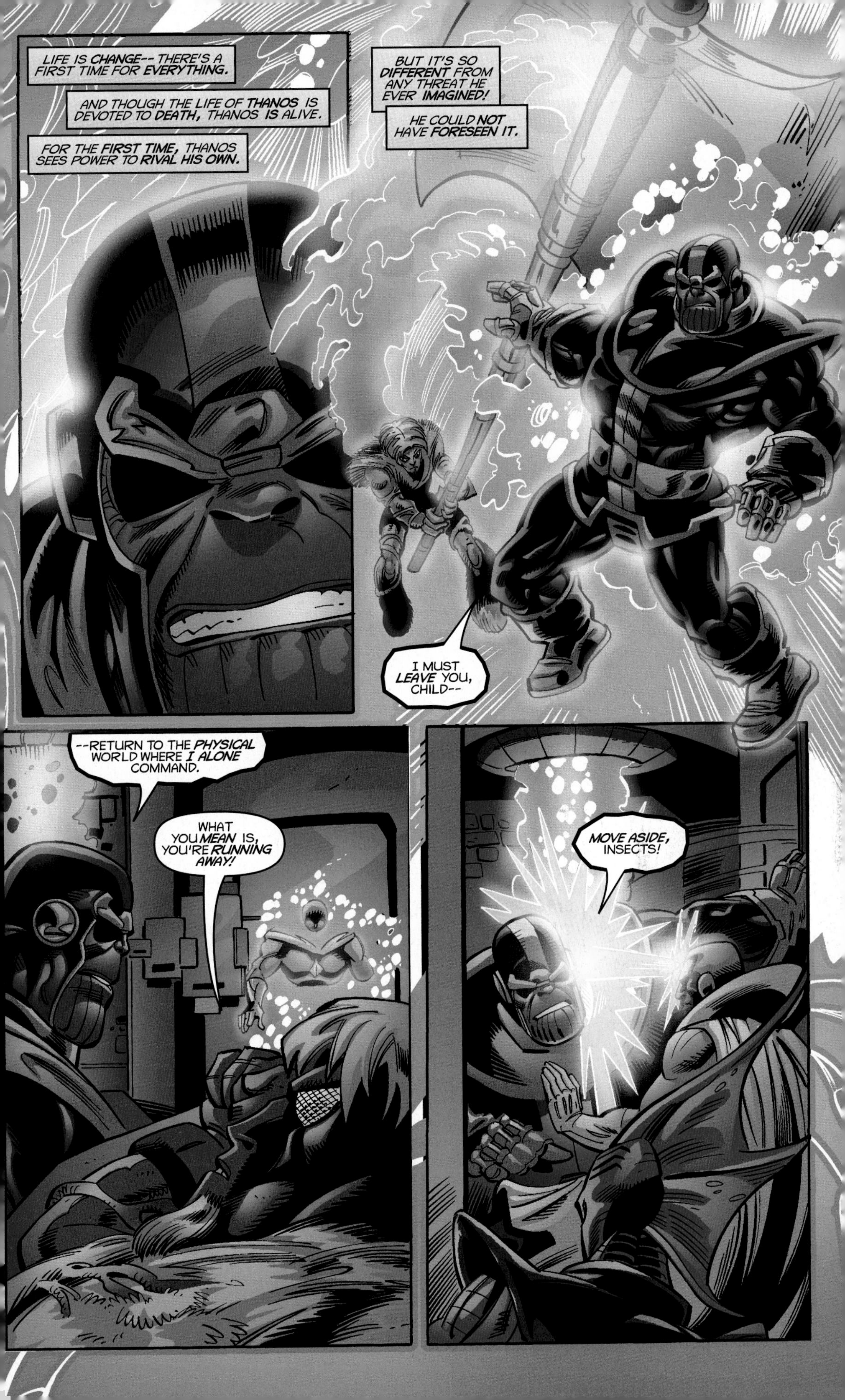

LIFE IS CHANGE-- THERE'S A FIRST TIME FOR EVERYTHING.
AND THOUGH THE LIFE OF THANOS IS DEVOTED TO DEATH, THANOS IS ALIVE.
FOR THE FIRST TIME, THANOS SEES POWER TO RIVAL HIS OWN.
BUT IT'S SO DIFFERENT FROM ANY THREAT HE EVER IMAGINED!
HE COULD NOT HAVE FORESEEN IT.
I MUST LEAVE YOU, CHILD--
--RETURN TO THE PHYSICAL WORLD WHERE I ALONE COMMAND.
WHAT YOU MEAN IS, YOU'RE RUNNING AWAY!
MOVE ASIDE, INSECTS!

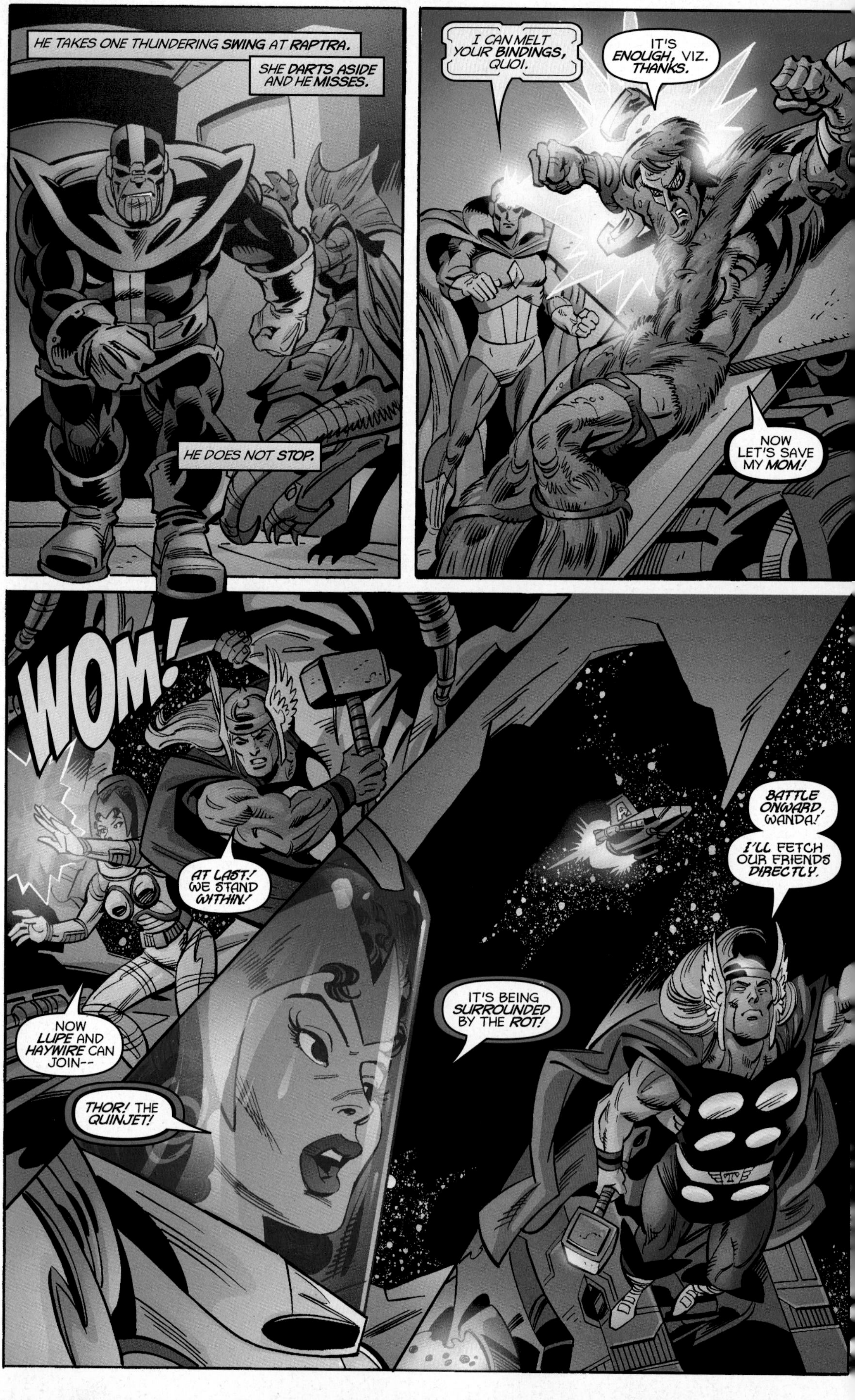
HE TAKES ONE THUNDERING SWING AT RAPTRA.
SHE DARTS ASIDE AND HE MISSES.
HE DOES NOT STOP.
I CAN MELT YOUR BINDINGS, QUOI.
IT'S ENOUGH, VIZ. THANKS.
NOW LET'S SAVE MY MOM!
WOM!
AT LAST! WE STAND WITHIN!
NOW LUPE AND HAYWIRE CAN JOIN--
THOR! THE QUINJET!
IT'S BEING SURROUNDED BY THE ROT!
BATTLE ONWARD, WANDA!
I'LL FETCH OUR FRIENDS DIRECTLY.

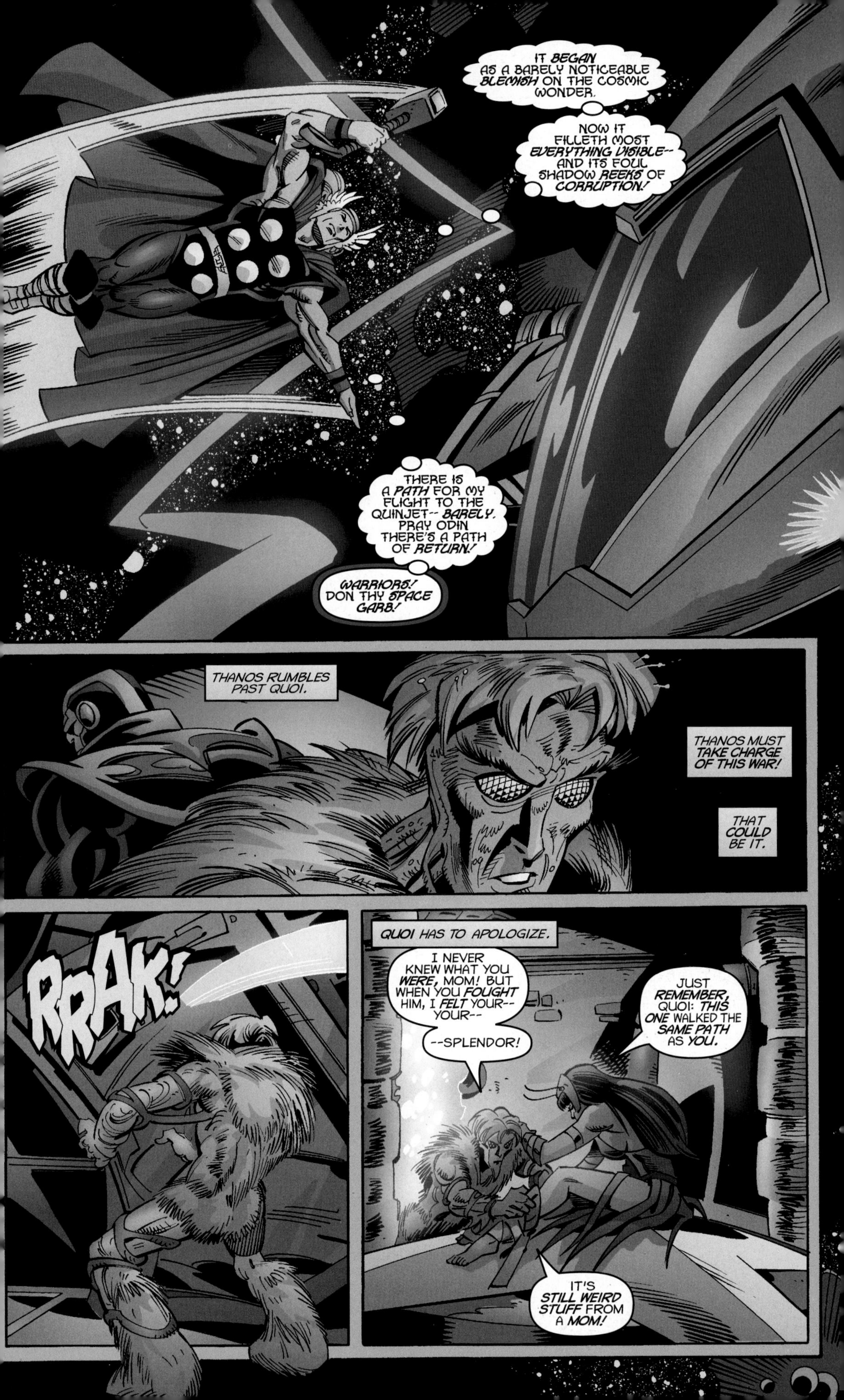
IT BEGAN AS A BARELY NOTICEABLE BLEMISH ON THE COSMIC WONDER.
NOW IT FILLETH MOST EVERYTHING VISIBLE-- AND ITS FOUL SHADOW REEKS OF CORRUPTION!
THERE IS A PATH FOR MY FLIGHT TO THE QUINJET-- BARELY. PRAY ODIN THERE'S A PATH OF RETURN!
WARRIORS! DON THY SPACE GARB!
THANOS RUMBLES PAST QUOI.
THANOS MUST TAKE CHARGE OF THIS WAR!
THAT COULD BE IT.
RRAK!
QUOI HAS TO APOLOGIZE.
I NEVER KNEW WHAT YOU WERE, MOM! BUT WHEN YOU FOUGHT HIM, I FELT YOUR-- YOUR--
--SPLENDOR!
JUST REMEMBER, QUOI: THIS ONE WALKED THE SAME PATH AS YOU.
IT'S STILL WEIRD STUFF FROM A MOM!

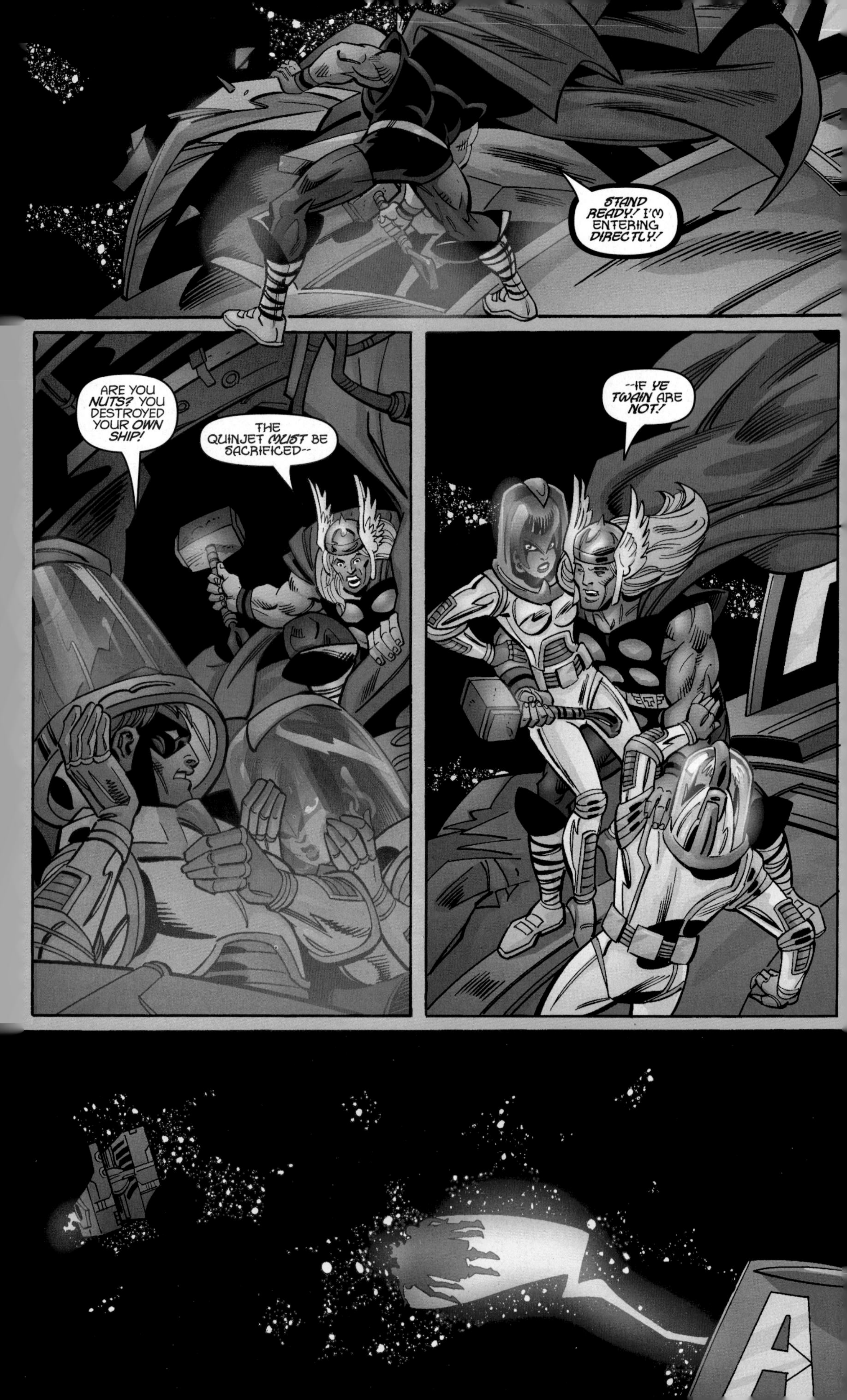
STAND READY! I'M ENTERING DIRECTLY!
ARE YOU NUTS? YOU DESTROYED YOUR OWN SHIP!
THE QUINJET MUST BE SACRIFICED--
--IF YE TWAIN ARE NOT!

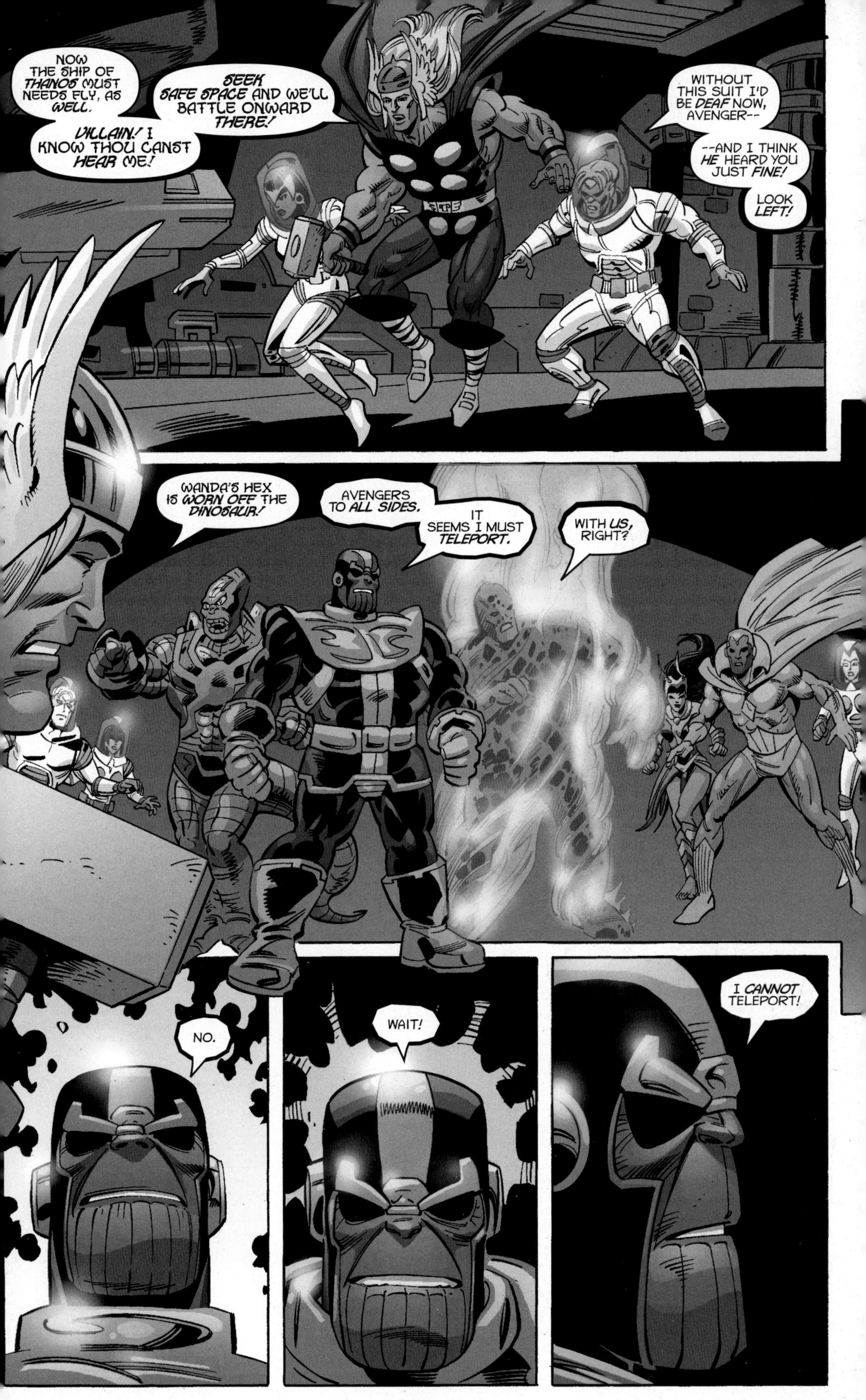
NOW THE SHIP OF THANOS MUST NEEDS FLY, AS WELL.
VILLAIN! I KNOW THOU CANST HEAR ME!
SEEK SAFE SPACE AND WE'LL BATTLE ONWARD THERE!
WITHOUT THIS SUIT I'D BE DEAF NOW, AVENGER--
--AND I THINK HE HEARD YOU JUST FINE!
LOOK LEFT!
WANDA'S HEX IS WORN OFF THE DINOSAUR!
AVENGERS TO ALL SIDES.
IT SEEMS I MUST TELEPORT.
WITH US, RIGHT?
NO.
WAIT!
I CANNOT TELEPORT!

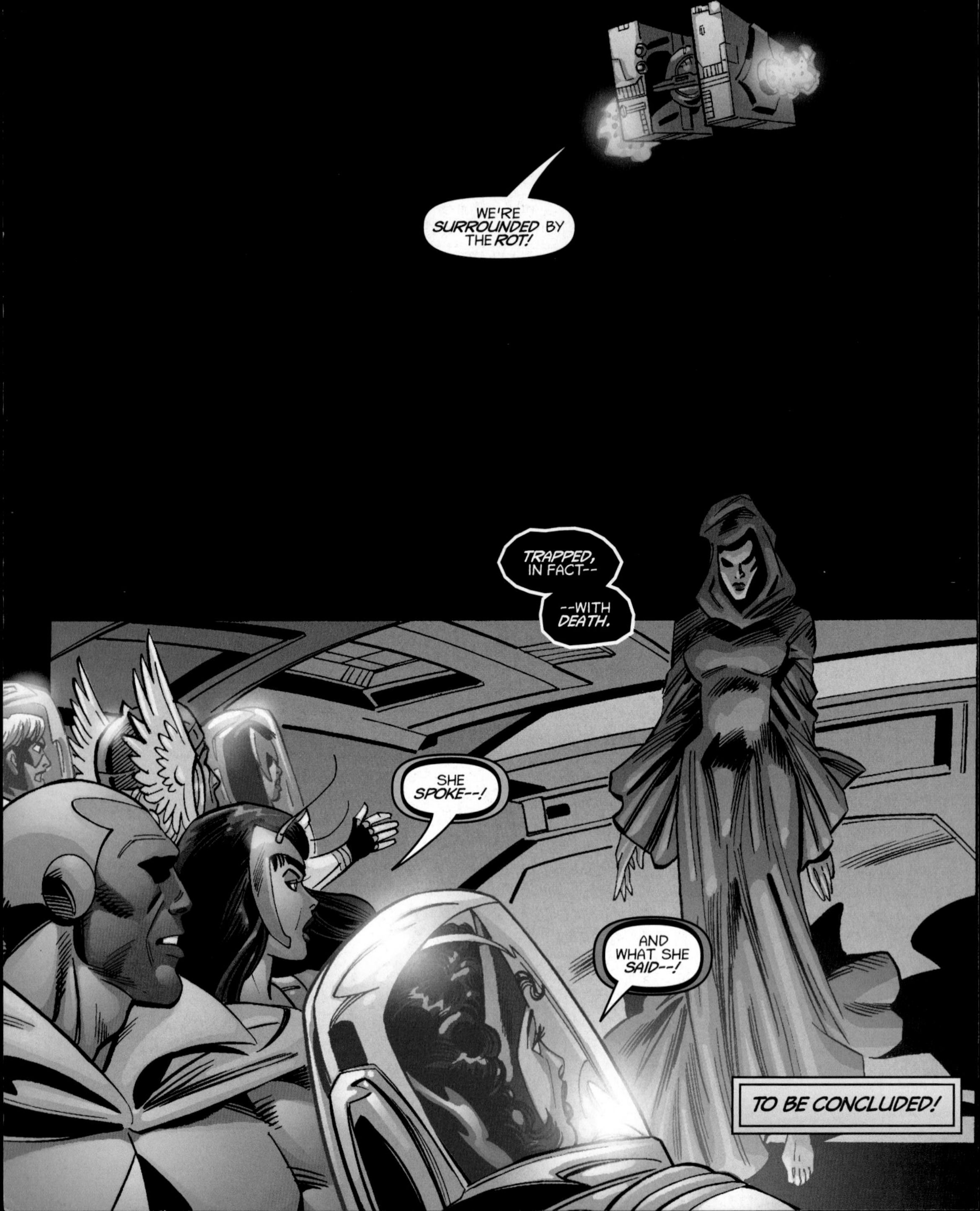
WE'RE SURROUNDED BY THE ROT!
TRAPPED, IN FACT--
--WITH DEATH.
SHE SPOKE--!
AND WHAT SHE SAID--!
TO BE CONCLUDED!

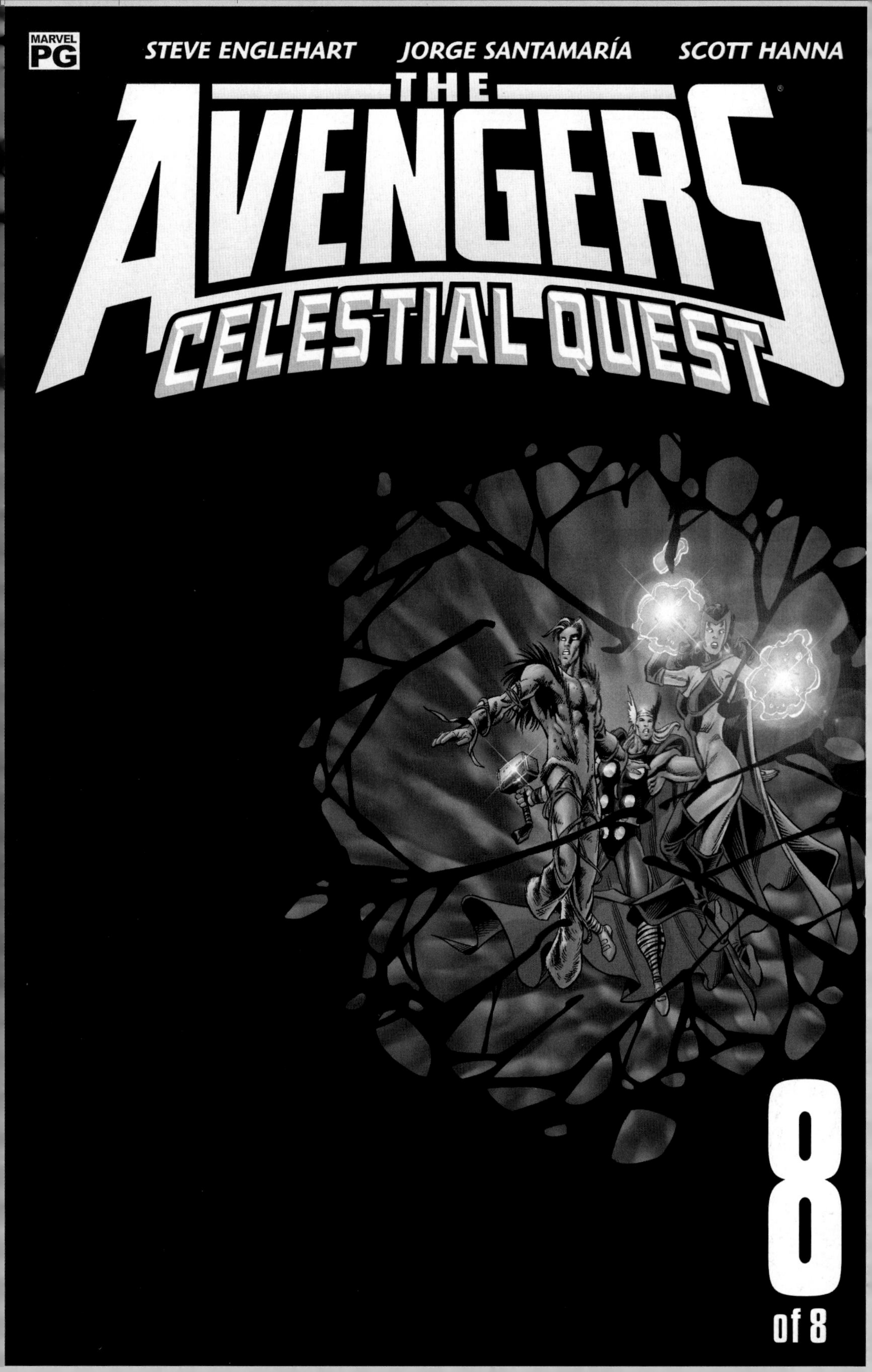
MARVEL PG
STEVE ENGLEHART
JORGE SANTAMARÍA
SCOTT HANNA
THE
AVENGERS
CELESTIAL QUEST
8
of 8

MANTIS! TRAINED ALMOST FROM BIRTH TO BE THE SUPREME EXAMPLE OF HUMANITY -- PHYSICALLY PERFECT, MENTALLY EXALTED! HER MIND WIPED BY THE PRIESTS OF PAMA, SHE WORKED AS A BAR GIRL, LIVING AMONG HUMANITY AT ITS WORST. THERE SHE MET THE BURNT-OUT **SWORDSMAN**, AND BEGAN A TWISTING JOURNEY THAT TOOK HER FIRST TO THE **AVENGERS**, AND THEN TO THE **UNIVERSE** -- AS MANTIS BECAME THE **CELESTIAL MADONNA**!

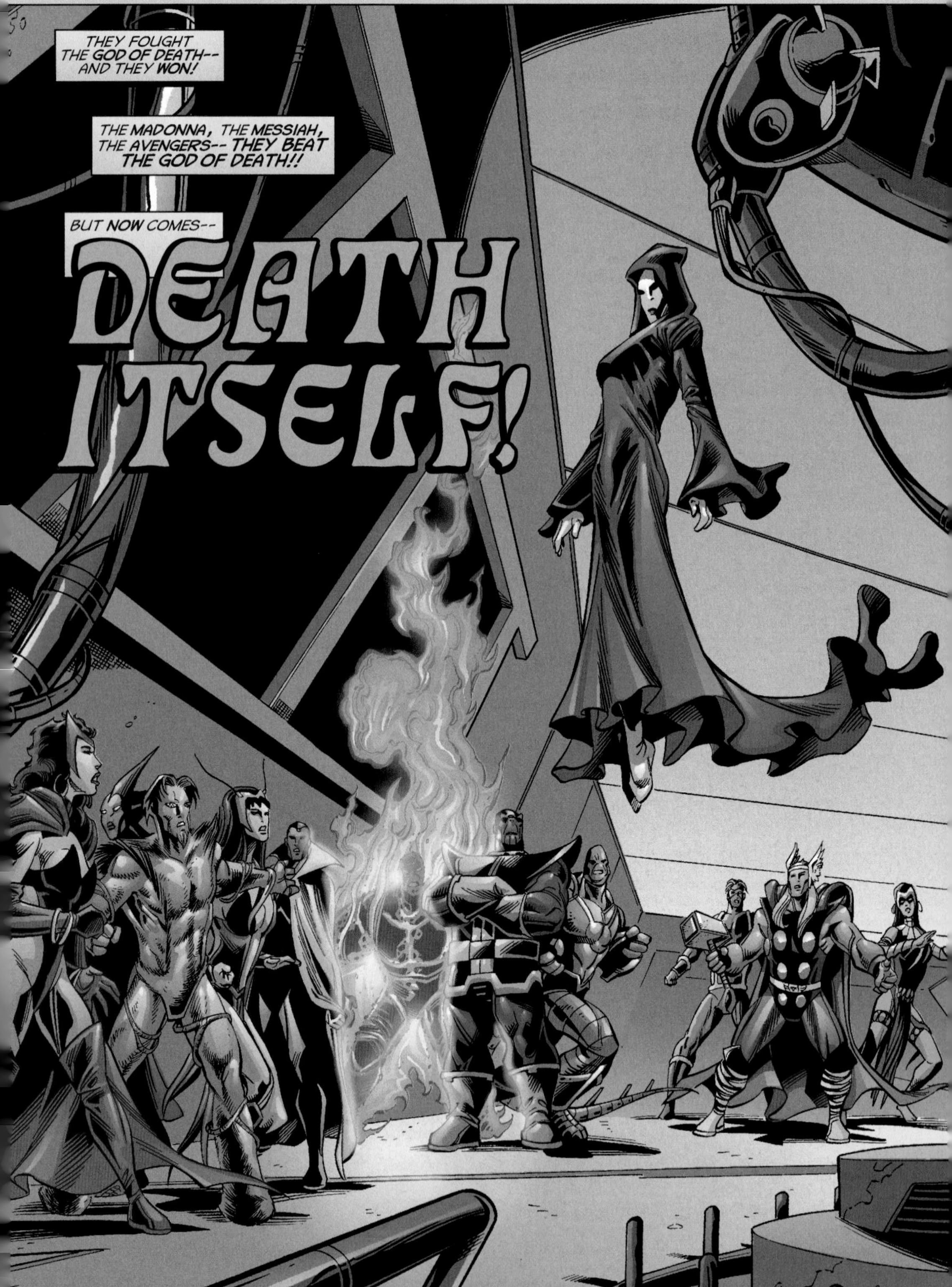
THEY FOUGHT THE GOD OF DEATH-- AND THEY WON!
THE MADONNA, THE MESSIAH, THE AVENGERS-- THEY BEAT THE GOD OF DEATH!!
BUT NOW COMES--
DEATH ITSELF!

STAINLESS STEVE ENGLEHART • AUTHOR   JORGE SANTAMARÍA, EL VALIENTE • PENCIL ARTIST
SCOTT HANNA • INK ARTIST   HIFI DESIGN • COLORIST   PAUL TUTRONE • LETTERER
MARC SUMERAK • ASSISTANT EDITOR   TOM BREVOORT • EDITOR   JOE QUESADA • EDITOR IN CHIEF
BILL JEMAS • PRESIDENT   JAMMIN' JIM STARLIN • CREATOR OF THANOS
FOR JIM, AL, FRANK, AND JAN.

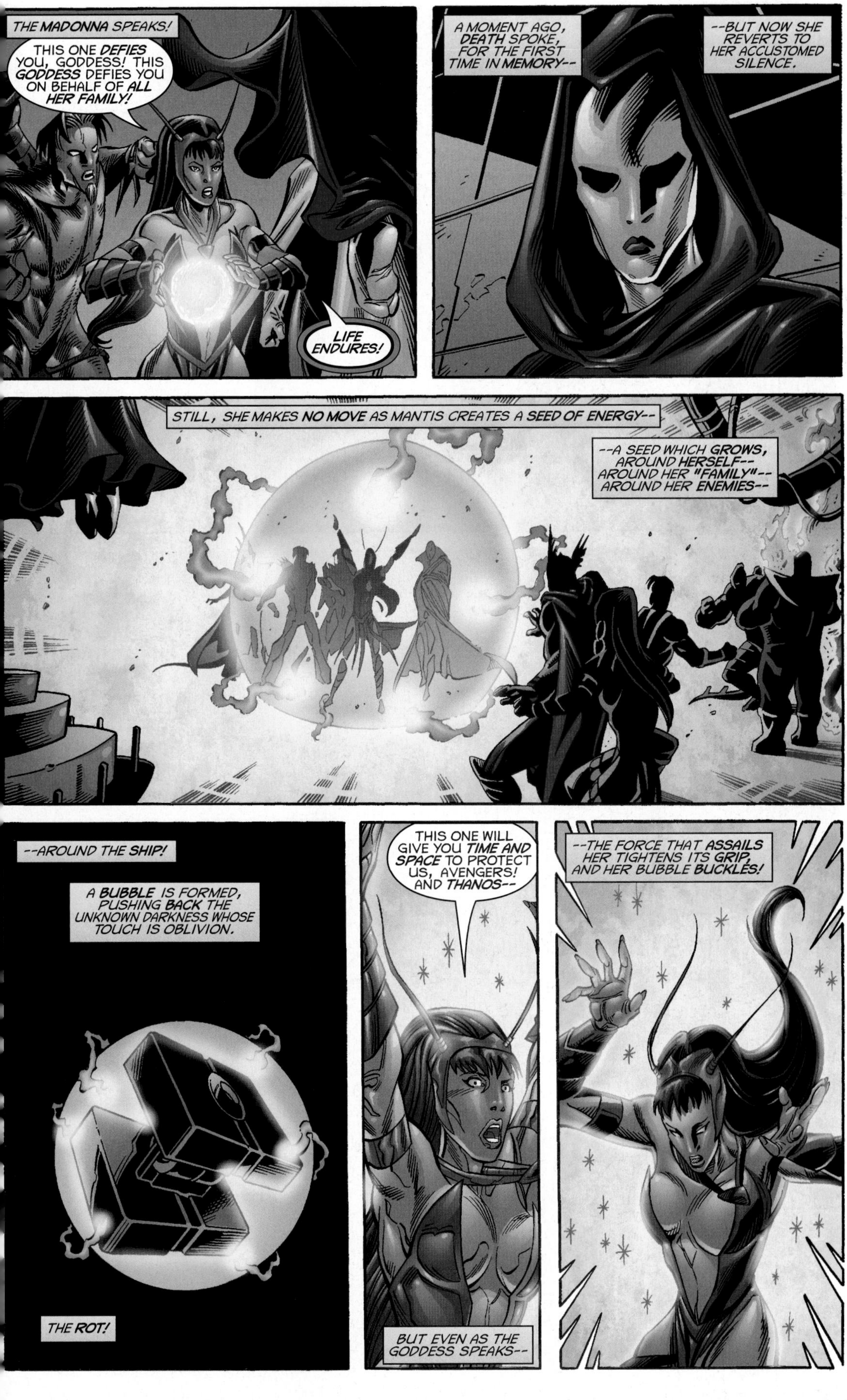
THE MADONNA SPEAKS!
THIS ONE DEFIES YOU, GODDESS! THIS GODDESS DEFIES YOU ON BEHALF OF ALL HER FAMILY!
LIFE ENDURES!
A MOMENT AGO, DEATH SPOKE, FOR THE FIRST TIME IN MEMORY--
--BUT NOW SHE REVERTS TO HER ACCUSTOMED SILENCE.
STILL, SHE MAKES NO MOVE AS MANTIS CREATES A SEED OF ENERGY--
--A SEED WHICH GROWS, AROUND HERSELF-- AROUND HER "FAMILY"-- AROUND HER ENEMIES--
--AROUND THE SHIP!
A BUBBLE IS FORMED, PUSHING BACK THE UNKNOWN DARKNESS WHOSE TOUCH IS OBLIVION.
THE ROT!
THIS ONE WILL GIVE YOU TIME AND SPACE TO PROTECT US, AVENGERS! AND THANOS--
BUT EVEN AS THE GODDESS SPEAKS--
--THE FORCE THAT ASSAILS HER TIGHTENS ITS GRIP, AND HER BUBBLE BUCKLES!

JUST FOR A MOMENT...

THE ROT'S THRUSTING *INTO THE SHIP!*

PRIMO--

--GET THE HELL AWAY FROM ME!

ARRRRr!!

BACK, FREAK OF NATURE!

PRIMO-- DISINTEGRATED, WITH *ONE TOUCH!*

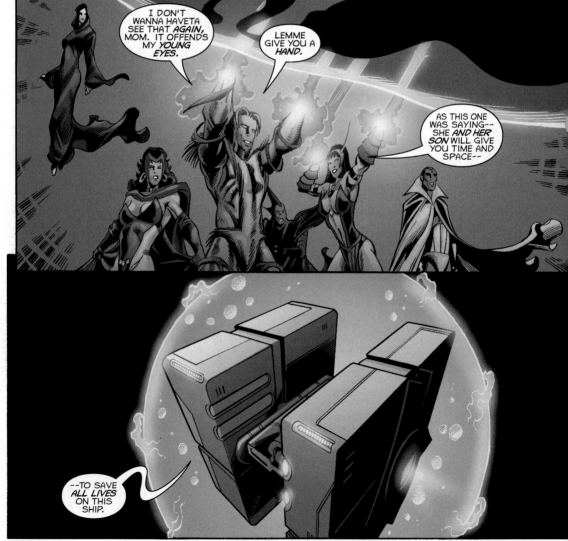

I DON'T WANNA HAVETA SEE THAT *AGAIN,* MOM. IT OFFENDS MY *YOUNG EYES.*

LEMME GIVE YOU A *HAND.*

AS THIS ONE WAS SAYING-- SHE *AND HER SON* WILL GIVE YOU TIME AND SPACE--

--TO SAVE *ALL LIVES* ON THIS SHIP.

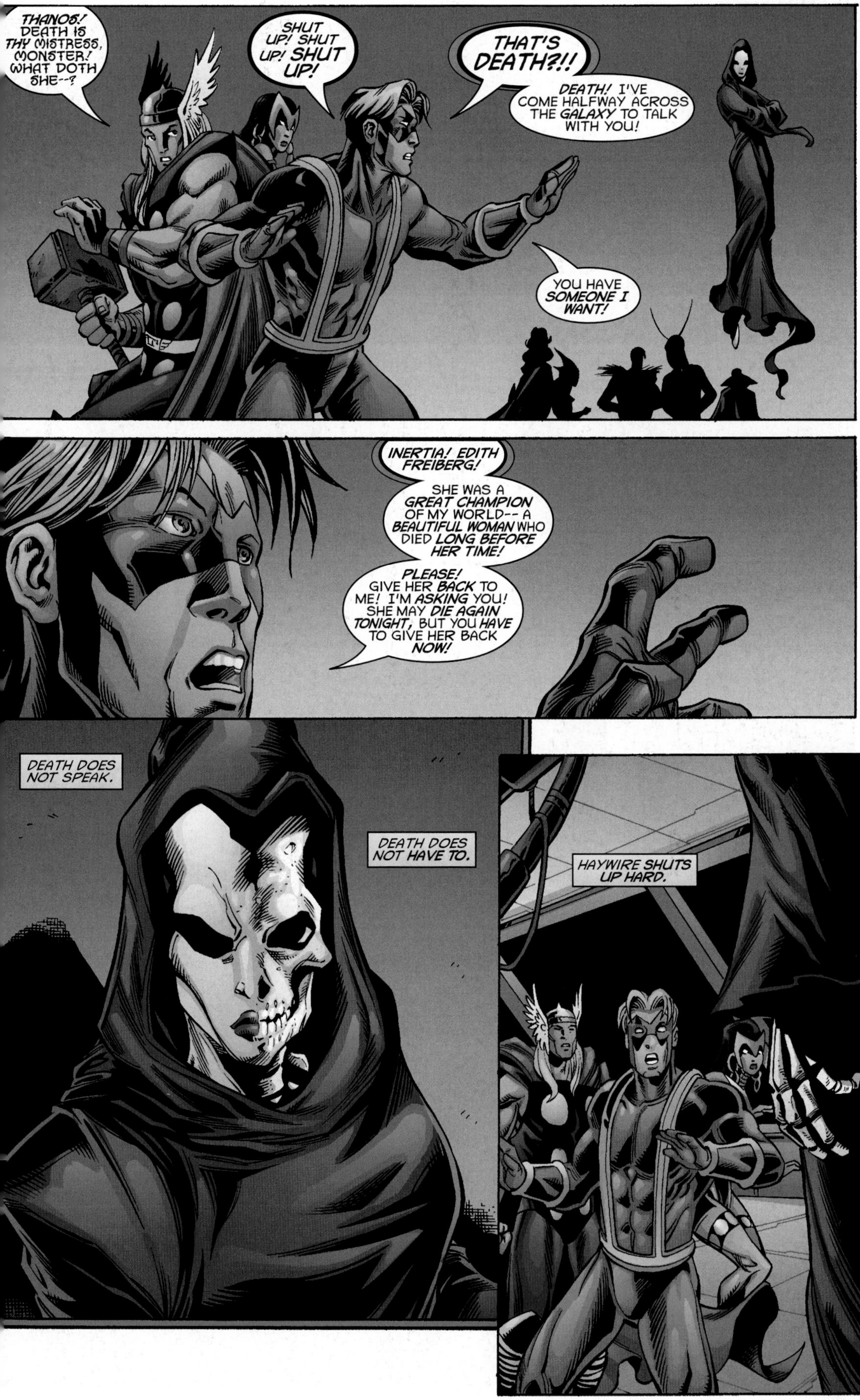
THANOS! DEATH IS THY MISTRESS, MONSTER! WHAT DOTH SHE--?
SHUT UP! SHUT UP! SHUT UP!
THAT'S DEATH?!!
DEATH! I'VE COME HALFWAY ACROSS THE GALAXY TO TALK WITH YOU!
YOU HAVE SOMEONE I WANT!
INERTIA! EDITH FREIBERG!
SHE WAS A GREAT CHAMPION OF MY WORLD-- A BEAUTIFUL WOMAN WHO DIED LONG BEFORE HER TIME!
PLEASE! GIVE HER BACK TO ME! I'M ASKING YOU! SHE MAY DIE AGAIN TONIGHT, BUT YOU HAVE TO GIVE HER BACK NOW!
DEATH DOES NOT SPEAK.
DEATH DOES NOT HAVE TO.
HAYWIRE SHUTS UP HARD.

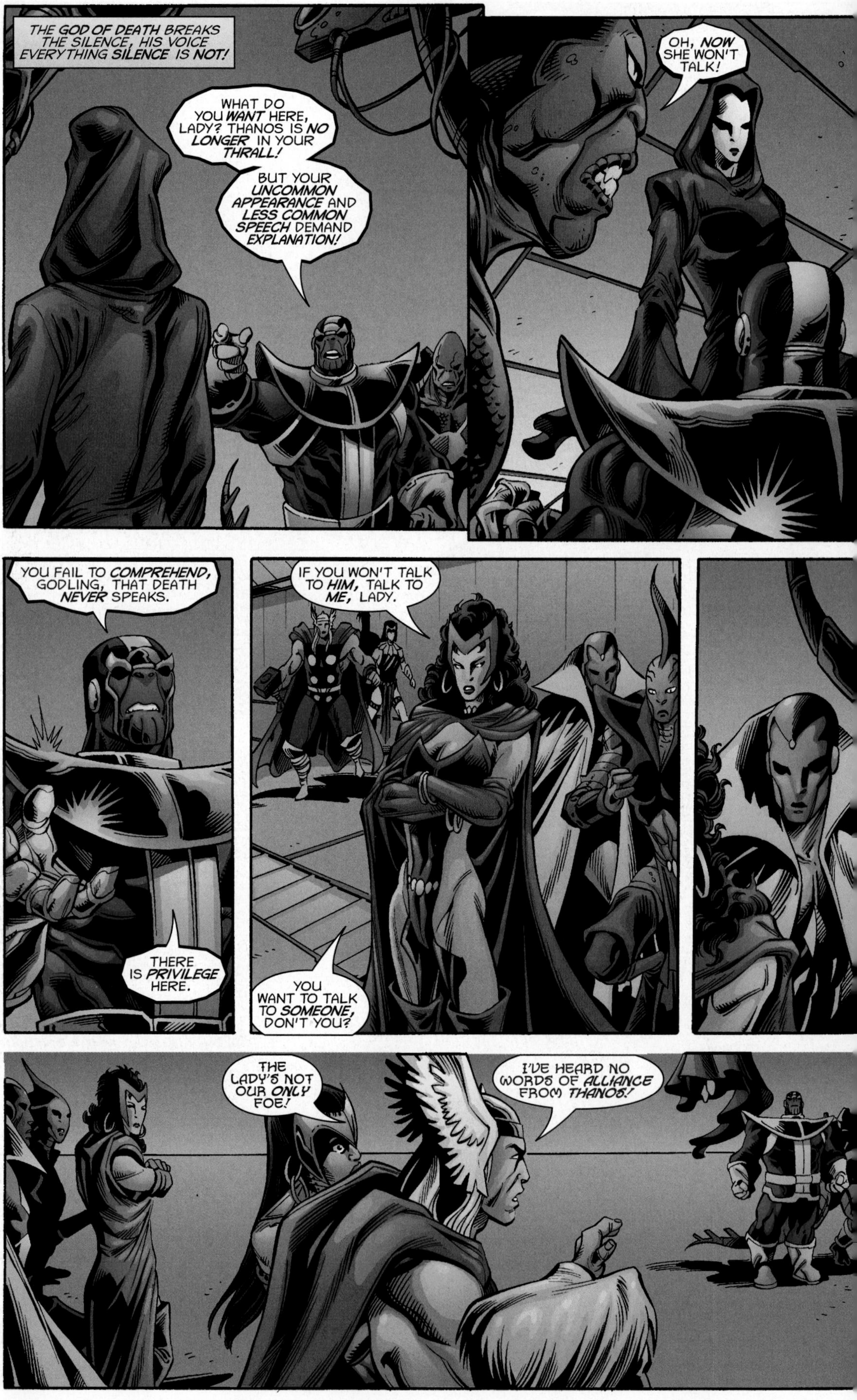
THE GOD OF DEATH BREAKS THE SILENCE, HIS VOICE EVERYTHING SILENCE IS NOT!
WHAT DO YOU WANT HERE, LADY? THANOS IS NO LONGER IN YOUR THRALL!
BUT YOUR UNCOMMON APPEARANCE AND LESS COMMON SPEECH DEMAND EXPLANATION!
OH, NOW SHE WON'T TALK!
YOU FAIL TO COMPREHEND, GODLING, THAT DEATH NEVER SPEAKS.
THERE IS PRIVILEGE HERE.
IF YOU WON'T TALK TO HIM, TALK TO ME, LADY.
YOU WANT TO TALK TO SOMEONE, DON'T YOU?
THE LADY'S NOT OUR ONLY FOE!
I'VE HEARD NO WORDS OF ALLIANCE FROM THANOS!

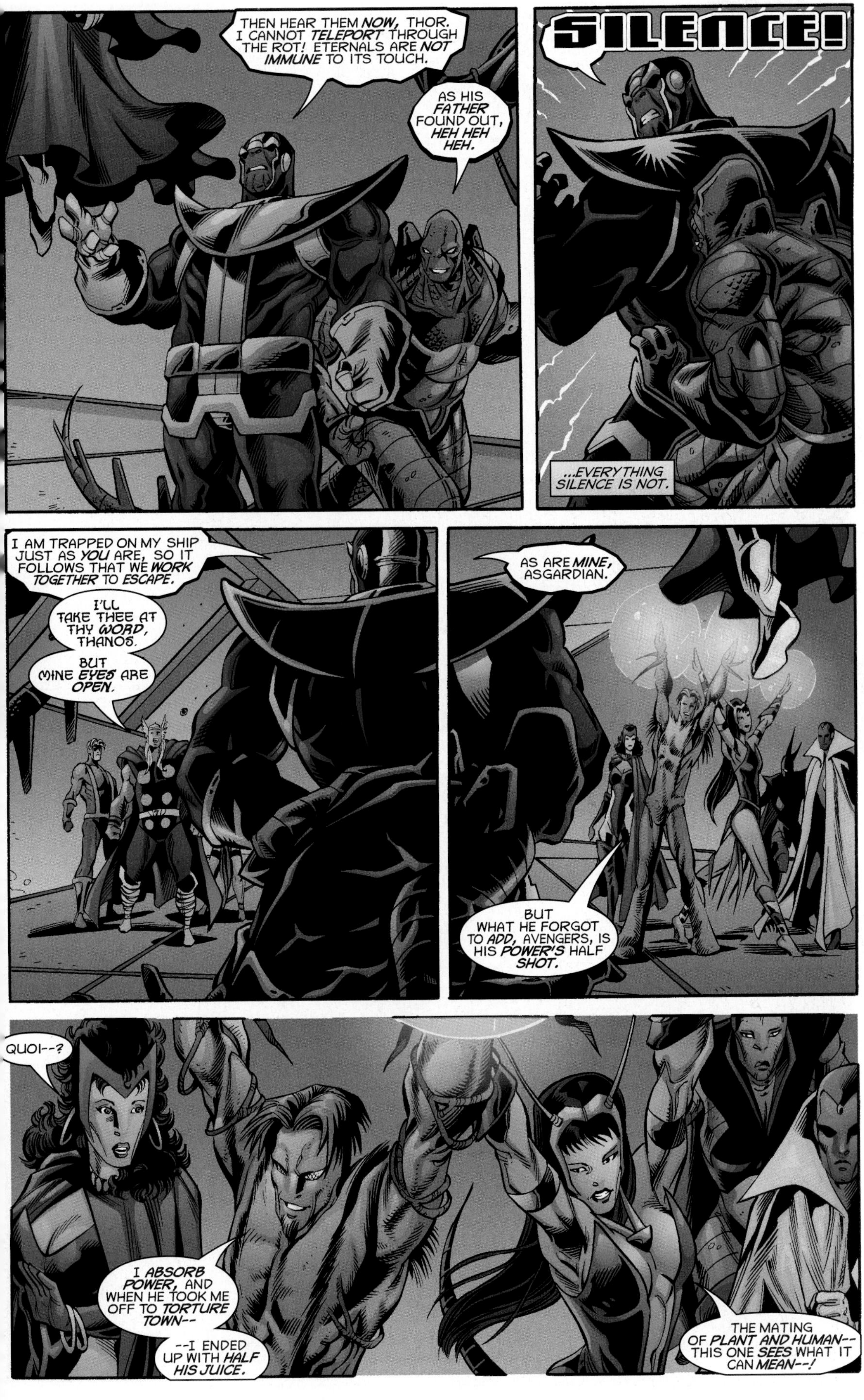
THEN HEAR THEM NOW, THOR. I CANNOT TELEPORT THROUGH THE ROT! ETERNALS ARE NOT IMMUNE TO ITS TOUCH.
AS HIS FATHER FOUND OUT, HEH HEH HEH.
SILENCE!
...EVERYTHING SILENCE IS NOT.
I AM TRAPPED ON MY SHIP JUST AS YOU ARE, SO IT FOLLOWS THAT WE WORK TOGETHER TO ESCAPE.
I'LL TAKE THEE AT THY WORD, THANOS.
BUT MINE EYES ARE OPEN.
AS ARE MINE, ASGARDIAN.
BUT WHAT HE FORGOT TO ADD, AVENGERS, IS HIS POWER'S HALF SHOT.
QUOI--?
I ABSORB POWER, AND WHEN HE TOOK ME OFF TO TORTURE TOWN--
--I ENDED UP WITH HALF HIS JUICE.
THE MATING OF PLANT AND HUMAN-- THIS ONE SEES WHAT IT CAN MEAN--!

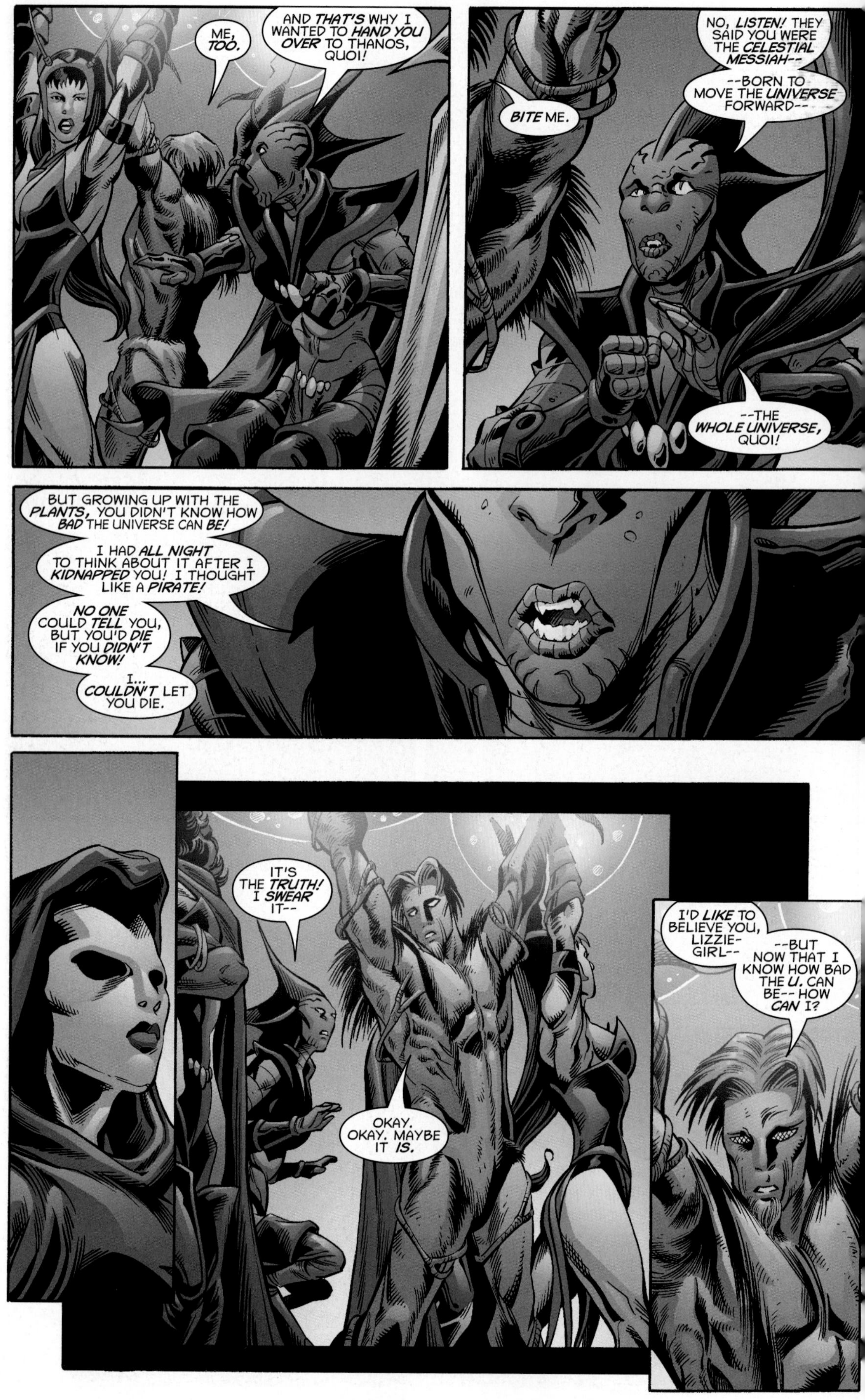
ME, *TOO.*
AND *THAT'S* WHY I WANTED TO *HAND YOU OVER* TO THANOS, QUOI!
NO, *LISTEN!* THEY SAID YOU WERE THE *CELESTIAL MESSIAH--*
BITE ME.
--BORN TO MOVE THE *UNIVERSE* FORWARD--
--THE *WHOLE UNIVERSE,* QUOI!
BUT GROWING UP WITH THE *PLANTS,* YOU DIDN'T KNOW HOW *BAD* THE UNIVERSE CAN *BE!*
I HAD *ALL NIGHT* TO THINK ABOUT IT AFTER I *KIDNAPPED* YOU! I THOUGHT LIKE A *PIRATE!*
NO ONE COULD *TELL* YOU, BUT YOU'D *DIE* IF YOU *DIDN'T KNOW!*
I... *COULDN'T* LET YOU DIE.
IT'S THE *TRUTH!* I *SWEAR* IT--
OKAY. OKAY. MAYBE IT *IS.*
I'D *LIKE* TO BELIEVE YOU, LIZZIE-GIRL--
--BUT NOW THAT I KNOW HOW BAD THE *U.* CAN BE-- HOW *CAN* I?

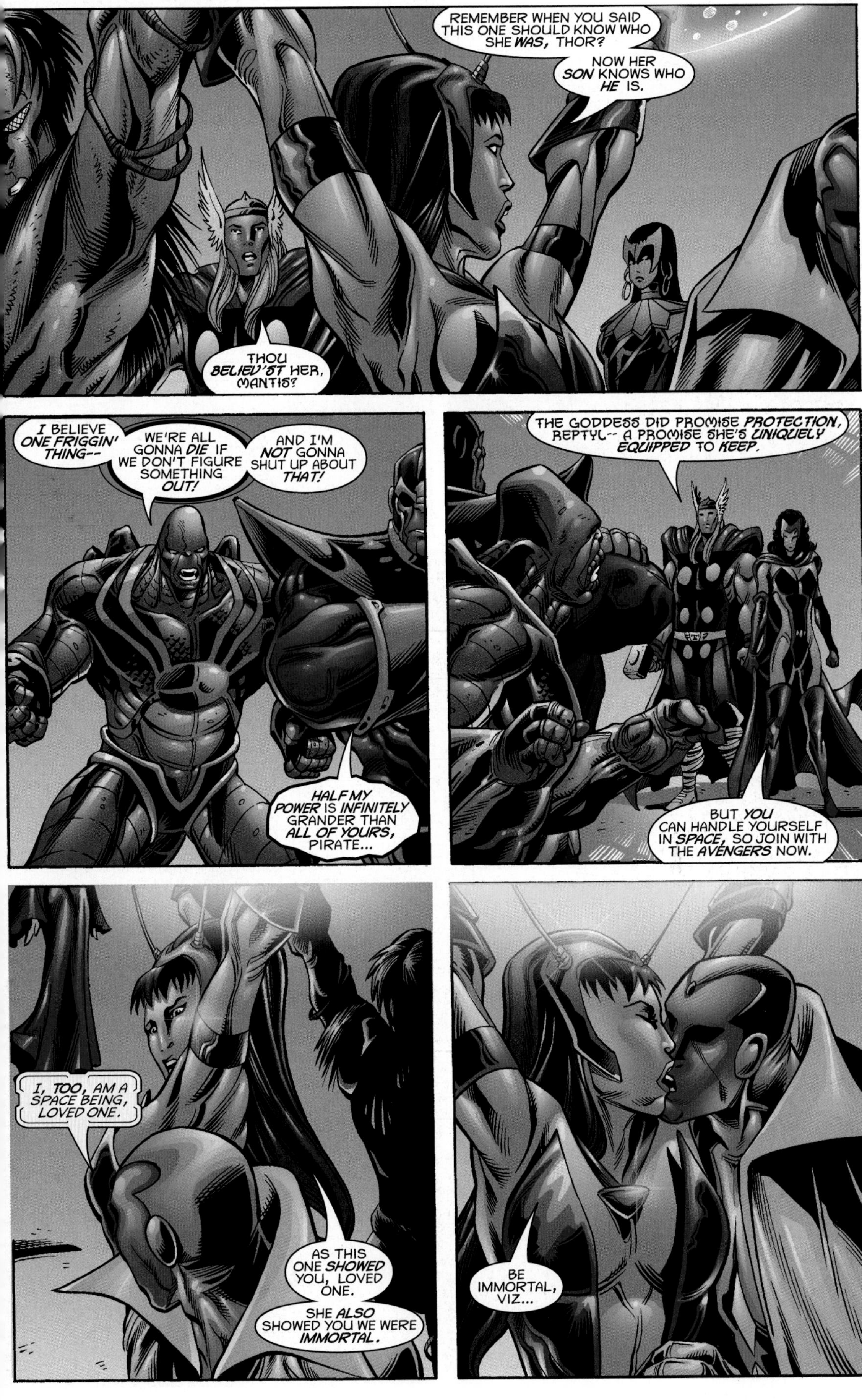

REMEMBER WHEN YOU SAID THIS ONE SHOULD KNOW WHO SHE *WAS*, THOR?
NOW HER *SON* KNOWS WHO *HE* IS.
THOU *BELIEV'ST* HER, MANTIS?
I BELIEVE *ONE FRIGGIN'* THING--
WE'RE ALL GONNA *DIE* IF WE DON'T FIGURE SOMETHING *OUT!*
AND I'M *NOT* GONNA SHUT UP ABOUT *THAT!*
HALF MY POWER IS *INFINITELY* GRANDER THAN *ALL OF YOURS,* PIRATE...
THE GODDESS DID PROMISE *PROTECTION,* REPTYL-- A PROMISE SHE'S *UNIQUELY EQUIPPED* TO *KEEP.*
BUT *YOU* CAN HANDLE YOURSELF IN *SPACE,* SO JOIN WITH THE *AVENGERS* NOW.
I, *TOO,* AM A SPACE BEING, LOVED ONE.
AS THIS ONE *SHOWED* YOU, LOVED ONE.
SHE *ALSO* SHOWED YOU WE WERE *IMMORTAL.*
BE IMMORTAL, VIZ...

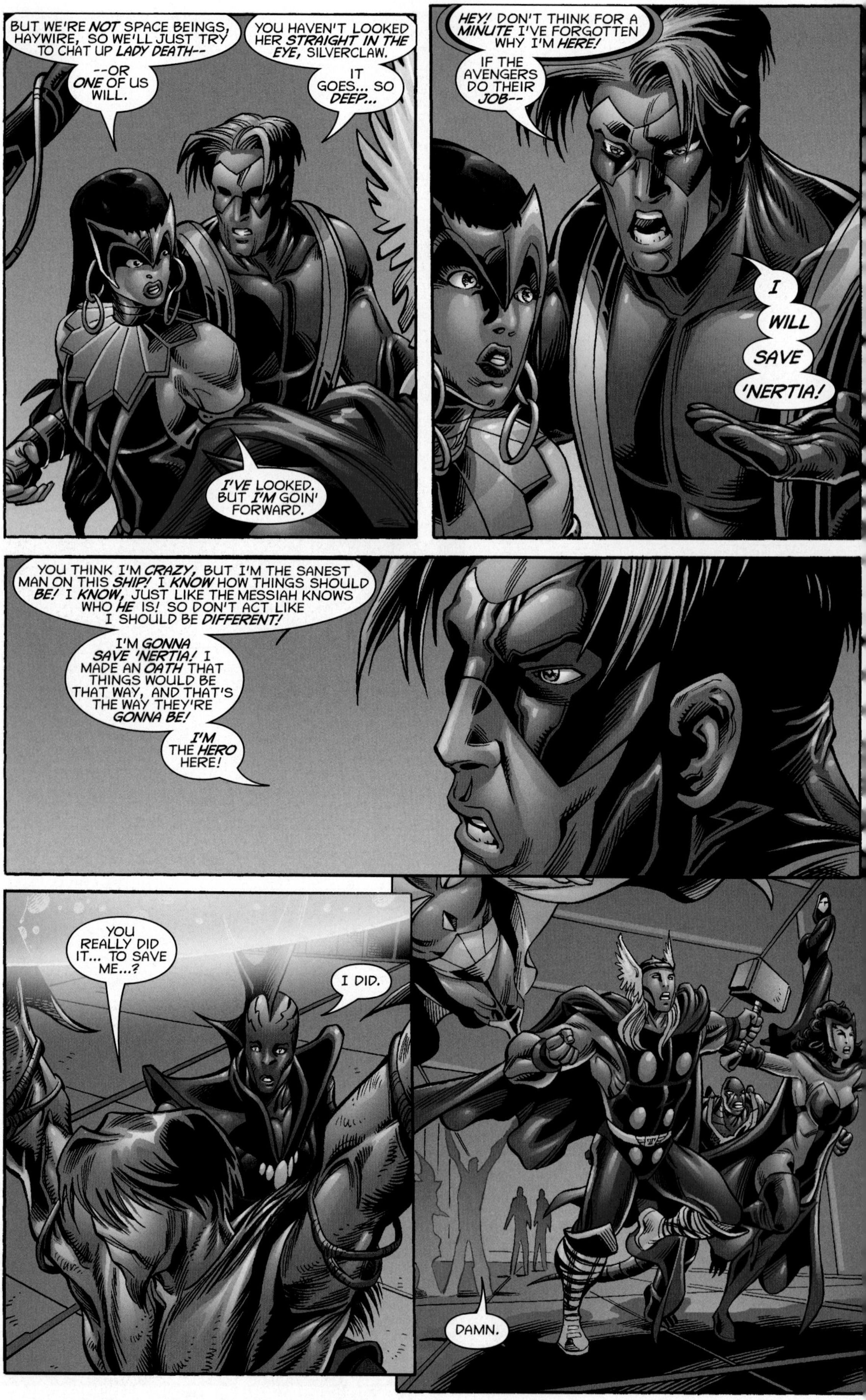

BUT WE'RE NOT SPACE BEINGS, HAYWIRE, SO WE'LL JUST TRY TO CHAT UP LADY DEATH--
--OR ONE OF US WILL.
YOU HAVEN'T LOOKED HER STRAIGHT IN THE EYE, SILVERCLAW.
IT GOES... SO DEEP...
I'VE LOOKED. BUT I'M GOIN' FORWARD.
HEY! DON'T THINK FOR A MINUTE I'VE FORGOTTEN WHY I'M HERE!
IF THE AVENGERS DO THEIR JOB--
I WILL SAVE 'NERTIA!
YOU THINK I'M CRAZY, BUT I'M THE SANEST MAN ON THIS SHIP! I KNOW HOW THINGS SHOULD BE! I KNOW, JUST LIKE THE MESSIAH KNOWS WHO HE IS! SO DON'T ACT LIKE I SHOULD BE DIFFERENT!
I'M GONNA SAVE 'NERTIA! I MADE AN OATH THAT THINGS WOULD BE THAT WAY, AND THAT'S THE WAY THEY'RE GONNA BE!
I'M THE HERO HERE!
YOU REALLY DID IT... TO SAVE ME...?
I DID.
DAMN.

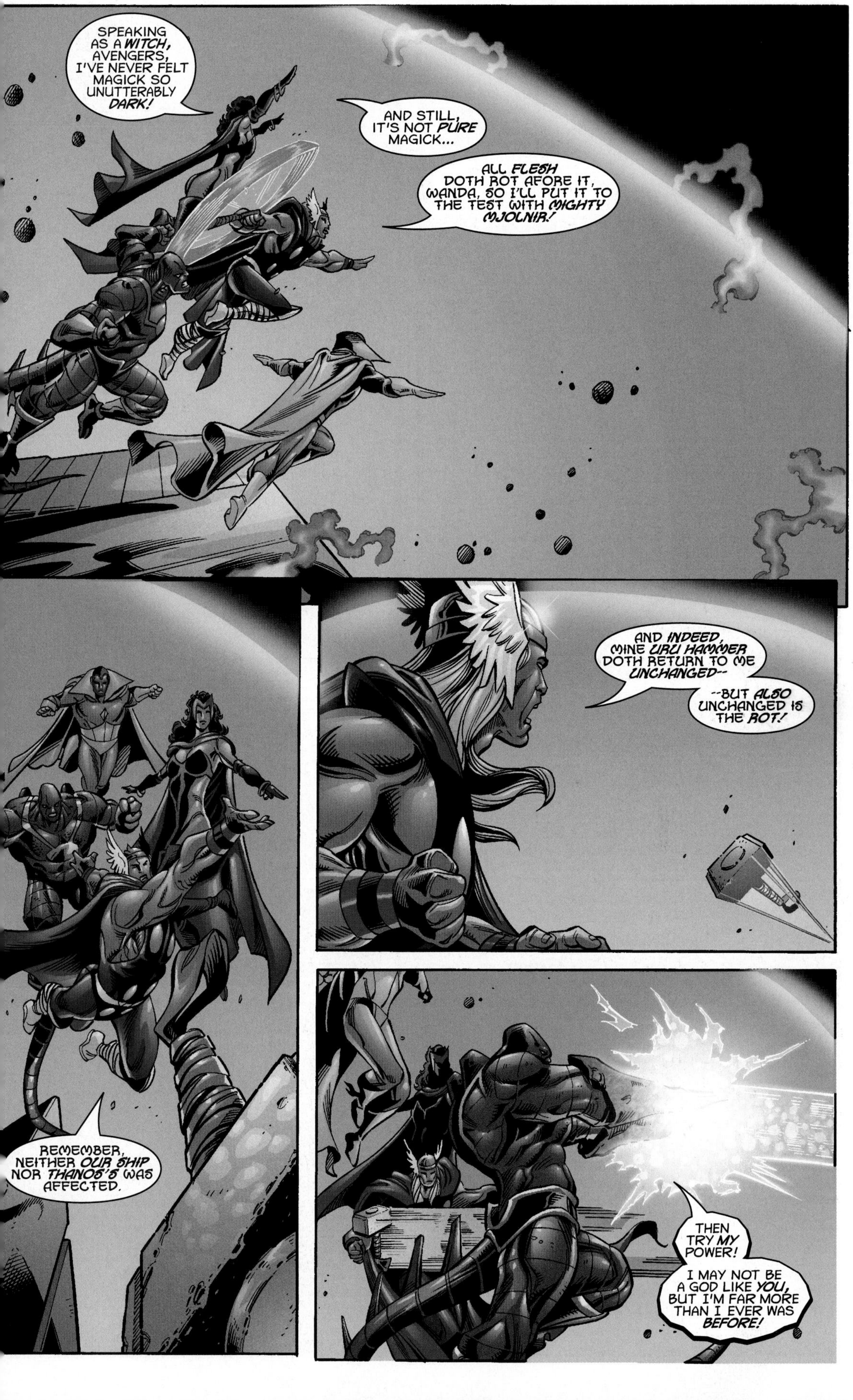

SPEAKING AS A WITCH, AVENGERS, I'VE NEVER FELT MAGICK SO UNUTTERABLY DARK!
AND STILL, IT'S NOT PURE MAGICK...
ALL FLESH DOTH ROT AFORE IT, WANDA, SO I'LL PUT IT TO THE TEST WITH MIGHTY MJOLNIR!
REMEMBER, NEITHER OUR SHIP NOR THANOS'S WAS AFFECTED.
AND INDEED, MINE URU HAMMER DOTH RETURN TO ME UNCHANGED--
--BUT ALSO UNCHANGED IS THE ROT!
THEN TRY MY POWER!
I MAY NOT BE A GOD LIKE YOU, BUT I'M FAR MORE THAN I EVER WAS BEFORE!

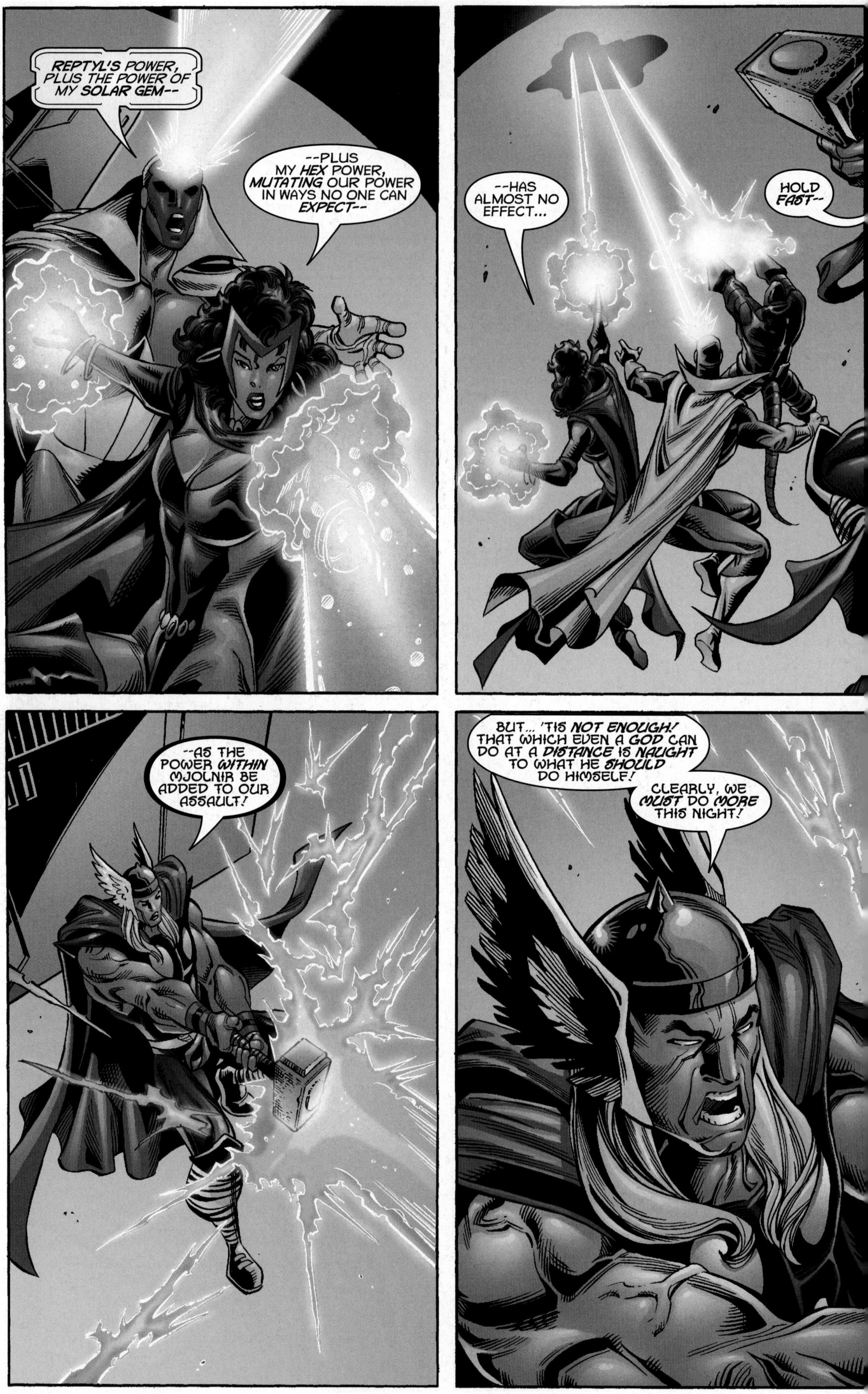
REPTYL'S POWER, PLUS THE POWER OF MY SOLAR GEM--
--PLUS MY HEX POWER, MUTATING OUR POWER IN WAYS NO ONE CAN EXPECT--
--HAS ALMOST NO EFFECT...
HOLD FAST--
--AS THE POWER WITHIN MJOLNIR BE ADDED TO OUR ASSAULT!
BUT... 'TIS NOT ENOUGH! THAT WHICH EVEN A GOD CAN DO AT A DISTANCE IS NAUGHT TO WHAT HE SHOULD DO HIMSELF!
CLEARLY, WE MUST DO MORE THIS NIGHT!

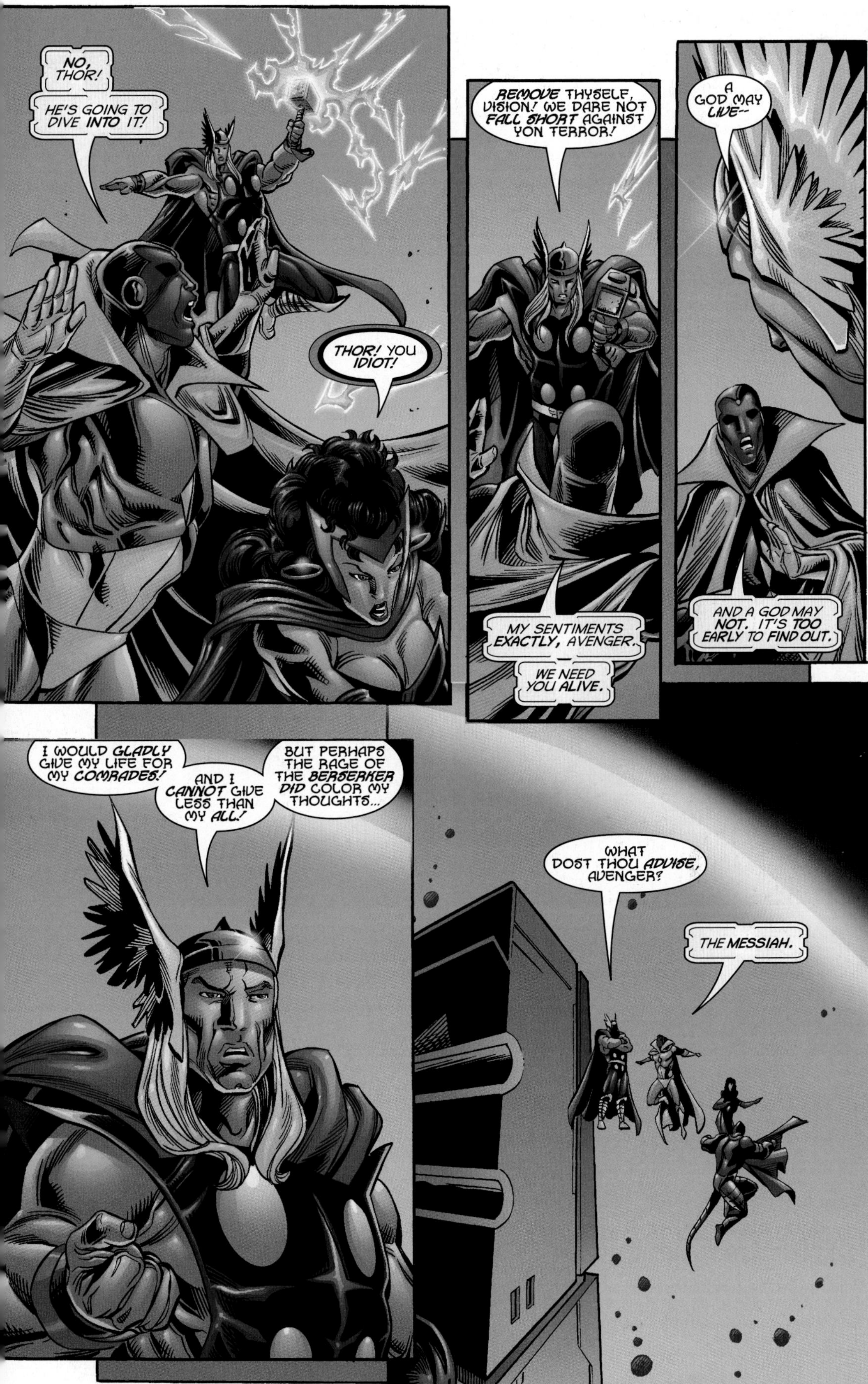
NO, THOR!
HE'S GOING TO DIVE INTO IT!
THOR! YOU IDIOT!
REMOVE THYSELF, VISION! WE DARE NOT FALL SHORT AGAINST YON TERROR!
MY SENTIMENTS EXACTLY, AVENGER.
WE NEED YOU ALIVE.
A GOD MAY LIVE--
AND A GOD MAY NOT. IT'S TOO EARLY TO FIND OUT.
I WOULD GLADLY GIVE MY LIFE FOR MY COMRADES!
AND I CANNOT GIVE LESS THAN MY ALL!
BUT PERHAPS THE RAGE OF THE BERSERKER DID COLOR MY THOUGHTS...
WHAT DOST THOU ADVISE, AVENGER?
THE MESSIAH.

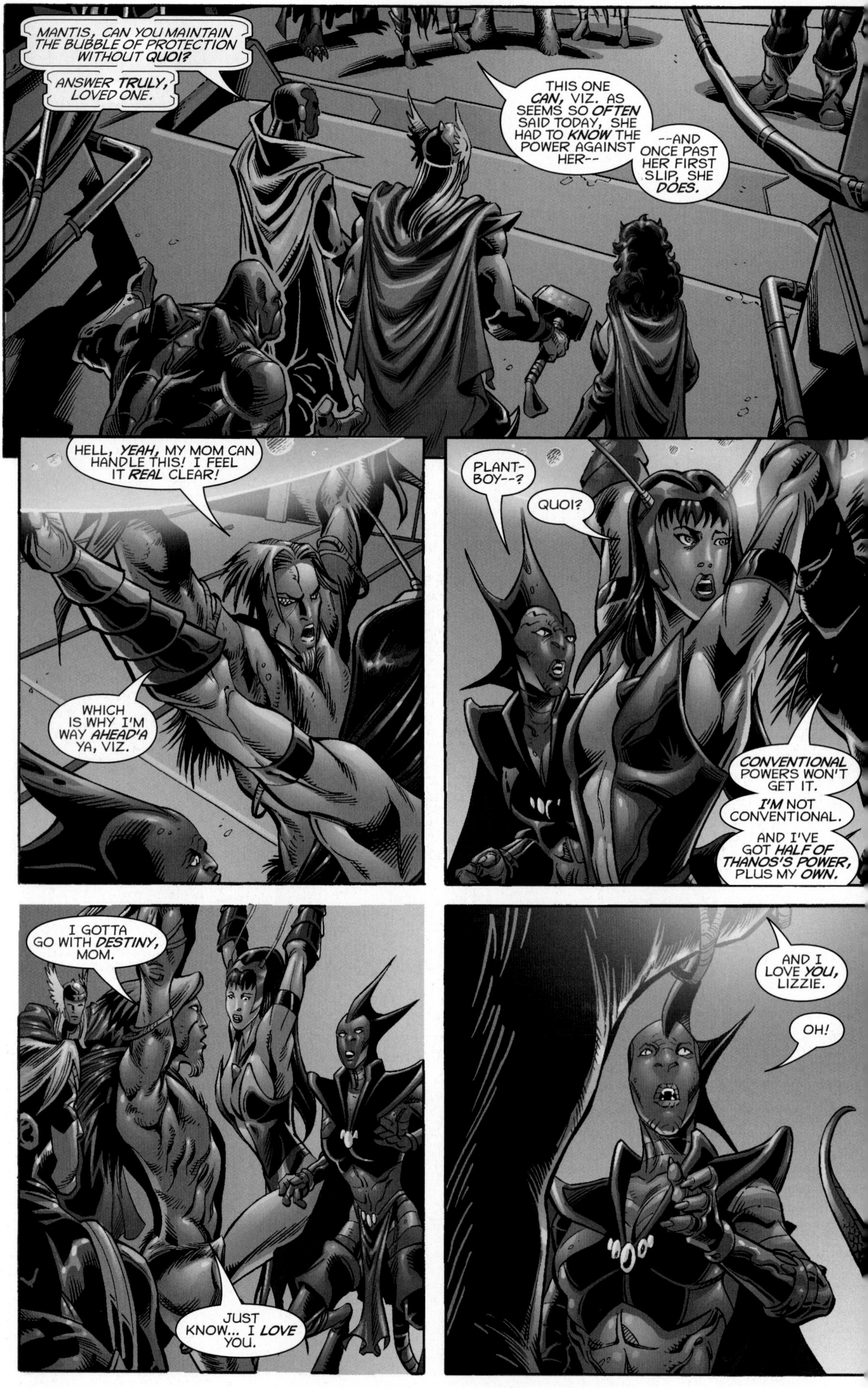
MANTIS, CAN YOU MAINTAIN THE BUBBLE OF PROTECTION WITHOUT QUOI?
ANSWER TRULY, LOVED ONE.
THIS ONE CAN, VIZ. AS SEEMS SO OFTEN SAID TODAY, SHE HAD TO KNOW THE POWER AGAINST HER--
--AND ONCE PAST HER FIRST SLIP, SHE DOES.
HELL, YEAH, MY MOM CAN HANDLE THIS! I FEEL IT REAL CLEAR!
WHICH IS WHY I'M WAY AHEAD'A YA, VIZ.
PLANT-BOY--?
QUOI?
CONVENTIONAL POWERS WON'T GET IT.
I'M NOT CONVENTIONAL.
AND I'VE GOT HALF OF THANOS'S POWER, PLUS MY OWN.
I GOTTA GO WITH DESTINY, MOM.
JUST KNOW... I LOVE YOU.
AND I LOVE YOU, LIZZIE.
OH!

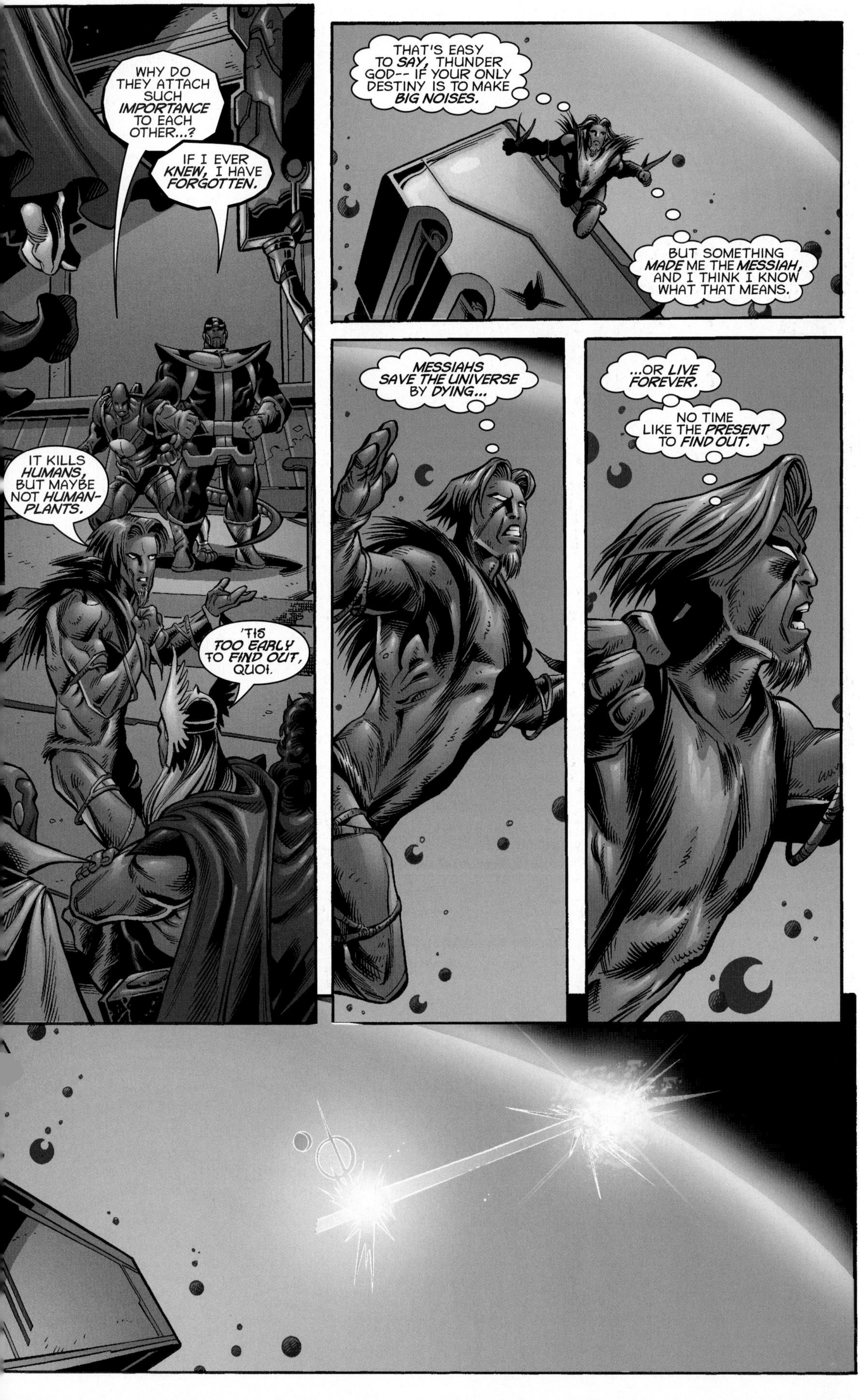
WHY DO THEY ATTACH SUCH IMPORTANCE TO EACH OTHER...?
IF I EVER KNEW, I HAVE FORGOTTEN.
IT KILLS HUMANS, BUT MAYBE NOT HUMAN-PLANTS.
'TIS TOO EARLY TO FIND OUT, QUOI.
THAT'S EASY TO SAY, THUNDER GOD-- IF YOUR ONLY DESTINY IS TO MAKE BIG NOISES.
BUT SOMETHING MADE ME THE MESSIAH, AND I THINK I KNOW WHAT THAT MEANS.
MESSIAHS SAVE THE UNIVERSE BY DYING...
...OR LIVE FOREVER.
NO TIME LIKE THE PRESENT TO FIND OUT.

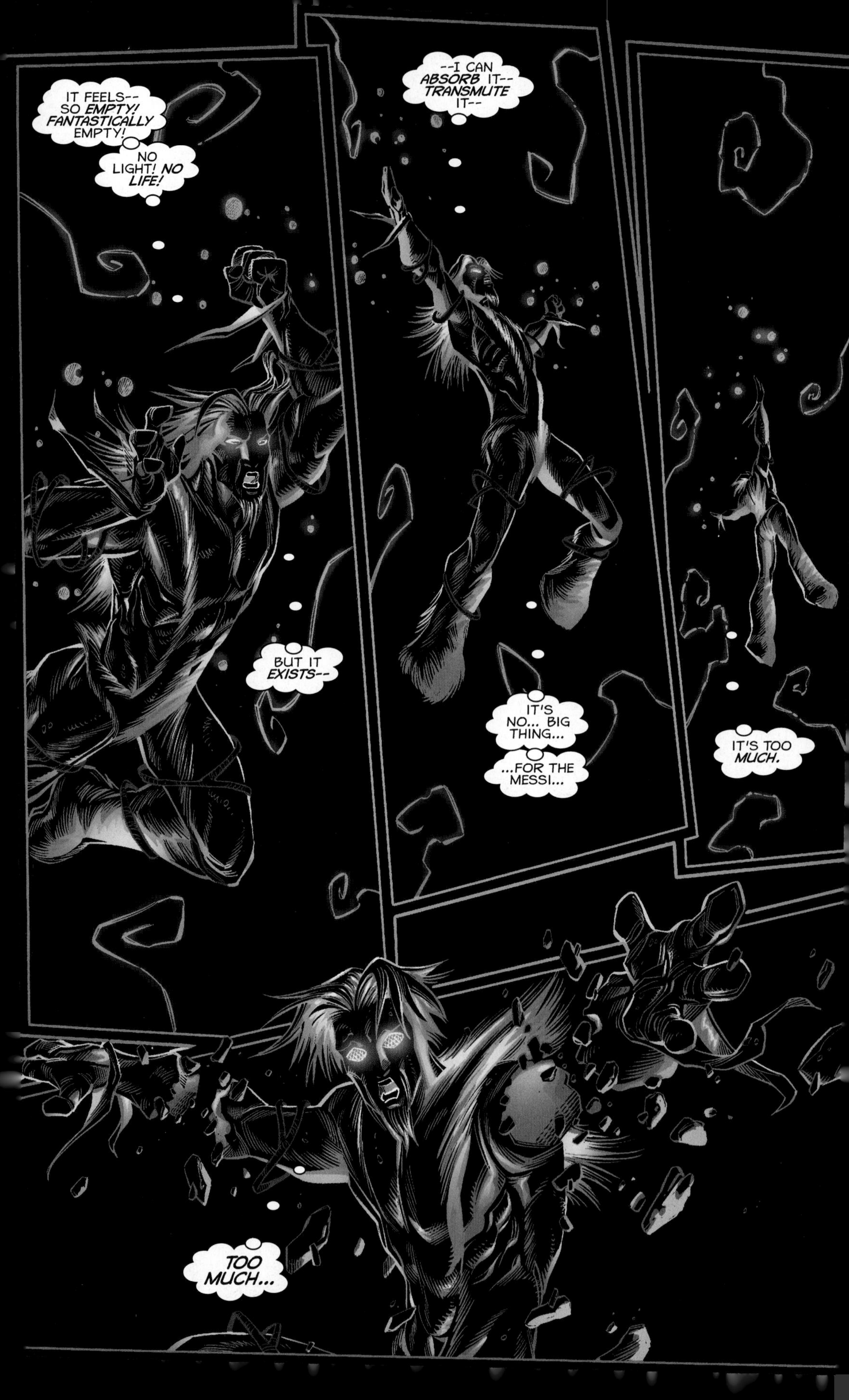
IT FEELS-- SO EMPTY! FANTASTICALLY EMPTY!
NO LIGHT! NO LIFE!
BUT IT EXISTS--
--I CAN ABSORB IT-- TRANSMUTE IT--
IT'S NO... BIG THING...
...FOR THE MESSI...
IT'S TOO MUCH.
TOO MUCH...

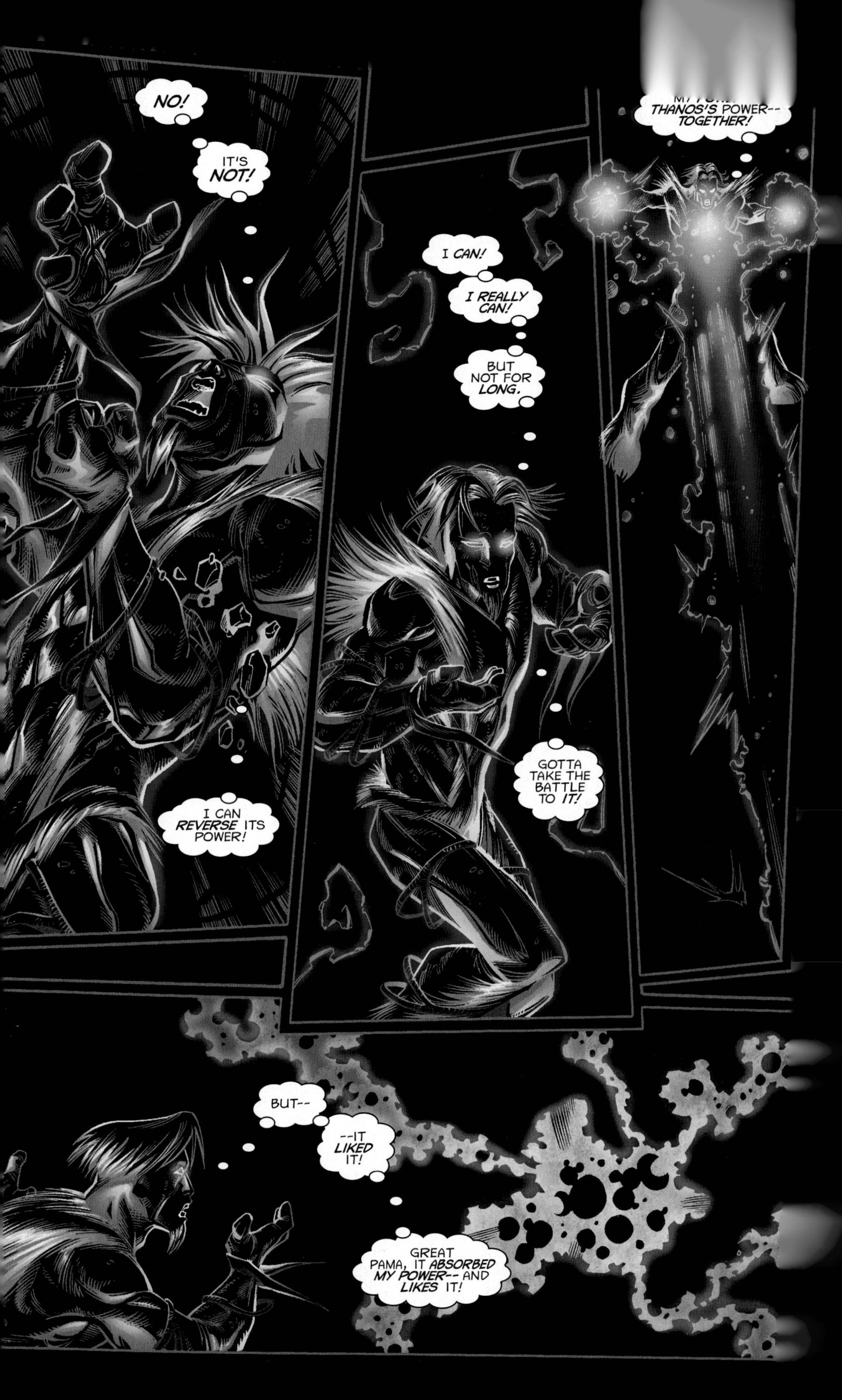
NO!
IT'S NOT!
I CAN REVERSE ITS POWER!
I CAN!
I REALLY CAN!
BUT NOT FOR LONG.
GOTTA TAKE THE BATTLE TO IT!
THANOS'S POWER-- TOGETHER!
BUT--
--IT LIKED IT!
GREAT PAMA, IT ABSORBED MY POWER-- AND LIKES IT!

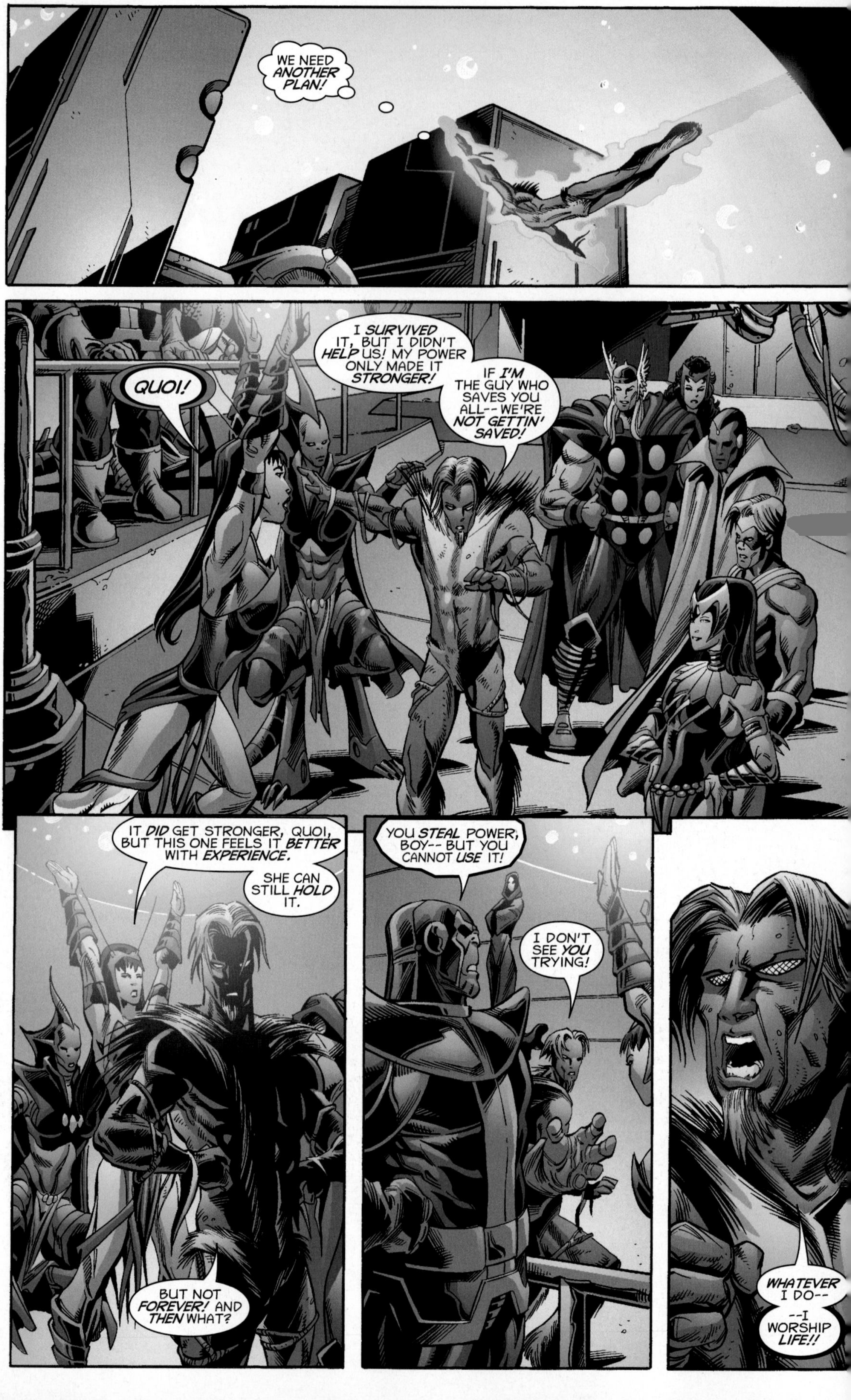
WE NEED ANOTHER PLAN!
QUOI!
I SURVIVED IT, BUT I DIDN'T HELP US! MY POWER ONLY MADE IT STRONGER!
IF I'M THE GUY WHO SAVES YOU ALL-- WE'RE NOT GETTIN' SAVED!
IT DID GET STRONGER, QUOI, BUT THIS ONE FEELS IT BETTER WITH EXPERIENCE.
SHE CAN STILL HOLD IT.
BUT NOT FOREVER! AND THEN WHAT?
YOU STEAL POWER, BOY-- BUT YOU CANNOT USE IT!
I DON'T SEE YOU TRYING!
WHATEVER I DO--
--I WORSHIP LIFE!!

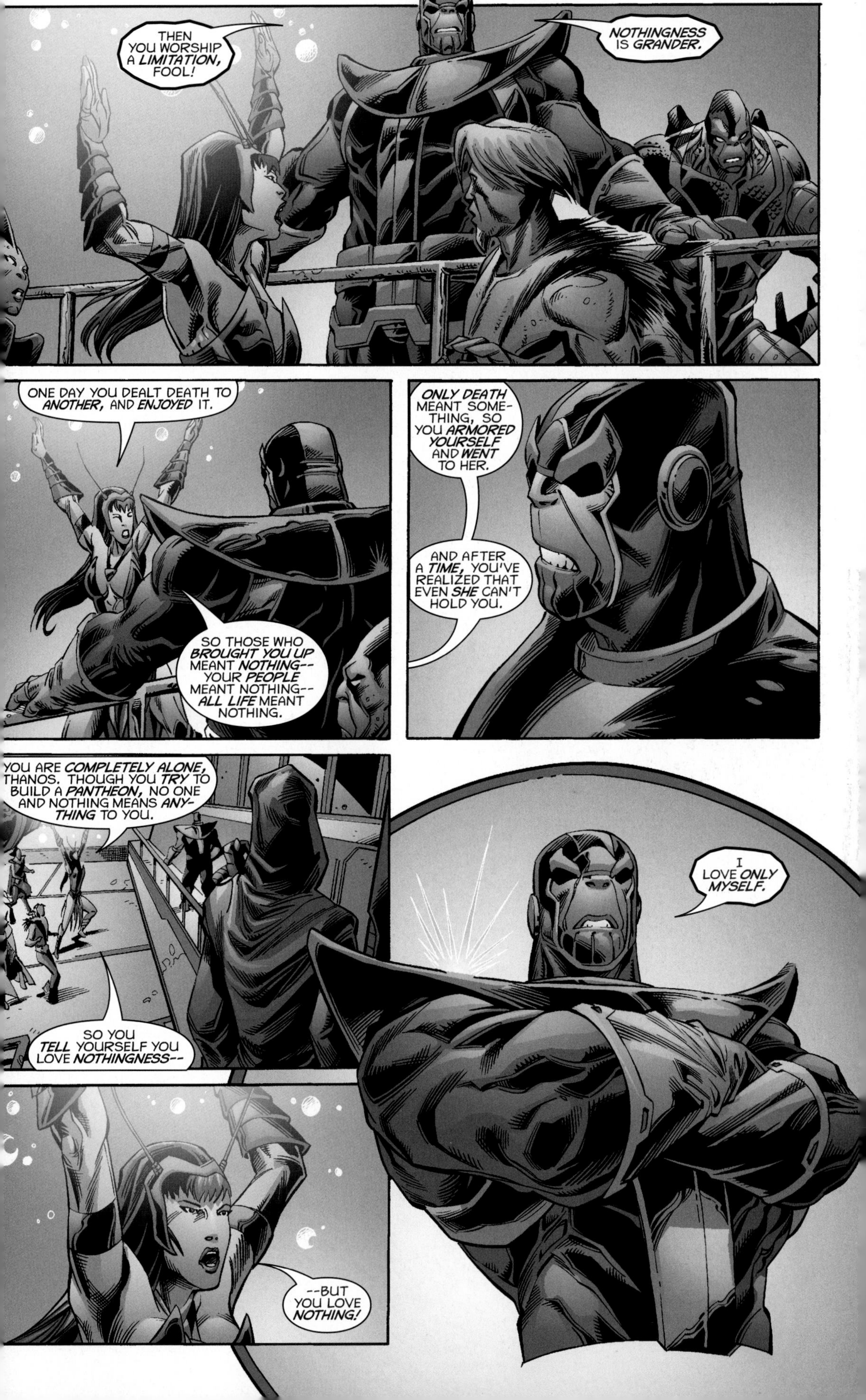
THEN YOU WORSHIP A LIMITATION, FOOL!
NOTHINGNESS IS GRANDER.
ONE DAY YOU DEALT DEATH TO ANOTHER, AND ENJOYED IT.
SO THOSE WHO BROUGHT YOU UP MEANT NOTHING-- YOUR PEOPLE MEANT NOTHING-- ALL LIFE MEANT NOTHING.
ONLY DEATH MEANT SOMETHING, SO YOU ARMORED YOURSELF AND WENT TO HER.
AND AFTER A TIME, YOU'VE REALIZED THAT EVEN SHE CAN'T HOLD YOU.
YOU ARE COMPLETELY ALONE, THANOS. THOUGH YOU TRY TO BUILD A PANTHEON, NO ONE AND NOTHING MEANS ANYTHING TO YOU.
SO YOU TELL YOURSELF YOU LOVE NOTHINGNESS--
--BUT YOU LOVE NOTHING!
I LOVE ONLY MYSELF.

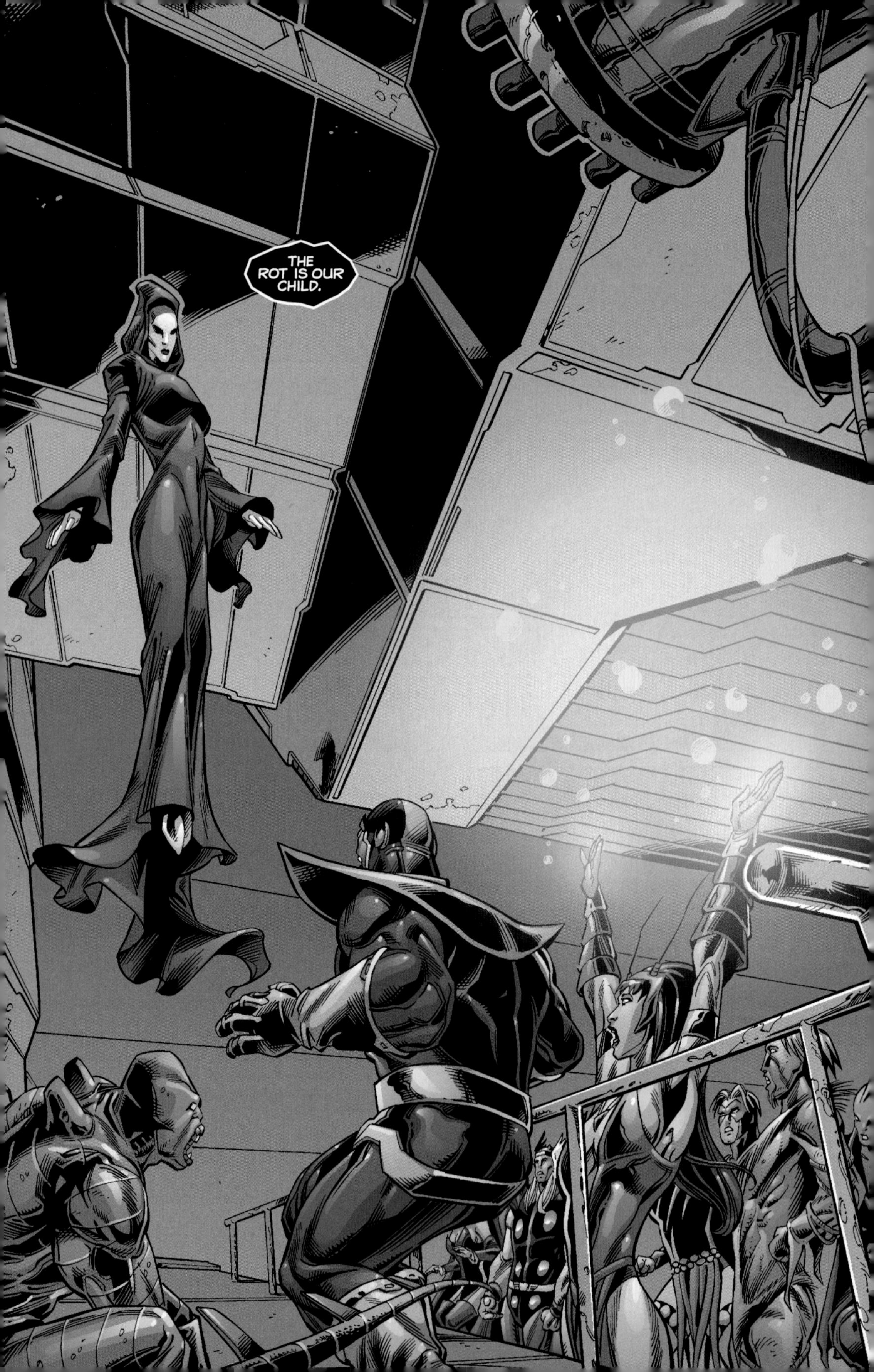
THE ROT IS OUR CHILD.

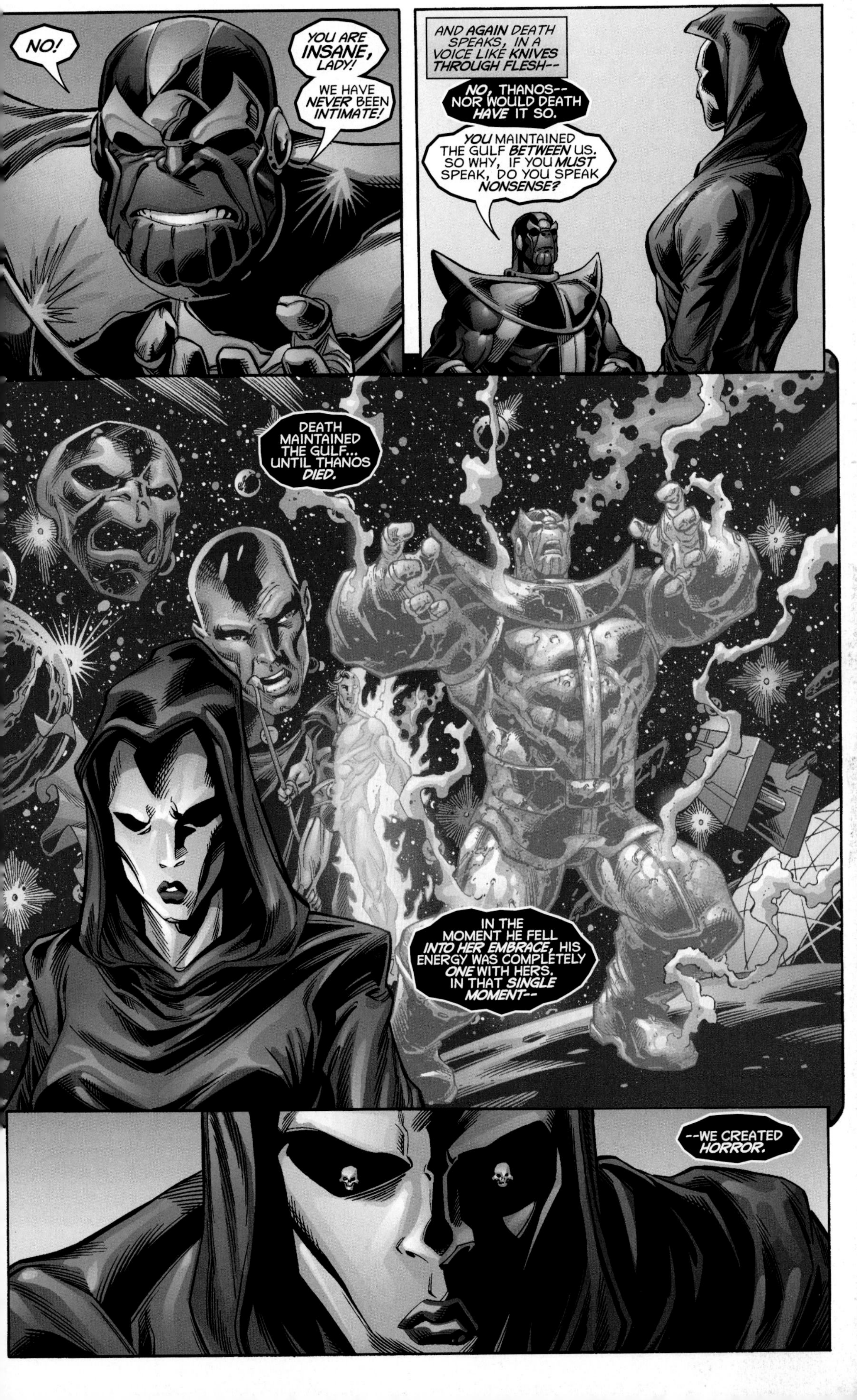
NO!
YOU ARE INSANE, LADY!
WE HAVE NEVER BEEN INTIMATE!
AND AGAIN DEATH SPEAKS, IN A VOICE LIKE KNIVES THROUGH FLESH--
NO, THANOS-- NOR WOULD DEATH HAVE IT SO.
YOU MAINTAINED THE GULF BETWEEN US. SO WHY, IF YOU MUST SPEAK, DO YOU SPEAK NONSENSE?
DEATH MAINTAINED THE GULF... UNTIL THANOS DIED.
IN THE MOMENT HE FELL INTO HER EMBRACE, HIS ENERGY WAS COMPLETELY ONE WITH HERS. IN THAT SINGLE MOMENT--
--WE CREATED HORROR.

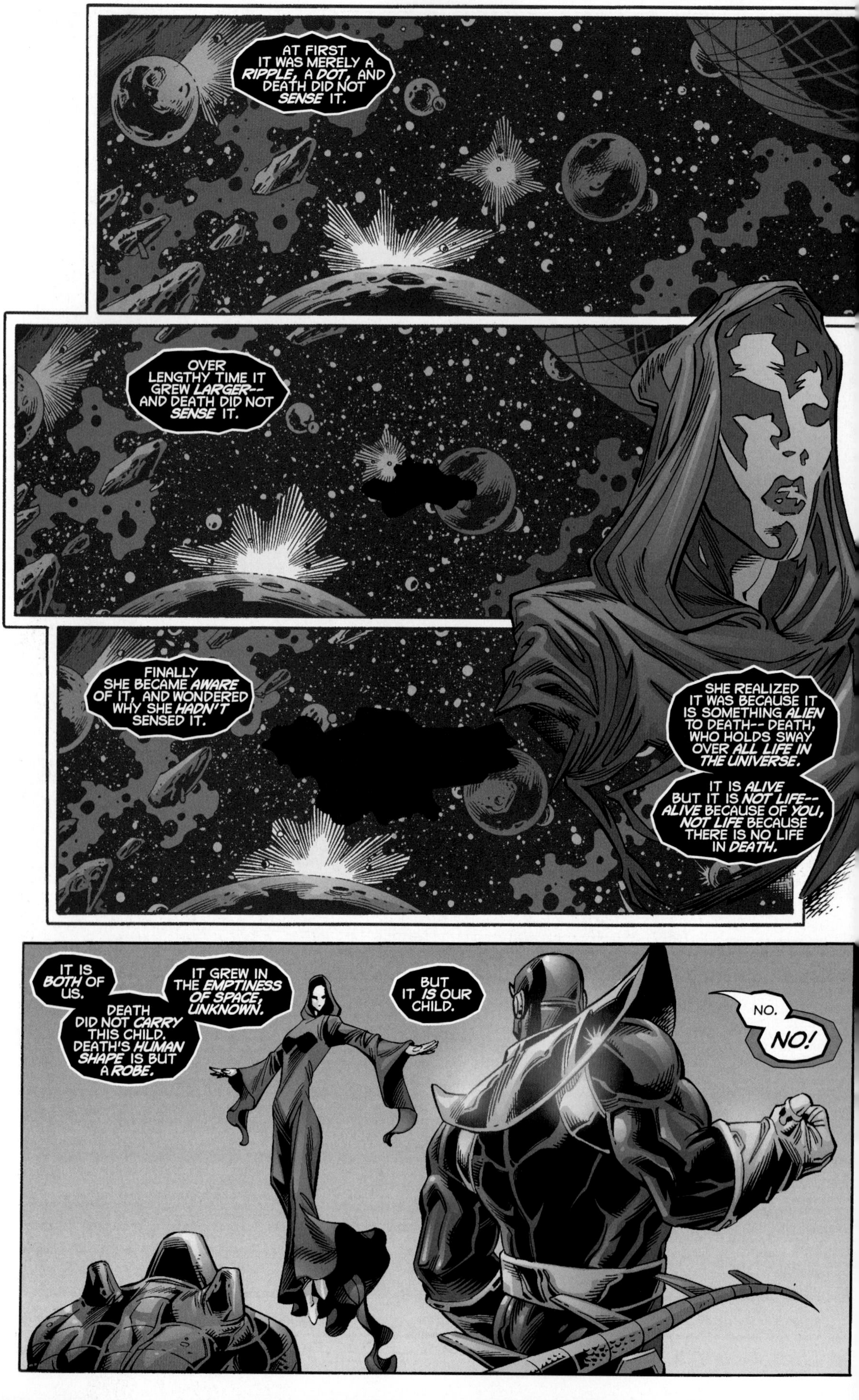

AT FIRST IT WAS MERELY A RIPPLE, A DOT, AND DEATH DID NOT SENSE IT.
OVER LENGTHY TIME IT GREW LARGER-- AND DEATH DID NOT SENSE IT.
FINALLY SHE BECAME AWARE OF IT, AND WONDERED WHY SHE HADN'T SENSED IT.
SHE REALIZED IT WAS BECAUSE IT IS SOMETHING ALIEN TO DEATH-- DEATH, WHO HOLDS SWAY OVER ALL LIFE IN THE UNIVERSE.
IT IS ALIVE BUT IT IS NOT LIFE-- ALIVE BECAUSE OF YOU, NOT LIFE BECAUSE THERE IS NO LIFE IN DEATH.
IT IS BOTH OF US.
DEATH DID NOT CARRY THIS CHILD. DEATH'S HUMAN SHAPE IS BUT A ROBE.
IT GREW IN THE EMPTINESS OF SPACE, UNKNOWN.
BUT IT IS OUR CHILD.
NO.
NO!

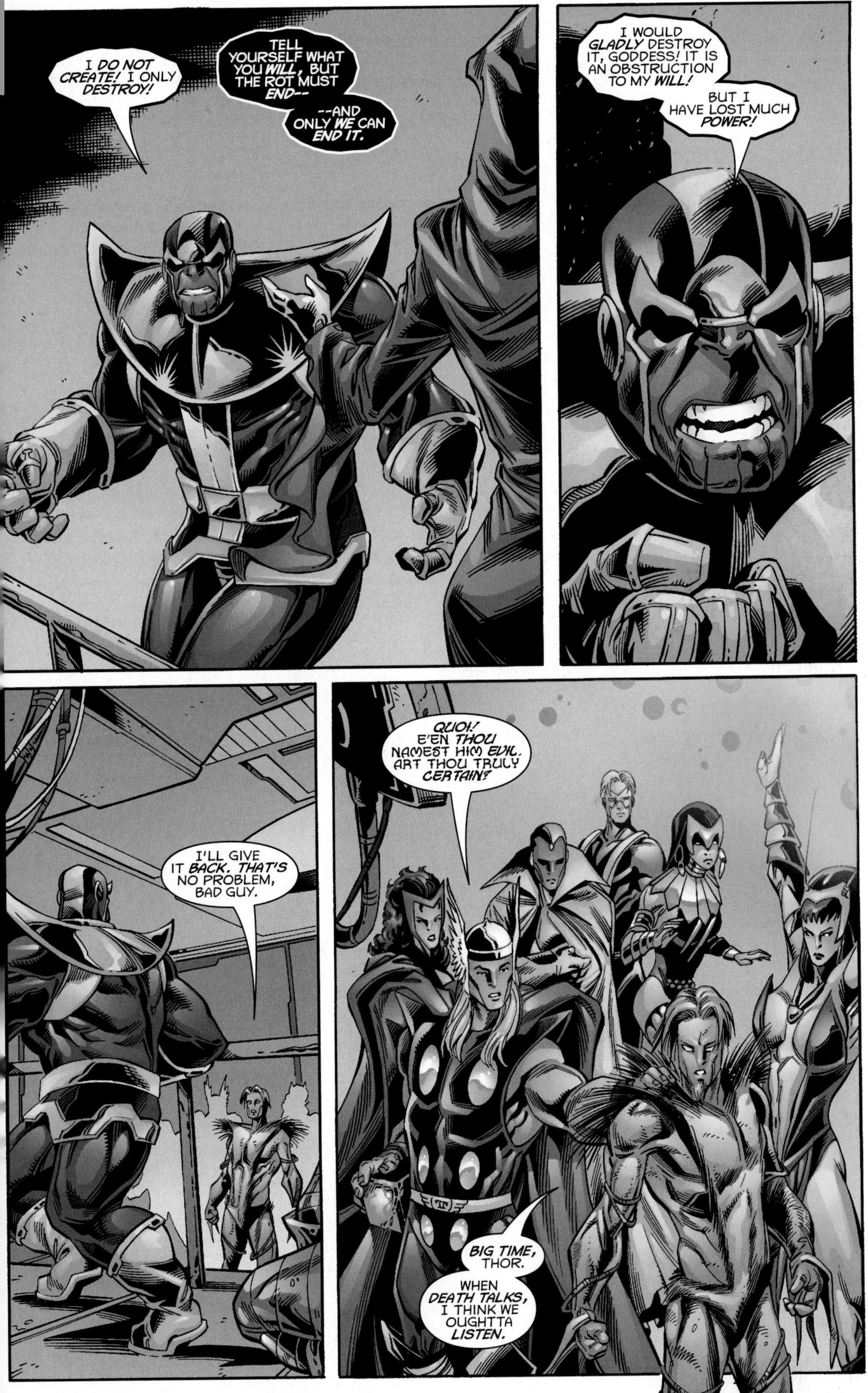
I DO NOT CREATE! I ONLY DESTROY!
TELL YOURSELF WHAT YOU WILL, BUT THE ROT MUST END--
--AND ONLY WE CAN END IT.
I WOULD GLADLY DESTROY IT, GODDESS! IT IS AN OBSTRUCTION TO MY WILL!
BUT I HAVE LOST MUCH POWER!
I'LL GIVE IT BACK. THAT'S NO PROBLEM, BAD GUY.
QUOI! E'EN THOU NAMEST HIM EVIL. ART THOU TRULY CERTAIN?
BIG TIME, THOR.
WHEN DEATH TALKS, I THINK WE OUGHTTA LISTEN.

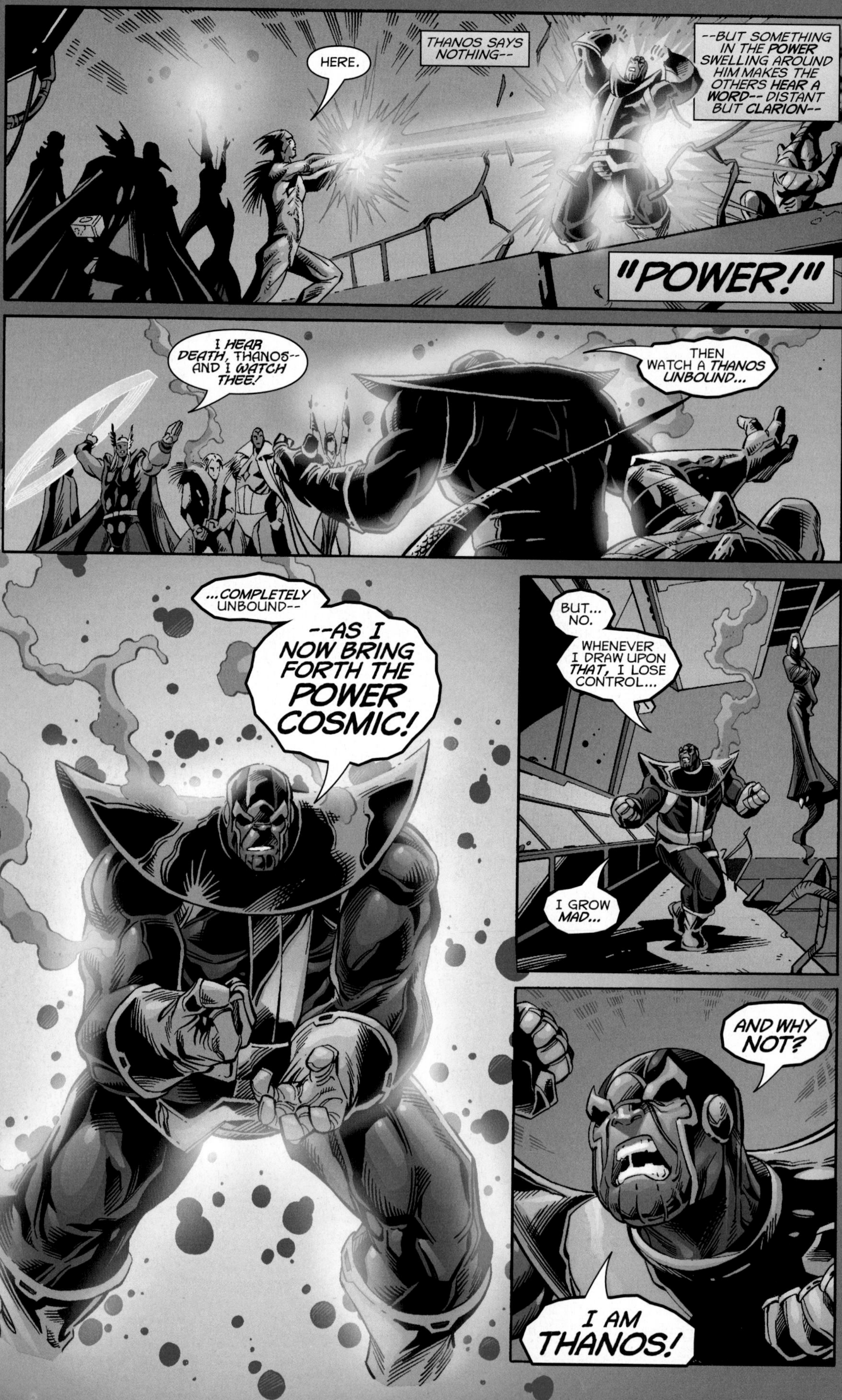
HERE.
THANOS SAYS NOTHING--
--BUT SOMETHING IN THE POWER SWELLING AROUND HIM MAKES THE OTHERS HEAR A WORD-- DISTANT BUT CLARION--
"POWER!"
I HEAR DEATH, THANOS-- AND I WATCH THEE!
THEN WATCH A THANOS UNBOUND...
...COMPLETELY UNBOUND--
--AS I NOW BRING FORTH THE POWER COSMIC!
BUT... NO.
WHENEVER I DRAW UPON THAT, I LOSE CONTROL...
I GROW MAD...
AND WHY NOT?
I AM THANOS!

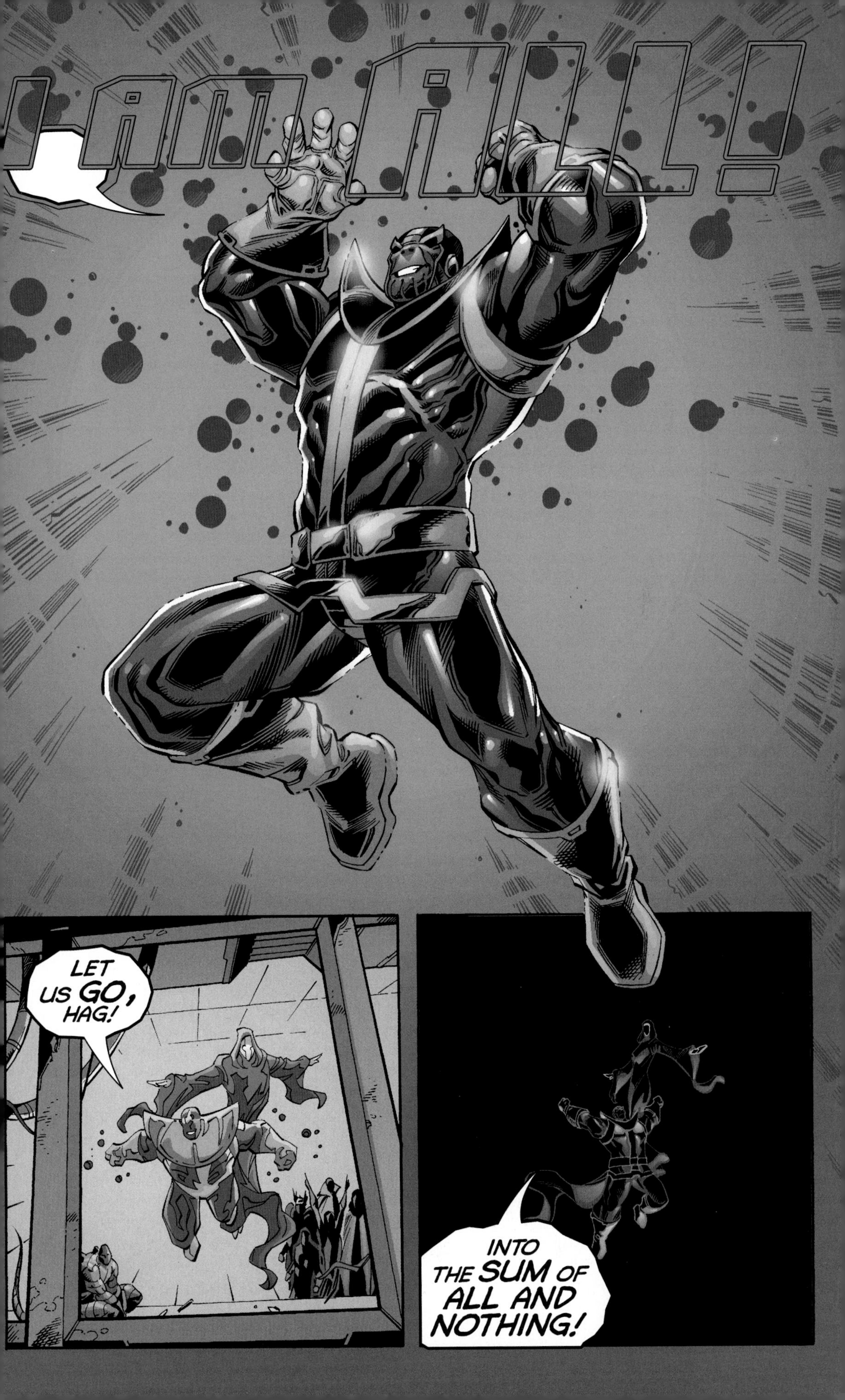
I AM ALL!
LET US GO, HAG!
INTO THE SUM OF ALL AND NOTHING!

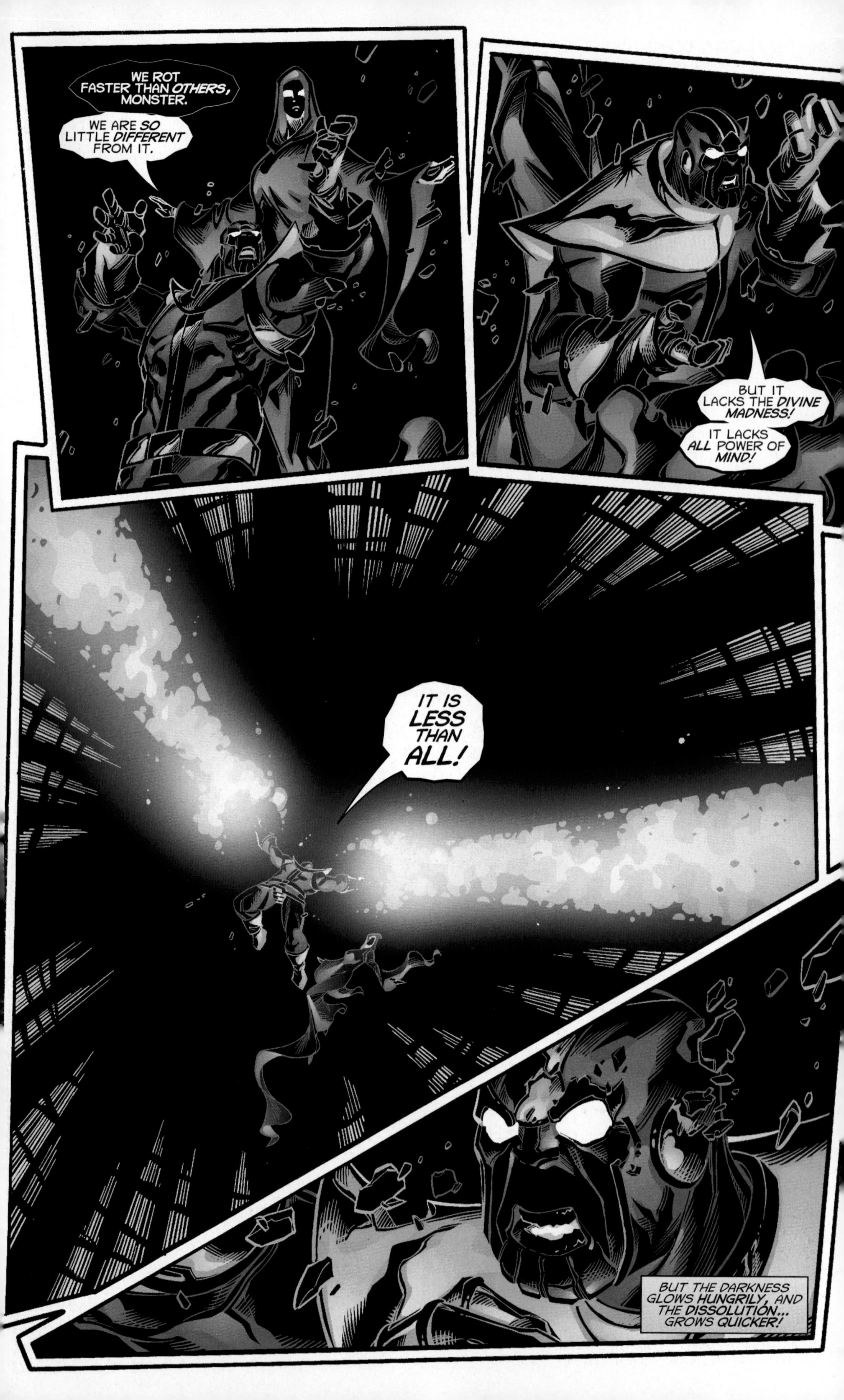
WE ROT FASTER THAN OTHERS, MONSTER.
WE ARE SO LITTLE DIFFERENT FROM IT.
BUT IT LACKS THE DIVINE MADNESS!
IT LACKS ALL POWER OF MIND!
IT IS LESS THAN ALL!
BUT THE DARKNESS GLOWS HUNGRILY, AND THE DISSOLUTION... GROWS QUICKER!

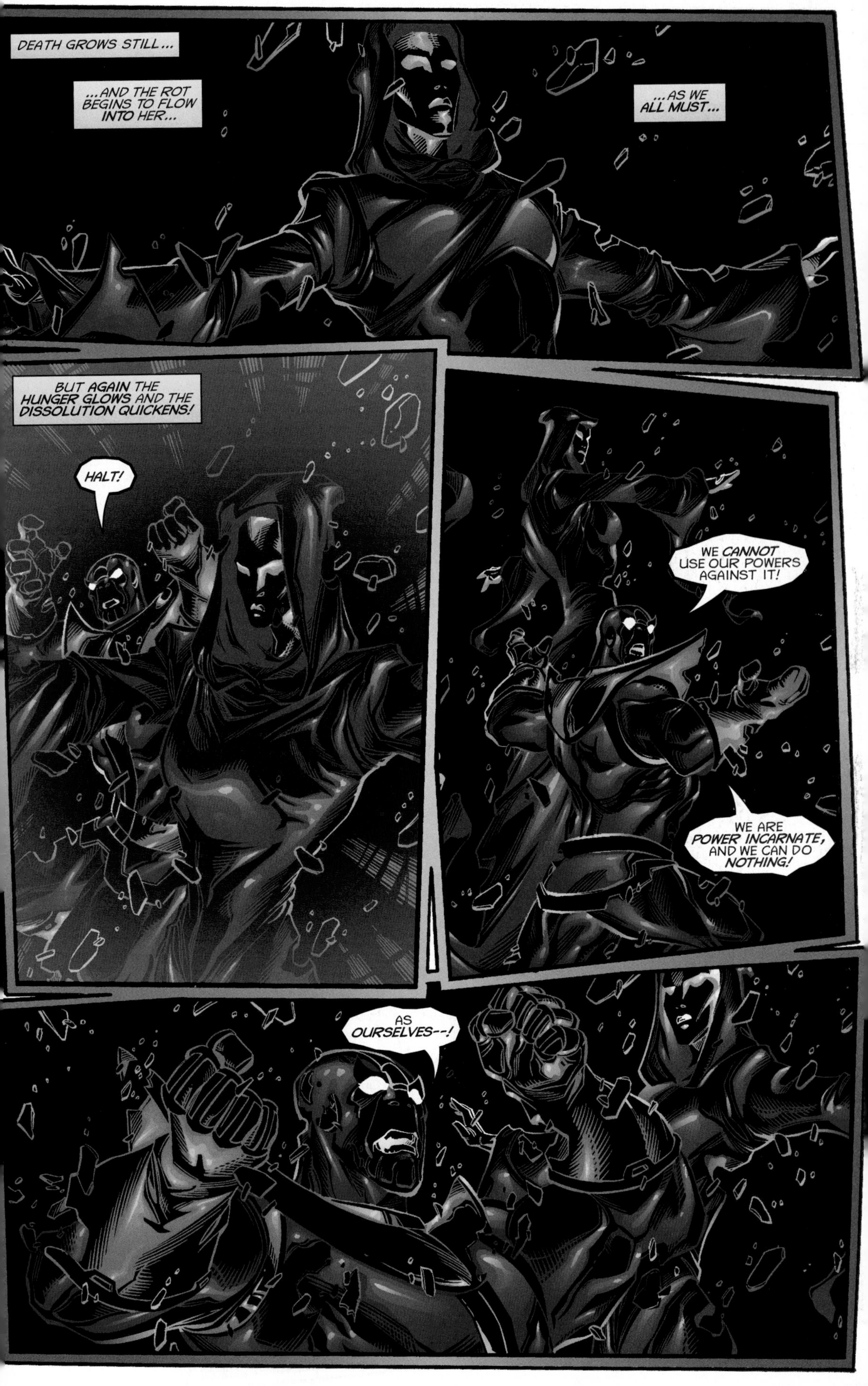
DEATH GROWS STILL...
...AND THE ROT BEGINS TO FLOW INTO HER...
...AS WE ALL MUST...
BUT AGAIN THE HUNGER GLOWS AND THE DISSOLUTION QUICKENS!
HALT!
WE CANNOT USE OUR POWERS AGAINST IT!
WE ARE POWER INCARNATE, AND WE CAN DO NOTHING!
AS OURSELVES--!

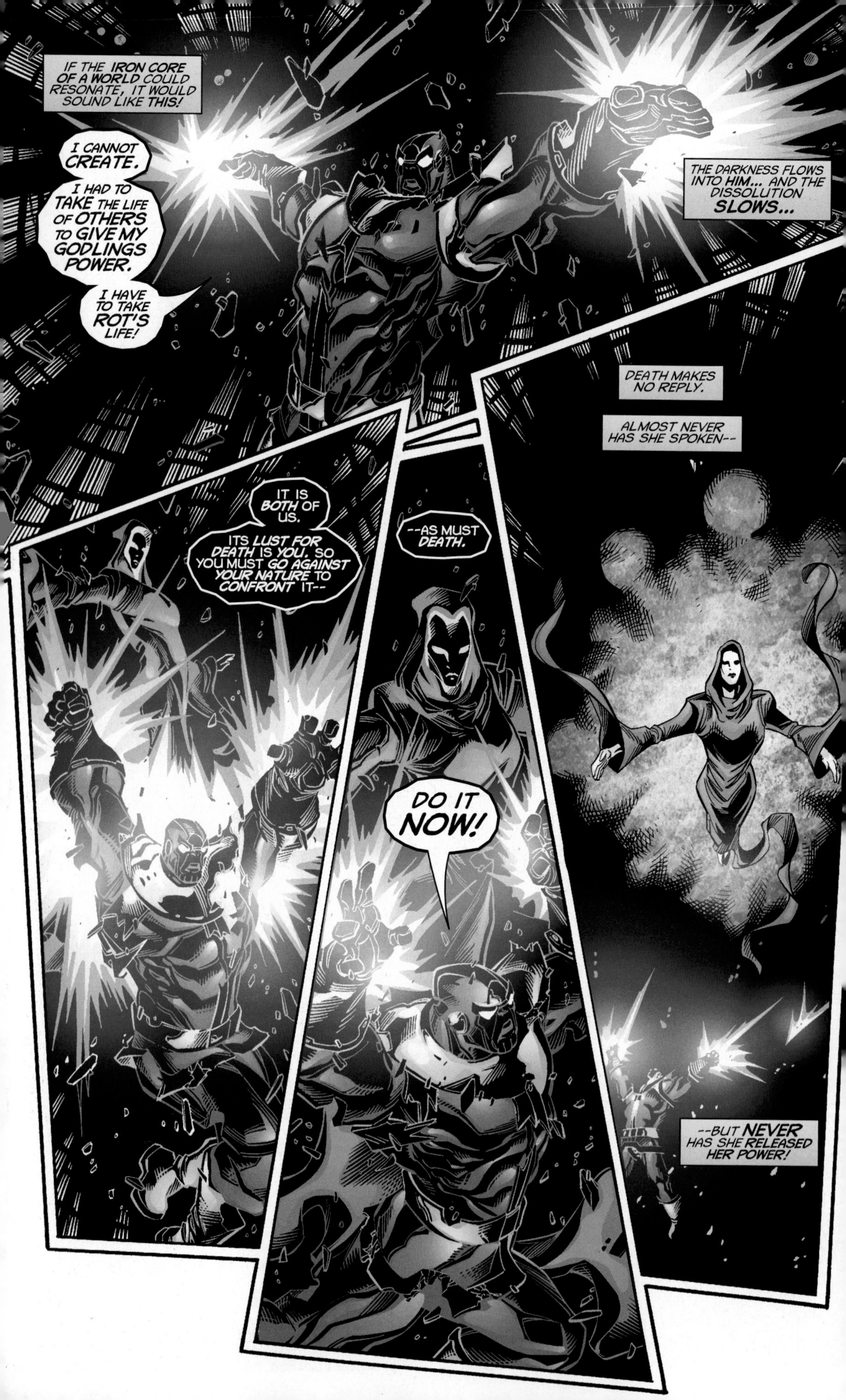
IF THE IRON CORE OF A WORLD COULD RESONATE, IT WOULD SOUND LIKE THIS!
I CANNOT CREATE.
I HAD TO TAKE THE LIFE OF OTHERS TO GIVE MY GODLINGS POWER.
I HAVE TO TAKE ROT'S LIFE!
THE DARKNESS FLOWS INTO HIM... AND THE DISSOLUTION SLOWS...
IT IS BOTH OF US.
ITS LUST FOR DEATH IS YOU. SO YOU MUST GO AGAINST YOUR NATURE TO CONFRONT IT--
--AS MUST DEATH.
DO IT NOW!
DEATH MAKES NO REPLY.
ALMOST NEVER HAS SHE SPOKEN--
--BUT NEVER HAS SHE RELEASED HER POWER!

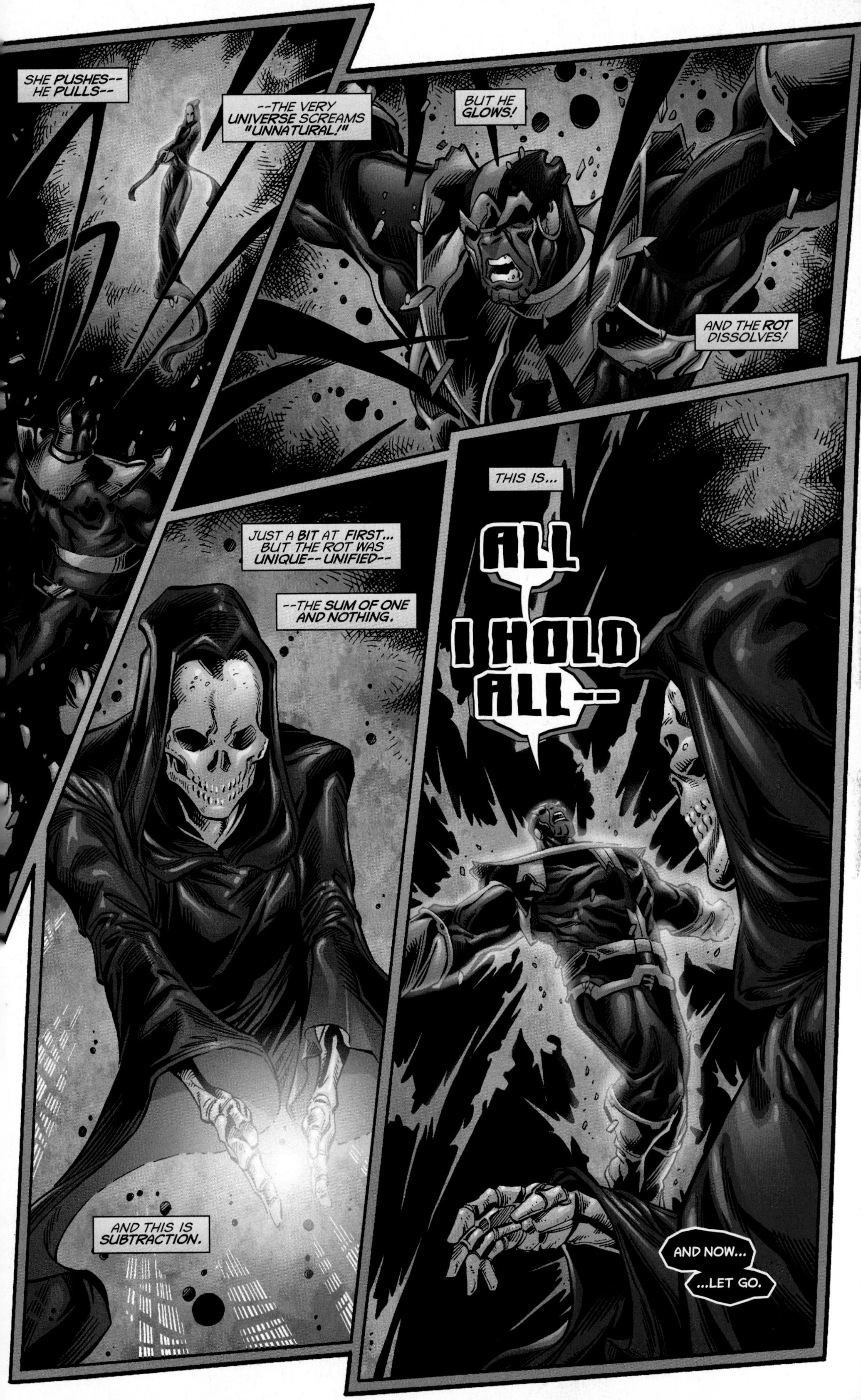

SHE PUSHES--
HE PULLS--
--THE VERY UNIVERSE SCREAMS "UNNATURAL!"
BUT HE GLOWS!
AND THE ROT DISSOLVES!
JUST A BIT AT FIRST... BUT THE ROT WAS UNIQUE--UNIFIED--
--THE SUM OF ONE AND NOTHING.
AND THIS IS SUBTRACTION.
THIS IS...
ALL
I HOLD ALL--
AND NOW...
...LET GO.

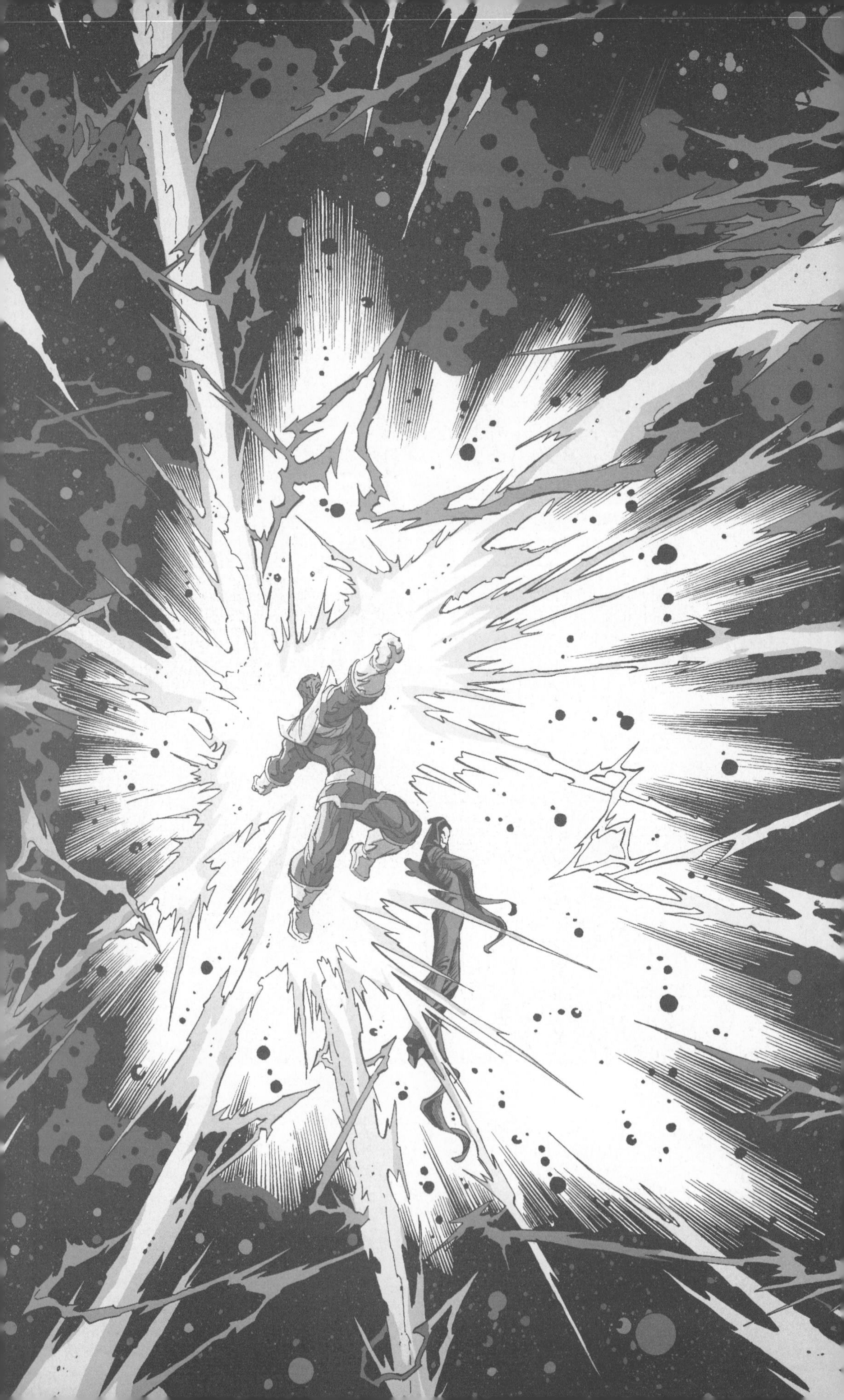

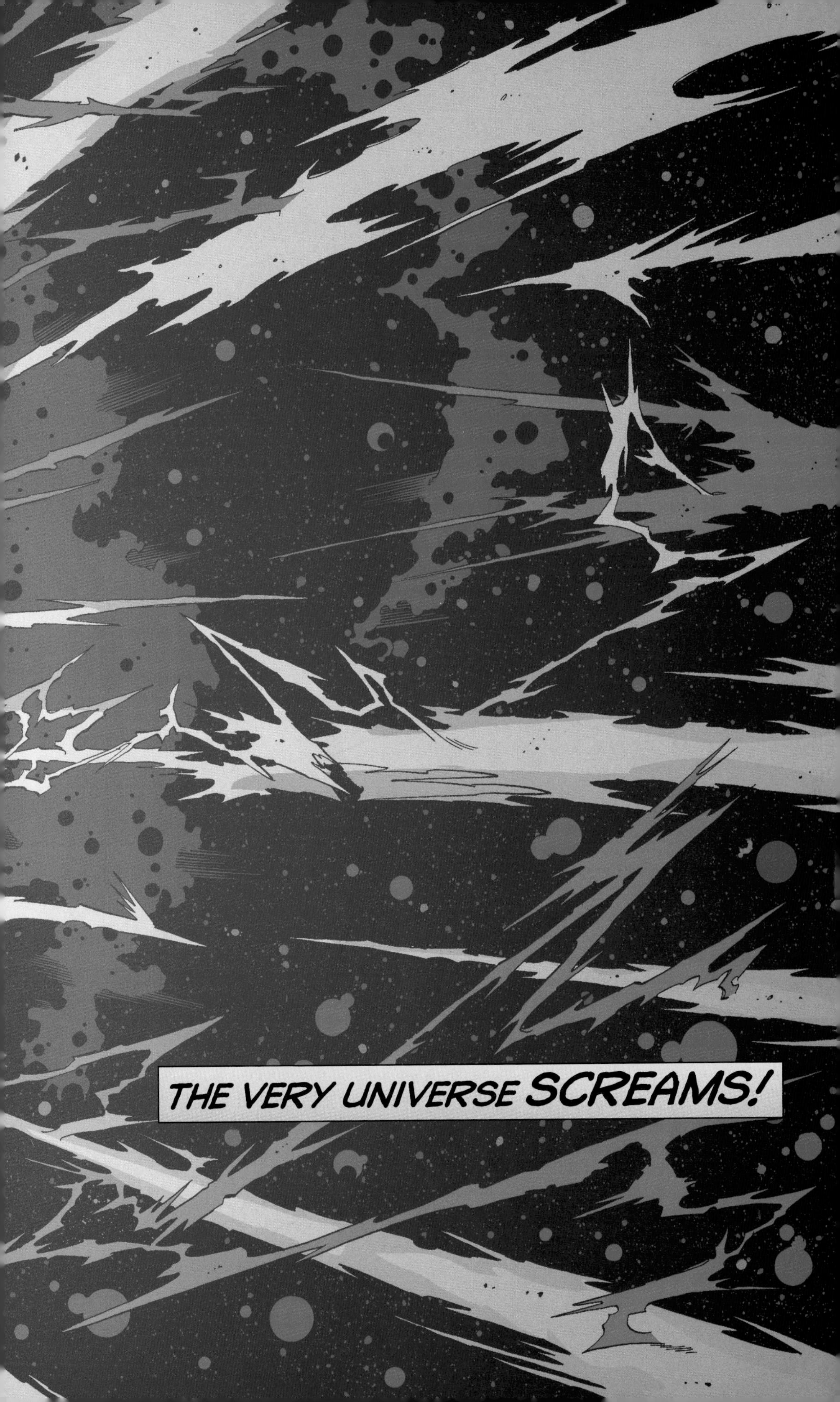
THE VERY UNIVERSE SCREAMS!

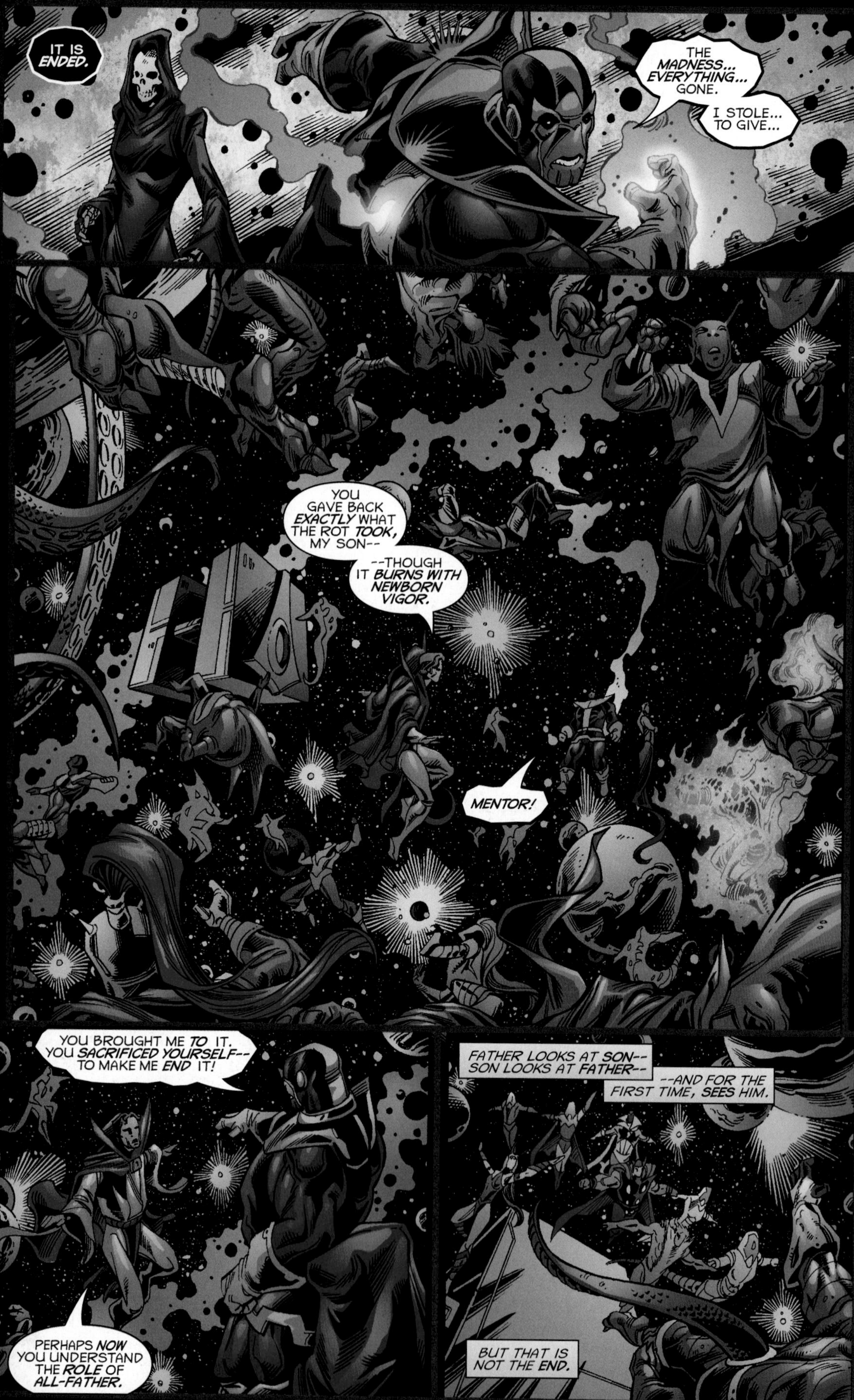
IT IS ENDED.
THE MADNESS... EVERYTHING... GONE.
I STOLE... TO GIVE...
YOU GAVE BACK EXACTLY WHAT THE ROT TOOK, MY SON--
--THOUGH IT BURNS WITH NEWBORN VIGOR.
MENTOR!
YOU BROUGHT ME TO IT. YOU SACRIFICED YOURSELF-- TO MAKE ME END IT!
PERHAPS NOW YOU UNDERSTAND THE ROLE OF ALL-FATHER.
FATHER LOOKS AT SON-- SON LOOKS AT FATHER--
--AND FOR THE FIRST TIME, SEES HIM.
BUT THAT IS NOT THE END.

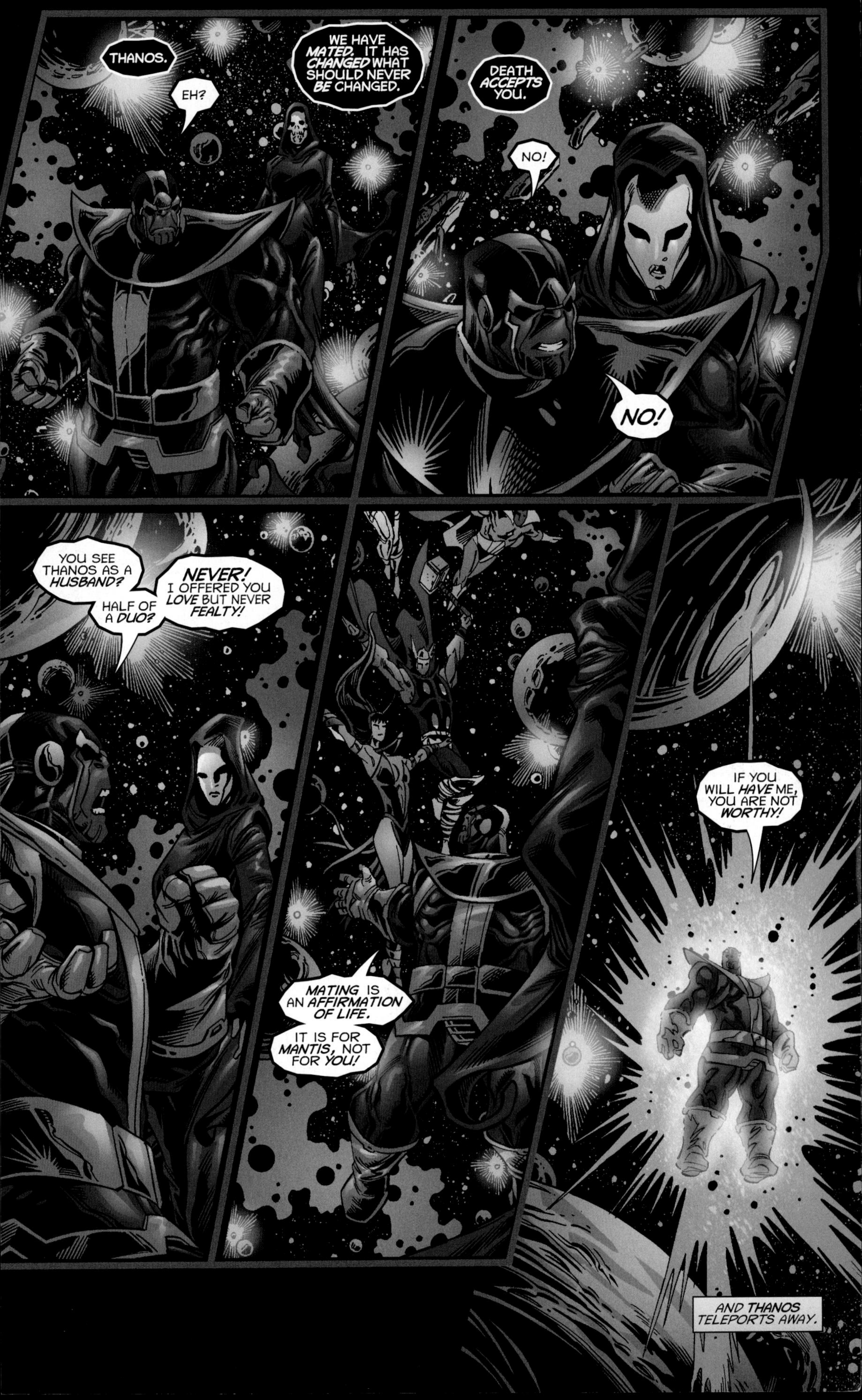
THANOS.
EH?
WE HAVE MATED. IT HAS CHANGED WHAT SHOULD NEVER BE CHANGED.
DEATH ACCEPTS YOU.
NO!
NO!
YOU SEE THANOS AS A HUSBAND?
HALF OF A DUO?
NEVER! I OFFERED YOU LOVE BUT NEVER FEALTY!
MATING IS AN AFFIRMATION OF LIFE.
IT IS FOR MANTIS, NOT FOR YOU!
IF YOU WILL HAVE ME, YOU ARE NOT WORTHY!
AND THANOS TELEPORTS AWAY.

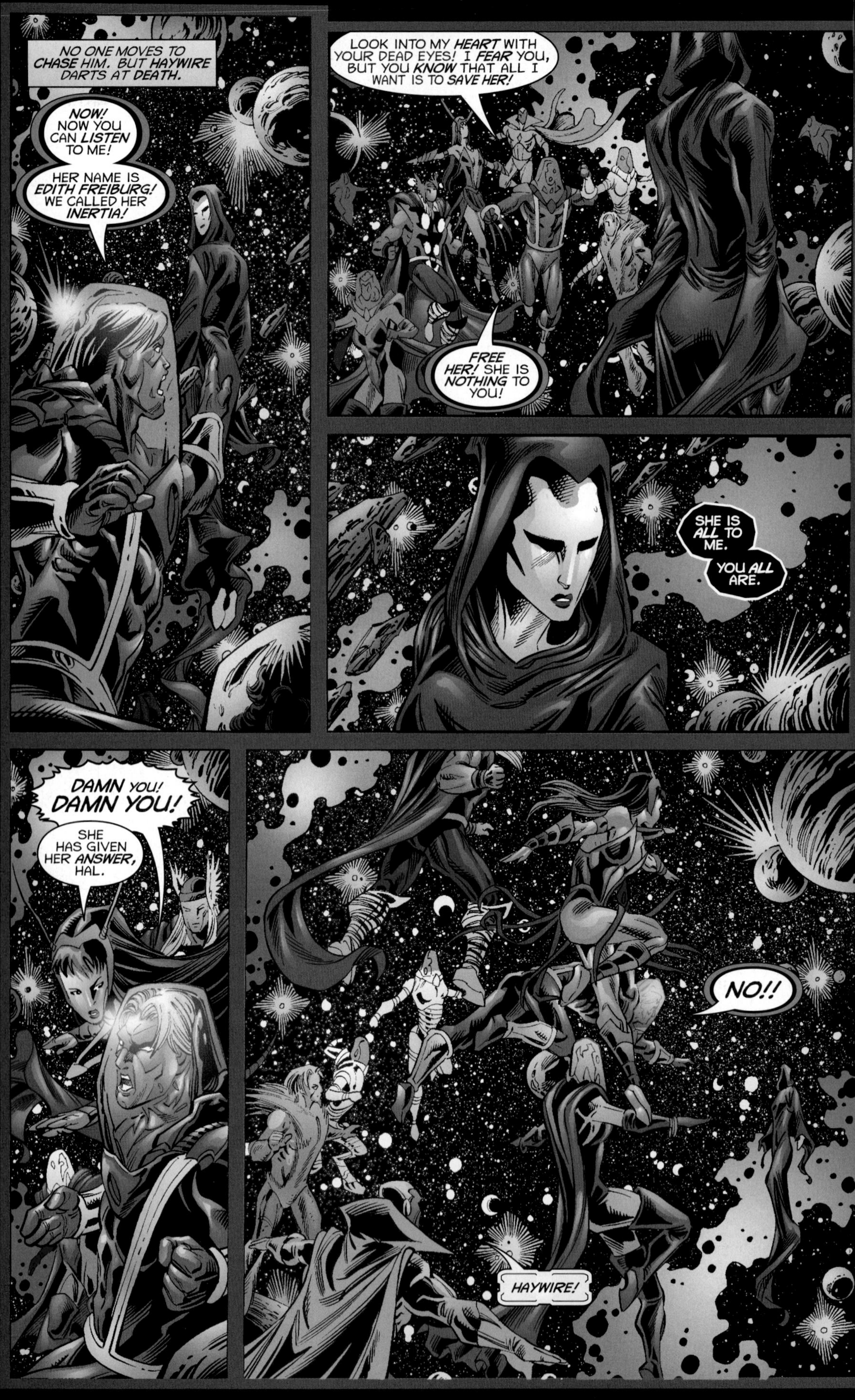

NO ONE MOVES TO CHASE HIM. BUT HAYWIRE DARTS AT DEATH.
NOW! NOW YOU CAN LISTEN TO ME!
HER NAME IS EDITH FREIBURG! WE CALLED HER INERTIA!
LOOK INTO MY HEART WITH YOUR DEAD EYES! I FEAR YOU, BUT YOU KNOW THAT ALL I WANT IS TO SAVE HER!
FREE HER! SHE IS NOTHING TO YOU!
SHE IS ALL TO ME.
YOU ALL ARE.
DAMN YOU! DAMN YOU!
SHE HAS GIVEN HER ANSWER, HAL.
NO!!
HAYWIRE!

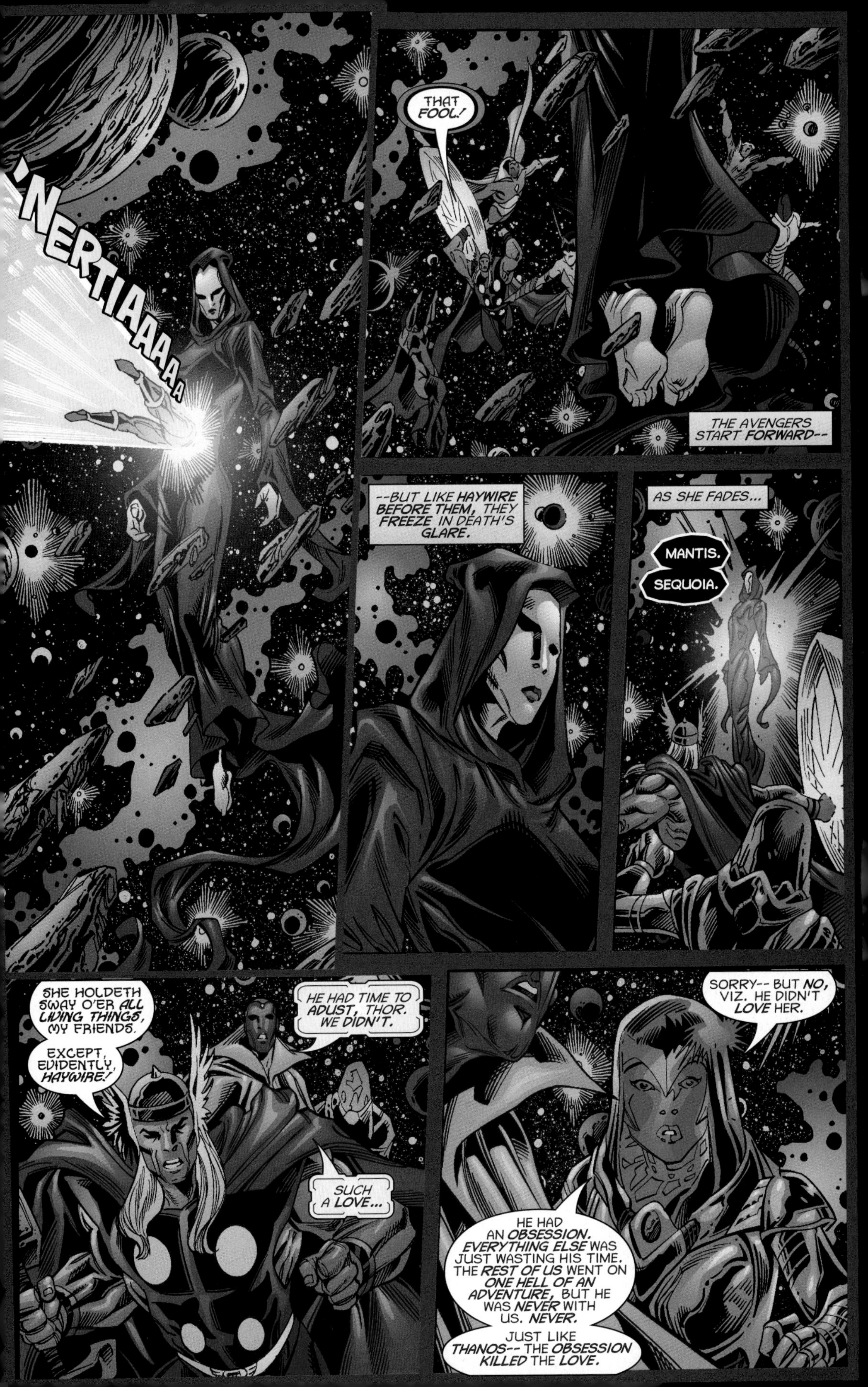
'NERTIAAAAAA
THAT FOOL!
THE AVENGERS START FORWARD--
--BUT LIKE HAYWIRE BEFORE THEM, THEY FREEZE IN DEATH'S GLARE.
AS SHE FADES...
MANTIS.
SEQUOIA.
SHE HOLDETH SWAY O'ER ALL LIVING THINGS, MY FRIENDS.
EXCEPT, EVIDENTLY, HAYWIRE!
HE HAD TIME TO ADUST, THOR. WE DIDN'T.
SUCH A LOVE...
SORRY-- BUT NO, VIZ. HE DIDN'T LOVE HER.
HE HAD AN OBSESSION. EVERYTHING ELSE WAS JUST WASTING HIS TIME. THE REST OF US WENT ON ONE HELL OF AN ADVENTURE, BUT HE WAS NEVER WITH US. NEVER.
JUST LIKE THANOS-- THE OBSESSION KILLED THE LOVE.

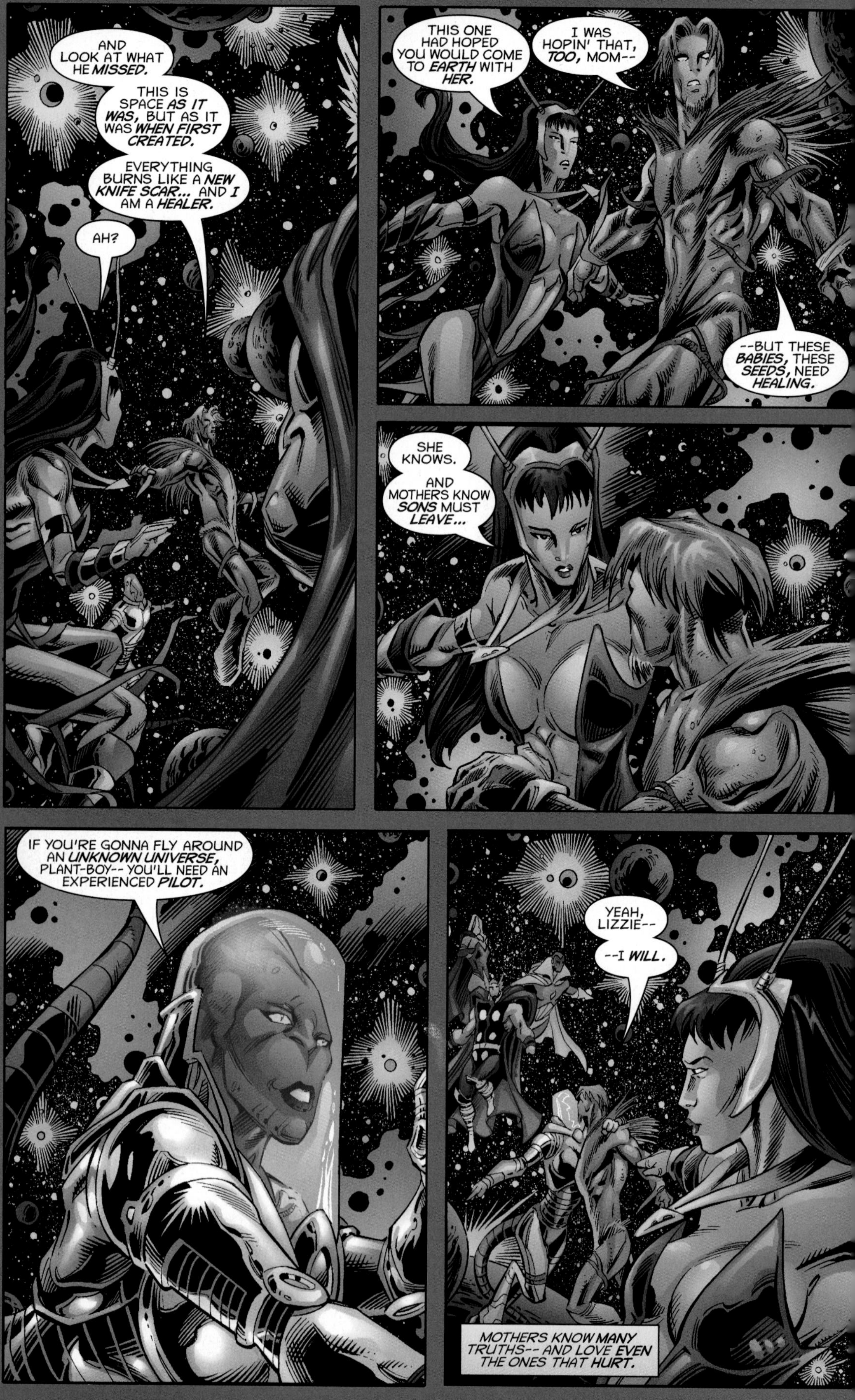
AND LOOK AT WHAT HE MISSED.
THIS IS SPACE AS IT WAS, BUT AS IT WAS WHEN FIRST CREATED.
EVERYTHING BURNS LIKE A NEW KNIFE SCAR... AND I AM A HEALER.
AH?
THIS ONE HAD HOPED YOU WOULD COME TO EARTH WITH HER.
I WAS HOPIN' THAT, TOO, MOM--
--BUT THESE BABIES, THESE SEEDS, NEED HEALING.
SHE KNOWS.
AND MOTHERS KNOW SONS MUST LEAVE...
IF YOU'RE GONNA FLY AROUND AN UNKNOWN UNIVERSE, PLANT-BOY-- YOU'LL NEED AN EXPERIENCED PILOT.
YEAH, LIZZIE--
--I WILL.
MOTHERS KNOW MANY TRUTHS-- AND LOVE EVEN THE ONES THAT HURT.

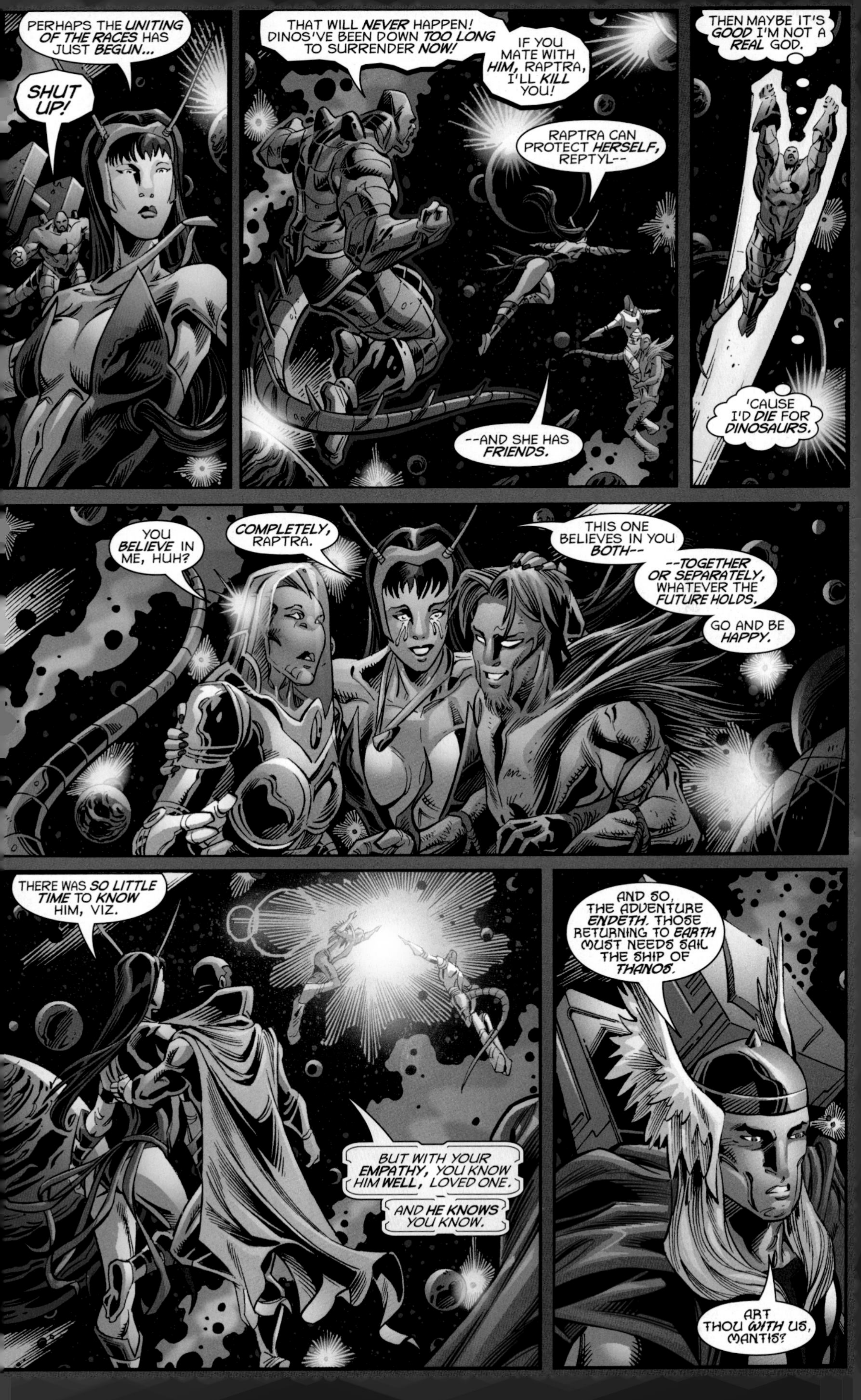
PERHAPS THE UNITING OF THE RACES HAS JUST BEGUN...
SHUT UP!
THAT WILL NEVER HAPPEN! DINOS'VE BEEN DOWN TOO LONG TO SURRENDER NOW!
IF YOU MATE WITH HIM, RAPTRA, I'LL KILL YOU!
RAPTRA CAN PROTECT HERSELF, REPTYL--
--AND SHE HAS FRIENDS.
THEN MAYBE IT'S GOOD I'M NOT A REAL GOD.
'CAUSE I'D DIE FOR DINOSAURS.
YOU BELIEVE IN ME, HUH?
COMPLETELY, RAPTRA.
THIS ONE BELIEVES IN YOU BOTH--
--TOGETHER OR SEPARATELY, WHATEVER THE FUTURE HOLDS.
GO AND BE HAPPY.
THERE WAS SO LITTLE TIME TO KNOW HIM, VIZ.
BUT WITH YOUR EMPATHY, YOU KNOW HIM WELL, LOVED ONE.
AND HE KNOWS YOU KNOW.
AND SO, THE ADVENTURE ENDETH. THOSE RETURNING TO EARTH MUST NEEDS SAIL THE SHIP OF THANOS.
ART THOU WITH US, MANTIS?

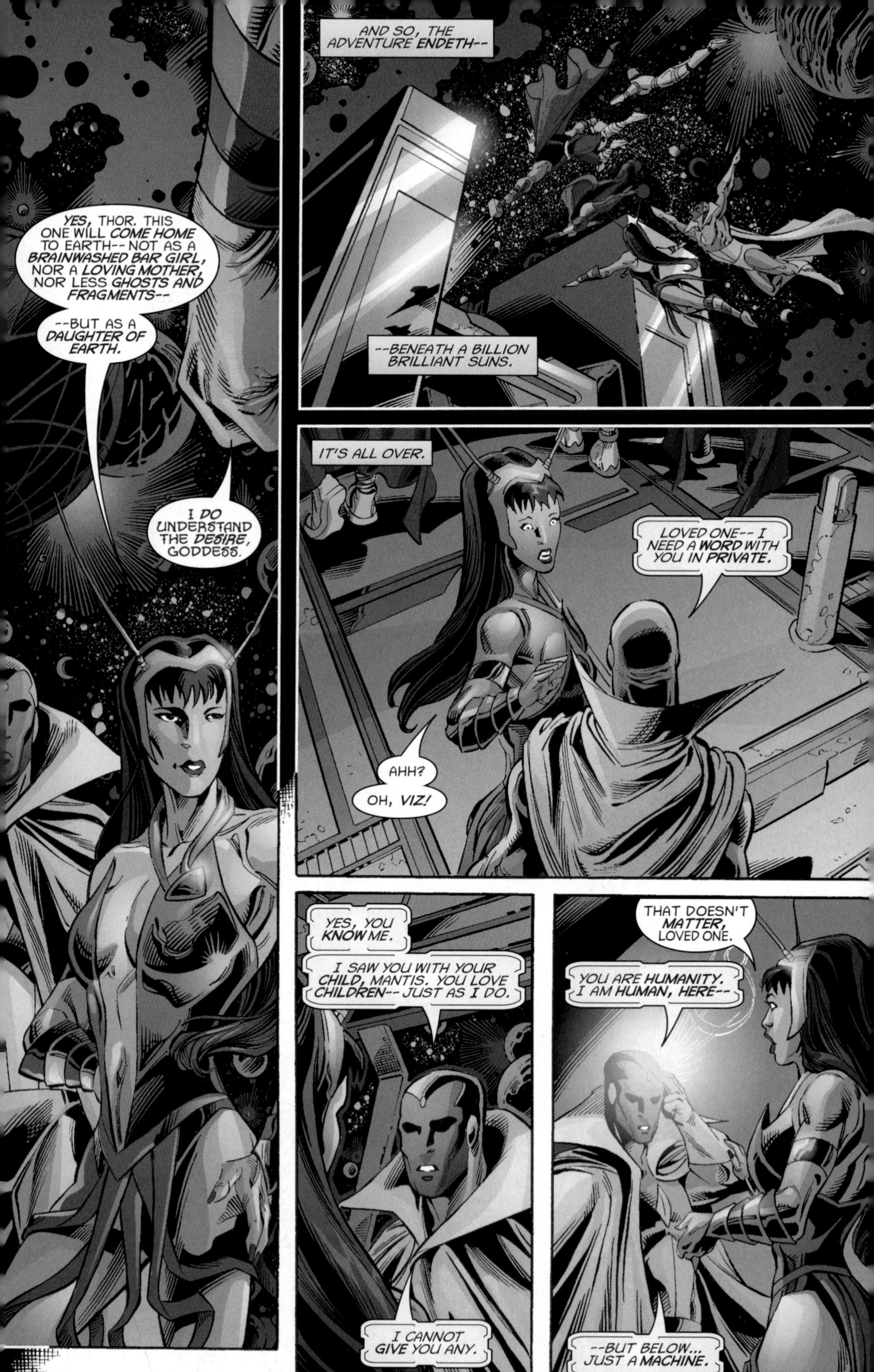
YES, THOR. THIS ONE WILL COME HOME TO EARTH--NOT AS A BRAINWASHED BAR GIRL, NOR A LOVING MOTHER, NOR LESS GHOSTS AND FRAGMENTS--
--BUT AS A DAUGHTER OF EARTH.
I DO UNDERSTAND THE DESIRE, GODDESS.
AND SO, THE ADVENTURE ENDETH--
--BENEATH A BILLION BRILLIANT SUNS.
IT'S ALL OVER.
LOVED ONE-- I NEED A WORD WITH YOU IN PRIVATE.
AHH?
OH, VIZ!
YES, YOU KNOW ME.
I SAW YOU WITH YOUR CHILD, MANTIS. YOU LOVE CHILDREN-- JUST AS I DO.
I CANNOT GIVE YOU ANY.
THAT DOESN'T MATTER, LOVED ONE.
YOU ARE HUMANITY. I AM HUMAN, HERE--
--BUT BELOW... JUST A MACHINE.

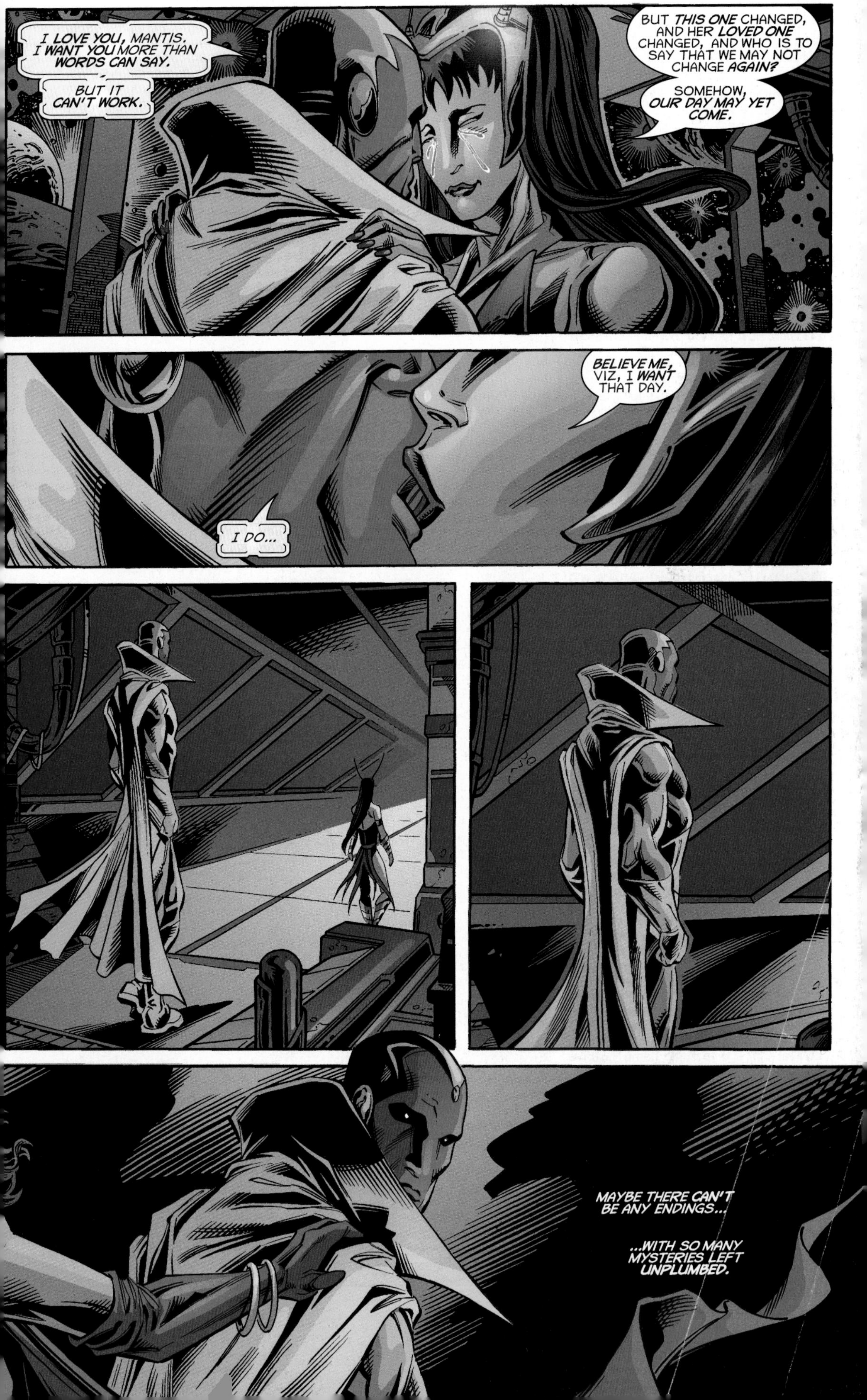
I LOVE YOU, MANTIS. I WANT YOU MORE THAN WORDS CAN SAY.
BUT IT CAN'T WORK.
BUT THIS ONE CHANGED, AND HER LOVED ONE CHANGED, AND WHO IS TO SAY THAT WE MAY NOT CHANGE AGAIN?
SOMEHOW, OUR DAY MAY YET COME.
BELIEVE ME, VIZ, I WANT THAT DAY.
I DO...
MAYBE THERE CAN'T BE ANY ENDINGS...
...WITH SO MANY MYSTERIES LEFT UNPLUMBED.

MANTIS

Real name: Unknown
Occupation: Barmaid, later adventuress, later Celestial Madonna
Identity: Secret
Legal status: Expatriate Vietnamese citizen, granted special visa to the United States on the request of the Avengers
Other aliases: The Celestial Madonna
Place of birth: Unknown village in Vietnam
Marital status: Married
Known relatives: Gustav Brandt (alias Lloyd Willoughby, father), Lua Brandt (mother, deceased), Khrull (uncle)
Group affiliation: Avengers
Base of operations: Temple of the Priests of Pama, Vietnam; later, Ho Chi Minh City (formerly Saigon), Vietnam; later, Avengers Mansion, New York City; currently unknown
First appearance: AVENGERS #112
Origin: AVENGERS #123–4, 133–5, GIANT-SIZE AVENGERS #4
History: Mantis was the daughter of Gustav Brandt, a German who fought in Indochina as a mercenary soldier, and his wife Lua, the sister of Monsieur Khrull, the leader of a local underworld organization. Khrull despised Europeans and was therefore infuriated by his sister's marriage. He was determined to kill both her and her husband. As a result the Brandts fled from one Indochinese village to another for nearly ten months. Towards the end, Mantis was born, and the Brandts decided to stop fleeing, but to remain in hiding. Nevertheless, Khrull and his men found them and used flamethrowers to set their home ablaze. Lua was killed. Badly burned and blinded, Gustav Brandt escaped with his infant daughter, who was unharmed. They both fled for days until they reached the temple of the Priests of Pama, a pacifistic sect of the humanoid alien Kree who established temples on various worlds to escape Kree persecution (see *Kree*). Because he was a soldier, the pacifistic Priests separated Brandt from his daughter so that they could raise her in their more peaceful ways. They tried to teach Brandt their philosophy as well, but succeeded only in teaching him how to "see" despite his blindness, presumably by psychic means. After a number of years Brandt left the temple and made his way to Honolulu, where he became a criminal under the alias of Lloyd Willoughby. Later, he joined the criminal cartel known as Zodiac under the name Libra (see *Zodiac, Appendix: Libra*).

The Priests educated Brandt's daughter, who they knew might someday become the Celestial Madonna, the woman who would mother the Celestial Messiah, a genetically perfect being of great power who would bring peace to the universe. She proved to be especially talented in her studies of the Kree pacifists' martial arts. It was because of her skill in defeating male opponents in combat that she took the name "Mantis" after the insect whose females kill the males. Mantis was also taught to communicate telepathically with the Cotati, an alien race of telepathic plant-beings, one of whom would father the Celestial Messiah (see *Alien Races: Cotati*). The priests had brought some of the Cotati to Earth. The growth of Mantis's telepathic rapport with the Cotati was the basis for her overall empathic nature.

When Mantis had completed her training, the Priests decided that she should be sent to live among humans so as to learn what it was to be a human. Therefore, on the night of Mantis's eighteenth birthday, two of the Priests took her, dressed in ordinary Viet-

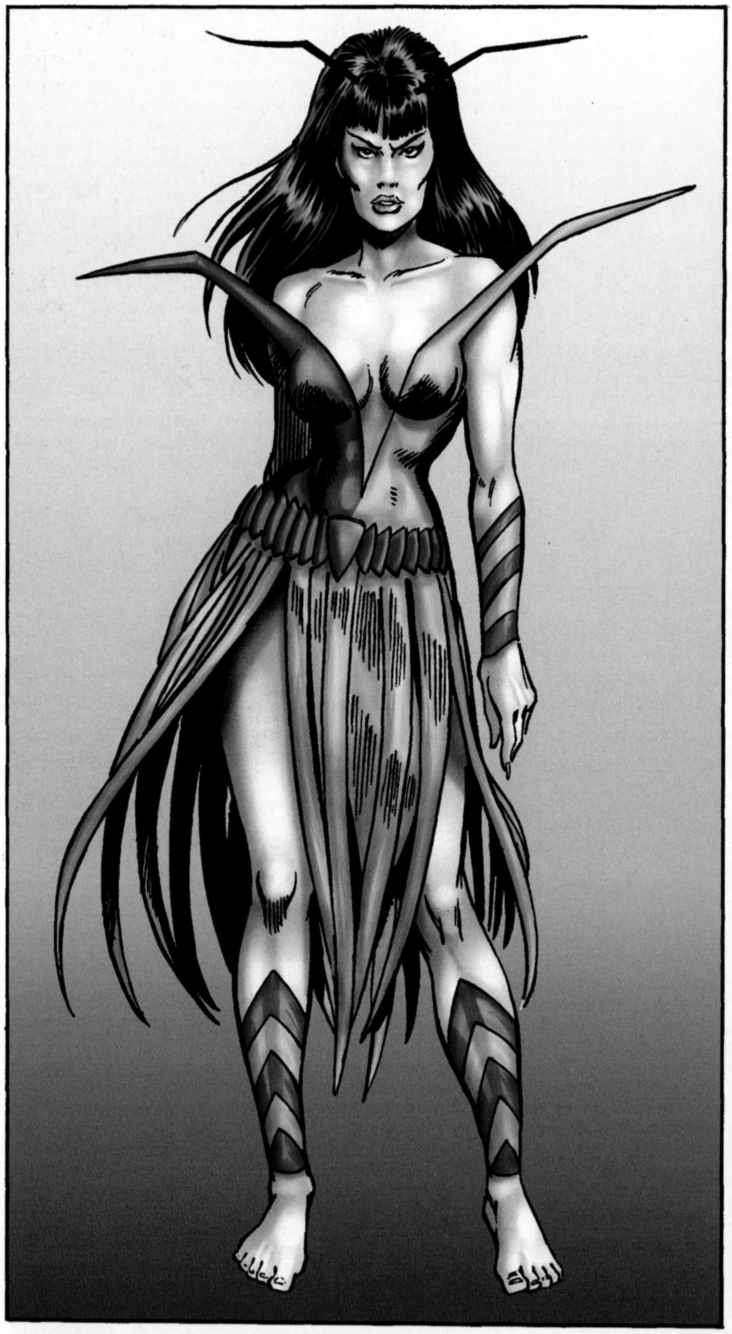

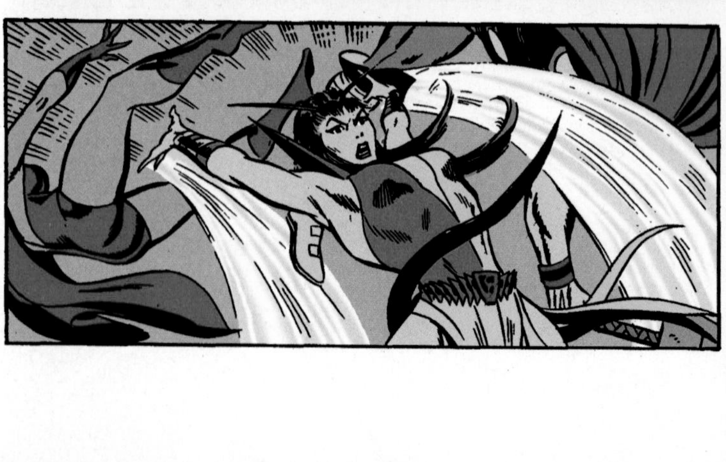

namese clothing, to Ho Chi Minh City (formerly Saigon) and left her there. The Priests of Pama had removed Mantis's memories of her life at their temple, and instead gave her false memories of growing up in Ho Chi Minh City as an orphan, struggling to survive.

Within hours, Mantis was taken to Monsieur Khrull; neither knew of his or her familial relationship to the other. Khrull forced her to work in a bar he owned as a barmaid. It was there that she eventually met the Swordsman, a costumed criminal who had come to Indochina because he was wanted by legal authorities through much of the rest of the world, and was now no more than an employee of Khrull's (see *Deceased: Swordsman*). Disgusted with his life, the Swordsman had become an alcoholic, but Mantis saw a buried nobility in him which made her recognize a similar spirit in herself, and made her dissatisfied with the way she was leading her own life. Mantis continually pleaded with the Swordsman to rehabilitate himself, and encouraged him to lead a life of which he could be proud. Finally, the Swordsman was wounded in an unsuccessful raid on a warehouse belonging to a mob that was a rival of Khrull's. Mantis found him and took him to her flat where she nursed him back to health. Now the Swordsman was ready to take her advice. He decided to reform, to return to America, and to offer his services to the Avengers (see *Avengers*). Mantis accompanied him, and when the Swordsman was readmitted to the Avengers, she was allowed to stay at Avengers Mansion as a courtesy to him. Mantis accompanied the Avengers on their missions and proved herself to be a valuable ally. However, while the Swordsman was deeply in love with Mantis, she believed she was not in love with him, and her disdain for his insecurities grew.

After the Avengers defeated Zodiac with her help, Libra revealed to Mantis that he was her father and told her how she had been raised in a temple, although he did not explain to her who the Priests of Pama really were. One day afterwards, the Avengers were attacked by their archenemy from the future, Kang the Conqueror, who had determined that one of the women then associated with the Avengers was the Celestial Madonna (see *Kang*). Kang knew of the prophecy that the Celestial Madonna's husband would be the "most powerful" being on Earth. It was for this reason that Kang had always attacked the 20th Century. Once he discovered who the Madonna was, Kang planned to father her child, thereby diverging an alternate reality in which he could rule the universe through the powers of his son, who would be the Celestial Messiah. Although Kang was thwarted in his plan, he discovered and revealed to Mantis and the Avengers that Mantis was the Celestial Madonna. In the course of these events, the Swordsman was killed by a stray blast from one of Kang's weapons. As the Swordsman died, Mantis realized that she did indeed love him. He was buried in the garden of the temple of the Priests of Pama, which Mantis and the Avengers had visited after their battle with Zodiac. The Priests were now all dead, having been killed by Khrull and his men.

Later, in the Priests' temple garden in Vietnam, Mantis and her Avenger comrades encountered Libra and the glowing, reanimated body of the Swordsman. It was the eldest Cotati on Earth, which now resembled a large tree in the garden, which animated and spoke through the Swordsman's body. The eldest Cotati told Mantis that she was the Celestial Madonna and that he was to be her husband. He had reanimated the Swordsman's body with part of his life force since he could not mate with

her in his tree-like form. Their child would be "a new life form" and would be the Celestial Messiah.

In honor of Mantis, the Avengers unanimously made her an Avenger. Immortus, master of time, officiated at the wedding of Mantis and the eldest Cotati (see *Immortus*). Once the ceremony was finished, the eldest Cotati (within the Swordsman's body) and Mantis both transformed themselves into pure energy and departed Earth. Mantis's present whereabouts are unknown.

Height: 5′ 6″
Weight: 115 lbs.
Eyes: Green
Hair: Black
Strength level: Mantis possessed the normal human strength of a woman of her age, height, and build who engages in intensive regular exercise.

Known superhuman powers: Thanks to her training by the Priests of Pama, Mantis had "complete control" over her body. Her agility was as great as any woman without superhuman powers could achieve. She was also capable of willing herself to recuperate quickly after being injured.

Mantis had extraordinary ability in the martial arts that have been developed and perfected over thousands of years by the Priests of Pama. These fighting methods place particular emphasis on the manipulation of pressure points and nerve endings on the bodies of one's opponents. Thus, by knowing the right areas of the body to strike, Mantis could stun even a being as powerful as Thor even though she herself had no superhuman strength.

Mantis had an empathic ability which enabled her to sense the emotions of others, which she felt as psychic "vibrations." ·

■

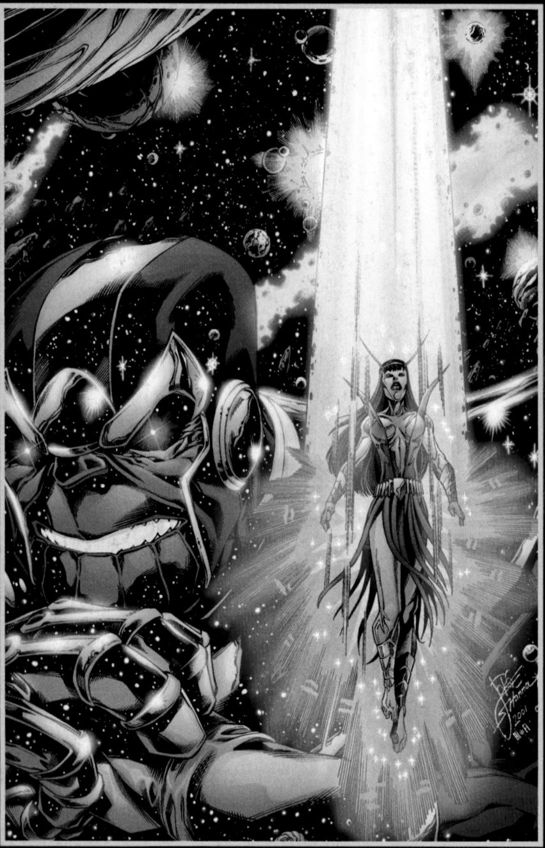
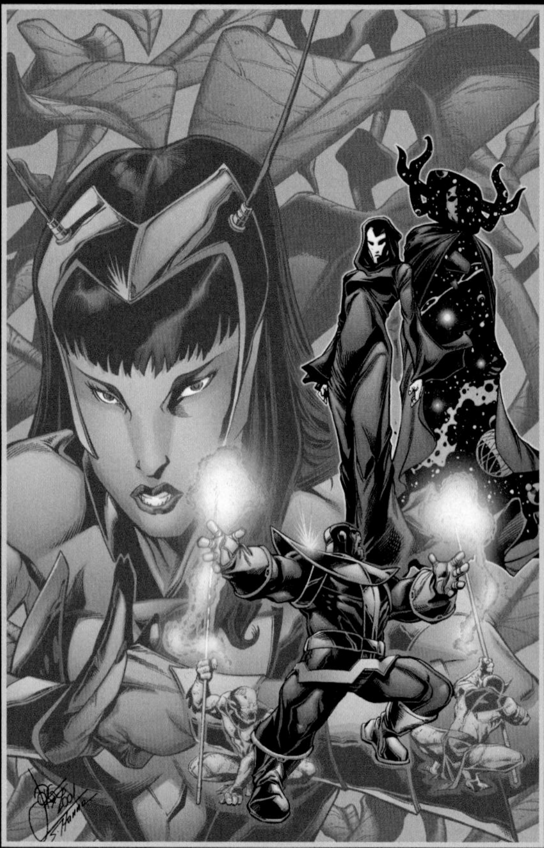
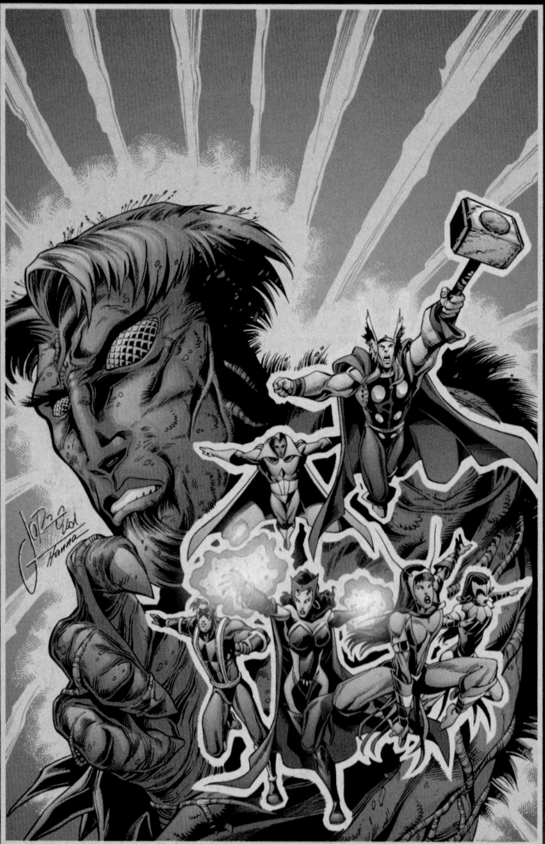
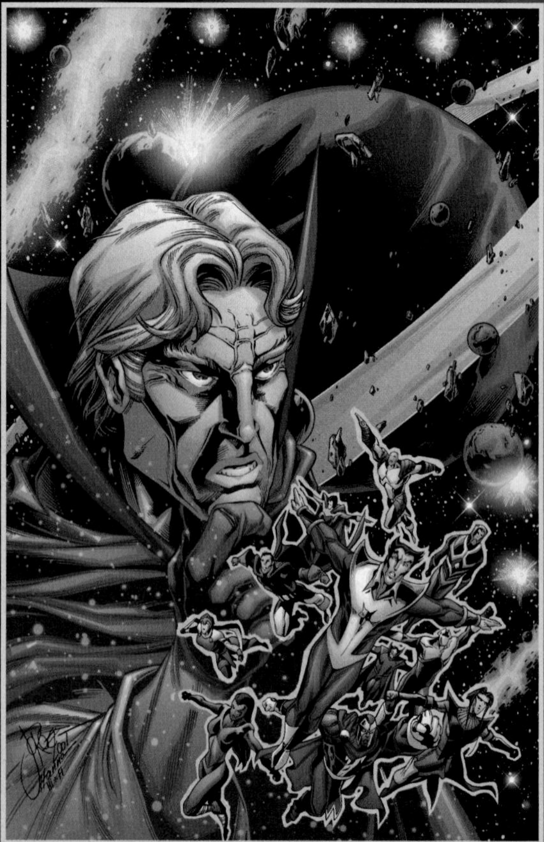

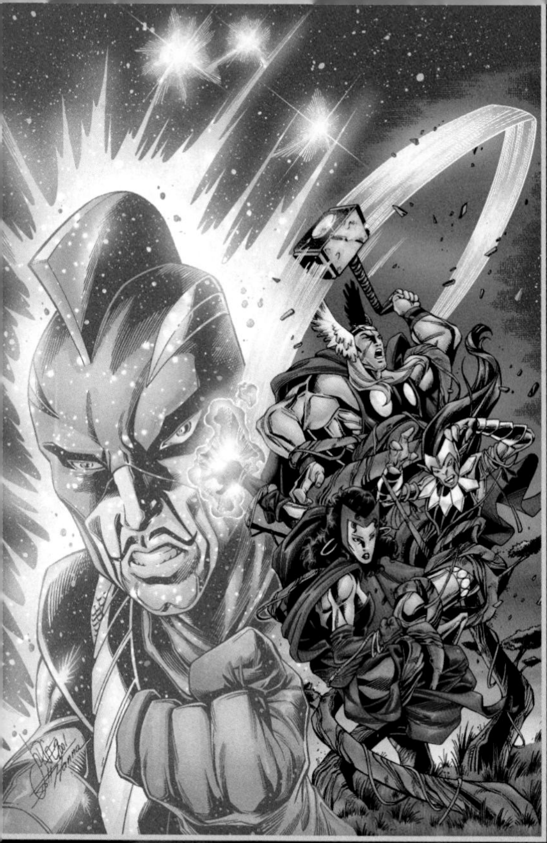

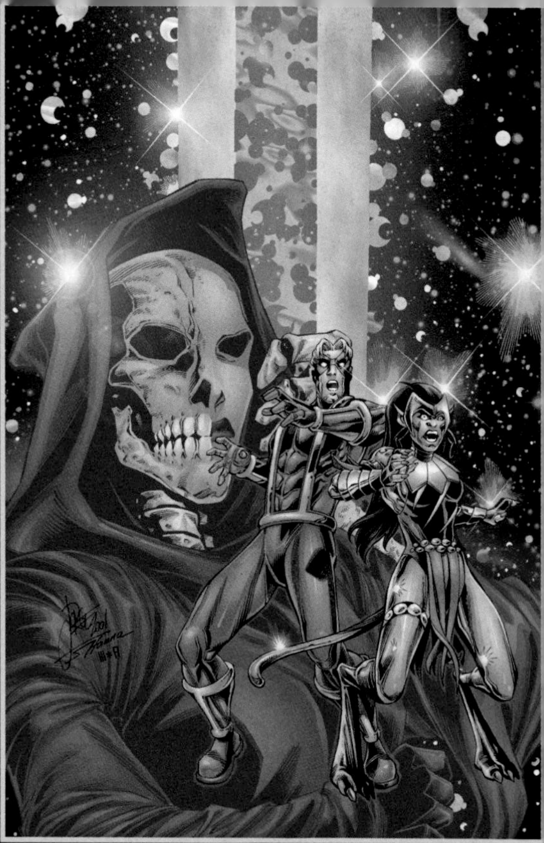

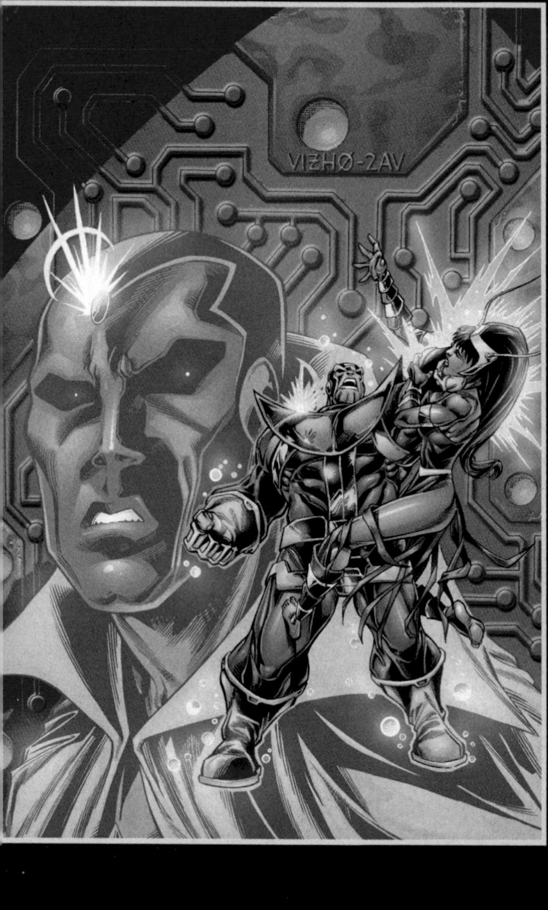
VIZHØ-2AV

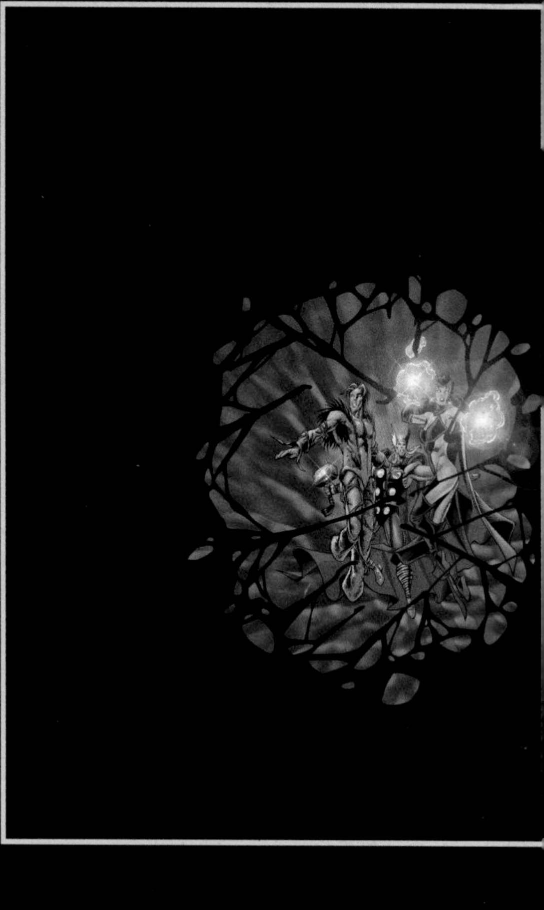